T0189187

Lecture Notes in Computer Science   10540

Commenced Publication in 1973
Founding and Former Series Editors:
Gerhard Goos, Juris Hartmanis, and Jan van Leeuwen

More information about this series at http://www.springer.com/series/7409

Giovanni Luca Ciampaglia · Afra Mashhadi
Taha Yasseri (Eds.)

Social Informatics

9th International Conference, SocInfo 2017
Oxford, UK, September 13–15, 2017
Proceedings, Part II

 Springer

Editors
Giovanni Luca Ciampaglia
Indiana University
Bloomington, IN
USA

Afra Mashhadi
University of Washington
Seattle, WA
USA

Taha Yasseri
University of Oxford
Oxford
UK

ISSN 0302-9743   ISSN 1611-3349 (electronic)
Lecture Notes in Computer Science
ISBN 978-3-319-67255-7   ISBN 978-3-319-67256-4 (eBook)
DOI 10.1007/978-3-319-67256-4

Library of Congress Control Number: 2017952387

LNCS Sublibrary: SL3 – Information Systems and Applications, incl. Internet/Web, and HCI

Printed on acid-free paper

This Springer imprint is published by Springer Nature
The registered company is Springer International Publishing AG
The registered company address is: Gewerbestrasse 11, 6330 Cham, Switzerland

Preface

This volume contains the proceedings of the 9th Conference on Social Informatics (SocInfo 2017), held in Oxford, UK on September 13–15, 2017. Continuing the tradition of this conference series, SocInfo 2017 brought together researchers from the computational and the social sciences with the intent of closing the chasm that has traditionally separated the two communities. The goal of the conference was in fact to provide a forum for practitioners from the two disciplines to define common research objectives and explore new methodological advances in both fields. The organizers welcomed a broad range of contributions, ranging from those that apply the methods of the social sciences in the study of socio-technical systems, to those that employ computer science methods to analyze complex social processes, as well as those that make use of social concepts in the design of information systems.

This year SocInfo received 142 submitted papers from a total of 451 distinct authors, located in 41 different countries covering 6 continents. We were glad to have a broad and diverse Program Committee of 218 experts with a strong interdisciplinary background from all over the world. The Program Committee reviewed all submissions and provided the authors with in-depth feedback on how to improve their work. In line with previous events, this year SocInfo continued to employ a single-blind peer review process. Papers received at least two reviews by the Program Committee; some submissions received up to five.

The Program Committee selected 40 submissions for oral presentation (28% acceptance rate) and 44 submissions to be presented as posters (30% acceptance rate). In line with the goal of fostering participation from fields with different publication practices than those of computer science, authors were given the chance to present their work without having it included in the proceedings. Four submissions opted out from the proceedings, taking the total number of contributions included in these volumes to 80.

In addition to posters and paper presentations, SocInfo 2017 hosted six great keynotes delivered by Licia Capra (University College London), Jennifer Golbeck (University of Maryland), Filippo Menczer (Indiana University), Gina Neff (University of Oxford), Daniele Quercia (Bell Labs), and Markus Strohmaier (RWTH Aachen University).

We would like to congratulate and thank all the authors and attendees for selecting this venue to present and discuss their research. We would like to thank everybody involved in the conference organization that helped us in making this event successful. We owe special thanks to the Steering Committee of this conference for their input and support, particularly Adam Wierzbicki, the chair of the Steering Committee.

The organizers are extremely grateful to all the reviewers and the members of the Program Committee for their tireless efforts in making sure that the contributions adhered to the highest standards of scientific rigor and originality. We thank our two hardworking program co-chairs Afra Mashhadi and Giovanni Luca Ciampaglia, who oversaw the process and put together a great program for this event. They both went out of their way to guarantee the quality of these proceedings and their support in other aspects of the conference organization was a great help to us. We are grateful to our publicity chair Julia Proskurnia, and our web chair Adam Tamer. This event would not have been possible without the generous support of the staff of the Oxford Internet Institute; in particular we would like to thank our sponsorship chair Victoria Nash, our finance chair Duncan Passey, and, last but not least, the local organizer Jordan Davies. We are extremely grateful to Wolfson College and in particular to Louise Gordon, who kindly provided us with the venue and amazing logistic support.

We are very thankful to our sponsors, particularly the Alan Turing Institute, Springer, and the American Association for the Advancement of Science.

September 2017   Taha Yasseri

The original version of the book was revised:
For detailed information please see Erratum.
The Erratum to these chapters is available at
https://doi.org/10.1007/978-3-319-67256-4_44

Organization

Program Committee

Palakorn Achananuparp	Singapore Management University, Singapore
Eytan Adar	University of Washington, USA
Thomas Ågotnes	University of Bergen, Norway
Luca Maria Aiello	Bell Labs, UK
Harith Alani	KMi, The Open University, UK
Merve Alanyali	University of Warwick, UK
Laura Maria Alessandretti	City University of London, UK
Fred Amblard	University of Toulouse, UK
Stuart Anderson	University of Edinburgh, UK
Pablo Aragón	Universitat Pompeu Fabra, Spain
Alex Arenas	URV, Spain
Yasuhito Asano	Kyoto University, Japan
Ching Man Au Yeung	Axon Labs Ltd., Hong Kong, China
Francois Bar	USC - Annenberg School, USA
Vladimir Barash	Graphika Inc., USA
Alain Barrat	CNRS, France
Dominik Batorski	University of Warsaw, Poland
Ginestra Bianconi	Queen Mary University, UK
Livio Bioglio	University of Turin, Italy
Arnim Bleier	GESIS-Leibniz Institute for the Social Sciences, Germany
Javier Borge-Holthoefer	Internet Interdisciplinary Institute (IN3-UOC), Spain
Ulrik Brandes	University of Konstanz, Germany
Colin Campbell	Washington College, USA
Nan Cao	IBM T.J. Watson Research Center, USA
Adrián Carro	INET, University of Oxford, UK
Claudio Castellano	Instituto dei Sistemi Complessi (ISC-CNR), Italy
Michael Castelle	University of Chicago, USA
James Caverlee	Texas A&M University, USA
Fabio Celli	University of Trento, Italy
Nina Cesare	University of Washington, USA
Meeyoung Cha	KAIST & Facebook, South Korea
Freddy Chong Tat Chua	Hewlett Packard Labs, USA
David Corney	Signal Media, UK
Michele Coscia	Harvard University, USA
Andrew Crooks	George Mason University, USA
Manlio De Domenico	Universitat Rovira i Virgili, Spain
Jean-Charles Delvenne	University of Leuven, Belgium

Bruce Desmarais	Pennsylvania State University, USA
Jana Diesner	University of Illinois at Urbana-Champaign, USA
Victor M. Eguiluz	IFISC (CSIC-UIB), Spain
Young-Ho Eom	University of Strathclyde, UK
Tim Evans	Imperial College London, UK
Katayoun Farrahi	Goldsmiths, University of London, UK
Rosta Farzan	University of Pittsburgh, USA
Diego Fregolente Mendes de Oliveira	Indiana University, USA
Seth Frey	Dartmouth College, USA
Vanessa Frias-Martinez	University of Maryland, USA
Gerhard Fuchs	University of Stuttgart, Germany
Matteo Gagliolo	Université libre de Bruxelles (ULB), Belgium
Bharath Ganesh	Oxford Internet Institute, UK
David Garcia	ETH Zurich, Switzerland
Ruth Garcia Gavilanes	Skyscanner, UK
Manuel Garcia-Herranz	UNICEF, USA
Floriana Gargiulo	CNRS and University of Paris Sorbonne, France
Carlos Gershenson	UNAM, Mexico
James Gleeson	University of Limerick, Ireland
Kwang-Il Goh	Korea University, South Korea
Jennifer Golbeck	University of Maryland, USA
Andreea Gorbatai	UC Berkeley, USA
Przemyslaw Grabowicz	Max Planck Institute for Software Systems, Germany
André Grow	KU Leuven, Belgium
Christophe Guéret	Accenture, Ireland
Scott Hale	University of Oxford, UK
Alex Hanna	University of Toronto, Canada
Tim Hannigan	University of Alberta, Canada
Mohammed Hasanuzzaman	ADAPT Centre, Dublin, Ireland
Takako Hashimoto	Chiba University of Commerce, Japan
Agnes Horvat	Northwestern University, USA
Yuheng Hu	University of Illinois at Chicago, USA
Baden Hughes	Glentworth Consulting, UK
Laurent Hébert-Dufresne	Santa Fe Institute, USA
Adam Jatowt	Kyoto University, Japan
Marco Alberto Javarone	University of Hertfordshire, UK
Mark Jelasity	University of Szeged, Hungary
Pablo Jensen	ENS Lyon, France
Hang-Hyun Jo	Pohang University of Science and Technology, South Korea
Andreas Kaltenbrunner	Eurecat - Technology Centre of Catalonia, Spain
Fariba Karimi	GESIS-Leibniz Institute for the Social Sciences, Germany
Kazuhiro Kazama	Wakayama University, Japan
Przemysław Kazienko	Wroclaw University of Technology, Poland

Pan-Jun Kim	Korea Advanced Institute of Science and Technology (KAIST), South Korea
Katharina Kinder-Kurlanda	GESIS Leibniz Institute for the Social Sciences, Germany
Mikko Kivela	Aalto University, Finland
Adam Kleinbaum	Tuck School of Business at Dartmouth, USA
Andreas Koch	University of Salzburg, Austria
Farshad Kooti	Facebook, USA
Renaud Lambiotte	University of Namur, Belgium
Walter Lamendola	University of Denver, USA
David Laniado	Eurecat, Spain
Georgios Lappas	Western Macedonia University of Applied Sciences, Greece
Deok-Sun Lee	Inha University, South Korea
Juyong Lee	National Institutes of Health, USA
Sang Hoon Lee	Korea Institute for Advanced Study, South Korea
Wonjae Lee	KAIST, South Korea
Sune Lehmann	Technical University of Denmark, Denmark
Akoglu Leman	CMU, USA
Zoran Levnajic	Faculty of Information Studies in Novo Mesto, Slovenia
Elisabeth Lex	Graz University of Technology, Austria
Vera Liao	University of Illinois at Urbana-Champaign, USA
David Liben-Nowell	Carleton College, USA
Ee-Peng Lim	Singapore Management University, Singapore
Yu-Ru Lin	University of Pittsburgh, USA
Huan Liu	Arizona State University, USA
Yabing Liu	Northeastern University, USA
Jiebo Luo	University of Rochester, USA
Mark Lutter	Max Planck Institute for the Study of Societies, Germany
Xiao Ma	Cornell Tech, USA
Matteo Magnani	Uppsala University, Sweden
Rosario Mantegna	Università di Palermo, Italy
Emanuele Massaro	EPFL, Switzerland
Naoki Masuda	University of Bristol, UK
Julian McAuley	UC San Diego, USA
Peter McMahan	University of Chicago, USA
Yelena Mejova	Qatar Computing Research Institute, Qatar
Rosa Meo	University of Turin, Italy
Stasa Milojevic	Indiana University, USA
Marija Mitrovic	Institute of Physics Belgrade, Serbia
Asako Miura	Kwansei Gakuin University, Japan
Hisashi Miyamori	Kyoto Sangyo University, Japan
Suzy Moat	University of Warwick, UK
John Mohr	University of California, Santa Barbara, USA

Jose Moreno	IRIT/UPS, France
Tsuyoshi Murata	Tokyo Institute of Technology, Japan
Mirco Musolesi	University College London, UK
Michael Mäs	ETH Zurich, Switzerland
Shinsuke Nakajima	Kyoto Sangyo University, Japan
Keiichi Nakata	University of Reading, UK
Mirco Nanni	KDD-Lab ISTI-CNR Pisa, Italy
Dong Nguyen	Alan Turing Institute, UK
Finn Årup Nielsen	Technical University of Denmark, Denmark
Laura Noren	NYU, USA
Carlos Nunes Silva	University of Lisbon, Portugal
Jason Nurse	University of Oxford, UK
Katherine Ognyanova	Rutgers University, USA
Nuria Oliver	Vodafone Research, Germany
Anne-Marie Oostveen	University of Oxford, UK
Daniela Paolotti	ISI Foundation, Italy
Mario Paolucci	Institute of Cognitive Sciences and Technologies, Italy
Symeon Papadopoulos	Information Technologies Institute, Greece
Luca Pappalardo	University of Pisa, Italy
Jaimie Park	KAIST, South Korea
Patrick Park	Northwestern University, USA
Leto Peel	Université catholique de Louvain, Belgium
Konstantinos Pelechrinis	University of Pittsburgh, USA
Orion Penner	École Polytechnique Fédérale de Lausanne, Switzerland
Matjaz Perc	University of Maribor, Slovenia
María Pereda	Universidad Carlos III de Madrid, Spain
Nicola Perra	University of Greenwich, UK
Alexander Petersen	University of California Merced, USA
Georgios Petkos	University of Macedonia, Greece
Giovanni Petri	ISI Foundation, Italy
Gregor Petrič	University of Ljubljana, Slovenia
Tobias Preis	University of Warwick, UK
Michal Ptaszynski	Kitami Institute of Technology, Japan
Hemant Purohit	George Mason University, USA
Giovanni Quattrone	Middlesex University, UK
Matthias R. Brust	University of Luxembourg, Luxembourg
Danica Radovanovic	University of Novi Sad, Serbia
Iyad Rahwan	Massachusetts Institute of Technology, USA
Jose J. Ramasco	IFISC (CSIC-UIB), Spain
Georgios Rizos	CERTH-ITI, Greece
Alice Robbin	Indiana University, USA
Luca Rossi	IT University of Copenhagen, Denmark
Martin Rosvall	Umeå Univeristy, Sweden
Giancarlo Ruffo	Università di Torino, Italy
Alessandra Sala	Bell Labs Ireland, UK

Mostafa Salehi	University of Tehran, Iran
Kazutoshi Sasahara	Nagoya University, Japan
Michael Schaub	Massachusetts Institute of Technology, USA
Maximilian Schich	The University of Texas at Dallas, USA
Rossano Schifanella	University of Turin, Italy
Harald Schoen	University of Mannheim, Germany
Ralph Schroeder	University of Oxford, UK
Frank Schweitzer	ETH Zurich, Switzerland
Amirhossein Shirazi	Shahid Beheshti University, Iran
Thanakorn Sornkaew	Ramkhamheang University, Thailand
Rok Sosic	Stanford University, USA
Viktoria Spaiser	University of Leeds, UK
Bogdan State	Stanford University, USA
Markus Strohmaier	University of Koblenz-Landau, Germany
Pål Sundsøy	Telenor ASA, Norway
Taro Takaguchi	National Institute of Information and Communications Technology, Japan
Katsumi Tanaka	Kyoto University, Japan
Maurizio Teli	Madeira Interactive Technologies Institute, Portugal
Xian Teng	University of Pittsburgh, USA
Rochelle Terman	UC Berkeley, USA
John Ternovski	Yale University, USA
Dimitrios Thilikos	National and Kapodistrian University of Athens, Greece
Bart Thomee	Google, USA
Michele Tizzoni	ISI Foundation, Italy
Klaus G. Troitzsch	University of Koblenz-Landau, Germany
Milena Tsvetkova	University of Oxford, UK
Lyle Ungar	University of Pennsylvania, USA
Carmen Vaca Ruiz	ESPOL, Ecuador
George Valkanas	University of Athens, Greece
Onur Varol	Northeastern University, USA
Julita Vassileva	University of Saskatchewan, Canada
Bertram Vidgen	University of Oxford, UK
Dani Villatoro	IIIA-csic, Spain
Daniele Vilone	National Research Council of Italy, Italy
Yana Volkovich	Appnexus, USA
Dylan Walker	Boston University, USA
Ning Wang	University of Oxford, UK
Wenbo Wang	GoDaddy Inc., USA
Ingmar Weber	Qatar Computing Research Institute, Qatar
Xidao Wen	University of Pittsburgh, USA
Tim Weninger	University of Notre Dame, USA
Adam Wierzbicki	Polish-Japanese Institute of Information Technology, Poland
Joss Wright	Oxford University, USA

Kevin S. Xu	University of Toledo, USA
Hayato Yamana	Waseda University, Japan
Pu Yan	University of Oxford, UK
Elad Yom-Tov	Microsoft Research, Israel
Hyejin Youn	MIT, USA
Burcu Yucesoy	Northeastern University, USA
Li Zeng	University of Washington, USA
Weining Zhang	University of Texas at San Antonio, USA
Arkaitz Zubiaga	University of Warwick, UK

Contents – Part II

Poster Papers: Network Science

Poster Papers: News, Misinformation, and Collective Sensemaking

Poster Papers: Opinions, Behavior, and Social Media Mining

Poster Papers: Proximity, Location, Mobility, and Urban Analytics

Poster Papers: Security, Privacy, and Trust

Poster Papers: Tools and Methods

Contents – Part I

Opinions, Behavior, and Social Media Mining

Proximity, Location, Mobility, and Urban Analytics

Security, Privacy, and Trust

Tools and Methods

Poster Papers: Economics, Science of Success, and Education

Mobile Social Media and Academic Performance

Fausto Giunchiglia[1](✉), Mattia Zeni[1](✉), Elisa Gobbi[2], Enrico Bignotti[1](✉), and Ivano Bison[2]

[1] Department of Information Engineering and Computer Science,
University of Trento, Via Sommarive 9, 38123 Trento, Italy
{fausto.giunchiglia,mattia.zeni.1,enrico.bignotti}@unitn.it
[2] Department of Sociology and Social Research, University of Trento,
Via Verdi 26, 38123 Trento, Italy
{elisa.gobbi,ivano.bison}@unitn.it

Abstract. Recent studies have shown that there is a negative correlation between social media and academic performance, since they can lead to behaviours that hurt students' careers, e.g., addictedness. However, these studies either focus on smartphones and social media addictedness *per se* or rely on sociological surveys, which only provide approximate estimations of the phenomena. We propose to bridge this gap by *(i)* parametrizing social media usage and academic performance and *(ii)* combining smartphones and time diaries to keep track of users' activities and their smartphone interaction. By analyzing the logs of social media apps while studying and attending lessons, and comparing them to students' GPA, we can quantify negative and positive correlations via smartphones.

Keywords: Social media · Academic performance · Smartphones · Time diaries

1 Introduction

Nowadays, social media and smartphones are intertwined, since smartphones are becoming more and more pervasive, especially in the student population.

In sociological literature, there is evidence of the negative impact of social media [9,16,17] and smartphone usage on academic performance [15,20]. For instance, [19] analyzed the behaviour and settings of study for 263 students, showing that students became distracted in less than 6 min before switching to technological distractions, e.g., social media. [8] notices that social networks can be used to predict smartphone addiction in users. In fact, smartphones lead to disruptive behaviors like multitasking [6], i.e., the use of social media while doing something else. [15] finds that the usage of smartphones from students with low self regulation affects their academic performance the most. [1] suggests that, among different demographics, gender and field of study, especially males and humanities students, may act as addiction predictors.

G.L. Ciampaglia et al. (Eds.): SocInfo 2017, Part II, LNCS 10540, pp. 3–13, 2017.
DOI: 10.1007/978-3-319-67256-4_1

4   F. Giunchiglia et al.

Studies that analyze smartphone usage and social media in students tend to focus on addictedness. They generally divide students in two groups (addicts and non addicts) based on the Smartphone Addiction Scale [12]. [14] extracted behavioural patterns from 95 students' smartphones, noting that addict risk groups tend to spend more time on apps providing instant gratifications. Similarly, [13] finds that, in a sample of 35 students monitored for 6 weeks, addicts strongly prefer social media. Students are also the main sample investigated in reality mining [4]. In terms of academic performance, the SmartGPA study [23] analyzed the impact of workload on several mental and physical aspects of students' life, e.g. mood, and sociability, to show that there is evidence of a link between students' GPA and their behaviour.

However, some research highlights how surveys used in sociology may be unreliable, leading to an approximation of actual usage [2,3,13]. One reason is that surveys are based on aggregate data from "stylized" questions [10], e.g., "How many times a day on average do you check your smartphone?" [6], which force users to recall activities and find an appropriate form of averaging [11]. On the other hand, works analyzing smartphone usage tend to focus on addictedness on its own [13,14] or do not correlate usage patterns to academic performance. In fact, [23] ignored social media usage, although this information was collected.

Thus there is a gap between work on addictedness and sociological surveys on academic performance. We bridge this gap by defining new metrics for representing social media usage and using smartphones to track usage and administer time diaries [22], a sociological tool for understanding people's time use. This innovative coupling allows us to isolate the time of specific activities related to academic performances and provide new insights on behavioural correlations.

We apply this approach on a subset of data about social media apps from the SmartUnitn project, which aims at correlating the time management of students and their academic performances. We extract social media usage from students' smartphones during specific academic activities, i.e., studying and attending lessons, and compare it with their GPA as a measure for academic performance. Results show that there is a negative correlation between the use of social media and academic performance, with different patterns depending on the activity.

The remainder of this paper is organized as follows. Section 2 describes our solution, while Sect. 3 explains the SmartUnitn dataset. Section 4 and Sect. 5 show our results on the correlation between social media usage and academic performance. Finally, Sect. 6 concludes the paper.

2 Social Media Usage and Academic Performance

Our proposed solution consists of two elements: *(i)* employing together time diaries and smartphones to establish the correlation between social media usage and academic performance and *(ii)* defining metrics for capturing the smartphone usage patterns in terms of social media.

Time diaries are logs where respondents are asked to detail how they allocated their time in terms of activities performed, locations visited and people encountered during their day [7]. In this work, we employ a time diary, shown in previous work [5], which asks users three questions: *(i)* "What are you doing?", i.e., activities like "shopping", *(ii)* "Where are you?", i.e., places like "home", and *(iii)* "Who is with you?", i.e., social relations like "family". The possible answers are a list of pre-defined labels, which minimizes coding, adapted from the ATUS time use survey [21]. Smartphones can enhance time diaries by administering them to users, which then can answer them in (almost) real time, while also performing sensor collection, e.g., GPS, Bluetooth, call logs, and running applications, among others. These two functionalities of smartphones can be exploited to match any given triple of reported activity, location, and social relation with the status of the smartphone as a proxy of the actual user behavior.

To represent social media usage and academic performance, we define three different parameters: *(i) social media, (ii) usage* and *(iii) academic performance*.

Social media (applications) are any technology used to share media, e.g., text and videos. We further divide social media applications, hence SM, in three categories: *Social Network Sites* (hence SNS), e.g., Facebook, *Instant Messaging Applications* (hence IM), e.g., Whatsapp, and *Browsers* (hence Web), e.g., Chrome. This distinction allows us to capture the fact that each type of social media requires different usage patterns and threatens students performances accordingly [9,15]. For instance, people use SNS for a longer period of time than IM [16] and both negatively affect students' performance, while browsers may be used to access both academic and non academic topics, e.g., going on Youtube vs going on Wikipedia.

To represent and evaluate *the usage of social media*, we distinguish between three types of interactions between students and their smartphone applications:

1. $\bar{S}$: the average number of occurrences of social media app usage, i.e., *sessions* of students checking social media;
2. $\bar{D}$: the average time of social media app usage (in seconds), i.e., the *duration* of the social media sessions, namely where any social media app is running;
3. $\bar{I}$: the average time in between app usage (in seconds), namely when there is known human interaction (swiping/typing) with an app, i.e., the duration of the *inactivity* of the phone

Notice that $\bar{S}$ and $\bar{D}$ extend and provide further structure to the notion of frequency from [2], which only accounts for frequency itself without considering its duration as parameter.

We represent *academic performance* with *Grade Point Average (GPA)*, i.e., the average of grade points a student obtained in a semester. Additionally, socio-demographic variables must be accounted for; in this paper, following [1], students' faculties (scientific and humanities) are treated as socio-demographic variables to predict the effect of social media on academic performance.

3 The Experiment

We validate our proposed solution on the data from the SmartUnitn project, which belongs to a family of projects called ƧMAЯTRAMS[1] that leverages on smartphones to extract behavioural patterns from people and develop systems that assist users in their everyday life. The SmartUnitn project aims at investigating how students' time allocations affects their academic performance.

The project relies on the i-Log mobile application [5,24] to provide the two functionalities needed from smartphones in our approach:

- **Data collection:** i-Log is designed to collect data from multiple sensors simultaneously, both hardware (e.g., GPS, accelerometer, gyroscope, among others) and software (e.g., in/out calls, application running on the device). A dedicated backend infrastructure manages the tasks of synchronizing and storing the streams of data from the smartphones.
- **Time diaries:** i-Log can administer the time diary from [5] as a question composed of three sub-question on activities, locations and social relations of students every 30 min. Every triple of questions can be answered within 150 min from its notification, with a maximum of 5 questions stacked in queue, otherwise it expires and treated as null. Questions appear as a silent notifications, shown in Fig. 1, in order to avoid bothering students and disrupt their activities too much.

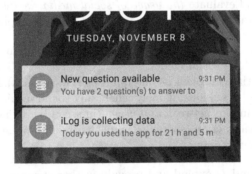

Fig. 1. I-Log notifications. The upper one shows the number of questions to be answered, while the bottom one notifies that the application running.

In SmartUnitn, 72 students used i-Log to answer to time diaries while also having their data collected for the first week; during the second week, they were only required to have the application running for the collection of data. Notice that one week of time diaries is considerably more than the conventional amount of days recorded in sociology, which is usually limited to two days (one weekday and one weekend) [18], and thus allowed us a bigger time window to extract

---

[1] See http://trams.disi.unitn.it for more information.

patterns from. Furthermore, the number of students is larger than other works in the area of computational social sciences, e.g., almost doubling SmartGPA [23] sample of 48 students. Given the involvement of students, the project is approved by the ethical committee of the University of Trento.

The SmartUnitn dataset amounts to 110 Gb, containing behavioural data from smartphones merged with socio-demographic characteristics of students obtained both through surveys and academic performance data provided by the University of Trento.

In terms of our parameters, SmartUnitn provides the following data:

- **Social media:** There are 32 SM apps used across our sample.
- **Usage:** To obtain usage information, i-Log collects running applications and the time at which their running every 5 s (on average). They are integrated with screen status information, since, due to Android operating system design, any application in the foreground keeps being logged for up to an hour; this allows us to achieve a more realistic usage result. We obtain a dataset of 135322 applications logging events covering the first week of the experiment, which is the time averaged for the usage parameters.
- **Academic performance:** Students' GPA is provided from the University of Trento. It concerns the final performance of students at the end of their first academic year (September 2016).

4   Quantifying Social Media Usage

We propose an analysis of the mean values of $\bar{S}$, $\bar{D}$, and $\bar{I}$ for all apps, focusing on SM apps, with respect to activities in general, Table 1a, while students were studying, Table 1b, and attending lessons, Table 1c. For each table, rows represent the type of activity (general, studying or attending lessons), the type of apps considered (all apps, SM apps as a whole, SNS, IM, and Web) and their respective parameters, while columns represent the parameters mean usage values (Mean), their standard deviation (Sd) and the number of students (N).

For general activities, $\bar{S}$ appears to be the most relevant parameter both for all apps and SM apps (1975.55, sd 798.31 and 664.25, sd 360.50), followed by $\bar{I}$ and $\bar{D}$. Within SM apps, IM are the most checked type of apps, with $\bar{S}$ almost 4 times the other apps (440, sd 282.58), but also the one with the highest value for $\bar{I}$ (180.89, sd 155,24), while SNS sessions last the longest ($\bar{D}$ of 120.25). This general pattern is also true for reported usage of smartphones both while studying and attending lessons, although with some differences. Firstly, SM apps are checked more frequently and for longer periods of time while studying than during lessons (higher values of $\bar{S}$ and $\bar{D}$ for SM and each app type). Notice that in the case of $\bar{D}$ of SNS and Web the values are nonetheless very close, unlike for IM, with 49.86, sd 30.57 for studying vs 36.65, sd 25.74 for attending lessons. Secondly, while $\bar{I}$ is lower when students are studying in terms of SM (121.69, sd 97.38), its values for IM apps are almost equal: for study the mean is 140.30 s (sd 127.88) and for lesson is 144.80 s (sd 200.07). Overall, these findings suggest the following:

Table 1. All social media usage with respect to our variables (parameters and apps) during:

(a) General activities

		Mean	Sd	N
All	$\bar{S}$	1975,55	798,31	67
	$\bar{D}$	47,67	50,79	67
	$\bar{I}$	236,37	136	67
SM	$\bar{S}$	664,25	360,50	67
	$\bar{D}$	69,13	22,65	67
	$\bar{I}$	157,80	143,65	67
SNS	$\bar{S}$	160,91	149,28	67
	$\bar{D}$	140,25	96,28	66
	$\bar{I}$	79,57	103,21	66
IM	$\bar{S}$	440	282,58	67
	$\bar{D}$	43,77	20,24	67
	$\bar{I}$	180,89	155,24	67
Web	$\bar{S}$	63,43	64,18	67
	$\bar{D}$	98,71	40,46	60
	$\bar{I}$	57,21	68,92	60

(b) Studying

		Mean	Sd	N
All	$\bar{S}$	296,37	228,99	67
	$\bar{D}$	44,52	20,88	64
	$\bar{I}$	198,64	148,06	64
SM	$\bar{S}$	108,44	96,94	67
	$\bar{D}$	70,57	34,13	64
	$\bar{I}$	121,69	97,38	64
SNS	$\bar{S}$	23,91	32,21	67
	$\bar{D}$	121,37	100,29	57
	$\bar{I}$	94,99	224,91	57
IM	$\bar{S}$	73,74	70,52	67
	$\bar{D}$	49,86	30,57	64
	$\bar{I}$	140,30	127,88	64
Web	$\bar{S}$	10,79	16,06	67
	$\bar{D}$	93,04	60,98	49
	$\bar{I}$	58,57	104,83	49

(c) Attending lessons

		Mean	Sd	N
All	$\bar{S}$	269,97	176,64	67
	$\bar{D}$	36,23	17,29	66
	$\bar{I}$	167,07	122,23	66
SM	$\bar{S}$	87,71	67,37	67
	$\bar{D}$	57,03	28,82	65
	$\bar{I}$	134,21	203,93	65
SNS	$\bar{S}$	19,76	26,28	67
	$\bar{D}$	117,50	111,11	57
	$\bar{I}$	66,65	87,27	57
IM	$\bar{S}$	57,22	48,98	67
	$\bar{D}$	36,65	25,74	65
	$\bar{I}$	144,80	200,07	65
Web	$\bar{S}$	10,73	14,31	67
	$\bar{D}$	90,38	73,59	51
	$\bar{I}$	87,82	280,39	51

(Row groups labelled vertically: General for (a), Study for (b), Lesson for (c).)

- On average, students check SM apps more frequently and for longer periods while studying than attending lessons (higher $\bar{S}$ and $\bar{D}$), but while in class these sessions occur in a longer window of time (higher $\bar{I}$);
- Within SM apps for both studying and attending lessons, IM apps are the most checked but with the longest window of time in between sessions, while SNS apps are the ones with the highest duration of usage.

5 Social Media Usage Vs GPA

Table 2 shows how $\bar{S}$, $\bar{D}$ and $\bar{I}$ are correlated to students' GPA by using Pearson's correlation because of the continuous nature of the variables. In Table 2, the darker the color of the cells whose parameters, considering columns and rows, obtain a significant value with respect to the correlation coefficient, the higher the value significance (p value). Rows represent $\bar{S}$, $\bar{D}$ and $\bar{I}$ for the combination of application type and activities from the Sect. 4. Columns represent the socio-demographic variables considered and the GPA. The socio-demographics are gender, faculties (distinguishing between scientific and humanities), and the combination of the two, i.e., male and female students from either faculties.

We expect a negative correlation in an increase of $\bar{S}$ and $\bar{D}$, since they would imply more smartphone usage and hence less time dedicated to academic activities. Conversely, we expect a higher value of $\bar{I}$ to be positively correlated with academic activity, since it would indicate less time dedicated to smartphones.

Table 2. Correlations of all apps and social media apps, with academic performance, based on overall activities plus studying and attending lessons.

Table is presented in its original (un-rotated) orientation. Columns are the GPA sub-groups (with N in parentheses); rows are the activity / app / parameter combinations. Values are correlation coefficients. Significance markers as in Notes.

GPA

Activity	App	Param	Hum.\M	Sci.\M	Hum.\F	Sci.\F	M	F	Sci.	Hum.	All
General	All	S	-0.0	-0.24	-0.31	0.29	-0.0	-0.13	0.02	-0.2	-0.05
General	All	D	-0.11	0.06	0.05	-0.4	-0.03	0.08	-0.06	0.07	0.07
General	All	I	-0.04	0.48	0.2	-0.69	0.21	0.14	0.14	0.14	0.16
General	SM	S	-0.25	-0.3*	-0.33	0.23	-0.1	-0.07	0.0	-0.32	-0.1
General	SM	D	0.31	0.19	-0.02	-0.7	0.19	-0.28	0.05	0.11	0.03
General	SM	I	-0.09	0.15	0.1	-0.37	0.04	0.14	0.14	0.08	0.07
General	SNS	S	0.12	-0.32*	-0.37	-0.23	-0.16**	-0.26	-0.31**	-0.18	-0.19
General	SNS	D	-0.03	0.08	0.08	-0.64	0.09	-0.03	0.06	-0.02	0.05
General	SNS	I	-0.38	-0.2	-0.22	-0.33	-0.17	-0.06	-0.19	-0.11	-0.16
General	IM	S	0.25	-0.27	-0.17	0.27	-0.11	0.03	0.06	-0.29	-0.07
General	IM	D	-0.05	0.04	-0.3**	-0.34	0.03	-0.32	0.06	0.08	-0.04
General	IM	I	-0.07	0.23	-0.09	0.26	0.26	0.18	0.11	0.12	0.12
General	Web	S	-0.0*	0.28	-0.23	-0.19	0.14	0.08	0.38	-0.06	0.19
General	Web	D	0.06	0.08	0.44	0.06	0.17	-0.23	0.09	-0.15**	-0.0
General	Web	I	-0.29*	0.38	-0.45	0.17	-0.04	0.31	0.25	-0.12	0.2
Study	All	S	0.21	-0.11	0.26	-0.17	-0.1	-0.09	-0.12	0.01	-0.04
Study	All	D	-0.06	0.04	0.33	0.02	0.37*	0.15	0.28*	0.29	0.02
Study	All	I	-0.08	0.57*	-0.33	-0.4	-0.11	-0.05	-0.14	-0.16	0.26*
Study	SM	S	0.12	-0.18	0.19	-0.22	0.06	0.06	0.18	-0.14*	-0.08
Study	SM	D	0.01	0.17	0.25	-0.54	0.2	0.06	0.2	-0.17	-0.04
Study	SM	I	-0.06	0.44	-0.39	-0.36	-0.12	-0.22	-0.41**	-0.13	0.11
Study	SNS	S	-0.24	0.33*	0.18	-0.11	0.12	-0.18	0.07	-0.12	-0.15
Study	SNS	D	-0.06	0.23	-0.21	0.09	0.07	-0.08	0.13	-0.12	0.02
Study	SNS	I	0.01	0.14	-0.2***	-0.33	-0.1	-0.0	-0.07	-0.08	0.0
Study	IM	S	0.23	-0.17	-0.05	-0.05	0.01	-0.3	0.06	0.17	-0.05
Study	IM	D	-0.17	0.02	-0.07	-0.09	0.35*	0.06	0.3*	-0.07*	-0.08
Study	IM	I	0.1	0.61**	0.43	-0.49	0.06	0.09	0.13	0.21	0.23
Study	Web	S	-0.02	0.19	-0.62	0.36	0.12	0.12	0.24	-0.26	0.03
Study	Web	D	0.06	0.1	-0.41	-0.2	0.15	0.15	0.41**	0.42	0.09
Study	Web	I	0.07	-0.07	0.64	0.09	-0.25	-0.25	0.17	-0.3	0.08
Lesson	Web	S	0.06	0.16	-0.49	0.27	-0.01	-0.25	-0.11	0.11	-0.03
Lesson	SM	D	0.07	0.65*	-0.35	-0.56	0.07	0.42	0.29	-0.21	-0.08
Lesson	SNS	I	0.14	-0.15	0.0	-0.36	0.05	-0.17	-0.2*	0.09	0.4***
Lesson	IM		-0.14	-0.01	-0.55	-0.36	0.31	-0.51*	0.08	-0.27	-0.01
Lesson	Web		0.31	0.44	0.45***	-0.3	-0.08	-0.11	0.25	-0.01	-0.11
Lesson			0.22	-0.23	-0.17	-0.52	-0.01	-0.46	-0.01	0.08	0.2
Lesson			0.43	-0.13	-0.26	-0.07	0.2	-0.34*	0.27	-0.37	-0.21
Lesson			0.14	0.1	-0.23	0.45	0.07	0.01	0.27	0.51	0.05
Lesson			0.31	-0.02	0.01	-0.3	0.05	-0.29	-0.06		0.05
Lesson			0.01	-0.08	0.13	-0.4	0.29	-0.14	0.36		0.18
Lesson			-0.28	0.03	-0.25	0.13	0.22	0.05			0.15
Lesson			0.26	0.43	-0.19	0.43	-0.14	-0.34			-0.19
Lesson			0.14	0.1	0.57		0.33	0.52*			0.3*
Lesson			-0.1	-0.13							
Lesson			-0.48	0.52							

Notes: $*\ p < .05$, $**\ p < .01$, $***\ p < .001$; Hum.=Humanities; Sci.=Scientific; F=Female; M=Male; G=Gender; (N)=N of students

5.1 Significant Values of Social Media Usage

Table 3a, Table 3b and Table 3c summarize the occurrence of significant values for $\bar{S}$, $\bar{D}$, and $\bar{I}$. Columns indicate the amount of significant values, divided according to their p value, and their total amount, while rows represent the type of activity (general, studying or attending lessons), the type of apps considered (all apps, SM apps as a whole, SNS, IM, and Web), their respective parameters, and their sum accounting for both the amount of values and their significance.

Table 3a shows that during general activities $\bar{S}$ and $\bar{D}$ have a relatively close amount of significant correlations (4 and 3, respectively), while $\bar{I}$ has only 1. Moreover, $\bar{S}$ of SNS is the parameter with the most significant values, reaching 3 values (2 with $p < .01$).

Table 3b and Table 3c indicate that studying provides slightly more occurrences than attending lessons (14 vs 11), but with similar occurrences of values per significance. Moreover, $\bar{I}$ is the parameter with the most occurrences of significant values for both activities, with a total of 13, followed by $\bar{D}$ with 9 and finally $\bar{S}$, only 3. Within SM, IM has the most significant values for

Table 3. Number of significant value occurrences from our variables in:

(a) General activities

General		$p<.05$	$p<.01$	$p<.001$	Total
All	$\bar{S}$	0	0	0	0
	$\bar{D}$	0	0	0	0
	$\bar{I}$	1	0	0	1
	Total	1	0	0	1
SM	$\bar{S}$	1	0	0	1
	$\bar{D}$	0	0	0	0
	$\bar{I}$	0	0	0	0
	Total	1	0	0	1
SNS	$\bar{S}$	1	2	0	3
	$\bar{D}$	0	0	0	0
	$\bar{I}$	0	0	0	0
	Total	1	2	0	3
IM	$\bar{S}$	0	0	0	0
	$\bar{D}$	0	1	0	1
	$\bar{I}$	0	0	0	0
	Total	0	1	0	1
Web	$\bar{S}$	0	0	0	0
	$\bar{D}$	1	1	0	2
	$\bar{I}$	0	0	0	0
	Total	1	1	0	2
Sum	$\bar{S}$	2	2	0	4
	$\bar{D}$	1	2	0	3
	$\bar{I}$	1	0	0	1
	Total	4	4	0	8

(b) Studying

Study		$p<.05$	$p<.01$	$p<.001$	Total
All	$\bar{S}$	0	0	0	0
	$\bar{D}$	1	0	0	1
	$\bar{I}$	4	0	0	4
	Total	5	0	0	5
SM	$\bar{S}$	0	0	0	0
	$\bar{D}$	2	0	0	2
	$\bar{I}$	0	0	0	0
	Total	2	0	0	2
SNS	$\bar{S}$	1	1	0	2
	$\bar{D}$	0	0	0	0
	$\bar{I}$	0	0	0	0
	Total	1	1	0	2
IM	$\bar{S}$	0	0	0	0
	$\bar{D}$	0	0	1	1
	$\bar{I}$	1	2	0	3
	Total	1	2	1	4
Web	$\bar{S}$	0	0	0	0
	$\bar{D}$	1	0	0	1
	$\bar{I}$	0	0	0	0
	Total	1	0	0	1
Sum	$\bar{S}$	1	1	0	2
	$\bar{D}$	4	0	1	5
	$\bar{I}$	5	2	0	7
	Total	10	3	1	14

(c) Attending lessons

Lesson		$p<.05$	$p<.01$	$p<.001$	Total
All	$\bar{S}$	0	0	0	0
	$\bar{D}$	0	0	0	0
	$\bar{I}$	2	1	1	4
	Total	2	1	1	4
SM	$\bar{S}$	0	0	0	0
	$\bar{D}$	1	0	0	1
	$\bar{I}$	0	0	0	0
	Total	1	0	0	1
SNS	$\bar{S}$	1	0	0	1
	$\bar{D}$	1	1	1	3
	$\bar{I}$	0	0	0	0
	Total	2	1	1	4
IM	$\bar{S}$	0	0	0	0
	$\bar{D}$	0	0	0	0
	$\bar{I}$	0	0	0	0
	Total	0	0	0	0
Web	$\bar{S}$	0	0	0	0
	$\bar{D}$	0	0	0	0
	$\bar{I}$	2	0	0	2
	Total	2	0	0	2
Sum	$\bar{S}$	1	0	0	1
	$\bar{D}$	2	1	1	4
	$\bar{I}$	4	1	1	6
	Total	7	2	2	11

studying (mainly for $\bar{I}$); however, there are no IM values for lessons. On the other hand, SNS provide the most values for establishing correlations in lessons, especially for $\bar{D}$.

Overall, these findings suggest that our parameters plus the time diary answers for academic activities allow us to effectively underline different patterns of SM app influence. Moreover:

- While studying, the average duration of usage of IM apps ($\bar{D}$ with negative p values) is the most harmful for academic performance; however, the longer students avoid them ($\bar{I}$ with positive p values) the higher their performances.
- The average duration of usage ($\bar{D}$ with negative p values) and the average occurrences of checking ($\bar{S}$ with negative p values) SNS while attending lessons negatively affect students' academic performance.

5.2 Significant Values for GPA

Table 4 show the total occurrences of significant values between our variables and GPA, i.e., 33. Columns indicate the type of variable considered: all, faculty (humanities and scientific), gender (females and males), the combination of the two (females and males in scientific and humanities faculties) and their sum. Rows represent the amount of significant values, divided according to their p value, and their total amount.

On average, the influence of SM apps on GPA appears to be stronger for scientific students than for students from humanities (7 vs 4), while gender differences seem to be less important, being almost equally distributed in our sample. In addition, distinguishing within each faculty suggests that being either a male student enrolled in a scientific faculty or being a female from humanities are the most "at risk" groups of a decrease of academic performance.

Table 4. Number of significant correlations for GPA.

		GPA							
	All	Hum.	Sci.	F	M	Sci.\F	Hum.\F	Sci.\M	Hum.\M	Sum
$p < .05$	1	3	3	2	3	0	1	5	2	20
$p < .01$	1	1	4	1	1	0	1	1	0	10
$p < .001$	1	0	0	0	0	0	2	0	0	3
Tot		3	4	7	3	4	0	4	6	2	33

Table 4 shows that, if we control for GPA without including demographics, $\bar{I}$ of all apps while both studying (0.26, $p < 0.05$) and attending lessons (0.40, $p < 0.001$) are positively associated with their GPA. Taking into account students' field of study, app usage significantly affects GPA while studying, with stronger effects for scientific students than humanities. Moreover, scientific students' GPA increases if they have higher $\bar{I}$ for all the apps (0.28, $p < 0.05$) and for IM apps (0.30, $p < 0.05$) and it decreases with higher level of $\bar{S}$ for SNS apps (-0.41, $p < 0.01$) while studying. The negative influence of social media app usage for females occurs while attending lessons. Indeed, $\bar{D}$ of social media apps in general (-0.51, $p < 0.05$) and of SNS in particular (-0.33, $p < 0.01$) affects females performance especially while they are in the classroom. Overall, these findings suggest that:

- While there is no major difference in terms of gender, academic performance of scientific students is more affected by their SM usage than students from humanities. Although this is an interesting finding, its causes are unclear and require further research.
- $\bar{S}$ and $\bar{D}$ are always correlated with lower GPA, while inactivity ($\bar{I}$) shows positive correlations.

6   Conclusions

In this paper, we proposed to overcome the current limitations of the state of the art in linking students' usage of social media on smartphones by coupling smartphones and time diaries, to then be able to match reports of time use with actual logs of SM apps. Based on the sample from the SmartUnitn project, we could corroborate the finding of sociological literature by using three parameters that pinpointed behavioural patterns that could either hurt academic performance, e.g., constantly messaging while studying or staying on SNS while in class, or improve it, e.g., limiting IM usage.

Acknowledgments. This work has been supported by QROWD (http:// qrowd-project.eu/), a Horizon 2020 project, under Grant Agreement N° 732194.

References

1. Al-Barashdi, H.S., Bouazza, A., Jabur, N.H.: Smartphone addiction among university undergraduates: a literature review. J. Sci. Res. Rep. **4**(3), 210–225 (2015)
2. Andrews, S., Ellis, D.A., Shaw, H., Piwek, L.: Beyond self-report: tools to compare estimated and real-world smartphone use. PLoS ONE **10**(10), e0139004 (2015)
3. Boase, J., Ling, R.: Measuring mobile phone use: self-report versus log data. J. Comput. Mediated Commun. **18**(4), 508–519 (2013)
4. Eagle, N., Pentland, A.S.: Reality mining: sensing complex social systems. Pers. Ubiquit. Comput. **10**(4), 255–268 (2006)
5. Giunchiglia, F., Bignotti, E., Zeni, M.: Personal context modelling and annotation. In: 2017 IEEE International Conference on Pervasive Computing and Communications Workshops (PerCom Workshops), pp. 117–122. IEEE (2017)
6. Gökçearslan, Ş., Mumcu, F.K., Haşlaman, T., Çevik, Y.D.: Modelling smartphone addiction: The role of smartphone usage, self-regulation, general self-efficacy and cyberloafing in university students. Comput. Hum. Behav. **63**, 639–649 (2016)
7. Hellgren, M.: Extracting more knowledge from time diaries? Soc. Indic. Res. **119**(3), 1517–1534 (2014)
8. Jeong, S.H., Kim, H., Yum, J.Y., Hwang, Y.: What type of content are smartphone users addicted to? SNS vs. games. Comput. Hum. Behav. **54**, 10–17 (2016)
9. Junco, R.: Too much face and not enough books: the relationship between multiple indices of facebook use and academic performance. Comput. Hum. Behav. **28**(1), 187–198 (2012)
10. Juster, F.T., Stafford, F.P.: Time, Goods, and Well-being. University of Michigan (1985)
11. Kan, M.Y., Pudney, S.: Measurement error in stylized and diary data on time use. Sociol. Methodol. **38**(1), 101–132 (2008)
12. Kwon, M., Lee, J.Y., Won, W.Y., Park, J.W., Min, J.A., Hahn, C., Gu, X., Choi, J.H., Kim, D.J.: Development and validation of a smartphone addiction scale (sas). PLoS ONE **8**(2), e56936 (2013)
13. Lee, H., Ahn, H., Nguyen, T.G., Choi, S.W., Kim, D.J.: Comparing the self-report and measured smartphone usage of college students: a pilot study. Psychiatry invest. **14**(2), 198–204 (2017)
14. Lee, U., Lee, J., Ko, M., Lee, C., Kim, Y., Yang, S., Yatani, K., Gweon, G., Chung, K.M., Song, J.: Hooked on smartphones: an exploratory study on smartphone overuse among college students. In: Proceedings of the 32nd Annual ACM Conference on Human Factors in Computing Systems, pp. 2327–2336. ACM (2014)
15. Lepp, A., Barkley, J.E., Karpinski, A.C.: The relationship between cell phone use and academic performance in a sample of us college students. Sage Open **5**(1), 1–9 (2015). 2158244015573169

16. Meier, A., Reinecke, L., Meltzer, C.E.: "Facebocrastination"? predictors of using facebook for procrastination and its effects on students well-being. Comput. Hum. Behav. **64**, 65–76 (2016)
17. Paul, J.A., Baker, H.M., Cochran, J.D.: Effect of online social networking on student academic performance. Comput. Hum. Behav. **28**(6), 2117–2127 (2012)
18. Romano., M.: Time use in daily life. a multidisciplinary approach to the time use's analysis. Technical report ISTAT No 35 (2008)
19. Rosen, L.D., Carrier, L.M., Cheever, N.A.: Facebook and texting made me do it: media-induced task-switching while studying. Comput. Hum. Behav. **29**(3), 948–958 (2013)
20. Samaha, M., Hawi, N.S.: Relationships among smartphone addiction, stress, academic performance, and satisfaction with life. Comput. Hum. Behav. **57**, 321–325 (2016)
21. Shelley, K.J.: Developing the american time use survey activity classification system. Monthly Lab. Rev. **128**, 3 (2005)
22. Sorokin, P.A., Berger, C.Q.: Time-Budgets of Human Behavior, vol. 2. Harvard University Press, Cambridge (1939)
23. Wang, R., Harari, G., Hao, P., Zhou, X., Campbell, A.T.: SmartGPA: how smartphones can assess and predict academic performance of college students. In: Proceedings of the 2015 ACM International Joint Conference on Pervasive and Ubiquitous Computing, pp. 295–306. ACM (2015)
24. Zeni, M., Zaihrayeu, I., Giunchiglia, F.: Multi-device activity logging. In: Proceedings of the 2014 ACM International Joint Conference on Pervasive and Ubiquitous Computing: Adjunct Publication, pp. 299–302. ACM (2014)

Towards Real-Time Prediction
of Unemployment and Profession

Pål Sundsøy[1]([⊠]), Johannes Bjelland[1], Bjørn-Atle Reme[1],
Eaman Jahani[2], Erik Wetter[3,4], and Linus Bengtsson[3,5]

[1] Telenor Group Research, Fornebu, Norway
sundsoy@gmail.com
[2] MIT Institute for Data, Systems and Society, Cambridge, USA
[3] Flowminder Foundation, Stockholm, Sweden
[4] Stockholm School of Economics, Stockholm, Sweden
[5] Department of Public Health Sciences,
Karolinska Institute, Stockholm, Sweden

Abstract. At a societal level unemployment is an important indicator of the performance of an economy and risks in financial markets. This study provides the first confirmation that individual employment status can be predicted from standard mobile phone network logs externally validated with household survey data. Individual welfare and households' vulnerability to shocks are intimately connected to employment status and professions of household breadwinners. By deriving a broad set of novel mobile phone network indicators reflecting users' financial, social and mobility patterns we show how machine learning models can be used to predict 18 categories of profession in a South-Asian developing country. The model predicts individual unemployment status with 70.4% accuracy. We further show how unemployment can be aggregated from individual level and mapped geographically at cell tower resolution, providing a promising approach to map labor market economic indicators, and the distribution of economic productivity and vulnerability between censuses, especially in heterogeneous urban areas. The method also provides a promising approach to support data collection on vulnerable populations, which are frequently under-represented in official surveys.

1 Introduction

Unemployment is a key economic indicator of labor market performance [1, 2]. When workers are unemployed, their families also get affected, while the nation as a whole loses their contribution to the economy in terms of the goods and services that could have been produced [3]. Unemployed workers also lose their purchasing power, which can lead to the unemployment for other workers, creating a cascading effect that ripples through the economy [4]. Additionally, unemployment has been shown to be a driver of interregional migration patterns [5]. Counting each and every unemployed person on a monthly basis would be a very expensive, time-consuming and impractical exercise. In many developed countries, including US, a monthly population survey is run to measure the extent of unemployment in the nation [6]. In developing countries such surveys often tend to have a low spatial and temporal frequency [7]. Lacking statistics

© Springer International Publishing AG 2017
G.L. Ciampaglia et al. (Eds.): SocInfo 2017, Part II, LNCS 10540, pp. 14–23, 2017.
DOI: 10.1007/978-3-319-67256-4_2

may lead to higher uncertainties in economic outlook, lower purchasing capacity and higher burden of debt. The problems of unemployment and poverty have always been major obstacles to economic development [8], and proper background statistics are important to change this trend. The increasing availability and reliability of new data sources, and the growing demand of comprehensive, up-to-date international employment data are therefore of high priority. Specifically, privately held data sources have been shown to hold great promise and opportunity for economic research, due to both high spatial and temporal granularity [9].

One of the most promising rich new data sources is mobile phone network logs [10, 11], which have the potential to deliver near real-time information of human behavior on individual and societal scale [12]. The prediction from mobile phone metadata are vast given that more than half of the world's population now own a mobile phone. Several research studies have used large-scale mobile phone metadata, in the form of call detail records (CDR) and airtime purchases (top-up) to quantify various socio-economic dimensions. On aggregated level mobile phone data have shown to provide proxy indicators for assessing regional poverty levels [13, 14], illiteracy [15], population estimates [16], human migration [17, 18] and epidemic spreading [19]. On individual level mobile phone data have been used to predict, among others, socio-economic status [20, 21], demographics [22, 23], personality [24] and product uptake [25].

Two previous papers analyze employment trends through cell phone data. The work by [26] argues that unemployment rates may be predicted two-to-eight weeks prior to the release of traditional estimates, and predict future rates up to four months ahead of official reports more accurately than using historical data alone. Another study [27] shows that mobile phone indicators are associated with unemployment and this relationship is robust when controlling for district area, population and mobile penetration rate. The results of these analyses highlight the importance of investigating the relationship between mobile phone data and employment data further.

Our work separates from [26, 27] in several ways:

(1) **Bottom-up approach:** We use individually matched mobile phone data and large-scale survey data. This approach allows us to predict employment status on the *individual* level to be able get a clean view of the drivers behind each profession. This is of relevance also as previous research has uncovered non-linear relationships between worker flows and job flows at the micro level, indicating a more complex relationship between the micro and macro levels of employment statistics than simple aggregation [5].
(2) **Geography:** We focus on a South-Asian developing country where employment statistics is almost non-existing and highly in demand.
(3) **Data:** In addition to CDR data we also include airtime purchases, as financial proxy, for our analysis. Airtime purchases have earlier shown to be among top predictors when measuring poverty and socioeconomic status from mobile phone data [14, 15].

The rest of this paper is organized as follows: In Sect. 2 we describe the methodological approach, including the features and modeling approach. In Sect. 3 we describe the results. In Sect. 4 we discuss the limitations from a holistic perspective, while we finally draw our conclusions.

2 Approach

2.1 Data

Household survey data: Data from two nationally representative cross-sectional household surveys of 200,000 individuals in a low-income South Asian country was analyzed. The data was collected for business intelligence purposes at spring and summer 2014 by an external survey company commissioned by the operator. The survey discriminated between 18 types of professions for the head of household, including currently being retired and unemployed. The head of household's was asked for their most frequently used phone number. 87% of households in the country has at least one mobile phone.

Mobile phone data: Mobile phone logs for 76 000 of the surveyed 200 000 individuals belonging to the leading operator were retrieved from a period of six months and de-identified by the operator. Individual level features were built from the raw mobile phone data and were subsequently matched with occupation data from surveys using the de-identified phone number for joining. The social features were extracted from a graph consisting of in total 113 million subscribers and 2.7 billion social ties. No content of messages or calls were accessible and all individual level data remained with the operator.

The following sub-sections describe the features and the machine learning algorithm used for our prediction.

2.2 Features and Labels

Input features: The input features are built entirely from the cell phone datasets. A structured dataset consisting of 160 novel mobile phone features are built from the raw CDRs and airtime purchases, and categorized into three dimensions: (1) financial (2) mobility and (3) social features (Table 1). The features are customized to be predictive of employment status and include various parameters of the corresponding distributions such as weekly or monthly median, mean and variance. In addition to basic features such as incoming and outgoing MMS, voice, SMS, internet and video calls we investigate more customized features such as the consumption rate of airtime purchases (spending speed), the amount time spent on each base station, the size of social circle, the time spent on different contacts and features related to the phone type owned by the customer.

Labels: The labels were built from the survey data. Since our aim is to separate one specific profession/employment status from the others we build 18 one-vs-rest binary classifiers – one for each profession (student vs non-student, employed vs unemployed and so forth). These classifiers are then trained separately.

Table 1. Sample of input features from mobile phone metadata used in model

Dimension	Input features
Financial	**Airtime purchases:** Recharge amount per transaction, Spending speed, fraction of lowest/highest recharge amount, coefficient of variation recharge amount etc. **Revenue:** Charge of outgoing/incoming SMS, MMS, voice, video, value added sevices, roaming, internet etc. **Handset:** Manufacturer, brand, camera enabled, smart/feature/basic phone etc.
Mobility	Home district/tower, radius of gyration, entropy of places, number of places visited etc.
Social	**Social Network:** Interaction per contact, degree, entropy of contacts etc. **General phone usage:** Out/In voice duration, SMS count, Internet volume/count, MMS count, video count/duration, value-added services duration/count etc.

2.3 Deep Neural Network Models

Based on the performance of several algorithms we propose a standard multi-layer feedforward neural network architecture where the weighted combination of the n input signals is aggregated, and an output signal f($\bullet$) is transmitted by the connected neuron. The function f used for the nonlinear activation is rectifier $f(\bullet) \approx \log(1 + e^{\cdot})$. To minimize the loss function we apply a standard stochastic gradient descent with the gradient computed via back-propagation. We use dropout as a regularization technique to prevent over-fitting [28]. Dropout secures that each training example is used in a different model which all share the same global parameters. For the input layer we use the value of 0.1 and 0.2 for the hidden layers. In total 18 models are built – one for each pre-classified profession type.

To compensate class imbalance, the minority class in the training set is up-sampled. The minority class is then randomly sampled, with replacement, to be of the same size as the majority class. In our set-up, each model is trained and tested using a 75%/25% (training/testing) split. The up-sampling is only applied to the training set. Commonly used performance metrics for classification problems [29], including overall accuracy, sensitivity and specificity, are reported for the test-set.

3 Results

3.1 Individual Employment Status

The average prediction accuracy for all 18 profession groups were 67.5%, with clerk being the easiest to predict with accuracy of 73.5%, and skilled worker the most difficult (accuracy: 61.9%) (Fig. 1).

Our unemployment model predicted whether phone users were unemployed with an accuracy of 70.4% (95% CI:70.1–70.6%). The accuracy difference between the training and test-set was 3.6%, which indicate our trained model has good generalization power. The true positive rate (sensitivity/recall) was 67% and true negative rate (specificity) 70.4%. Given the original baseline of 2.1%, the model predicts unemployment on average 30 times better than random.

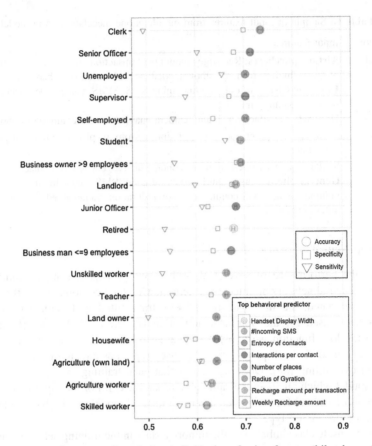

Fig. 1. Test-set performance of predicting individual profession from mobile phone data. For each profession accuracy ●, sensitivity ▽ and specificity ☐ are reported. Top behavioral predictors are indicated with colors (excluding most used tower (lon, lat))

Each cross-validated model was subsequently restricted to use its 20 most important predictors (applying Gedeon method [30]). An investigation of the five most important predictors for each profession is given in Fig. 2. This network shows how the professions are linked together via common predictors. We observe that several features are predictive across multiple professions – indicated by high in-degree in the network. Predictors that are superior across multiple professions include the most frequently used cell tower (longitude and latitude): in the case of unemployed (red node) this signal indicates that the model may catch regions of low economic development status, e.g. slum areas where unemployment is high. Other cross-profession predictors include number of visited places, the radius of gyration (how far the person usually travels from his home tower) and recharge amount per transaction. These indicators have earlier been shown to be important financial proxy indicators for household income in underdeveloped Asian markets [21]. Furthermore, unemployed people tend to have few interactions with their friends, generate more voice calls at

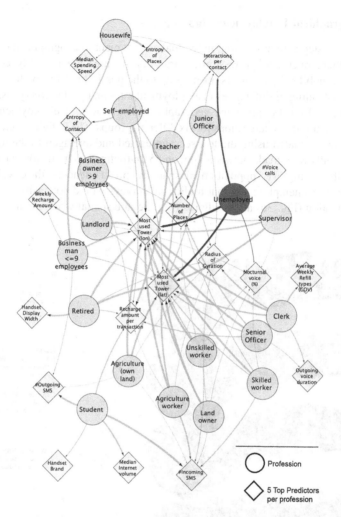

Fig. 2. Network of professions linked via common predictors. Each profession links to their 5 most important predictors. The link width is proportional to the scaled relative importance of the current predictor. For example the most important predictors for being unemployed (highlighted in red node color) are most used cell tower (lon, lat), interaction per contact, nocturnal voice (%) and number of voice calls.

night (when calls are cheaper) and make less voice calls. They also tend to top-up with the lowest recharge amount per transaction (sixth predictor) - a feature that also occurs as a predictor of low household income [21]. As seen in the figure, students have the most unique predictive signal, when it comes to few overlapping predictors with other groups. Interestingly they are not the easiest group to predict, which indicate the Deep Learning models have found stronger non-linear relationships in other categories of profession.

3.2 Geographical Employment Mapping

A natural next step is to move from individual employment to geographical distribution of employment rates and professions. Large Asian cities are typically covered by thousands of mobile phone towers opening up to the possibility of providing a detailed spatial understanding of differences in employment rates and profession types. In Fig. 3 we have mapped out the predicted geographical distribution of employment rate per home tower, in one of the large cities for six different groups. The individual employment rates are here calculated using the test set, aggregated and averaged to the tower from which most calls were made between 7pm and 5am (defined as home tower). Figure 3a shows that the unemployed population are spatially spread out across the city, indicating many pockets of unemployment that traditional surveys would not easily pick up. The retired population (Fig. 3d) and landlords (Fig. 3c) are spatially more concentrated.

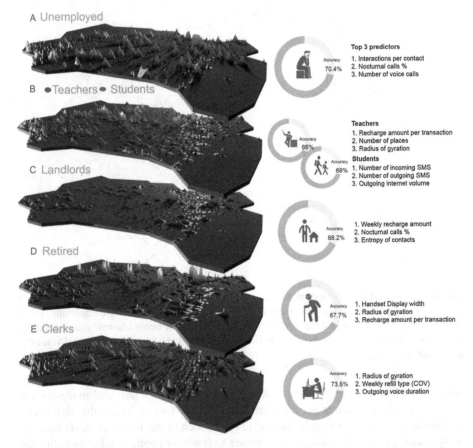

Fig. 3. Geographical distributions of employment status and profession categories per base station in one of the larger Asian cities with over 1,500 cell towers and 18 million people. Employment rates are calculated by using the out-of-sample test set, aggregated and averaged to their respective home tower. Individual prediction accuracy and top three predictors are given to the right for (A) Unemployed (B) Teachers and students (C) Landlords (D) Retired (E) Clerks.

By investigating the top 3 most important behavioral predictors we interestingly observe that the physical width of handset is the most important for the retired people. The elderly in this market tends to have older and smaller phones than the younger generation. This in contrast to Scandinavian markets where larger handsets are marketed especially towards elderly people. We also notice that SMS and mobile Internet consumption are the best indicators for being a student (Fig. 3b). The most important predictor of Clerks (Fig. 3e) is a low radius of gyration (or mobility radius – reflecting static office jobs). They also tend to have more advanced consumption patterns (more variation in top-up refill types) and longer voice duration. We also notice that airtime purchase information is among top predictors for several professions, stressing the importance to include such datasets in future research.

4 Discussion

This study shows how individual employment status can be predicted from mobile phone metadata, and further mapped geographically on cell tower level. An important policy application of this work is the prediction of regional and individual employment rates in developing countries where official statistics is limited or non-existing. Our framework can provide an alternative source of timely information to traditional census methods at a fraction of the cost, and opens-up the way to large-scale and low-cost labeling of mobile phone datasets and their use in research, economic policy making and humanitarian applications.

References

1. Lovati, J.: The unemployment rate as an economic indicator. Federal reserve bank of st.louis (1976)
2. Keynes, M.: The General Theory of Employment, Interest and Money. Palgrave Macmillan, Basingstoke, Hampshire (2009). ISBN 0-230-00476-8
3. International Labour Organization: Global Unemployment Trends. (2013)
4. Garegnani, P.: Heterogeneous capital, the production function and the theory of distribution. Rev. Econ. Stud. **37**(3), 407–436 (1970)
5. Faberman, D., Haltiwanger, J.: The flow approach to labor markets: new data sources and micro-macro links. J. Econ. Perspect. **20**(3), 3–26 (2006)
6. U.S. Bureau of Labor Statistics: How the Government Measures Unemployment. (2014)
7. International Labour Organization: World Employment Social Outlook. (2017)
8. Economy Watch: Unemployment and Poverty (2010). http://www.economywatch.com/unemployment/poverty.html
9. Einav, L., Levin, J.: Economics in the age of big data. Science **346**(6210) (2014). DOI:10.1126/science.1243089
10. Lokanathan, S. Gunaratne, R.L.: Behavioral insights for development from Mobile Network Big Data: enlightening policy makers on the State of the Art (2014). http://dx.doi.org/10.2139/ssrn.2522814
11. Sundsøy, P.: Big Data for Social Sciences: Measuring patterns of human behavior through large-scale mobile phone data. PHD Thesis, arXiv:1702.08349 [cs.CY] (2017)

12. Lazer, D., Pentland, A., Adamic, L., Aral, S., Barabasi, A.L., Brewer, D., Christakis, N.: Computational social science. Science **323**(5915), 721–723 (2009)
13. Blumenstock, C.: Predicting poverty and wealth from mobile phone metadata. Science **350** (6264), 1073–1076 (2015)
14. Steele, J. E., Sundsøy, P., Pezzulo, C., Alegana, V., Bird, T., Blumenstock, J., Bjelland, J., Engø-Monsen, K., de Montjoye, Y. A., Iqbal, A., Hadiuzzaman, K., Lu, X., Wetter, E., Tatem, A., Bengtsson, L.: Mapping poverty using mobile phone and satellite data. J. R. Soc. Interface **14**(127), (2017). 20160690
15. Sundsøy, P.: Mitigating the risks of financial exclusion: Predicting illiteracy with standard mobile phone logs. In: SBP-BRiMS 2017 International Conference on Social Computing, Behavioral-Cultural Modeling & Prediction and Behavior Representation in Modeling and Simulation (2017)
16. Deville, P., Linard, C., Martin, S., Gilbert, M., Stevens, F.R., Gaughan, A.E., Blondel, V.D., Tatem, A.J.: Dynamic population mapping using mobile phone data. In: PNAS, pp. 15888–15893 (2014). doi:10.1073/pnas.1408439111
17. Lu, X., Wrathall, D.J., Sundsøy, P.R., Nadiruzzaman, M., Wetter, E., Iqbal, A., Qureshi, T., Tatem, A.J., Canright, G.S., Engø-Monsen, K., Bengtsson, L.: Detecting climate adaptation with mobile network data in Bangladesh: anomalies in communication, mobility and consumption patterns during cyclone Mahasen. Clim. Change **138**(3), 505–519 (2016)
18. Lu, X., Wrathall, D.J., Sundsøy, P.R., Nadiruzzaman, M., Wetter, E., Iqbal, A., Qureshi, T., Tatem, A.J., Canright, G.S., Engø-Monsen, K., Bengtsson, L.: Unveiling hidden migration and mobility patterns in climate stressed regions: A longitudinal study of six million anonymous mobile phone users in Bangladesh. Glob. Environ. Change **38**, 1–7 (2016)
19. Wesolowski, A., Qureshi, T., Boni, M.F., Sundsøy, P.R., Johansson, M.A., Rasheed, S.B., Engø-Monsen, K., Buckee, C.O.: Impact of human mobility on the emergence of dengue epidemics in Pakistan. Proc. Nat. Acad. Sci. **112**(38), 11887–11892 (2015)
20. Guitierrrez, Krings, Blondel: Evaluating socio-economic state of a country analyzing airtime credit and mobile phone datasets. arXiv preprint arXiv:1309.4496 (2013)
21. Sundsøy, P., Bjelland, J., Reme, B., Iqbal, A., Jahani, E.: Deep learning applied to mobile phone data for Individual income classification. In: ICAITA 2016 International Conference on Artificial Intelligence and applications (2016)
22. Felbo, B., Pentland, S., Sundsøy, P., Montjoye, Y., Lehmann, S.: Using Deep Learning to predict demographics from mobile phone metadata. arXiv:1511.06660v4 (2016)
23. Jahani, E., Sundsøy, P., Bjelland, J., Pentland, A., Bengtsson, L.M.: Improving official statistics in emerging markets using machine learning and mobile phone data. EPJ Data Sci. **6**(1), 3 (2017)
24. Montjoye, Y.-A., Quoidbach, J., Robic, F., Pentland, A(.: Predicting Personality Using Novel Mobile Phone-Based Metrics. In: Greenberg, Ariel M., Kennedy, William G., Bos, Nathan D. (eds.) SBP 2013. LNCS, vol. 7812, pp. 48–55. Springer, Heidelberg (2013). doi:10.1007/978-3-642-37210-0_6
25. Sundsøy, P., Bjelland, J., Iqbal, A.M., de Montjoye, Y.A.: Big data-driven marketing: how machine learning outperforms marketers' gut-feeling. In: International Conference on Social Computing, Behavioral-Cultural Modeling, and Prediction, pp. 367–374 (2014)
26. Toole, J., Lin, Y.-r., Muehlegger, E., Shoag, D., Gonzalez, M., Lazer, D.: Tracking employment shocks using mobile phone data. J. R. Soc. Interface **12**(107) (2015)
27. Almaatouq, A., Prieto-Castrillo, F., Pentland, A.: Mobile communication signatures of unemployment. In: International Conference on Social Informatics, pp. 407–418 (2016)
28. Dahl, G.: Improving Deep Neural Networks for LVCSR using Rectified Linear Units and Dropout. In: ICASSP, pp. 8609–8613 (2013)

29. Koyejo, O.: Consistent Binary Classification with Generalized Performance Metrics. NIPS (2014)
30. Gedeon, T.: Data Mining of inputs: analysing magnitude and functional measures. Int. J. Neural Syst. **8**(2), 209–218 (1997)
31. OECD: Main Economic Indicators (2016)
32. Ciccone, A., Hall, R.: Productivity and density of economic activity. Am. Econ. Rev. **86**(1), 54–70 (1996)

The Digital Flynn Effect: Complexity of Posts on Social Media Increases over Time

Ivan Smirnov[✉]

Institute of Education,
National Research University Higher School of Economics, Moscow, Russia
ibsmirnov@hse.ru

Abstract. Parents and teachers often express concern about the extensive use of social media by youngsters. Some of them see emoticons, undecipherable initialisms and loose grammar typical for social media as evidence of language degradation. In this paper, we use a simple measure of text complexity to investigate how the complexity of public posts on a popular social networking site changes over time. We analyze a unique dataset that contains texts posted by $942,336$ users from a large European city across nine years. We show that the chosen complexity measure is correlated with the academic performance of users: users from high-performing schools produce more complex texts than users from low-performing schools. We also find that complexity of posts increases with age. Finally, we demonstrate that overall language complexity of posts on the social networking site is constantly increasing. We call this phenomenon the digital Flynn effect. Our results may suggest that the worries about language degradation are not warranted.

Keywords: Social media · Language complexity · Academic performance

1 Introduction

Media reports often express concern about the extensive use of social media by young people [1]. One major concern is that texting style typical for social media leads to poor language skills. However, no clear links between texting practices and literacy were discovered (see [2,3] for a review of the topic). As social media are constantly evolving, it might also be important to account for potential changes in language practices of its users. Does the complexity of texts posted on social media decrease, indicating the language degradation that parents and educators are afraid of? We address this question by using a large longitudinal dataset.

We investigate the changes in complexity of public posts made by users on a popular social networking site across nine years. We use data from VK, the largest European social networking site, that provides functionality similar to Facebook. The dataset contains $1,320,572,032$ words posted by $942,336$ users from Saint-Petersburg, Russia whose ages range from 15 to 60. In their profiles,

G.L. Ciampaglia et al. (Eds.): SocInfo 2017, Part II, LNCS 10540, pp. 24–30, 2017.
DOI: 10.1007/978-3-319-67256-4_3

users indicate the high school in which they study or which they graduated from. In addition to post content, information about average academic performance of graduates from these schools is also available (see Methods for details).

We use average word length as the measure of text complexity. The traditional measures of text complexity are readability indices that are based on average word length, average sentence length or number of complex words in the text [4,5]. The same features were successfully used for single-sentence readability prediction in the Russian language [6]. In the online context, average word length was shown to be shorter for the simple English Wikipedia than for the main English Wikipedia [7]. In this paper, we limit ourselves to average word length (see Methods for details). It is worth mentioning that automatic determination of sentence length is more problematic in the social media context than in traditional texts. For example, people often neglect to capitalize the first letter of a sentence, and emoticons can be used to indicate the end of a sentence but may appear in the middle of a sentence as well.

Measuring text complexity is a challenging task. One might even argue that using shorter words means that authors have found a clever way to communicate the same amount of content more efficiently. In order to justify our measuring system, we compare average word length in posts made by users with different academic performance. We expect that users with higher academic performance produce more complex posts. We also expect to see age-related differences in the posts' complexity. It was previously reported that the average word length in texts increases with the age of their authors [8,9].

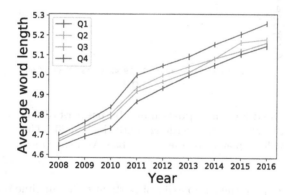

Fig. 1. Average word length in posts of graduates from different schools. Users from top-performing schools (Q1) produce more complex posts than users from middle- or low-performing schools. However, there is no significant difference between middle-high (Q2) and middle-low (Q3) performing schools. Vertical bars are standard errors.

2 Results

For each school in our dataset, we assign a quartile ranking based on the average academic performance of its graduates. Q1 denotes the top-performing schools and Q4 the low-performing schools. We find that the complexity of posts is correlated with users' academic performance (Fig. 1): users from high-performing schools (Q1) produce more complex texts than those from middle-performing schools (Q2, Q3), and users from middle-performing schools produce more complex texts than those from low-performing schools (Q4). However, we find no significant difference between middle-high (Q2) and middle-low (Q3) performing schools.

We find that the complexity of posts increases with age until the late 20s (Fig. 2). It is relatively stable through the 30s and increases again starting from the early 40s. The latter·fact is potentially explained by the sample bias. While VK use is ubiquitous among young people, the proportion of older people who use the social networking site is significantly lower. Less than half of users are in their 40s (124, 830) compared to those in their 30s (287, 641) in the dataset.

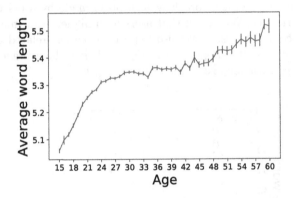

Fig. 2. Average word length in posts made by users of different ages in 2016. The average word length increases with age until the late 20s. The increase after the early 40s is potentially explained by the sample bias. Vertical bars are standard errors.

Finally, we compare the complexity of posts at different time points. We find that complexity increases over time (Fig. 3). This increase cannot be explained by aging alone: 15-year-old users in 2016 wrote more complex posts than users of any age in 2008. We call this phenomenon the digital Flynn effect by analogy with the so-called Flynn effect — the massive increase in IQ test scores over the course of the twentieth century [10–12].

Intriguingly, the observed growth cannot be explained by differences in characteristics of users who joined the social networking site at different time points. The average word length follows the same line, regardless of the year when the first post on VK was made (see Fig. 4).

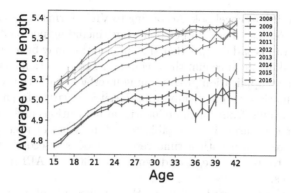

Fig. 3. The digital Flynn effect. The complexity of posts on a social networking site increases over time. Each line represents posts made by users of different ages in a given year. Vertical bars are standard errors.

These results are summarised in Table 1. A multiple linear regression was calculated to predict the average word lengths of posts made by a group of users based on their age (0 corresponds to 15 years old), the time since their first post in years and the time passed since the launch of VK in years (0 corresponds to 2008 in both cases). The regression was calculated for 15- to 23-year-old users, the period when we observe linear growth in post complexity.

Table 1. Coefficients from the regression model. Both age and year since the launch of VK correlate with complexity, however time since site adoption does not.

Parameter	Estimate	Std. Err
Intercept	4.734***	0.009
Age	0.022***	0.001
Year since site adoption	-0.002	0.002
Year since launch of VK	0.050***	0.001

*** - p-value $< 10^{-3}$. $R^2 = 0.828$

The largest increase in text complexity occurs between 2010 and 2011. We track changes in complexity with higher time resolution and find that the largest gain in average word length was between October 2010 and November 2010. This is probably related to the major change in site functionality on the 20th of October of that year. On this day, the News Feed and Wall were consolidated (a similar change in functionality was made by Facebook in 2008).

3   Methods

VK is the largest European social networking site, with more than 100 million active users. It was launched in September 2006 in Russia and provides functionality similar to Facebook. According to VK's Terms of Service: "Publishing any content on his / her own personal page, including personal information, the User understands and accepts that this information may be available to other Internet users taking into account the architecture and functionality of the Site".

VK provides an application programming interface (API) that enables downloading of information systematically from the site. In particular, it is possible to download user profiles from certain educational institutions and within selected age ranges. For each user, it is possible to obtain a list of their public posts. Posting times are known with a time resolution of one second. VK's support team confirmed to us that the data downloaded via their API may be used for research purposes.

Using specially-developed software, the profiles of all users from Saint-Petersburg were downloaded. We excluded users who have no VK friends from the same educational institution that was indicated in their profile. It was previously shown that this is an effective way to remove fake user profiles [13].

High school graduates are obliged to pass the standardized examination (Unified State Examination or USE) in Russia. The information about average USE scores of graduates for each school in Saint-Petersburg is publicly available for certain years. We use the distribution of these scores to assign to each school a corresponding quartile, splitting them into four groups: high-performing schools, middle-high-performing schools, middle-low-performing schools, and low-performing schools. The results for one cohort of students (born in 1993) to which the data is available are shown in Fig. 1. The relationship between time of site adoption and complexity growth in Fig. 4 is shown for the same cohort. Similar results were obtained for other cohorts.

We define a word as a sequence of Cyrillic letters. Words preceded by the pound sign (#) were excluded because hashtags typically contain multiple words without spaces between them. We also excluded words that contain the same

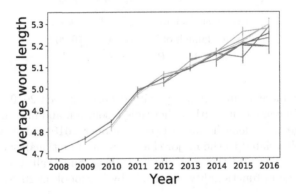

Fig. 4. Time of site adoption and post complexity. Each line corresponds to users who started to post on the social networking site in a given year. The observed growth in text complexity cannot be explained by time of site adoption by different groups of users. Vertical bars are standard errors.

letter three or more times in a row, in order to account for potential differences in word-lengthening practices among different groups of users. All posts written by a given user during a year were combined in one text, with the average length of words (mean value) in this text then being computed. We excluded users who wrote less than five posts in a given year. We also excluded all posts which contain a URL, in order to account for potential automatic posting by applications or websites. Only the original content written by users (not reposts of content written by someone else) were included in the dataset.

4 Discussion

We use average word length to measure language complexity of posts on a popular social networking site. We show that this measure is consistent with the assumed cognitive complexity of the posts: average word length increases with age and correlates with academic performance of users. We find that the complexity of posts is constantly increasing, and that this increase cannot be explained by aging alone. We call this phenomenon the digital Flynn effect.

Our results suggest that social media do not lead to language degradation. Instead, users change their language practices in this environment to produce more sophisticated texts than in previous years. It remains unclear whether the observed changes are specific to the particular social networking site, or reflect broader changes of language practices in online or even real-world settings. While there is not enough evidence to suggest a specific explanation of the observed changes, our results indicate that the way texts in social media are produced is constantly evolving. It might be important to investigate these changes in detail and to account for them in future research.

References

1. Drouin, M.A.: College students' text messaging, use of textese and literacy skills. J. Comput. Assist. Learn. **27**(1), 67–75 (2011)
2. Wood, C., Kemp, N., Plester, B.: Text Messaging And Literacy-the Evidence. Routledge, London (2013)
3. Zebroff, D.: Youth texting: Help or hindrance to literacy? Education and Information Technologies 1–16 (2017). doi:10.1007/s10639-017-9606-1
4. Gunning, R.: The Technique of Clear Writing. McGraw-Hill, New York (1952)
5. Flesch, R.F.: How To Write Plain English: A Book For Lawyers And Consumers. HarperCollins, New York (1979)
6. Karpov, N., Baranova, J., Vitugin, F.: Single-Sentence Readability Prediction in Russian. In: Ignatov, D.I., Khachay, M.Y., Panchenko, A., Konstantinova, N., Yavorskiy, R.E. (eds.) AIST 2014. CCIS, vol. 436, pp. 91–100. Springer, Cham (2014). doi:10.1007/978-3-319-12580-0_9
7. Yasseri, T., Kornai, A., Kertész, J.: A practical approach to language complexity: a wikipedia case study. PloS One **7**(11), e48386 (2012)
8. Nguyen, D.P., Gravel, R., Trieschnigg, R.B., Meder, T.: "How Old Do You Think I Am?" A Study Of Language And Age In Twitter (2013)

9. Pennebaker, J.W., Stone, L.D.: Words of wisdom: language use over the life span. J. Pers. Soc. Psychol. **85**(2), 291 (2003)
10. Flynn, J.R.: The mean iq of americans: Massive gains 1932 to 1978. Psychol. Bull. **95**(1), 29 (1984)
11. Flynn, J.R.: Massive iq gains in 14 nations: What iq tests really measure. Psychological bulletin **101**(2), 171 (1987)
12. Flynn, J.R.: What Is Intelligence?: Beyond The Flynn Effect. Cambridge University Press, Cambridge (2007)
13. Smirnov, I., Sivak, E., Kozmina, Y.: In search of lost profiles: the reliability of vkontakte data and its importance for educational research. Educ. Stud. Moscow **4**, 106–122 (2016)

An Exploration of Wikipedia Data as a Measure of Regional Knowledge Distribution

Fabian Stephany[1]([✉])[iD] and Fabian Braesemann[2][iD]

[1] Vienna University of Economics and Business, Vienna, Austria
fabian.stephany@wu.ac.at
[2] Oxford Internet Institute, University of Oxford, Oxford, UK
fabian.braesemann@oii.ox.ac.uk

Abstract. In today's economies, knowledge is the key ingredient for prosperity. However, it is hard to measure this intangible asset appropriately. Standard economic models mostly rely on common measures such as enrollment rates and international test scores. However, these proxies focus rather on the quality of education of pupils than on the distribution of knowledge among the whole population, which is increasingly defined by alternative sources of education such as online learning platforms. As a consequence, the economically relevant stock of knowledge in a region is only roughly approximated. Furthermore, they are abstract in content, and both capital-, and time-consuming in census. This paper proposes to explore Wikipedia data as an alternative source of capturing the knowledge distribution on a narrow geographical scale. Wikipedia is by far the largest digital encyclopedia worldwide and provides data on usage and editing publicly. We compare Wikipedia usage worldwide and edits in the U.S. to existing measures of the acquisition and stock of knowledge. The results indicate that there is a significant correlation between Wikipedia interactions and knowledge approximations on different geographical scales. Considering these results, it seems promising to further explore Wikipedia data to develop a reliable, inexpensive, and real-time proxy of knowledge distribution around the world.

JEL Classification: C 55 · C 82 · I 21

Keywords: Mining of big social data · Wikipedia · Knowledge geographies

1 Introduction

The stock of knowledge is a strong determinant for economic growth and the vast majority of economic forecasting models includes some kind of approximation for it. Most commonly, enrollment rates in tertiary education and standardized international education scores, such as the Programme for International Student Assessment (PISA) are used to capture the distribution of knowledge in economic

---

F. Stephany and F. Braesemann—Both authors contributed equally to this work.

G.L. Ciampaglia et al. (Eds.): SocInfo 2017, Part II, LNCS 10540, pp. 31–40, 2017.
DOI: 10.1007/978-3-319-67256-4_4

modeling. While the availability of these standard measures has increased over the last decades, these indicators are usually not available below the country level. Moreover, due to the complex process of data collection, they often lag significantly behind in time.

When it comes to relating knowledge or know-how to economic growth, particular knowledge in specific domains is most relevant. Scholars have argued that, from an economic point of view, increased enrollment in some subjects show higher return on investment than others. Most prominently, the acquisition of knowledge in natural and computer science, mathematics, as well as in engineering, seems to boost economic growth to a sizable extent [1]. The increasing digitalisation in many economic sectors suggests that this trend will continue in the future. At the same time, it remains questionable if assessments like PISA can reflect the complex distribution of knowledge across different disciplines. The capability of performing well in reading and calculus is certainly a basic requirement for the acquisition of further skills, but it does not represent the much higher stock of knowledge that is relevant for innovation and competitiveness in todays' high-tech economies. Additionally, international test scores only focus on a small reference group, in most cases students, while neglecting the knowledge distribution among the rest of the population.

At the same time, the education sector gets more and more digitized [2]. Massive open online course (MOOC) providers like *Coursera* and *Khan Academy* bring high-level education to people all over the world. While these technologies indisputable help individuals to acquire important knowledge, classical measurements like enrollment rates do not capture their effect on the stock of knowledge in a region.

As an alternative to other knowledge measurements, this work therefore proposes the exploration the world's largest on-line encyclopedia, Wikipedia, as a source for retrieving data about knowledge distribution on a global and narrow geographical scale.

Wikipedia data has the following properties that are appealing to use it as a source to measure knowledge: first, its predominance as general reference work makes it a first stop for many who seek information online; it is thus an important provider of knowledge.[1] Secondly, the content production is a collaborative project. Everyone is invited to contribute to the articles. Indeed, millions of users worldwide provide content to the different language versions of Wikipedia.[2] Thirdly, while consuming Wikipedia articles is a process that increases knowledge, editing articles is even more associated with personal learning [4–6]. Similar to the online learning activities described above, the contribution to Wikipedia content can thus be considered as a learning process related to domain-specific knowledge. Finally, Wikipedia data are publicly available.

---

[1] Wikipedia provides over 40 million articles in 250 languages worldwide and is ranked among the top-ten most popular websites, see [3].

[2] According the [3] the English language version alone has more than 30 million registered editors and additionally a large number of not-registered editors.

Usage data are published every month on country level.[3] The edit history of all articles can be collected via an SQL interface.[4] Since the articles are semi-hierarchically organised into categories, it is possible to assign edits into different domains of knowledge. Taking all this together, Wikipedia appears to be a valuable data source that allows to map the global distribution of knowledge. While it takes the macro-perspective of standardized knowledge assessments, it features the timeliness and availability of online data sources.

This article explores the feasibility of Wikipedia data to measure the stock of knowledge on different geographic scales by relating usage and edit data to common measures globally and in the United States.

2 Literature Review

As outlined in the introduction, the primary underlying assumption of this work is that engagement on Wikipedia, via usage and editing, reflects learning and the knowledge base of individuals and, as a consequence, of societies as a whole. Previous studies about topical editing on Wikipedia have found strong evidence for the assumption ([4–6]) that editing Wikipedia articles deepens the contributors' understanding of the articles' topic. Other scholars confirm that editors feel confident with the subject they are contributing to, as reported by Collier and Bear [7]. The authors also report some of the results of the Wikipedia user survey that has taken place in 2008. From 22,000 readers of the English Wikipedia that took part in the survey, more than 50% are students. The participating contributors report on average 14.7 years of education, which is slightly higher than the overall U.S. or U.K. average. Thus, the relation between domain knowledge and editing behaviour has been proven relevant on an individual level, but no large scale investigation on the relation between Wikipedia and knowledge measures has been undertaken so far.

Most studies that employ Wikipedia data, utilize the network of different language versions for each article. Examples are studies that focus on similarities between cultures [8–10] or the global influence of languages [11].

Additionally, the global scope of the online encyclopedia has encouraged the investigation on research questions with a geographical background. Yasseri et al. [12], for example, examine the geographical and linguistic similarities and differences between controversial topics on Wikipedia in so-called "edit wars". Their findings show that Wikipedia should be considered as more than "just" an encyclopedia, for it contains also information about socio-spatial patterns of interest groups, which can be observed as they develop over time. A similar study has been conducted by Borra et al. [13] who provide a tool that gives insights into the development of controversial topics on Wikipedia.

Similarly, Wikipedia activities can be used to mirror geographical circumstances. For instance, Graham et al. [14] show, in analysing all geocoded articles of the English Wikipedia, that regional imbalances in broadband connections

---

[3] http://bit.ly/PageViewsPerCountry.
[4] http://bit.ly/WikiSQL.

match the activity rates on Wikipedia. Analog to the physical world, the researchers map the participation patterns on Wikipedia. They underline the importance of access to knowledge, via Wikipedia, and advocate the democratization of the digital space in order to overcome existing "analog" inequalities. Other studies on participation and the geographical distribution of Wikipedia articles find spatial clusters in the knowledge production which lead to a digital underrepresentation of certain parts of the World ([15,16], and [17]).[5]

In summary, past contributions on Wikipedia have proven that a second use of its' data can help to answer specific research questions from the social sciences. However, to our best knowledge, there are no large-scale investigations on the applicability of Wikipedia data as a measure of knowledge distribution available so far.

3   Scope and Methodology

3.1   Access to Wikipedia and Knowledge Measures

Wikipedia is by far the largest online encyclopedia. The English Wikipedia alone counts roughly 3,000 views per second. Surely, the share of people that have regular access to the internet and as a consequence may visit Wikipedia varies significantly around the world. While large parts of the population in high-income countries use the internet on a daily basis, this is not the case for many developing countries.

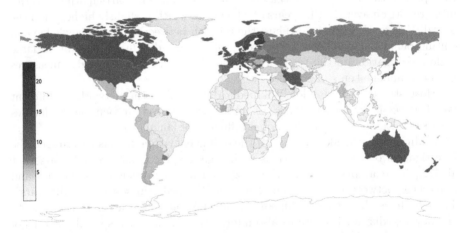

Fig. 1. Monthly Wikipedia clicks per internet user (averaged on the period 2011 to 2017) - Wikipedia is substantially more often visited in high income countries than in developing countries. China is an outlier with very few clicks per user.

As shown in Fig. 1, the clicks to Wikipedia per internet user are highest for high-income countries, lower for emerging economies and lowest for poor

---

[5] Visualiszations of these information geographies can be found here: [18,19].

countries, particularly in Africa. The map moreover shows that this pattern is largely consistent with only two major outliers. China, with more than 650 million internet users counts on average only 0.2 monthly Wikipedia clicks per user. This is a clear indication of the distorted internet access in China. The other outlier is Iran with more than 10 monthly Wikipedia clicks per user on average. These examples show that one needs to be cautious in making far-fetched claims on the general inference of results gained by the big data analysis of Wikipedia. However, the rates of usage across high-income countries indicate the prevalence of Wikipedia across the populations of these countries.

It is one of the main assertions in this article that the distribution of Wikipedia usage does not only reflect economic circumstances, but that it is rather related to differences in the stock of knowledge in the respective economies. If one consults Wikipedia especially in the process of learning or acquiring knowledge about a specific topic, then it should be expected that classical measures like student enrollment rates are related to Wikipedia clicks. In order to investigate this hypothesis, we collect tertiary enrollment rates as well as economic control variables on a country level from the World Bank.[6] The Wikipedia usage level is collected from the Wikimedia Foundation.[7]

3.2   Wikipedia Edit Data

While Wikipedia usage data is only available on a very aggregated level, information about the edits to Wikipedia can be collected in much more detail. This is true for the geographical dimension, as many editors are identified by their IP-address which can be geolocated on a narrow geographical scale (at least for many developed countries), as well as for the topic of contribution. The edits are displayed for each single article. The articles themselves are summarised into categories and sub-categories. Following the tree-like structure of the categories starting by a relatively broad one, it is thus possible to collect a lot of data on the geographical origin of edits in a specific domain.

To test the feasibility of the proposed approach, we concentrate in this article on one specific category of Wikipedia articles: all pages that are linked to the category "Computer Science" and its subcategories to a depth of two subcategory-layers.[8] Moreover, the analysis is limited to the English version of Wikipedia. In total, the edits of 12,669 Wikipedia pages that are linked to 203 subcategories of the category "Computer Science" have been collected via the SQL-interface provided by the Wikimedia Foundation.[9] This leads to 467,896 edits (date of data collection: 26th June 2017) with an IP-address. After geocoding the IP-addresses

---

[6] http://data.worldbank.org/.

[7] http://bit.ly/PageViewsPerCountry.

[8] Thus we include all articles that link to the category "Computer Science" itself (level 1), to the subcategories that link to the "Computer Science" (level 2) and to their subcategories (level 3). This number of layers has been chosen to avoid the collection of edit data that are only very weakly related to computer science.

[9] http://bit.ly/WikiSQL.

using the *freegeoip.net*-API, we end up with 60,326 individual IP-addresses in the United States that are considered as individual editors contributing to the domain "Computer Science".

4 Findings

The results on the relation between Wikipedia usage and tertiary enrollment rates on a country level are summarised in model (1) in Table 1. Wikipedia click rates per internet user are available for the years 2011 to 2016. The World Bank provides information on tertiary enrollment for 127 countries. In total, 492 country-year observations are included in a simple regression model that relates the Wikipedia clicks per users to the share of urban population, GDP per capita, and the tertiary gross enrollment rate. Even on this very aggregate level, the regression shows a highly significant relation between tertiary enrollment, a classical knowledge measure commonly applied in economic models, and Wikipedia usage. Moreover, and as expected from the illustration in Fig. 1, Wikipedia clicks are also highly correlated with GDP per capita. This result can be considered as a first indication in favour of the hypothesis that, on a macro level, Wikipedia interactions are related to the acquisition of knowledge. However, since usage data are not available on a more narrow level, the potential of this type of analysis is limited.

More revealing results with respect to the relation between the stock of specific knowledge and Wikipedia interactions can be gained by considering editing data. Figure 2 shows the number of "editors" (individual geolocated IP-addresses) in computer science per state and for the 307 largest cities with more than 100,000 population in the United States. We focus on the U.S. in order to avoid effects of the different language versions of Wikipedia. Moreover, the U.S. are culturally largely homogeneous and many data about the economy and education are available, even on a city level. The darker the contour of the state, the more editors per 100,000 population. The share of editors in computer science on the city level is captured by the size of the circle at the location of the city.[10] The colour represents the presence of an academic computer science department in the city.

Interestingly, the more urban states at the coasts show a higher level of editors than the more rural states in the center of the United States. Particularly revealing is however the relation between cities with and without an academic computer science department. Obviously, there are more large dark circles than large bright circles, indicating a difference in the number of editors between both types of cities. While the cities with computer science department count on average 51.1 editors, the cities without computer science department have on average 18.2 computer science editors. Prominent examples in the map are Cambridge in Massachusetts, as well as Berkley, Pasadena and Seattle.

---

[10] An interactive version of the map can be accessed via the online dashboard that provides supplementary information to this article: http://bit.ly/Wiki_Dashboard.

Table 1. Regression results on three different models on the relation between knowledge indicators and Wikipedia usage/editing - In all three models the relative number of Wikipedia usage in general/ Editors in computer science is related to control variables and indicators of knowledge.

	(1)	(2)	(3)
Dimension	Country-Year	U.S. states	U.S. cities
Dep. Variable (log. values)	Clicks per User[a]	Editors in CS.	per 100,000 Population
Observations	492	51	160
Intercept	−11.72 (1.83)***	0.36 (0.25)	2.01 (0.21)***
% Urban Pop	0.00 (0.01)	0.22 (0.13)	
GDP per capita[b]	1.56 (0.25)***	−0.00 (0.01)	
Tertiary gross enrollment	0.07 (0.01)***		
% Internet users		1.85 (0.35)***	
% Advanced degree		2.85 (0.79)***	
Pop. Density			0.001 (0.00)**
Med. Age			0.009 (0.01)
Med. Income			0.000 (0.00)
Share of Students			2.952 (0.47)***
CS Department			0.589 (0.11)***
Adj. R^2	0.49	0.30	0.29

[a] 127 countries from 2011–2016
[b] For model (1) as log of PPP current international USD

These descriptive results are confirmed by the inferential models presented in Table 1. Model (2) relates the share of editors per 100,000 population on a state level (50 states and the District of Columbia) to the share of urban population, GDP per capita, the share of internet users and the share of individuals with an advanced degree (Master or PhD).[11] Both the portion of internet users and the share of advanced degree holders, indicating the stock of knowledge, are significantly related to the number of editors in computer science.

On an even more granular level, model (3) shows that the number of editors is significantly correlated to the number of students and the presence of a computer science department in the city.[12]

These results confirm the hypothesis, at least for the example of computer science, that Wikipedia data is suitable to capture the stock of knowledge on a very granular geographical level.

---

[11] The data stems from the U.S. census: https://www.census.gov/.

[12] Data on the number of students stems from http://www.stateuniversity.com/. City-level covariates are collected from http://www.city-data.com// and a list of academic computer science departments is available on Wikipedia: http://bit.ly/CS_Departments.

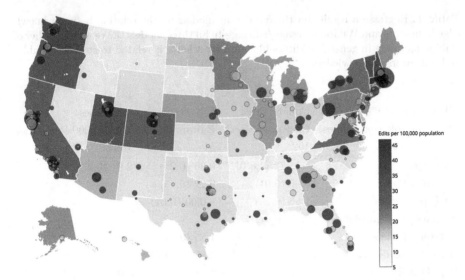

Fig. 2. Computer science edits per 100,000 population on U.S. state and city level - On a regional level, edits in computer science differ substantially across the United States, particularly between the more urban states at east and west coast and the more rural states in the center. Moreover, even larger differences are evident on a city level, as displayed by the circles for the 307 U.S. cities with more than 100,000 population. The color represents the presence of an academic computer science department in the city (dark gray: Department = 1, light gray: No Department = 0). Those cities with an computer science department have on average significantly more computer science edits per 100,000 population than those cities without such an institute: $\bar{x}_1 = 51.1, \bar{x}_0 = 18.2$. (Color figure online)

5   Conclusion and Future Work

The goal of this exploratory analysis is to test the feasibility of Wikipedia as a data source to measure the stock of knowledge. The initial findings confirm, first, that it is feasible to establish a robust relationship between Wikipedia data and traditional metrics of knowledge. Page views correlate to a sizable extent with tertiary education rates on a country level. For specific fields of knowledge this association is shown to be even more pronounced when compared to domain-specific Wikipedia engagement. For the case of Wikipedia editors in computer science, it can be shown on a fine-grained geographical level that they are significantly correlated with real-world entities of knowledge production, namely the presence of an academic computer science department on a city level. This relation is robust on top of the share of student population per city, which is incorporated into the inferential model as control variable. The most prominent cities with respect to computer science edits per capita are the places of top universities in the United States. It is an astonishing that the approach of simply counting the number of IP-addresses in the editing history of specific Wikipedia articles reveals exactly this result.

This study sheds some light on the enormous potential of Wikipedia as a data source to proxy the stock of knowledge. In order to investigate how robust and generalisable the results are, more Wikipedia data from more domains should be analysed. Moreover, it would be interesting to investigate whether Wikipedia edit data can actually be employed to accurately predict the presence of a specific academic department in a city. For this purpose, more sophisticated data science algorithms should be used.

Nonetheless, it can be summarised that the access to data with both a precise geographical and contextual focus opens a vast horizon for exploring domain-specific regional knowledge distribution via Wikipedia.

Acknowledgements. The authors are thankful for the feedback this work received on the brown-bag seminar at the Oxford Internet Institute and the SIS Statistics and Data Science conference in Florence, both taken place in June 2017. Particularly helpful comments have been made by Scott Hale, Otto Kässi, and Taha Yasseri.

References

1. Benos, N., Zotou, S.: Education and economic growth: a meta-regression analysis. World Dev. **64**, 669–689 (2014). doi:10.1016/j.worlddev.2014.06.034
2. Mayer-Schönberger, V., Cukier, K.: Learning with Big Data: The Future of Education. Houghton Mifflin Harcourt, New York (2014)
3. Wikimedia, Wikipedia (2017). https://en.wikipedia.org/wiki/Wikipedia
4. Moy, C.L., Locke, J.R., Coppola, B.P., McNeil, A.J.: Improving science education and understanding through editing Wikipedia. J. Chem. Educ. **87**(11), 1159–1162 (2010). doi:10.1021/ed100367v
5. Ebner, M., Kickmeier-Rust, M., Holzinger, A.: Utilizing Wiki-Systems in higher education classes: a chance for universal access? Univ. Access Inf. Soc. **7**(4), 199 (2008). doi:10.1007/s10209-008-0115-2
6. Cain, J., Fox, B.I.: Web 2.0 and pharmacy education. Am. J. Pharm. Educ. **73**(7), 120 (2009). doi:10.5688/aj7307120
7. Collier, B., Bear, J.: Conflict, criticism, or confidence: an empirical examination of the gender gap in Wikipedia contributions. In: Proceedings of the ACM 2012 Conference on Computer Supported Cooperative Work, pp. 383–392. ACM (2012)
8. Gloor, P., De Boer, P., Lo, W., Wagner, S., Nemoto, K., Fuehres, H.: Cultural Anthropology Through the Lens of Wikipedia-A Comparison of Historical Leadership Networks in the English, Chinese, Japanese and German Wikipedia, arXiv preprint arXiv:1502.05256
9. Eom, Y.-H., Aragón, P., Laniado, D., Kaltenbrunner, A., Vigna, S., Shepelyansky, D.L.: Interactions of cultures and top people of Wikipedia from ranking of 24 language editions. PloS one **10**(3), e0114825 (2015)
10. Laufer, P., Wagner, C., Flöck, F., Strohmaier, M.: Mining cross-cultural relations from Wikipedia: a study of 31 European food cultures. In: Proceedings of the ACM Web Science Conference, p. 3. ACM (2015)
11. Ronen, S., Gonçalves, B., Hu, K.Z., Vespignani, A., Pinker, S., Hidalgo, C.A.: Links that speak: the global language network and its association with global fame. Proc. Nat. Acad. Sci. **111**(52), E5616–E5622 (2014)
12. Yasseri, T., Spoerri, A., Graham, M., Kertész, J.: The most controversial topics in Wikipedia: a multilingual and geographical analysis. arXiv:1305.5566 [physics]

13. Borra, E., Weltevrede, E., Ciuccarelli, P., Kaltenbrunner, A., Laniado, D., Magni, G., Mauri, M., Rogers, R., Venturini, T.: Societal controversies in Wikipedia articles. In: Proceedings of the 33rd Annual ACM Conference on Human Factors in Computing Systems, pp. 193–196. ACM (2015)

14. Graham, M., Straumann, R.K., Hogan, B.: Digital divisions of labor and informational magnetism: mapping participation in Wikipedia. Ann. Assoc. Am. Geogr. **105**(6), 158–1178 (2015). doi:10.1080/00045608.2015.1072791

15. Graham, M., Hogan, B., Straumann, R.K., Medhat, A.: Uneven geographies of user-generated information: patterns of increasing informational poverty. Ann. Assoc. Am. Geogr. **104**(4), 746–764 (2014)

16. Graham, M., De Sabbata, S., Zook, M.A.: Towards a study of information geographies: (im) mutable augmentations and a mapping of the geographies of information. Geo: Geogr. Environ. **2**(1), 88–105 (2015)

17. Hardy, D., Frew, J., Goodchild, M.F.: Volunteered geographic information production as a spatial process. Int. J. Geogr. Inf. Sci. **26**(7), 1191–1212 (2012)

18. Graham, M., De Sabbata, S.: Information Geographies at the Oxford Internet Institute (2014). http://geography.oii.ox.ac.uk/

19. Liao, H.-T., Hogan, B., Graham, M., Hale, S.A., Ford, H.: Wikipedia's Networks and Geographies: Representation and Power in Peer-Produced Content (2010). https://www.oii.ox.ac.uk/research/projects/wikipedias-networks-and-geographies/

Differential Network Effects on Economic Outcomes: A Structural Perspective

Eaman Jahani[1(✉)], Guillaume Saint-Jacques[2], Pål Sundsøy[3],
Johannes Bjelland[3], Esteban Moro[4,5], and Alex 'Sandy' Pentland[1,5]

[1] Institute for Data, Systems and Society, MIT, Cambridge, USA
eaman@mit.edu
[2] Sloan School of Management, MIT, Cambridge, USA
[3] Telenor Group Research, Fornebu, Norway
[4] Universidad Carlos III de Madrid, Madrid, Spain
[5] Media Lab, MIT, Cambridge, USA

Abstract. In a study of about 33,000 individuals in a south Asian country, we find that structural diversity, measured as the fraction of open triads in an ego-network, shows a relatively strong association with individual income. After including all the relevant control variables, the effect of structural diversity becomes exclusive to the highly educated individuals. We hypothesize these results are due to concentrated distribution of economic opportunities among the highly educated social strata combined with homophily among members of the same group. This process leads to two important societal consequences: extra network advantages for the highly educated, similar to the rich club effect, and inadequate diffusion of economic opportunities to the low educated social strata.

Keywords: Ego-networks · Structural diversity · Income · Social status

1 Introduction

The impact of social networks on individual performance has been the subject of much interest in sociology and economics. The role of social ties on outcomes has been studied in various contexts such as health [4], education [7], productivity in firms [18,19], knowledge transfer [20] and regional prosperity [5]. Within the sociology literature, most of the attention has centered on the effect of informal social networks on the economic outcomes, and in particular job search. The foundational work by Granovetter [9,10] demonstrated that economic activity, and in particular job search, is embedded in informal social networks. Therefore, the local network influences the access to high quality employment opportunities. Later studies have built more context to the original theory of Granovetter and shown how use of social networks affects youth unemployment [1], varies by the category of the job right after college [16], interacts with education and

---

The original version of this chapter was revised: An acknowledgement has been added. The erratum to this chapter is available at https://doi.org/10.1007/978-3-319-67256-4_44

G.L. Ciampaglia et al. (Eds.): SocInfo 2017, Part II, LNCS 10540, pp. 41–50, 2017.
DOI: 10.1007/978-3-319-67256-4_5

leads to different outcomes depending on the extent of social isolation [6]. Nevertheless, there have been few studies on the relationship between *local network* characteristics and the most important economic outcome, namely *income*.

The closest outcome variable to income appears in the work of Lin et al. [13], which demonstrates that the social status of local contacts in the informal social network has a strong impact on the prestige of the attained job. However the prestige of the attained job as measured by Blau-Duncans SEI score [2] is too coarse since it does not capture the variations within a single occupation. A recent paper [15] did investigate the link between income and position in the global network and found that centrality of individuals is highly correlated with personal economic status. While such macro-level measures are excellent for prediction, they are too coarse for studying the flow of economic opportunities from local contacts, hence provide little sociological insight on the effect of personal social choices in the socio-economical status of individuals. Therefore in this work, we directly measure the connection between the capacity of an *individual's ego-network in terms of access to diverse information sources among the local contacts* and their *income*. This allows us to account for all the observable variation in the economic outcomes at an individual level, hence generalizing the results of [13]. Furthermore by focusing our attention on local contacts, we are able to develop insights into local network processes that provide access to economic opportunities and how the efficiency of these processes interact with other variables, such as social status.

As noted by [11], the effect of informal ego-networks on economic outcomes, and in particular job search, can be explained by four mechanisms of employer, worker, and most importantly *contact and relational heterogeneity*. Most of the previous studies on the effect of networks on economic outcomes have focused on contact heterogeneity: the variation in endowments or the micro characteristics of contacts in the network, such as their education or gender, as different manifestations of social capital. For example, [17] looked at the number of unique occupations and the proportion of white males present among the contacts and its effect of job leads. Similarly, Elliott [6] investigates how race and neighborhood location and the strength of a tie determine the level of social isolation and consequently how insulated an individual is from the labor market. Lin, Vaughn and Ensel [14] look at outcomes in job referrals and report that the occupational status of the contact, as a measure of social resources, has a strong impact on the prestige of the obtained job.

The *relational information on contacts* in an ego-network is more general than information on contact characteristics, since relational variation depends on the overall structure of the ego-network, and not only the characteristics of individual contacts. The theoretical underpinning for the impact of relational variation on economic outcomes revolves around the Granovetter weak tie theory [8]. The strong ties are associated with dense networks and triadic closures and as a result exhibit high levels of information redundancy. In contrast, weak ties tend to be bridges to diverse communities, hence have superior information novelty. With the exception of work by Burt [3] which investigated managerial success, there has not been any studies that examine the link between the full structure of the ego-network and economic outcomes, and as in our case income. Most works on the effect of relational heterogeneity have instead focused on the strength of the ties to information sources. In this study, we examine the effect of overall ego-network structure, namely its *structural diversity*, as a measure of relational heterogeneity on economic outcomes using about 33,000 surveyed individuals, a much larger scale compared to previous studies.

We have three empirical contributions in this paper. First, we examine the effect of the structural diversity of ego-networks on economic outcomes. Structural diversity is a relational characteristic that is an indication of the level of information novelty among the contacts based on their connections to each other. Second, we use income as our measure of economic outcome instead of the prestige of the jobs obtained through informal referral. By using income rather than job prestige, we generalize previous findings on network effects which have been mainly limited to labor-market outcomes. Furthermore, we believe income is an explicit measure of economic well-being which can be directly used in policy analysis. Finally, we provide evidence for the differential effects of structural diversity across different educational levels. We show that individuals with high educational status receive larger benefits from the same level of structural diversity when compared to individuals with low educational status. This result is most similar to findings in [13,14] in which the status of the informal contact had a direct and large effect on the status of the attained job. When considered along with homophily and stratification across social status, the results of [13,14] suggest that high status individuals receive larger benefits from their social contacts than low status individuals. This observation is in agreement with our findings. However there is an important difference between the observation of Lin et al and our findings, since in their case the differential effects are due to heterogeneity in contact characteristics. In contrast, we report the same phenomena from a relational perspective: *high status individuals have differential advantages stemming from the structure of their ego-networks, regardless of the characteristics of their contacts.*

2   Data

We use an anonymized mobile phone dataset containing one month of standard metadata in a developing country in South Asia. Our goal is to study the relationship between individual income and local structural characteristics of the network. In particular we focus on a local view of the network called ego-network. The focal node of interest is called the ego whereas all ego's connections are called alters. In addition to ego-alter edges, the ego-network includes all the edges between the alters, thus enabling us to study structural factors that are not directly controlled by the ego.

2.1   Income Data

The income categories for a random selection of more than 270,000 individuals across the country were obtained through three sequential large-scale market research household surveys. 101,500 of these surveyed individuals were customers of our phone carrier. Out of these initial 101,500 individual surveys, we restricted our data to those who are employed (no students, housewives, unemployed or retired) and are at least 25 years old. Furthermore, to prevent our results from getting biased by inactive egos without enough communication data, we limited our data only to those individuals who had a phone communication with more than 5 unique individuals over the one month period of the phone data (Approximately 20% of individuals have *degree* ≤ 5). This smaller subset of surveys accounted for 32,870 subscribers who we treated as the egos in our analysis. Information about income was directly asked from the respondents, who were requested to place themselves within pre-defined income bins. Several other demographic characteristics such as education, gender, age and occupation were obtained through the same survey. Survey participants were distributed across 220 sales territories proportional to their population so that there were overall about 400 surveyed households in each sales territory. Systematic sampling was undertaken by selecting every fourth household, starting from a randomly selected geographic reference point and direction within each sub-territory. Respondents within the household were selected via the Kish grid method [12] among those who were eligible. Eligibility was defined as individuals with their own phone, between 15 and 65 years of age. The monthly income values were coded as ordinal categories from 1–13. Table 1 summarizes the correspondence between the income categories and their actual monetary value after conversion to US dollars. Figure 1 illustrates the income distribution among our egos. The Pearson correlation between the projected average income per region based on the survey results and their actual values published in official statistics is 0.925.

2.2   Social Network Data

We used one month of raw Call Detail Records (CDR) for all carrier subscribers to construct a large-scale undirected call graph, in which two individuals are connected if there is a call between the two in both direction during the observation period. Raw CDR records for each user contain the following metadata:

1. Interactions type (SMS or Call)
2. Correspondent ID (The unique identifier of the contact)
3. Direction (Incoming or Outgoing)
4. Date and time of the interaction
5. Duration of Interaction (Only valid for calls)
6. Location of cell tower serving the subscriber (Latitude and Longitude)

Edges in the call graph are weighted by the total number of phone calls between the two individuals during the observation period. From the full call graph, we extracted individual undirected ego-networks corresponding to the surveyed individuals for whom we also have income and demographics information. It is important to note that the ego-networks only contain the reciprocal links to avoid spurious one-time contacts (e.g. telemarketing) to influence our results.

Table 1. Survey relationship between household income categories and corresponding range in US dollars.

Income Category	Monthly Household Income ($)	Frequency
1	0-33	1895
2	33-78	9351
3	78-130	29718
4	130-195	28532
5	195-260	17841
6	260-325	9995
7	325-390	4536
8	390-455	3752
9	455-520	2341
10	520-585	929
11	585-651	999
12	651-1301	966
13	1301+	274

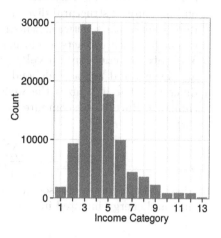

Fig. 1. Income Distribution of Egos

3 Variables

Dependent Variable: As mentioned in Sect. 2, we obtained income data for a subset of about 33,000 egos through surveys. Since income is not observed as a continuous variable, we use the middle income value in each category as representing its actual income value. As confirmed in Fig. 1, the raw income values exhibits a log-normal distribution. Therefore, middle income value of the category in USD converted to the log-scale will serve as our dependent variable.

Independent Variable: Structural diversity serves as our main independent variable. To ensure our results are robust, we perform the analysis using three different operatinalizations of structural diversity:

1. **Density** measures the completeness of the local network, and is defined as the fraction of ties from a fully-connected network that exist in the ego network. Sparsity in the ego network is an indication of structural holes and that the ego acts as a bridge between the alters, who belong to different communities. Low density also means that there is little redundancy in the ego network and most alters act as novel sources of information. Since lower values of density correspond to sparsity, we use (1-density) as our first measure of structural diversity.
2. **Clustering Coefficient** measures the fraction of closed triads in the ego network. Similar to the explanation above for density, lower values of clustering coefficient indicate diversity, non-redundancy and independence

among the contacts. Therefore, we use (1 - clustering coefficient) as our second measure of structural diversity. This would effectively measure the fraction of alter pairs between whom ego acts as a bridge which indicates the extent to which ego acts a information broker in their network.

3. **Weighted Structural Novelty** also measures the extent to which the alters are diverse and act as independent sources of information, with the main difference that it utilizes the weights of the edges. Following an argument similar to Burt [3], we compute the fraction of novelty among alters of an ego i as:

$$M_i = \frac{\sum_{j \in N(i)}(1 - \sum_{q \in N(j) \cap N(i)} p_{iq}p_{qj})}{|N(i)|} \quad i \neq j \neq q \quad (1)$$

where $N(k)$ denotes the set of k neighbors, p_{ij} is the proportion of ego i's time and energy invested in the tie with contact j:

$$p_{ij} = \frac{z_{ij}}{\sum_{q \in N(i)} z_{iq}} \quad i \neq j \quad (2)$$

where z_{ij} denote the strength of the tie or the edge weight (number of phone calls) between i and j. The term $\sum_{q \in N(j) \cap N(i)} p_{iq}p_{qj}$ in Eq. 1 represents redundancy or the extent to which information held by alter j can reach ego i through other pathways.

In addition to structural diversity, we use the level of education to demonstrate the differential effect of diversity across different social strata. The country of our interest experiences an excessive level of hereditary stratification and for this reason we believe education serves as a sufficient proxy for social status. Education will be coded as a binary variable, with high corresponding to high school, Bachelors or Masters and low corresponding to illiterate, primary school or middle school.

Control Variables: In order to control for possible confounders with income, we will include profession (a categorical variable), gender, level of education (a binary variable), age (an interval variable) and the home location of each ego on a 5×5 grid over the country (a categorical variable) as control variables in our regression analysis. Including age ensures we compare income values along the same career phases and allows us to control for long-term changes in communication patterns that are associated with variation in income. By controlling for location fixed effects, we obtain a more justified comparison of income opportunities between individuals across vastly different geographical areas (e.g. urban vs. rural). The log degree of the ego must be present as another control variable in the model, because various measures of structural diversity (e.g. density) are correlated with degree and have different scales or reasonable ranges as the ego network grows larger. For example, as the degree of the ego increases, a fully connected ego-network, corresponding to a density of 1, becomes more unlikely since the edges between alters are not independent and in particular depend on the size of the ego-network. The clustering coefficient and log degree have a correlation of 0.4 in our data.

4 Results and Discussion

Our goal is to study the effect of informal networks on career success measured in terms of income, therefore before performing the regression analysis, we excluded those egos who do not hold a valid occupation (student or housewife or retired or unemployed).

Model Specification: The equation below demonstrates the model we will use in the regression analysis:

$$Y = \beta_0 + \beta_1 * I_{high} + \beta_2 * SD + \beta_3 * SD * I_{high} + C + \epsilon \qquad (3)$$

where Y and SD corresponds to income and structural diversity respectively and I_{high} is an indicator variable taking a value of 1 when ego belongs to the high education group and 0 otherwise and C corresponds to the control variables. We have three main hypothesis:

1. More structurally diverse networks are associated with higher income: $\beta_2 > 0$
2. Everything being equal, individuals with low education level have a *deficit* in their economic outcomes: $\beta_1 > 0$.
3. Individuals from a high education level have a larger *return* to the structural diversity of their networks: $\beta_3 > 0$. Note that the *return* refers to the marginal effect of structural diversity.

Table 2 shows our regression results where structural diversity is measured as clustering coefficient and in each column we successively add more control variables. We make two main observations from the results. First, all three hypothesis are validated in all models, with the exception of hypothesis 1 in model 6. Second, in model 6 which includes all the control variables, structural diversity provides no return on income for the group with low education. Effectively, only individuals with high education benefit from access to structurally diverse sources of information. We obtained similar results using the other two operationalizations of structural diversity, which points to the robustness of these observed effects. It should be noted that females in our data tend to have higher income than men; because while women in our country of study are generally housewives, those women who are employed disproportionately hold better paying jobs such as teacher or government worker.

These results confirm our main argument that information and economic opportunities are not distributed uniformly across the social network and high status individuals have an advantage in terms of their returns to networking. A potential mechanism that explains the differential returns to structural diversity relies on homophily. When the concentration of information about economic opportunities within high status and influential social strata is combined with strongly homophilous ties among individuals from the same social strata, the result is differential benefits of high status individuals from networking.

To strengthen the external validity of our findings, we plan to replicate this study on a similar data set from a different country as future work. Finally, we

Table 2. Full Regression Results. Each column successively adds more controls variables to the model. High Education and Gender are binary indicator variables. Age, Profession and Location are all categorical variables and not shown among the control variables, but their corresponding rows indicate in which models they are included. Structural diversity is measured by clustering coefficient, but the results for other operationalizations of structural diversity are similar. Degree exhibits a power law distribution, thus it is transformed to log scale. Both Structural diversity and degree are standardized.

	Log Income					
	(1)	(2)	(3)	(4)	(5)	(6)
Structural Diversity	0.037***	0.019***	0.019***	0.019***	0.008**	−0.003
	(0.004)	(0.004)	(0.004)	(0.004)	(0.004)	(0.004)
Structural Diversity:	0.037***	0.033***	0.035***	0.034***	0.033***	0.025***
High Education	(0.007)	(0.007)	(0.007)	(0.007)	(0.006)	(0.006)
High Education	0.500***	0.489***	0.482***	0.487***	0.305***	0.291***
	(0.007)	(0.007)	(0.007)	(0.007)	(0.009)	(0.008)
Degree		0.047***	0.048***	0.048***	0.033***	0.036***
		(0.004)	(0.004)	(0.004)	(0.003)	(0.003)
Gender Female			0.081***	0.094***	0.095***	0.072***
			(0.012)	(0.012)	(0.012)	(0.011)
Age Included	No	No	No	Yes	Yes	Yes
Profession Included	No	No	No	No	Yes	Yes
Location Included	No	No	No	No	No	Yes
Number of Variables	4	5	6	13	29	44
Observations	32,870	32,870	32,870	32,870	32,870	32,870
R^2	0.153	0.158	0.159	0.168	0.243	0.301
Adjusted R^2	0.153	0.158	0.159	0.167	0.242	0.300
Residual Std. Error	0.583	0.581	0.581	0.578	0.551	0.530
F Statistic	1,980.9***	1,537.8***	1,241.0***	551.9***	376.2***	329.3***

Note: $^*p<0.1$; $^{**}p<0.05$; $^{***}p<0.01$

should mention that our claims are in no way causal since for establishing the causality we need an appropriate instrumental variable in place of structural diversity and social status. Nevertheless, we believe the observation of such differential effects, matching our theoretical expectation, renders the possibility of confounding effects unlikely.

5   Conclusion

In this study, we define the concept of *structural diversity as the extent to which the structure of a local network lacks information redundancy* and displays potential for access to diverse and independent sources of economic opportunity. We show that structural diversity, measured as the fraction of open triads in an ego-network, has a significant association with economic outcomes, mainly income, even after controlling for education, occupation, age and gender. We do this by using the ego-networks of about 33,000 individuals derived from mobile phone communication meta data matched with income and demographic variables at the individual level collected through surveys. Our findings suggest that structural diversity generally has a positive effect on income, but the benefits of structural diversity are larger for individuals with high education. This result is in agreement with a previous related study [13] in which the social status of the informal contacts determined the prestige of the obtained job. We believe this phenomenon is due to two factors: homophily and the concentrated distribution of economic opportunities among the highly educated social strata. A negative consequence of this process is the insufficient diffusion of economic opportunities to the low educated social strata.

Acknowledgement. This material is based upon work supported by the National Science Foundation Graduate Research Fellowship under Grant No. 1122374. Any opinion, findings, and conclusions or recommendations expressed in this material are those of the authors(s) and do not necessarily reflect the views of the National Science Foundation.

References

1. Åberg, Y., Hedström, P.: Youth unemployment : a self-reinforcing process?. In: Demeulenaere, P. (ed.) Analytical Sociology and Social Mechanisms, p. 201. Cambridge University Press, New York (2011)
2. Blau, P.M., Duncan, O.D.: The American Occupational Structure, vol. 33 (1968)
3. Burt, R.S.: Structural holes and good ideas. Am. J. Sociol. **110**(2), 349–399 (2004)
4. Christakis, N., Fowler, J.: The collective dynamics of smoking in a large social network. N. Engl. J. Med. **21358**(22), 2249–2258 (2007)
5. Eagle, N., Macy, M., Claxton, R.: Network diversity and economic development. Science **335**, 1215–1220 (2012)
6. Elliott, J.R.: Social isolation and labor market insulation: network and neighborhood effects on less-educated urban workers. Sociol. Q. **40**(2), 199–216 (1999)
7. Epple, D., Romano, R.E.: Peer effects in education: a survey of the theory and evidence. Handb. Soc. Econ. **1**(1B), 1053–1163 (2011)
8. Granovetter, M.: The strength of weak ties. J. Sociol. **78**(6), 1360–1380 (1973)
9. Granovetter, M.: Economic action and social structure: the problem of embeddedness. Am. J. Sociol. **91**(3), 481–510 (1985)
10. Granovetter, M.S.: Getting a Job: A Study of Contacts and Careers, vol. 25. University of Chicago Press, Chicago (1996)
11. Ioannides, Y.M., Datcher, L.: Job information networks, neighborhood effects, and inequality. J. Econ. Lit. **42**(4), 1056–1093 (2004)
12. Kish, L.: A procedure for objective respondent selection within the household. J. Am. Stat. Assoc. **44**(247), 380 (1949)
13. Lin, N., Ensel, W.M., Vaughn, J.C.: Social resources and strength of ties : structural factors in occupational status attainment. Am. Sociol. Rev. **46**(4), 393–405 (1981)

14. Lin, N., Ensel, W.M., Vaughn, J.C.: Social resources and occupational status attainment. Am. Sociol. Rev. **59**(46), 393–405 (1981)
15. Luo, S., Morone, F., Sarraute, C., Travizano, M., Makse, H.A.: Inferring personal economic status from social network location. Nat. Commun. **8** (2017). 15227
16. Marmaros, D., Sacerdote, B.: Peer and social networks in job search. Eur. Econ. Rev. **46**(4–5), 870–879 (2002)
17. McDonald, S., Lin, N., Ao, D.: Networks of opportunity: gender, race, and job leads. Soc. Probl. **56**(3), 385–402 (2009)
18. Reagans, R., Mcevily, B.: Source network structure and knowledge transfer: the effects of cohesion and range. Adm. Sci. Q. **48**(2), 240–267 (2012)
19. Reagans, R., Zuckerman, E.W.: Networks, diversity, and productivity: the social capital of corporate R&D teams. Organ. Sci. **12**(4), 502–517 (2001)
20. Wu, L., Waber, B., Brynjolfsson, E., Pentland, A.S.: Mining face-to-face interaction networks using socimetric badges: predicting productivity in an ITC configuation task. In: ICIS. pp. 1–19 (2008)

Poster Papers: Health and Behaviour

Stance Classification in Out-of-Domain Rumours: A Case Study Around Mental Health Disorders

Ahmet Aker[1,2(✉)], Arkaitz Zubiaga[3], Kalina Bontcheva[1], Anna Kolliakou[4], Rob Procter[3,5], and Maria Liakata[3,5]

[1] University of Sheffield, Sheffield, UK
a.aker@is.inf.uni-due.de
[2] University of Duisburg-Essen, Duisburg, Germany
[3] University of Warwick, Coventry, UK
[4] King's College London, London, UK
[5] Alan Turing Institute, London, UK

Abstract. Social media being a prolific source of rumours, stance classification of individual posts towards rumours has gained attention in the past few years. Classification of stance in individual posts can then be useful to determine the veracity of a rumour. Research in this direction has looked at rumours in different domains, such as politics, natural disasters or terrorist attacks. However, work has been limited to in-domain experiments, i.e. training and testing data belong to the same domain. This presents the caveat that when one wants to deal with rumours in domains that are more obscure, training data tends to be scarce. This is the case of mental health disorders, which we explore here. Having annotated collections of tweets around rumours emerged in the context of breaking news, we study the performance stability when switching to the new domain of mental health disorders. Our study confirms that performance drops when we apply our trained model on a new domain, emphasising the differences in rumours across domains. We overcome this issue by using a little portion of the target domain data for training, which leads to a substantial boost in performance. We also release the new dataset with mental health rumours annotated for stance.

Keywords: Social media · Stance classification · Veracity · Rumours · Mental health

1 Introduction

Social media are known to be rife with rumours, where along with the circulation of valuable information and fresh news, users also post about and spread information that is yet to be verified [21]. Twitter has become one of the main online platforms to access information that is updated in real time. However, the fact that it is not moderated and anyone can post and share tweets gives rise to rumours [17].

© Springer International Publishing AG 2017
G.L. Ciampaglia et al. (Eds.): SocInfo 2017, Part II, LNCS 10540, pp. 53–64, 2017.
DOI: 10.1007/978-3-319-67256-4_6

An approach that is increasingly being used to alleviate the effect of rumours is stance classification, which aims to determine the stance of individual posts discussing a rumour, defined as a classification problem that classifies each post as supporting, denying, querying or commenting on the rumour. While stance classification has been increasingly studied in recent years, previous work assumes that sufficient training data is available in the target domain, and therefore have trained and tested in the same domain.

Previous research on rumour stance classification for tweets has mostly focused on rumours about politics, natural disasters or terrorist attacks [7, 12, 14, 15, 17, 20, 22]. The fact that it is relatively easy to retrieve large amounts of data for these domains has enabled them to use in-domain data for training. However, one may not be able to retrieve as much training data for more obscure domains for which collection of data is harder. Here we document our work on performing rumour stance classification in the domain of mental health disorders, where the dearth of sufficient training data required us to look into the use of out-of-domain data for training. Leveraging out-of-domain rumour data within the context of breaking news, available from previous work, we study different classifiers to determine the stance of tweets discussing rumours in the context of mental health disorders, looking particularly at a rumoured case of depression that led to a pre-meditated plane crash. Our study contributes with analyses about how classifiers trained on out-of-domain data perform on mental health rumours where the shortage of training data makes it more difficult to build a model for the classification. We also investigate alternative ways of boosting the performance by adding a proportion of the testing data into the training process. Our results show that the domain switch from breaking news to mental health is bound with a performance loss when it comes to rumours. However, the addition of a small proportion of the mental health data to the training process leads to remarkable improvements.

2   Related Work

One of the pioneering studies in this task is reported by Mendoza et al. [15]. In this study they have manually looked into rumours with established veracity levels to understand the stance Twitter users take with respect to true and false rumours. They analysed seven rumours which were later proven true and seven rumours which had been debunked. They manually labelled the tweets with the stance categories "affirms" (supports), "denies" and "questions". They showed encouraging results correlating stance and veracity, with 95% of the tweets associated with true rumours labelled as "affirming", and 38% of the tweets associated with false rumours labelled as "denying".

The first study that tackles the stance classification automatically is reported by Qazvinian et al. [17]. With a dataset containing 10K tweets and using a Bayesian classifier and three types of features categorised as "content", "network" and "Twitter specific memes", the authors achieved an accuracy of 93.5%. Similar to them, Hamidian and Diab [7] perform rumour stance classification by applying supervised machine learning using the data set reported by Qazvinian et al. [17]. However, instead of Bayesian classifiers the authors use J48 decision tree implemented within the Weka platform [6]. The features from Qazvinian et al. [17] are adopted and extended with time related information and hastag itself instead of the content of the hashtag as used by [17]. In addition to the feature categories introduced above Hamidian and Diab [7] introduce another feature category namely "pragramatic". The pragmatic features include named entity, event, sentiment and emoticons. The evaluation of the performance is casted as either 1-step problem containing a 6 class classification task (not rumour, 4 classes of stance and not determined by the annotator) or 2-step problem containing first a 3 class classification task (non-rumour or rumour, not determined) and then 4 class classification task (stance classification). Better performances are achieved using the 2-step approach leading to 82.9% F-1 measure compared to 74% with the 1-step approach. The authors also report that the best performing features were the content based features and the least performing ones the network and twitter specific features. In their recent paper Hamidian and Diab [8] introduce the Tweet Latent Vector (TLV) approach that is obtained by applying the Semantic Textual Similarity model proposed by Guo and Diab [5]. The authors compare the TLV approach to their own earlier system as well as to original features of Qazvinian et al. [17] and show that the TVL approach outperforms both baselines.

Liu et al. [12] follow the resulting investigations about stances in rumours made by Mendoza et al. [15] and use stance as additional feature to those reported by related work to tackle the veracity classification problem. On the stance classification the authors adopt the approach of Qazvinian et al. [17] and compare it with a rule-based method briefly outlined by the authors. They claim that their rule-based approach performed better than the one adopted from related work and thus use the rule-based stance classification as additional component on the veracity problem. The experiments were performed on the data set reported by Qazvinian et al. [17]. Unfortunately the authors do not provide detailed analysis about the performance of their rule-based stance classification.

More recently, Zeng et al. [20] enriches the feature sets investigated by earlier studies by features determined through the Linguistic Inquiry and Word Count (LIWC) dictionaries [19]. They investigate supervised approaches using Logistic Regression, naïve Bayes and Random Forest classification. The authors use their own manually annotated data to classify them by stance. However, unlike previous studies Zeng et al. consider only two classes: affirm and deny. Best results are reported with Random Forest leading to 87% precision, 96.9% recall, 91.7% F1-measure and 88.4% accuracy.

Unlike related work we test all reported machine learning techniques on the same data set. This helps to compare their performance better. In addition, we evaluate the best performing model using out-of-domain data. This gives reliable indication about how portable a model is when used in an unseen environment.

3   Rumour Data

We use two types of datasets, both related and unrelated to mental health:

3.1   Mental Health Data

For our scenario studying mental health related rumours, we collected a dataset from Twitter during the Germanwings plane crash in March 2015. Following the approach described in Zubiaga et al. [23], we sampled tweets related to the rumour that the co-pilot had been diagnosed with depression, and randomly selected a subset of 31 tweet conversations (tweets discussing a rumour and replies to those) to annotate for stance, amounting to a total of 401 tweets. More details about the different stance distributions are shown in Table 1.

Owing to the small size of this dataset, we opted for obtaining out-of-domain data that would expand the data available for training.

Table 1. Counts of tweets with supporting, denying or questioning labels in each event collection from our 6 datasets. S: supporting, D: denying, Q: querying, C: commenting.

Dataset	Rumours	S	D	Q	C
Health data					
Depression	1	85	67	14	235
Non-health data					
Ottawa shooting	58	161	76	64	481
Ferguson riots	46	192	83	94	685
Germanwings crash	68	177	12	28	169
Charlie Hebdo	74	236	56	51	710
Sydney siege	71	89	4	99	713

3.2   Out-of-Domain Data

The out-of-domain data is reported by Zubiaga et al. [23], who made it publicly available. The authors identify rumours associated with events, collect conversations sparked by those rumours in the form of replies and annotate each of the tweets in the conversations for stance. These data consist of tweets from 5 different events: Ottawa shooting, Ferguson riots, Germanwings crash, Charlie Hebdo and Sydney siege. Each dataset has a different number of rumours where each rumour contains tweets marked with annotations for stance. These 5 datasets contain a total of 2,758 tweets and each post is annotated as one of "supporting", "questioning", "denying" or "commenting". Different from the mental health data, these 5 datasets are collected in the early stages of breaking news, where rumours are related to the reporting of the event and unrelated to mental health disorders. Examples of rumours in the out-of-domain-data include stories such as *"Suspected shooter has been killed/is dead"* or *"There were three separate shooting incidents"*. A summary of the data is given in Table 1.

4   Experimental Setup

In keeping with prior work, our experiments assume that incoming tweets already belong to a particular rumour, e.g. a user is tracking tweets related to a certain rumour.

Using the out-of-domain data we follow two scenarios during training and testing: (1) training and testing are performed on isolated data, i.e. we train our models on n-1 non-health rumours and test them on the nth non-health rumour, and (2) introducing a proportion of the nth rumour in the training data. In (1) the classifier is trained on all rumours except the one that is used for testing. In (2) the training data is enriched with first 10%, 20%, 30%, 40%, 50% and 60% tweets from the rumour set that builds the testing data i.e. from the nth rumour data. Note that in setting (2) we exclude from the testing data whatever is included in the training data. We use setting (1) to determine the best performing classifier. We use this best classifier and run it using scenario (2) on the non-health rumours.

For the mental health related rumours we use all the non-health rumors to train the classifiers and test them on the health data. However, similar to the above setting (2), we also introduce 10–60% tweets from the health rumours in the non-health training data. Again like above the tweets included from the testing set to the training one are excluded from the testing data. We report performance results in accuracy. However, in some cases accuracy can be biased if there is an unbalanced number of class instances. Therefore we also report results in macroaveraged F1 scores – the harmonic mean between precision and recall, computed first for each class and then averaged across all classes; this enables a complementary evaluation for an imbalanced problem like this.

Classifiers. We experiment with five different classifiers: (1) Support Vector Machines (SVMs) using the RBF kernel [2], (2) the J48 Tree, (3) Random Forests, (4) Naïve Bayes, and (5) an Instance Based classifier.

Features. Prior work on stance classification investigated various features varying from syntactical, semantical, indicator, user-specific, message-specific, etc. types [7,12,14,15,17,20,22]. This paper adopts the features from these papers, coupled with experiments with a wide range of machine learning classifiers. All in all, we use a range of 33 different features, which we describe in detail in Appendix A.

5   Results

On the non-health data we run each of the classifiers using the setting (1). The results are shown in Table 2.

From the results in Table 2 we can see that the worst performing classifier is the SVM and the best the J48. This is the case both in terms of the accuracy and F1 metrics. We think SVM does not perform well because our training data is imbalanced in terms of class instances. As shown in Table 1 there are far more

Table 2. Different classifier performances on setting (1). IBk is the Instance Based Learning classifier. The F1 figures are weighted over the 4 classes (support, deny, question and comment).

Classifier	Accuracy	F1
SVM	64.59	52.13
Random Forest	70.07	62.99
IBk	71.82	72.95
Bayes	73.14	68.83
J48	**75.84**	**73.37**

commenting instances than the other 3 classes. The J48 Tree is not affected to the same extent by this as it can handle imbalanced data. In the following we use J48 to report detailed results in both non-health and health related data. The results for the non-health rumours for the best performing classifier – J48 Tree – are shown in Table 3.

Table 3. Classification results in accuracy and F1 obtained using the J48 Tree.

In domain tweets	Accuracy	F1
0%	75.84	73.37
10%	75.66	71.42
20%	76.64	72.67
30%	76.86	73.25
40%	77.5	73.74
50%	78.9	75.64
60%	80.1	76.86

The row with 0% shown in Table 3 represents the set-up scenario (1) discussed above. From the results we can see inclusion of testing data (instances from the rumour that is under test) in the training improves the results in both accuracy and F1 cases. Furthermore, we can see that the more testing data is included the better is the overall performance (except from 0% to 10%).

The results shown in Table 4 are obtained by the classifiers trained using the entire non-health data without inclusion of any health-rumours. This simulates the scenario of applying a classifier to out-of-domain data. From these results we can see that there is a performance drop of all classifiers when applied on a different domain. In terms of accuracy we can see that the largest drop in performance happens with the Random Forest classifier. The smallest drop can be observed with the SVM and J48 classifiers. In terms of F1 score, again Random Forest is affected with the largest drop. The least affected classifier for the F1 score is the instance based classifier. However, the overall picture is that again

Table 4. Stance classification results for the health rumours in accuracy and weighted F1 over the 4 classes.

Classifier	Accuracy	F1
SVM	59.27	46.18
Random Forest	57.89	29.8
IBk	65.22	60.42
Bayes	63.22	58.31
J48	**69.45**	**65.45**

J48 is the best performing classifier based on both accuracy and F1 metrics. The worst performing one is the Random Forest classifier.

Table 5. Classification results in accuracy and F1 obtained using the J48 Tree.

In domain tweets	Accuracy	F1
0%	69.45	65.45
10%	70.77	65.83
20%	72.41	66.79
30%	73.12	67.69
40%	74.67	70.06
50%	72.89	70.08
60%	75.87	73.54

Using the best performing classifier, the J48 tree, we replicated the (2) scenario experiment with the health data, i.e. 10–60% of health rumours were injected into the entire non-health data for training purposes. The results of this experiment are shown in Table 5. From this table we can see that the inclusion of in-domain data to the training process increases the results gradually (except for 50% for the accuracy case) both for accuracy and F1 measures and so demolishes the performance loss. In fact, these results suggest that inclusion of in-domain data in this scenario with little annotated data is much more crucial than in the non-health scenario; we see for instance that in the non-health scenario the use of 30% in-domain data leads to 1% improvement, while the same amount of in-domain data leads to nearly 4% improvement in the new domain.

Finally, to test the real impact of the out-domain data on the health data we trained and tested our classifier only on the health data. Because of the size of the data we performed 50% till 80% reservations for training purposes and the remaining for testing. Results are shown in Table 6.

Table 6. Classification results in accuracy and F1 obtained using the J48 Tree. The results are obtained using only in domain data for training.

In domain tweets	Accuracy	F1
50%	44.55	37.45
60%	46.15	41.64
70%	51.02	48.57
80%	59.95	59.27

From Table 6 we can see that, by performing training and testing on the in-domain data, we achieve significantly lower results than when the training process is augmented with out-domain data. This also shows that the out-domain data has substantial contribution on boosting the results.

6 Conclusions

We have tackled the rumour stance classification task leveraging out-of-domain data for training for the first time. While previous research utilised in-domain data for training in scenarios with large datasets available, such as breaking news, here we studied the classification in more obscure scenarios, which is the case of mental health disorders. We experimented with various classifiers and reported the performance of different classifiers on the same dataset. We also performed experiments on domain transfer, applying models trained from the non-health domain on the health-related rumours. We showed that the best performing classifier is the J48 decision tree. It outperformed all other classifiers on the non-health rumours and also achieved the best results after domain transfer. We also observed that the domain transfer is in general bound with a loss in performance. For instance, J48 dropped from an accuracy of 75% to 69% when switching from the non-health to the health domain. Our results showed that the Random Forest classifier has undergone the worst performance loss among all other methods. However, we also reported that inclusion of some proportion of the in-domain data to the training process helps boost the performance. Finally, we reported training and testing on the in-domain data only and showed that the results are substantially lower compared to the case when the training data is augmented with the out-domain data.

Our rumour stance classifier applied to new, obscure domains with shortage of training data has numerous applications that we aim to explore in the near future, such as rumours around bullying and suicide [9], or disputed perceptions around psychoactive substances [10]. Further improving our classifier, in future work we also aim to perform a more detailed analysis underpinning the reasons for the performance drop. For instance, we plan to investigate the stability of features during a domain transfer.

Acknowledgements. This work was partially supported by the European Union under grant agreement No. 654024 SoBigData, PHEME project under the grant agreement No. 611223 and by the Deutsche Forschungsgemeinschaft (DFG) under grant No. GRK 2167, Research Training Group "User-Centred Social Media". Rob Procter and Maria Liakata were supported by the Alan Turing Institute.

A   Appendix: Complete Set of Features

- **BOW (Bag of words):** For this feature we first create a dictionary from all the tweets in the out-of-domain dataset. Next each tweet is assigned the words in the dictionary as features. For words occurring in the tweet the feature values are set to the number of times they occur in the tweet. For all other words "0" is used.
- **Brown Cluster:** Brown clustering is a hard hierarchical clustering method and we use it to cluster words in hierarchies. It clusters words based on maximising the probability of the words under the bigram language model, where words are generated based on their clusters [11]. In previous work it has been shown that Brown clusters yield better performance than directly using the BOW features [13]. Brown clusters are obtained from a bigger tweet corpus that entails assignments of words to brown cluster ids. We used 1000 clusters, i.e. there are 1000 cluster ids. All 1000 ids are used as features however only, ids that cover words in the tweet are assigned a feature value "1". All other cluster id feature values are set to "0".
- **POS tag:** The BOW feature captures the actual words and is domain dependent. To create a feature that is not domain dependent we added Part of Speech (POS) tags as additional feature. Similar to the BOW feature we created a dictionary of POS tags from the entire corpus (excluding the health data) and used this dictionary to label each tweet with it – binary, i.e. whether a POS tag is present.[1] However, instead of using just single POS tag we created sequences containing bi-gram, tri-gram and 4-gram POS tags. Feature values are the frequencies of POS tag sequences occurring in the tweet.
- **Sentiment:** This is another domain independent feature. Sentiment analysis reveals the sentimental polarity of the tweet such as whether it is positive or negative. We used the Stanford sentiment [18] tool to create this feature. The tool returns a range from 0 to 4 with 0 indicating "very negative" and 4 "very positive". First, we used this as a categorical feature but turning it to a numeric feature gave us better performance. Thus each tweet is assigned a sentiment feature whose value varies from 0 to 4.
- **NE:** Named entity (NE) is also domain independent. We check for each tweet whether it contains *Person, Organization, Date, Location* and *Money* tags and for each tag in case of presence we add "1" otherwise "0".

---

[1] We also experimented with frequencies of POS tags, i.e. counting how many times a particular POS tag occurs in the tweet. The counts then have been normalized using mean and standard deviation. However, the frequency based POS feature negatively affected the classification accuracy so that we omitted it from the feature set.

- **Reply:** This feature is a binary feature and assigns "1" if the tweet is a reply to a previous one or not and otherwise "0". The reply information is extracted from the tweet metadata. Again this feature is domain independent.
- **Emoticon:** We created a dictionary of emoticons using Wikipedia[2]. In Wikipedia those emoticons are grouped by categories. We use the categories as the feature. If any emoticon from a category occurs in the tweet we assign for that category feature the value "1" otherwise "0". Again similar to the previous features this feature is domain independent.
- **URL:** This is again domain independent. We assign the tweet "1" if it contains any URL otherwise "0".
- **Mood:** Mood detection analyses a textual content using different view points or angles. We use the tool described by [3] to perform the mood detection. This tools looks from 5 different angles to each tweet: amused, disappointed, indignant, satisfied and worried. For each of this angles it returns a value from -1 to $+1$. We use the different angles as the mood features and the returned values as the feature value.
- **Originality score:** Is the count of tweets the user has produced, i.e. the "statuses count" in the Twitter API.
- **isUserVerified(0-1):** Whether the user is verified or not.
- **NumberOfFollowers:** Number of followers the user have.
- **Role score:** Is the ratio between the number of followers and followees (i.e. NumberOfFollowers/NumberOfFollowees).
- **Engagement score:** Is the number of tweets divided by the number of days the user has been active (number of days since the user account creation till today).
- **Favourites score:** The "favourites count" divided by the number of days the user has been active.
- **HasGeoEnabled(0-1):** User has enabled geo-location or not.
- **HasDescription(0-1):** User has description or not.
- **LenghtOfDescription in words:** The number of words in the user description.
- **averageNegation:** We determine using the Stanford parser [4] the dependency parse tree of the tweet, count the number of negation relation ("neg") that appears between two terms and divide this by the number of total relations.
- **hasNegation(0-1):** Tweet has negation relationship or not.
- **hasSlangOrCurseWord(0-1):** A dictionary of key words[3] is used to determine the presence of slang or curse words in the tweet.
- **hasGoogleBadWord(0-1):** Same as above but the dictionary of slang words is obtained from Google.[4]
- **hasAcronyms(0-1):** The tweet is checked for presence of acronyms using a acronym dictionary.[5]

---

[2] https://en.wikipedia.org/wiki/List_of_emoticons.
[3] www.noswearing.com/dictionary.
[4] http://fffff.at/googles-official-list-of-bad-words.
[5] www.netlingo.com/category/acronyms.php.

- **averageWordLength:** Average length of words (sum of word character counts divided by number of words in each tweet).
- **surpriseScore:** We collected a list of surprise words such as "amazed", "surprised", etc. We use this list to compute a cumulative vector using word2Vec [16] – for each word in the list we obtain its word2Vec representation, add them together and finally divide the resulting vector by the number of words to obtain the cumulative vector. Similarly a cumulative vector is computed for the words in the tweet – excluding acronyms, named entities and URLs. We use cosine to compute the angle between those two cumulative vectors to determine the surprise score. Our word embeddings comprise the vectors published by Baroni et al. [1].
- **doubtScore:** Similar to the *surpriseScore* but use instead a list of doubt words such as "doubt", "uncertain", etc.
- **noDoubtScore:** As in *doubtScore* but use instead words which stand for certainty such as "surely", "sure", "certain", etc.
- **hasQuestionMark(0-1):** The tweet has "?" or not.
- **hasExclamationMark(0-1):** The tweet has "!" or not.
- **hasDotDotDot(0-1):** Whether the tweet has "..." or not.
- **numberOfQuestionMark:** Count of "?" in the tweet.
- **NumberOfExclamationMark:** Count of "!" in the tweet.
- **numberOfDotDotDot:** Count of "..." in the tweet.
- **Binary regular expressions applied on each tweet:** .*(rumor?—debunk?).*, .*is (that—this—it) true.*, etc. In total there are 10 features covering regular expressions.

References

1. Baroni, M., Dinu, G., Kruszewski, G.: Don't count, predict! a systematic comparison of context-counting vs. context-predicting semantic vectors. In: Proceedings of ACL, pp. 238–247 (2014)
2. Buhmann, M.D.: Radial Basis Functions: Theory and Implementations. Cambridge Monographs on Applied and Computational Mathematics, vol. 12, pp. 147–165 (2003)
3. Celli, F., Ghosh, A., Alam, F., Riccardi, G.: In the mood for sharing contents: emotions, personality and interaction styles in the diffusion of news. Inf. Process. Manag. **52**(1), 93–98 (2016)
4. Chen, D., Manning, C.D.: A fast and accurate dependency parser using neural networks. In: Proceedings of EMNLP, pp. 740–750 (2014)
5. Guo, W., Diab, M.: Modeling sentences in the latent space. In: Proceedings of ACL, pp. 864–872. Association for Computational Linguistics (2012)
6. Hall, M., Frank, E., Holmes, G., Pfahringer, B., Reutemann, P., Witten, I.H.: The weka data mining software: an update. ACM SIGKDD Explor. Newsl. **11**(1), 10–18 (2009)
7. Hamidian, S., Diab, M.: Rumor detection and classification for twitter data. In: Proceedings of SOTICS, pp. 71–77 (2015)
8. Hamidian, S., Diab, M.T.: Rumor identification and belief investigation on twitter. In: Proceedings of NAACL-HLT, pp. 3–8 (2016)

9. Hinduja, S., Patchin, J.W.: Bullying, cyberbullying, and suicide. Arch. Suicide Res. **14**(3), 206–221 (2010)
10. Kolliakou, A., Ball, M., Derczynski, L., Chandran, D., Gkotsis, G., Deluca, P., Jackson, R., Shetty, H., Stewart, R.: Novel psychoactive substances: An investigation of temporal trends in social media and electronic health records. Eur. Psychiatry **38**, 15–21 (2016)
11. Liang, P.: Semi-supervised learning for natural language. Ph.D. thesis, Massachusetts Institute of Technology (2005)
12. Liu, X., Nourbakhsh, A., Li, Q., Fang, R., Shah, S.: Real-time rumor debunking on twitter. In: Proceedings of CIKM, pp. 1867–1870. ACM (2015)
13. Lukasik, M., Cohn, T., Bontcheva, K.: Classifying tweet level judgements of rumours in social media. In: Proceedings of the 2015 Conference on Empirical Methods in Natural Language Processing, EMNLP 2015, pp. 2590–2595 (2015)
14. Lukasik, M., Srijith, P.K., Vu, D., Bontcheva, K., Zubiaga, A., Cohn, T.: Hawkes processes for continuous time sequence classification: an application to rumour stance classification in twitter. In: Proceedings of the 54th Meeting of the Association for Computational Linguistics, pp. 393–398. Association for Computer Linguistics (2016)
15. Mendoza, M., Poblete, B., Castillo, C.: Twitter under crisis: can we trust what we rt? In: Proceedings of the Workshop on Social Media Analytics, pp. 71–79. ACM (2010)
16. Mikolov, T., Sutskever, I., Chen, K., Corrado, G.S., Dean, J.: Distributed representations of words and phrases and their compositionality. In: Advances in Neural Information Processing Systems, pp. 3111–3119 (2013)
17. Qazvinian, V., Rosengren, E., Radev, D.R., Mei, Q.: Rumor has it: Identifying misinformation in microblogs. In: Proceedings of EMNLP, pp. 1589–1599 (2011)
18. Socher, R., Perelygin, A., Wu, J.Y., Chuang, J., Manning, C.D., Ng, A.Y., Potts, C.: Recursive deep models for semantic compositionality over a sentiment treebank. In: Proceedings of EMNLP, vol. 1631, p. 1642. Citeseer (2013)
19. Tausczik, Y.R., Pennebaker, J.W.: The psychological meaning of words: liwc and computerized text analysis methods. J. Lang. Soc. Psychol. **29**(1), 24–54 (2010)
20. Zeng, L., Starbird, K., Spiro, E.S.: # unconfirmed: classifying rumor stance in crisis-related social media messages. In: Proceedings of ICWSM (2016)
21. Zubiaga, A., Aker, A., Bontcheva, K., Liakata, M., Procter, R.: Detection and resolution of rumours in social media: a survey (2017). arXiv preprint: arXiv:1704.00656
22. Zubiaga, A., Kochkina, E., Liakata, M., Procter, R., Lukasik, M.: Stance classification in rumours as a sequential task exploiting the tree structure of social media conversations. In: Proceedings of COLING (2016)
23. Zubiaga, A., Liakata, M., Procter, R., Wong Sak Hoi, G., Tolmie, P.: Analysing how people orient to and spread rumours in social media by looking at conversational threads. PLoS ONE **11**(3), 1–29 (2016)

Predicting Multiple Risky Behaviors via Multimedia Content

Yiheng Zhou$^{(\boxtimes)}$, Jingyao Zhan, and Jiebo Luo

University of Rochester, Rochester, NY 14627, USA
{yzhou49,jzhan}@u.rochester.edu, jiebo.luo@gmail.com

Abstract. Risky behaviors pose a growing threat to our society. In the case of drug consumption, according to National Survey on Drug Use and Health, "substance abuse costs our society more than 484 billion dollars a year", which is about thrice of what we spend on cancer. Researchers have started studying risky behaviors through big data from social media. However, to our best knowledge, most of the existing schemes focus on only one risky behavior, despite that the research in public health and psychology has shown us that there exist correlations among risky behaviors. In this work, in order to exploit such correlation, we select five risky behaviors, namely drug consumption, drinking, sleep disorder, depression, and eating disorder. Furthermore, we propose a deep learning neural network constructed by combining recurrent neural networks (RNN) and convolutional neural networks (CNN) to effectively predict whether an Instagram user will conduct which kind of risky behaviors in the near future.

Keywords: Multimedia · Social media · Risky behaviors · Multi-task learning · Prediction · Health informatics

1 Introduction

Traditionally, researchers use online surveys, telephone surveys, and hard-copy surveys to study risky behaviors. However, collecting data by surveys is time-consuming, and suffers from sample noise and small scale. Moreover, people may not answer the survey questions truthfully on sensitive topics [2]. Therefore, an alternative way to collect data is needed. Social media has become a popular data source among data science researchers, as it has not only various kinds of data such as captions, comments, images and videos, but also a very large number of active users [2]. Instagram is our choice of data source because it had a very convenient API for researchers to fetch data based on tags, usernames, or locations.

Risky behavior remains a major problem in public health. While some people with mental illness receive proper treatments on time, many patients are unaware of their mental conditions, which results in delay in treatment. Therefore, it's very crucial to detect and intervene with risky behaviors before they deteriorate. In this paper, we want to employ machine learning algorithms and social media data to intervene with risky behaviors.

One of the problems of studying multiple risky behaviors is how to exploit correlations among risky behaviors. According to National Institute on Drug Abuse (NIDA) [3], "Many people who regularly abuse drugs are also diagnosed with mental

© Springer International Publishing AG 2017
G.L. Ciampaglia et al. (Eds.): SocInfo 2017, Part II, LNCS 10540, pp. 65–73, 2017.
DOI: 10.1007/978-3-319-67256-4_7

disorders and vice versa. The high prevalence of this comorbidity has been documented in multiple national population surveys since the 1980s." The approach we take, multi-task learning (MTL) [4], is a possible solution to our concern.

Choosing Instagram as a data source provides us with enough data to analyze not only text, but also other medias. In order to utilize multimedia, a pretrained ConvNet (convolutional Neural Networks) was retrained (transfer learning), and integrated into our multi-task learning network as a feature extractor.

The main contributions of this study are summarized below:

1. Employing Instagram as a reliable data source to study risky behaviors;
2. Discovering and exploiting correlations among risky behaviors to increase prediction accuracy;
3. Applying SVM (support vector machine) to build a reliable text classifier to determine which risky behavior(s) an Instagram post is related to;
4. Utilizing recurrent and convolutional neural networks to predict whether an Instagram user will conduct what kind of risky behaviors in the near future..

2 Related Work

2.1 Applications of Social Media Data

In the light of easier access to social media data, many researchers focus on mining social media data to solve real-life problems. For example [5], in public health, Munmun and her group proposed a method to detect and diagnose major depression by mining tweets from the Twitter users who were diagnosed with clinical depression. In drug consumption studies, Cody and Jennifer summarized statistics about drug-related tweets on Twitter, in terms of time and location [6]; Yiheng and his group did studies on drug abuse on Instagram [2]. Finally, some researchers study drinking on Twitter: monitoring underage drinking on Twitter [7], and analyzing alcohol-related promotions on Twitter [8].

2.2 Multiple Risky Behaviors

One of the technical challenges we faced is collecting a sample that contains enough information about all the targeted risky behaviors. In Germain's study [9], they investigated the distinctions between direct and indirect forms of non-suicidal self-injury. Second challenge is how to take advantage of the correlations among risky behaviors. MIT Media Lab used multi-task learning to predict health, stress, and happiness [10].

3 Methods

3.1 Data Collection

Instagram offered a Tag-Search API (deprecated in Nov. 2015.), which allows us to fetch all the posts with one specified hashtag at a rate limit of 5000 posts per hour. In this paper, we focus on utilizing images and captions for our predictions.

Since Tag-Search API only supports single hashtag search, we cannot fetch posts related to multiple risky behaviors. To solve this problem, first, we chose to obtain a group of users that have conducted at least one kind of risky behaviors, then find other risky behavior related posts in that user pool. Drug consumption was the initial risky behavior we selected. By applying the fetching methods used in [2], we end up with 2362 potential drug users with all their posts since Instagram launched in 2010.

After the data of our initial user pool was fetched, we decided to also get demographic information, an important feature for training neural network. Because Instagram does not require users to enter their demographic information, we employed facial identification technique to derive age and gender information. For each user in our dataset, we extracted all the posts with selfie-related hashtags including 'selfie', 'weedselfie', 'selfportrait', and 'selfy'. Then, we fed those selfie-related posts to the face identification API, Project Oxford [12], from Microsoft to calculate face attributes (age and gender).

Figure 1 shows the age and gender distribution of our Instagram users. Most of our users are between 20 and 40 years old. In the younger population, we have more female than male users. In the older population, there are more male than female users.

3.2 Convolutional Neural Network

Every Instagram post must be uploaded with either an image or a video, which allows us to evaluate each post with not only its text information, but also images. Before integrating our image classifier into multi-task learning network, we designed a convolutional network first.

In this work, we only focus on drinking-related images for several reasons. First, due to our collaboration with Diligence Lab, a local startup, we received some high-quality and drinking-related pictures for our transfer learning. Second, owning to the correlations between drinking and other risky behaviors, correctly identifying drinking images can not only help train drinking predictor, but also others. Table 1 shows the information of our drinking-related dataset from Diligence Lab.

Table 1. The information of drinking-related images from Diligence Lab

	Positive	Negative		
Type	Drinking	Christmas	Thanksgiving	Birthday
# of image	1176	884	930	910

Because of very limit number of positive images, it is impractical to train ConvNet from sketch, which would cost considerable amount of time. Therefore, we decided to use transfer learning to save time and avoid overfitting. Pretrained VGG16 [13] (Very Deep Convolutional Networks) on ImageNet [14] was selected as a fully trained convolutional network. Finally, we manually labeled some negative images to solve class imbalance problem, as shown in Table 1.

Training process is described in Fig. 2. First, we resized our input images to $224 \times 224 \times 3$. Then, we fed the resized image matrix to VGG16, which returns an

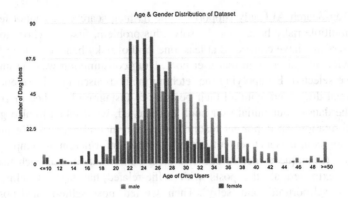

Fig. 1. Age and gender distributions of our dataset.

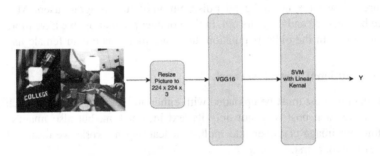

Fig. 2. Structure of our convolutional network.

output vector with length of 1,000. Finally, we put the output of VGG16 model along with a target value (one-hot vector, [1,0] if positive, [0,1] if negative) to our linear support vector machine [16]. Table 2 shows 5-fold cross validation results.

3.3 Text Classifier

After acquiring a dataset of drug users, we started to identify the positive risky behavior posts within our drug users' posts. Two filters were used to get the final positive risky behaviors posts: one is hashtag filter; the other is our text classifier. The overall procedure is shown in Fig. 3. For this subsection, we focus on explaining "Preprocessing 1" "1st filter", and "2nd filters".

Table 2. 5-fold cross validation of our convolutional network

Fold	1	2	3	4	5
ACC	0.816	0.822	0.805	0.803	0.8
AVE	**0.809**				
STDEV	0.0093				

3.3.1   1st Filter

As for the hashtags filter, we obtained a list of hashtags for each risky behavior. For drug consumption, the hashtags are from [2]. We considered the posts with five or more drug-related hashtags as potentially drug-related. For drinking, we adopted the hashtags from [7]. We deemed the post with five or more drinking-related hashtags as potentially drinking-related. For depressive disorder, we employed the related-hashtag-fetching algorithm from [2]. For eating disorder and sleep disorder, the same related-hashtag-fetching process was conducted as for depression. Additionally, sentiment analysis [17] was conducted for depressive disorder and sleep disorder. If the sentiment analysis for a post has positive valence, this post is removed from our depression/sleep-related posts list.

Before feeding the data to the text classifier (2nd filter), we needed to label our data first. Therefore, we designed a web interface for medical and psychology workers to label our posts. This interface was installed for both the medical workers at our school's Medical Center, and the professors at the Department of Clinical and Social Sciences in Psychology to help us label the posts (each risky behavior has approximately 1500 labeled posts except eating disorder, which we have only 542 posts in total).

3.3.2   Preprocessing 1

After obtaining a list of labeled posts for each risky behavior, we started preprocessing the posts. For each risky behavior, the following steps have been done. First, we created a single text file by extracting all the captions from all the posts and concatenating them together separated by '<eos>' symbol (short for "the end of sentence").

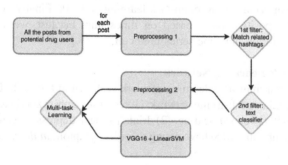

Fig. 3. Diagram of the proposed framework.

Second, we calculated the top 80% frequent unique words in the text file and replaced the bottom 20% frequent unique words by '<unk>' symbol. Third, a python 'emoji' package was employed to replace all the emoji in the text file by English words. Fourth, the non-letter symbols were removed as well. Finally, word2vec [18] from Google's project was applied. One important thing about using word2vec is that it successfully captures the relationship among different words, which can be used to feed our text classifier.

Linear Support Vector Machine [16] was our choice of text classifier.

3.4   Multi-task Learning

After feeding all the posts in our user pool to the text classifier in Sect. 3.3, we obtained a list of positive posts for each user. Table 3 shows the number of positive posts for each risky behavior in our user pool.

Table 3. Number of positive posts for each risky behavior.

Depression	Drug	Drink	Sleep disorder	Eating disorder
18,203	138,021	4,979	4,758	234

3.4.1   Preprocessing 2

After we have a list of positive posts for each user, we need to reformat the data to put into our multi-task learning network. First, we extracted timestamp for each positive post, and used one-hot vector to represent which risky behavior this post represents. For example, in Fig. 4, the one-hot vector is embedded in the list from the second feature to the sixth one: [0, 0, 0, 0, 1]. Second, because the value of timestamp is overly large compared with other features in the input vector, we normalized all the timestamps in our positive posts by subtracting each of them by 1286323200, which is the date when Instagram launched, and dividing the time difference by 3600 to get the hour difference. Third, earlier in the paper, we mentioned the importance of demographics. Therefore, we put age and gender attributes into the input vector. In Fig. 4, the seventh feature represents the age of this user, and the eighth feature represents the gender of this user. Moreover, the last feature in the input vector is from our image classifier. For each positive post, we passed its image to our image classifier, and concatenated the results to the input vector of our multi-task learning network. Finally, for each user, we sorted all his/her positive posts based on timestamp, because we want to employ time-series data to train our time-series predictor.

3.4.2   Multi-task Learning Network

The structure of our multi-task learning network is shown in Fig. 5. In Fig. 5, there are five tasks in our multi-task learning network: Given a user's past experiences, whether this Instagram user will (1) consume drug, (2) drink, (3) have depression symptom, (4) have sleep disorder symptom, or (5) have eating disorder symptom *in the next 30 days*?

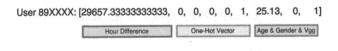

User 89XXXX: [29657.33333333333, 0, 0, 0, 0, 1, 25.13, 0, 1]

| Hour Difference | One-Hot Vector | Age & Gender & Vgg |

Fig. 4.   Sample input data for multi-task learning.

To be specific, Fig. 4 shows a sample input. Each user in our user pool has a list of positive posts, each of which has a format like the sample input vector in Fig. 4. X_{drug}, X_{drink}, $X_{depress}$, X_{eating}, X_{sleep} are defined to be the input vectors that represent drug consumption, drinking, depression, eating disorder, and sleep disorder respectively. The way we generated input-target pair is shown in Fig. 6. In Fig. 6, "User1" has a timeline with risky behavior events on it. First, we input X_{drug}, since it's the first event on the timeline. Then, for *each of our five risky behaviors*, we search for the next earliest one *within 30 days*. Finally, the target vector consists of five binary bits, each of which represents whether a certain risky behavior event can be found within 30 days from the current input event.

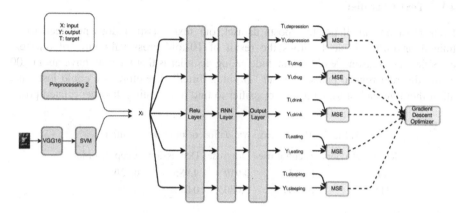

Fig. 5. Procedure of multi-task learning.

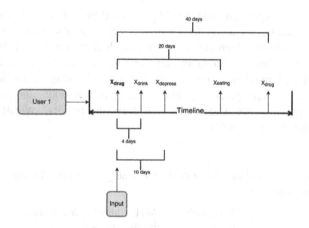

Fig. 6. Sample input data for multi-task learning.

TensorFlow [20] was our choice of implementing multi-task learning network. As shown in Fig. 5, for each risky behavior, our network consists of 3 layers in total. "Relu Layer" takes an input vector to multiply a weight tensor variable of shape (9,9), add to a bias tensor variable of shape (9,1), and finally apply the rectifier. "RNN layer" consists of two layers of 9 LSTM (Long Short-Term Memory) [21] cells and each cell has an input (and output) drop-out probability of 0.7. "Output Layer" takes an output vector from "RNN layer", multiples it with a weight tensor variable of shape (9,5), adds it to a bias tensor variable of shape (5, 1), and finally applies sigmoid function to it. Finally, we utilized traditional MSE (mean square error) to calculate the loss and applied gradient descent to the loss function as an optimizer.

4   Experimental Results

4.1   Text Classifier

Because of our small positive posts dataset, our text classifier does not need to be trained on GPU. Table 4 shows the result of 10-fold cross validation of our text classifier. The reason we did not include eating disorder is that we only have about 500 eating disorder related posts after our "Hashtag Filter". Therefore, we could just label all of them instead of utilizing text classifier to find more eating disorder related posts.

Table 4. 10-fold cross validation of our text classifier

Risky behaviors	Alcohol use	Drug use	Depression	Sleep disorder
AVE	**0.613**	**0.919**	**0.985**	**0.930**
STDEV	0.0897	0.0805	0.011	0.100

4.2   Multi-task Learning

Training the multi-task learning on GTX TITAN 6 GB took about 2 days and training a single task took about half a day for each risky behavior. As shown in Table 5, the accuracy of the multi-task learning is significantly higher than that of the single-task learning, suggesting that the correlations among different risky behaviors help improve the performance of prediction. Finally, in Table 5, our image classifier does help increase the accuracies for predicting drinking, drug consumption, and depression, but not for sleep disorder and eating disorder. Nevertheless, the overall accuracy is increased by our image classifier.

Table 5. 10-fold cross validation for Multi-Task Learning with image classifier and Multi-Task Learning without image classifier

	MTL with image classifier		MTL without image classifier		Single-Task	
Behaviors	AVE	STDEV	AVE	STDEV	AVE	STDEV
Alcohol use	0.885	0.0446	0.739	0.00358	0.864	0.0591
Drug use	0.873	0.0223	0.757	0.0364	0.863	0.0459
Depression	0.877	0.0561	0.727	0.00083	0.867	0.0242
Sleep disorder	0.846	0.0440	0.613	0.00223	0.856	0.0588
Eating disorder	0.969	0.0227	0.903	0.0272	0.981	0.0199
AVE	**0.890**		0.748		0.886	

References

1. National Survey on Drug Use and Health (2014)
2. Zhou, Y., Sani, N., Luo, J.: Understanding Illicit Drug Use Behaviors by Mining Social Media. SBP-BRiMS, Washington DC (2016)
3. National Institute on Drug Abuse. NIDA (2015)
4. Caruana, R.: Multi-Task Learning. Machine Learning (1997)
5. Choudhury, M., Gamon, M., Counts, S., Horvitz, E.: Predicting Depression via Social Media (2013)
6. Buntain, C., Golbeck, J.: This is your Twitter on drugs. any questions? In: Proceedings of the 24th International Conference on World Wide Web (WWW) (2015)
7. Pang, R., Baretto, A., Kautz, H., Luo, J.: Monitoring adolescent alcohol use via multimodal analysis in social multimedia. In: IEEE Big Data Conference (2015)
8. Menon, A., Farmer, F., Whalen, T., Hua, B., Najib, K., Gerber, M.: Automatic identification of alcohol-related promotions on Twitter and prediction of promotion spread. In: Systems and Information Engineering Design Symposium (SIEDS) (2014)
9. Germain, S., Hooley, J.: Direct and Indirect Forms of Non-suicidal Self-injury: Evidence for a Distinction. Psychiatry Research (2011)
10. Jaques, N., Taylor, S., Nosakhare, E., Sano, A., Picard, R.: NIPS 2016 Workshop on Machine Learning for Health (2016)
11. Mike, B.: Instagram statistics (2014)
12. Face API, version 1.0, Project Oxford, Microsoft
13. Simonyan, K., Zisserman, A.: Very deep convolutional networks for large-scale image recognition. In: International Conference on Learning Representations (ICLR) (2015)
14. Russakovsky*, O., Deng*, J., Su, H., Krause, J., Satheesh, S., Ma, S., Huang, Z., Karpathy, A., Khosla, A., Bernstein, M., Berg, A.C., Fei-Fei, L.: (* = equal contribution) ImageNet Large Scale Visual Recognition Challenge. In: IJCV (2015)
15. Zhou, Y., Glenn, C., Luo, J.: Understanding and predicting multiple risky behaviors from social media. In: AAAI 2017 Joint Workshop on Health Intelligence, San Francisco, CA, February 2017
16. Hsieh, C., Chang, K., Lin, C., Keerthi, S., Sundararajan, S.: A dual coordinate descent method for large-scale linear svM. In: Proceedings of the 25th International Conference on Machine Learning, ICML 2008, pp. 408–415. ACM, New York (2008). doi:10.1145/1390156.1390208. ISBN 978-1-60558-205-4
17. Hutto, C.J., Gilbert, E.: VADER: a parsimonious rule-based model for sentiment analysis of social media text. In: Eighth International Conference on Weblogs and Social Media (ICWSM-14) (2014)
18. Mikolov, T., Sutskever, I., Chen, K., Corrado, G.S., Dean, J.: Distributed representations of words and phrases and their compositionality. In: Advances in Neural Information Processing Systems (NIPS) (2013)
19. Agrawal, R.; Srikant, R; 1994. Fast algorithms for mining association rules in large databases. Proceedings of the 20th International Conference on Very Large Data Bases, VLDB, pages 487–499, Santiago, Chile, September 1994
20. Harp, A., Irving, G., et al.: TensorFlow: Large-Scale Machine Learning on Heterogeneous Distributed Systems (2015)
21. Zaremba, W., Sutskever, I., Vinyals, O.: Recurrent neural network regularizations. In: ICLR (2015)

On the Role of Political Affiliation in Human Perception The Case of Delhi OddEven Experiment

Tahar Zanouda[✉], Sofiane Abbar, Laure Berti-Equille, Kushal Shah,
Abdelkader Baggag, Sanjay Chawla, and Jaideep Srivastava

Qatar Computing Research Institute, HBKU, Doha, Qatar
{tzanouda,sabbar,lberti,kshah,abaggag,schawla,jsrivastava}@hbku.edu.qa

Abstract. In an effort to curb air pollution, the city of Delhi (India), known to be one of the most populated, polluted, and congested cities in the world has run a trial experiment in two phases of 15 days intervals. During the experiment, most of four-wheeled vehicles were constrained to move on alternate days based on whether their plate numbers ended with odd or even digits. While the local government of Delhi represented by A. Kejriwal (leader of AAP party) advocated for the benefits of the experiment, the prime minister of India, N. Modi (former leader of BJP) defended the inefficiency of the initiative. This later has led to a strong polarization of public opinion towards OddEven experiment. This real-world urban experiment provided the scientific community with a unique opportunity to study the impact of political leaning on humans perception at a large-scale. We collect data about pollution and traffic congestion to measure the real effectiveness of the experiment. We use Twitter to capture the public discourse about the experiment in order to study people's opinion within different dimensions: time, location, and topics. Our results reveal a strong influence of political affiliation on how people perceived the outcomes of the experiment. For instance, AAP supporters were significantly more enthusiastic about the success of OddEven compared to BJP supporters. However, taking into account location of people revealed that personal experience is able to overcome political bias.

Keywords: Urban big data analytics · Urban policy making · Computational social science · Political science

1 Introduction

Context. Delhi, the home of more than twenty millions inhabitants, is one of the world's most densely populated cities [24]. The city has grown rapidly, and expanded geographically in the last years. This increase has enlarged the challenges for the urban transport systems, resulting critical air quality levels, endless traffic congestion, and alarming accident rates [20]. Thus, political leaders and decision makers are striving to take the lead in combating these challenges to

G.L. Ciampaglia et al. (Eds.): SocInfo 2017, Part II, LNCS 10540, pp. 74–88, 2017.
DOI: 10.1007/978-3-319-67256-4_8

improve the accessibility and enhance the livability in the city. As a practical step towards crystallizing this goal, the city of Delhi has launched an urban initiative to reduce air pollution. With more than nine million registered vehicles in Delhi, Aam Aadmi Party (AAP) led an initiative coined as OddEven experiment [1] to tackle the issue by allowing *non-transport four-wheeled vehicles* to move on alternate days based on whether their registration number ends with odd or even digits. The first phase of the 15-day pilot took place in Delhi from January 1st to January 15th, 2016. It is important to notice that over 20 categories were exempted from this rules. Examples for such omissions are women only vehicles, vehicles belonging to some government agencies, and vehicles occupied by handicapped persons. Full description of the experiment as per the official notification can be found in this document [3].

The urban experiment. Air pollution is a major problem in many cities around the world. This problem is tightly associated with road traffic and congestion [25]. OddEven experiment is one of the urban experiments that cities adopted in order to cut congestion and control the number of cars circuling in the city [12].

Understanding the succes factors and the impact of these urban experiments would effectively lead to design better public strategies and policies. However, assessing the success of these experiments is often hard and tedious as many parameters need be controlled. For instance, the success of an experiment can be measured by looking at the strict impact it had on the expected outcome. Doing so, we might be missing important secondary effects on people's daily lives that we did not anticipate. Therefore, it is importance to consider people's opinion in such circumstances. Delhi OddEven experiment provides a unique opportunity to study the political bias and preconceptions affecting human perceptions toward the outcomes of a large-scale and real-life experiment. In fact, while Delhi state government led by Arvin Kejriwal, *leader of the AAP party*, claimed that OddEven experiment would result in an improved air quality and eventually a decreased traffic congestion, the principal opposition party in Delhi *BJP, previously led by India PM*, argued that the experiment will have no impact but disturbing people's daily commute in the city. In order to track the public discourse toward this experiment, we propose to distinguish three major phases (1) Two weeks before the experiment (Anticipation) (2) Two weeks during the experiment (Experience) and (3) Two weeks after the experiment (Recollection).

Literature review. Although OddEven took place in Delhi, the experiment attracted national and international attention. In our study, we are interested in understanding people's opinion with a focus on political and spatio-temporal factors that shaped the public discourse. This paper contributes to a growing body of literature on exploiting social media platforms to better understand human behavior that lies at the intersection of social, political, and urban sciences. Researchers in these areas have focused on studying human social interactions on twitter to better understand their opinions in general and their political views in particular. While there are few papers that study the political influence of a large-scale urban experiment, many researchers used the platform to analyze people's political views [4,6,7,9,11,14,16]. Barber [4] has developed a *Bayesian spatial following* model that takes into account users' Twitter network to estimate the ideological position of average citizens in several countries. The main finding of the author was an efficient inference of users political leaning based solely on Twitter structural network. Another work by Barber [5] builds on 12 political and non-political events to understand the role of social media in the formation of polarized groups as well as user opinion. The key finding is that during certain political-driven events, individuals with similar political orientation tend to engage in discussions and share similar opinions, creating what is known as *echo chamber*. Other attempts to infer the political leaning of users include Golbeck and Hansen work of using Twitter following relationships to infer political preferences [13], and Colleoni et al. who use a combination of machine learning and social network analysis to categorize users as Democrats or Republicans based on what they share on social networks [8].

Research Questions. The current literature does not offer a comprehensive overview on using social interactions to assess the impact of political bias in how large scale urban initiatives are perceived by people.

The objective of this paper is to understand the political factors that contribute to citizens' perception towards the urban initiative. The main research questions are summarized as follows:

- **RQ1** Does political affiliation influence people perception and opinion about real-life experiment?
- **RQ2** Does personal experience have any impact on reducing political bias and preconceptions?
- **RQ3** Is there enough publicly available data that one could use to address such inquiries?

Approach and contributions. To run this study, we use Twitter to sense the public discourse toward `OddEven` experiment. A list of relevant keywords has been manually created and was continuously curated to catch relevant tweets. The obtained collection consists of more than 300 K tweets posted by 64 K different users. It spans from December 17th, 2015 to February 5th, 2016 covering most of the three phases of the experiment: Anticipation, Experience, and Eecollection. We collect the contextual urban data about the experiment to quantify the actual impact of `OddEven` on air quality and traffic congestion. Our findings were similar to other studies [15,18,19,21] in that the experiment has had a positive impact of traffic congestion and no impact at all on air quality. These findings are used as a ground truth in our study.

We use Twitter data (Content) to infer the political leaning of users as well as their locations. Users are then clustered based on these two dimensions. For each cluster, we use sentiment analysis to assess the overall opinion of groups toward different topics (air quality & traffic congestion) during the three phases of the experiments. Our analysis reveals the following key findings:

- Overall, political formation plays a significant role in the way people perceive the outcome of natural experiments. Interestingly enough, we found that even people who live outside Delhi and India, had strong opinions about the success & failure of the experiment.
- Personal experience is able to overcome political bias. This was the case when we limited the analysis on those who live inside Delhi, i.e., people who have had a personal experience of OddEven.

Roadmap. In what follows, we start by describing the different datasets that we used to study people's opinion. Then, we introduce the methods that have been used to sense people's opinion as well as quantifying the political affiliation of twitter users. Next, we question and study our finiding based on different contextual dimensions.

2 Data

In order to study the impact of the experiment, we have collected data from twitter to track public opinion about OddEven whereas we collected data on air quality and traffic congestion to estimate the actual outcomes of the experiment. We describe in the following the processes by which data is collected and curated from different sources.

2.1 Twitter

Collecting relevant tweets. The data collection process was carried out using the Twitter Streaming API. First, we build a list of seed hash-tags that are used during experiment. Then, we expand this list to identify more tweets that could be potentially used during the experiment. The final list contains the following keywords/hashtags: OddEven, *Odd Even, ToxicDelhi, ICantBreathe, Delhi, Even-OddFormula, DelhiChokes, LetDelhiBreathe, NationalGreenTribunal, DelhiOddEvenLogic, DelhiPollution, pollutionfreeDelhi, IPledgeForOddEven, IamWithOddEven, EvenYourOdds, OddEvenMovement, OddEvenPlan, OddEvenFormula,* and *EvenOddPlan.* Finally, we employ various techniques to clean the data. The cleaning step includes the removal of irrelevant tweets, and identifying bots that use trending hashtags to publish irrelevant tweets.

The collection process spans across six weeks, starting from December 17th, 2015 to February 5th, 2016, covering two weeks before, during and after the experiment. The result of our dataset after filtering the non relevant data is 320,450 tweets, posted by 63,988 unique users. Figure 1 shows the volume of tweets as well as the number of active users over time.

Collecting network data. We identified Twitter accounts that authored at least one tweet related to OddEven experiment and collect their network information (followers and followees) as well as up to 3,200 of the latest tweets that they authored or re-tweeted. Note that as per Twitter policy, it is not possible to retrieve more than 3,200 per user.

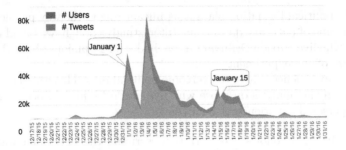

Fig. 1. Distribution of tweets and users discussing #OddEven experiment. Most of Twitter traffic took place during the experience. We observe that the recollection period was quite active compared to the anticipation period.

2.2 Air Quality

In order to measure the success of the experiment with respect to air quality improvement, we collected environmental data to sense pollution levels in the city. Our exploration allowed us to identify and compare different data sources that offer Air Quality datasets. Examples of such open platforms include: U.S. Embassy air Quality Monitoring Station[1], and CPCB Program[2]. Figure 2(a) shows the distribution of Air Quality stations. The figure also shows the important number of industries inside and surrounding the city of Delhi that may have a significant impact on the air quality regardless of OddEven experiment.

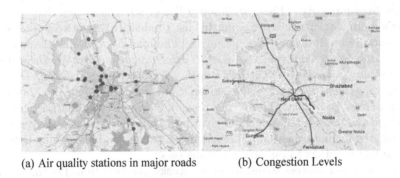

(a) Air quality stations in major roads   (b) Congestion Levels

Fig. 2. Illustration of Odd even impact on Traffic Congestion and Air Quality. The right panel showcases congestion levels in major highways linking the city of Delhi to its neighboring suburbs. The left panel showcases Air Quality stations, Dwarka and Shadipur (light blue) in Delhi industrial areas (purple spots) (Color figure online).

---

[1] http://newdelhi.usembassy.gov/airqualitydata.html.
[2] http://www.cpcb.gov.in/.

2.3   Road Traffic Congestion

With the help of Delhi-born scientists, we have manually and carefully identified a short list of road segments (origin-destination pairs) reputed to be of the most congested in Delhi. We also identified the main surrounding agglomerations of Delhi and created routes from-to Delhi to those cities. Figure 2(b) shows the selected routes for a visual inspection. We use Google Maps API to request the timely details about the traffic status for the list of road segments every 15 min. The collected data has been used to track Travel Time (TT) for each origin-destination route at different times of the day, different days of the week; before, within, and after the experiment.

3   Methods

Recall that our main objective is to verify whether or not political affiliation influences human perception in real life urban experiments such as OddEven.

The first task is to identify the political leaning of users. We use Twitter's data, which is composed of tweets, hashtags, mentions, user biographies, and social links (friends and followers) in order to train different multi-class classifiers to infer one of the four political labels: (1) AAP supporters, (2) BJP supporters, (3) Bi-political, and (4) Apolitical. We manually labeled a training set by looking at users who mentioned their political affinities in their Twitter biographies. Surprisingly enough, we found that the political leaning of users can be accurately inferred by looking at people and accounts they follow. More details and discussions will be reported in the next section.

The second task is to mine the opinion of different users and political camps (the four aforementioned labels) toward OddEven experiment. To do so, we use sentiment analysis as a mean to quantify people's opinion [17]. We are mainly interested in measuring whether people and groups expressed positive, negative, or neutral opinions. We use a tool introduced by Thelwall et al. called "Sentistrength" to score the sentiment of individual tweets [23]. This method is reported to be effective and has been specifically designed to deal with short-text shared on social media platforms. We also use LabMT to assess the sentiment trend of different political groups [10]. LabMT is known to perform better and more accurately for large pieces of text, which is the case when we concatenate all tweets posted by the members of a given political camp. We also introduce the concept of opinionated users as opposed to neutral users. For us, a user is labeled as opinionated if she has authored more positive and negative tweets than neutral tweets. For both cases, we compute sentiments over time (on daily basis) and for different topics related to OddEven experiment, namely: air quality, and traffic congestion. It is important to recall that as per the official notification of OddEven [3], the objective was to curb air pollution and no mentions were made to improving traffic congestion. However, one would expect that people will observe the "corollary" impact of the experiment on traffic congestion as the number of cars allowed to drive in the city is reduced.

4   Results and Discussion

We report in this section the main findings of our analysis. We first present the ground reality to identify how biased people are. Then, we explain how did we infer the political leaning of users using different types of data from Twitter and different methods. Finally, we analyze opinion and sentiment trends observed in different configurations of time, geographical location and topics.

4.1   The Ground Reality

In order to understand the perception of Twitter users toward the experiment, it is important to assess the ground reality and measure the extend to which *OddEven* succeeded in fulfilling its main goal of reducing air pollution, as well as its impact on traffic congestion. We analyzed the time series of collected air quality readings before, during and after the experiment. We analyzed also Google Traffic data for the predefined representative pairs of origin-destination routes in Delhi. Our findings were aligned with those of the Indian Energy and Resources Institute (TERI) listed in [18,19] and with other studies [15,21] that focus on analyzing the impact of the experiment of both air quality and traffic congestion.

There was a consensus among all these studies according to which OddEven has significantly improved traffic congestion (e.g., 21% reduction in cars and 18% increase in average speed [19]). However, the air quality in the city of Delhi – which was the primary goal of the experiment – did not improve.

4.2   Inferring Political Leaning

The first task was to infer the political leaning of users on Twitter. By mining biographies – a short text used by Twitter users to describe themselves and their interest on Twitter – we identify users who publicly expressed their political affiliation and we use them for training. Using biographies to identify users' political affiliation is widely used [22]. Note that biographies are only used to create the set of labeled users whereas features to identify the political leaning of users could include other data such as tweets authors, hashtags, mentions, followers and followees, etc. Among the set of 64 K users that we have, we searched for all those who mentioned AAP, BJP, or any other term related to these two political parties (e.g., names of prominent personalities) in the biography field of their Twitter accounts. Next, we manually read the selected biographies and manually labeled them as belonging to one of the classes of interest. This step was important to discard users who may mention political camps related terms but do not endorse them. This is for instance the case of a user who would express that he dislikes a given political personality. Thus, we obtained 3,300 Twitter accounts, 944 are labeled as AAP supporters (AAP is ruling the state of Delhi) and 2,381 labeled as BJP supporters (BJP is ruling India.)

Next, we built a multi-class Support Vector Machine (SVM) classifier to classify users into four different political camps: AAP supporters, BJP supporters,

Table 1. Performance of the multi-class SVM classifier in predicting the political camp of users using different features

Features	# Features	Accuracy	Precision	Recall	F1
Hashtags (H)	1181	0.685	0.722	0.617	0.665
Friends (F)	2455	0.716	0.735	0.685	0.709*
Mentions (M)	2307	0.700	0.728	0.649	0.686
H & F	3636	0.718	0.744	0.671	0.705
H & M	3488	0.716	0.746	0.658	0.699
F & M	4762	0.735	0.761	0.662	0.708
Dir. Fri	-	0.951	0.966	0.973	0.959

bi-political, apolitical. Given the known difficulty of inferring the political leaning of users [7], we tested the classifier with different feature combinations: (1) Hashtags (2) Friendship network (3) Mention network (4) Hashtags & Friends. (5) Hashtags & Mentions. (6) Friends & Mentions. For every set, we consider top 10% shared features (example: top 10% shared Hashtags) used by all users.

Table 1 summarizes the obtained results for every classifier. Clearly, the Friends features-set outperforms all other combinations in terms of F1 score. Yet, the eye scanning of the results revealed they are not as good as one would expect. Thus, inspired by the predictive power of the friendship network (recall that friends are people that a user follows on Twitter) we used another intuitive approach to determine the political affiliation of users (Direct Friendship). We first identified political leaders from both parties: BJP and AAP. Next, we use a simple heuristic to label users into one of the four political camps we created. Users who only follow the BJP leaders on Twitter are labeled as BJP supporters and users who only follow AAP leaders are labeled as AAP supporters. Similarly, users who follow leaders from both parties are labeled as Bi-political whereas those who do not follow any of the leaders are labeled as Apolitical. The last row in Table 1 shows that the intuitive and straightforward method outperforms all SVM based classifiers.

4.3 Political Bias vs. Personal Experience in Shaping Human Perception

At this point, and based on our ground reality analysis, we can say the OddEven experiment missed its objective in reducing air pollution, but the road traffic congestion which was not the main target of the experiment did improve. One of the co-authors did visit Delhi during the experience and has confirmed to us this observation.

The question now is to know what supporters of different camps said about the experiment in general, and about air pollution and traffic congestion in particular. Recall that OddEven was subject to political polarization as AAP who implemented the experiment claimed its usefulness whereas BJP has put it in doubt.

We started by associating every tweet authored by a user to a political camp to which she belongs. For every camp, we aggregate the sentiment of its members per time intervals of one day. We use LabMT for this task. Figure 3a illustrates different camps sentiment over time. Sentiment scores ranges in [1,9] interval with 1 being the less positive value and 9 the most positive one. The visual inspection reveals a clearly that AAP supporters are more positive (enthusiastic) about OddEven compared to their BJP counterparts. The Pearson correlation between the sentiment time series if AAP and BJP supporters is equal to 0.1465.

However, when we limited the analysis to only users living in Delhi to remove noise from people expressing opinions without having a personal experience of OddEven, we found the the differences in opinion were less significant as shown in Fig. 3b. Thus, we recomputed the Pearson correlation score between the sentiment time series of the two camps, by considering only members living in Delhi, we found that it jumped to 0.2587. This means that the global trends of opinion for BJP were driven by the mass of users who did not experience OddEven and yet decided to align with the positions of their political party.

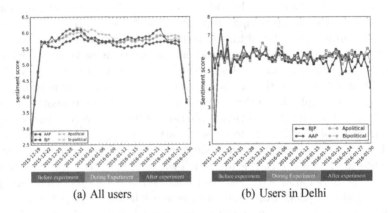

| (a) All users | (b) Users in Delhi |

Fig. 3. Overall sentiment over time of the four different political camps. Panel (a) showcases the sentiment distribution of all users who interacted with OddEven. Panel (b) showcases the sentiment distribution of users living in Delhi.

To enable a fine grained analysis, we used SentiStrength[3] tool to label individual tweets as positive, negative, or neutral. Thus, we could aggregate sentiment at the level of individual users and have it tracked over time. Table 2 shows the distribution of the number of positive and negative tweets by camp and time. We refer to these tweets as opinionated tweets (in contrast to neutral tweets.) We can see that number of opinionated tweets during the experiment (experience phase) is high in both camps varying between 3 K and 5K tweets, but this burst faded out after this period. Moreover, we can see that the overall volume of opinionated tweets lay inside bi-political and apolitical camps.

---

[3] http://sentistrength.wlv.ac.uk/.

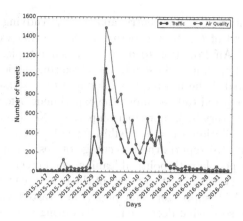

Fig. 4. Distribution of tweets about Air Quality and Traffic Congestion over time

Table 2. Number of positive/negative tweets posted by each camp over time. Most of the tweets lay in the apolitical and bi-political camps.

Camp/Time	Anticipation	Experience	Recollection
AAP	$103(41\%)^+/144(59\%)^-$	$3470(59\%)^+/2319(41\%)^-$	$1256(63\%)^+/722(36\%)^-$
BJP	$74(38\%)^+/120(62\%)^-$	$1746(52\%)^+/1617(48\%)^-$	$374(42\%)^+/504(58\%)^-$
Apolitical	$321(38\%)^+/506(62\%)^-$	$14490(64\%)^+/8117(36\%)^-$	$3327(59\%)^+/2274(41\%)^-$
Bi-political	$2137(44\%)^+/2641(56\%)^-$	$62692(55\%)^+/50900(45\%)^-$	$22482(60\%)^+/14706(40\%)^-$

Figure 4 illustrates the distribution over time of tweets volume corresponding to different topics. We use manually curated keyword dictionaries related to different topics in order to classify tweets into: air pollution, and traffic congestion. Note that one tweet can belong to different topics if its content match keywords from different lists. Interestingly, we found that all topics received most of their contributions at the beginning of the experiment. For instance, one of the most noticeable burst is on the first three days of OddEven that were off days (concatenation of a long weekend and beginning of year's holidays.) Another interesting observation is that air quality was the main discussed topic in the anticipation phase, followed by congestion. This is mainly due to the fact that the main reason for implementing OddEven was to reduce air pollution.

Next, we will share our findings regarding the two topics separately. For each topic, we report the volume of opinionated users as well as the negativity and positivity in each camp in order to capture the evolution of users engagement in the six weeks of the study. In addition, we introduce the location dimension to have a closer inspection on the opinion of users who had personal experience of OddEven.

Air Quality. We start our topic-centric analysis by studying tweets about Air Quality in the context of *OddEven* experiment. Notice that we interchangeably use Air Quality and Air Pollution to refer to the same topic. Figure 5(a) illustrates the number of opinionated users in the three time periods. A user is considered as opinionated if she has more opinionated tweets than neutral tweets. We see that people started talking about the experiment before it took place as the expectations were very high (anticipation period). Needless to say, the media has focused on the pollution aspect as Delhi is one of the most polluted cities in the world [2]. Figure 5(b) reports the percentage of positive users over different periods of time. For people with political leaning, the percentage of positivity in general has increased during the two weeks of the experiment. More specifically, the expectations of AAP supporters were high (they started with 37% of positive tweets), but this has somewhat decreased to 15% during the first week of the recollection period. BJP supporters on the other side remained skeptical throughout the experiment. Indeed, we see that during all the periods, positive tweets varied between 12% and 18% only. Generally speaking, people with no political drive have had a negative opinion about Air Quality. For instance, during the experiment, the percentage of positive tweets was as low as 12%. Despite the huge difference in the number of users in bi-political and apolitical groups, we found that they share similar views, which are well aligned with the ground truth.

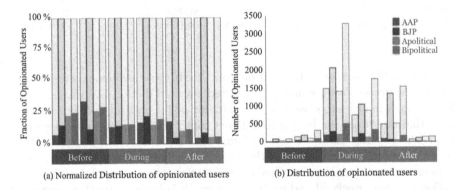

(a) Normalized Distribution of opinionated users   (b) Distribution of opinionated users

Fig. 5. Distribution of opinionated users discussing Air Quality. Panel(a) presents the volume of opinionated users, Panel(b) presents the percentage of opinionated users.

Next, we introduced the location dimension to capture the effect of personal experience of reality. Location of users is extracted from the "location" attribute of their Twitter profiles. We distinguish three different locations: Inside Delhi, Inside India (but not in Delhi), and Outside India. In Fig. 6(a) that illustrates the number of users who are discussing Air Quality in Delhi over time period together with their sentiment, we see that AAP and BJP supporters are equally negative about the topic. However, when we looked at people who live in India but outside Delhi (Fig. 6(b)), we found the number of BJP supporters who discussed air

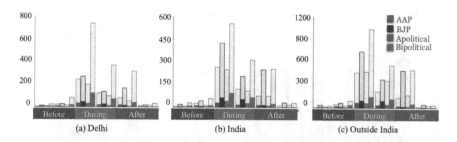

Fig. 6. Fraction of opinionated users in Delhi, India, and outside India discussing Air Quality topic over time

quality to be more than the number of AAP supporters. This is related to the fact that BJP is a national and an old party, while AAP is a new party promising to bring change to the traditional political system. The same pattern is outlined in Fig. 6(c) for people living outside India.

Traffic Congestion. After Air Quality, we analyze the traffic congestion topic in the context of OddEven experiment. Figure 7(a) illustrates the number of opinionated users at different phases of the experiment. The figure shows that bipolitical group is over taking other groups in terms of volume of positive tweets. Having the distribution of tweets is interesting in this case to highlight the fact that the topic was not a main focus during the "anticipation" period (with a maximum of one hundred unique engaged users in all camps). However, congestion has popped up during the experiment where the number of users varied between 550 and 2000 users in different camps. Figure 7(b) reports the percentage of opinionated users over time periods. As the number of tweets was very low before the experiment, it is difficult to generalize any observed pattern, even though one can see that most of the tweets were positive. The percentage of positive users varied between 50% and 60% in AAP camp, more than any other one. BJP supporters were skeptical, only 40% of users in this camp were positive about the improvement in traffic congestion. Another observation that can be made is that traffic congestion is a very localized problem that varies from a neighborhood to another. This is different from air quality where people in the same city breath "almost" the same air. Thus, opinion on traffic can vary from neighborhood to another. As we do not have enough geo-coded tweets, we could not deepen our analysis to provide high-resolution spatial analysis.

Similarly to the previous analysis, we introduce the location dimension in our analysis to see how people who have witnessed the experiment reacted compared to the outsiders. Figure 8 presents the number of users who engaged with traffic topic in Delhi. We see that bi-political camp was the most engaged among other camps. In terms of sentiment, we see that AAP supporters were more positive in Delhi. The figure also shows that BJP supporters in India engaged in the discourse about traffic more than those in Delhi, due to the fact that BJP is a big national party. BJP engagement was negative. Surprisingly, we found that the number of

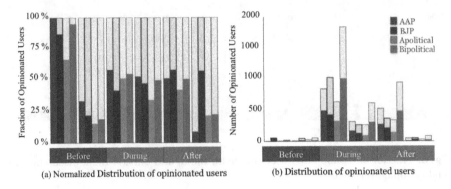

(a) Normalized Distribution of opinionated users
(b) Distribution of opinionated users

Fig. 7. Distribution of opinionated users discussing Traffic congestion. Panel(a) presents the volume of opinionated users, Panel(b) presents the percentage of opinionated users.

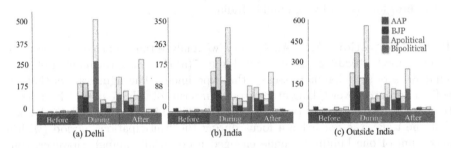

(a) Delhi   (b) India   (c) Outside India

Fig. 8. Fraction of opinionated users in Delhi, India and outside India discussing Traffic topic over time.

BJP supporters living outside India who engaged in the discussion was higher than those living in India which reveals the international echo of OddEven.

5 Conclusion

We present in this paper our findings about the role of political affiliation on human perception. Our case study was OddEven, a live real-world and large-scale experiment that took place in Delhi. To conduct the study, we mined twitter data to capture the public discourse. We used also Delhi's air quality stations' data to measure the effectiveness of the experiment in reducing air pollution, and used Google Traffic API data to estimate the impact on traffic congestion. Our findings were aligned with other studies that focused on analyzing the impact of Odd Even experiment. We used state of the art machine learning techniques to infer the political leaning and sentiment analysis to understand people's opinion.

Our findings reveal a strong alignment between people perceptions and positions of the political parties to which they belong. This is particularly amplified in cases where people are not exposed to the realities on the ground. We found also that personal experience does help people formulate objective opinion and overcome political biases. For instance, BJP supporters living in Delhi tended to be less skeptical about OddEven when compared to their fellows in BJP who live outside Delhi. This analysis shows demonstrated the use of social media to analyze urban experiments and design better urban policy strategies.

References

1. Delhi government's notification (2015). http://it.delhigovt.nic.in/writereaddata/egaz20157544.pdf
2. Delhi's cars and the odd-even formula (2016). www.aljazeera.com/news/2016/01/delhi-cars-odd-formula-india-pollution-160103075511009.html
3. Oddeven official notification (2016). http://it.delhigovt.nic.in/writereaddata/egaz20157544.pdf
4. Barber, P.: Birds of the same feather tweet together: Bayesian ideal point estimation using Twitter data. Polit. Anal. 23(1), 76–91 (2015)
5. Barberá, P., Jost, J.T., Nagler, J., Tucker, J.A., Bonneau, R.: Tweeting from left to right: Is online political communication more than an echo chamber? Psychol. Sci. 26, 1531–1542 (2015)
6. Barberá, P., Rivero, G.: Understanding the political representativeness of Twitter users. Soc. Sci. Comput. Rev. 33, 712–729 (2014). 0894439314558836
7. Cohen, R., Ruths, D.: Classifying political orientation on Twitter: it's not easy!. In: Proceedings of ICWSM 2013 (2013)
8. Colleoni, E., Rozza, A., Arvidsson, A.: Echo chamber or public sphere? predicting political orientation and measuring political homophily in Twitter using big data. J. Commun. 64(2), 317–332 (2014)
9. Conover, M.D., Gonçalves, B., Ratkiewicz, J., Flammini, A., Menczer, F.: Predicting the political alignment of Twitter users. In: Proceedings of the 2011 IEEE Third International Conference on Privacy, Security, Risk and Trust (PASSAT) and 2011 IEEE Third Inernational Conference on Social Computing (SocialCom), pp. 192–199 (2011)
10. Dodds, P.S., Clark, E.M., Desu, S., Frank, M.R., Reagan, A.J., Williams, J.R., Mitchell, L., Harris, K.D., Kloumann, I.M., Bagrow, J.P., et al.: Human language reveals a universal positivity bias. Proc. Natl. Acad. Sci. 112(8), 2389–2394 (2015)
11. Fowler, J.H., Heaney, M.T., Nickerson, D.W., Padgett, J.F., Sinclair, B.: Causality in political networks. Am. Polit. Res. 39(2), 437–480 (2011)
12. Gehl, J.: Cities for People. Island press, Washington, D.C. (2013)
13. Golbeck, J., Hansen, D.: A method for computing political preference among Twitter followers. Soc. Netw. 36, 177–184 (2014)
14. Himelboim, I., McCreery, S., Smith, M.: Birds of a feather tweet together: Integrating network and content analyses to examine cross-ideology exposure on Twitter. J. Comput.-Med. Commun. 18(2), 40–60 (2013)
15. Kumar, P., Gulia, S., Harrison, R.M., Khare, M.: The influence of odd-even car trial on fine and coarse particles in delhi. Environ. Pollut. 225, 20–30 (2017)
16. Makazhanov, A., Rafiei, D., Waqar, M.: Predicting political preference of Twitter users. Soc. Netw. Anal. Min. 4(1), 1–15 (2014)
17. Pang, B., Lee, L., et al.: Opinion mining and sentiment analysis. Found. Trends® Inf. Retr. 2(1–2), 1–135 (2008)

18. Sehgal, M., Gautam, S.K.: Odd even story of delhi traffic and air pollution. Int. J. Environ. Stud. **73**(2), 170–172 (2016)
19. Sharma, S., Malik, J., Suresh, R., Ghosh, P.: Analysis of odd-even scheme-full report. TERIIN Institute (2016). http://www.teriin.org/odd-even-scheme/
20. Singh, S.K.: Scenario of Urban transport in Indian cities: challenges and the way forward. In: Dev, S.M., Yedla, S. (eds.) Cities and Sustainability. SPBE, pp. 81–111. Springer, New Delhi (2015). doi:10.1007/978-81-322-2310-8_5
21. Singhania, K., Girish, G., Vincent, E.N.: Impact of odd-even rationing of vehicular movement in Delhi on air pollution levels. Low Carbon Econ. **7**(04), 151 (2016)
22. Tan, C., Lee, L., Tang, J., Jiang, L., Zhou, M., Li, P.: User-level sentiment analysis incorporating social networks. In: Proceedings of the 17th ACM SIGKDD International Conference on Knowledge Discovery and Data Mining, pp. 1397–1405. ACM (2011)
23. Thelwall, M., Buckley, K., Paltoglou, G., Cai, D., Kappas, A.: Sentiment strength detection in short informal text. J. Am. Soc. Inform. Sci. Technol. **61**(12), 2544–2558 (2010)
24. WHO: WHO Global Urban Ambient Air Pollution Database (2014). www.who.int/phe/health_topics/outdoorair/databases/cities/en/
25. Zheng, Y., Liu, F., Hsieh, H.P.: U-air: when urban air quality inference meets big data. In: Proceedings of the 19th ACM SIGKDD International Conference on Knowledge Discovery and Data Mining, pp. 1436–1444. ACM (2013)

Discovering the Typing Behaviour of Parkinson's Patients Using Topic Models

Antony Milne[1(✉)], Mihalis Nicolaou[1,2], and Katayoun Farrahi[1]

[1] Goldsmiths, University of London, London, UK
antony.milne@gmail.com
[2] Imperial College London, London, UK

Abstract. Sensing health-related behaviours in an unobtrusive, ubiquitous and cost-effective manner carries significant benefits to healthcare and patient management. In this paper, we focus on detecting typing behaviour that is characteristic of patients suffering from Parkinson's disease. We consider typing data obtained from subjects with and without Parkinson's, and we present a framework based on topic models that determines the differing behaviours between these two groups based on the key hold time. By learning a topic model on each group separately and measuring the dissimilarity between topic distributions, we are able to identify particular topics that emerge in Parkinson's patients and have low probability for the control group, demonstrating a clear shift in terms of key stroke duration. Our results further support the utilisation of key stroke logs for the early onset detection of Parkinson's disease, while the method presented is straightforwardly generalisable to similar applications.

Keywords: Health behaviour models · Topic models · Latent Dirichlet Allocation

1 Introduction

Early diagnosis of progressive neurodegenerative disease plays a crucial role in maximising the impact of medication and preventing (as far as possible) further progression of the disease. In particular, Parkinson's disease is considered a slow progressing neurodegenerative disease. While diagnosis is usually performed by considering the patient's symptoms as well as a physical examination, a main characteristic of Parkinson's disease lies in the manifestation of motor symptoms during the early stage of the disease. Since the cost of constantly monitoring motor signs can be prohibitive for healthcare systems, a possible alternative is to study the daily behaviours of patients. Typing behaviour can be indicative of degenerative motor signs during the early stages of the disease. This constitutes an unobtrusive, ubiquitous, transparent and inexpensive approach, since data can be collected while subjects perform their daily routines.

Motivated by the above, in this paper we study the typing behaviour of Parkinson's patients in an unsupervised setting, and contrast results to a

© Springer International Publishing AG 2017
G.L. Ciampaglia et al. (Eds.): SocInfo 2017, Part II, LNCS 10540, pp. 89–97, 2017.
DOI: 10.1007/978-3-319-67256-4_9

control group. To this end, we consider topic models, and in particular Latent Dirichlet Allocation (LDA) [2], a statistical generative model that has been successfully employed in human behaviour mining problems in various contexts [4, 7–9,11]. LDA discovers semantically coherent latent *topics* in a collection of data (called a *corpus*), with low-level features (or *words*) being generated from a distribution of topics. Considering a recently released dataset of typing data [5], we present an approach where LDA models are trained on each of the Parkinson's and control groups. We consider a typing session to be analogous to a *document*, with the key hold durations corresponding to words. We show that discovered topics are heavily shifted towards long key hold times in the Parkinson's patient group, and that discovering topics containing long key press durations is likely to be an indicator of the disease. While key hold times are the dominant feature considered in this paper, the methodology proposed can easily extend to words encoding multiple features. We further validate our findings by computing the similarity between topics across groups with the Bhattacharyya coefficient. The results of this analysis indicate which topics, and therefore which words and co-occurrence of words, have the highest probability of being associated with Parkinson's disease.

2   Related Work

Machine learning techniques have previously been used to monitor and automatically detect the severity of Parkinson's symptoms considering speech data [6,15]. Home monitoring systems for Parkinson's patients have also been developed using accelerometer data [3] as well as gyroscope data sensing upper body activities [13]. Wearable sensor data has been used to estimate the severity of Parkinson's symptoms, such as tremor, bradykinesia and dyskinesia from accelerometer data features [12]. While most works in the wearable sensing community consider Parkinson's monitoring using upper body sensors, shoe worn sensors have also been used to assess locomotion for early diagnosis [10]. Bachlin et al. [1] use wearable technology to study gait, particularly freezing of gait by using accelerometer sensors attached to the belt and lower body.

Giancardo et al. [12] recently proposed to use typing data for the detection of Parkinson's disease. This is the first study to consider typing data and it has the major advantage of "transparency" and ubiquitousness. Giancardo et al. propose a neuroQWERTY index (nQi) based on key hold times in order to classify Parkinson's vs. control patients. In this work, we consider a very different approach to the problem, one based on unsupervised learning, and the goal is to discover the precise patterns which may be discriminative of Parkinson's disease. Our proposed approach is generalisable to new features that can be obtained by typing and to other similar problems.

3   Methodology

All the analysis performed in this paper uses the datasets MIT-CS1PD and MIT-CS2PD associated with Ref. [5]. Subjects in Madrid, Spain performed typing tests by transcribing a folk tale on a word processor for 15 min with key stroke data being recorded. Some subjects completed two such typing tests. For our purposes, the key strokes from each individual typing test form a *document*. In total there are 116 documents, of which $D^P = 60$ correspond to Parkinson's sufferers and $D^C = 56$ to control subjects. These two collections of documents correspond to our groups of Parkinson's and control. Using the language of LDA [2], each collection of documents forms a *corpus*.

The documents are preprocessed to keep only key presses corresponding to alphabetic and the space, comma, period and return keys. Thus any extraneous key presses such as shift, accents and backspaces are removed. To filter out erroneously recorded data (e.g., arising from simultaneous or overlapping key strokes) we keep only key strokes whose duration is between 0 and 0.5 s, and whose travel time to the following key is between 0.02 and 20 s. Following this data cleaning procedure, the average number of key strokes in a document is 1240 (standard deviation 470).

We next convert each document into a collection of *words* that will be analysed by the topic model. Again, we emphasise that a 'word' in this context does not describe the actual Spanish word typed, but instead relates to the duration for which each key is pressed. Combining the control and Parkinson's corpora, we find a set of boundaries that will allocate each key press duration into one of 50 bins. These boundaries are calculated so that there is a roughly equal number of key strokes in each bin across the two corpora. Owing to the distribution of key press durations, the bin widths are not uniform. For example, bin number 5 corresponds to a key press between 0.0615 and 0.0645 s, whilst bin number 45 corresponds to a key press between 0.1697 and 0.1771 s. The word that labels each key stroke is given by the number of the key press duration bin to which it is allocated. We therefore have a vocabulary $\mathcal{V} = \{1, 2, \ldots, 50\}$, where the word 1 corresponds to the shortest time bin and the word 50 corresponds to the longest time bin. A document d then consists of a sequence of N_d words drawn from $\mathcal{V}$.

We train a separate LDA model on each of the two corpora independently. Each model is trained on all documents in the corpus in order to infer the underlying distributions. In particular, the inference identifies latent topics that describe documents, where each document can be thought of as a random mixture over topics; for document d, the probability distribution $\Theta_d(t)$ gives the probability of drawing a word from topic t. Each topic will itself consist of a distribution over words; for topic t, the probability distribution $\Phi_t(w)$ gives the probability of drawing word $w \in \mathcal{V}$ from the topic t. Note that since we are applying LDA to the two groups independently, we will discover different distributions for the control and Parkinson's corpora, which we label with the appropriate superscript. We instruct LDA to discover $T = 50$ topics for each corpus using $\alpha = 50/T = 1$ and $\beta = 0.1$ for the hyperparameters that describe the underlying prior Dirichlet distributions for $\Theta^{C,P}$ and $\Phi^{C,P}$ respectively. These values are chosen heuristically and follow the guidance given in Ref. [14]. The procedure of building LDA models from the datasets is illustrated in Fig. 1.

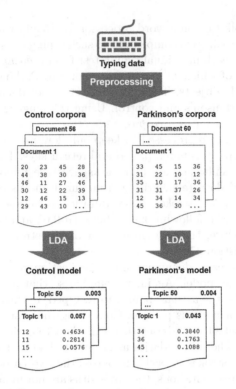

Fig. 1. An outline of the procedure: typing data is preprocessed to form a control corpus and a Parkinson's corpus. Each corpus consists of a set of documents (typing sessions) formed from a sequence of words (key stroke durations). LDA then infers 50 latent topics for each corpus.

4   Results

4.1   Topic Discovery on Parkinson's and Control Groups

The LDA models trained on the control and Parkinson's groups are visualized in Figs. 2 and 3. We emphasise that the words are common between the two datasets (i.e., $w = 23$, for example, will always refer to key presses of the same duration), whilst the meaning of the topics is different for the control and Parkinson's datasets (i.e., the control topic $t^C = 23$, for example, does *not* contain the same words as the Parkinson's topic $t^P = 23$). Figure 2 shows the composition of documents as a mixture of topics, and Fig. 3 shows the word content of each of the topics.

Note that, within each corpus, topics are ordered according to their probabilities. Thus $t^{C,P} = 1$ corresponds to the topic that is most likely to be drawn for generating a document, $t^{C,P} = 2$ is the next most likely, and so on (the least likely topic is $t^{C,P} = 50$). The ordering of documents has no particular significance.

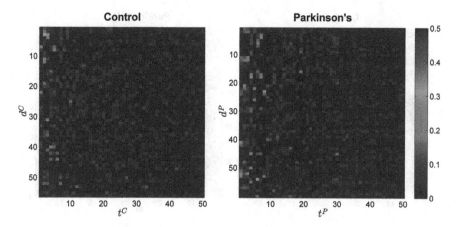

Fig. 2. The distribution of topics discovered in each document, $\Theta^{C}_{d^C}(t^C)$ and $\Theta^{P}_{d^P}(t^P)$. Results for the control corpus are shown on the left, and results for the Parkinson's corpus are shown on the right. The same colour scale has been used for both plots, and each row sums to 1. The points at $(t^C, d^C) = (7, 48)$ and $(1, 54)$ have been clipped to the limit of the colour scale.

Figure 2 shows that each document is indeed generated by a probabilistic mixture of a range of topics. As expected from the labelling, the most probable topics are towards the left of each plot. Although there are some particularly high density data points for the control corpus (indicating that a document is composed of just a few topics), there is no clear distinction between the control and Parkinson's corpora in terms of the distribution of topics over documents. In other words, both a control and Parkinson's typing session can be modelled using a similar distribution of topics. In order to discriminate between control and Parkinson's typing data, we turn to the content of these latent topics.

Figure 3 demonstrates that the words discovered in each topic are noticeably different for the control and Parkinson's corpora. There is a clear tendency towards Parkinson's topics containing words with higher labels, which correspond to longer key press durations. In particular, we might highlight $t^P = 4, 6$, which contain high density points around long key press durations, as particularly indicative. These topics are relatively likely to be drawn when generating a Parkinson's document, and no similar topics exist for the control corpus. They could thus be regarded as potential signatures for Parkinson's disease.

It is also worth noting that there appears to be some quite similar topics for the control and Parkinson's corpora, although the topic label (and hence relative probability) may be different, e.g., compare $t^C = 1$ with $t^P = 8$. In both corpora, a topic tends to be composed of words clustered around a certain label. This indicates that for both the control and Parkinson's subjects, similar length key press durations tend to co-occur in a given document. From our results the clearest signature of Parkinson's is the content of topics discovered by LDA;

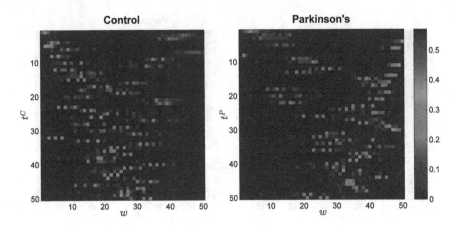

Fig. 3. The distribution of words discovered in each topic, $\Phi^C_{t^C}(w)$ and $\Phi^P_{t^P}(w)$. Results for the control corpus are shown on the left, and results for the Parkinson's corpus are shown on the right. The same colour scale has been used for both plots, and each row sums to 1. The point at $(w, t^P) = (50, 7)$ has been clipped to the limit of the colour scale.

in particular, topics which show long key press durations seem to be strongly indicative of Parkinson's disease.

4.2 Topic Similarity Analysis to Discover Parkinson's Behaviour

We now systematise the detection of signature Parkinson's topics by computing the similarity between topics discovered for the control group and those for the Parkinson's group. In particular, for each control topic t^C and Parkinson's topic t^P we compute the Bhattacharyya coefficient

$$\rho(t^C, t^P) = \sum_{w \in \mathcal{V}} \sqrt{\Phi^C_{t^C}(w)\, \Phi^P_{t^P}(w)}, \tag{1}$$

where the summation runs over all words in the vocabulary. This gives a measure of the overlap between the distribution $\Phi^C_{t^C}$ and $\Phi^C_{t^C}$. As a measure of the "uniqueness" of a given Parkinson's topic t^P, we then compute the average Bhattacharyya coefficient,

$$\bar{\rho}(t^P) = \frac{1}{T} \sum_{t^C=1}^{T} \rho(t^C, t^P). \tag{2}$$

A small value of $\bar{\rho}(t^P)$ indicates that there is on average little overlap between the content of topic t^P and the control topics, and hence that t^P is a signature of Parkinson's disease.

Figure 4 shows the Bhattacharyya coefficient for each pairing (t^C, t^P) and the average Bhattacharyya coefficient $\bar{\rho}(t^P)$. Identifying the Parkinson's topics with

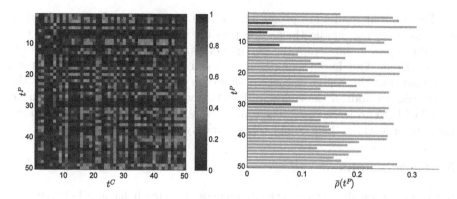

Fig. 4. Identification of signature Parkinson's topics. Left: the Bhattacharyya coefficient $\rho(t^C, t^P)$ gives a measure of the similarity between a control topic and a Parkinson's topic. Right: the average Bhattacharyya coefficient $\bar{\rho}(t^P)$ indicates which Parkinson's topics are on average the most dissimilar from the control topics. We have highlighted the five topics with the lowest $\bar{\rho}(t^P)$; these topics are signatures for Parkinson's disease.

$t^P = 4$		$t^P = 6$		$t^P = 7$		$t^P = 11$		$t^P = 30$	
w	$\Phi_{t^P}^P(w)$	w	$\Phi_{t^P}^P(w)$	w	$\Phi_{t^P}^P(w)$	w	$\Phi_{t^P}^P(w)$	w	$\Phi_{t^P}^P(w)$
49	0.483	48	0.390	50	0.964	49	0.365	47	0.358
50	0.369	47	0.243	44	0.013	48	0.294	48	0.277
48	0.108	49	0.230	46	0.008	47	0.201	49	0.187
47	0.033	44	0.115	42	0.007	46	0.126	44	0.065
44	0.003	40	0.017	28	0.003	39	0.008	45	0.062

Fig. 5. The content of the topics discovered that signify Parkinson's disease. For each topic the most likely 5 words are shown, together with the corresponding probabilities.

the smallest $\bar{\rho}(t^P)$ confirms our above interpretation of $t^P = 4, 6$ as signature topics for Parkinson's disease and also identifies $t^P = 7, 11, 30$. The content of the topics is shown in Fig. 5, which indicates that they are dominated by words that correspond to long key press durations.

4.3   Discussion

In preparing this paper we also considered a number of features which are not discussed here, including the travel time between key strokes as well as the hand (left vs. right). We found the key press duration time to reveal the most interesting differences between the two groups. However, considering more features related to typing activity such as key pressed, keyboard row, or even smartphone key and holding information, is an avenue for further work.

These initial results are promising and the approach can be generalised to other datasets and applications. One possible limitation with the approach is that the topics found across the two corpora are different, although the words are consistent. Our initial experiments learned a topic model on both corpora combined, but the topics discovered showed a mixture of behaviours and the results did not address the task well. In future work, extensions to the graphical model of LDA to learn consistent topics across two groups without combining the data or learning them completely separately will be considered.

5   Conclusions

In this paper, we aimed to find the differences in typing behaviour between people who have Parkinson's disease and those who do not. Considering a dataset of 116 typing sessions each of 15 min duration, we formulated an approach based on topic models to identify the patterns that are much more probable in the group with Parkinson's disease than in the control group. These patterns corresponded to longer key hold times. The novelty of this work stems from the ability to display the word distributions from topics which correspond to the actual behaviour of interest. This is particularly useful when considering more complex typing features, as well as multi-modal typing features (e.g., hand, key and hold time).

Several future directions arise based on this work. The most elementary of these is to consider more features and fuse them appropriately in order to obtain more intricate behaviour differences between the two groups. Experiments on other datasets to validate the generalisation of the results would also be important. We also plan to utilise generative models that learn keystroke dynamics and further evaluate the discovered topics in order to detect signatures of Parkinson's disease in key stroke logs.

References

1. Bachlin, M., Plotnik, M., Roggen, D., Maidan, I., Hausdorff, J.M., Giladi, N., Troster, G.: Wearable assistant for Parkinson's disease patients with the freezing of gait symptom. IEEE Trans. Inf. Technol. Biomed. **14**(2), 436–446 (2010)
2. Blei, D.M., Ng, A.Y., Jordan, M.I.: Latent Dirichlet allocation. J. Mach. Learn. Res. **3**(Jan), 993–1022 (2003)
3. Chen, B.R., Patel, S., Buckley, T., Rednic, R., McClure, D.J., Shih, L., Tarsy, D., Welsh, M., Bonato, P.: A web-based system for home monitoring of patients with Parkinson's disease using wearable sensors. IEEE Trans. Biomed. Eng. **58**(3), 831–836 (2011)
4. Farrahi, K., Gatica-Perez, D.: Discovering routines from large-scale human locations using probabilistic topic models. ACM Trans. Intell. Syst. Technol. **2**(1), 3:1–3:27 (2011). http://doi.acm.org/10.1145/1889681.1889684
5. Giancardo, L., Sanchez-Ferro, A., Arroyo-Gallego, T., Butterworth, I., Mendoza, C.S., Montero, P., Matarazzo, M., Obeso, J.A., Gray, M.L., Estépar, R.S.J.: Computer keyboard interaction as an indicator of early Parkinson's disease. Sci. Rep. **6**, 34468 (2016)

6. Hazan, H., Hilu, D., Manevitz, L., Ramig, L.O., Sapir, S.: Early diagnosis of Parkinson's disease via machine learning on speech data. In: 2012 IEEE 27th Convention of Electrical & Electronics Engineers in Israel (IEEEI), pp. 1–4. IEEE (2012)
7. Huynh, T., Fritz, M., Schiele, B.: Discovery of activity patterns using topic models. In: Proceedings of the 10th International Conference on Ubiquitous Computing, pp. 10–19. ACM (2008)
8. Lin, C., He, Y.: Joint sentiment/topic model for sentiment analysis. In: Proceedings of the 18th ACM Conference on Information and Knowledge Management, pp. 375–384. ACM (2009)
9. Madan, A., Farrahi, K., Gatica-Perez, D., Pentland, A.S.: Pervasive sensing to model political opinions in face-to-face networks. In: Lyons, K., Hightower, J., Huang, E.M. (eds.) Pervasive 2011. LNCS, vol. 6696, pp. 214–231. Springer, Heidelberg (2011). doi:10.1007/978-3-642-21726-5_14
10. Mariani, B., Jiménez, M.C., Vingerhoets, F.J., Aminian, K.: On-shoe wearable sensors for gait and turning assessment of patients with Parkinson's disease. IEEE Trans. Biomed. Eng. 60(1), 155–158 (2013)
11. Mei, Q., Ling, X., Wondra, M., Su, H., Zhai, C.: Topic sentiment mixture: modeling facets and opinions in weblogs. In: Proceedings of the 16th International Conference on World Wide Web, pp. 171–180. ACM (2007)
12. Patel, S., Lorincz, K., Hughes, R., Huggins, N., Growdon, J., Standaert, D., Akay, M., Dy, J., Welsh, M., Bonato, P.: Monitoring motor fluctuations in patients with Parkinson's disease using wearable sensors. IEEE Trans. Inf. Technol. Biomed. 13(6), 864–873 (2009)
13. Salarian, A., Russmann, H., Wider, C., Burkhard, P.R., Vingerhoets, F.J., Aminian, K.: Quantification of tremor and bradykinesia in Parkinson's disease using a novel ambulatory monitoring system. IEEE Trans. Biomed. Eng. 54(2), 313–322 (2007)
14. Steyvers, M., Griffiths, T.: Probabilistic topic models. Handb. Latent Semant. Anal. 427(7), 424–440 (2007)
15. Tsanas, A.: Accurate telemonitoring of Parkinson's disease symptom severity using nonlinear speech signal processing and statistical machine learning. University of Oxford, Diss (2012)

Poster Papers: Network Science

Effects of Contact Network Models
on Stochastic Epidemic Simulations

Rehan Ahmad and Kevin S. Xu$^{(\boxtimes)}$

EECS Department, University of Toledo, Toledo, OH 43606, USA
Rehan.Ahmad@rockets.utoledo.edu, Kevin.Xu@utoledo.edu

Abstract. The importance of modeling the spread of epidemics through
a population has led to the development of mathematical models for
infectious disease propagation. A number of empirical studies have collected and analyzed data on contacts between individuals using a variety
of sensors. Typically one uses such data to fit a probabilistic model of
network contacts over which a disease may propagate. In this paper,
we investigate the effects of different contact network models with varying levels of complexity on the outcomes of simulated epidemics using
a stochastic Susceptible-Infectious-Recovered (SIR) model. We evaluate
these network models on six datasets of contacts between people in a
variety of settings. Our results demonstrate that the choice of network
model can have a significant effect on how closely the outcomes of an
epidemic simulation on a simulated network match the outcomes on the
actual network constructed from the sensor data. In particular, preserving degrees of nodes appears to be much more important than preserving
cluster structure for accurate epidemic simulations.

Keywords: Network model · Stochastic epidemic model · Contact network · Degree-corrected stochastic block model

1 Introduction

The study of transmission dynamics of infectious diseases often involves simulations using stochastic epidemic models. In a compartmental stochastic epidemic
model, transitions between compartments occur randomly with specified probabilities. For example, in a stochastic Susceptible-Infectious-Recovered (SIR)
model [4,10], a person may transition from S to I with a certain probability
upon contact with an infectious person, or a person may transition from I to R
with a certain probability to simulate recovering from the disease.

The reason for the spread of infection is contact with the infectious individual. Hence, the contact network in a population is a major factor in the
transmission dynamics. Collecting an actual contact network over a large population is difficult because of limitations in capturing all the contact information.
This makes it necessary to represent the network with some level of abstraction,
e.g. using a statistical model. A variety of statistical models for networks have

© Springer International Publishing AG 2017
G.L. Ciampaglia et al. (Eds.): SocInfo 2017, Part II, LNCS 10540, pp. 101–110, 2017.
DOI: 10.1007/978-3-319-67256-4_10

been proposed [9]; such models can be used to simulate contact networks that resemble actual contact networks.

Our aim in this paper is to evaluate different models for contact networks in order to find the best model to use to simulate contact networks that are close to an actual observed network. We do this by comparing the disease dynamics of a stochastic SIR model over the simulated networks with the disease dynamics over the actual network. One commonly used approach is to compare the epidemic size at the end of the simulation, i.e. what fraction of the population caught the disease [19,25]. A drawback of this approach is that it only considers the steady-state outcome and not the dynamics of the disease as it is spreading.

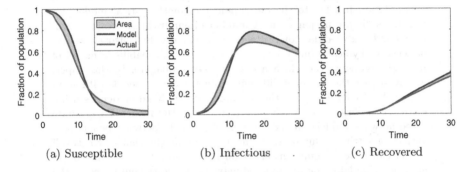

(a) Susceptible   (b) Infectious   (c) Recovered

Fig. 1. For each of the susceptible (S), infectious (I), and recovered (R) compartments, the mean curve for simulations on the model (shown in blue) is compared to the mean curve for simulations on the actual network (shown in red). The closeness between the model and actual network is given by the sum of the shaded areas between the curves for each compartment (smaller is better). (Color figure online)

We propose to compare the dynamics at each time instant in the simulation by calculating the area between the mean SIR curves for the epidemic over the simulated and actual networks, shown in Fig. 1. A small area indicates that the dynamics of the epidemic over the simulated contact networks are close to those of the actual network. We use this approach to compare four contact network models (in increasing order of number of parameters): the Erdős-Rényi model, the degree model, the stochastic block model, and the degree-corrected stochastic block model. Our experiment results over six different real network datasets suggest that the degree-corrected stochastic block model provides the closest approximation to the dynamics of an epidemic on the actual contact networks. Additionally, we find that preserving node degrees appears to be more important than preserving community structure for accuracy of epidemic simulations.

2   Related Work

A significant amount of previous work deals with the duration [23], frequency [17], and type [6,24] of contacts in a contact network. These findings are often incorporated into simulations of epidemics over different types of contact models. The R package EpiModel [13] allows for simulation of a variety of epidemics over temporal exponential random graph models for contact networks and has been used in studies of various different infectious diseases including HIV [14].

There has also been prior work simulating the spread of disease over a variety of contact network models with the goal of finding a good approximation to the actual high resolution data in terms of the epidemic size, i.e. the final number of people infected [19,25]. Such work differs from our proposed area metric, which considers the dynamics as the disease is spreading and not just the steady-state outcome. In [3], the authors use the squared differences between the I curves (fraction of infectious individuals) of an epidemic model on simulated contact networks and on an actual contact network to calibrate parameters of the epidemic model when used on simulated contact networks. Although this metric does consider the dynamics of the epidemic, our proposed metric also involves the S and R curves for a more complete evaluation of population dynamics.

Table 1. Summary statistics from datasets used in this study.

	HYCCUPS	Friends & Family	High school	Infectious	Primary school	HOPE
Number of nodes	43	123	126	201	242	1178
Sensor type	Wi-Fi	Bluetooth	RFID	RFID	RFID	RFID
Proximity range	N/A	5 m	1–1.5 m	1–1.5 m	1–1.5 m	Room
Graph density	0.326	0.228	0.217	0.0328	0.285	0.569
Clustering coefficient	0.604	0.496	0.522	0.459	0.480	0.748
Average degree	14.0	27.8	27.1	6.56	68.7	671
Maximum degree	28	73	55	21	134	1072

3 Datasets

We consider a variety of contact network datasets in this paper. Table 1 shows summary statistics for each dataset along with the sensor type. The HYCCUPS dataset was collected at the University Politehnica of Bucharest in 2012 using a background application for Android smartphones that captures a device's encounters with Wi-Fi access points [20]. The Friends & Family (F&F) dataset was collected from the members of a residential community nearby a major research university using Android phones loaded with an app that records many features including proximity to other Bluetooth devices [2]. The High School (HS) dataset was collected among students from 3 classes in a high school in Marseilles, France [7] using wearable sensors that capture face-to-face proximity for more than 20 seconds. The Infectious dataset was collected at a science gallery in Dublin using wearable electronic badges to sense sustained face-to-face proximity between visitors. [12]. We use data for one arbitrarily selected day (April 30) on which 201 people came to visit. The Primary School (PS) dataset was collected over 232 students and 10 teachers at a primary school in Lyon, France in a similar manner to the HS dataset [8]. Lastly, the HOPE dataset is collected from the Attendee Meta-Data project at the seventh Hackers on Planet Earth (HOPE) conference [1]. We create a contact network where the attendees at each talk form a clique; that is, each person is assumed to be in contact with every other person in the same room, hence why this network is much denser.

4   Methods

We construct actual networks from the datasets by connecting the individuals (nodes) with an edge if they have a contact at any point of time. We evaluate the quality of a contact network model for simulations of epidemics by conducting the following steps for each dataset:

1. Simulate 5,000 epidemics over the actual network.
2. Fit contact network model to actual network.
3. Simulate 100 networks from contact network model. For each simulated network, simulate 50 epidemics over the network for 5,000 epidemics total.
4. Compare the results of the epidemic simulations over the actual network with those over the simulated networks.

These steps are repeated for each contact network model that we consider. We describe the stochastic epidemic model we use to simulate epidemics in Sect. 4.1 and the contact network models we use in Sect. 4.2. To get a fair evaluation of the dynamics of epidemics spreading over different contact network models, all of the parameters which are not related to the contact network model, e.g. probability of infection and probability of recovery are kept constant. Our aim is to single out the effect of using a particular contact network model while simulating an epidemic.

4.1   Stochastic Epidemic Model

An actual infection spread in a population experiences randomness in several factors which may aggravate or inhibit the spread. This is considered in stochastic epidemic models. The initial condition is, in general, to have a set of infectious individuals, while the rest of the population is considered susceptible. We consider a discrete-time process, where at each time step, the infectious individuals can spread the disease with some probability of infection to susceptible individuals they have been in contact with. Also, the infectious individuals can recover from the disease with some probability independent of the individuals' contacts with others. This model is known as the stochastic SIR model and is one of the standard models used in epidemiology [4,10].

We randomly choose 1 infectious individual from the population as the initial condition and simulate the epidemic over 30 time steps. We set the probability of infection for every interaction between people to be 0.025. The probability of recovery is also set to be 0.025. Note that the rate at which the disease spreads across the population is dependent not only on the infection probability but also the topology of the contact network; thus, by fixing these probabilities, we are exploring only the effects of the contact network.

4.2   Contact Network Models

In practice, it is extremely difficult to obtain accurate contact network data. An alternative is to simulate a contact network by using a statistical network model. We consider several such models, which we briefly describe in the following. We refer interested readers to the survey by Goldenberg et al. [9] for details.

Erdős-Rényi (E-R) Model. In the E-R model, an edge between any two nodes is formed with probability p independent of all other edges. To fit the E-R model to a network, set the single parameter, the estimated edge probability $\hat{p} = M/\binom{N}{2}$, where N and M denote the number of nodes and edges in the actual network, respectively. By doing so, the expected number of edges in the E-R model will be $\binom{N}{2}\hat{p} = M$, the number of edges in the actual network.

Degree Model. In several network models, including the configuration model and preferential attachment models, the edge probability depends upon the degrees of the nodes it connects [21]. We consider a model that preserves the expected rather than actual degree of each node, often referred to as the Chung-Lu model [5]. In this model, the probability of an edge between two nodes is proportional to the product of their node degrees, and all edges are formed independently. The model has N parameters, the expected degrees of each node.

To fit the degree model to a network, we compute the degrees of all nodes to obtain the degree vector $\mathbf{d}$. We then set the estimated edge probabilities $\hat{p}_{ij} = \alpha d_i d_j$, where the constant α is chosen so that the sum of all edge probabilities (number of expected edges) is equal to the number of edges in the actual network.

Stochastic Block Model (SBM). In the SBM [11], the network is divided into disjoint sets of individuals forming K communities. The probability of edge formation between two nodes depends only upon the communities to which they belong. This model takes as input a vector of community assignments $\mathbf{c}$ (length N) and a matrix of edge formation probabilities Φ (size $K \times K$), where ϕ_{ab} denotes the probability that a node in community a forms an edge with a node in community b, independent of all other edges. For an undirected graph, Φ is symmetric so the SBM has $N + \binom{K+1}{2}$ parameters in total.

To estimate community assignments, we use a regularized spectral clustering algorithm [22] that is asymptotically consistent and has been demonstrated to be very accurate in practice. We select the number of communities using the eigengap heuristic [18]. Once the community assignments $\hat{\mathbf{c}}$ are estimated, the edge probabilities can be estimated by $\hat{\phi}_{ab} = m_{ab}/n_{ab}$, where m_{ab} denotes the number of edges in the block formed by the communities a, b in the observed network, and n_{ab} denotes the number of possible edges in the block [16].

Degree-Corrected Stochastic Block Model (DC-SBM). The DC-SBM is an extension to the SBM in a way that incorporates the concepts of the degree model within an SBM [16]. The parameters of the DC-SBM are the vector of community assignments **c** (length N), a node-level parameter vector $\boldsymbol{\theta}$ (length N), and a block-level parameter matrix Ω (size $K \times K$). In a DC-SBM, an edge between a node $i \in a$ (meaning node i is in community a) and node $j \in b$ is formed with probability $\theta_i \theta_j \omega_{ab}$ independent of all other edges. Ω is symmetric, so the DC-SBM has $2N + \binom{K+1}{2}$ parameters in total.

To fit the DC-SBM to an actual network, we first estimate the community assignments in the same manner as in the SBM using regularized spectral clustering. We then estimate the remaining parameters to be $\hat{\theta}_i = d_i / \sum_{j \in a} d_j$, for node $i \in a$, and $\hat{\omega}_{ab} = m_{ab}$ [16]. Using these estimates, we arrive at the estimated edge probabilities $\hat{p}_{ij} = \hat{\theta}_i \hat{\theta}_j \hat{\omega}_{ab}$.

5 Results

To evaluate the quality of a contact network model, we compare the mean SIR curves resulting from epidemic simulations on networks generated from that model to the mean SIR curves from epidemic simulations on the actual network. If the two curves are close, then the network model is providing an accurate representation of what is likely to happen on the actual network.

To measure the closeness of the two sets of mean SIR curves, we use the sum of the areas between each set of curves as shown in Fig. 1. By measuring the area between the curves rather than just the final outcome of the epidemic simulation (e.g. the fraction of recovered people after the disease dies out as in [19,25]), we capture the difference in transient dynamics (e.g. the rate at which the infection spreads) rather than just the difference in final outcomes.

The area between the SIR curves for each model over each dataset is shown in Fig. 2a. According to this quality measure, the DC-SBM is the most accurate model on F&F, HS, and PS; the degree model is the most accurate on HYCCUPS and HOPE; and the SBM is most accurate on Infectious. However, the SBM appears to be only slightly more accurate than the E-R model overall, despite having $N + \binom{K+1}{2}$ parameters compared to the single parameter E-R model. The contact network models were most accurate on the HOPE network, which is the densest, causing the epidemics to spread rapidly.

We compute also the log-likelihood for each contact network model on each dataset, shown in Fig. 2b. To normalize across the different sized networks, we compute the log-likelihood per node pair. Since all of the log-likelihoods are less than 0, we show the negative log-likelihood (i.e. lower is better) in Fig. 2b. Unsurprisingly, the DC-SBM, with the most parameters, also has the highest log-likelihood, whereas the relative ordering of the log-likelihoods of the degree model

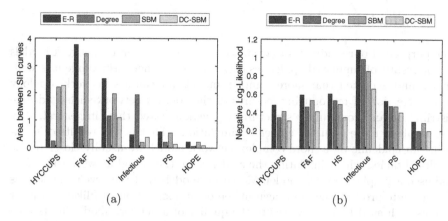

Fig. 2. Comparison of (a) area between SIR curves of each model with respect to actual network for each dataset and (b) negative log-likelihood per node pair for each model (lower is better for both measures). The DC-SBM model appears to be the best model according to both quality measures, but the two measures disagree on the quality of the degree model compared to the SBM.

Table 2. Quality measures (lower is better) averaged over all datasets for each model. Best model according to each measure is shown in bold.

Quality Measure	E-R	Degree	SBM	DC-SBM
Area between SIR curves	1.82	0.73	1.43	**0.71**
Negative log-likelihood per node pair	0.597	0.496	0.504	**0.385**
Number of parameters	**1**	319	328	647

and SBM, both with roughly the same number of parameters, vary depending on the dataset.

Both the proposed area between SIR curves and the log-likelihood can be viewed as quality measures for a contact network model. A third quality measure is given by the number of parameters, which denotes the simplicity of the model. A simpler model is generally more desirable to avoid overfitting. These three quality measures for each model (averaged over all datasets) are shown in Table 2. The DC-SBM achieves the highest quality according to the area between SIR curves and the log-likelihood at the expense of having the most parameters. On the other hand, the E-R model has only a single parameter but is the worst in the other two quality metrics. Interestingly, the degree model and SBM appear to be roughly equal in terms of the number of parameters and log-likelihood, but the area between SIR curves for the two models differs significantly. This suggests that the degree model may be better than the SBM at reproducing features of contact networks that are relevant to disease propagation.

6 Discussion

The purpose of our study was to evaluate the effects of contact network models on the results of simulated epidemics over the contact network. While it is well-known and expected that more complex models for contact network topology do a better job of reproducing features of the contact network such as degree distribution and community structure, we demonstrated that, in general, they also result in more accurate epidemic simulations. That is, the results of simulating an epidemic on a more complex network model are usually closer to the results obtained when simulating the epidemic on the actual network than if we had used a simpler network model. Moreover, models that preserve node degrees are shown to produce the most accurate epidemic simulations. Unlike most prior studies such as [19,25], we measure the quality of a network model by its area between SIR curves compared to the SIR curve of the actual network, which allows us to capture differences while the disease is still spreading rather than just the difference in the final outcome, i.e. how many people were infected.

Our findings suggest that the degree-corrected stochastic block model (DC-SBM) is the best choice of contact network model in epidemic simulations because it resulted in the minimum average area between SIR curves. Interestingly, using the degree model resulted in an average area between SIR curves to be only slightly larger than the DC-SBM despite having less than half as many parameters, as shown in Table 2. The SBM (without degree correction) also has half as many parameters as the DC-SBM, but has over twice the area between SIR curves. We note that the difference between the degree model and the SBM *cannot* be observed using log-likelihood as the quality measure, as both models are very close in log-likelihood. This leads us to believe that preserving degree has a greater effect on accuracy of epidemic simulations than preserving community structure. Furthermore, this finding demonstrates that one cannot simply evaluate the accuracy of a contact network model for epidemic simulations only by examining goodness-of-fit on the actual contact network!

In practice, one cannot often collect high-resolution contact data on a large scale, so having accurate contact network models is crucial to provide realistic network topologies on which we can simulate epidemics. In this paper, we estimated the parameters for each contact network model using the contact network itself, which we cannot do in practice because the contact network is often unknown. As a result, one would have to estimate the model parameters from prior knowledge or partial observation of the contact network, which introduces additional error that was not studied in this paper. It would be of great interest to perform this type of sensitivity analysis to identify whether the DC-SBM and degree model are still superior even when presented with less accurate parameter estimates. Also, there is a risk of overfitting in more complex models which should be examined in a future extension of this work. Both issues could potentially be addressed by considering hierarchical Bayesian variants of network models such as the degree-generated block model [27], which add an additional generative layer to the model with a smaller set of hyperparameters.

Another limitation of this study is our consideration of static unweighted networks. Prior work [15,19,23,25] has shown that it is important to consider the time duration of contacts between people, which can be reflected as weights in the contact network, as well as the times themselves, which can be accommodated by using models of dynamic rather than static networks, such as dynamic SBMs [26]. We plan to expand this work in the future by incorporating models of weighted and dynamic networks to provide a more thorough investigation.

References

1. aestetix, Petro, C.: CRAWDAD dataset hope/amd, 07 August 2008 (2008). http://crawdad.org/hope/amd/20080807
2. Aharony, N., Pan, W., Ip, C., Khayal, I., Pentland, A.: Social fMRI: Investigating and shaping social mechanisms in the real world. Pervasive Mob. Comput. **7**(6), 643–659 (2011)
3. Bioglio, L., Génois, M., Vestergaard, C.L., Poletto, C., Barrat, A., Colizza, V.: Recalibrating disease parameters for increasing realism in modeling epidemics in closed settings. BMC Infect. Dis. **16**(1), 676 (2016)
4. Britton, T.: Stochastic epidemic models: a survey. Math. Biosci. **225**(1), 24–35 (2010)
5. Chung, F., Lu, L.: The average distances in random graphs with given expected degrees. Proc. Natl. Acad. Sci. **99**(25), 15879–15882 (2002)
6. Eames, K.: Modeling disease spread through random and regular contacts in clustered populations. Theor. Popul. Biol. **73**(1), 104–111 (2008)
7. Fournet, J., Barrat, A.: Contact patterns among high school students. PLoS ONE **9**(9), e107878 (2014)
8. Gemmetto, V., Barrat, A., Cattuto, C.: Mitigation of infectious disease at school: targeted class closure vs school closure. BMC Infect. Dis. **14**(1), 695 (2014)
9. Goldenberg, A., Zheng, A.X., Fienberg, S.E., Airoldi, E.M.: A survey of statistical network models. Found. Trends Mach. Learn. **2**(2), 129–233 (2010)
10. Greenwood, P., Gordillo, L.: Stochastic epidemic modeling. In: Chowell, G., Hyman, J.M., Bettencourt, L.M.A., Castillo-Chavez, C. (eds.) Mathematical and Statistical Estimation Approaches in Epidemiology, pp. 31–52. Springer, Dordrecht (2009)
11. Holland, P.W., Laskey, K.B., Leinhardt, S.: Stochastic blockmodels: first steps. Soc. Netw. **5**(2), 109–137 (1983)
12. Isella, L., Stehl, J., Barrat, A., Cattuto, C., Pinton, J., Van den Broeck, W.: What's in a crowd? analysis of face-to-face behavioral networks. J. Theor. Biol. **271**(1), 166–180 (2011)
13. Jenness, S., Goodreau, S.M., Morris, M.: EpiModel: mathematical modeling of infectious disease (2017), http://epimodel.org/
14. Jenness, S.M., Goodreau, S.M., Rosenberg, E., Beylerian, E.N., Hoover, K.W., Smith, D.K., Sullivan, P.: Impact of the centers for disease control's HIV preexposure prophylaxis guidelines for men who have sex with men in the United States. J. Infect. Dis. **214**(12), 1800–1807 (2016)
15. Karimi, F., Holme, P.: Threshold model of cascades in empirical temporal networks. Phys. A **392**(16), 3476–3483 (2013)
16. Karrer, B., Newman, M.E.J.: Stochastic blockmodels and community structure in networks. Phys. Rev. E **83**, 016107 (2011)

17. Larson, R.C.: Simple models of influenza progression within a heterogeneous population. Eur. J. Oper. Res. **55**(3), 399–412 (2007)
18. von Luxburg, U.: A tutorial on spectral clustering. Stat. Comput. **17**(4), 395–416 (2007)
19. Machens, A., Gesualdo, F., Rizzo, C., Tozzi, A.E., Barrat, A., Cattuto, C.: An infectious disease model on empirical networks of human contact: bridging the gap between dynamic network data and contact matrices. BMC Infect. Dis. **13**(1), 185 (2013)
20. Marin, R.C., Dobre, C., Xhafa, F.: Exploring predictability in mobile interaction. In: Proceedings of the 3rd International Conference on Emerging Intelligent Data and Web Technologies, pp. 133–139 (2012)
21. Newman, M.: Networks: An Introduction. Oxford University Press Inc., New York (2010)
22. Qin, T., Rohe, K.: Regularized spectral clustering under the degree-corrected stochastic blockmodel. In: Advances in Neural Information Processing Systems, vol. 26, pp. 3120–3128 (2013)
23. Smieszek, T.: A mechanistic model of infection: why duration and intensity of contacts should be included in models of disease spread. Theor. Biol. Med. Model. **6**(1), 25 (2009)
24. Smieszek, T., Fiebig, L., Scholz, R.W.: Models of epidemics: when contact repetition and clustering should be included. Theor. Biol. Med. Model. **6**(1), 11 (2009)
25. Stehlé, J., Voirin, N., Barrat, A., Cattuto, C., Colizza, V., Isella, L., Régis, C., Pinton, J.F., Khanafer, N., Van den Broeck, W., Vanhems, P.: Simulation of an SEIR infectious disease model on the dynamic contact network of conference attendees. BMC Med. **9**(1), 87 (2011)
26. Xu, K.S., Hero III, A.O.: Dynamic stochastic blockmodels for time-evolving social networks. IEEE J. Sel. Top. Sign. Process. **8**(4), 552–562 (2014)
27. Zhu, Y., Yan, X., Moore, C.: Oriented and degree-generated block models: generating and inferring communities with inhomogeneous degree distributions. J. Complex Netw. **2**(1), 1–18 (2014)

From Relational Data to Graphs: Inferring Significant Links Using Generalized Hypergeometric Ensembles

Giona Casiraghi$^{(\boxtimes)}$ ⓘ, Vahan Nanumyan ⓘ, Ingo Scholtes ⓘ, and Frank Schweitzer ⓘ

Chair of Systems Design, ETH Zürich, 8092 Zürich, Switzerland
gcasiraghi@ethz.ch
http://sg.ethz.ch/

Abstract. The inference of network topologies from relational data is an important problem in data analysis. Exemplary applications include the reconstruction of social ties from data on human interactions, the inference of gene co-expression networks from DNA microarray data, or the learning of semantic relationships based on co-occurrences of words in documents. Solving these problems requires techniques to infer significant links in noisy relational data. In this short paper, we propose a new statistical modeling framework to address this challenge. The framework builds on *generalized hypergeometric ensembles*, a class of generative stochastic models that give rise to analytically tractable probability spaces of directed, multi-edge graphs. We show how this framework can be used to assess the significance of links in noisy relational data. We illustrate our method in two data sets capturing spatio-temporal proximity relations between actors in a social system. The results show that our analytical framework provides a new approach to infer significant links from relational data, with interesting perspectives for the mining of data on social systems.

Keywords: Statistical analysis · Graph theory · Network inference · Statistical ensemble · Relational data · Graph mining · Graph analysis · Network analysis · Social network · Social network analysis · Community structures · Data mining · Social interactions

1 Motivation

Advances in data sensing and collection give rise to an increasing volume of data that capture *dyadic relations* between elements or actors in social, natural, and technical systems. While it is common to apply *graph mining* and *network analysis* to such relational data, it is often questionable whether the application of these techniques is actually justified. Consider, for instance, various forms of *time series data*, which not only tell us which elements of a complex system are related but also when or in which order relations occur. Such data give rise to *temporal*

© Springer International Publishing AG 2017
G.L. Ciampaglia et al. (Eds.): SocInfo 2017, Part II, LNCS 10540, pp. 111–120, 2017.
DOI: 10.1007/978-3-319-67256-4_11

networks, which question the application of widely used network-based modeling and data mining techniques [13,24,26,27,30]. Apart from temporal information, we often have access to data that capture multiple types of relations or interactions. The resulting *multi-layer network topologies* give rise to complications that threaten standard techniques, e.g., to infer and analyze social networks, detect community structures, or to model and control dynamical processes in networked systems [3,7,16,28,35].

The challenges outlined above are due to the growing availability of *additional information* – such as time-stamped, sequential or multi-dimensional relational data – which must be incorporated into network-based techniques to model and analyze relational data. However, we are often confronted with situations in which we *lack information* that is needed to interpret observed relations. Consider, for instance, data sets that capture the simultaneous presence of two users at the same location, the joint expression of two genes in a DNA microarray, or the co-occurrence of two words in the same document. Each of these observed relations can either be due to an underlying social tie, a functional relationship between genes, a semantic link between two words, or it could simply have occurred by mere chance. Rather than naïvely analyzing such data from the perspective of graphs or networks, we should thus treat them as *noisy observations* that may or may not indicate true *relations* between a system's elements.

Principled and efficient methods to solve this *network inference problem* are of major importance for the modeling and analysis of social networks, the reconstruction of biological networks, and the mining of semantic structures in information systems. The problem has received significant attention from the data mining and machine learning community, as well as from researchers in graph theory and network science. Especially in the latter community, the problem is commonly addressed using *statistical ensembles*, i.e., generative stochastic models of graphs that can be used for inference, learning and modeling tasks. A common issue of these techniques is that the underlying statistical ensembles are not analytically tractable, thus requiring time-consuming numerical simulations and Monte-Carlo sampling techniques.

To address this problem, in this short paper we propose *generalized hypergeometric ensembles* (gHypE), a novel framework of statistical ensembles to infer significant links in relational data. The framework can be viewed as generalization of the configuration model, which is commonly used to generate random graph topologies with a given sequence of node degrees. Our framework extends this state-of-the-art graph-theoretic approach in two ways. First, it provides *analytically tractable* probability spaces of directed and undirected multi-edge graphs, eliminating the need for expensive numerical simulations. Second, it allows to account for known factors that influence the occurrence of interactions, such as known group structures, similarities between elements, or other forms of biases. We demonstrate our framework in two real-world data sets that capture spatio-temporal proximities of actors in a social system. The results show that our framework provides interesting new perspectives for the mining and learning in graphs.

2   Background and Related Work

The problem of inferring *significant* links in relational data has been addressed in a number of works. In the following, we coarsely categorize them into three lines of research.

Applying predictive analytics techniques, a first set of works studied the problem from the perspective of *link prediction* [17]. In [29], a supervised learning technique is used to predict *types* of social ties based on unlabeled interactions. The authors of [25] show that tensor factorization techniques allow to infer international relations from data that capture how often two countries co-occur in news reports. In [33], a link-based latent variable model is used to predict friendship relations using data on social interactions.

Using the special characteristics of time-stamped social interactions or geographical co-occurrences, a second line of works has additionally accounted for *spatio-temporal information*. Studying data on time-stamped proximities of students at MIT campus, the authors of [8] show that the temporal and spatial distribution of proximity events allows to infer social ties with high accuracy. In [5], a model that captures location diversity, regularity, intensity and duration is used to predict social ties based on co-location events. An entropy-based approach taking into account the diversity of interactions' locations has been used in [22].

Addressing scenarios where neither training data nor spatio-temporal information is available, a third line of works is based on *generative models for random graphs*. Such models can be used as *null models* for observed dyadic interactions, which help us to assess whether the relations between a given pair of elements occur significantly more often than expected. Existing works in this area typically rely on standard modeling frameworks, such as *exponential random graphs* [4,23], or the *configuration model* for graphs with given degree sequence or distribution [18]. On the one hand, these approaches provide statistically principled network inference and learning methods for general relational data [2,12,19,32]. On the other hand, the underlying generative models are often not analytically tractable, thus requiring expensive numerical simulations [19,23]. Proposing a framework of analytically tractable generative models for directed and undirected multi-edge graphs, in this work we close this research gap.

3   Generalized Hypergeometric Ensembles

In the following we introduce our framework step by step. For this, let us first consider a data set consisting of repeated dyadic interactions (i, j), which have been observed between two nodes i and j. Such a data set can be represented as a *multi-edge*, or *weighted*, network $G = (V, E)$, where V is a set of n nodes, and $E \subseteq V \times V$ is a multi-set of (directed or undirected) edges. Let us further define an adjacency matrix $\hat{\mathbf{A}}$, where entries $\hat{A}_{ij} \in \mathbb{N}_0$ capture the *weight* of an edge $(i, j) \in V \times V$, i.e., the multiplicity of an edge (i, j) in the multiset E. For each node $i \in V$ we further define the (weighted) in-degree $\hat{k}_{in}(i) := \sum_{j \in V} \hat{A}_{ji}$ and the (weighted) out-degree $\hat{k}_{out}(i) := \sum_{j \in V} \hat{A}_{ij}$.

Rather than directly applying graph mining and learning techniques to such a weighted graph G, in the following we are interested in a crucial question: Which of the links between nodes are *significant*, i.e., which of the observed weights A_{ij} go beyond what is expected at random, given (i) the total number of observed interactions, and (ii) the number of times individual nodes engage in interactions? To answer this question, we take the common approach of defining a *stochastic model* that generates a so-called *statistical ensemble*, i.e., a probability space of graphs. Different from existing approaches, where link weights are assumed to be continuous (e.g. [1,6]), we are interested in a statistical ensemble that (i) can handle directed and multi-edge graphs, (ii) is analytically tractable, and (iii) thus allows us to assess the significance of links in a theoretically principled way.

Our construction of a statistical ensemble follows the general idea of the Molloy-Reed configuration model, which is to randomly shuffle the topology of a given network G while preserving the observed node degrees. For this, the configuration model generates edges between randomly sampled pairs of nodes in such a way that the *exact* observed degrees of all nodes are preserved. Different from this approach, we assume a sampling of m multi-edges such that the sequence of *expected* degrees of nodes is preserved. For this, for each pair of nodes i and j, we first define the maximum number Ξ_{ij} of multi-edges that can possibly exist between nodes i and j as $\Xi_{ij} := \hat{k}_{\text{out}}(i)\hat{k}_{\text{in}}(j)$ (cf. [15,20]). The maximally possible numbers of links between all pairs of nodes can then be conveniently represented in matrix form as $\mathbf{\Xi} := (\Xi_{ij})_{i,j \in V}$.

Our statistical ensemble is then defined by the following sampling procedure: For each pair of nodes i,j, we sample edges from a set of Ξ_{ij} possible multi-edges uniformly at random. This can be viewed as an *urn problem* [14] where the edges to be sampled are represented by balls in an urn. By representing edges connecting different pairs of nodes (i,j) as balls having $n^2 = |V \times V|$ different colours, we obtain an urn with a total of $M = \sum_{i,j} \Xi_{ij}$ differently colored balls. With this, the sampling of a network according to our model corresponds to drawing exactly m balls from this urn. Each adjacency matrix $\mathbf{A}$, with entries A_{ij} such that $\sum_{i,j} A_{ij} = m$, corresponds to one particular realization drawn from this ensemble. The probability to draw exactly $\mathbf{A} = \{A_{ij}\}_{i,j \in V}$ edges between each pair of nodes is given by the *multivariate* hypergeometric distribution[1]

$$\Pr(\mathbf{A}) = \binom{M}{m}^{-1} \prod_{i,j} \binom{\Xi_{ij}}{A_{ij}}. \tag{1}$$

For each pair of nodes $i,j \in V$, the probability to draw exactly $\hat{A}_{ij}$ edges between i and j is given by the marginal distributions of the multivariate hypergeometric distribution. We thus arrive at a *hypergeometric statistical ensemble*, which (i) generalizes the configuration model to directed, multi-edge graphs, (ii) has a fixed sequence of *expected* degrees, and (iii) is analytically tractable.

---

[1] Note that we do not distinguish between the $n \times n$ adjacency matrix $\mathbf{A}$ and the $n^2 \times 1$ vector obtained by stacking.

Moreover, it provides a framework to generalize other random graph models like, e.g., the multi-edge version of the Erdös-Rényi model [10], where only n and m are fixed, while there are no constraints on the degree sequence. This corresponds to a definition of Ξ with $\Xi_{ij} = m^2/n^2 = $ const. which directly results from $\langle k_{\text{in}}(i) \rangle = \langle k_{\text{out}}(i) \rangle = m/n$.

The sampling procedure above gives a stochastic model for weighted, directed graph in which (i) the expected weighted in- and out-degree sequence is fixed, and (ii) interactions between nodes are generated at random. This provides a null model in which the probability for a particular pair of nodes to be connected by an edge is only influenced by combinatorial effects, and thus only depends on the node degrees. For scenarios where we have additional information on factors that influence the formation of edges, we can further generalize the ensemble above as follows: We introduce a matrix $\mathbf{\Omega}$ whose entries Ω_{ij} capture relative *dyadic propensities*, i.e., the tendency of a node i to form an edge *specifically* to node j. These propensities Ω_{ij} bias the edge sampling process described above. This implies that entry Ω_{ij} only captures the propensity that goes *beyond* the tendency of a node i to connect to a node j that is due to combinatorial effects, i.e., the in-degree of j and the out-degree of i. In analogy to the urn model, here a biased sampling implies that the probability of drawing balls of a given color (representing all possible edges between a given pair of nodes) does not only depend on their number but also on the respective relative propensities. The probability distribution resulting from such a biased sampling process is given by the multivariate *Wallenius' non-central hypergeometric distribution* [11,31]:

$$\Pr(\mathbf{A}) = \left[\prod_{i,j} \binom{\Xi_{ij}}{A_{ij}} \right] \int_0^1 \prod_{i,j} \left(1 - z^{\frac{\Omega_{ij}}{S_\Omega}} \right)^{A_{ij}} dz \tag{2}$$

with $S_\Omega = \sum_{i,j} \Omega_{ij}(\Xi_{ij} - A_{ij})$.

Similar to the unbiased sampling described above, the probability to observe a particular number $\hat{A}_{ij}$ of edges between a pair of nodes i and j can again be calculated from the marginal distribution as

$$\Pr(A_{ij} = \hat{A}_{ij}) = \binom{\Xi_{ij}}{\hat{A}_{ij}} \binom{M - \Xi_{ij}}{m - \hat{A}_{ij}} \cdot$$
$$\int_0^1 \left[\left(1 - z^{\frac{\Omega_{ij}}{S_\Omega}} \right)^{\hat{A}_{ij}} \left(1 - z^{\frac{\bar{\Omega}_{\backslash(i,j)}}{S_\Omega}} \right)^{m - \hat{A}_{ij}} \right] dz \tag{3}$$

where $\bar{\Omega}_{\backslash(i,j)} = (M - \Xi_{ij})^{-1} \sum_{(l,m) \in V \times V \backslash (i,j)} \Xi_{lm} \Omega_{lm}$.

Note that for the special case of a uniform dyadic propensity matrix $\mathbf{\Omega} \equiv$ const, we recover Eq. 1 for the unbiased case, i.e., where all dyadic propensities are identical. We thus obtain a general framework of statistical ensembles which (i) allows to encode arbitrary a priori tendencies of nodes to interact, and (ii) provides an analytical expression for the probability to observe a given number of interactions between any pair of nodes.

4 Inferring Significant Social Ties

In the following, we demonstrate how our framework can be used to infer significant links in two relational data sets: (RM) captures time-stamped proximities between students and faculty at MIT [9] recorded via smart devices. (ZKC) covers frequencies of self-reported encounters between members of a university Karate club collected by Wayne Zachary [34]. We denote the weighted adjacency matrix capturing observed dyadic interactions as $\hat{A}$. For a given significance threshold α, we then identify significant links by filtering matrix $\hat{A}$ by a threshold $\Pr(A_{ij} \leq \hat{A}_{ij}) > 1 - \alpha$ based on Eq. 3. This can be seen as assigning p-values to dyads (i, j), obtaining a *high-pass* noise filter for entries in the adjacency matrix.

To illustrate our approach, Fig. 1(a) shows the entries of the (original) adjacency matrix $\mathbf{A}$ for (RM). The high-pass noise filter resulting from our methodology (using $\alpha = 0.01$) is shown in Fig. 1(b), where black entries correspond to

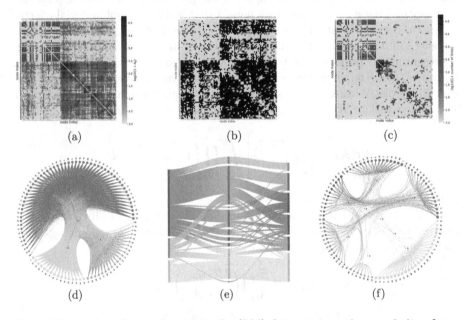

(a)   (b)   (c)

(d)   (e)   (f)

Fig. 1. Illustration of our approach in the (RM) data set capturing proximity of students and staff at MIT campus. For the observed weighted adjacency matrix (a) and a given significance threshold, our framework allows to establish a high-pass noise filter matrix (b), which can be used to obtain a filtered adjacency matrix containing only significant links (c). A visual comparison of the output of a community detection algorithm on the unfiltered (d) and filtered (f) graphs shows that detected partitions in the filtered one better correspond to ground truth lab affiliations and classes (e). **(a)** Unfiltered weighted adjacency matrix. **(b)** High-pass noise filter matrix. **(c)** Filtered adjacency matrix containing only significant links. **(d)** Unfiltered graph. **(e)** Comparison of ground truth lab affiliations (center column) vs. detected communities in the unfiltered (left column) and filtered (right column) graph. **(f)** Filtered graph.

pairs of nodes with non-significant links. The application of this filter to the original matrix yields the noise-filtered matrix shown in Fig. 1(c). While in the full network there are 721, 889 observed multi-edges amounting to 2, 952 distinct links, after filtering there are 626 (21.2%) significant links left (617, 069 multi-edges, 85.5% of the original). We validate the benefit of filtering the original interactions in (RM) by comparing the output of a standard community detection algorithm – the degree-corrected block model [21] – in (i) the original, unfiltered graph shown in Fig. 1(d), and (ii) the filtered, significant graph shown in Fig. 1(f). Using known classes of students and affiliations of staff members as ground truth allows us to compare the quality of the community detection. Figure 1(e) shows the set overlaps between the ground truth labels (middle column) and detected partitions in the unfiltered (left column) and filtered graph (right column). Due to the high number of non-significant links in the unfiltered graph, the algorithm only detects three partitions, each spanning multiple labs and classes. In contrast, applying the algorithm to the filtered graph yields six partitions that better capture the ground truth lab and class structure (cf. Fig. 1(e)). As expected, detected partitions do not perfectly correspond to the ground truth, since labs and classes are likely not the only driving force behind observed proximities.

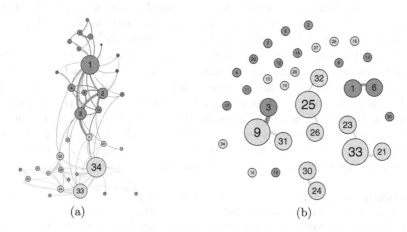

(a)   (b)

Fig. 2. Observed (a) and filtered (b) weighted graphs for the (ZKC) data set, capturing encounters between members of a Karate club. The filtered graph shows that most of the observed encounters can be explained by random effects resulting from the club members' separation into two classes.

A major advantage of gHypEs is that, by specifying a non-uniform matrix Ω, we can additionally encode known factors that influence the occurrence of interactions between nodes, while still obtaining an analytically tractable ensemble. In our second illustrative example, we use this to encode the known structure of two separate Karate classes in the (ZKC) data. These two classes naturally influence the frequency of encounters between actors beyond what would be expected "at random". We incorporate this prior knowledge via a block matrix Ω that assigns higher dyadic propensities to pairs of actors in the same class (cf. [3]). This approach allows to establish a "random baseline" accounting both (i) for combinatorial effects due to heterogeneous node degrees, and (ii) the known group structure in the data. Using a significance threshold of $\alpha = 0.01$, for (ZKC) this yields the striking result that only 8 out of 78 observed links are significant ($\sim$ 90% of 231 observed multi-edges are filtered out, cf. Fig. 2). In other words, taking into account the partitioning of members in two classes for (ZKC) almost all encounters between club members can simply be explained by random effects. Figure 2 compares the original weighted network, illustrated in Fig. 2(a), and the filtered network, in Fig. 2(b).

5   Conclusion

In this short paper we introduce gHypEs, a broad class of statistical ensembles of graphs that can be used to infer significant links from noisy data. Our work makes three important contributions: First, we provide an analytically tractable statistical model of directed and undirected multi-edge graphs that can be used for inference and learning tasks. Second, the formulation of our ensemble highlights a – to the best of our knowledge – previously unknown relation between random graph theory and Wallenius'non-central hypergeometric distribution. And finally, different from existing statistical ensembles such as, e.g., the configuration model, our framework can be used to encode prior knowledge on factors that influence the formation of relations. This flexible approach allows for a tuning of the "random baseline", opening perspectives for a statistically principled network inference that accounts for effects that are not purely random. We thus argue that our work advances the theoretical foundation for the mining of relational data on social systems. It further highlights that principled model selection and hypothesis testing are crucial prerequisites that should precede the application of network-based data mining and modeling techniques.

Acknowledgments. The authors acknowledge support from the Swiss State Secretariat for Education, Research and Innovation (SERI), Grant No. C14.0036, the MTEC Foundation project "The Influence of Interaction Patterns on Success in Socio-Technical Systems", and EU COST Action TD1210 KNOWeSCAPE. The authors thank Rebekka Burkholz, Giacomo Vaccario, and Simon Schweighofer for helpful discussions.

References

1. Aicher, C., Jacobs, A.Z., Clauset, A.: Learning latent block structure in weighted networks. J. Complex Netw. **3**(2), 221–248 (2015). https://academic.oup.com/comnet/article-lookup/doi/10.1093/comnet/cnu026
2. Anand, K., Bianconi, G.: Entropy measures for networks: toward an information theory of complex topologies. Phys. Rev. E **80**, 045102 (2009)

3. Casiraghi, G.: Multiplex network regression: how do relations drive interactions? arXiv preprint arXiv:1702.02048, February 2017. http://arxiv.org/abs/1702.02048
4. Cimini, G., Squartini, T., Garlaschelli, D., Gabrielli, A.: Systemic risk analysis on reconstructed economic and financial networks. Sci. Rep. 5(1), 15758 (2015). http://arxiv.org/abs/1411.7613%0A, http://dx.doi.org/10.1038/srep15758, http://www.nature.com/articles/srep15758
5. Cranshaw, J., Toch, E., Hong, J., Kittur, A., Sadeh, N.: Bridging the gap between physical location and online social networks. In: Proceedings of the 12th ACM International Conference on Ubiquitous Computing, UbiComp 2010, pp. 119–128. ACM, New York (2010)
6. De Choudhury, M., Mason, W.A., Hofman, J.M., Watts, D.J.: Inferring relevant social networks from interpersonal communication. In: Proceedings of the 19th International Conference on World Wide Web, WWW 2010, pp. 301–310. ACM, New York (2010)
7. De Domenico, M., Lancichinetti, A., Arenas, A., Rosvall, M.: Identifying modular flows on multilayer networks reveals highly overlapping organization in interconnected systems. Phys. Rev. X 5(1), 011027 (2015)
8. Eagle, N., Pentland, A.S., Lazer, D.: Inferring friendship network structure by using mobile phone data. Proc. Nat. Acad. Sci. 106(36), 15274–15278 (2009)
9. Eagle, N., (Sandy) Pentland, A.: Reality mining: sensing complex social systems. Pers. Ubiquit. Comput. 10(4), 255–268 (2006)
10. Erdős, P., Rényi, A.: On random graphs I. Publ. Math. Debrecen 6, 290–297 (1959)
11. Fog, A.: Calculation methods for wallenius' noncentral hypergeometric distribution. Commun. Stat. - Simul. Comput. 37(2), 258–273 (2008)
12. Gemmetto, V., Cardillo, A., Garlaschelli, D.: Irreducible network backbones: unbiased graph filtering via maximum entropy, June 2017. http://arxiv.org/abs/1706.00230
13. Holme, P.: Modern temporal network theory: a colloquium. Europ. Phys. J. B 88(9), 1–30 (2015)
14. Jacod, J., Protter, P.E.: Probability Essentials. Springer Science & Business Media, Heidelberg (2003)
15. Karrer, B., Newman, M.E.J.: Stochastic blockmodels and community structure in networks. Phys. Rev. E 83, 016107 (2011)
16. Kivelä, M., Arenas, A., Barthelemy, M., Gleeson, J.P., Moreno, Y., Porter, M.A.: Multilayer networks. J. Complex Netw. 2(3), 203–271 (2014)
17. Liben-Nowell, D., Kleinberg, J.: The link-prediction problem for social networks. J. Am. Soc. Inform. Sci. Technol. 58(7), 1019–1031 (2007)
18. Molloy, M., Reed, B.: A critical point for random graphs with a given degree sequence. Random Struct. Algorithms 6(2–3), 161–180 (1995)
19. Newman, M.E.J., Peixoto, T.P.: Generalized communities in networks. Phys. Rev. Lett. 115, 088701 (2015)
20. Newman, M.E.J.: Modularity and community structure in networks. Proc. Nat. Acad. Sci. 103(23), 8577–8582 (2006)
21. Peixoto, T.P.: Efficient monte carlo and greedy heuristic for the inference of stochastic block models. Phys. Rev. E 89, 012804 (2014)
22. Pham, H., Shahabi, C., Liu, Y.: EBM: an entropy-based model to infer social strength from spatiotemporal data. In: Proceedings of the 2013 ACM SIGMOD International Conference on Management of Data, SIGMOD 2013, pp. 265–276. ACM (2013)
23. Robins, G., Pattison, P., Kalish, Y., Lusher, D.: An introduction to exponential random graph (p*) models for social networks. Soc. Netw. 29(2), 173–191 (2007)

24. Rosvall, M., Esquivel, A.V., Lancichinetti, A., West, J.D., Lambiotte, R.: Memory in network flows and its effects on spreading dynamics and community detection. Nat. Commun. **5**, 4630 (2014)
25. Schein, A., Paisley, J., Blei, D.M., Wallach, H.: Bayesian poisson tensor factorization for inferring multilateral relations from sparse dyadic event counts. In: Proceedings of the 21th ACM SIGKDD International Conference on Knowledge Discovery and Data Mining, KDD 2015. ACM (2015)
26. Scholtes, I.: When is a network a network? multi-order graphical model selection in pathways and temporal networks. In: KDD 2017 - Proceedings of the 23rd ACM SIGKDD International Conference on Knowledge Discovery and Data Mining, February 2017, to appear
27. Scholtes, I., Wider, N., Garas, A.: Higher-order aggregate networks in the analysis of temporal networks: path structures and centralities. Europ. Phys. J. B **89**(3), 1–15 (2016). http://link.springer.com/article/10.1140:2016-60663-0
28. Szell, M., Lambiotte, R., Thurner, S.: Multirelational organization of large-scale social networks in an online world. Proc. Natl. Acad. Sci. **107**(31), 13636–13641 (2010)
29. Tang, J., Lou, T., Kleinberg, J.: Inferring social ties across heterogenous networks. In: Proceedings of the Fifth ACM International Conference on Web Search and Data Mining, WSDM 2012, pp. 743–752. ACM, New York (2012)
30. Vidmer, A., Medo, M.: The essential role of time in network-based recommendation. EPL (Europhy. Lett.) **116**(3), 30007 (2016)
31. Wallenius, K.T.: Biased Sampling: The Noncentral Hypergeometric Probability Distribution. Ph.D. thesis, Stanford University (1963)
32. Wilson, J.D., Wang, S., Mucha, P.J., Bhamidi, S., Nobel, A.B.: A testing based extraction algorithm for identifying significant communities in networks. Ann. Appl. Stat. **8**(3), 1853–1891 (2014)
33. Xiang, R., Neville, J., Rogati, M.: Modeling relationship strength in online social networks. In: Proceedings of the 19th International Conference on World Wide Web, WWW 2010, pp. 981–990. ACM, New York (2010)
34. Zachary, W.W.: An information flow model for conflict and fission in small groups. J. Anthropol. Res. **33**(4), 452–473 (1977)
35. Zhang, Y., Garas, A., Schweitzer, F.: Value of peripheral nodes in controlling multilayer scale-free networks. Phys. Rev. E **93**, 012309 (2016). https://journals.aps.org/pre/abstract/10.1103/PhysRevE.93.012309

DepthRank: Exploiting Temporality to Uncover Important Network Nodes

Nikolaos Bastas$^{(\boxtimes)}$, Theodoros Semertzidis, and Petros Daras

Centre for Research and Technology Hellas, Thessaloniki, Greece
{nimpasta,theosem,daras}@iti.gr

Abstract. Identifying important network nodes is very crucial for a variety of applications, such as the spread of an idea or an innovation. The majority of the publications so far assume that the interactions between nodes are *static*. However, this approach neglects that real-world phenomena evolve in time. Thus, there is a need for tools and techniques which account for evolution over time. Towards this direction, we present a novel graph-based method, named *DepthRank* (DR) that incorporates the temporal characteristics of the underlying datasets. We compare our approach against two baseline methods and find that it efficiently recovers important nodes on three real world datasets, as indicated by the numerical simulations. Moreover, we perform our analysis on a modified version of the DBLP dataset and verify its correctness using ground truth data.

Keywords: Influence detection · Network analysis · Temporal awareness

1 Introduction

In everyday life, humans communicate with each other in various ways: face-to-face [20], through mobile devices [18], facebook posts [24] or tweets [6], to name a few. Graph theory is a valuable tool for investigating these relations because it provides analytic capabilities, meaningful representations and easy visualization of the results [15]. In this setting, humans are considered as nodes and their communication as links. In various applications, it is important to find those nodes that play a dominant role in the interconnection of the graph and the exchange of information: examples are the stability of power grid supply [17], the diffusion of ideas or innovations [3], the delay of an epidemic outbreak [5]. We are interested in those nodes that maximize the spread of information, known as influence maximization [7]. There is a vast amount of research in this direction using either network topology, network functionality or both, on static representations. For a recent review, the reader is refered to [11] and references therein.

The static representations neglect the evolution over time of the real world networks which may seriously affect the outcome. For example, in Fig. 1, users A and W appear at different time steps (denoted by the separate planes in Fig. 1 (a)).

© Springer International Publishing AG 2017
G.L. Ciampaglia et al. (Eds.): SocInfo 2017, Part II, LNCS 10540, pp. 121–137, 2017.
DOI: 10.1007/978-3-319-67256-4_12

They exhibit the same connectivity pattern (i.e. A(W) → B → C and A(W) → B → D). This is captured by the static representation in Fig. 1(b). According to the latter, the two users are symmetric with respect to user B and there is no difference on how their influence is passed through it. However, A appears earlier in this sequence (Fig. 1(a)) and thus its "influence" should have decayed compared to the "influence" exerted by W on the same set of subsequent users. This cannot be captured by the "static" representation.

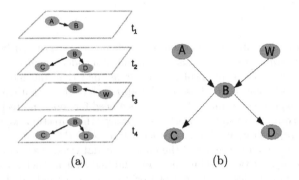

(a)   (b)

Fig. 1. (a) An example of a temporal network and (b) its static representation. In (a) A and W appear at different time steps (t_1 and t_3, respectively), having the same connectivity pattern. Thus, it is expected that their "influence" on the rest of the nodes should not be the same due to aging effects. In (b) the connectivity pattern is retained but the time ordering is neglected; this representation indicates an equal behavior for both A and W, which biases the outcome.

In the last few years, there has been an increasing interest for tools and techniques that preserve the temporal properties of the graphs. In [1], the authors formulate stochastic evolutionary equations for information spreading on a time varying network. A similar approach was used in the field of epidemic spreading [16]. In [25], the authors exploit the in-degree of the nodes on an evolving network, to determine the set of users that maximize the spread of influence under the Independent Cascade (IC) model [7]. In [13], the authors divide the dataset into two parts, using the first part for the identification of possible seed sets, and the second part for the evaluation of the spreading ability of the seed sets under a temporal Linear Threshold (LT) model [7]. In [19], the influence maximizing set is evaluated by preserving the dynamic nature of the underlying network and developing an efficient update scheme. In [10], a ranking method is proposed based on communicability [4] combined with an aging function, which is called "dynamic centrality". A similar approach is used on opportunistic mobile social networks [2]. In [12], the authors define the *temporal delta-centrality* to measure the importance of each node as time passes.

In this paper, we propose a novel method which calculates the ability of each node to transmit information by sequentially processing fixed time windows and incorporating an aging factor. The outcome of the proposed method is a ranking of the network nodes which indicates their strength in influencing other nodes within the evolving graph.

The rest of the paper is organized as follows: In Sect. 2, we briefly outline our approach which is fully described in Appendix A. In Sect. 3 we present in short the baseline methods and the evaluation process with the details left for Appendices B and C. In Sect. 4 we illustrate the obtained results, while in Sect. 5, we provide a summary and propose future directions.

2 Method

Here, we briefly present our proposed method (for more see Appendix A). We assume that the sequence of interactions of the form (u, v, t) is mapped onto a set of directed unweighted graphs G_i, $i = 1, ..., M$ - called layers - by aggregating them within user-defined time windows. Each layer G_i corresponds to a time step t_i. *DepthRank* is a two level procedure, incorporating (a) the calculation of the "influence score" update for each node in consecutive time steps and (b) the application of a monotonically decreasing function to account for the influence decay as time passes. With respect to (b), we introduce three variants of *DepthRank*: with no forgetting mechanism (DR), with forgetting mechanism $(DR - F)$ and with forgetting mechanism with normalization $(DR - NF)$. The "influence score" S of a node s taking into account all the interactions in the dataset is given by the following set of equations in the case of DR-F:

$$\Delta H(s, G_i) = \sum_{w \in G_{i+d}} H(w, G_{i+d} | s, G_i) \qquad (1)$$

$$S(s, G_i) = \Delta H(s, G_i) + S(s, G_j) \cdot e^{-(t_i - t_j^s)} \qquad (2)$$

$$S(s) = S(s, G_j) \cdot e^{-(T - t_j^s)} \qquad (3)$$

In the previous equations, $H(w, G_{i+d} | s, G_i)$ is the product of incoming and outgoing links to node w in layer G_{i+d}, given that there is a path from node s at layer G_i (see Appendix A). $\Delta H(s, G_i)$ refers to the update of the "influence score" of node s rooted in layer G_i and $S(s, G_j)$ is the score acquired after the most recent update of S at time step t_j^s, corresponding to layer G_j. Note that $t_j^s < t_i$. The final "influence score" for node s is calculated in Eq. (3). T is the maximum time step in the aggregated data. The rest of the cases (DR and DR-NF), along with the notations and algorithmic implementation are described in Appendix A.

3 Experimental Setup

Our experiments were performed using a Ubuntu 14.04 LTS desktop PC with Intel(R) Core(TM) i5-2500K CPU at 3.30 GHz and 16 GB RAM. For comparison, we have employed two popular and widely used methods, namely k-shell (kS) [9] and Collective Influence (CI) [14] (see Appendix B). To assess the spreading ability of the important network nodes uncovered by each method, we apply a temporal implementation of the SIR model, called *Temporal Gillespie Algorithm* [23], using as an indicator the maximum number of infected nodes within the time limits of the dataset $I_{max} = \max_{1 \leq t \leq T} I(t)$. The correctness of the ordering is evaluated by incorporating the τ-Kendall measure [8]. More details on the evaluation metrics can be found in Appendix B.

The methods were applied to the following publicly available real world datasets: CollegeMsg, Facebook and Data Mining (DM) temporal citation network (refer to Appendix C for details). Each of them consists of (u, v, t) tuples, where u is the sender of a message or the author being cited and v the receiver of the message or the author citing an article at time t. In order to apply k-shell and CI methods, we aggregate the interactions in a static unweighted graph.

4   Results

In this section, we present the results obtained for each of the datasets of Sect. 3.

4.1   CollegeMsg

We have aggregated the timestamped dataset using a one day interval. We have also applied the DR variants using time windows dt of $1, 2$ or 3 days.

In Fig. 2, we present I_{max} for the $m = 50$ most important (top) nodes, with $\beta = 0.02$ (Fig. 2(a)) and $\beta = 0.05$ (Fig. 2(b)), keeping $\gamma = 0.01$ fixed in both cases. We observe that for β very close to the epidemic threshold (which is calculated as $\beta_c = 0.017$ for $\gamma = 0.01$ using the method described in [22]), CI performs the best, followed by kS, DR-NF ($dt = 1$), DR-NF ($dt = 3$) and DR ($dt = 1$). DR-F behaves overall poorly. However, the case is different for $\beta = 0.05$ (Fig. 2(b)). Now, both DR-NF and DR-F are the best methods, with the latter outperforming the former. These results suggest a positive correlation between β and the spreading efficiency of the seed sets uncovered with our method.

To investigate the preservation of the ordering for the different methods, we have used the τ-Kendall measure, as described in Sect. 3. In Fig. 3, we plot the results for one parameter value per method, to make the comparisons more clear. For a complete list of the methods refer to Fig. 9 in the Appendix D. In Fig. 3(a), we observe that, even though CI($l = 2$) has been identified as the best method for $\beta = 0.02$ and $\gamma = 0.01$, it exhibits poorer ordering preservation compared to DR-F($dt = 2$). The latter is very robust within the range $10 \leq m \leq 50$. For larger values of β (Fig. 3(b)), DR-NF($dt = 2$) and DR-F($dt = 2$) rapidly increase their ability to preserve the ordering as the number of the most important (top) nodes taken into account increases, closely following each other for $m \geq 30$.

In conclusion, DR-F and DR-NF variants increase their efficiency both in terms of uncovering important nodes as well as preserving the ranking ordering as β increases. Also, for the specific case of $m = 50$ most important nodes, DR-F outperforms DR-NF with respect to both I_{max} and τ-Kendall values.

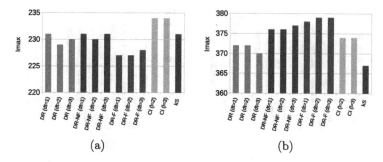

Fig. 2. Plot of the I_{max} for the CollegeMsg dataset, for $\gamma = 0.01$ and (a) $\beta = 0.02$ and (b) $\beta = 0.05$. The results are obtained for seed sets comprised of the $m = 50$ top nodes and are averages of 10,000 runs. The methods are indicated in the horizontal axis. In the parentheses, we include the parameters used per method.

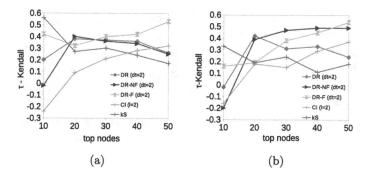

Fig. 3. Plot of the τ-Kendall as a function of the number of top nodes for the CollegeMsg dataset, for $\gamma = 0.01$ and (a) $\beta = 0.02$ and (b) $\beta = 0.05$. The methods are shown in the legends. In the parentheses, we include the parameters used per method. For a complete comparison of the methods refer to Appendix D.

4.2 Facebook

In the case of Facebook dataset, we have chosen to aggregate the timestamps in an hour interval. We have also selected the values of dt to be $1, 2$ and 3 hours for the DR variants.

In Fig. 4, we present I_{max}, for the $m = 50$ most important nodes, for fixed $\beta = 0.15$ and two values of γ which differ by an order of magnitude. In the case of $\gamma = 0.01$ (Fig. 4(a)), DR-NF behaves slightly better than kS, with DR-F following closely the first two methods. DR-NF continues to be the best method for the case of $\gamma = 0.001$ (Fig. 4(b)). Now, DR-F climbs in the second place and kS becomes the worst method.

In Fig. 5, we plot the evolution of τ-Kendall as a function of the number m of top ranked nodes. For the case of $\gamma = 0.01$ (Fig. 5(a)), we observe that DR-NF($dt = 2$), DR-F($dt = 2$) and kS preserve the ranking ordering. The behavior continues to be the same for DR-F($dt = 2$) and kS for $\gamma = 0.001$ (Fig. 5(b)).

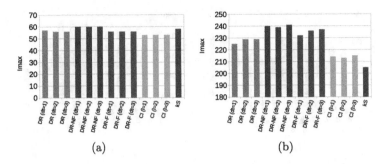

Fig. 4. Plot of the I_{max} for Facebook dataset, for $\beta = 0.15$ and (a) $\gamma = 0.01$ and (b) $\gamma = 0.001$. The results are obtained for seed sets comprised of the $m = 50$ top nodes and are averages of 10,000 runs. The methods are indicated in the horizontal axis. In the parentheses, we include the parameters used per method.

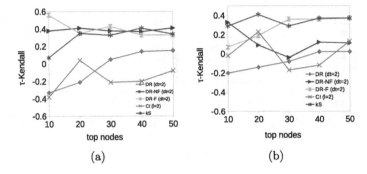

Fig. 5. Plot of the τ-Kendall as a function of the number of top nodes for Facebook dataset, for $\beta = 0.15$ and (a) $\gamma = 0.01$ and (b) $\gamma = 0.001$. The methods are shown in the legends. In the parentheses, we include the parameters used per method. For a complete comparison of the methods refer to Appendix D.

In conclusion, DR variants display the best performance in terms of spreading efficiency, which increases as γ decreases. In terms of ranking preservation, only DR-F exhibits an overall stable behavior among the variants.

4.3   DM Temporal Citation Network

Finally, we investigate the DM temporal citation network (see Sect. 3). We maintain the resolution of the dataset to one year and use dt values of $1, 2$ and 3 years for the DR variants.

In Fig. 6, we present I_{max} for the $m = 50$ most important nodes. We observe that DR variants closely follow kS as the best performing method for $\beta = 0.004$ and $\gamma = 0.05$. However, all DR variants are top performing for $\beta = 0.04$ and $\gamma = 0.05$. Interestingly, DR performs better than DR-NF and DR-F for the latter set of parameters.

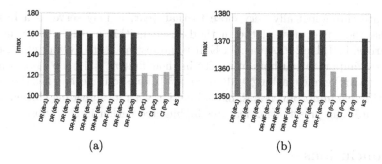

Fig. 6. Plot of the I_{max} for DM temporal citation network, for $\gamma = 0.05$ and (a) $\beta = 0.004$ and (b) $\beta = 0.04$. The results are obtained for seed sets comprised of the $m = 50$ top nodes and are averages of 10,000 runs. The methods are indicated in the horizontal axis. In the parentheses, we include the parameters used per method.

In Fig. 7, we monitor the behavior of τ-Kendall for the different methods as a function of the number of top ranked nodes. In Fig. 7(a), we observe that kS is the best method with respect to the rank ordering preservation. DR variants are stable and have a constant τ value for $m \geq 20$, but behave worse than the kS. In Fig. 7(b), kS and DR variants are generally indistinguishable and display a relative high value of τ.

In terms of spreading efficiency and ranking ordering preservation, the DR variants behave better than the rest of the methods and improve their performance as β increases, which has also been observed for the *CollegeMsg* dataset (Sect. 4.1).

For the DM dataset, we are also able to test our rankings against ground truth data. This is a list of the 10 most important authors on DM topic up to 2012[1].

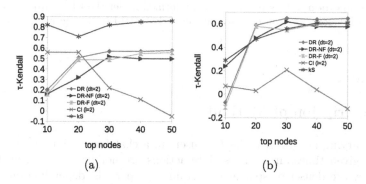

Fig. 7. Plot of the τ-Kendall as a function of the number of top nodes for DM temporal citation network, for $\gamma = 0.05$ and (a) $\beta = 0.004$ and (b) $\beta = 0.04$. The methods are shown in the legends. In the parentheses, we include the parameters used per method. For a complete comparison of the methods refer to Appendix D.

---

[1] http://www.kdnuggets.com/2012/03/top-10-in-data-mining.html.

As we are chronologically very close to that year, it may serve as a baseline to assess the correctness of the methods used in this paper. The results are summarized in Table 2 in Appendix E. It is interesting that DR variants discover 5/10 most important authors in reality in their first $m = 10$ top ranked nodes (50% accuracy) while reaching 9/10 for $m = 50$. Thus, our method has the ability to identify real important nodes, in conjunction with its spreading efficiency and ranking ordering preservation features highlighted earlier in this subsection.

5   Conclusions

The research on influence maximization in the field of graph theory has long focused on static representations. However, nodes and links appear and disappear through time and thus, the consideration of the temporal dimension is crucial.

In this paper, we have developed a family of methods called DepthRank (DR), able to discover important nodes in evolving networks. The results indicate that DR variants are efficient in terms of spreading and ranking ordering preservation. Using the DM temporal citation network, we were able to demonstrate that DepthRank is capable of identifying nodes that are "influential" in reality.

As a rule of thumb, we may provide the following guidelines for the application of the method: (a) dt should not exceed the dataset's resolution more than a factor of 3 and (b) the utilization of the absolute forgetting mechanism (DR-F) is the most robust.

In the future, we plan to investigate the effects of the incorporation of other types of information (text similarity, sentiments etc.), as it is expected to enhance the identification of important network nodes and provide results that consider the semantic gap, as our current method takes into account only the topological interactions between users and not the interplay between topology and content.

Acknowledgement. This research was performed under the EU's project "Trusted, Citizen - LEA collaboration over sOcial Networks(TRILLION)" (grant agreement No 653256).

Appendix

A   Description of Method

In time-varying networks, nodes (i.e. users in a chat forum) interact with each other at given timestamps. These interactions are not homogeneously distributed; they are denser or sparser in certain time periods, depending on various factors (i.e. type of media, occurrence of an important event etc.). In the following, we proceed by aggregating these interactions using appropriate time windows with the exact values per dataset presented in Sect. 4. We denote by t the time step in the aggregated data.

After the aggregation, data are transformed into a set of directed unweighted graphs G_i, $i = 1...M$, which are called layers. A part of them is shown in Fig. 8 (left). In this setting, there are two types of links: intra-links that connect two nodes in the same layer and inter-links that connect identical nodes in consecutive layers.

Next, we present the method for ranking important network nodes by evaluating their "influence score" S. This is a two level procedure, incorporating (a) the calculation of the "influence score" update for each node in consecutive time steps and (b) the application of a monotonically decreasing function to account for the influence decay as time passes.

We denote with $\Delta H(s, G_i)$ the "influence score" update which refers to a node s residing in layer G_i. It is calculated as follows: starting from G_i, we specify the number of subsequent layers d within the time range $[t_i, t_i + dt]$, with dt the (fixed) length of the time window and t_i the timestep corresponding to layer G_i.[2] Then, we construct every possible path from node s in layer G_i to any node w in layer G_{i+d}, which passes through nodes in the intermediate layers (Fig. 8(right)). Note that we take into account both the inter and intra-links during path construction.

Each node w in layer G_{i+d} has $r^{out}_{(w,G_{i+d})}$ outgoing links and $r^{in}_{(w,G_{i+d-1})}$ incoming links in layer G_{i+d-1}. We introduce the following relation:

$$H(w, G_{i+d}|s, G_i) = \begin{cases} r^{in}_{(w,G_{i+d-1})} \cdot r^{out}_{(w,G_{i+d})}, & \text{if } dist((w, G_{i+d}), (s, G_i)) < 2 \cdot d + 1 \\ 0, & \text{otherwise} \end{cases}$$

which couples path diversity ($r^{in}_{(w,G_{i+d-1})}$) and transmission efficiency ($r^{out}_{(w,G_{i+d})}$), to denote the portion of the update ΔH attributed to node w. Thus, $\Delta H(s, G_i)$ is given by:

$$\Delta H(s, G_i) = \sum_{w \in G_{i+d}} H(w, G_{i+d}|s, G_i)$$

Referring to Fig. 8 (right), we have at layer $i + 3$ (i is the top layer): $H(2, G_{i+3}|1, G_i) = 2 \cdot 1 = 2$, $H(1, G_{i+3}|1, G_i) = 2 \cdot 2 = 4$, $H(3, G_{i+3}|1, G_i) = 2 \cdot 1 = 2$, $H(4, G_{i+3}|1, G_i) = 1 \cdot 1 = 1$, $H(5, G_{i+3}|1, G_i) = 2 \cdot 1 = 2$ and $H(6, G_{i+3}|1, G_i) = 1 \cdot 2 = 2$. Thus, for node $s = 1$ in layer G_i, the update is $\Delta H(1, G_i) = 13$.

The "influence score" $S(s, G_i)$ of node s up to layer G_i is the sum of the update $\Delta H(s, G_i)$ and its previous value $S(s, G_j)$ in layer G_j - which corresponds to the time step t^s_j of its most recent update - weighted using a forgetting function $g(t_i - t^s_j)$ to account for aging effects:

$$S(s, G_i) = \Delta H(s, G_i) + S(s, G_j) \cdot g(t_i - t^s_j)$$

In the following, we consider three different variants: no forgetting mechanism ($g(t_i - t^s_j) = 1$), forgetting mechanism ($g(t_i - t^s_j) = e^{-(t_i - t^s_j)}$) and forgetting

---

[2] The number of layers d within time window dt is not fixed because the layers may not be equally spaced.

Table 1. List of notations used in the text

Symbol	Notation
t	Time step of the aggregated dataset
T	Maximum time in the aggregated dataset
dt	Time window for the calculation of the "influence score" update
G_i	Directed unweighted graph (layer)
t_i	Time step corresponding to layer G_i
d	Number of layers in the time range $[t_i, t_i + dt]$
M	Total number of layers
s	Node in layer G_i for which "influence score" update is calculated
w	Node in layer G_{i+d}
G_j	The most recent layer in which node s has updated its "influence score"
t_j^s	Time step corresponding to layer G_j in which the "influence score" of node s has been recently updated
$r^{in}_{(w,G_{i+d-1})}$	Number of incoming edges to node w in layer G_{i+d-1} (including self-links)
$r^{out}_{(w,G_{i+d})}$	Number of outgoing edges from node w in layer G_{i+d} (including self-links)
$H(w, G_{i+d}\|s, G_i)$	Product between r^{in} and r^{out} for node w in layer G_{i+d}, which is connected through a path to node s in layer G_i
$\Delta H(s, G_i)$	Update of the "influence score" of node s residing in layer G_i
$g(t_i - t_j^s)$	Forgetting function
$S(s, G_i)$	"Influence score" of node s up to layer G_i
$S(s)$	"Influence score" of node s
m	Number of important (top) nodes

mechanism with normalization $(g(t_i - t_j^s) = e^{-(t_i-t_j^s)/T})$, with T the maximum time step of the aggregated dataset.[3] Thus, the score $S(s, G_i)$, can be formulated as follows:

– No forgetting mechanism

$$S(s, G_i) = \Delta H(s, G_i) + S(s, G_j) \qquad (4)$$

– Forgetting mechanism:

$$S(s, G_i) = \Delta H(s, G_i) + S(s, G_j) \cdot e^{-(t_i-t_j^s)} \qquad (5)$$

– Forgetting mechanism with normalization:

$$S(s, G_i) = \Delta H(s, G_i) + S(s, G_j) \cdot e^{-(t_i-t_j^s)/T} \qquad (6)$$

---

[3] The exponential decay function is commonly used in many applications, however we can replace it with any other monotonically decreasing function.

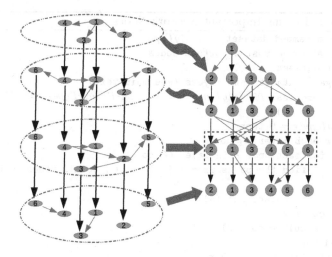

Fig. 8. Path construction for the DepthRank method. Left panel: nodes populate the layers (denoted by the blue dashed ellipses) according to their time ordering. Red arrows indicate the interactions between nodes in the same layer and black arrows the links between the same nodes on subsequent layers. Right panel: we start from node 1 as a source node and draw connections between the source node and its nearest neighbors in layer G_i (corresponding to time step t_i). For each node (including the source node), we proceed in the same manner for the subsequent layers, until reaching the last one within the time window $[t_i, t_i + dt]$. Red arrows stand for the directed connections between nodes in the same layer and black arrows for the connections between the identical nodes in subsequent layers ("self-links"). The dashed box indicate the level at which we perform the calculations (see text).

The procedure ends when we reach the last layer for which $t \leq T - dt$. The overall "influence score" S for node s in the underlying dataset is given by (remember that G_j denotes the layer of the most recent update):

- No forgetting mechanism:
$$S(s) = S(s, G_j) \tag{7}$$

- Forgetting mechanism:
$$S(s) = S(s, G_j) \cdot e^{-(T-t_j^s)} \tag{8}$$

- Forgetting mechanism with normalization:
$$S(s) = S(s, G_j) \cdot e^{-(T-t_j^s)/T} \tag{9}$$

We finally rank the nodes in descending order according to their S value. In Algorithm 1, we provide the pseudo-code for our method, including the three variants defined previously: DepthRank (DR), where we do not impose any forgetting mechanism (Eqs. (4) and (7)), DepthRank with forgetting mechanism (DR-F) (Eqs. (5) and (8)) and DepthRank where we impose normalization (DR-NF) (Eqs. (6) and (9)).

Algorithm 1. Finding Important Network Nodes

Input: timestamped dataset, dt, $algType$
Output: List of m most important nodes
1. Import dataset
2. Aggregate dataset into layers (see main text)
3. Choose process: DR ($algType == 0$), $DR\text{-}F$ ($algType == 1$) or $DR\text{-}NF$ ($algType == 2$).
4. if $algType == 0$ then
5.   for each layer G_i do
6.   for each node s in layer G_i do
7.   find the paths from s in layer G_i to all nodes w in layer G_{i+d}
8.   calculate eq. (4)
9.   end for
10.   calculate eq. (7)
11.   end for
12. else if $algType == 1$ then
13.   for each layer G_i do
14.   for each node s in layer G_i do
15.   find the paths from s in layer G_i to all nodes w in layer G_{i+d}
16.   calculate eq. (5)
17.   end for
18.   calculate eq. (8)
19.   end for
20. else if $algType == 2$ then
21.   for each layer G_i do
22.   for each node s in layer G_i do
23.   find the paths from s in layer G_i to all nodes w in layer G_{i+d}
24.   calculate eq. (6)
25.   end for
26.   calculate eq. (9)
27.   end for
28. end if
29. Rank nodes according to their ''influence score'' S in descending order and output the first m nodes.

B   Baseline Methods and Evaluation Metrics

In this section, we present the baseline methods along with the evaluation metrics. For the former, we have chosen k-shell (kS) and Collective Influence (CI) methods because they are widely employed in the context of graph-based techniques.

k -shell is broadly used for ranking purposes. Given a graph G, it proceeds as follows: every isolated node is considered as being in the 0-shell. For the rest of the nodes with connectivity $k \geq 1$, one first removes the links from every node with $k = 1$. The residual graph may consist of nodes with connectivity $k = 1$; thus, the same procedure is repeated until no nodes with $k \leq 1$ remain. We say that these nodes constitute the 1-shell. The rest of the shells are uncovered in the same way. The nodes belonging to the highest shells are the most important [9].

Collective Influence is based on optimal percolation. According to [14], it takes the form:

$$CI(i) = (r_i - 1) \sum_{j \in \partial Ball(i,l)} (r_j - 1) \qquad (10)$$

where, r_i is the degree of the node i, $\partial Ball(i, l)$ the front of a sphere centered at the i-th node with radius l (in terms of shortest path distance). We follow the suggestions of the authors in [14] and set $l = 2$ and 3 in the calculations.

To assess the spreading ability of the important network nodes uncovered by each method, we apply a temporal implementation of the SIR model, called *Temporal Gillespie Algorithm* [23] (we choose the Poisson homogeneous version), to account for the time-varying interactions in real-world networks. We have slightly modified the process in order to start from a set of initially infected nodes rather than a single one. These sets coincide with the ordered sets identified by the methods used. The efficiency of spreading is evaluated by using the maximum number of infected nodes within the whole dataset, $I_{max} = \max_{1 \leq t \leq T} I(t)$. β and γ are the infection and recovery rates, respectively. Except for the case of the small CollegeMsg dataset, where we have calculated the epidemic threshold for a fixed γ value as in [22], for the rest of the datasets this was done heuristically, by searching for those values of β and γ for which considerable amount of spreading is observed. The exact values are displayed in the figure captions in Sect. 4.

We are also interested in the correct ordering of the ranking methods. A suitable measure is the τ-Kendall [8], which evaluates the concordance of two ordered lists. We exploit it in the following way:

- We collect all the nodes tagged as important from every method o. We calculate I_{max} for each one and rank them according to this value. This will be the overall "ground-truth" ranking list, L.
- We select the m first nodes according to each method ranking, R_o, and find their position in L. This will be the method specific "ground-truth" ranking list, L_o.
- We calculate the τ-Kendall between L_o and R_o.

This evaluation is applied for various lengths m of the most important nodes lists (see respective figures in Sect. 4).

C   Datasets

We have performed the experiments using the following publicly available real world datasets:

- **CollegeMsg**[4]: It is a small temporal network corresponding to a private messaging facility at the University of California, Irvine. It consists of 1899 users and 59835 temporal edges. The timestamps are in UNIX time (seconds).
- **Facebook**[5]: It consists of 855542 facebook wall posts between 45813 unique users. The timestamps are in UNIX time (seconds).
- **Data Mining (DM) temporal citation network:** We have used the DBLP dataset of [21] which consists of all the papers in computer science up to 2010. The timestamps are in years.

The preparation of the DM dataset was performed as follows: we have selected the papers that contain one or more authors from a list of DM experts[6]. Each article record contains a set of indexes to other articles which cite the current one. We use this information to create the connections between the authors citing a paper and those of the cited paper per year of citation. For example, assume that we pick a record of the form: (title1, author1, author2, author3, 2009) which cites among other papers the following: (title2, cauthor1, cauthor2, 1993). We formulate the authors temporal interaction patterns as: (cauthor1, author1, 2009), (cauthor1, author2, 2009), (cauthor1, author3, 2009), (cauthor2, author1, 2009), (cauthor2, author2, 2009), (cauthor2, author3, 2009). Each tuple means that the first author influenced the second author in year 2009. In this way, we construct the temporal citation network for the years 1993–2010.

Each of the previous datasets comes into the form (u, v, t), where u is the sender of a message or the author being cited and v the receiver of the message or the author citing an article at time t. In order to apply k-shell and CI methods, we aggregate the interactions in a static unweighted graph.

D   Detailed Results for τ-Kendall

In this section, we provide more detailed plots for the τ-Kendall, by incorporating all the methods and parameters used (Figs. 9, 10 and 11).

---

[4] https://snap.stanford.edu/data/CollegeMsg.html.
[5] http://konect.uni-koblenz.de/networks/facebook-wosn-wall.
[6] https://static.aminer.org/lab-datasets/expertfinding/datasets/Data-Mining.txt.

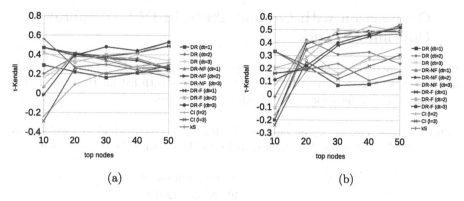

Fig. 9. Plot of the τ-Kendall as a function of the number m of the most important (top) nodes for the CollegeMsg dataset, for $\gamma = 0.01$ and (a) $\beta = 0.02$ and (b) $\beta = 0.05$. The methods are shown in the legends.

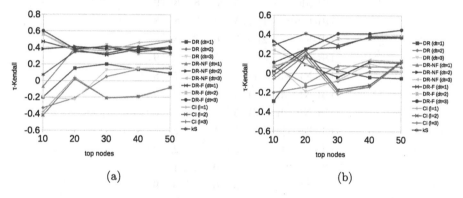

Fig. 10. Plot of the τ-Kendall as a function of the number m of the most important (top) nodes for Facebook dataset, for $\beta = 0.15$ and (a) $\gamma = 0.01$ and (b) $\gamma = 0.001$. The methods are shown in the legends.

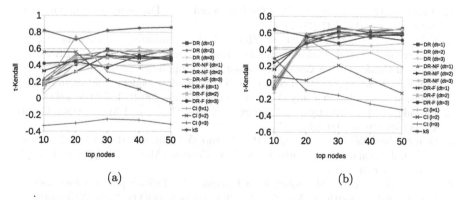

Fig. 11. Plot of the τ-Kendall as a function of the number m of the most important (top) nodes for DM temporal citation network, for $\gamma = 0.05$ and (a) $\beta = 0.004$ and (b) $\beta = 0.04$. The methods are shown in the legends.

E   Comparison with Ground-Truth in DM Temporal Citation Network

In Table 2, we present the number of important network nodes identified by each method that are common with those in the ground-truth list for the case of DM temporal citation network (see Sect. 4), as m increases.

Table 2. Number of important authors identified by the methods used compared to the top-10 DM authors list (see main text) for the DM temporal citation network.

Method	# of top authors m				
	10	20	30	40	50
DR (dt = 1)	5	6	7	8	8
DR (dt = 2)	5	6	7	8	9
DR (dt = 3)	5	6	8	8	9
DR-F (dt = 1)	5	6	7	8	8
DR-F (dt = 2)	5	6	7	8	9
DR-F (dt = 3)	5	5	8	8	9
DR-NF (dt = 1)	5	7	7	7	8
DR-NF (dt = 2)	5	6	7	8	9
DR-NF (dt = 3)	5	5	7	8	8
CI (l = 1)	1	1	2	2	3
CI (l = 2)	2	2	2	2	3
CI (l = 3)	0	0	1	1	1
kS	3	6	7	9	9

References

1. Aggarwal, C.C., Lin, S., Yu, P.S.: On Influential Node Discovery in Dynamic Social Networks, pp. 636–647 (2012)
2. Cai, Q., Sun, L., Niu, J., Liu, Y., Zhang, J.: Disseminating real-time messages in opportunistic mobile social networks: a ranking perspective. In: 2015 IEEE International Conference on Communications (ICC), pp. 3228–3233 (2015)
3. van Eck, P.S., Jager, W., Leeflang, P.S.H.: Opinion leaders' role in innovation diffusion: a simulation study. J. Prod. Innov. Manag. **28**(2), 187–203 (2011)
4. Estrada, E.: The Structure of Complex Networks: Theory and Applications. Oxford University Press, Oxford (2011)
5. Gómez-Gardeñes, J., Echenique, P., Moreno, Y.: Immunization of real complex communication networks. Euro. Phys. J. B - Condens. Matter Complex Syst. **49**(2), 259–264 (2006)
6. Jansen, B.J., Zhang, M., Sobel, K., Chowdury, A.: Twitter power: tweets as electronic word of mouth. J. Am. Soc. Inf. Sci. Technol. **60**(11), 2169–2188 (2009)
7. Kempe, D., Kleinberg, J., Tardos, E.: Maximizing the spread of influence through a social network. In: Proceedings of the Ninth ACM SIGKDD International Conference on Knowledge Discovery and Data Mining, KDD 2003, New York, NY, USA, pp. 137–146 (2003)

8. Kendall, M.G.: A new measure of rank correlation. Biometrika **30**(1–2), 81 (1938)
9. Kitsak, M., Gallos, L., Havlin, S., Liljeros, F., Muchnik, L., Stanley, H., Makse, H.: Identification of influential spreaders in complex networks. Nat. Phys. **6**(11), 888–893 (2010)
10. Laflin, P., Mantzaris, A.V., Ainley, F., Otley, A., Grindrod, P., Higham, D.J.: Discovering and validating influence in a dynamic online social network. Soc. Netw. Anal. Min. **3**(4), 1311–1323 (2013)
11. Lü, L., Chen, D., Ren, X.L., Zhang, Q.M., Zhang, Y.C., Zhou, T.: Vital nodes identification in complex networks. Phys. Rep. **650**, 1–63 (2016)
12. Magnien, C., Tarissan, F.: Time evolution of the importance of nodes in dynamic networks. In: 2015 IEEE/ACM International Conference on Advances in Social Networks Analysis and Mining (ASONAM), pp. 1200–1207 (2015)
13. Michalski, R., Kajdanowicz, T., Bródka, P., Kazienko, P.: Seed selection for spread of influence in social networks: temporal vs. static approach. New Gener. Comput. **32**(3), 213–235 (2014)
14. Morone, F., Makse, H.: Influence maximization in complex networks through optimal percolation. Nature **524**(7563), 65–68 (2015)
15. Newman, M.: Networks: An Introduction. Oxford University Press, New York (2010)
16. Rocha, L., Masuda, N.: Individual-based approach to epidemic processes on arbitrary dynamic contact networks. Scientific Reports 6 (2016)
17. Rosas-Casals, M., Valverde, S., Solé, R.V.: Topological vulnerability of the European power grid under errors and attacks. Int. J. Bifurcat. Chaos **17**(07), 2465–2475 (2007)
18. Saramäki, J., Moro, E.: From seconds to months: an overview of multi-scale dynamics of mobile telephone calls. Euro. Phys. J. B **88**(6), 164 (2015)
19. Song, G., Li, Y., Chen, X., He, X., Tang, J.: Influential node tracking on dynamic social network: an interchange greedy approach. IEEE Trans. Knowl. Data Eng. **29**(2), 359–372 (2017)
20. Stehlé, J., Voirin, N., Barrat, A., Cattuto, C., Isella, L., Pinton, J.F., Quaggiotto, M., van den Broeck, W., Régis, C., Lina, B., Vanhems, P.: High-resolution measurements of face-to-face contact patterns in a primary school. PLoS ONE **6**(8), e23176 (2011)
21. Tang, J., Zhang, J., Yao, L., Li, J., Zhang, L., Su, Z.: ArnetMiner: extraction and mining of academic social networks. In: Proceedings of the 14th ACM SIGKDD International Conference on Knowledge Discovery and Data Mining, KDD 2008, New York, NY, USA, pp. 990–998 (2008)
22. Valdano, E., Ferreri, L., Poletto, C., Colizza, V.: Analytical computation of the epidemic threshold on temporal networks. Phys. Rev. X **5**, 021005 (2015)
23. Vestergaard, C., Génois, M.: Temporal gillespie algorithm: fast simulation of contagion processes on time-varying networks. PLoS Comput. Biol. **11**(10), e1004579 (2015)
24. Viswanath, B., Mislove, A., Cha, M., Gummadi, K.P.: On the evolution of user interaction in Facebook. In: Proceedings of the 2nd ACM Workshop on Online Social Networks, WOSN 2009, New York, NY, USA, pp. 37–42 (2009)
25. Zhuang, H., Sun, Y., Tang, J., Zhang, J., Sun, X.: Influence maximization in dynamic social networks. In: 2013 IEEE 13th International Conference on Data Mining, pp. 1313–1318 (2013)

Poster Papers: News, Misinformation, and Collective Sensemaking

On Early-Stage Debunking Rumors on Twitter: Leveraging the Wisdom of Weak Learners

Tu Ngoc Nguyen[1(✉)], Cheng Li[2], and Claudia Niederée[1]

[1] L3S Research Center, Leibniz Universität Hannover, Hanover, Germany
{tunguyen,niederee}@L3S.de
[2] SAP S/4 Hana Cloud Foundation, Shanghai, China
cheng.li@SAP.com

Abstract. Recently a lot of progress has been made in rumor modeling and rumor detection for micro-blogging streams. However, existing automated methods do not perform very well for early rumor detection, which is crucial in many settings, e.g., in crisis situations. One reason for this is that aggregated rumor features such as propagation features, which work well on the long run, are - due to their accumulating characteristic - not very helpful in the early phase of a rumor. In this work, we present an approach for early rumor detection, which leverages Convolutional Neural Networks for learning the hidden representations of individual rumor-related tweets to gain insights on the credibility of each tweets. We then aggregate the predictions from the very beginning of a rumor to obtain the overall event credits (so-called *wisdom*), and finally combine it with a time series based rumor classification model. Our extensive experiments show a clearly improved classification performance within the critical very first hours of a rumor. For a better understanding, we also conduct an extensive feature evaluation that emphasized on the early stage and shows that the low-level credibility has best predictability at all phases of the rumor lifetime.

1 Introduction

Widely spreading rumors can be harmful to the government, markets and society and reduce the usefulness of social media channel such as Twitter by affecting the reliability of their content. Therefore, effective method for detecting rumors on Twitter are crucial and rumors should be detected as early as possible before they widely spread. As an example, let us recall of the shooting incident that happened in the vicinity of the Olympia shopping mall, Munich; in a summer day, 2016. Due to the unclear situation at early time, numerous rumors about the event did appear and they started to circulate very fast over social media. The city police had to warn the population to refrain from spreading related news on Twitter as it was getting out of control: *"Rumors are wildfires that are difficult to put out and traditional news sources or official channels, such as police departments, subsequently struggle to communicate verified information to the public, as it gets lost under the flurry of false information."*[1] Fig. 1 shows the rumor *sub-events* in

---

[1] Deutsche Welle: http://bit.ly/2qZuxCN.

G.L. Ciampaglia et al. (Eds.): SocInfo 2017, Part II, LNCS 10540, pp. 141–158, 2017.
DOI: 10.1007/978-3-319-67256-4_13

the early stage of the event Munich shooting. The first *terror-indicating* "news" –
The gunman shouted 'Allahu Akbar'– was widely disseminated on Twitter right
after the incident by an unverified account. Later the claim of three gunmen also
spread quickly and caused public tension. In the end, all three information items
were falsified.

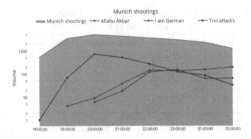

Fig. 1. The *Munich shooting* and its sub-events burst after the first 8 h, y-axis is English
tweet volume.

We follow the rumor definition [24] considering a rumor (or fake news) as a
statement whose truth value is unverified or deliberately false. A wide variety of
features has been used in existing work in rumor detection such as [6,11,13,18–
20,23,30,31]. Network-oriented and other aggregating features such as propagation pattern have proven to be effective for this task. Unfortunately, the
inherently accumulating characteristic of such features, which require some time
(and Twitter traffic) to mature, does not make them very apt for early rumor
detection. A first semi-automatic approach focussing on early rumor detection
presented by Zhao et al. [32], thus, exploits rumor signals such as enquiries that
might already arise at an early stage. Our fully automatic, cascading rumor
detection method follows the idea on focusing on early rumor signals on text
contents; which is the most reliable source before the rumors widely spread.
Specifically, we learn a more complex representation of single tweets using Convolutional Neural Networks, that could capture more hidden meaningful signal
than only enquiries to debunk rumors. [7,19] also use RNN for rumor debunking.
However, in their work, RNN is used at *event-level*. The classification leverages
only the deep data representations of aggregated tweet contents of the whole
event, while ignoring exploiting other –in latter stage–effective features such
as user-based features and propagation features. Although, tweet contents are
merely the only reliable source of clue at early stage, they are also likely to
have doubtful perspectives and different stands in this specific moment. In addition, they could relate to rumorous sub-events (see e.g., the Munich shooting).
Aggregating all relevant tweets of the event at this point can be of noisy and
harm the classification performance. One could think of a sub-event detection
mechanism as a solution, however, detecting sub-events at real-time over Twitter
stream is a challenging task [22], which increases latency and complexity. In this
work, we address this issue by deep neural modeling only at single tweet level.

Our intuition is to leverage the "wisdom of the crowd" theory; such that even a certain portion of tweets at a moment (mostly early stage) are weakly predicted (because of these noisy factors), the ensemble of them would attribute to a stronger prediction.

In this paper, we make the following contributions with respect to rumor detection:

- We develop a machine learning approach for modeling tweet-level credibility. Our CNN-based model reaches 81% accuracy for this novel task, that is even hard for human judgment. The results are used to debunk rumors in an ensemble fashion.
- Based on the credibility model we develop a novel and effective cascaded model for rumor classification. The model uses time-series structure of features to capture their temporal dynamics. Our model clearly outperforms strong baselines, especially for the targeted early stage of the diffusion. It already reaches over 80% accuracy in the first hour going up to over 90% accuracy over time.

2   Related Work

A variety of issues have been investigated using data, structural information, and the dynamics of the microblogging platform Twitter including event detection [16], spam detection [1,29], or sentiment detection [4]. Work on rumor detection in Twitter is less deeply researched so far, although rumors and their spreading have already been investigated for a long time in psychology [2,5,26]. Castillo et al. researched the information credibility on Twitter [6,11]. The work, however, is based solely on people's attitude (trustful or not) to a tweet not the credibility of the tweet itself. In other words, a false rumor tweet can be trusted by a reader, but it might anyway contain false information. The work still provides a good start of researching rumor detection.

Due to the importance of information propagation for rumors and their detection, there are also different simulation studies [25,27] about rumor propagations on Twitter. Those works provide relevant insights, but such simulations cannot fully reflect the complexity of real networks. Furthermore, there are recent work on propagation modeling based on epidemiological methods [3,13,17], yet over a long studied time, hence how the propagation patterns perform at early stage is unclear. Recently, [30] use unique features of Sina Weibo to study the propagation patterns and achieve good results. Unfortunately Twitter does not give such details of the propagation process as Weibo, so these work cannot be fully applied to Twitter.

Most relevant for our work is the work presented in [20], where a time series model to capture the time-based variation of social-content features is used. We build upon the idea of their *Series-Time Structure*, when building our approach for early rumor detection with our extended dataset, and we provide a deep analysis on the wide range of features change during diffusion time. Ma et al. [19]

used Recurrent Neural Networks for rumor detection, they batch tweets into time intervals and model the time series as a RNN sequence. Without any other hand-crafted features, they got almost 90% accuracy for events reported in Snope.com. As the same disadvantage of all other deep learning models, the process of learning is a black box, so we cannot envisage the cause of the good performance based only on content features. The model performance is also dependent on the tweet retrieval mechanism, of which quality is uncertain for stream-based trending sub-events.

3   Single Tweet Credibility Model

Before presenting our Single Tweet Credibility Model, we will start with an overview of our overall rumor detection method. The processing pipeline of our classification approach is shown in Fig. 2. In the first step, relevant tweets for an event are gathered. Subsequently, in the upper part of the pipeline, we predict tweet credibilty with our pre-trained credibility model and aggregate the prediction probabilities on single tweets (CreditScore). In the lower part of the pipeline, we extract features from tweets and combine them with the creditscore to construct the feature vector in a time series structure called Dynamic Series Time Model. These feature vectors are used to train the classifier for rumor vs. (non-rumor) news classification.

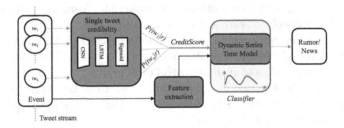

Fig. 2. Pipeline of our rumor detection approach.

Early in an event, the related tweet volume is scanty and there are no clear propagation pattern yet. For the credibility model we, therefore, leverage the signals derived from tweet contents. Related work often uses aggregated content [18,20,32], since individual tweets are often too short and contain slender context to draw a conclusion. However, content aggregation is problematic for hierarchical events and especially at early stage, in which tweets are likely to convey doubtful and contradictory perspectives. Thus, a mechanism for carefully considering the 'vote' for individual tweets is required. In this work, we overcome the restrictions (e.g., semantic sparsity) of traditional text representation methods (e.g., bag of words) in handling short text by learning low-dimensional tweet embeddings. In this way, we achieve a rich hidden semantic representation for a more effective classification.

3.1   Exploiting Convolutional and Recurrent Neural Networks

Given a tweet, our task is to classify whether it is associated with either a news or rumor. Most of the previous work [6,11] on tweet level only aims to measure the *trustfulness* based on human judgment (note that even if a tweet is trusted, it could anyway relate to a rumor). Our task is, to a point, a reverse engineering task; to measure the probability a tweet refers to a *news* or *rumor* event; which is even trickier. We hence, consider this a weak learning process. Inspired by [33], we combine CNN and RNN into a unified model for tweet representation and classification. The model utilizes CNN to extract a sequence of higher-level phrase representations, which are fed into a long short-term memory (LSTM) RNN to obtain the tweet representation. This model, called CNN+RNN henceforth, is able to capture both local features of phrases (by CNN) as well as global and temporal tweet semantics (by LSTM) (see Fig. 3).

Representing Tweets: Generic-purpose tweet embedding in [9,28] use character-level RNN to represent tweets that in general, are noisy and of idiosyncratic nature. We discern that tweets for rumors detection are often triggered from professional sources. Hence, they are linguistically clean, making word-level embedding become useful. In this work, we do not use the pre-trained embedding (i.e., *word2vec*), but instead learn the word vectors from scratch from our (large) rumor/news-based tweet collection. The effectiveness of fine-tuning by learning task-specific word vectors is backed by [15]. We represent tweets as follows: Let $x_i \in \mathscr{R}$ be the k-dimensional word vector corresponding to the i-th word in the tweet. A tweet of length n (padded where necessary) is represented as: $x_{1:n} = x_1 \oplus x_2 \oplus \cdots \oplus x_n$, where $\oplus$ is the concatenation operator. In general, let $x_{i:i+j}$ refer to the concatenation of words $x_i, x_{i+1}, ..., x_{i+j}$. A convolution operation involves a filter $w \in \mathscr{R}^{hk}$, which is applied to a window of h words to produce a feature. For example, a feature c_i is generated from a window of words $x_{i:i+h-1}$ by: $c_i = f(w \cdot x_{i:i+h-1} + b)$.

Here $b \in \mathscr{R}$ is a bias term and f is a non-linear function such as the hyperbolic tangent. This filter is applied to each possible window of words in the tweet $\{x_{1:h}, x_{2:h+1}, ..., x_{n-h+1:n}\}$ to produce a feature map: $c = [c_1, c_2, ..., c_{n-h+1}]$ with $c \in \mathscr{R}^{n-h+1}$. A max-over-time pooling or dynamic k-max pooling is often applied to feature maps after the convolution to select the most or the k-most important features. We also apply the 1D max pooling operation over the time-step dimension to obtain a fixed-length output.

Using Long Short-Term Memory RNNs: RNN are able to propagate historical information via a chain-like neural network architecture. While processing sequential data, it looks at the current input x_t as well as the previous output of hidden state h_{t-1} at each time step. The simple RNN hence has the ability to capture context information. However, the length of reachable context is often limited. The gradient tends to vanish or blow up during the back propagation. To address this issue, LSTM was introduced in [12]. The LSTM architecture has a range of repeated modules for each time step as in a standard RNN. At each time step, the output of the module is controlled by a set of gates in $\mathscr{R}^d$ as a

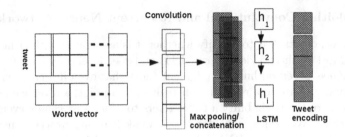

Fig. 3. CNN+LSTM for tweet representation.

function of the old hidden state h_{t-1} and the input at the current time step x_t: forget gate f_t, input gate i_t, and output gate o_t.

3.2   CNN+LSTM for Tweet-Level Classification

We regard the output of the hidden state at the last step of LSTM as the final tweet representation and we add a softmax layer on top. We train the entire model by minimizing the cross-entropy error. Given a training tweet sample $x^{(i)}$, its true label $y_j^{(i)} \in \{y_{rumor}, y_{news}\}$ and the estimated probabilities $\tilde{y}_j^{(i)} \in [0..1]$ for each label $j \in \{rumor, news\}$, the error is defined as:

$$L(x^{(i)}, y^{(i)}) = 1\{y^{(i)} = y_{rumor}\}log(\tilde{y}_{rumor}^{(i)}) + 1\{y^{(i)} = y_{news}\}log(\tilde{y}_{news}^{(i)}) \quad (1)$$

where 1 is a function converts boolean values to $\{0, 1\}$. We employ stochastic gradient descent (SGD) to learn the model parameters.

4   Time Series Rumor Detection Model

As observed in [19,20], rumor features are very prone to change during an event's development. In order to capture these temporal variabilities, we build upon the Dynamic Series-Time Structure (DSTS) model (time series for short) for feature vector representation proposed in [20]. We base our credibility feature on the time series approach and train the classifier with features from diffent high-level contexts (i.e., users, Twitter and propagation) in a cascaded manner. In this section, we first detail the employed Dynamic Series-Time Structure, then describe the high and low-level ensemble features used for learning in this pipeline step.

4.1   Dynamic Series-Time Structure (DSTS) Model

For an event E_i we define a time frame given by $timeFirst_i$ as the start time of the event and $timeLast_i$ as the time of the last tweet of the event in the observation time. We split this event time frame into N intervals and associate each tweet to one of the intervals according to its creation time. Thus, we can generate a vector $V(E_i)$ of features for each time interval. In order to capture the changes of feature over time, we model their differences between two time intervals. So the model of DSTS is represented as: $V(E_i) = (\mathbf{F}_{i,0}^D, \mathbf{F}_{i,1}^D, ..., \mathbf{F}_{i,N}^D, \mathbf{S}_{i,1}^D, ..., \mathbf{S}_{i,N}^D)$, where $\mathbf{F}_{i,t}^D$ is the feature vector in time interval t of event E_i. $\mathbf{S}_{i,t}^D$ is the difference between $\mathbf{F}_{i,t}^D$ and $\mathbf{F}_{i,t+1}^D$. $V(E_i)$ is the time series feature vector of the event E_i. $\mathbf{F}_{i,t}^D = (\widetilde{f}_{i,t,1}, \widetilde{f}_{i,t,2}, ..., \widetilde{f}_{i,t,D})$. And $\mathbf{S}_{i,t}^D = \frac{\mathbf{F}_{i,t+1}^D - \mathbf{F}_{i,t}^D}{Interval(E_i)}$. We use Z-score to normalize feature values; $\widetilde{f}_{i,t,k} = \frac{f_{i,t+1,k} - \overline{f}_{i,k}}{\sigma(f_{i,k})}$ where $f_{i,t,k}$ is the k-th feature of the event E_i in time interval t. The mean of the feature k of the event E_i is denoted as $\overline{f}_{i,k}$ and $\sigma(f_{i,k})$ is the standard deviation of the feature k over all time intervals. We can skip this step, when we use Random Forest or Decision Trees, because they do not require feature normalization.

4.2 Features for the Rumor Detection Model

In selecting features for the rumor detection model, we have followed two rationales: (a) we have selected features that we expect to be useful in early rumor detection and (b) we have collected a broad range of features from related work as a basis for investigating the time-dependent impact of a wide variety of features in our time-dependence study. In total, we have constructed over 50 features[2] in the three main categories i.e., *Ensemble, Twitter* and *Epidemiological* features. We refrained from using network features, since they are expected to be of little use in early rumor detection [8], since user networks around events need time to form. Following our general idea, none of our features are extracted from the content aggregations. Due to space limitation, we describe only our main features as follows.

Ensemble Features. We consider two types of Ensemble Features: features accumulating crowd wisdom and averaging feature for the Tweet credit Scores. The former are extracted from the surface level while the latter comes from the low dimensional level of tweet embeddings; that in a way augments the sparse crowd at early stage.

CrowdWisdom: Similar to [18], the core idea is to leverage the public's common sense for rumor detection: If there are more people denying or doubting the truth of an event, this event is more likely to be a rumor. For this purpose, [18] use an extensive list of bipolar sentiments with a set of combinational rules. In contrast to mere *sentiment* features, this approach is more tailored *rumor* context (difference not evaluated in [18]). We simplified and generalized the "dictionary" by keeping only a set of carefully curated *negative words*. We call them "debunking words" e.g., *hoax, rumor* or *not true*. Our intuition is, that the attitude of doubting or denying events is in essence sufficient to distinguish rumors from news. What is more, this generalization augments the size of the

---

[2] details are listed in the Appendix.

crowd (covers more 'voting' tweets), which is crucial, and thus contributes to the quality of the crowd wisdom. In our experiments, "debunking words" is an high-impact feature, but it needs substantial time to "warm up"; that is explainable as the crowd is typically sparse at early stage.

CreditScore: The sets of single-tweet models' predicted probabilities are combined using an *ensemble averaging*-like technique. In specific, our pre-trained $CNN + LSTM$ model predicts the credibility of each tweet tw_{ij} of event E_i. The *softmax* activation function outputs probabilities from 0 (rumor-related) to 1 (news). Based on this, we calculate the average prediction probabilities of all tweets $tw_{ij} \in E_i$ in a time interval t_{ij}. In theory there are different sophisticated ensembling approaches for averaging on both training and test samples; but in a real-time system, it is often convenient (while effectiveness is only affected marginally) to cut corners. In this work, we use a sole training model to average over the predictions. We call the outcome CreditScore.

5   Experimental Evaluation

5.1   Data Collection

To construct the training dataset, we collected rumor stories from online rumor tracking websites such as snopes.com and urbanlegends.about.com. In more detail, we crawled 4300 stories from these websites. From the story descriptions we manually constructed queries to retrieve the relevant tweets for 270 rumors with high impact. Our approach to query construction mainly follows [11]. For the news event instances (non-rumor examples), we make use of the manually constructed corpus from Mcminn et al. [21], which covers 500 real-world events. In [21], tweets are retrieved via Twitter firehose API from 10th of October 2012 to 7th of November 2012. The involved events are manually verified and relate to tweets with relevance judgments, which results in a high quality corpus. From the 500 events, we select top 230 events with the highest tweet volumes (as a criteria for event impact). Furthermore, we have added 40 other news events, which happened around the time periods of our rumors. This results in a dataset of 270 rumors and 270 events. The dataset details are shown in Table 1. To serve our learning task. we then constructs two distinct datasets for (1) single tweet credibility and (2) rumor classification.

Table 1. Tweet Volume of News and Rumors

Type	Min volume	Max volume	Total	Average
News	98	17414	345235	1327.82
Rumors	44	26010	182563	702.06

Training data for single tweet classification. Here we follow our assumption that an event might include sub-events for which relevant tweets are rumorous. To deal with this complexity, we train our single-tweet learning model only with manually selected *breaking and subless*[3] events from the above dataset. In the end, we used 90 rumors and 90 news associated with 72452 tweets, in total. This results in a highly-reliable large-scale ground-truth of tweets labelled as *news*-related and *rumor*-related, respectively. Note that the labeling of a tweet is inherited from the event label, thus can be considered as an semi-automatic process.

5.2   Single Tweet Classification Experiments

For the evaluation, we developed two kinds of classification models: traditional classifier with handcrafted features and neural networks without tweet embeddings. For the former, we used 27 distinct surface-level features extracted from single tweets (analogously to the Twitter-based features presented in Sect. 4.2). For the latter, we select the baselines from NN-based variations, inspired by state-of-the-art short-text classification models, i.e., Basic tanh-RNN, 1-layer GRU-RNN, 1-layer LSTM, 2-layer GRU-RNN, FastText [14] and CNN+LSTM [33] model. The hybrid model CNN+LSTM is adapted in our work for tweet classification.

Single Tweet Model Settings. For the evaluation, we shuffle the 180 selected events and split them into 10 subsets which are used for 10-fold cross-validation (we make sure to include near-balanced folds in our shuffle). We implement the 3 non-neural network models with Scikit-learn[4]. Furthermore, neural networks-based models are implemented with TensorFlow[5] and Keras[6]. The first hidden layer is an embedding layer, which is set up for all tested models with the embedding size of 50. The output of the embedding layer are low-dimensional vectors representing the words. To avoid overfitting, we use the 10-fold cross validation and dropout for regularization with dropout rate of 0.25.

Single Tweet Classification Results. The experimental results of are shown in Table 2. The best performance is achieved by the CNN+LSTM model with a good accuracy of 81.19%. The non-neural network model with the highest accuracy is RF. However, it reaches only 64.87% accuracy and the other two non-neural models are even worse. So the classifiers with hand-crafted features are less adequate to accurately distinguish between rumors and news.

Discussion of Feature Importance For analyzing the employed feature, we rank them by importances using RF (see Table 3). The best feature is related to sentiment polarity scores. There is a big bias between the sentiment associated to rumors and the sentiment associated to real events in relevant tweets.

---

[3] the terminology *subless* indicates an event with no sub-events for short.
[4] scikit-learn.org/.
[5] https://www.tensorflow.org/.
[6] https://keras.io/.

Table 2. Single Tweet classification performance

Model	Accuracy
CNN+LSTM	**0.8119**
2-layer GRU	0.7891
1-layer GRU	0.7644
1-layer LSTM	0.7493
Basic RNN with tanh	0.7291
FastText	0.6602
Random Forest	**0.6487**
SVM	0.5802
Decision Trees	0.5774

Table 3. Top features importance

Feature	Importance
PolarityScores	0.146
Capital	0.096
LengthOfTweet	0.092
UserTweets	0.087
UserFriends	0.080
UserReputationScore	0.080
UserFollowers	0.079
NumOfChar	0.076
Stock	0.049
NumNegativeWords	0.030
Exclamation	0.023

In specific, the average polarity score of news event is -0.066 and the average of rumors is -0.1393, showing that rumor-related messages tend to contain more negative sentiments. Furthermore, we would expect that verified users are less involved in the rumor spreading. However, the feature appears near-bottom in the ranked list, indicating that it is not as reliable as expected. Also interestingly, the feature "IsRetweet" is also not as good a feature as expected, which means the probability of people retweeting rumors or true news are similar (both appear near-bottom in the ranked feature list).

It has to be noted here that even though we obtain reasonable results on the classification task in general, the prediction performance varies considerably along the time dimension. This is understandable, since tweets become more distinguishable, only when the user gains more knowledge about the event.

5.3 Rumor Datasets and Model Settings

We use the same dataset described in Sect. 5.1. In total –after cutting off 180 events for pre-training single tweet model – our dataset contains 360 events and 180 of them are labeled as rumors. Those rumors and news fall comparatively evenly in 8 different categories, namely *Politics, Science, Attacks, Disaster, Art, Business, Health* and *Other*. Note, that the events in our training data are not necessarily subless, because it is natural for high-impact events (e.g., *Missing MH370* or *Munich shooting*) to contain sub-events. Actually, we empirically found that roughly 20% of our events (mostly news) contain sub-events. As a rumor is often of a long circulating story [10], this results in a rather long time span. In this work, we develop an event identification strategy that focuses on the first 48 h after the rumor is peaked. We also extract 11,038 domains, which are contained in tweets in this 48 h time range.

Rumor Detection Model Settings. For the time series classification model, we only report the best performing classifiers, SVM and Random Forest, here. The parameters of SVM with RBF kernel are tuned via grid search to $C = 3.0$, $\gamma = 0.2$. For Random Forest, the number of trees is tuned to be 350. All models are trained using 10-fold cross validation.

5.4 Rumor Classification Results

We tested all models by using 10-fold cross validation with the same shuffled sequence. The results of these experiments are shown in Table 4. Our proposed model (*Ours*) is the time series model learned with Random Forest including all ensemble features; $TS - SVM$ is the baseline from [20], and $TS - SVM_{all}$ is the $TS - SVM$ approach improved by using our feature set. In the lower part of the table, RNN_{el} is the RNN model at event-level [19]. As shown in the Table 4 and as targeted by our early detection approach, our model has the best performance in all case over the first 24 h, remarkably outperforming the baselines in the first 12 h of spreading. The performance of RNN_{el} is relatively low, as it is based on aggregated *contents*. This is expected as the news (non-rumor) dataset used in [19] are crawled also from snopes.com, in which events are often of small granularity (aka. subless). As expected, exploiting contents solely at event-level is problematic for high-impact, evolving events on social media. We leave a deeper investigation on the sub-event issue to future work.

Table 4. Performance of different models over time (bold for best accuracy, underlined for second-to-best). TS indicates time-series structure; we separate the TS models (upper) with the static ones (lower).

Model	Accuracy in hours								
	1	6	12	18	24	30	36	42	48
Ours	**0.82**	**0.84**	**0.84**	<u>0.84</u>	**0.87**	<u>0.87</u>	**0.88**	<u>0.89</u>	**0.91**
$TS - SVM_{all}$	<u>0.76</u>	0.79	<u>0.83</u>	0.83	<u>0.87</u>	**0.88**	0.86	0.89	<u>0.90</u>
$TS - SVM_{Credit}$	0.73	<u>0.80</u>	0.83	**0.85**	0.85	0.86	<u>0.88</u>	**0.90**	0.90
$TS - SVM$ [20]	0.69	0.76	0.81	0.81	0.84	0.86	0.87	0.88	0.88
RNN_{el} [19]	0.68	0.77	0.81	0.81	0.84	0.83	0.81	0.85	0.86
$SVM_{static} + Epi$ [13]	0.60	0.69	0.71	0.72	0.75	0.78	0.75	0.78	0.81
$SVM_{static} + SpikeM$ [17]	0.58	0.68	0.72	0.73	0.77	0.78	0.78	0.79	0.77
SVM_{static} [31]	0.62	0.70	0.70	0.72	0.75	0.80	0.79	0.78	0.77

CreditScore and CrowdWisdom. As shown in Table 5, *CreditScore* is the best feature in overall. In Fig. 4 we show the result of models learned with the full feature set with and without *CreditScore*. Overall, adding *CreditScore* improves the performance, especially for the first 8–10 h. The performance of *all-but-CreditScore* jiggles a bit after 16–20 h, but it is not significant. *CrowdWisdom*

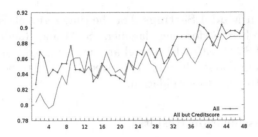

Fig. 4. Accuracy: All features with and without CreditScore.

Table 5. Importance ranking of CreditScore, CrowdWisdom and PolarityScores over time; 0 indicates the best rank.

Features	Ranks									
Hours	1	6	12	18	24	30	36	42	48	AVG
CreditScore	1	0	0	0	0	0	0	0	0	0.08
CrowdWisdom	34	38	21	14	8	5	5	2	2	13.18
PolarityScores	12	15	23	28	33	33	34	31	32	28

is also a good feature which can get 75.8% accuracy as a single feature. But its performance is poor (less than 70%) in the first 32 h getting better over time (see Table 5). Table 5 also shows the performance of *sentiment* feature (*PolarityScores*), which is generally low. This demonstrates the effectiveness of our *curated* approach over the *sentiments*, yet the crowd needs time to unify their views toward the event while absorbing different kinds of information.

Case Study: Munich Shooting. We showcase here a study of the Munich shooting. We first show the event timeline at an early stage. Next we discuss some examples of misclassifications by our "weak" classifier and show some analysis on the strength of some highlighted features. The rough event timeline looks as follows.

- At 17:52 CEST, a shooter opened fire in the vicinity of the Olympia shopping mall in Munich. 10 people, including the shooter, were killed and 36 others were injured.
- At 18:22 CEST, the first tweet was posted. There might be some certain delay, as we retrieve only tweets in English and the very first tweets were probably in German. The tweet is *"Sadly, i think there's something terrible happening in #Munich #Munchen. Another Active Shooter in a mall. #SMH"*.
- At 18:25 CEST, the second tweet was posted: *"Terrorist attack in Munich????"*.
- At 18:27 CEST, traditional media (BBC) posted their first tweet. *"'Shots fired' in Munich shopping centre* - http://www.bbc.co.uk/news/world-europe-36870800a02026 *@TraceyRemix gun crime in Germany just doubled"*.
- At 18:31 CEST, the first misclassified tweet is posted. It was a tweet with shock sentiment and swear words: *"there's now a shooter in a Munich shopping centre.. What the f*** is going on in the world. Gone mad"*. It is classified as *rumor-related*.

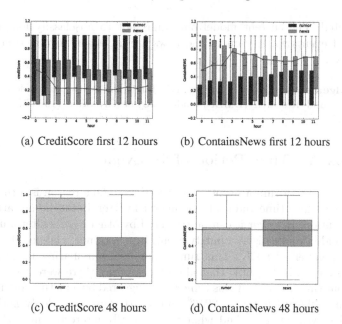

(a) CreditScore first 12 hours   (b) ContainsNews first 12 hours

(c) CreditScore 48 hours   (d) ContainsNews 48 hours

Fig. 5. Creditscore and ContainsNews for *Munich shooting* in red lines, compared with the corresponding average scores for *rumor* and *news*. (Color figure online)

We observe that at certain points in time, the volume of rumor-related tweets (for sub-events) in the event stream surges. This can lead to *false positives* for techniques that model events as the aggregation of all tweet contents; that is undesired at critical moments. We trade-off this by debunking at single tweet level and let each tweet vote for the credibility of its event. We show the *CreditScore* measured over time in Fig. 5(a). It can be seen that although the credibility of some tweets are low (rumor-related), averaging still makes the *CreditScore* of Munich shooting higher than the average of news events (hence, close to a *news*). In addition, we show the feature analysis for ContainNews (percentage of URLs containing news websites) for the event *Munich shooting* in Fig. 5(b). We can see the curve of *Munich shooting* event is also close to the curve of average news, indicating the event is more news-related.

6 Conclusion

In this work, we propose an effective cascaded rumor detection approach using deep neural networks at tweet level in the first stage and wisdom of the "machines", together with a variety of other features in the second stage, in order to enhance rumor detection performance in the early phase of an event. The proposed approach outperforms state of the art methods for early rumor detection. There is, however, still considerable room to improve the effectiveness of the rumor detection method. The support for events with rumor sub-events is still limited. The current model only aims not to misclassify long-running, multi-aspect events where rumors and news are mixed and evolve over time as false positive.

Acknowledgements. This work was partially funded by the German Federal Ministry of Education and Research (BMBF) under project GlycoRec (16SV7172) and K3 (13N13548).

Appendix A   Time Period of an Event

The time period of a rumor event is hard to define. One reason is a rumor may be created for a long time and kept existing on Twitter, but it did not attract the crowd's attention. However it can be triggered by other events after a uncertain time and suddenly spreads as a bursty event. E.g., a rumor[7] claimed that Robert Byrd was member of KKK. This rumor has been circulating in Twitter for a while. As shown in Fig. 6(a) that almost every day there were several tweets talking about this rumor. But this rumor was triggered by a picture about Robert Byrd kissing Hillary Clinton in 2016[8] and Twitter users suddenly noticed this rumor and it was bursted. And what we are really interested in is the tweets which are posted in hours around the bursty peak. We defined the hour with the most tweets' volume as t_{max} and we want to detect the rumor event as soon as possible before its burst, so we define the time of the first tweet before t_{max} within 48 h as the beginning of this rumor event, marked as t_0. And the end time of the event is defined as $t_{end} = t_0 + 48$. We show the tweet volumes in Fig. 6 of the above rumor example.

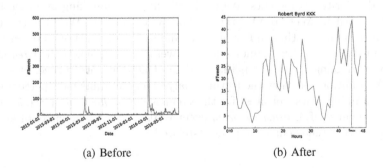

(a) Before   (b) After

Fig. 6. tweet volume of the rumor event of Robert Byrd at full scale and after selected time period

---

[7] http://www.snopes.com/robert-byrd-kkk-photo/.
[8] http://www.snopes.com/clinton-byrd-photo-klan/.

Appendix B   Full FeaturesTime Period of an Event

See Table 6.

Table 6. Features of Time Series Rumor Detection Model

Category	Feature	Description
Twitter features	Hashtag	% tweets contain #hashtag [6,11,18,18,24]
	Mention	% tweets mention others @user [6,11,18,18,24]
	NumUrls	# URLs in the tweet [6,11,18,24,31]
	Retweets	Average # retweets [18]
	IsRetweet	% tweets are retweeted from others [6,11]
	ContainNEWS	% tweets contain URL and its domain's catalogue is News [18]
	WotScore	Average WOT score of domain in URL [11]
	URLRank5000	% tweets contain URL whose domain's rank less than 5000 [6]
	ContainNewsURL	% tweets contain URL whose domain is News Website
Text features	LengthofTweet	Average tweet lengths [6,11]
	NumOfChar	Average # tweet characters [6,11]
	Capital	Average fraction of characters in Uppercase [6]
	Smile	% tweets contain $:->,:-),;->,;-)$ [6,11]
	Sad	% tweets contain $:-<,:-(,;->,;-($ [6,11]
	NumPositiveWords	Average # positive words [6,11,18,31]
	NumNegativeWords	Average # negative words [6,11,18,31]
	PolarityScores	Average polarity scores of the Tweets [6,18,31]
	Via	% of tweets contain via [11]
	Stock	% of tweets contain $ [6,11]
	Question	% of tweets contain ? [6,18]
	Exclamation	% of tweets contain ! [6,18]
	QuestionExclamation	% of tweets contain multi Question or Exclamation mark [6,18]
	I	% of tweets contain first pronoun like I, my, mine, we, our [6,11,18]
	You	% of tweets contain second pronoun like U, you, your, yours [6]
	He/She	% of tweets contain third pronoun like he, she, they, his, etc. [6]

Table 6. (*Continued*)

Category	Feature	Description
User features	UserNumFollowers	Average number of followers [6,11,18]
	UserNumFriends	Average number of friends [6,11,18]
	UserNumTweets	Average number of users posted tweets [6,11,18,31]
	UserNumPhotos	Average number of users posted photos [31]
	UserIsInLargeCity	% of users living in large city [18,31]
	UserJoinDate	Average days since users joining Twitter [6,18,31]
	UserDescription	% of user having description [6,18,31]
	UserVerified	% of user being a verified user [18,31]
	UserReputationScore	Average ratio of #Friends over (#Followers + #Friends) [18]
Epidemiological features	β_{SIS}	Parameter β of Model SIS [13]
	α_{SIS}	Parameter α of Model SIS [13]
	β_{SEIZ}	Parameter β of Model SEIZ [13]
	b_{SEIZ}	Parameter b of Model SEIZ [13]
	l_{SEIZ}	Parameter l of Model SEIZ [13]
	p_{SEIZ}	Parameter p of Model SEIZ [13]
	ε_{SEIZ}	Parameter ε of Model SEIZ [13]
	ρ_{SEIZ}	Parameter ρ of Model SEIZ [13]
	R_{SI}	Parameter R_{SI} of Model SEIZ [13]
SpikeM model features	P_s	Parameter P_s of Model Spike [17]
	P_a	Parameter P_a of Model SpikeM [17]
	P_p	Parameter P_p of Model SpikeM [17]
	Q_s	Parameter Q_s of Model SpikeM [17]
	Q_a	Parameter Q_a of Model SpikeM [17]
	Q_p	Parameter Q_p of Model SpikeM [17]
Crowd wisdom	CrowdWisdom	% of tweets containing "Debunking Words" [18,32]
CreditScore	CreditScore	Average CreditScore

References

1. Ahmed, F., Abulaish, M.: An MCL-based approach for spam profile detection in online social networks. In: Proceedings of TrustCom, pp. 602–608. IEEE (2012)
2. Allport, G.W., Postman, L.: The Psychology of Rumor (1947)
3. Bao, Y., Yi, C., Xue, Y., Dong, Y.: A new rumor propagation model and control strategy on social networks. In: Proceedings of ICWSM, pp. 1472–1473. ACM (2013)
4. Barbosa, L., Feng, J.: Robust sentiment detection on Twitter from biased and noisy data. In: Proceedings of ACL, pp. 36–44 (2010)
5. Borge-Holthoefer, J., Moreno, Y.: Absence of influential spreaders in rumor dynamics. Phys. Rev. E **85**(2), 026116 (2012)
6. Castillo, C., Mendoza, M., Poblete, B.: Information credibility on Twitter. In: Proceedings of WWW, pp. 675–684. ACM (2011)
7. Chen, T., Wu, L., Li, X., Zhang, J., Yin, H., Wang, Y.: Call attention to rumors: deep attention based recurrent neural networks for early rumor detection. arXiv preprint arXiv:1704.05973 (2017)
8. Conti, M., Lain, D., Lazzeretti, R., Lovisotto, G., Quattrociocchi, W.: It's always April fools' day! on the difficulty of social network misinformation classification via propagation features. CoRR, abs/1701.04221 (2017)
9. Dhingra, B., Zhou, Z., Fitzpatrick, D., Muehl, M., Cohen, W.W.: Tweet2Vec: character-based distributed representations for social media. arXiv preprint arXiv:1605.03481 (2016)
10. Friggeri, A., Adamic, L.A., Eckles, D., Cheng, J.: Rumor cascades (2014)
11. Gupta, A., Kumaraguru, P., Castillo, C., Meier, P.: TweetCred: real-time credibility assessment of content on Twitter. In: Aiello, L.M., McFarland, D. (eds.) SocInfo 2014. LNCS, vol. 8851, pp. 228–243. Springer, Cham (2014). doi:10.1007/978-3-319-13734-6_16
12. Hochreiter, S., Schmidhuber, J.: Long short-term memory. Neural Comput. **9**(8), 1735–1780 (1997)
13. Jin, F., Dougherty, E., Saraf, P., Cao, Y., Ramakrishnan, N.: Epidemiological modeling of news and rumors on Twitter. In: Proceedings of SNA-KDD (2013)
14. Joulin, A., Grave, E., Bojanowski, P., Mikolov, T.: Bag of tricks for efficient text classification. arXiv preprint arXiv:1607.01759 (2016)
15. Kim, Y.: Convolutional neural networks for sentence classification. arXiv preprint arXiv:1408.5882 (2014)
16. Kimmey, D.: Twitter event detection (2015)
17. Kwon, S., Cha, M., Jung, K., Chen, W., Wang, Y.: Prominent features of rumor propagation in online social media. In: Proceedings of ICDM (2013)
18. Liu, X., Nourbakhsh, A., Li, Q., Fang, R., Shah, S.: Real-time rumor debunking on Twitter. In: Proceedings of CIKM, pp. 1867–1870. ACM (2015)
19. Ma, J., Gao, W., Mitra, P., Kwon, S., Jansen, B.J., Wong, K.-F., Cha, M.: Detecting rumors from microblogs with recurrent neural networks
20. Ma, J., Gao, W., Wei, Z., Lu, Y., Wong, K.-F.: Detect rumors using time series of social context information on microblogging websites. In: Proceedings of CIKM (2015)
21. McMinn, A.J., Moshfeghi, Y., Jose, J.M.: Building a large-scale corpus for evaluating event detection on Twitter. In: Proceedings of CIKM (2013)

22. Meladianos, P., Nikolentzos, G., Rousseau, F., Stavrakas, Y., Vazirgiannis, M.: Degeneracy-based real-time sub-event detection in Twitter stream. In: Proceedings of ICWSM (2015)
23. Mendoza, M., Poblete, B., Castillo, C.: Twitter under crisis: can we trust what we RT? In: Proceedings of the First Workshop on Social Media Analytics, pp. 71–79. ACM (2010)
24. Qazvinian, V., Rosengren, E., Radev, D.R., Mei, Q.: Rumor has it: identifying misinformation in microblogs. In: Proceedings of EMNLP (2011)
25. Seo, E., Mohapatra, P., Abdelzaher, T.: Identifying rumors and their sources in social networks. In: SPIE (2012)
26. Sunstein, C.R.: On Rumors: How Falsehoods Spread, Why we Believe Them, and What can be Done. Princeton University Press, Princeton (2014)
27. Tripathy, R.M., Bagchi, A., Mehta, S.: A study of rumor control strategies on social networks. In: Proceedings of CIKM, pp. 1817–1820. ACM (2010)
28. Vosoughi, S., Vijayaraghavan, P., Roy, D.: Tweet2Vec: learning tweet embeddings using character-level CNN-LSTM encoder-decoder. In: Proceedings of the 39th International ACM SIGIR Conference on Research and Development in Information Retrieval, pp. 1041–1044. ACM (2016)
29. Wang, A.H.: Don't follow me: spam detection in Twitter. In: Proceedings of SECRYPT, pp. 1–10. IEEE (2010)
30. Wu, K., Yang, S., Zhu, K.Q.: False rumors detection on Sina Weibo by propagation structures. In: Proceedings of ICDE, pp. 651–662. IEEE (2015)
31. Yang, F., Liu, Y., Yu, X., Yang, M.: Automatic detection of rumor on Sina Weibo. In: Proceedings of MDS. ACM (2012)
32. Zhao, Z., Resnick, P., Mei, Q.: Enquiring minds: early detection of rumors in social media from enquiry posts. In: Proceedings of WWW (2015)
33. Zhou, C., Sun, C., Liu, Z., Lau, F.: A C-LSTM neural network for text classification. arXiv preprint arXiv:1511.08630 (2015)

Convergence of Media Attention
Across 129 Countries

Jisun An[✉], Hassan Aldarbesti, and Haewoon Kwak

Qatar Computing Research Institute, Hamad Bin Khalifa University, Doha, Qatar
{jisun.an,haewoon}@acm.org, aldarbesti@outlook.com

Abstract. The objective of this study is to assess the longitudinal
trends of media similarity and dissimilarity on the international scale.
As news value has well-established political, cultural, and economic consequences, the degree to which media coverage and content is converging
across countries has implications for international relations. To study
this convergence, we use the daily data of the 100 topics that were over-
reported in each country, compared to other countries, from March 7
to October 9, 2016. The results of this analysis indicate that two complementary patterns–globalization and domestication–explain the media
attention across the countries. We conclude that this attention can
be driven not only by geographical closeness but also by more complex dimensions, such as historical relationships. Also, although a group
of countries often have common media attention, their similarity level
depends on time and topic.

Keywords: Media convergence · Media attention · Globalization ·
Domestication · Unfiltered News · Tensor factorization

1 Introduction

Media plays a significant role in determining what events are important and providing information to audiences on those events [11]. In the era of technological
advancement and globalization, there is a growing interest in the impact of these
factors on the media–on media globalization and convergence [8]. While early
studies of these concepts focused on the systematic flow of media from international sources to advance our understanding of the factors that influence domestic coverage of foreign events [9], globalization and technology have increased the
flow of news between countries, as well as our access to that information. There
is a long tradition in media studies looking at the systemic determinants of news
content and coverage of international news topics and events [17], but there is a
lack of empirical evidence on how much the manner in which the media presents
events across countries is converging.

As "transnational information flow is a reflection and a constituent of the
larger global system" [16], understanding the similarity of media values and
content across countries has significant political, economic, and cultural implications. To this effect, this study evaluates the over and under-emphasis of news

© Springer International Publishing AG 2017
G.L. Ciampaglia et al. (Eds.): SocInfo 2017, Part II, LNCS 10540, pp. 159–168, 2017.
DOI: 10.1007/978-3-319-67256-4_14

topics over time and determines how this compares by country in order to assess if there is, in fact, a pattern of convergence at the international scale. We assess the homogenization of media attention over time using Unfiltered News and 100 media topics and hypothesize that, through globalization forces, media content is, in fact, converging.

2   Related Work

The gap in research that this study fills has been identified through a review of the extant literature on media content, convergence, and scale. The dominant theme is the literature on media attention and similarity on an international level, which is the comparison of multiple countries to assess how a selected event or topic has been covered (c.f., [16]). Media convergence occurs when sources become more similar. Regarding scale, it is important to understand if this convergence is happening at the domestic level, at the international level, or both. The structures of media content and attention are assessed through this review of the extant literature. News convergence is defined as an increase in the similarity of content over time and scale (i.e., domestic and international).

With increased attention to both media content and globalization, there is growing concern in the academic community that media content is converging. One side of the debate hypothesizes that agency copy within the media [4] results in cultural imperialism by which US news, culture, and values are shared and adopted international through media [7]. However, there is another side of literature that presents empirical evidence challenges this claim. In fact, Nielsen (2013) presents enduring differences and divergences across media. Flew and Waisbord (2015) makes a similar argument for national media politics [8]. News coverage and convergence of this coverage is of interest for their meaning as "news values." These are values that give meaning to modern society. As there are millions of events that occur everyday in the world, news values dictate those stories that are most salient [10]. The question remains as to whether these news values are converging.

While there are arguments both for and against news convergence, no studies to date have measured the direct changes in the homogenization of news coverage over time. Although conducting a quantitative analysis of how media covered the Israeli-Palestinian conflict over a decade [3], the research presented herein covers a wide range of topics. We note that Baden and Tenenboim-Weinblatt (2016) conclude that cultural and language affinity is the underlying factor of media content selection patterns, but that these findings only relate to the conflict of study and, as so, cannot be generalized to speak to media convergence more broadly [3]. Our study, however, presents a more generalizable assessment of news convergence through looking at the similarity of media content more broadly over time.

Most of the studies have conducted with limitations of studying a handful number of countries, news articles, or topics. Privileged in the digital era and the emergence of advanced machine learning techniques, we overcome all these limitations and provide a data-driven analysis of media attention of 196 countries during 211 days.

3   Data Collection

Unfiltered News offers two kinds of indexed data for each country: topics mentioned more than other topics (In the rest of the paper, we simply say "topics mentioned more") and topics mentioned less than other countries do (we say "topics mentioned less"). The former represents what media pay attention, and the latter reflects what media do not pay attention. In this work, we focus only on the topics mentioned more that encode media attention. A deeper analysis of media attention (topics mentioned more) and media disregard (topics mentioned less) together is available in [12]. We collect the data from 7 March to 9 October 2016.

3.1   Data Description and Notation

Unfiltered News ideally provides the 100 topics mentioned more for each country; however, it sometimes has missing data. For a fair comparison across the countries, we filter out such incomplete data.

We denote by $C = \{c_1, c_2, ..., c_n\}$ a set of n countries and $D = \{d_1, d_2, ..., d_m\}$ a set of m days available in our data. We denote by $M_{d_j}^{c_i}(k)$ a set of k topics mentioned more in the country c_i on the day d_j. For example, $M_{20160101}^{Korea}(10)$ is a set of the top 10 most frequently mentioned topics in Korea on 1 January 2016. We then refine the data in the following ways:

1. We set the threshold k ($0 < k \leq 100$).
2. For each country $c_i \in C$, we check whether at least k topics mentioned more are available on $\forall d_i \in D$. If so, we add c_i to a set C^k.
3. Let us say $C^k = \{c_1^k, c_2^k, ..., c_l^k\}$.
4. Then, the final datasets of the topics mentioned more with k, $M(k)$, is:
$$M(k) = \{(M_{d_1}^{c_1^k}(k), M_{d_2}^{c_1^k}(k), ..., M_{d_m}^{c_1^k}(k)), \ (M_{d_1}^{c_2^k}(k), \ M_{d_2}^{c_2^k}(k), \ ..., \ M_{d_m}^{c_2^k}(k)), \ ...,$$
$$(M_{d_1}^{c_l^k}(k), \ M_{d_2}^{c_l^k}(k), \ ..., \ M_{d_m}^{c_l^k}(k))\}.$$

When we do not have any constraint ($k = 0$), the number of countries in C^0 is 196. With the weakest condition ($k = 10$), $|C^{10}|$ quickly decreases to 129. The number of countries in C^k monotonically decreases with growing k and reaches at 88 when $k = 90$. We conducted all our experiments with different k and found that the overall trend stays the same with some variations in numbers. Thus, in this work, we report the result with specific k (usually 10) and omit other results due to lack of space.

4   Similarity and Dissimilarity of Media Attention Across the Countries

4.1   Globalization and Domestication of Media

As we mentioned in the Related work section, there are several reasons why the media attention of different countries is expected to converge: (1) News published on the Web can have a worldwide audience, overcoming geographical limitations; thus, the media chooses news topics that appeal to as many people as possible; and (2) The role of a global news agency becomes more and more important. For financial reasons, it is impossible to have offices all over the world. Instead, the media relies on global news agencies, such as Reuters or AP, for foreign news. The fact that news coverage of foreign disasters is heavily dependent on whether it is reported by global news agencies [11] shows this trend.

By comparing the topics mentioned more often in each of the countries, we measure the similarities in media attention among the countries. We begin with how many countries mention the same topic every day.

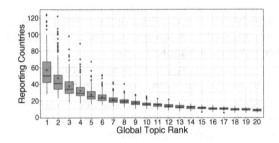

Fig. 1. How many countries report the globally popular topics

For each of 211 days, we count how many countries report each of the top global topics on the same day. Figure 1 shows how many countries mentioned the global top topics on a certain day, where $k = 10$. The variance becomes small, and the number of countries reporting the global topic decreases. The topics ranked first and second received media attention from 57 and 47 countries (out of 129 countries) as a median, respectively. The fact that tens of the countries share the top global topics every day shows a high level of globalization in the world.

As we manually look into which topic is the most widely mentioned in the world every day, we find some common topical characteristics: sports (e.g., Rio Olympics or UEFA Champions League), terror in the Western world (e.g., France, Germany, or Belgium), big natural disasters (e.g., earthquakes in Italy), airplane crash (e.g., EgyptAir crash), and big political events (e.g., coup in Turkey).

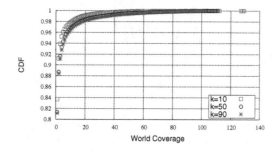

Fig. 2. Cumulative distribution of the number of countries that mention the same topic

In Fig. 2, by contrast, the rest of the media attention is highly unique. For clarity, we define the attention diversity as the union of the topics more mentioned and denoted it by $U(k) = \bigcup\limits_{c_j}^{C^k} \bigcup\limits_{d_i}^{D} M_{d_i}^{c_j}(k)$ as in [1]. Then, we find that 83.7% of all the topics in $U(10)$ appears in a single country. When testing with different ks, the proportion of the topics that get attention from a single country stays high (81.1% in $U(90)$). This uniqueness of media attention in each country demonstrates that media continues shaping news for domestic readers [3].

In summary, two complementary patterns–globalization and domestication–explain the media attention across the countries.

4.2 Countries Sharing Media Attention in a Long-Term

We begin with vectorizing media attention. We create a $|U(k)|$-d vector space, $\mathbf{V}(k)$, where each dimension is mapping into each topic $t \in \{t_1, t_2, ..., t_{|U(k)|}\}$. In $\mathbf{V}(k)$, we can locate a country c_i as a vector whose n-th element is the number of days ($|\forall d_j|$) that the topic $t_n \in M_{d_j}^{c_i}(k)$. We build a distance matrix among country vectors and apply a hierarchical clustering method using Ward's method [14].

Figure 3 is the dendrogram to show the attention similarity among countries. In the figure, we clearly see the regional groups, which are consistent with our intuition: the Eastern Europe (at 12 o'clock), the Western and Northern Europe (at 2 o'clock), the MENA region (at 4 o'clock), Latin America (at 6 o'clock), and Asia and North America (at 9 o'clock). Seeing the leaf level, which is the direct connection between two countries, we find that most of them are neighboring countries, such as Cyprus and Greece, Belgium and France, Austria and Germany, Qatar and Kuwait, Ireland and the United Kingdom, the United States and Canada, and so on.

Some historical colonial ties are also closely located in the dendrogram. Even though Spain and Mexico are far apart geographically, they directly connect to each other on the tree. Singapore and Malaysia connect to the United Kingdom at the lower level rather than other Asian countries. Similarly, Philippines connects to the tree that contains the United States. These colonial ties do not only

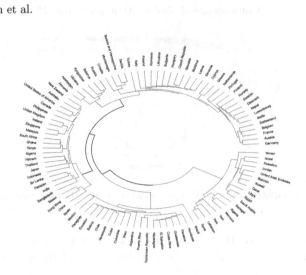

Fig. 3. [Zoomable in PDF] Attention similarity between countries regarding the topics more mentioned

remain in past relationships but have also been developed as strong economic and political relationships. Therefore, it is understandable that the news media in these countries share similar attention.

We can also see a block-level association in the dendrogram. There are several regional clusters in Europe (Northern, Eastern, Southern, and Western), and they are more similar to each other than other regions. Europe connects to North America, Asia, Latin America, and the MENA region. In other words, the MENA region is the most different from the rest of the world regarding the topics more mentioned by local media.

4.3   Country Blocks Having Common Media Attention

We found that there are a few topics that attract media attention from multiple countries. Are there any patterns in these "multiple" countries? To answer this question, we must systematically identify country blocks that have common media attention.

Instead of using an aggregated data, we build a 3-way tensor, $T(k) \in \mathbb{R}^{N \times N \times S}$, where N is the number of countries in C^k, and S is the number of days in D, to represent the attention similarity among countries for each day; τ_{ijk} is the attention similarity between country c_i and c_j on day d_k, defined as cosine similarity between $M_{d_k}^{c_i}(k)$ and $M_{d_k}^{c_j}(k)$. This allows us to incorporate the timing of the media attention in measuring the similarity between countries.

By representing a tensor as a product of lower-dimensional factors, we can uncover its latent structure. Out of several techniques, we use PARAFAC decomposition for its simplicity and comparable performance [5]. A detailed discussion of the advantages and disadvantages of PARAFAC, versus its alternatives, such as Tucker3 and two-way PCA, is available in [5]. We also apply a constraint, with the non-negativity of elements, in the resulting matrices for ease of interpretation. We use N-way Toolbox 3.31 for MATLAB [2] for the actual computation.

The PARAFAC decomposition of a 3-way tensor, $\mathcal{T} \in \mathbb{R}^{N \times N \times S}$, results in three matrices, $\mathbf{A}$, $\mathbf{B}$, and $\mathbf{C}$, whose dimensions are $N \times R$, $N \times R$, and $S \times R$, respectively, and $R \ll min(rank(\mathcal{T})) = min(N, N, S)$ to benefit from the decomposition. Then, an element of $\mathcal{T}$ can be written as following:

$$\tau_{ijk} = \sum_{r=1}^{R} a_{ir} b_{jr} c_{kr} + \epsilon_{ijk} \qquad (1)$$

In Eq. (1), R is the number of components that encode the level of detail. A higher R gets a more detailed latent structure but has the risk of over-fitting, and a lower R overlooks the latent structure but is resilient to noise. We use the core consistency that is proposed in [6], to systematically determine the best R. We run the PARAFAC model from 2 to 10 and compute the core consistency. By the scree plot and the rule of thumb, that core consistency higher than 0.5 is generally acceptable, we choose $R = 5$ (core consistency $= 0.560$). In other words, by the PARAFAC decomposition of $\mathcal{T}$, we get the five components from $\mathbf{A}$ and $\mathbf{B}$. As the attention similarity matrix among countries is symmetric, $\mathbf{A}$ is the same as $\mathbf{B}$.

Table 1. Top 10 countries (with the highest loading factors) in each component

CP	Countries
1	France, Belgium, Switzerland, Luxembourg, Austria, Germany, Slovakia, Czech Republic, Slovenia, Denmark
2	Saudi Arabia, Egypt, Kuwait, United Arab Emirates, Palestine, Yemen, Jordan, Qatar, Bahrain, Libya
3	Russia, Belarus, Ukraine, Kyrgyzstan, Azerbaijan, Moldova, Latvia, Bulgaria, Lebanon, Iran
4	Australia, United States of America, Singapore, South Africa, United Kingdom, Malaysia, New Zealand, Pakistan, China, Thailand
5	Venezuela, Colombia, Chile, Ecuador, Peru, Panama, Bolivia, Nicaragua, Costa Rica, Argentina

The resulting components are presented in Table 1. Interestingly, with the exception of one component (CP4), geographically close countries are well grouped together, such as the Western European countries (CP1), the Middle East and North African (MENA) countries (CP2), the Eastern European countries (CP3), and the Latin American countries (CP5). Since geographical proximity is known to be associated with culture, language, and ethnicity affinity, and also lead to strong economic and political relations, it is reasonable that countries in the same regional block share media attention. The CP4, which has both neighboring countries and distant countries together, is an interesting mixture of geographical proximity (Asian countries) and colonial ties with the United Kingdom (the former British Empire). The result shows that the similar media attention of countries can be driven not only by geographical closeness but also by more complex dimensions, such as historical relationships.

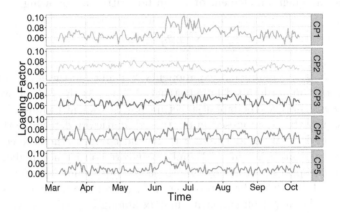

Fig. 4. Activate patterns of identified components

The remaining matrix, **C**, encodes the activate patterns of the identified components (i.e., when do countries in each component become more similar to each other?). Figure 4 shows constant fluctuations in the activation of each component. It means that, within each of components, the similarity of media attention among countries continuously changes. For example, the media attention of countries in CP1 become more similar around June and July, during the Brexit referendum, compared to other months. In other words, although the component we found is a group of countries who often have common media attention, their similarity level depends on time and topic.

5   Conclusion

Media is consistent in its roles of socialization and communication [11] but constantly evolving in in its technological basis and its impact [8]. Globalization, technological advancements, and a changing understanding of the role that media plays in the presentation of and access to information have warranted this study on media similarity and dissimilarity on an international scale.

Thus far, scholars have focused on understanding the current global divides and power structures through news coverage [15,16]. In understanding the factors relating to foreign news coverage based on limited data, studies have shown inconsistent results because of cultural, regional, or political differences [13].

While the determinants of news coverage have been studied at an international level, this work is the first empirical study of the convergence of media coverage of events globally. We have evaluated the over-emphasis of news topics by country to assess whether there is a convergence of topic coverage at the international level by evaluating the longitudinal homogenization of media attention. Using Unfiltered News and 100 topics, we began with the hypothesis that globalization is, in fact, resulting in the convergence of news coverage across countries. Our results confirm the convergence of news coverage on a global scale, but we find that this is not the only pattern of convergence. In addition to a pattern of globalization, we find that coverage is also converging at the country level, as a form of domestication. As we estimate the press freedom index of a country on the basis of the topic diversity of news media in that country in our previous work [1], it would be possible to make the "globalization index" or "domestication index" in terms of the topic overlap among countries on the basis of what we did in this work. We will leave this for future research directions. Interestingly, we also find similarity patterns in the similarity across countries that can be traced to historical colonial ties. For instance, the dendrogram depicts similarity and shows direct links between Spain and Mexico; it also links Malaysia and Singapore to the United Kingdom and the Philippines to the United Kingdom. This demonstrates that the economic and political legacy of colonialism is evident in the current media coverage across countries. Finally, we find geographical proximity in convergence. At the block-level association in the dendrogram, we see regional clusters, such as European countries, which exhibit similarity.

References

1. An, J., Kwak, H.: Data-driven approach to measuring the level of press freedom using media attention diversity from Unfiltered News. In: The Workshops of the Eleventh International AAAI Conference on Web and Social Media AAAI Technical Report WS-17-17: News and Public Opinion (NECO), pp. 739–742 (2017)
2. Andersson, C.A., Bro, R.: The N-way toolbox for MATLAB. Chemometr. Intell. Lab. Syst. **52**(1), 1–4 (2000)
3. Baden, C., Tenenboim-Weinblatt, K.: Convergent news? A longitudinal study of similarity and dissimilarity in the domestic and global coverage of the Israeli-Palestinian conflict. J. Commun. **67**(1), 1–25 (2017)
4. Boumans, J.: Outsourcing the news? An empirical assessment of the role of sources and news agencies in the contemporary news landscape (2016)
5. Bro, R.: PARAFAC tutorial and applications. Chemometr. Intell. Lab. Syst. **38**(2), 149–171 (1997)
6. Bro, R., Kiers, H.A.: A new efficient method for determining the number of components in parafac models. J. Chemometr. **17**(5), 274–286 (2003)
7. Clausen, L.: Localizing the global: 'domestication' processes in international news production. Media Cult. Soc. **26**(1), 25–44 (2004)
8. Flew, T., Waisbord, S.: The ongoing significance of national media systems in the context of media globalization. Media Cult. Soc. **37**(4), 620–636 (2015)
9. Galtung, J., Ruge, M.H.: The structure of Foreign news the presentation of the Congo, Cuba and Cyprus crises in four Norwegian newspapers. J. Peace Res. **2**(1), 64–90 (1965)
10. Harcup, T., O'neill, D.: What is news? Galtung and Ruge revisited. J. Stud. **2**(2), 261–280 (2001)

11. Kwak, H., An, J.: A first look at global news coverage of disasters by using the GDELT dataset. In: Aiello, L.M., McFarland, D. (eds.) SocInfo 2014. LNCS, vol. 8851, pp. 300–308. Springer, Cham (2014). doi:10.1007/978-3-319-13734-6_22

12. Kwak, H., An, J.: Multiplex media attention and disregard network among 129 countries. In: Proceedings of the IEEE/ACM International Conference on Advances in Social Networks Analysis and Mining (ASONAM 2017) (2017)

13. Peterson, S.: Foreign news gatekeepers and criteria of newsworthiness. J. Q. **56**(1), 116–25 (1979)

14. Rokach, L., Maimon, O.: Clustering Methods. Springer, Boston (2005)

15. Sreberny-Mohammadi, A.: The "world of the news" study. J. Commun. **34**(1), 121–134 (1984)

16. Wu, H.D.: Systemic determinants of international news coverage: a comparison of 38 countries. J. Commun. **50**(2), 110–130 (2000)

17. Wu, H.D.: Homogeneity around the world? Comparing the systemic determinants of international news flow between developed and developing countries. Int. Commun. Gaz. **65**(1), 9–24 (2003)

Attention Please!

Exploring Attention Management on Wikipedia in the Context of the Ukrainian Crisis

Jon Roozenbeek$^{(\boxtimes)}$ and Mariia Terentieva

University of Cambridge, Cambridge, UK
{jjr51,mt667}@cam.ac.uk

Abstract. This study investigates the behaviour of Ukrainian, Russian and English Wikipedia contributors in terms of their attention management, which Pierre Lévy casts as the initial stage of personal knowledge management. We analyse the salience of the Ukrainian crisis of 2013-14 as a topic of public discussion on the national, regional and international level, as well as the changing intensity of discussions between Ukrainian-speaking, Russian-speaking and English-speaking communities of Wikipedia contributors. We propose a meta-driven methodology to identify and track multi-faceted topics of public discussion rather than individual articles, which is common practice in Wikipedia scholarship. We develop a 'discussion intensity' metric to trace the salience of topics related to the Ukrainian crisis among Wikipedia contributors over time and to detect which aspects of this topic fuel discussions and direct attention. This method allows for a comparison across different language versions of Wikipedia and enables the identification of major differences in the attention management of different communities of Wikipedia creators and the role of the encyclopaedia in the development of collective knowledge. We observe three distinct patterns of collective attention management, which we characterize as intense attention, dispersed attention, and focused attention.

Keywords: Wikipedia · Ukrainian crisis · Collective intelligence · Attention management

1 Introduction

Wikipedia is often the first place people end up when searching for information on the internet, including for news events. As Clay Shirky observed, "Wikipedia was designed as encyclopaedia but has also become critical for breaking global news" [1].

With a corpus of 42 million articles, Wikipedia still grows by about 20,000 articles per month, as a result of the contributions of over 31,000,000 volunteers worldwide. According to Pierre Lévy, Wikipedia is "a striking example of the power of collective

The original version of this chapter was revised: In sections 3.2 and 3.3, the last paragraphs were corrected. The erratum to this chapter is available at https://doi.org/10.1007/978-3-319-67256-4_44

© Springer International Publishing AG 2017
G.L. Ciampaglia et al. (Eds.): SocInfo 2017, Part II, LNCS 10540, pp. 169–191, 2017.
DOI: 10.1007/978-3-319-67256-4_15

intelligence emerging from civilised creative conversations" [2]. "A sense of duty towards society" [3] motivates Wikipedia creators to systematically process abundant information flows, turning them into universally accessible knowledge, which can then be further discussed and edited by other contributors. Wikipedia itself imposes a number of restraints that are meant to guide discussions and keep the site encyclopaedic in nature. An important example of this is the 'Neutral Point of View' (NPOV)-rule, which means "representing fairly, proportionately, and, as far as possible, without editorial bias, all of the significant views that have been published by reliable sources on a topic.[1]"

Studying the behaviour of Wikipedia contributors allows us to gain insight into the creation of collective knowledge. Lévy suggests that on the individual level the process of knowledge creation (which he calls 'personal knowledge management') consists of a few steps: focusing attention; collecting, filtering, recording and sharing information; getting feedback; and starting the process all over again [2]. After this, other participants will discuss and evaluate the relevance and validity of individual inputs and integrate the received information into their personal knowledge management practices. This will, in the end, transform their practice. In this way, Wikipedia illustrates "how a creative conversation constructs a common memory and is in turn constructed through the relationship to that memory" [2]. Taking into consideration this formative function of Wikipedia, exploration of this global archive of collective knowledge allows us to obtain insights into public knowledge and memory about important, newsworthy events.

Thus, by looking at the collective efforts of Wikipedia contributors to bring news topics to the public's attention, we gain insight into the interplay between individual and collective attention management; As Lévy points out, attention management is about "defin[ing] interests, order[ing] priorities, identify[ing] areas of effective competency, and determin[ing] the knowledge and know-how [one wishes] to acquire" [2]. Individual Wikipedia contributors go through this process to control their attention and decide on which article(s) to edit. When aggregated, communities of contributors manage their attention to broader topics or relevant events. As such, collective attention management is the first step in the creation of collective intelligence. In this article, we will take this first step, using the Ukrainian crisis as a guiding topic.

From December 2013, the Euromaidan Revolution in Ukraine garnered world headlines. In February 2014, it led to the ouster of President Viktor Yanukovych in February and the instalment of a new, pro-European government in Kyiv. Shortly thereafter, the Russian Federation annexed Ukraine's Autonomous Republic of Crimea and helped spark public unrest and military conflict in two of Ukraine's eastern regions, which led to the emergence of the self-declared Luhansk and Donetsk People's Republics (LNR and DNR). The downing of Malaysian Airlines flight MH17 above the territory of these self-styled statelets in July 2017 exacerbated the crisis even further, and the situation remains highly volatile to this day.

Our article explores how the Ukrainian, Russian and English-speaking Wikipedia communities were focusing their attention in discussions on issues related to the Ukrainian crisis. It also investigates which events were particularly important for

---

[1] Taken from: https://en.wikipedia.org/wiki/Wikipedia:Neutral_point_of_view.

motivating people to contribute to Wikipedia, and which global developments were the most important factors of distraction. We ask:

- What trends can be discerned regarding the editing activity among contributors on English, Russian and Ukrainian Wikipedia concerning the Ukrainian crisis between December 2013 and August 2014?
- How are these trends informed and shaped by contributors' attention to the crisis?
- How can we classify the differences in the discussion process that we observe across different language versions?
- What does this say about attention management in the context of personal and collective knowledge management?

We posit that there are significant differences in how the Wikipedia editing process occurs on the Russian, Ukrainian and English versions of the website. It is important to note that contributors to both national and global versions of Wikipedia do not represent specific national so much as linguistic communities. For example, since most or all Ukrainians are proficient in spoken and written Russian, Ukrainian contributors are often able to edit Russian-language Wikipedia pages. The reverse is not true: the majority of citizens of the Russian Federation is not equipped to write proficiently in Ukrainian. In addition, a significant number of Ukrainians, as well as Russians, is proficient in English. Seeing as the English-language version of Wikipedia is by far the most widely read worldwide and oftentimes ends up at the top of Google search results, Ukrainian as well as Russian editors have an incentive to contribute to global Wikipedia to share unique knowledge or make sure their preferred narrative becomes dominant on the 'cosmopolitan' online encyclopaedia.

In this article, we propose a meta-driven method of measuring the intensity of Wikipedia discussions on a broadly defined 'topic' across different language versions of Wikipedia [4]. We develop the 'discussion intensity' metric, a qualitative approach to analysing a news topic's salience among contributors.

This methodology is likely the first to enable researchers to look at the salience of geopolitical topics that stretch across different Wikipedia articles over a defined time period. It also takes into consideration how statistical data can pinpoint the most important points of Wikipedia contributors' interests, which can be to some extent indicative of the most important ongoing discussions in the public arena.

2 Literature Review

Wikipedia is a popular object of scholarly research, partially because of the website's popularity and partially because of its policy of making its statistical and meta-data openly available. For example, many scholars have attempted to assess the degree of bias present on the platform, e.g. [5–8]. Others have sought to find methods to detect vandalism on Wikipedia articles, e.g. [9–13]. Despite the lofty stated motivations by contributors for taking part in the editing process (see [3]), bias, vandalism and prolonged editing conflicts among contributors appear unavoidable.

Roughly speaking, there are four different groups of models that are used to analyse editing processes on Wikipedia. (see [14] for an overview). The first group is agent-based, meaning that they focus on the behaviour of and interactions between editors [15–20] or readers themselves (see [21]). The second group of models is content-based, meaning that they focus on the revision histories and discussion pages, rather than contributors or readers [14, 22–27]. The third group of models is pattern-driven. Here, researchers look at patterns of revisions rather than revision content, such as mutual reverts [28, 29]. The final group is meta-driven models [14, 30, 31]. Here, researchers extract a set of numerical statistics from an article's revision history and/or its discussion page. These statistics can then be combined into a score, or otherwise introduced to a machine learning system as meta-classifiers.

In terms of Wikipedia's role as a nexus of knowledge creation, a number of scholars have tackled the encyclopaedia's role in knowledge management [32–34] (including personal knowledge management, see [35]), as a vector for collaborative knowledge [35, 36], and collective intelligence [38, 39]. The opportunities for using Wiki technology (which Wikipedia is based on) for knowledge management have been explored as well [37, 40]. Lévy's ideas [2, 41] have not yet been applied to Wikipedia research. Furthermore, attention management among Wikipedia contributors is yet to be examined as well.

Scholarly work on Wikipedia that pertains to the Ukrainian crisis in some way is sparse. Hélène Dounaevsky looked at edit warring between Ukrainians and Russians on a number of controversial pages, although not in a quantitative manner [42]. Other than this interesting contribution, there is no other work available that looks at Wikipedia dynamics in the context of Russia, Ukraine or the Ukrainian crisis.

3 Methodology

The main conceptual problem with analysing attention management to news events among Wikipedia contributors is that a newsworthy topic is rarely fully covered by one Wikipedia entry. For example, if one wants to measure the salience of the 2016 Olympic Games in Rio de Janeiro, it does not suffice to analyse the revision history or visitor statistics of the main Wikipedia article '2016 Summer Olympics'. To get a clear picture of the interests of contributors, one needs to take into account the editing process of articles closely related to the main article, for example '2016 Summer Olympics opening ceremony' or '2016 Summer Olympics medal table'.

However, since we are measuring salience, which in our case we define as the relative popularity of a topic among contributors, we need not include every individual article about a given topic. It would be sufficient to limit our data set to a list of the most popular articles for a given time period, identify which topics occur on the list, and see which articles pertain to that topic, in order to get a decent picture of the salience of that topic. This works especially well for major contemporary geopolitical events that play out on a longer time scale and have multiple entries dedicated to them, such as the war in Syria, the European refugee crisis, or the Ukrainian crisis. In this paper, we develop a meta-driven method based mainly on page statistics, that can trace discussion intensity, and by extension topical salience, over time.

There are two challenges inherent in this method. The first is defining what exactly is meant by 'topic'. While Wikipedia's own categorisation system (which has main topic classifications such as arts, culture, games and so on) makes sense for structuring such a massive, sprawling encyclopaedia [4], it is unhelpful for identifying newsworthy topics. By 'topic' we mean a series of interconnected articles complex enough to warrant multiple Wikipedia entries over an extended period of time. A topic can sometimes be divided into sub-topics: the Ukrainian crisis, for instance, has sub-topics such as Euromaidan and the Crimea annexation. In our approach, it is up to the researcher to decide which articles are included in a topic and which are not. As we will see, however, the classification method based on this definition is fairly simple and straightforward, and rarely leads to a large degree of ambiguity.

3.1 Data Set

Our data set consists of the lists of titles of the 25 articles that had the most contributors in each month, between December 2013 and August 2014, for the English-, Russian- and Ukrainian-language versions of Wikipedia[2]. Since we look at 9 months of the crisis and three language versions, the total number of articles is 25 * 9 * 3 = 675. We complement this list with the number of contributors per each article, as well as the number of edits made to each article in that month[3]. Using this meta-data makes it possible to measure the salience of a topic among contributors in a certain language over a given time span[4]: what one has to do is define a measurement for this intensity per time unit and language, and track it over time. The result is an estimate of discussion intensity.

3.2 The Variables and Their Relation

Based on the above, we propose that the intensity of discussion for a given topic, within the confines of our data set, depends on a number of variables:

- The number of articles on the list of the top 25 articles with the most contributors per month that are connected to the topic (i.e. the Ukrainian crisis), and the number of articles that are not related to the topic.
- The total number of edits made in topic-related articles, and
- The total number of edits made in non-topic-related articles on the list.

In our definition, discussion intensity is higher when fewer contributors are making more edits on fewer topic-related articles. The variables have to relate in such a way that there is no bias in favour of languages with more contributors; a higher absolute number of total edits or contributions on a page must not raise the overall discussion intensity, meaning that a language with a high absolute number of edits cannot always have a higher intensity score than a language with a low number of edits. This prevents the English-language Wikipedia from being 'rewarded' too much for having more contributors. Non-topic-related articles are factored into the equation in order to measure

---

[2] The source of this data is found here: https://stats.wikimedia.org/EN/TablesPageViewsMonthly.htm.

[3] The number of edits per article per month can be obtained by using this tool: https://tools.wmflabs.org/xtools-articleinfo/.

[4] The full tables and lists of articles can be found in appendices 1, 2 and 3.

how intensely a topic was discussed vis-à-vis non-topic-related articles. Thus, a normalised discussion intensity score of 1 for a topic means that the topic is discussed as intensely as non-topic-related articles; a score higher than 1 means it was discussed more intensely, and so on. Peaks in discussion intensity indicate points of interests where individual articles take on a high degree of relevance. We will discuss this in Sect. 4.

As a supplement to the 'discussion intensity' metric, we will also include a metric called editors' concentration. We define this as the number of contributors contributing to topic-related articles compared to the number of contributors contributing to non-topic related articles. Together with the discussion intensity, these metrics form a way of quantifying the aforementioned concept of attention management.

- The number of edits on topic-related articles;
- The number of contributors on topic-related articles;
- The number of edits on non-topic-related articles;
- The number of contributors on non-topic-related articles.

Finally, we will also make use of a simple calculation of the proportion of Ukraine-related edits versus non-Ukraine-related edits per month.

3.3   Equations

We measure discussion intensity per given month by taking the proportion of Ukraine-related edits per Ukraine-related article and divide it by the proportion of non-Ukraine-related edits per non-Ukraine-related article. See Eq. (1).

$$I_m^d = \frac{E_t}{N_t} \div \frac{E_n}{N_n} = \frac{E_t N_n}{E_n N_t} \tag{1}$$

In which I_m^d is the intensity of discussion among contributors in a given month; E_t is the number of topic-related edits; E_n is the number of edits on non-topic related articles; N_m is the number of non-topic-related articles; and N_t is the number of articles on the topic. As stated, high discussion intensity is indicative of a high proportion of on-topic edits versus off-topic edits, as well as a low proportion of on-topic versus off-topic articles. That is to say, the discussion intensity will be higher when more edits are made in fewer articles, and therefore is indicative of the degree to which contributors' attention was focused on a single topic in a given month.

We measure editors' concentration as the number of contributors working on Ukraine-related articles over the number of contributors working on non-Ukraine-related articles. See Eq. (2):

$$C_m^e = C_t/N_t \div C_n/N_n = (C_t * N_n)/(N_t * C_n) \tag{2}$$

In which C_m^e is the editors' concentration in a given month; C_t is the number of contributors working on topic-related articles; N_t is the number of articles on topic; C_n is the number of contributors working on off-topic articles; and N_n is the number of non-topic-related articles.

4   Results and Discussion

In this section, we will first describe general trends for Ukrainian, Russian and English Wikipedia, respectively. We will do this using the discussion intensity metric as a guideline, and discuss specific articles, issues, and trends along the way. More details can be found in the appendices.

The discussion intensity of the issues related to Ukrainian crisis is graphically represented in Fig. 1. The ordinate on the graph indicates how many times more or fewer edits were – on average – dedicated to the Ukrainian crisis for each language. The line of abscissae demonstrates this dynamic over time between December 2013 and August 2014. Ordinate 1 means that articles related to Ukrainian crisis were edited as intensively as other popular articles on Wikipedia. The proportion of edits on the Ukrainian crisis versus the total number of edits per month can be found in Fig. 2. Figure 3 displays the editors' concentration. Here too, ordinate 1 indicates that the average number of edits per contributor to on-topic articles equals the average editors' concentration for all other topics on the list.

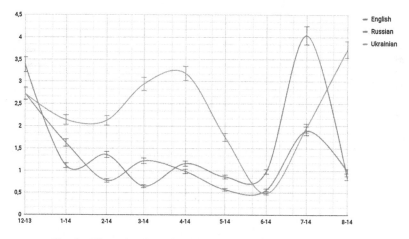

Fig. 1. Discussion intensity for English, Russian and Ukrainian.

From Fig. 1 we can discern that Ukrainian Wikipedia saw a consistently high discussion intensity, save for a dip in May, June, and July 2014. Especially March, April, and August 2014 stand out. Compared to Russian and English, however, the Ukrainian version shows very few peaks and valleys.

Articles about the crisis attracted on average 2.3 times more edits compared to the average number of edits on non-crisis-related articles on the list. This factor can be explained by the continuing relevance of crisis-related articles, regardless of their novelty or newsworthiness.

The first sub-topic of note is 'Euromaidan'. The main article for these events remained on the list until April 2014, a month and a half after the culmination of the Euromaidan events. Other related articles, such as 'chronology and geography of

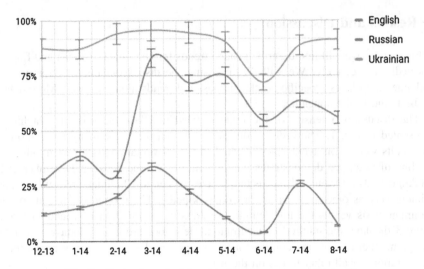

Fig. 2. Proportion of crisis-related edits versus unrelated edits

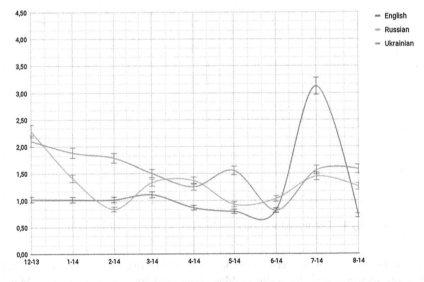

Fig. 3. Editors' concentration

Euromaidan' and 'List of detainees and missing activists on Euromaidan', also appear. The second sub-topic is the annexation of Crimea, which picks up steam in March and remains somewhat relevant until August. The third sub-topic is the war in Donbas, which began to be relevant in April (when 2 articles, 'War in Eastern Ukraine' and 'pro-Russian interventions in Ukraine in 2014') were both high on the list. This issue remained the dominant sub-topic until August. Not only the main article 'War in Eastern Ukraine' was edited heavily throughout articles on individual battalions, battles, and uprisings in various Ukrainian cities were also on the list. The only radical drop in editing intensity, in June, is explained by the high average number of edits in non-crisis related articles, which were mostly dedicated to the 2014 FIFA World Cup. This brings us back to Lévy's notion of attention management: despite escalating warfare in Eastern Ukraine, the Ukrainian Wikipedia community did not stay focused exclusively on Ukrainian crisis, but was distracted by a major sports event. This idea is supported in Fig. 3: in general, the editors' concentration is higher than for Russian or English, with the mean index being around 1,5. We suggest that in the case of Ukraine, such behaviour of Wikipedia editors indicates an augmented interest in contributing to collective knowledge. This implores contributors to suggest new edits when new information about unfolding events becomes available.

On Ukrainian Wikipedia, an average of 88.9% of edits made to the top-25 articles to between December 2013 and August 2014 was related to the Ukrainian crisis. The peak was in February 2014, with 93%. Other important months were March, April and May 2014 (92%, 87%, and 89% respectively. These months overlap with the Crimea annexation, the start of the war in Donbas and the emergence of the DNR and LNR. This overlap is indicative of the large degree of public interest in crisis-related information among Ukrainian-speaking audiences. It is possible that this editing process was grounded in a collective interest in the topic and a need to update information continuously, even when the crisis seemed to recede from view for international audiences. This implies that the Ukrainian crisis was the principal point of discussion for the Ukrainian Wikipedia community. This is also indicative of a level of emotional involvement in the events unfolding, and a need to catalogue historical moments in real time. Indeed, one could argue that Ukrainian Wiki-pedia offers support for Baytiyeh & Pfaffmann's conclusion that the most common stated motivation for people to contribute to Wikipedia is altruism or a sense of duty towards society [3].

What is further noteworthy is the apparent abandonment of Wikipedia's neutral point of view principle (NPOV) when it comes to naming the articles. Some examples of non-neutral article titles include 'Dictatorship Laws of January 16th', 'Repressions against Euromaidan', 'Putin is a dick!', and 'Victims of the Russian Invasion into Ukraine 2014-2016'. This is indicative of a lack of ideological conflict among contributors: since the NPOV is enforced by editors, there can be a degree of leeway in terms of what editors see as neutral. In this case, it is clear that title wording on Ukrainian Wikipedia was less strict than on the other two language versions.

On Russian Wikipedia, we see a different pattern emerge. The sub-topics that are the most relevant are the same as for the Ukrainian version: Euromaidan, the Crimea annexation, and the war in Donbas. All had multiple articles that remained relevant over time. Additionally, the article 'Catastrophe with the Boeing 777 in Donetsk Oblast' (also known as Malaysia Airlines Flight 17) was also relevant, especially in July 2014, the month of the catastrophe.

An average of 55.5% of edits in the top 25 articles on the Russian language version related to Ukraine. The Ukrainian crisis was still by far the most significant topic being discussed on Wikipedia in this time period. Especially March (83%), April (71.7%), May 2014 (75.1%) and July (64%) 2014 stand out as important months, similar to the Ukrainian version. Quite surprisingly, however, Russian Wikipedia does not reveal a particularly high average discussion intensity on Ukraine-related articles. Discussion intensity starts out high in December 2013, due to the relevance of Euromaidan. It then declines in January and February 2014, then flatlines before peaking in July and going down again in August 2014m. In February, April, May, June and August 2014, discussion intensity is 1 or lower, indicating that the Ukrainian crisis was as or less intensely discussed in a public sphere than other topics. Crisis-related articles attracted on average 1.3 times more edits per contributor than any other unrelated article on the list, lower than for both English and Ukrainian. This is explained by two dynamics: first, the large influx of contributors to relevant articles making relatively few edits, and second, the large variety of articles that related to Ukraine that made it onto the top 25 article list. Both dynamics meant that attention was spread out across different articles and hence less focused. Interestingly, the topics that offset the relevance of the Ukrainian crisis mostly related to sports (the same as for Ukrainian), e.g. the Sochi Olympic Games, the FIFA World Cup and the world ice hockey championships. While the topic stayed highly relevant over time (as witnessed by the high percentage of crisis-related articles on the list, especially in March, April, and May 2014), editors' concentration hovered around index 1, except in December 2013.

While the Ukrainian crisis was highly relevant to Russian-language Wikipedia contributors, attention was focused on individual articles that had a large number of both contributors and edits. The points of high editors' concentration were connected to Euromaidan, the annexation of Crimea, the emergence of the so-called LNR and DNR, and the MH17 tragedy (all three with the indices around 1.4, which is slightly above average). The most important of these are 'The Crimea crisis', 'The entry of Russian troops into Ukraine', 'Protests in South-eastern Ukraine (2014)', 'Armed conflict in Eastern Ukraine', and the aforementioned 'Catastrophe with the Boeing 777 in Donetsk Oblast'. Interestingly, these individual articles saw untypically high editors' concentration. For example, in the case of Euromaidan, each two editors made nearly five edits, which indicates that some small group of people was actively engaged in editing articles concerning Euromaidan. We also observe that the NPOV is more enforced than on the Ukrainian version; the use of the word 'entry' (*vvod* in Russian) instead of, say, 'intervention' (*vmeshatel'stvo*) or 'invasion' (*vtorzhenie*) is an indicative example of this.

On the English-language version, we see yet another pattern. On average, Ukraine-related articles were discussed 1.6 times more intensely than other topics. The most salient sub-topics overlap with the Ukrainian and especially Russian Wikipedia: Euromaidan, the Crimea annexation, the Russian intervention in eastern Ukraine, and flight MH17. The proportion of edits about the Ukrainian crisis was, on average, 16.8%. The months that stand out are March (33.8%), April (22.5%) and July (26%). In other months, this average was not very high and remained limited to a small number of articles. What stands out, however, is the high intensity of attention in case of selected individual articles. This becomes especially visible in the high peaks in December 2013 and July 2014. These peaks are almost entirely explained by two individual articles: 'Euromaidan' in December and 'Malaysia Airlines Flight 17' in July, both of which had a large number of edits and a relatively small number of contributors. Figure 3 illustrates this point: the trend line fluctuates around an average index of 1, except for a radical spike in July 2014. Together with the same spike visible in Fig. 2, we can observe that July 2014 was a month in which the editing process on the English language page was highly focused and very intense: a small number of editors made a large number of edits on the topic, far outpacing any other topic or an individual article. This only occurred on highly newsworthy articles. This implies that a small community of contributors interested in Ukraine was working on Ukraine-related pages. This community then clashed with outside contributors on articles that were heavily covered by the news.

5 Conclusion

This article investigated the first stage of the cycle of knowledge management – attention management – among contributors to English, Russian and Ukrainian Wikipedia between December 2013 and August 2014.

The trends discussed above indicate three patterns of collective attention management. The first, which we will call 'intense', suggests a state where a community of contributors is committed to exploring every aspect of a topic, continuously adding new information and creating new articles. The discussion intensity is consistently higher than 1, although individual articles stand out as being subjected to a particularly high discussion intensity. A high proportion of popular articles is dedicated to the topic.

The second pattern can be labelled as 'dispersed'. The topic enjoys moments of high salience, with individual articles receiving large amounts of edits in times of newsworthiness. Fewer individual articles related to the topic pop up, although the number of topic-related articles is still large when a topic's newsworthiness is at a peak. The average discussion intensity is low due to a relatively large number of contributors making relatively few edits across a rather large number of articles. Attention is given to a multitude of articles, without a great deal of convergence towards a single one.

The third pattern can be described as 'focused'. A small community may be working on the topic from time to time, contributing new information in a relatively conflict-free environment. In total, only a few popular articles are related to the topic, but in times of great newsworthiness, they become platforms for intense discussion. The average discussion intensity is therefore low to medium, but with a high variance. This may lead to, for example, prolonged discussions about article title wording and NPOV, as controversial articles attract large numbers of contributors who are only interested in one article or aspect of a topic. We suggest that this is likely to happen because these individuals seek to establish the dominance of their preferred narrative in times when the topic is highly newsworthy, so as to be ahead of the curve when casual internet users try to find information about the topic.

The suggested metrics open up a way for further qualitative or quantitative research in other aspects of knowledge management – filtering, reshaping, sharing and internalising knowledge. In addition, one could look into the issue of edit warring and bot activities, as well as propaganda efforts, all of which may influence attention management and knowledge production to a significant extent.

Appendix A: Contributor Table

Rank	dec.13 Eng	dec.13 Rus	dec.13 Ukr	jan-14 Eng	jan-14 Rus	jan-14 Ukr	feb-14 Eng	feb-14 Rus	feb-14 Ukr	mrt-14 Eng	mrt-14 Rus	mrt-14 Ukr	apr-14 Eng	apr-14 Rus	apr-14 Ukr	mei-14 Eng	mei-14 Rus	mei-14 Ukr	jun-14 Eng	jun-14 Rus	jun-14 Ukr	jul-14 Eng	jul-14 Rus	jul-14 Ukr	aug-14 Eng	aug-14 Rus	aug-14 Ukr
1	267	97	101	201	83	58	216	123	96	814	166	67	190	104	32	169	118	36	317	95	49	666	165	56	357	107	49
2	245	47	52	159	50	42	196	92	48	410	125	49	176	83	30	167	91	30	173	90	42	378	114	48	273	51	36
3	243	45	28	115	33	41	189	64	46	235	95	32	160	47	28	163	68	20	166	59	26	193	52	30	241	45	20
4	150	39	26	102	29	32	151	53	46	195	91	30	160	44	26	161	67	19	164	59	24	171	49	28	229	40	18
5	112	37	23	92	28	22	137	46	46	194	81	29	120	38	24	159	66	18	163	44	24	157	45	22	220	39	17
6	111	35	22	90	24	19	131	42	21	189	72	26	112	32	22	131	64	18	132	42	21	131	44	22	195	38	17
7	106	34	16	88	24	18	126	40	20	155	63	23	110	31	21	129	60	17	122	37	21	121	40	21	184	34	17
8	100	31	16	86	21	16	121	39	20	115	62	23	108	31	19	122	46	17	122	36	20	119	37	20	150	33	16
9	98	29	16	86	20	15	103	37	20	113	61	22	103	30	18	116	46	17	110	35	18	116	36	18	136	32	15
10	93	28	15	83	20	15	96	36	17	110	58	21	97	29	17	112	53	16	106	32	18	114	35	18	121	32	13
11	88	27	14	82	20	14	96	35	17	101	56	21	97	29	16	106	51	15	105	32	16	108	32	17	115	31	13
12	87	23	13	79	19	13	91	31	17	95	56	19	95	29	16	98	49	14	98	31	16	100	32	15	113	31	13
13	83	22	12	78	18	13	84	30	16	90	55	16	88	28	15	95	47	13	94	28	15	99	29	15	113	31	12
14	77	20	12	74	18	12	82	29	15	89	52	16	86	28	14	93	46	13	94	28	15	98	29	14	108	30	12
15	76	20	11	71	18	12	82	29	14	89	49	16	79	26	13	88	45	13	93	26	14	96	28	12	98	26	11
16	76	19	11	71	18	11	81	29	14	84	48	16	79	25	13	84	40	12	91	25	14	93	26	12	89	26	10
17	75	19	11	67	18	10	80	29	13	83	45	16	78	24	13	82	35	12	90	24	13	93	25	12	89	26	10
18	73	18	11	64	17	10	79	26	13	78	44	16	74	24	12	80	34	12	85	24	13	92	24	12	83	25	10
19	69	17	11	64	17	10	75	26	13	76	42	15	71	24	12	79	31	11	84	23	12	89	24	12	80	24	9
20	65	17	10	62	17	10	72	26	12	74	42	15	69	23	11	79	26	11	82	23	11	86	23	12	79	24	9
21	64	17	10	62	16	10	72	25	12	74	42	14	69	23	11	78	26	11	77	22	11	84	22	11	79	24	9
22	64	17	10	61	16	9	67	24	12	73	42	14	65	23	11	77	26	10	75	20	11	83	22	11	78	22	9
23	63	16	10	60	16	9	65	23	12	72	40	14	64	21	10	72	25	10	75	19	10	82	21	11	74	21	9
24	60	16	9	58	16	9	63	22	11	71	40	14	62	21	10	71	25	10	74	19	10	82	21	11	73	21	9
25	60	16	9	58	15	9	62	22	11	70	39	13	59	19	9	71	25	10	72	19	10	81	21	11	73	20	9
Sum	2605	706	481	2113	587	439	2617	978	579	3749	1564	554	2471	836	386	2690	1210	386	2864	892	446	3532	996	472	3450	833	365
Sum (topic)	106	168	406	106	171	208	423	313	41	1744	1317	508	438	651	335	262	1003	392	94	612	361	755	570	407	202	512	293
Mean	104,2	28,24	19,24	84,52	23,48	17,56	104,68	39,12	23,16	149,96	62,56	22,16	98,84	33,44	15,44	107,6	48,4	17,6	114,56	35,68	17,84	141,28	39,84	18,88	138	33,32	14,6
Median	83	22	12	78	18	13	84	30	16	90	55	16	88	28	13	55	46	16	94	28	15	99	29	15	113	31	12
St. Dev	59,43	17,17	19,34	32,75	14,55	12,53	43,61	23,35	19,32	157,80	29,92	19,32	36,85	19,51	6,16	33,46	22,40	6,16	52,46	20,32	9,58	125,22	32,20	11,36	75,33	17,21	9,21

Appendix B: Edits Table

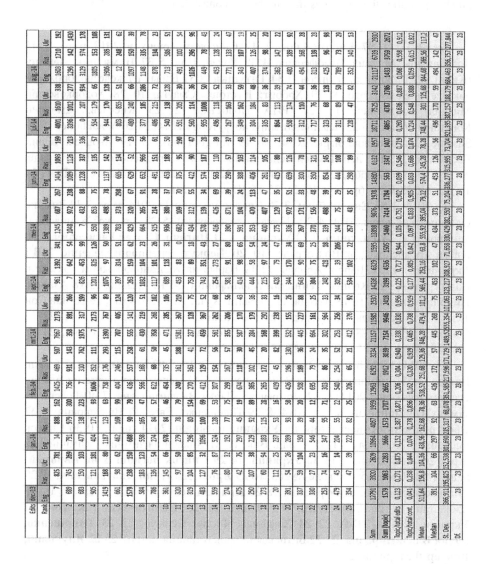

Appendix C: Article List Per Month

Below is a list of the 25 Wikipedia pages that had the highest number of people contributed to them, per month, from December 2013 to August 2014. This is given for the Russian, English and Ukrainian-language versions of Wikipedia. Articles that pertain to the Ukrainian crisis are highlighted. The first number indicates the rank; the number just after that indicates the number of contributors[5].

Russian

Dec 2013: 1 **97 Евромайдан**, 2 47 Список умерших в 2013 году, 3 45 Калашников, Михаил Тимофеевич, 4 39 Уокер, Пол, 5 **37 Памятник Ленину (Киев)**, 6 35 Мандела, Нельсон, 7 **34 Титушки**, 8 31 Взрыв на железнодорожном вокзале в Волгограде, 9 29 Хоббит: Пустошь Смауга, 10 28 Ходорковский, Михаил Борисович, 11 27 РИА Новости, 12 23 Киселёв, Дмитрий Константинович, 13 22 Чемпионат мира по футболу 2014, 14 20 YotaPhone, 15 20 Зимние Олимпийские игры 2014, 16 19 Яя (остров), 17 19 Яковлев, Юрий Васильевич, 18 18 Гней Помпей Великий, 19 17 Взрыв троллейбуса в Волгограде, 20 17 Крейсер «Аврора», 21 17 Волгоград, 22 17 Россия, 23 16 Чан Сон Тхэк, 24 16 Доктор Живаго (фильм, 1965), 25 16 Шумахер, Михаэл

Jan 2014: 1 **83 Евромайдан**, 2 50 Список умерших в 2014 году, 3 33 Зимние Олимпийские игры 2014, 4 29 Шерлок (телесериал), 5 28 Фриске, Жанна Владимировна, 6 **24 Титушки**, 7 **24 Украина**, 8 **21 Нигоян, Сергей Гагикович**, 9 20 Взрыв троллейбуса в Волгограде, 10 **20 Беркут (спецподразделение МВД Украины)**, 11 20 Шарон, Ариэль, 12 19 Взрыв на железнодорожном вокзале в Волгограде, 13 **18 Кернес, Геннадий Адольфович**, 14 18 Армяне, 15 **18 Азаров, Николай Янович**, 16 18 Латвия, 17 17 Мата, Хуан, 18 17 2014 год, 19 16 Чан Сон Тхэк, 20 16 Блокада Ленинграда, 21 16 Сталин, Иосиф Виссарионович, 22 16 Санкт-Петербург, 23 16 Союз Советских Социалистических Республик, 24 15 Список умерших в 2013 году, 25 15 This is Хорошо

Feb 2014: 1 123 Зимние Олимпийские игры 2014, 2 **92 Евромайдан**, 3 64 Ан, Виктор, 4 53 Липницкая, Юлия Вячеславовна, 5 46 Церемония открытия зимних Олимпийских игр 2014, 6 42 Домрачева, Дарья Владимировна, 7 40 Россия на зимних Олимпийских играх 2014, 8 39 Плющенко, Евгений Викторович, 9 **37 Обострение противостояния на Украине (февраль 2014 года)**, 10 36 Список умерших в 2014 году, 11 35 Уайлд, Вик, 12 31 Хоккей на зимних Олимпийских играх 2014 (мужчины), 13 **30 Украина**, 14 **29 Список погибших на Евромайдане**, 15 29 Стрельба в школе № 263, 16 **29 Ярош, Дмитрий Анатольевич**, 17 29 Сотникова, Аделина Дмитриевна, 18 **26 Правый сектор**, 19 26 Джексон, Томас Джонатан, 20 26 Бьёрндален, Уле-Эйнар, 21 **25 Политический кризис на Украине (2013—2014)**, 22 24 Хоффман, Филип Сеймур, 23 **23 Тимошенко, Юлия Владимировна**, 24 22 Битцевский парк (станция метро), 25 **22 Янукович, Виктор Фёдорович** 21

Mar 2014: 1 **166 Крымский кризис**, 2 **125 Референдум о статусе Крыма (2014)**, 3 **95 Севастополь**, 4 **91 Ввод российских войск на Украину**, 5 **80 Протесты на Юго-Востоке Украины (2014)**, 6 **72 Республика Крым (независимое государство)**, 7 **63 Россия**, 8 **62 Автономная Республика Крым**, 9 **61 Поклонская, Наталья Владимировна**, 10 **58 Присоединение Крыма к Российской Федерации**, 11 **56 Евромайдан**, 12 **56 Украина**, 13 **55 Аксёнов, Сергей**

---

[5] The source of this data is found here: https://stats.wikimedia.org/EN/TablesPageViewsMonthly.htm.

Валерьевич, 14 **52 Республика Крым**, 15 **49 Военно-морские силы Украины**, 16 48 Музычко, Александр Иванович, 17 **45 Субъекты Российской Федерации**, 18 44 Рейс 370 Malaysia Airlines, 19 42 **Политический кризис на Украине (2013 —2014)**, 20 **42 Ярош, Дмитрий Анатольевич**, 21 **42 Симферополь**, 22 **41 Янукович, Виктор Фёдорович**, 23 40 Список умерших в 2014 году, 24 **40 История Крыма**, 25 39 Кухня (телесериал)

Apr 2014: 1 **104 Протесты на Юго-Востоке Украины (2014)**, 2 **83 Донецкая Народная Республика**, 3 **47 Крымский кризис**, 4 44 Список умерших в 2014 году, 5 **38 Украина**, 6 **32 Противостояние в Славянске**, 7 **31 Присоединение Крыма к Российской Федерации**, 8 **31 Президентские выборы на Украине (2014)**, 9 **30 Вейдер, Дарт Алексеевич**, 10 **29 Дело о киевских снайперах**, 11 **29 Аксёнов, Сергей Валерьевич**, 12 **29 Севастополь**, 13 **28 Референдум о статусе Крыма (2014)**, 14 28 Кухня (телесериал), 15 **26 Царёв, Олег Анатольевич**, 16 **25 Евромайдан**, 17 **24 Поклонская, Наталья Владимировна**, 18 **24 Республика Крым**, 19 24 Гарсиа Маркес, Габриэль, 20 **23 Санкции в связи с украинскими событиями 2014 года**, 21 23 Леньков, Александр Сергеевич, 22 **23 Славянск**, 23 21 Физрук, 24 **21 Россия**, 25 **19 Стрелков, Игорь Иванович**

May 2014: 1 **118 Донецкая Народная Республика**, 2 **91 Противостояние в Одессе (2013—2014)**, 3 **68 Противостояние в Славянске**, 4 67 Чемпионат мира по хоккею с шайбой 2014, 5 **66 Вооружённый конфликт на востоке Украины**, 6 **64 Стрелков, Игорь Иванович**, 7 **60 Протесты на Юго-Востоке Украины (2014)**, 8 **56 Референдум о самоопределении Донецкой Народной Республики**, 9 **56 Президентские выборы на Украине (2014)**, 10 **53 Новороссия (конфедерация)**, 11 **51 Луганская Народная Республика**, 12 49 Кончита Вурст, 13 **47 Украина**, 14 46 Евровидение-2014, 15 45 Список умерших в 2014 году, 16 **40 Порошенко, Пётр Алексеевич**, 17 **35 Противостояние в Мариуполе**, 18 **34 Крымский кризис**, 19 **31 Референдум о самоопределении Луганской Народной Республики**, 20 **26 Пожар в одесском Доме профсоюзов**, 21 **26 Автономная Республика Крым**, 22 **26 Новороссия**, 23 25 Антитеррористическая операция на востоке Украины, 24 25 Губарев, Павел Юрьевич (ДНР), 25 25 Донецк

Jun 2014: 1 **95 Вооружённый конфликт на востоке Украины**, 2 90 Чемпионат мира по футболу 2014, 3 **59 Протесты на Юго-Востоке Украины (2014)**, 4 **59 Порошенко, Пётр Алексеевич**, 5 **44 Луганская Народная Республика**, 6 **42 Донецкая Народная Республика**, 7 37 Сборная России по футболу, 8 36 Список умерших в 2014 году, 9 35 **Катастрофа Ил-76 в Луганске**, 10 **32 Авиаудар по зданию Луганской областной государственной администрации 2 июня 2014 года**, 11 32 Дещица, Андрей Богданович, 12 **31 Новороссия (конфедерация)**, 13 **28 Противостояние в Мариуполе**, 14 28 Псаки, Дженнифер, 15 **26 Стрелков, Игорь Иванович**, 16 **25 Янукович, Виктор Фёдорович**, 17 24 Филипп VI (король Испании), 18 **24 Кличко, Виталий Владимирович**, 19 **23 Противостояние в Славянске**, 20 **23 Су-25**, 21 **22 Ан-30**, 22 20 Чемпионат мира по футболу 2014 (составы), 23 **19 Азов (полк)**, 24 **19 Противостояние в Луганской области (2014)**, 25 **19 Крымский кризис**

Jul 2014: 1 **165 Катастрофа Boeing 777 в Донецкой области**, 2 **114 Вооружённый конфликт на востоке Украины**, 3 52 Чемпионат мира по футболу 2014, 4 49 Новодворская, Валерия Ильинична, 5 **45 Стрелков, Игорь Иванович**,

6 44 Список умерших в 2014 году, 7 40 Реал Мадрид (футбольный клуб), 8 **37 Противостояние в Славянске**, 9 36 Катастрофа в Московском метрополитене (2014), 10 **35 Донецкая Народная Республика**, 11 32 Родригес, Хамес, 12 **32 Бук (зенитный ракетный комплекс)**, 13 29 Операция «Нерушимая скала», 14 29 Сборная Бразилии по футболу, 15 **28 Ракетная атака под Зеленопольем**, 16 26 Бородай, Александр Юрьевич, 17 25 Навас, Кейлор, 18 24 Футбольный матч Бразилия — Германия (2014), 19 24 Сборная Германии по футболу, 20 23 Трансформеры: Эпоха истребления, 21 **22 Санкции в связи с украинскими событиями 2014 года**, 22 22 Клозе, Мирослав, 23 21 Павлов, Арсен Сергеевич, 24 21 Финал чемпионата мира по футболу 2014, 25 **21 Луганская Народная Республика**

Aug 2014: 1 **107 Вооружённый конфликт на востоке Украины**, 2 **51 Катастрофа Boeing 777 в Донецкой области**, 3 45 Список умерших в 2014 году, 4 **40 Стрелков, Игорь Иванович**, 5 39 Уильямс, Робин, 6 **38 Бои за Саур-Могилу (2014)**, 7 **34 Донецкая Народная Республика**, 8 **33 Санкции в связи с украинскими событиями 2014 года**, 9 **32 Южный котёл**, 10 32 Орёл и решка (телепередача), 11 31 Ice Bucket Challenge, 12 **31 Бои за Иловайск**, 13 **31 Новороссия (конфедерация)**, 14 30 Геморрагическая лихорадка Эбола, 15 26 Стражи Галактики (фильм), 16 **26 Саур-Могила**, 17 26 Спартак (станция метро), 18 25 Бородай, Александр Юрьевич, 19 24 Эпидемия лихорадки Эбола в Западной Африке, 20 24 Лига Европы УЕФА 2014/2015, 21 24 Ди Мария, Анхель, 22 **22 Противостояние в Донецке (2014—2016)**, 23 **21 76-я гвардейская десантно-штурмовая дивизия**, 24 **21 Украина**, 25 20 Ревизорро

English
Dec 2013: 1 267 Deaths in 2013, 2 245 Nelson Mandela, 3 243 Paul Walker, 4 150 Death of Nelson Mandela, 5 112 Beyoncé (album), 6 111 The Hobbit: The Desolation of Smaug, 7 **106 Euromaidan**, 8 100 Bitcoin, 9 98 Frozen (2013 film), 10 93 Furious 7, 11 88 Peter O'Toole, 12 87 Jang Sung-taek, 13 83 The Time of the Doctor, 14 77 South Sudanese Civil War, 15 76 December 2013 Volgograd bombings, 16 76 Devyani Khobragade incident, 17 75 Alan Turing, 18 73 2014 FIFA World Cup, 19 69 Chang'e 3, 20 65 The Doctor (Doctor Who), 21 64 Abdul Quader Molla, 22 64 Jacoby Ellsbury, 23 63 Phil Robertson, 24 60 Edward Snowden, 25 60 American Hustle

Jan 2014: 1 201 Deaths in 2014, 2 159 Early 2014 North American cold wave, 3 115 Ariel Sharon, 4 102 Super Bowl XLVIII, 5 92 Fort Lee lane closure scandal, 6 90 Royal Rumble (2014), 7 88 Frozen (2013 film), 8 86 The Wolf of Wall Street (2013 film), 9 86 Juan Mata, 10 **83 Euromaidan**, 11 82 56th Annual Grammy Awards, 12 79 2014 Winter Olympics, 13 78 2014 Australian Open, 14 **74 2014 Hrushevskoho Street riots**, 15 71 Justin Bieber, 16 71 2014, 17 67 James Avery (actor), 18 64 Richard Sherman (American football), 19 64 The Everly Brothers, 20 62 Chris Christie, 21 62 Pete Seeger, 22 61 Bitcoin, 23 60 Stan Wawrinka, 24 58 South Sudanese Civil War, 25 58 American Hustle

Feb 2014: 1 216 Philip Seymour Hoffman, 2 196 2014 Winter Olympics, 3 189 Deaths in 2014, 4 151 **2014 Ukrainian revolution**, 5 137 The Lego Movie, 6 131 Super Bowl XLVIII, 7 126 Flappy Bird, 8 121 Satya Nadella, 9 103 2014 Winter Olympics medal table, 10 **96 Euromaidan**, 11 **96 Ukraine**, 12 91 Shirley Temple,

13 84 Frozen (2013 film), 14 82 WhatsApp, 15 82 Harold Ramis, 16 81 Ice hockey at the 2014 Winter Olympics – Men's tournament, 17 **80 Viktor Yanukovych**, 18 79 Sochi, 19 75 2014 Winter Olympics opening ceremony, 20 72 Gunday, 21 72 Joaquín Guzmán, 22 67 2014–17 Venezuelan protests, 23 65 Twitch Plays Pokémon, 24 63 List of Bollywood films of 2014, 25 62 Winter Olympic Games

Mar 2014: 1 814 Malaysia Airlines Flight 370, 2 **410 2014 Crimean crisis**, 3 **235 Russian military intervention in Ukraine (2014–present)**, 4 195 Deaths in 2014, 5 **194 Crimean status referendum, 2014**, 6 **189 Autonomous Republic of Crimea**, 7 **155 Ukraine**, 8 **115 Republic of Crimea**, 9 **113 Republic of Crimea (country)**, 10 110 86th Academy Awards, 11 101 2014 ICC World Twenty20, 12 95 Fred Phelps, 13 **90 Sevastopol**, 14 89 2014 Kunming attack, 15 **89 2014 Ukrainian revolution**, 16 84 Frozen (2013 film), 17 83 Noah (2014 film), 18 **78 Russia**, 19 **76 Crimea**, 20 74 Lupita Nyong'o, 21 74 Group of Eight, 22 73 2014 NCAA Men's Division I Basketball Tournament, 23 72 300: Rise of an Empire, 24 71 Cosmos: A Spacetime Odyssey, 25 70 Eurovision Song Contest 2014

Apr 2014: 1 190 Heartbleed, 2 176 Deaths in 2014, 3 160 Sinking of MV Sewol, 4 160 Malaysia Airlines Flight 370, 5 **120 Donetsk People's Republic**, 6 112 Peaches Geldof, 7 110 Donald Sterling, 8 **108 2014 pro-Russian unrest in Ukraine**, 9 103 Bundy standoff, 10 97 WrestleMania XXX, 11 97 The Ultimate Warrior, 12 95 Extreme Rules (2014), 13 88 Indian general election, 2014, 14 **86 Ukraine**, 15 79 Captain America: The Winter Soldier, 16 79 The Amazing Spider-Man 2, 17 78 Mickey Rooney, 18 74 Pope John Paul II, 19 71 Narendra Modi, 20 69 Paige (wrestler), 21 69 Bitcoin, 22 **65 2014 Crimean crisis**, 23 64 Gabriel García Márquez, 24 62 Last Forever, 25 **59 Russian military intervention in Ukraine (2014–present)**

May 2014: 1 169 X-Men: Days of Future Past, 2 167 Godzilla (2014 film), 3 163 Deaths in 2014, 4 161 Eurovision Song Contest 2014, 5 159 2014 Isla Vista killings, 6 131 European Parliament election, 2014, 7 129 2014 FIFA World Cup squads, 8 122 Indian general election, 2014, 9 116 Narendra Modi, 10 **112 2014 pro-Russian unrest in Ukraine**, 11 106 2014 Southeast Europe floods, 12 98 The Amazing Spider-Man 2, 13 95 Xscape (album), 14 93 Soma mine disaster, 15 88 Frozen (2013 film), 16 84 2014 NFL Draft, 17 82 Watch Dogs, 18 80 Malaysia Airlines Flight 370, 19 79 Conchita Wurst, 20 79 Boko Haram, 21 **79 Ukraine**, 22 78 UK Independence Party, 23 77 Eurovision Song Contest 2015, 24 72 Chibok schoolgirls kidnapping, 25 **71 Petro Poroshenko**

Jun 2014: 1 317 2014 FIFA World Cup, 2 173 Islamic State of Iraq and the Levant, 3 166 Money in the Bank (2014), 4 164 Deaths in 2014, 5 163 Northern Iraq offensive (June 2014), 6 132 2014 FIFA World Cup squads, 7 122 Bowe Bergdahl, 8 122 Telangana, 9 110 Felipe VI of Spain, 10 106 Seth Rollins, 11 105 Rik Mayall, 12 98 The Fault in Our Stars (film), 13 94 Dave Brat, 14 **94 2014 pro-Russian unrest in Ukraine**, 15 93 Transformers: Age of Extinction, 16 91 Juan Carlos I of Spain, 17 90 Swift (programming language), 18 85 Casey Kasem, 19 84 Ultraviolence (album), 20 82 Edge of Tomorrow, 21 77 Luis Suárez, 22 75 Gopinath Munde, 23 75 Andhra Pradesh, 24 74 Maleficent (film), 25 72 Roman Reigns

Jul 2014: 1 **666 Malaysia Airlines Flight 17**, 2 378 2014 Israel–Gaza conflict, 3 193 Deaths in 2014, 4 171 2014 FIFA World Cup, 5 157 Brazil v Germany (2014 FIFA World Cup), 6 131 Air Algérie Flight 5017, 7 121 Germany national football team, 8 119 Brazil national football team, 9 116 2014 FIFA World Cup Final, 10 114 Dawn of the Planet of the Apes, 11 108 2014 kidnapping and murder of Israeli teenagers, 12 100 SummerSlam (2014), 13 99 Islamic State of Iraq and the Levant, 14 98 Kick (2014 film), 15 96 LeBron James, 16 93 West African Ebola virus epidemic, 17 93 Malaysia Airlines Flight 370, 18 92 Transformers: Age of Extinction, 19 **89 War in Donbas**, 20 86 2014 FIFA World Cup knockout stage, 21 84 Miroslav Klose, 22 83 Big Brother 16 (U.S.), 23 82 Nash Grier, 24 82 James Garner, 25 81 FIFA World Cup

Aug 2014: 1 357 Robin Williams, 2 273 Ice Bucket Challenge, 3 241 Shooting of Michael Brown, 4 229 West African Ebola virus epidemic, 5 220 2014 Israel–Gaza conflict, 6 195 Deaths in 2014, 7 184 Islamic State of Iraq and the Levant, 8 150 SummerSlam (2014), 9 136 Ebola virus disease, 10 121 James Foley (journalist), 11 115 Lauren Bacall, 12 **113 War in Donbas**, 13 113 Guardians of the Galaxy (film), 14 108 Yazidis, 15 98 Big Brother 16 (U.S.), 16 89 Anaconda (Nicki Minaj song), 17 89 **Malaysia Airlines Flight 17**, 18 83 Reflection (Fifth Harmony album), 19 80 Bang Bang (Jessie J, Ariana Grande and Nicki Minaj song), 20 79 Ferguson unrest, 21 79 Kick (2014 film), 22 78 Maryam Mirzakhani, 23 74 2014 MTV Video Music Awards, 24 73 FIFA 15, 25 73 Teenage Mutant Ninja Turtles (2014 film)

Ukrainian
Dec 2013: 1 **101 Євромайдан**, 2 **52 Тітушки**, 3 **28 Силовий розгін Євро-майдану в Києві**, 4 **26 Повалення пам'ятника Леніну в Києві**, 5 **23 Чорновол Тетяна Миколаївна**, 6 22 **Пам'ятник Леніну (Київ)**, 7 16 **Події біля Адмініс-трації Президента України 1 грудня 2013 року**, 8 **16 Хронологія та географія Євромайдану**, 9 **16 Беркут (спецпідрозділ)**, 10 **15 Корчинський Дмитро Олександрович**, 11 **14 Янукович Віктор Федорович**, 12 **13 Всеукраїнське об'єднання «Майдан»**, 13 **12 Антимайдан**, 14 12 Пол Вокер, 15 **11 Слісаренко Ігор Юрійович**, 16 **11 Євромайдан у регіонах України**, 17 **11 Список журналістів, побитих під час Євромайдану**, 18 11 Кепи, 19 **11 Чечетов Михайло Васильович (депутат приймав диктаторські закони у січні 2014)**, 20 11 Медведчук Віктор Володимирович, 21 10 Чебишев В'ячеслав Олексійович, 22 10 День святого Миколая, 23 **10 Азаров Микола Янович**, 24 10 **Україна**, 25 9 **Список пам'ятних знаків жертвам ОУН і УПА**

Jan 2014: 1 **58 Євромайдан**, 2 **42 Диктаторські закони 16 січня**, 3 **41 Протистояння на Грушевського**, 4 **32 Нігоян Сергій Гагікович**, 5 **22 Вербицький Юрій Тарасович (викрадений активіст Євромайдану)**, 6 **19 Про-тести в областях України у січні 2014**, 7 **18 Небесна сотня**, 8 **16 Жизневський Михайло Михайлович (активіст Майдану затриманий)**, 9 **15 Правий сек-тор**, 10 **15 Тітушки**, 11 **14 Бойкот Партії регіонів**, 12 **13 Беркут (спецпідрозділ)**, 13 **13 Кличко Віталій Володимирович**, 14 12 Список померлих 2014, 15 12 Радянська анексія західноукраїнських земель, 16 **11 Янукович Вік-тор Федорович**, 17 **10 Список затриманих і зниклих безвісти активістів Євромайдану**, 18 **10 Чорний четвер (Україна)**, 19 10 Погляди Тараса Шевченка щодо релігії, 20 10 Шевченко Тарас Григорович, 21 **10 Україна**, 22 9 **Булатов Дмитро Сергійович**, 23 **9 Репресії проти Євромайдану**, 24 9 Кепи, 25 **9 Чорновол Тетяна Миколаївна**

Feb 2014: 1 **96 Небесна сотня**, 2 **48 Євромайдан**, 3 **46 Ленінопад**, 4 **46 Янукович Віктор Федорович**, 5 44 **Протистояння в Україні 18—21 лютого 2014 року**, 6 **21 Бойкот Партії регіонів**, 7 **20 Беркут (спецпідрозділ)**, 8 **20 Турчинов Олександр Валентинович**, 9 **20 Яценюк Арсеній Петрович**, 10 **17 Костенко Ігор Ігорович**, 11 **17 Самооборона Майдану**, 12 17 Зимові Олімпійські ігри 2014, 13 16 **Вибори Президента України 2014**, 14 **15 Тітушки**, 15 **14 Революція гідності**, 16 **14 Україна**, 17 **13 Булатов Дмитро Сергійович**, 18 **13 Тимошенко Юлія Володимирівна**, 19 **12 Список загиблих силовиків під час Євромайдану**, 20 12 Таблиця медалей зимових Олімпійських ігор 2014, 21 **12 Захарченко Віталій Юрійович**, 22 12 Майкон Перейра ді Олівейра, 23 **12 Аваков Арсен Борисович**, 24 **11 Парасюк Володимир Зіновійович**, 25 11 Сольчаник Богдан Зіновійович

Mar 2014: 1 **67 Російська інтервенція до Криму (2014)**, 2 **49 Кримська криза**, 3 **32 Небесна сотня**, 4 **30 Автономна Республіка Крим**, 5 **29 Євромайдан**, 6 **26 Республіка Крим**, 7 **23 Музичко Олександр Іванович (Правий Сектор)**, 8 **23 Янукович Віктор Федорович**, 9 **22 Референдум про статус Криму 2014**, 10 **21 Березовський Денис Валентинович (український військовий в Криму, перейшов на бік Росії)**, 11 **21 Вибори Президента України 2014**, 12 **19 Правий сектор**, 13 **16 Рашизм**, 14 **16 Аксьонов Сергій Валерійович**, 15 **16 Стрілкове (місце вторгнення російський військ в Крим)**, 16 16 Вітовт, 17 16 Шевченко Тарас Григорович, 18 **15 Севастополь**, 19 **15 Україна**, 20 14 Коваль Михайло Володимирович, 21 **14 Ленінопад**, 22 **14 Путін Володимир Володимирович**, 23 **14 Росія**, 24 **13 Угода про асоціацію між Україною та Європейським Союзом**, 25 13 Фірташ Дмитро Васильович

Apr 2014: 1 **36 Війна на сході України**, 2 **30 Путін Володимир Володимирович**, 3 **20 Проросійські виступи в Україні 2014**, 4 **19 Вибори Президента України 2014**, 5 **18 Небесна сотня**, 6 **18 Російська інтервенція до Криму (2014)**, 7 **17 Анексія Криму Росією (2014)**, 8 **17 Євромайдан**, 9 **17 Янукович Віктор Федорович**, 10 **16 Автономна Республіка Крим**, 11 15 OROCHI, 12 14 GOTHIKA, 13 **13 Царьов Олег Анатолійович**, 14 **13 Турчинов Олександр Валентинович**, 15 **13 Тимошенко Юлія Володимирівна**, 16 12 Візитка Яроша, 17 **12 Богомолець Ольга Вадимівна**, 18 **12 Україна**, 19 11 Weua.info, 20 **11 Аксьонов Сергій Валерійович**, 21 **11 Мустафа Джемілєв (голова Меджелісу Криму)**, 22 11 Габрієль Гарсія Маркес, 23 **10 Кримська криза**, 24 10 Фірташ Дмитро Васильович, 25 **10 Республіка Крим**

May 2014: 1 **49 Вибори Президента України 2014**, 2 **42 Донецька народна республіка**, 3 **26 Війна на сході України**, 4 **24 Порошенко Петро Олексійович**, 5 **21 Протистояння в Одесі 2 травня 2014**, 6 **21 Жертви російського вторгнення в Україну 2014—2016 років**, 7 **20 Проросійські виступи в Україні 2014**, 8 **18 Референдуми на Донеччині та Луганщині 2014**, 9 **18 Путін Володимир Володимирович**, 10 **16 Небесна сотня**, 11 16 Пісенний конкурс Євробачення 2014, 12 **15 Кульчицький Сергій Петрович**, 13 **15 Російська інтервенція до Криму (2014)**, 14 **14 Луганська народна республіка**, 15 **14 Гіркін Ігор Всеволодович**, 16 **13 Новоросія (конфедерація)**, 17 **13 Тимошенко Юлія Володимирівна**, 18 12 Георгіївська стрічка, 19 **11 Анексія Криму Росією (2014)**, 20 **11 Ленінопад**, 21 **11 Республіка Крим**, 22 10 Модель вільних електронів,

23 10 Футбольний матч Росія — Україна (1999), 24 10 Weua.info, 25 **10 Референдум про статус Криму 2014**

Jun 2014: 1 **46 Війна на сході України**, 2 **39 Путін — хуйло!**, 3 28 Чемпіонат світу з футболу 2014, 4 **24 Порошенко Петро Олексійович**, 5 **21 Проросійські виступи в Україні 2014**, 6 **17 Збиття Іл-76 у Луганську**, 7 **17 Жертви російського вторгнення в Україну 2014—2016 років**, 8 **17 Російська інтервенція до Криму (2014)**, 9 **17 Дещиця Андрій Богданович**, 10 16 Гонтарева Валерія Олексіївна, 11 **16 Втрати силових структур внаслідок російського вторгнення в Україну**, 12 **16 Луганська народна республіка**, 13 16 Плющ Іван Степанович, 14 **15 2-й батальйон спеціального призначення НГУ «Донбас»**, 15 **14 Небесна сотня**, 16 **14 Донецька народна республіка**, 17 **13 24-й окремий штурмовий батальйон «Айдар»**, 18 13 Спеціальна поліція Нацполіції України, 19 **13 Путін Володимир Володимирович**, 20 **13 Кличко Віталій Володимирович**, 21 13 Україна, 22 **12 Кульчицький Сергій Петрович**, 23 **12 Російсько-українські війни**, 24 **12 Турчинов Олександр Валентинович**, 25 12 Європейський Союз

Jul 2014: 1 **56 Збиття Boeing 777 біля Донецька**, 2 **48 Війна на сході України**, 3 **30 Втрати силових структур внаслідок російського вторгнення в Україну**, 4 **28 Путін — хуйло!**, 5 **22 24-й окремий штурмовий батальйон «Айдар»**, 6 **22 Путін Володимир Володимирович**, 7 **21 Російська інтервенція до Криму (2014)**, 8 **20 Російська збройна агресія проти України (2014—2017)**, 9 **18 Донецька народна республіка**, 10 18 Чемпіонат світу з футболу 2014, 11 **17 Небесна сотня**, 12 **15 Новоросія (конфедерація)**, 13 **15 Гелетей Валерій Вікторович**, 14 **14 Луганська народна республіка**, 15 12 Юп Ланге, 16 **12 Семенченко Семен Ігорович**, 17 **12 2-й батальйон спеціального призначення НГУ «Донбас»**, 18 **12 Протистояння у Слов'янську 2014 року**, 19 **12 Су-25**, 20 12 Новодворська Валерія Іллівна, 21 **12 Савур-могила**, 22 **11 Референдуми на Донеччині та Луганщині 2014**, 23 **11 Російська пропаганда**, 24 **11 Ленінопад**, 25 11 Мальтійські конвої

Aug 2014: 1 **49 Війна на сході України**, 2 **36 Втрати силових структур внаслідок російського вторгнення в Україну**, 3 **20 Ленінопад**, 4 **18 Російська збройна агресія проти України (2014—2017)**, 5 **17 Громадяни Російської Федерації, що загинули внаслідок російського вторгнення в Україну (2014)**, 6 17 Онуфрій (Березовський), 7 **16 Збиття Boeing 777 біля Донецька**, 8 **15 24-й окремий штурмовий батальйон «Айдар»**, 9 **13 Путін — хуйло!**, 10 **13 Міхнюк Олег Іванович**, 11 13 Робін Вільямс, 12 **12 Добровольчий український корпус**, 13 12 Ukraine Today, 14 11 Белькевич Валентин Миколайович, 15 10 Кубок України з футболу 2014—2015, 16 **10 Ватник (сленг)**, 17 **10 Анексія Криму Росією (2014)**, 18 **10 Костенко Ігор Ігорович**, 19 9 Савченко Надія Вікторівна, 20 **9 Хронологія війни на сході України (квітень-червень 2014)**, 21 **9 Парламентські вибори в Україні 2014**, 22 **9 Ватник**, 23 **9 Сухопутні війська Збройних Сил України**, 24 **9 Іловайськ**, 25 **9 Ясинувата (бої за Ясинувату)**

References

1. Shirky, C.: Cognitive Surplus: Creativity and Generosity in a Connected Age. Penguin Books, New York (2010)
2. Levy, P.: The creative conversation of collective intelligence. In: Delwiche, A., Henderson, J. (eds.) The Participation of Culture Handbook, pp. 99–108. Routledge, London (2013)
3. Baytiyeh, H., Pfaffman, J.: Volunteers in Wikipedia: why the community matters. J. Educ. Technol. Soc. **13**, 128–140 (2010)
4. Halavais, A., Lackaff, D.: An analysis of topical coverage of Wikipedia. J. Comput. Commun. **13**, 429–440 (2008). doi:10.1111/j.1083-6101.2008.00403.x
5. Stvilia, B., Twidale, M., Gasser, L., Smith, L.: Information quality discussions in Wikipedia. In: Knowledge Management: Nurturing Culture, Innovation, and Technology - Proceedings of the 2005 International Conference on Knowledge Management, pp. 101–113. Graduate School of Library and Information science, University of Illinois at Urbana-Champaign, Urbana, IL (2005)
6. Kuznetsov, S.: Motivations of contributors to Wikipedia. SIGCAS Comput. Soc. **36**(2) (2006). doi:10.1145/1215942.1215943
7. Brown, A.R.: Wikipedia as a data source for political scientists: accuracy and completeness of coverage. PS Polit. Sci. Polit. **44**, 339–343 (2011). doi:10.1017/S1049096511000199
8. Greenstein, S., Zhu, F.: Is Wikipedia biased? Am. Econ. Rev. **102**, 343–348 (2012)
9. Adler, B.T., De Alfaro, L., Pye, I.: Detecting Wikipedia vandalism using WikiTrust: lab report for PAN at CLEF 2010. In: CEUR Workshop Proceedings (2010)
10. Chang, T., Lin, H., Lin, Y.: Feature transformation method enhanced vandalism detection in Wikipedia (2012)
11. Tang, X., Zhou, G., Fu, Y., Gan, L., Yu, W., Li, S.: Detecting Wikipedia vandalism with a contributing efficiency-based approach (2012)
12. Alfonseca, E., Garrido, G., Delort, J.-Y., Peñas, A.: WHAD: Wikipedia historical attributes data: historical structured data extraction and vandalism detection from the Wikipedia edit history. Lang. Resour. Eval. **47**, 1163–1190 (2013)
13. Heindorf, S., Potthast, M., Stein, B., Engels, G.: Vandalism detection in Wikidata. In: Proceedings of the International Conference on Information and Knowledge Management, pp. 327–336 (2016)
14. Sepehri Rad, H., Barbosa, D.: Towards identifying arguments in Wikipedia pages. In: Proceedings of the 20th International Conference Companion on World Wide Web, WWW 2011 (2011)
15. Kittur, A., Suh, B., Pendleton, B.A., Chi, E.H.: He says, she says: conflict and coordination in Wikipedia. In: Proceedings of the International Conference on Human Factors in Computing Systems (2007)
16. Yasseri, T., Sumi, R., Rung, A., Kornai, A., Kertész, J.: Dynamics of conflicts in Wikipedia. PLoS ONE **7**, e38869 (2012). doi:10.1371/journal.pone.0038869
17. Gandica, Y., Sampaio Dos Aidos, F., Carvalho, J.: The dynamic nature of conflict in Wikipedia. EPL. **108**, 1–6 (2014). doi:10.1209/0295-5075/108/18003
18. Sepehri-Rad, H., Barbosa, D.: Identifying controversial Wikipedia articles using editor collaboration networks. ACM Trans. Intell. Syst. Technol. **6**, 1–24 (2015). doi:10.1145/2630075
19. Kalyanasundaram, A., Wei, W., Carley, K.M., Herbsleb, J.D.: An agent-based model of edit wars in Wikipedia: how and when is consensus reached. In: Proceedings of the Winter Simulation Conference (2016)

20. DeDeo, S.: Conflict and computation on Wikipedia: a finite-state machine analysis of editor interactions. Futur. Internet. **8**, 31 (2016). doi:10.3390/fi8030031
21. Jankowski-Lorek, M., Nielek, R., Wierzbicki, A., Zieliński, K.: Predicting controversy of Wikipedia articles using the article feedback tool. In: ACM International Conference Proceeding Series (2014)
22. Brandes, U., Lerner, J.: Is editing more rewarding than discussion? A statistical framework to estimate causes of dropout from Wikipedia. In: Proceedings of the 1st International Workshop on Motivation and Incentives on the Web, Webcentives 2009, co-located with WWW 2009, Innsbruck (2009)
23. Sumi, R., Yasseri, T., Rung, A., Kornai, A., Kertesz, J.: Edit wars in Wikipedia. In: Proceedings of the 2011 IEEE International Conference on Privacy, Security, Risk and Trust and IEEE International Conference on Social Computing, PASSAT/SocialCom 2011 (2011)
24. Borra, E., Kaltenbrunner, A., Mauri, M., Weltevrede, E., Laniado, D., Rogers, R., Ciuccarelli, P., Magni, G., Venturini, T.: Societal controversies in Wikipedia articles. In: Proceedings of the International Conference on Human Factors in Computing Systems (2015)
25. Bykau, S., Korn, F., Srivastava, D., Velegrakis, Y.: Fine-grained controversy detection in Wikipedia. In: Proceedings of the International Conference on Data Engineering (2015)
26. Li, H., Ma, J.: A novel method for identifying controversial contents of Wikipedia articles based on revision history. J. Comput. Inf. Syst. **11**, 5697–5707 (2015). http://or.nsfc.gov.cn/bitstream/00001903-5/354778/1/1000014423263.pdf
27. Rudas, C., Surányi, O., Yasseri, T., Török, J.: Understanding and coping with extremism in an online collaborative environment: a data-driven modeling. PLoS ONE **12**, e0173561 (2017). doi:10.1371/journal.pone.0173561
28. Jurgens, D., Lu, T.: Temporal motifs reveal the dynamics of editor interactions in Wikipedia. In: Breslin, J.G., Ellison, N.B., Shanahan, J.G., Tufekci, Z. (eds.) ICWSM. The AAAI Press (2012)
29. Jang, M., Allan, J.: Improving automated controversy detection on the web. In: SIGIR 2016 - Proceedings of the 39th International ACM SIGIR Conference on Research and Development in Information Retrieval (2016)
30. Sepehri Rad, H., Makazhanov, A., Rafiei, D., Barbosa, D.: Leveraging editor collaboration patterns in Wikipedia. In: Proceedings of the 23rd ACM Conference on Hypertext and Social Media, pp. 13–22. ACM, New York (2012)
31. Rad, H.S., Barbosa, D.: Identifying controversial articles in Wikipedia: a comparative study. In: WikiSym 2012 Conference Proceedings - 8th Annual International Symposium on Wikis and Open Collaboration (2012)
32. Ghimpu, A.-G.: New media and the knowledge management: The Wikipedia project. Philobiblon, XIX, pp. 357–366 (2014)
33. Sun, D., Park, S., Jung, H.: Knowledge management using Wikipedia. In: CEUR Workshop Proceedings (2009)
34. Hepp, M., Siorpaes, K., Bachlechner, D.: Harvesting wiki consensus: using Wikipedia entries as vocabulary for knowledge management. IEEE Internet Comput. **11**, 54–65 (2007). doi:10.1109/MIC.2007.110
35. Yang, H.-L., Lai, C.-Y.: Understanding knowledge-sharing behaviour in Wikipedia. Behav. Inf. Technol. **30**, 131–142 (2011). doi:10.1080/0144929X.2010.516019
36. Niederer, S., van Dijck, J.: Wisdom of the crowd or technicity of content? Wikipedia as a sociotechnical system. New Media Soc. **12**, 1368–1387 (2010). doi:10.1177/1461444810365297
37. Wagner, C.: Wiki: a technology for conversational knowledge management and group collaboration. Commun. Assoc. Inf. Syst. **13**, 265–289 (2004)

38. Bonabeau, E.: Decisions 2.0: the power of collective intelligence. MIT Sloan Manag. Rev. **50**, 45–52 (2009)
39. Kittur, A., Lee, B., Kraut, R.E.: Coordination in collective intelligence: the role of team structure and task interdependence. In: Proceedings of the SIGCHI Conference on Human Factors in Computing Systems, pp. 1495–1504. ACM, New York (2009)
40. Oren, E., Völkel, M., Breslin, J.G., Decker, S.: Semantic wikis for personal knowledge management. In: Bressan, S., Küng, J., Wagner, R. (eds.) DEXA 2006. LNCS, vol. 4080, pp. 509–518. Springer, Heidelberg (2006). doi:10.1007/11827405_50
41. Lévy, P.: Collective Intelligence: Mankind's Emerging World in Cyberspace. Persus Books, Cambridge (1997)
42. Dounaevsky, H.: Building wiki history: between consensus and edit-warring. In: Rutten, E., Zvereva, V. (eds.) Memory, Conflict and New Media: Web Wars in Post-Socialist States, pp. 130–142. Routledge, London (2013)

I Read It on Reddit: Exploring the Role of Online Communities in the 2016 US Elections News Cycle

Jon Roozenbeek[1($\boxtimes$)] and Adrià Salvador Palau[2]

[1] Department of Slavonic Studies, Faculty of Modern and Medieval Languages, University of Cambridge, Cambridge CB39DA, UK
jjr51@cam.ac.uk
[2] Department of Engineering, Institute for Manufacturing, University of Cambridge, Cambridge CB30FS, UK

Abstract. Reddit has developed into a significant platform for political discussion among Millennials. In this exploratory study, we examine subscription trends on three political sub-forums on Reddit during the 2016 US presidential elections: /The_Donald, /SandersForPresident, and /HillaryClinton. As a theoretical framework, we draw from work on online communities' group identity and cohesion. Concretely, we investigate how subscription dynamics relate to positive, negative and neutral news events occurring during the election cycle. We classify news events using a sentiment analysis of event-related news headlines. We observe that users who supported Sanders displayed no consolidation of support for Clinton after she won the Democratic Party's presidential nomination. Secondly, we show that negative news events affected Sanders and Clintons subscription trends negatively, while showing no effect for Donald Trump. This gives empirical credence to Trump's controversial claim that he could "stand in the middle of 5th Avenue and shoot somebody and not lose any voters". We offer a number of explanations for the observed phenomena: the nature of the content of the three subreddits, their cultural dynamics, and changing dynamics of partisanship. We posit that the 'death of expertise' expresses itself on Reddit as a switch in persuasion tactics from a policy-based to an emotions-based approach, and that group members' agreement on policy proved a weak marker for online communities' group identity and cohesion. We also claim that strong partisanship coupled with weak party affiliation among Millennials contributed to the low levels of Democratic support consolidation after Clinton won the nomination.

Keywords: Electoral politics · US elections 2016 · Social media · Reddit · Millennial generation

1 Introduction

Since Donald Trump's electoral victory in the US presidential elections on November 8 of 2016, many have sought to explain Secretary of State

© Springer International Publishing AG 2017
G.L. Ciampaglia et al. (Eds.): SocInfo 2017, Part II, LNCS 10540, pp. 192–220, 2017.
DOI: 10.1007/978-3-319-67256-4_16

Hillary Clinton's loss to Donald Trump, as well as the insurgent candidacy of Senator Bernie Sanders during the Democratic primaries [7,11,13,39]. In 2016, the Millennial generation (people born between 1981 and 1997) was seen as a crucial demographic by Republican as well as Democratic party strategists [46], even more so than in the 2008 and 2012 elections [14,34]. In order to attract these Millennials, campaigns have actively engaged with young voters through social media activity such as Facebook, Twitter and Instagram [12,27].

This has prompted scholars of political communication and electoral campaigns to focus on the growing role of social media in US elections. Pancer and Maxwell [50] look at what kinds of political messages are shared on social media during the 2016 elections. Lee and Lim [37] investigate the differences in the ways Trump and Clinton communicated with their supporters on social media. Alashri et al. [2] look at Facebook dynamics, and specifically commentator sentiments with regards to candidates' social media engagement. Hu et al. [29] employ a similar approach for user sentiments on Twitter. Effing et al. [24] show that politicians with higher social media engagement received more preference votes within their political parties. Groshek and Koc-Michalska [28] explore if social media use was linked to increased support for 'populist' candidates Bernie Sanders and Donald Trump. Their findings suggest that political social media use was linked to less support for Republican candidates, including Trump, but to more support for Sanders. In terms of the methodology used in these and similar studies, social network analytics and big data continue to provide insight into this interplay between the youngest voting generation, political campaigns, and online media [41,43].

Facebook and Twitter have received the bulk of attention in the above-mentioned studies. However, other social media outlets are increasingly asserting themselves as hubs of political engagement. One such platform is Reddit (www.Reddit.com), a social news aggregation and discussion site. The site is divided into sub-fora, commonly called 'subreddits'. On these subreddits, users discuss topics that can range from music, film and politics to sex, practical advice and product reviews. During the 2016 presidential election cycle, several candidates actively used Reddit in their campaign strategy; for example, both Bernie Sanders and Donald Trump held 'Ask me Anything'-sessions on the site, during which Reddit users could pose questions directly to them. As such, Reddit has become an important political platform where mostly young voters exchange ideas and events, raise funds for candidates, and work out strategies. Its role in the 2016 US presidential elections, however, has thus far remained unexplored by scholars.

In this study, we look at subreddit subscription trends for three subreddits dedicated to three 2016 presidential candidates: /The_Donald (Donald Trump), /SandersForPresident (Bernie Sanders), and /HillaryClinton. These three subreddits were by far the most popular out of all presidential candidates, with approximately 366.000, 215.000 and 40.000 subscribers, respectively, as of January 15, 2017. There are several reasons why we chose to focus on subscription dynamics and not content or traffic numbers. First of all, all three subreddits have a policy of allowing only subscribers to place comments. Furthermore, they only allow actual supporters to write posts, and ban or remove users who post content critical of the candidate. In addition, both /The_Donald and /HillaryClinton have hidden the downvote-buttons by means of a skin, which means that even subscribers would find it hard to vote down a particular thread. Therefore, especially for Trump's and Clinton's subreddits, we assume that most subscribers are actually supporters of the candidate, as there is no rationale to subscribe from a non-supporter point of view. We extend this assumption to /SandersForPresident. Traffic numbers, on the other hand, also include non-subscribing visitors, who may or may not support a candidate. Second, we do not quantitatively analyse the content of the posts, although we do cite illustrative examples in Sect. 4. The reason for this is that the number of active Reddit users (defined as people who post three or more posts on a given subreddit) is disproportionately low compared to the number of visitors: approximately 6 in 10 Reddit users who posted at least one comment only posted *one* comment, and only a quarter of commenters posted three or more comments in total. This means that the level of active participation is quite low, but passive participation among subscribers (meaning reading but not commenting) can be very high [8]. Thus, subscription dynamics are the most effective way of mapping not only active, but also passive participation, while at the same time staying confined within the body of Reddit users that can be seen as actual supporters rather than visitors.

Our study is the first to marry Reddit subscription dynamics with news events occurring during electoral campaigns. To do so, we run a sentiment analysis algorithm to establish the average polarity of headlines on 3 major news outlets. This allows us to classify events as positive, neutral or negative for a particular candidate.

We place our study within the theoretical framework of online group identity and cohesion [51]. The difference in definition between these two concepts is that group cohesion is defined as how much group members like the other individuals in the group, whereas group identity refers to how much group members like the group's purpose. This framework predicts that the ability of an online community to keep its members together and grow larger is dependent on fostering members' interdependence, social interactions and interpersonal attraction. Furthermore, intergroup comparisons, social categorisation and setting common goals are key factors in determining the strength of an online community. In this paper, we consider the three subreddits as separate online communities. In terms of theoretical development, we study how communities interact with a relevant news cycle, and what factors determine any observed differences in the reception of positive and negative news.

Concretely, we ask the following research questions: First, to which extent does the positivity or negativity of news events affect Reddit subscription dynamics? Second, what differences can we discern among the three candidates' subreddits? Third, how do we explain the observed differences? And fourth, how can these observations be placed within the context of the role of social media in electoral campaigns?

Answering these questions enables researchers as well as analysts working for electoral campaigns to investigate which types of news events resonate with social media users, and gain insight into how online political communities operate. Additionally, this opens up opportunities to build a more general framework on how news cycles and social media affect one another.

2   Methods

This paper's data set consists of two main components: Reddit visitor and subscriber metrics, and a list of news events relevant during the 2016 US elections. In this section, we describe the methodology used in order to analyse the visitor and subscriber trends, and to classify the news events. Additionally, we discuss Reddit demographics as a proxy for broader political trends among Millennials.

2.1   Visitor Trends

The primary data set consists of monthly visitor and daily subscriber numbers for /SandersForPresident, /The_Donald, and /HillaryClinton. It covers the period between the announcement of Bernie Sanders' presidential campaign on April 30th, 2015, and November 9th, 2016, the day after the elections. This data was provided by a Reddit administrator team upon request by the authors, and complemented with data from www.redditmetrics.com

We define two inter-related indicators; subscriber growth, or ΔS and accumulated subscribers, $S(T)$. Their relation can be simply stated as follows:

$$S(T) = \sum_{t=0}^{N(T)} \Delta S_t. \tag{1}$$

where $t = 0$ corresponds to the date when the subreddit was created and $N(T)$ to the number of days until the time T. Note that ΔS_t can be both positive (subscriber increase) or negative (subscriber loss).

The reason for using subscriber metrics and not page views, comments or other indicators, is discussed in Sect. 2.4.

The ideal indicator of the relation between subreddit subscription and subscriber support would be individual user subscription data. Unfortunately, such data is not available, since Reddit does not keep track of it. Therefore subscriber indicators remain the best available metrics for Reddit user support.

2.2   News Event Classification

In order to analyse the relation between news events occurring during the 2016 election campaign and subscriber variations on Reddit, we look at the association between positive, neutral and negative news events and subscriber trends. The list with these events was compiled using different timelines of the 2016 primary and general elections that are available online [5, 26, 36, 64].

We selected those news events that were of direct political relevance to the election (such as primary elections, debates, party conventions, candidates' speeches, et cetera) or particularly newsworthy otherwise (such as terrorist attacks and political scandals). We have allowed for a deviation from the day of the news event by one day; for example, a traffic bounce that occurs one day before or after a party convention is considered to be associated with this convention. In case of unplanned or unpredictable events, the previous days are not considered.

Our method for determining if a news event is positive, negative or neutral relies primarily on a sentiment analysis of the headlines on these events on 3 major news outlets. For this, we used TextBlob, an open-source pre-trained Python library for processing natural language. We extracted the headlines for articles about each event in our data set from the New York Times, CNN and Wall Street Journal websites. These outlets were chosen based on their audiences' place on the ideological spectrum: according to a Pew Research survey from 2014, the New York Times' audience is predominantly somewhat liberal, CNN's is rather in the centre, and the Wall Street Journal's audience leans somewhat to the right [10].

By drawing from ideologically diverse sources, we sought to eliminate the possibility of a consistent ideological slant in the sentiment analysis sample as much as possible. In cases where there was more than one article per website about an event, we chose only one. We also disregarded any op-eds and editorials. Next, we ran Textblob's 'sentiment'-property over the three headlines to return an average event polarity between -1 and 1. We classified a polarity between -1 and -0.15 as a negative event; between -0.15 and $.15$ as a neutral event; and between 0.15 and 1 as a positive event.

Sentiment analysis, however, has its limitations. For example, Ted Cruz winning the Iowa primary is rather obviously a negative event for Donald Trump. Nonetheless, the algorithm returns a positive value, because the headlines in our data set emphasise Cruz' victory rather than Trump's loss. In order to smooth out such discrepancies, we therefore compared the sentiment analysis polarities to our independent classification. We individually classified each event as positive, negative or neutral to each candidate, and then compared our answers. In case a difference occurred, we discussed it and settled on a compromise.

After this, we compared the sentiment analysis classification to our own. In the majority of cases, the two overlapped. In cases such as the one mentioned above, where the algorithm is unambiguously wrong, we went with our classification. In all other cases, we gave the benefit of the doubt to the algorithm.

The full list of positively, negatively and neutrally classified news events can be found in the Appendix A.

In order to quantify the influence of news events on traffic and subscriber dynamics, we perform a linear fit with dummy nominal variables. We compare two equations, first a simple model for news events in general:

$$\Delta S = \beta_1 n + k. \tag{2}$$

Where ΔS is the total subscriber change, β_1 is the slope of the fit and k is the intercept. n is a dummy nominal variable, in other words, n is 1 when a relevant news event occurs and 0 when it does not. The standard error of the fit and the adjusted R^2 will give us an estimate of the predictive power of news events.

We compare this with a model that takes into account news categorised as positive and negative:

$$\Delta S = \beta_+ n_+ + \beta_- n_- + \gamma. \tag{3}$$

Where ΔS is the total subscriber change, β_+ is the slope related to positive news events and β_- the slope related to negative news events. n_+ and n_- are set to 0 except in the case when a positive or negative news event occurs in which they are correspondingly set to 1. γ is the intercept. The fits were all performed using the fitlm-function of the MATLAB mathematical computing software.

2.3   Reddit Demographics

We argue that Reddit's demographic make-up makes it a decent proxy for the Millennial population in the United States. There are three reports available on Reddit user demographics: a SurveyMonkey poll, a PingDom.com survey, and a Pew Research report. Their conclusions can be found in Fig. 4. This is a fairly limited data set, and it comes with a few caveats.

First, according to US census data, 61.6% of Americans consider themselves white, 17.6% non-white Hispanic, 13.3% black, 5.8% Asian or Pacific Islander, and 1.2% Native American. However, whereas Hispanics comprise 17.6% of the total US population [63], they form 24.4% of the population under 18 years of age [16]. The age pyramid for minorities in the US (particularly for Hispanics) is therefore skewed towards young people more so than for whites [19]. Since young people are more likely to use Reddit, it is possible that there is a certain amount of over-representation of Hispanics among US Reddit users. This, however, cannot be said for sure.

Furthermore, in terms of education levels, 9% of the Pew Research report's respondents without a high school diploma reported to use Reddit (n = 99), more than those with a college degree (7%, n = 79), some college education (6%, n = 517) and a high school degree (4%, n = 473). The finding by Pew Research that non-high school graduates are the most likely to use Reddit is rather counter-intuitive (Fig. 4). Considering especially the small number of non-high school graduates in the sample, this should be seen as statistically suspicious.

Overall, the available surveys indicate that Reddit demographics are not fully representative of the US Millennial population as a whole. The website's user base somewhat skewed towards male, white, English-speaking users, although there are a few issues of statistical reliability and a lack of available data that make it difficult to state this definitively. In terms of ethnic origin, the only demographic within the US which can be safely assumed to be underrepresented in Reddit's user base is the black population; it is possible that whites and Asians are overrepresented on Reddit, but this cannot be said for sure. It is important to bear this imbalance in mind when using Reddit data to draw broader conclusions about Millennial political involvement.

Nonetheless, despite this somewhat skewed sample, Reddit's user base is certainly young and to a large extent politically engaged. Furthermore, considering the popularity of the platform and the growing relevance of online communities and social media in political campaigning [24,33,55], using Reddit could offer a new route to understanding Millennial online political participation.

2.4 Limitations

There are a number of limitations to our approach. First, we only look at one social media platform that is not used by a very large share of the US population. Therefore, drawing general conclusions about the 2016 elections should be done with care. Furthermore, as was mentioned above, Reddit as a platform is not fully representative of the US Millennial population. Therefore, the data set is not to be seen as a representative sample of Millennials in general. Nonetheless, the trends observed can be to some extent indicative of broader sentiments among members of this group, once the demographic differences are weighted. Furthermore, since social media plays an important role in modern election campaigns, the dynamics and trends visible within social media hubs are increasingly likely to reflect broader electoral dynamics, and as such are of value to researchers, campaign managers, and so on.

Second, our sentiment analysis does not measure audiences' perception of headlines or events. This is a common limitation for sentiment analysis [38]. Without looking at how individual Reddit users received and internalised a particular event and aggregating this data, it is difficult to draw firm conclusions about how news events affect group identity and candidates' levels of support. We nonetheless maintain that there is a measurable difference in the effects of positive and negative headlines that can inform substantial analysis.

Third, we limit ourselves mainly to subscription dynamics, which (as discussed above) we argue is the best available proxy for measuring true support for a candidate. However, there is a significant degree of active user overlap between /SandersForPresident and /HillaryClinton. We analysed this using the Reddit Subreddit Similarity and Algebra-tool developed by Trevor Martin at Short Tails [42]. Both subreddits have a subreddit similarity scoring (calculated as the cosine distance between positive pointwise mutual information vectors) of 0,74 (it is much lower for /The_Donald). This indicates that a significant number of active commenters were active on both threads. However, as we previously discussed, the number of active users on Reddit is low compared to the total number of subscribers. Furthermore, it is important to acknowledge the difference in total number of subscribers between /SandersForPresident and /HillaryClinton. Nonetheless, we should be careful in our analysis to take this overlap into account.

3 Results

The accumulated subscriber data set against time can be divided into three different consecutive periods (see Fig. 1).

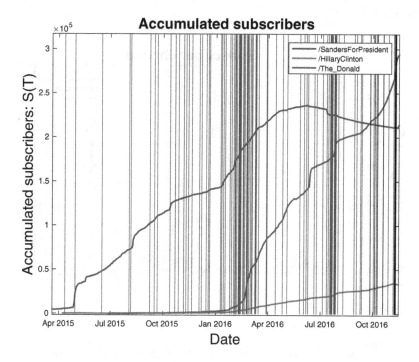

Fig. 1. Accumulated subscribers $S(T)$ per subreddit. The blue line shows the total number of subscribers for /SandersForPresident, the red line for /The_Donald and the pink line for /HillaryClinton. The vertical lines indicate relevant news events. Blue lines represent events mostly related to the Democratic candidates, and red lines to their Republican counterparts. Black lines are events that were classified as affecting both equally. The vertical axis is given in scientific notation. (Color figure online)

The first period, between May 2015 and January 4th, 2016, is characterised by /HillaryClinton and /The_Donald being stagnant at low subscription rates and /SandersForPresident growing linearly. The second period, between January 2016 and 20th of February 2016, shows a strong growth of /The_Donald, coupled with /SandersForPresident maintaining an even higher growth rate than before, and /HillaryClinton growing at a much smaller pace. Finally, the third period, starting on the 20th of February 2016, consists of a decline in the growth of /SandersForPresident from its peak value of 236745 subscribers. In the same period /The_Donald overcomes /SandersForPresident between the 24th and 25th of September 2016. /HillaryClinton follows roughly the same ascending trend during the second and third period. Sanders was the most popular candidate among Reddit users up until February 2016, when the total amount of views on The Donald first exceeded those on SandersForPresident (the total amount of subscribers for The Donald only first exceeded those on SandersForPresident in September 2016).

Second, subscriber change can be divided into the same three consecutive periods (see Fig. 2).

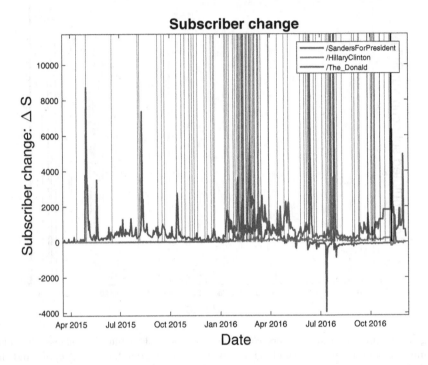

Fig. 2. Subscriber change, ΔS, per subreddit. The blue line shows the subscriber change for /SandersForPresident, the red line for /The_Donald and the pink line for /HillaryClinton. The vertical lines show relevant news events. Blue lines represent events mostly related to the Democratic candidates, and red lines to their Republican counterparts. Black lines are events that were classified as affecting both equally. (Color figure online)

The average daily subscriber change within the first period was of 16.1 ± 22.6 for /The_Donald, 4.8 ± 4.6 for /HillaryClinton and 186.9 ± 562.8 for /SandersForPresident. It must be noted that the values of the standard deviations are high, indicating strong variability. For the second period, the average daily subscriber change increases for all subreddits: 297.8 ± 342 for /The_Donald, 64.9 ± 48.5 for /HillaryClinton and 1011.2 ± 727.5 for /SandersForPresident. In the third period, we see an abrupt decrease in the average growth of /SandersForPresident, which shows an average of 83.4 ± 447.5, while the other two subreddits witness an increase. /HillaryClinton has an average subscriber growth of 100.3 ± 95.73

and /The_Donald has an average of 1035.9 ± 1212.1. In reality, these standard deviations must not be treated under the typical Gaussian assumption, as the subscriber change rarely hits negative values and the variables do not seem to conform to any stable probability distribution. The standard deviation here stands simply as a measure of the sample variance, with no further assumption of any properties of the subscriber change variables. We use the unbiased estimator definition:

$$\sigma = \sqrt{\frac{1}{N-1} \sum_{i=1}^{N} |\Delta S - \mu|^2}. \tag{4}$$

Where μ is the mean of the sample and N is the number of elements.

To further analyse the influence of new effects in subreddit subscriber change, we performed a linear fit as described in Eqs. (2) and (3). The results show that in all cases, Eq. (2) predicted a statistically significant increment in subscriber growth. Concretely, in the case of /The_Donald, the extrapolated average subscriber growth with the presence of news events was 592±90, compared with 397± 53 for the case of non-existent relevant news events. Similarly, /HillaryClinton and /SandersForPresident showed a clear difference between the presence and absence of news events, with 392 ± 44 compared to 127 ± 18 in the case of /SandersFor President, and 60±7 compared to 37±4 for /HillaryClinton. Equation (3), which considers separately positive and negative news events, explains the data significantly better than Eq. (2) for the case of /SandersForPresident and /Hillary Clinton, with respective adjusted R^2 of 0.24 and 0.16 compared to 0.07 and 0.11 from the one parameter linear model. In the case of /The_Donald, classifying news events as positive and negative did not change the adjusted R^2, which was low at a constant 0.07. An alternative way to evaluate the mathematical soundness of this approach is to compare the fit parameters β_+ and β_- and their standard deviations. If the hypothesis of positive and negative influence of new events holds for a candidate, β_- is expected to be smaller than β_+, as a negative event is expected to add less subscribers to the subscriber count. In Table 1 we show how /The_Donald does not follow this behaviour as the other two subreddits do.

Table 1. Weight of positive and negative news events away from the mean

	/SandersForPresident	/HillaryClinton	/The_Donald
β_+	1474 ± 81	102 ± 9	694 ± 117
β_-	−456 ± 130	8 ± 15	572 ± 177

Figure 3 shows the total views by subreddit per month, where the three time periods are again apparent.

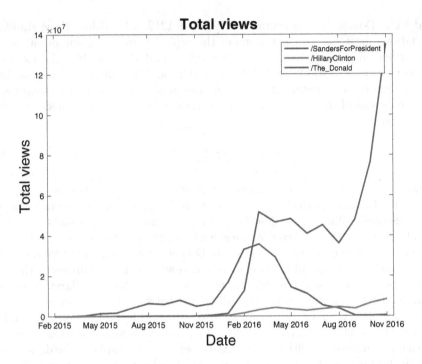

Fig. 3. Total monthly views per subreddit. The blue line shows the total views for /SandersForPresident, the red line for /The_Donald and the pink line for /HillaryClinton. News events are not shown because the data is given per month. The vertical axis is given in scientific notation. (Color figure online)

4   Discussion

4.1   General Trends

First, Fig. 1 shows that interest in the general election began to pick up steam around February of 2016. This is explained by the fact that the first primary elections, in Iowa and New Hampshire, were held on February 1st and February 9th, respectively. Bernie Sanders' subreddit, however, had been rather popular and growing continuously since April of 2015, when he declared his interest in running for president. /SandersForPresident remained the most popular subreddit of the three until September of 2016, two months after he lost the primary race and endorsed Hillary Clinton.

Second, Table 3 (see Appendix A) shows that the news events described in Sect. 2 coincide with the fifteen days with the highest subscriber change in descending order. The most important news events for each candidate's subreddit are: the Orlando shooting for /The_Donald (June 12th, 2016), the third day of the Democratic National Convention for /HillaryClinton (July 28th, 2016), and the announcement of Bernie Sanders' candidacy for /SandersForPresident (April 30th, 2015). Only Bernie Sanders has a negative subscriber growth day in the list, July 7th, 2016, a date that coincides with Sanders' endorsement of Hillary Clinton before the Democratic National Convention. The events that showed a correlation with more than one candidate are marked in blue in the table. Peaks in Sanders' and Trump's subreddits are correlated with the afore-mentioned Wikileaks revelations of supposedly "rigged" primaries in the case of Sanders, and Trump's Reddit Ask Me Anything-session in the case of Trump. Trump's subreddit seems to be more affected by the Democratic convention than by the Republican one, perhaps explained by the fact that Trump was fairly dominant during the primaries, resulting relatively in low levels of interest in the Republican convention. The Democratic primaries were more of a tight contest between Clinton and Sanders, and speculation of a possible contested convention, as well as anger over the DNC email leak scandal, may have peaked Reddit users' interest [54,58].

Third, the data in Figs. 1 and 3 shows an unexpectedly large difference between /HillaryClinton and /The_Donald and /SandersForPresident. Both /The_Donald and /SandersForPresident were very popular compared to /HillaryClinton, particularly after the first primary elections were held in February of 2016. We know that Clinton's support among young voters was lower than Barack Obama's in both 2008 and 2012, with many Millennials preferring Sanders or third party candidates [35]. This lack of enthusiasm was thus reflected in Clinton's lower levels of online community engagement. However, her support among Millennials is not so low as to explain the full width of the subscription and visitor gaps visible in the data. In fact, according to exit polls, Hillary received 55% of the votes from citizens younger than 29, compared to 37% in the case of Donald Trump [35].

Fourth, the data does not show a clear transfer of traffic and subscriptions from /SandersForPresident to /HillaryClinton after Clinton obtained the Democratic Party's nomination, despite the fact that the total number of accumulated subscribers to /SandersForPresident went down after July 2016 (see Fig. 1). This indicates that Clinton did not manage to consolidate support among Democratic-leaning Reddit users after it became clear that she was going to be the nominee. This is not in line with polling data showing that Clinton enjoyed a typical amount of support from likely Democratic voters (of any age) [25,30]. For example, support for Clinton among Sanders supporters was higher in 2016 than support for Barack Obama was among Clinton supporters in 2008 (after Obama had won the nomination over Clinton; see [61]).

We propose three possible explanations for the observations mentioned above: skewed demographics, differences in subreddit cultures, and a decline in party affiliation paired with increased partisanship.

Skewed Demographics. The hypothesis of skewed demographics has been reviewed in Sect. 2. The underrepresentation of minority groups on Reddit lends credence to the idea that Reddit would be more supportive of Trump than Clinton (compared to the average Millennial population), since Clinton drew more support from minority communities and women than Trump. Additionally, this hypothesis could help explain the lack of popularity of /HillaryClinton, since young women are underrepresented on Reddit. However, this sample skewing is not sufficient to explain the more than sevenfold difference between subscribers to Donald Trump's subreddit and subscribers to Hillary Clinton's. In fact, even if we only look at white male Millennials, Hillary Clinton would be expected to have roughly the same demographic support as Donald Trump [46]. Therefore, the skewed demographics hypothesis is not sufficient to explain the lack of support for Clinton on Reddit.

Differences in Subreddit Culture. Internet fora are known to develop unique subcultures [47]. From its inception, /SandersForPresident was characterised by an energetic spirit, mixing ideas such as universal health care and raising taxes on the rich with an additional focus on social issues such as racial discrimination and LGBT rights [44]. The general tone of the discussion was optimistic; users created posts with personal stories of how they further contributed to the cause, and asked other users to match them in their efforts. This created a culture among /SandersForPresident subscribers where contributing to Sanders' political cause was encouraged [51,53].

Donald Trump's subreddit showed a markedly different culture. It is unclear if the forum was initially conceived ironically, or as a serious support group for Trump. Whichever is the case, the general tone was humorous and playful, with a penchant for criticising more establishment-friendly Republican and Democratic primary candidates. Many /The_Donald posts made fun of the attitude present in /SandersForPresident, for example: *I have just donated $0 to Donald Trump's campaign, match me if you can!* [3].

On /The_Donald, users posted memes, jokes, video mashups and Trump quotes. These tropes grew in popularity with time. This may have attracted passive users that were not overt Trump supporters [27]. As we mentioned in Sect. 2.4, however, this is somewhat unlikely, since /The_Donald does not allow non-Trump supporters to post on the forum. Thus, /The_Donald's popularity is most likely best explained by the fact that it managed to become an attractive place for not only Trump supporters, but also the politically disaffected or disengaged, who were drawn in by the subreddit's humorous bent.

/HillaryClinton, which had fewer subscribers than the other two subreddits, generally struck a more policy-focused tone, with some attempts at replicating the mischievous nature of /The_Donald. An example of this is a post by the user name "Deceptiveideas" in June 2016 titled "Hillary engaging in the meme war" followed by a photo of an exasperated Hillary Clinton in front of the text *"Q: Saying [a judge] can't do his job because of his race - is that not the definition of racism? Trump: No."* [20].

In general, the mood among /HillaryClinton users was mostly optimistic in nature, due in part to her good standing in many national election polls. As a social platform of support, however, /HillaryClinton had an insignificant amount of subscribers compared to other online support groups such as the "secret" pro-Clinton Facebook group PantsuitNation, which as of February 2017 had accumulated over 2.5 million users [18]. It is therefore likely that Clinton's supporters did not choose Reddit as their main avenue of expression, but instead preferred other online channels. In addition, /HillaryClinton did not see a spike in accumulated subscribers after /SandersForPresident's numbers began to drop after July 2016. This implies that /HillaryClinton did not absorb a significant number of Sanders supporters after Sanders dropped out of the race.

As the primary elections advanced, the sentiment in /The_Donald and /SandersForPresident subreddits evolved, with the former denying Sanders' primary loss against Clinton and, following Wikileaks revelations that appeared to indicate that the Democratic National Committee (DNC) had been biased against Sanders' candidacy, a sense of betrayal towards Clinton and the DNC. Meanwhile, /The_Donald started a campaign to assimilate /SandersForPresident supporters. One post, published in March 2016, "The Reformed BernieBot's Guide on Assimilation", outlines the steps that Bernie supporters must follow in order to integrate into the r/The_Donald community [4]. Another post from May 2016 was titled "RIP BERNIE — CONVERT NOW" and featured an image portraying Donald Trump as the priest of the Disciples of Christ-church, blessing a coffin where an image of Bernie Sanders was photoshopped into [40]. The most upvoted comment on this particular thread was a direct quote by Donald Trump: *"Bernie Sanders is being treated very badly by the Democrats, the system is rigged against him"*.

Thus, the subreddit culture explanation for the observed trends states that users were more attracted to /The_Donald and /SandersForPresident due to their more humorous, ironic, or anti-establishment nature. The content of the posts in these subreddits was perhaps simply considered funnier or of better quality than in /HillaryClinton, and therefore was more successful at constructing a group identity and group cohesion [51]. The same goes for Clinton support groups outside of Reddit, such as the aforementioned PantSuitNation. We posit that /HillaryClinton remained relatively unpopular due in part to its excessive focus on 'boring' or serious topics. Content analysis should reveal more about this proposed negative relation between online political community popularity and the level of focus on policy.

Furthermore, the attempts undertaken by /The_Donald to assimilate Sanders supporters can be seen as a way to overcome /SandersForPresident's group identity by pointing to shared experiences and a common adversary [51]. This, in turn, affected group cohesion, as /SandersForPresident began to abandon the group. This is particularly noteworthy considering that Trump and Sanders have little in common politically, which is a strong indicator that online political communities do not see politics and policy as a primary driver for constructing and maintaining group identity. As such, these assimilation attempts are in line with what Tom Nichols has dubbed the "death of expertise": the authority of experts, especially when it comes to political topics, is becoming less and less relevant. This development, he claims, occurred in tandem with the rise of the internet and the ubiquitous availability of media resources [48]. We put forward that policy and political ideology were not as relevant for group identity and cohesion as entertainment value. Nichols' 'death of expertise' thus expressed itself as a switch in persuasion tactics from a policy-based to an emotions-based approach.

Partisanship and Declining Party Affiliation. There are several factors pointing at the possibility that Millennials may have voted in a higher proportion for Donald Trump than was indicated by election polls. This, again, would not suffice to explain the sevenfold difference in subscribers between Trump's and Clinton's reddits, but in conjunction with the aforementioned skewed demographics may have had a non-zero effect. This is in line with observations by Twenge et al. [62], who argue that the Millennial generation is more positively inclined towards conservative ideas than the Boomer and Gen X-generations were at the same age. This may have lowered the threshold to go from voting Democratic to voting Republican.

The relatively large number of Millennials who do not identify as Democrats forms part of the explanation for the popularity of /The_Donald. Furthermore, /SandersForPresident's popularity does not seem to have translated into loyalty to the Democratic Party or Hillary Clinton after Sanders' primary loss. One particular day in the data set is indicative of this. On July 12th, 2016, Sanders officially endorsed Clinton during a rally they both attended in Portsmouth, New Hampshire. On this day, /SandersForPresident lost 3947 subscribers, indicating a degree of disappointment among Sanders supporters for his decision to endorse Clinton. On the same day, /The_Donald gained 411 subscribers, and /HillaryClinton gained 136. Thus, it is safe to say that there was no transfer from /SandersForPresident to /HillaryClinton to speak of, and a slightly larger but still quite small transfer to /The_Donald.

It is therefore possible that a significant portion of /SandersForPresident subscribers did not, by and large, base their subreddit subscriptions on party identification or shared viewpoints on political issues [1,17,57]. This phenomenon can be explained by looking at trends of partisanship versus party affiliation. Julia Azari argues that the influence of party organisations and the interest groups that constitute parties (such as the NRA, the US Chamber of Commerce or environmental groups) has waned, both because voters do not have to listen to elites and because elites do not have to listen to each other [6]. This opens up avenues for non-traditional candidates such as Donald Trump and Bernie Sanders to do unexpectedly well in electoral cycles, in apparent violation of the idea that 'the Party decides' who is an acceptable (enough) candidate to win the party's primary elections. [15,22,60]. At the same time, partisanship is strong, as witnessed by increased congressional as well as societal polarisation and growing self-identification at the outer edges of the political spectrum. Thus, parties can no longer control whom they nominate, but voters and elites are prepared to support the eventual candidate. This is especially true for those who get the majority of their news from online sources; as Nie et al. [49] argue, consumers of internet news sources are likely to hold more extreme political views, while being interested in a wider range of political topics, than those who mostly watch TV or read newspapers. Reddit users can be seen to fit within this framework.

However, Azari's idea predicts more consolidation in favour of Clinton after she clinched the nomination than the data is able to show. Instead, we see almost no increase in subscriptions and page visits for Clinton's subreddit, despite a persistent decline in Sanders' after his loss. We therefore propose that it is important to take into account how negative news events affected subscription trends for both Clinton and Sanders. We explore this in the next section.

4.2   News Event Dynamics

The analysis of the relation between news events and Reddit activity shown in Sect. 3, adds weight to the hypothesis that subreddit subscriber count relates to specific news events rather than being mostly determined by common activity trends. Only one event shows up as significant for all candidates: the Democratic National Convention, which was expected to have an important effect on voter enthusiasm, for example by way of a convention bounce [56].

Generally speaking, most of the traffic and subscription spikes correspond to news events expected to be of interest during a political campaign (such as primary elections, inter- and intra-party debates, and party conventions), and 'Ask me Anything'-events in the case of Sanders and Trump. Three data points warrant special mention. First, 12 June 2016, the day of the Orlando mass shooting, was the day with the largest increase in subscribers on /The_Donald. Second, /SandersForPresident witnessed a traffic spike on August 8, 2015. This was the day a Sanders rally was interrupted by Black Lives Matter activists. And finally, one data point appears to be absent: on October 8, 2016, a tape was leaked of Donald Trump making controversial comments about women. This scandal dominated the news cycle for a number of days, and one would expect a spike in /The_Donald's traffic or subscriptions because of it. However, this did not occur: /The_Donald grew by a total of 1337 subscribers between October 8 and 9, and /HillaryClinton by a total of 566. This corresponds to a small local bump for both candidates. A content-analytical approach of Reddit posts on these days may reveal some insights about this ostensible paradox.

Finally, we will make a few broader observations about the relation between subscription dynamics and news events. As explained in Sect. 3, our linear fit model found in 3 shows that the impact of positive and negative news events on subscriber and traffic dynamics are significant for /HillaryClinton and /SandersForPresident, but not for /The_Donald (see also Table 1). Broadly speaking, albeit with significant statistical caveats (explained in Sect. 3), our observations support the idea that Donald Trump's candidacy was not adversely affected by negative news events in the same way as other candidates. Whereas Hillary Clinton and especially Bernie Sanders experienced significant Reddit traffic and subscription dips during or briefly after some negative news events, this association does not exist for Donald Trump. Our observations are therefore in line with the idea that Trump's candidacy was helped by his continuous domination of the news cycle and social media activity [32]. His presence online allowed him to run a low-cost campaign that relied on controversy to generate support [59]. This finding is also corroborated by Effing, Van Hillegersberg and

Huibers [24], who argue that increased social media participation by politicians can increase preference voting. Additionally, there is the possibility that Trump's supporters on /The_Donald simply did not care about news events perceived as negative to Trump's campaign by what they saw as the "mainstream media" [9,45]. The perception that many media outlets were biased against Trump may have led to a sense that whatever report came out about his candidacy either did not matter, was taken out of context or was just as bad as other candidates' campaign hiccups. /The_Donald developed an immunity against negative news that /HillaryClinton and /SandersForPresident did not possess. Further research into /The_Donald's group dynamics and identity could shed light onto how this immunity emerged. We posit that looking at the content of posts on /The_Donald within the context of positive and negative news events could offer insight into how this immunity came to be.

5   Conclusion

In this paper, we have sought to understand social media dynamics in the 2016 US presidential election, particularly concerning Millennial voters, by measuring Reddit metrics and election-related news events. From the analysis of subscriber trends for Trump's, Clinton's and Sanders' subreddits, no consolidation of support was observed for Hillary Clinton after her victory in the primaries. Additionally, Hillary Clinton had much less Reddit support than Donald Trump. We show how this deficit is unlikely to be caused by skewed demographics in Reddit, as the skewing is much smaller than the recorded difference in subscribers. We discuss three possible explanations of the observed phenomena: the difference of the quality of content produced on /HillaryClinton, /The_Donald, and /SandersForPresident; the efforts by /The_Donald subscribers to assimilate Sanders supporters not through policy but through emotional appeals; and high partisanship paired with low party identification in the United States. We suggest that a combination of these factors three explains candidates' different levels of popularity on Reddit.

The correlation between news events during the electoral cycle and subscriber change on Reddit was also studied. We observe that positive and negative news events explains our observations better than just news events in general in the case of Sanders' and Clinton's subreddits. However, this was not the case for Donald Trump, whose subreddit seems to be affected positively by both positive and negative news events. In fact, one of the elections' major scandals, Trump's *Grab 'em by the pussy*-comments, did not seem to affect the number of /The_Donald subscribers in any significant way. Our findings thus provide support for Trump's remark that he could "stand in the middle of Fifth Avenue and shoot somebody and not lose any voters" [21,24].

A   Appendix

Table 2 contains the list of news events used in this paper and their classification. The relevant variables are set in columns, starting by labels which we describe as follows:

- **Year, Month, Day:** The date of the news event.
- **Label:** A label describing the news event(s) in the given day.
- **Party:** A numerical label used to draw the vertical lines in the figures. If equal to 0, represents a new event mostly relevant for the Republican party, if equal to 1, it represents a news event relevant for the Democratic party. If equal to 2 it represents a news event equally relevant for both.
- **PositiveH:** A numerical label used to classify news events positive to Hillary Clinton's campaign as described in Sect. 2. If equal to 1, the event is considered as positive. If equal to 0 as neutral.
- **NegativeH:** A numerical label used to classify news events negative to Hillary Clinton's campaign as described in Sect. 2. If equal to 1, the event is considered as negative. If equal to 0 as neutral.
- **PositiveT:** A numerical label used to classify news events positive to Donald Trump's campaign as described in Sect. 2. If equal to 1, the event is considered as positive. If equal to 0 as neutral.
- **NegativeT:** A numerical label used to classify news events negative to Donald Trump's campaign as described in Sect. 2. If equal to 1, the event is considered as negative. If equal to 0 as neutral.
- **PositiveS:** A numerical label used to classify news events positive to Bernie Sanders campaign as described in Sect. 2. If equal to 1, the event is considered as positive. If equal to 0 as neutral.
- **NegativeS:** A numerical label used to classify news events negative to Bernie Sanders campaign as described in Sect. 2. If equal to 1, the event is considered as negative. If equal to 0 as neutral.

Table 2. News events considered for the analysis of subscriber and visitor trends.

Year	Month	Day	Label	Party	PositiveH	NegativeH	PositiveT	NegativeT	positiveS	negativeS	Comparison	Verdict
2015	4	12	Hillary Clinton formally announces her candidacy for the presidential nomination of the Democratic Party	1	1	0	0	0	0	0	Different	Human
2015	4	30	Bernie Sanders, of Vermont, formally announces his candidacy for the presidential nomination of the Democratic Party	1	0	0	0	0	1	0	Different	Human
2015	6	16	Donald Trump, of New York, officially declares his candidacy for the presidential nomination of the Republican Party	0	0	0	1	0	0	0	Same	Same
2015	8	3	First presidential forum, featuring 14 Republican candidates, was broadcast on C-SPAN	0	0	0	0	1	0	0	Different	Algorithm
2015	8	6	First official presidential debate, featuring 10 Republican candidates, is held in Cleveland, Ohio	0	0	0	1	0	0	0	Different	Human
2015	9	8	Hillary Clinton apologises for her emails	1	0	1	0	0	0	0	Same	Same
2015	9	16	Second Republican debate is held in Simi Valley, California	0	0	0	1	0	0	0	Same	Same
2015	10	13	First Democratic debate	1	1	0	0	0	1	0	Same	Same
2015	10	22	Hillary Clinton's hearing on Benghazi	1	0	1	1	0	0	0	Different	Algorithm
2015	10	28	Third Republican debate is held in Boulder	0	0	0	0	0	0	0	Different	Algorithm
2015	11	10	Fourth Republican debate is held in Milwaukee, Wisconsin	0	0	0	0	0	0	0	Different	Algorithm
2015	11	14	Second Democratic debate is held in Des Moines, Iowa	1	1	0	0	0	1	0	Same	Same
2015	12	3	The Republican Jewish Coalition Presidential Candidates	0	0	0	1	0	0	0	Same	Same
2015	12	7	Trump calls for Muslim ban	0	0	0	0	0	0	0	Different	Algorithm
2015	12	15	Fifth Republican debate is held in Las Vegas	0	0	0	1	0	0	0	Same	Same
2015	12	19	Third Democratic debate is held in Manchester	1	1	0	0	0	1	0	Same	Same
2016	1	9	The Republican Kemp Forum is held in Columbia	0	0	0	0	0	0	0	Different	Algorithm
2016	1	11	Third Democratic forum is held in Des Moines	1	1	0	0	0	1	0	Same	Same
2016	1	14	Sixth Republican debate is held in North Charleston	0	0	0	1	0	0	0	Different	Human

(continued)

Table 2. (*continued*)

Year	Month	Day	Label	Party	PositiveH	NegativeH	PositiveT	NegativeT	positiveS	negativeS	Comparison	Veredict
2016	1	17	Fourth Democratic debate is held in Charleston, South Carolina	1	1	0	0	0	1	0	Same	Same
2016	1	25	A Democratic forum, a Town Hall event, is held in Des Moines	1	1	0	0	0	1	0	same	same
2016	1	28	Seventh Republican debate is held in Des Moines, Iowa. Trump does not participate	0	0	0	1	0	0	0	same	same
2016	2	1	The Iowa Democratic caucus is won by Hillary Clinton	1	1	0	0	0	1	0	Same	Same
2016	2	1	The Iowa Republican caucus is won by Ted Cruz	0	0	0	1	0	0	0	Different	Same
2016	2	3	A Democratic Town Hall forum event is held in Derry, New Hampshire	1	1	0	0	0	1	0	Same	Same
2016	2	4	Fifth Democratic debate is held in Durham	1	1	0	0	0	1	0	Same	Same
2016	2	6	Eighth Republican debate is held in Manchester	0	0	0	0	0	0	0	Different*	Algorithm
2016	2	9	The New Hampshire Republican primary is won by Donald Trump	0	0	0	0	1	0	0	Same	Same
2016	2	9	The New Hampshire Democratic primary is won by Bernie Sanders	1	0	1	0	0	1	0	Same	Same
2016	2	11	Sixth Democratic debate is held in Milwaukee	1	1	0	0	0	1	0	Different*	Human
2016	2	13	Ninth Republican debate is held in Charleston, South Carolina	0	0	0	0	0	0	0	Different	Algorithm
2016	2	17	CNN Republican town halls are held in Greenville	0	0	0	1	0	0	0	Nodata	Human
2016	2	18	CNN Republican town halls are held in Greenville	0	0	0	1	0	0	0	Nodata	Human
2016	2	18	Democratic Town Hall forum event is held in Las Vegas	1	1	0	0	1	1	0	Nodata	Human
2016	2	18	Trump fights the Pope	0	0	0	0	0	0	0	Different	Algorithm
2016	2	20	Trump wins South Carolina	0	0	0	1	0	0	0	Same	Same
2016	2	23	Nevada Republican caucuses are won by Donald Trump	0	0	0	1	0	0	0	Same	Same
2016	2	23	CNN Democratic town hall is held in Columbia	1	1	0	0	0	1	0	Same	Same
2016	2	24	Republican town hall is held in Houston	0	0	0	1	0	0	0	Nodata	Human
2016	2	25	10th Republican debate is held in Houston	0	0	0	0	0	0	0	Different	Algorithm
2016	2	27	South Carolina Democratic primary is won by Hillary Clinton	1	1	0	0	0	1	1	Same	Same

(continued)

Table 2. (*continued*)

Year	Month	Day	Label	Party	PositiveH	NegativeH	PositiveT	NegativeT	positiveS	negativeS	Comparison	Verdict
2016	3	1	Super Tuesday, big win for Trump	0	0	0	1	0	0	0	Same	Same
2016	3	3	11th Republican debate. Rubio jokes about Trump's tiny penis	0	0	0	0	1	0	0	Same	Same
2016	3	9	Eighth and final Democratic debate is held in Miami	1	1	0	0	0	1	0	Same	Same
2016	3	10	Twelfth Republican debate is held in Miami, Florida	0	0	0	1	0	0	0	Same	Same
2016	3	11	Corey Lewandowski (Trump's campaign manager) accused of assault	0	0	0	0	1	0	0	Different	Human
2016	3	15	Trump wins Florida, Illinois, Missouri, North Carolina. Kasich wins Ohio	0	1	0	1	0	0	0	Same	Same
2016	3	29	Republican town hall	0	1	0	1	0	0	0	Different	Human
2016	3	30	Trump says women should be punished for having abortions	0	0	0	0	1	0	0	Different	Human
2016	4	14	Ninth Democratic debate is held in Brooklyn	1	1	0	0	0	1	0	Same	Same
2016	4	26	Trump wins Connecticut, Delaware, Maryland, Rhode Island, Pennsylvania	0	0	0	1	0	0	0	Same	Same
2016	5	26	Donald Trump passes 1237 pledged delegates	0	1	0	1	0	0	0	Different*	Human
2016	6	2	Paul Ryan says he'll vote for Trump	0	1	0	1	0	0	0	Different	Human
2016	6	6	Hillary Clinton passes 2383 pledged delegates	1	0	0	0	0	0	1	Same	Same
2016	6	9	Obama endorses Clinton	1	1	0	0	0	0	1	Same	Same
2016	6	20	Trump fires Corey Lewandowski	0	0	0	0	0	0	0	Different	Algorithm
2016	6	24	Trump goes to Scotland the day after Brexit vote	0	0	0	0	0	0	0	Different	Algorithm
2016	7	5	FBI director James Comey recommends not indicting Clinton	1	1	0	0	0	0	0	Same	Same
2016	7	12	Bernie Sanders endorses Hillary Clinton	1	1	0	0	0	0	1	Same	Same
2016	7	15	Republican presumptive nominee Donald Trump announces Indiana governor Mike Pence as his vice presidential running mate	0	1	0	0	0	0	0	Different	Human
2016	7	18	Republican National Convention is held in Cleveland, Ohio. Donald Trump and Mike Pence are formally nominated for President	0	0	0	0	0	0	0	Different	Algorithm
2016	7	19	Republican National Convention is held in Cleveland, Ohio. Donald Trump and Mike Pence are formally nominated for President	0	0	0	1	0	0	0	Different	Human

(*continued*)

Table 2. (continued)

Year	Month	Day	Label	Party	PositiveH	NegativeH	PositiveT	NegativeT	positiveS	negativeS	Comparison	Verdict
2016	7	20	Republican National Convention is held in Cleveland, Ohio. Donald Trump and Mike Pence are formally nominated for President	0	0	0	1	0	0	0	Same	Same
2016	7	21	Republican National Convention is held in Cleveland, Ohio. Donald Trump and Mike Pence are formally nominated for President	0	0	0	1	0	0	0	Same	Same
2016	7	22	Democratic presumptive nominee Hillary Clinton announces Tim Kaine as her vicepresidential candidate	1	1	0	0	0	0	0	Same	Same
2016	7	22	Wikileaks leaks 20,000 emails from the Democratic National Committee, revealing a systematic bias against Bernie Sanders	1	0	1	0	0	1	0	Same	Same
2016	7	25	Democratic National Convention is held in Philadelphia	1	1	0	0	0	0	1	Same	Same
2016	7	26	Democratic National Convention is held in Philadelphia, Pennsylvania	1	1	0	0	0	0	1	Same	Same
2016	7	27	Democratic National Convention is held in Philadelphia, Pennsylvania	1	1	0	0	0	0	1	Same	Same
2016	7	28	Democratic National Convention is held in Philadelphia, Pennsylvania	1	1	0	0	0	0	1	Same	Same
2016	8	1	Trump feuds with Khizr Khan, parent of dead soldier	0	1	0	0	0	0	0	Same	Same
2016	8	10	Leaked emails show Clinton Foundations ties with State Department	1	0	1	1	0	0	0	Different	Human
2016	8	29	New sexting scandal with Anthony Wiener & Huma Abedin	1	0	1	1	0	0	0	Different	Human
2016	9	2	FBI releases more Clinton emails, Trump lashes onto them	1	0	1	1	0	0	0	same	same
2016	9	9	Clinton calls half of Trump supporters deplorables	1	0	1	1	0	0	0	Same	Same
2016	9	11	Clinton faints	1	0	1	1	0	0	0	Same	Same
2016	9	26	First presidential general election debate was held at Hofstra University in Hempstead, New York	2	1	0	0	1	1	0	Same	Same
2016	10	2	NYT report suggests Trump paid no federal income tax for 20 years	0	1	0	1	1	0	0	Different	Algorithm

(continued)

Table 2. (*continued*)

Year	Month	Day	Label	Party	PositiveH	NegativeH	PositiveT	NegativeT	positiveS	negativeS	Comparison	Verdict
2016	10	4	Only vice presidential general election debate was held at Longwood University in Farmville, Virginia	2	0	1	1	0	0	0	Different*	Human
2016	10	7	Tapes are leaked out from Access Hollywood showing Donald Trump and Billy Bush bragging about sexual exploits in 2005	0	1	0	0	1	0	0	Same	Same
2016	10	7	Hillary Clinton's transcripts of speeches to Wall Street bankers are leaked	1	1	0	1	0	0	0	Different	Algorithm
2016	10	9	Second presidential general election debate was held at Washington University in St. Louis, Missouri	2	0	1	0	1	0	0	Different	Algorithm
2016	10	19	The third and final presidential debate between the two major candidates was held at the University of Nevada	2	1	0	1	0	0	0	Same	Same
2016	10	28	James Comey announces that the FBI will be investigating newly discovered emails pertinent to Hillary Clinton	1	0	1	1	0	0	0	Different	Human
2016	11	6	James Comey tells Congress there is no evidence in the recently discovered emails that Clinton should face charges	1	1	0	0	1	0	0	Same	Same
2016	11	9	Election day	2	0	1	1	0	0	0	Same	Same
2016	11	10	Day after the election	2	0	1	1	0	0	0	Same	Same
2016	6	13	Donald Trump's national security and terrorism speech after Orlando massacre. He repeats his call to ban Muslim immigration	0	1	0	1	0	0	0	Different	Algorithm
2016	6	14	Donald Trump turns 70. Barack Obama, in a speech, denounces Trump's plan to stop immigration to the US from Muslim countries	0	0	0	0	1	0	0	Same	Same
2016	3	17	Trump claims there will be riots if he is not named the GOP nominee, in an interview with CNN	0	1	0	0	1	0	0	Same	Same
2016	5	3	Bernie Sanders wins Indiana primary. Ted Cruz drops out of the presidential race, effectively handing Trump the nomination	1	0	1	1	0	1	0	Same	Same
2016	3	16	day after Clinton wins primaries in Florida, Ohio, Illinois and North Carolina	1	1	0	0	0	0	1	Same	Same

(*continued*)

Table 2. (*continued*)

Year	Month	Day	Label	Party	PositiveH	NegativeH	PositiveT	NegativeT	positiveS	negativeS	Comparison	Verdict
2016	5	4	Day after Indiana primary. News states the race is now effectively between Trump and Clinton	1	1	0	0	0	0	1	Same	Same
2016	7	30	Clinton takes 10-point lead over Trump in polls in first poll after DNC convention	1	0	0	0	1	0	0	Same	Same
2016	3	6	Day after Democratic debate (CNN)	1	1	0	0	0	1	0	Same	Same
2015	10	8	Bernie Sanders admits he was insensitive to African-American issues and Black Lives Matter in an interview with Ebony Magazine	1	1	0	0	0	0	1	Same	Same
2015	8	10	Bernie Sanders rally in Portland is interrupted by Black Lives Matter activists	1	1	0	0	0	0	1	Different	Algorithm
2015	4	28	Bernie Sanders announces his candidacy for the Democratic Party nomination for President	0	0	0	1	0	1	0	Different	Human
2015	4	29	Day after Sanders announces his candidacy for president	0	0	0	1	0	1	0	Different	Human
2016	2	2	Day after Iowa Caucus, in which Bernie Sanders loses to Clinton by a tiny margin	1	1	0	0	0	1	0	Same	Same
2016	5	19	Day after Nevada Democratic National Convention chaos breaks out	1	1	0	0	0	0	1	Different	Human
2016	2	1	Day of Iowa caucus	1	0	1	1	1	1	0	Different	Human
2016	5	2	Day after Sanders appears on CBS Face the Nation. Day before Indiana primary	1	0	0	0	0	0	0	Different	Algorithm
2016	5	1	Day of Sander's appearance on CBS Face the Nation. May 1 st is also Labour Day	1	0	0	0	0	0	0	Different	Algorithm
2015	10	14	Day after first Democratic Party debate	1	1	0	0	0	1	0	Same	Same
2016	2	10	Day after Bernie Sanders wins New Hampshire primary	1	0	1	0	0	1	0	Same	Same
2015	8	12	Bernie Sanders is ahead of Clinton in New Hampshire primary poll. First time Sanders is ahead of Clinton in any poll	1	0	1	0	0	1	0	Same	Same
2015	10	15	Two days after first Democratic debate	1	1	0	0	0	1	0	Nodata	Human
2016	6	12	Orlando Shooting	0	0	0	1	0	0	0	Nodata	Human
2016	2	20	Clinton wins Nevada'	1	1	0	0	0	0	1	Nodata	Human
2016	3	12	Marco Rubio wins District of Columbia	0	0	0	0	1	0	0	Same	Same
2016	4	26	Clinton wins 4, Sanders 1	1	1	0	0	0	0	1	Same	Same

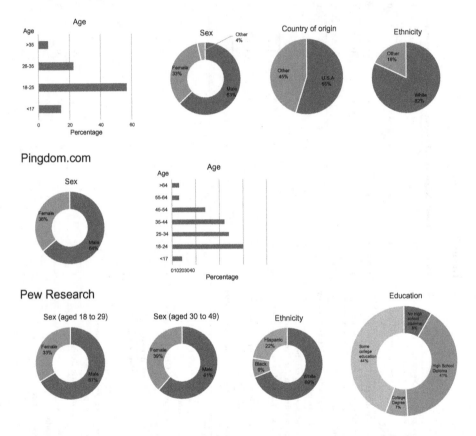

Fig. 4. Graphical representation of Reddit demographics according to different sources
[23, 31, 52]

Table 3. News event occurrence versus subscriber change, per candidate

Donald Trump			Hillary Clinton			Bernie Sanders		
Date	Event	ΔS	Date	Event	ΔS	Date	Event	ΔS
2016-6-12	Orlando shooting	11712	2016-7-28	Dem. National Convention	534	2015-4-30	Sanders announces candidacy	8735
2016-7-27	Dem. Nat. Convention Trump's Reddit AMA	6914	2016-9-27	1 Pres. Debate.Aftermath	451	2015-8-10	BLM interrupts Sanders rally	7370
2016-11-10	Day after election	6335	2016-7-27	Dem. National Convention	441	2016-7-12	Sanders endorses Clinton	-3947
2016-11-9	Election day	6335	2016-7-29	Hillary accepts nomination	418	2015-4-28	Sanders Announces Candidacy	3795
2016-11-8	Day before election	6335	2016-7-26	Dem. National Convention	388	2015-4-29	Sanders Announces Candidacy +1	3772
2016-2-24	Nevada primary caucus	5664	2016-7-25	Dem. National Convention	372	2016-2-2	Day after IO Caucus	3609
2016-11-30	Trump illegal vote claim	4947	2016-10-9	Second presidentialdebate	358	2015-5-19	Sanders' Reddit AMA	3512
2016-6-13	Trump Speech on Orlando	4864	2016-9-26	First presidentialdebate	343	2016-2-1	Iowa caucus	3374
2016-2-23	CNN Dem. town hall	4618	2016-5-3	Sanders wins Indiana	335	2015-5-2	Two days after announcing candidacy	3249
2016-7-25	Dem. National Convention	3625	2016-3-16	Clinton won OH,IL,NC	324	2015-5-1	Sanders in CBS	3047
2016-2-22	South Car. Primary	3027	2016-3-9	Eighth and finalDem. debate	321	2015-10-14	After first Dem. debate	2751
2016-2-21	Trump in CBS	3023	2016-5-4	Hillary secures nomination	281	2016-2-10	Day after NH primary	2477
2016-6-14	Obama Speech vs Trump	2956	2016-7-30	Dem. Conventionrebound (+10)	274	2015-8-12	NH poll: Sanders overtakes Clinton	2421
2016-3-17	Trump warns of riots	2611	2016-6-9	Obama endorsesClinton	260	2015-10-15	Two days after 1st Dem. deb	2094
2016-2-28	Trump in CBS	2589	2016-3-6	Aftermath Dem. Debate	260	2016-2-9	New Hampshire Primary	2048

References

1. Aelst, P.V., Walgrave, S.: New media, new movements? The role of the internet in shaping the anti-globalization' movement. Inf. Commun. Soc. **5**(4), 465–493 (2002)
2. Alashri, S., Kandala, S.S., Bajaj, V., Ravi, R., Smith, K.L., Desouza, K.C.: An analysis of sentiments on facebook during the 2016 U.S. presidential election. In: Proceedings of the 2016 IEEE/ACM International Conference on Advances in Social Networks Analysis and Mining, ASONAM 2016, pp. 795–802 (2016)
3. Anonymous. For Every Upvote I Will Donate Exactly $0 to Donald Trump's Campaign!!! Be High Energy!!!! Make Reddit Great Again!!!!!, 2 February 2016. Reddit.com
4. Anonymous. The Reformed BernieBot's Guide on Assimilation! (2016). Reddit.com
5. AOL.com. Timeline: election. AOL (2016)
6. Azari, J.R.: Weak parties and strong partisanship are a bad combination, 3 November 2016. Vox.com
7. Ball, M.: Why Hillary Clinton Lost. The Atlantic, 15 November 2016
8. Barthel, M.: How the 2016 presidential campaign is being discussed on Reddit. Pew research center: Factank, 26 May 2016
9. Bateman, O.L.: Trump Supporters Were Hiding In Plain Sight In Online Comment Sections, 14 November 2016. Vice.com
10. Center, P.R., Polarization, P., Habits, M.: Ideological placement of each sources audience, 20 October 2014. Journalism.org
11. Choma, B.L., Hanoch, Y.: Cognitive ability and authoritarianism: understanding support for Trump and Clinton. Personality Individ. Differ. **106**, 287–291 (2017)
12. Chou, L.-C., Fu, C.-Y.: The influence of Internet on politics: the impact of Facebook and the Internet penetration on elections in Taiwan. Appl. Econ. Lett. **24**(7), 494–497 (2017)
13. Cillizza, C.: One of Hillary Clinton's top aides nailed exactly why she lost. The Washington Post, 1 November 2016
14. Circle. At Least 80 Electoral Votes Depended on Youth. The Center For Information & Research On Civic Learning and Engagement, 7 November 2012
15. Cohen, M., McGrath, M.C., Aronow, P., Zaller, J.: Ideologically extreme candidates in U.S. presidential elections, 1948–2012. Ann. Am. Acad. Polit. Soc. Sci. **667**(1), 126–142 (2016)
16. Colby, S.L., Ortman, J.M.: Projections of the Size, Composition of the U.S. Population: 2014 to 2060. US Census: Population Estimates and Projections, 10 March 2015
17. Conway, J.M.: Anti-Globalization Movements. The Wiley Blackwell Encyclopedia of Gender and Sexuality Studies (2016)
18. Correal, A.: Pantsuit Nation, a Secret' Facebook Hub, Celebrates Clinton. The New York Times, New York (2016)
19. Sandefur, G.D., Matrin, M., Eggerling-Boeck, J., Mannon, S.E., Meier, A.M.: 3: an overview of racial and ethnic demographic trends. In: America Becoming: Racial Trends and Their Consequences, vol. 1. The National Academic Press, p. 48 (2001)
20. Deceptiveideas. Hillary engaging in the meme war (2016). Reddit.com
21. Diamond, J.: Trump: I could 'shoot somebody and I wouldn't lose voters'. CNN, 24 January 2016
22. Dowdle, A.: The party decides: presidential nominations before and after reform by Marty Cohen, David Karol, Hanes Noel, and John Zaller. Polit. Sci. Q. **124**(3), 550–551 (2009)

23. Duggan, M., Smith, A.: 6% of Online Adults are reddit Users. Pew Research Center, 3 July 2013

24. Effing, R., van Hillegersberg, J., Huibers, T.: Social media and political participation: are Facebook, Twitter and Youtube democratizing our political systems? In: Tambouris, E., Macintosh, A., de Bruijn, H. (eds.) ePart 2011. LNCS, vol. 6847, pp. 25–35. Springer, Heidelberg (2011). doi:10.1007/978-3-642-23333-3_3

25. Enten, H.: GOP Voters Are Rallying Behind Trump As If He Were Any Other Candidate. fivethirtyeight, 1 June 2016

26. Gambino, L., Pankhania, M.: How we got here: a complete timeline of 2016's historic US election. The Guardian, 8 November 2016

27. Gilman, H.R., Stokes, E.: The Civic and Political Participation of Millennials. New America, pp. 57–60 (2014)

28. Groshek, J., Koc-Michalska, K.: Helping populism win? Social media use, filter bubbles, and support for populist presidential candidates in the 2016 US election campaign. Inf. Commun. Soc. **20**, 9 (2017)

29. Hu, G., Kodali, S., Padamati, A.: Sentiment analysis of tweets on 2016 US presidential election candidates. In: 29th International Conference on Computer Applications in Industry and Engineering, CAINE 2016, pp. 219–226 (2016)

30. HuffPostPollster. Custom Chart: 2016 General Election: Trump vs. Clinton. The Huffington Post (2016)

31. HurricaneXriks. Results Of The Reddit Demographics Survey 2016, 11 October 2016. Reddit.com

32. Boczkowski, P.J.: Has election 2016 been a turning point for the influence of the news media? Nieman Labs, 8 November 2016

33. Jungherr, A.: Twitter use in election campaigns: a systematic literature review. J. Inf. Technol. Polit. **13**(1), 72–91 (2016)

34. Keeter, S., Tyson, J., Horowitz, A.: Young Voters in the 2008 Election. Pew Research Center, Washington, D.C. (2008)

35. Khalid, A., Rose, J.: Millennials Just Didn't Love Hillary Clinton The Way They Loved Barack Obama. NPR, 1 November 2016

36. Kurtzleben, D.: The Most 'Unprecedented' Election Ever? 65 Ways It Has Been. NPR, 3 July 2016

37. Lee, J., Lim, Y.-S.: Gendered campaign tweets: the cases of Hillary Clinton and Donald Trump. Public Relat. Rev. **42**(5), 849–855 (2016)

38. Liu, B.: Sentiment Analysis and Opinion Mining. Morgan & Claypool Publishers, San Rafael (2012)

39. Long, R.: Why did Hillary Clinton lose? Simple. She ran a bad campaign. Chicago Tribune, 1 November 2016

40. LorezMaster. RIP Bernie—Convert Now, 7 June 2016. Reddit.com

41. Maldonado, M., Sierra, V.: Twitter predicting the 2012 US presidential election? Lessons learned from an unconscious value co-creation platform. J. Organ. End User Comput. **28**(3), 10–30 (2016)

42. Martin, T.: Interactive Map of Reddit and Subreddit Similarity Calculator. Short Tails, 28 November 2016

43. Mirowski, T., Roychoudhury, S., Zhou, F., Obradovic, Z.: Predicting poll trends using Twitter and multivariate time-series classification. In: Spiro, E., Ahn, Y.-Y. (eds.) SocInfo 2016. LNCS, vol. 10046, pp. 273–289. Springer, Cham (2016). doi:10.1007/978-3-319-47880-7_17

44. Montellaro, Z.: Bernie Sanders is Dominating the Reddit Primary. The Atlantic, 5 October 2015

45. Morin, R.: Trump says social media was the key to victory. Politico, 12 November 2016
46. Mosendz, P.: What this Election Taught Us About Millennial Voters. Bloomberg, 9 November 2016
47. Muggleton, D., Weinzierl, R.: The Post-Subcultures Reader, 1st edn. Berg Publisheres, Oxford (2003)
48. Nichols, T.: The Death of Expertise: The Campaign against Established Knowledge, and Why It Matters. Oxford University Press, Oxford (2017)
49. Nie, N.H., Miller III, D.W., Golde, S., Butler, D.M., Winneg, K.: The World Wide Web and the U.S. political news market. Am. J. Polit. Sci. **54**(2), 428–439 (2010)
50. Pancer, E., Poole, M.: The popularity and virality of political social media: hashtags, mentions, and links predict likes and retweets of 2016 U.S. presidential nominees' tweets. Soc. Influence **11**(4), 259–270 (2016)
51. Panconesi, G., Guida, M.: Handbook of Research on Collaborative Teaching Practice in Virtual Learning Environments. IGI Global, Hershey (2017)
52. Pingdom. Report: Social network demographics in 2012, 21 August 2012. Pingdom.com
53. Pollack, L.: How Reddit has boosted Bernie Sanders' US campaign. Financial Times, 29 March 2016
54. Reilly, K.: Bernie Sanders: Democratic Convention Will Be Contested. Time Magazine, 4 June 2016
55. Rothmund, T., Otto, L.: The changing role of media use in political participation. J. Media Psychol. **28**(3), 97–99 (2016)
56. Saad, L.: Average Convention "Bounce" Since 1964 Is Six Points. Gallup News Service, 26 July 2000
57. Saull, R.: Capitalism, crisis and the far-right in the neoliberal era. J. Int. Relat. Dev. **18**(1), 25–51 (2015)
58. Siddiqui, S., Gambino, L., Roberts, D.: DNC apologizes to Bernie Sanders amid convention chaos in wake of email leak. The Guardian, 25 July 2016
59. Silver, N.: How Trump Hacked the Media. Fivethirtyeight, 30 March 2016
60. Steger, W.P.: Polls and elections: two paradigms of presidential nominations. Presidential Stud. Q. **43**(2), 377–387 (2013)
61. Sumner, M.: Sanders voters moving to Clinton much faster than Clinton voters moved to Obama. Daily Kos, 27 June 2016
62. Twenge, J.M., Honeycutt, N., Prislin, R., Sherman, R.A.: More polarized but more independent: political party identification and ideological self-categorization among U.S. adults, college students, and late adolescents, 1970–2015. Personal. Soc. Psychol. Bull. **42**(10), 1364–1383 (2016)
63. United States Census Bureau. United Status Census: Quick Facts (2017). Census.gov
64. Wikipedia. United States presidential election, 2016 timeline (2016)

How do eyewitness social media reports reflect socio-economic effects of natural hazards?

Nataliya Tkachenko[1,2(✉)], Rob Procter[1,2,3], and Stephen Jarvis[1,2,3]

[1] Warwick Institute for the Science of Cities, University of Warwick, Coventry, UK
{nataliya.tkachenko,rob.procter,stephen.jarvis}@warwick.ac.uk
[2] Department of Computer Science, University of Warwick, Coventry, UK
[3] The Alan Turing Institute, The British Library, London, UK

Abstract. Recent years have seen a remarkable proliferation of studies attempting to establish relationships between observable online human behaviour and various types of crisis (social, political, economic and natural). Methods utilizing user generated content (UGC) have been already applied to various environmental hazards, such as floods, wildfires, earthquakes, tsunamis and other kinds of emergencies. However, what is currently lacking are more detailed insights into differences between the ways people use social media to report various natural hazard events. In this study we make use of the YFCC100M dataset in order to verify whether statistically robust relationships exist between the volumes of uploaded content during different natural hazards and estimated human and economic losses in the affected countries. Our findings demonstrate that Flickr reflect impacts of events with the highest frequency of occurrence (such as floods or storms) and/or with the recurring spatial structure (such as landslides or earthquakes).

Keywords: Hazard analytics · Socio-economics · Data mining · Eyewitness media · Flickr

1 Introduction

Scientific evidence continues to accumulate that global climate change is real and provoking more frequent and intensified environmental emergencies [1–3]. According to [4], during the past decade the occurrence of natural disasters have increased six times as compared to the 1960s, with the increase being mainly accounted for by regional and country-scale disasters [5]. Apart from the difficulty of efficiently predicting such events [6], what is an even more challenging task is sensing their intensity [7], which can cause widespread destruction and interruption of the daily routine for months or years [8].

Where hazards impact estimation is concerned, different experts use various terms to describe and measure impact [5,9]. As a consequence, assessing and comparing disaster impact has been traditionally been very challenging as systematic data or studies are hard to come by or data from different sources cannot be compared across zones or over time. For example, impact measurement may

© Springer International Publishing AG 2017
G.L. Ciampaglia et al. (Eds.): SocInfo 2017, Part II, LNCS 10540, pp. 221–229, 2017.
DOI: 10.1007/978-3-319-67256-4_17

involve market-based and non-market valuation techniques. The former would include destruction to property and reduction in income and sales; the latter would include loss of life, various environmental consequences and psychological effects suffered by individuals affected [1,5,9].

One of the emerging methods in event analytics where human or economic impacts are concerned involves the use of social media data [11–13,15]. Such methods extend *posteriori* valuation to *ex post* ('now') or even *ex ante* (i.e., before the event's outbreak) impact [10,19]. The main idea behind this method is that instead of basing impact evaluation on the number of directly measured characteristics, which may only become available months or even years after the event, a number of relative (or indirect) indicators recording people's reactions to their surroundings may enable impact estimation during the event or even before it started.

Natural hazard analytics using online activity traces and eyewitness accounts as additional or alternative data sources has been already applied to individual hazards, for example, flood impact prediction [7] and semantic event forecasting [6]). However, we argue that what is currently lacking from this emerging domain of analytics is records of how various hazards are represented in user generated content (UGC) sourced from social media platforms and whether it is possible to use UGC from the same platform to estimate impacts of different kinds of hazards. To answer this and related questions, we mined the entire content of the YFCC100m dataset [14] in order to extract georeferenced entries for the main hazard keywords ('landslide', 'earthquake', 'flood', 'storm' and 'volcano/eruption') and these were benchmarked against the official, globally normalized estimates of socio-economic impacts contained in the EM-DAT dataset [4].

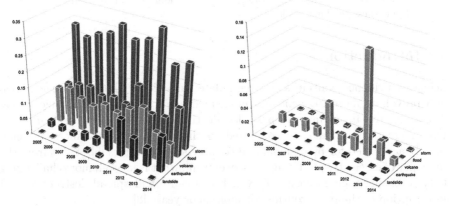

Fig. 1. Fractions of hazard-related image and video material uploaded to the Yahoo! Flickr platform worldwide (2005–2014): normalized to total posted (left) and normalized to total posted and by number of events (right)

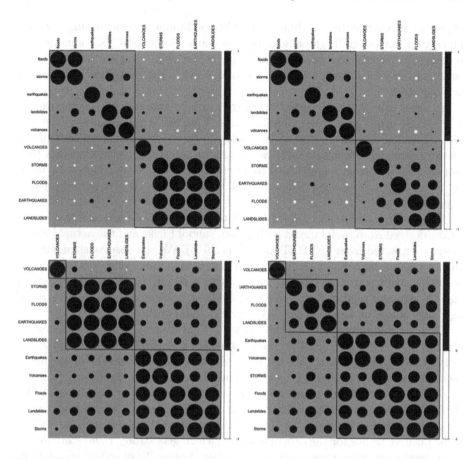

Fig. 2. Expanded version of the FII matrices, calculated for the entire 2005–2014 period across all countries, between official EM-DAT metrics of socio-economic impact due to natural hazards (in capitals) and the volume of social media activity (top row) or its spatial density (bottom row), where left and right hand columns correspond to human losses and infrastructure damage respectively.

2 Results

In order to compare social media data with official impact indicators (Economic losses (incl. Damage to infrastructure) and Number of people affected (incl. Dead, Injured and Homeless)), we used fractional metrics, which indicated the proportion of the keywords 'flood', 'storm', 'volcano/eruption', 'earthquake' and 'landslide' to the total amount of UGC uploaded to the platform over the same time interval (See Appendix).

Figure 1 illustrates annual fractions of worldwide hazard-tagged image and video material uploaded to Yahoo! Flickr platform during 2005–2014 (a.k.a. *semantic volume*), with the figure on the left-hand side depicting total volume and that on the right-hand side depicting volume normalized by the number of events in each corresponding year. This preliminary data mining exercise illustrated that, overall, global geotagged hazard-related UGC is dominated by reporting of storm and flood events, which, however, once normalized, show similar average patterns to other hazards – with the exception of volcanic activity [18].

In order to capture the potential hazard impact signal in social media, we ran a series of feature interaction identifications (FIIs; See Appendix), with the aim of establishing empirical relationships between eyewitness media uploads to the platform and official impact metrics: (a) across annual temporal transects [16], worldwide, (b) across countries, throughout the entire 10-year period (*semantic volume*), (c) across countries, throughout the entire 10-year period (*spatial density*).

The results presented in Table 1 illustrate relationships between all three indicators derived from social media activity on Yahoo! Flickr and the actual impact metrics extracted from EM-DAT dataset (v.2016). We can observe straightaway that social media activity indicators do not exhibit any consistent behaviour across all five hazards within the scope of this study. However, we do observe a slightly stronger relation between social media activity and infrastructure damage costs across all three scenarios in our FII framework.

As per results illustrated in Table 1, we did not observe much consistency for the scenario where global data is analyzed across the selected time period 2005–2014. Thus, if we try to capture a statistical relationship worldwide on an annual basis across each individual hazard we find no statistically significant relationship for people affected, apart from the case of landslides ($r = 0.508$, $p < 0.1$). Although statistically insignificant, we do observe negative correlation trends between direct human losses for the cases of earthquakes and storms, as well as some positive trends for the case of flooding, which gets stronger and statistically more significant when measuring infrastructure losses. We observed no relationship between direct human impact on an annual basis for the incidents of volcanic activity worldwide. We also observe no relationship between human losses and infrastructure damage, although we do find some statistically significant correlations for the cases of flooding, landslides and earthquakes when trying to establish relationships between real-world indicators of infrastructure/economic damage. In general, the strongest potential for this scenario was demonstrated for landslides and floods.

If we change our perspective and look into how relationships form across individual countries during the period 2005–2014, we find no strong or statistically significant correlation whatsoever; This may be indicative of the fact that damage to national infrastructures and direct human loss of life due to the same type of hazard varies from country to country and can be linked to local conditions such as, for example, age of infrastructure, social preparedness and other resilience measures, as well as the nature of the hazard itself. To account for the spatial distribution of eyewitness reporting, we introduced the corrective metric of spatial density of the social media postings (See Appendix) in order to explore how both distribution and semantic volume of UGC changes the relationships presented above. Here, we observe that the correction makes a difference for cases of infrastructure damage during floods and storms only. Some positive correlation trends can still be observed for the cases of landslides and earthquakes (however, much weaker than during the first scenario).

Figure 2 provides an expanded version of the FII matrices, calculated for the entire 2005–2014 period across all countries, between official EM-DAT metrics of socio-economic impact due to natural hazards (in capitals) and the volume of social media activity (top row) or its spatial density (bottom row), where left and right hand columns correspond to human loss of life and infrastructure damage respectively. Here, first of all, we do observe some obvious clusters between the impact due to groups of hazards 'STORMS-FLOODS-EARTHQUAKES-LANDSLIDES' ('Human losses' component of the EM-DAT dataset) and 'EARTHQUAKES-FLOODS-LANDSLIDES' ('Infrastructure damage' component of the EM-DAT dataset). For the case where UGC intensity is analyzed without accounting for geographic distribution (top row), we can see two main clusters, where 'storms' correlate strongly with 'floods' and 'landslides' with volcanic activity, as signaled by UGC uploaded to the platform across countries and throughout the entire study period 2005–2014. We also observe very weak general correlations *between* the official EM-DAT data and the Yahoo! Flickr UGC. The bottom row represents the same correlation analyses, however, this time accounting for spatial compactness of the uploaded UGC. Here, more interesting patterns emerge, notably within and between groups of hazard-tagged social media activity data and the official EM-DAT indicators. Within groups, social media thematic tags correlate very strongly between themselves, across all five hazards (in case of the 'human losses' component) and with the 'STORMS' component (in case of 'infrastructure damage' component).

Table 1. Comparison of the statistical relationships between uploaded online image and video materials during each individual type of hazard event and correspondingly aggregated socio-economic losses

	Landslide	Earthquake	Volcano	Flood	Storm
Worldwide, each year 2005–2014					
Total affected	0.508*	−0.262	−0.034	0.204	−0.318
Total damage	0.656**	0.522*	−0.207	0.564*	0.171
Across countries, entire 2005–2014 period (volume)					
Total affected	−0.007	0.064	0.040	−0.004	−0.018
Total damage	0.001	0.064	0.023	−0.004	−0.005
Across countries, entire 2005–2014 period (density)					
Total affected	0.227	0.123	0.052	0.245	0.285
Total damage	0.217	0.121	0.080	0.399*	0.499*

Statistical significance: (**):p<0.05, (*):p<0.1, ():not significant.

Finally, we ran the same principle FIIs, but this time adapted to countries present in the EM-DAT dataset. This is done in order to extend the previously identified knowledge on candidate hazards to the candidate locations for applications of impact estimation using UGC. Figure 3 illustrates the strength and

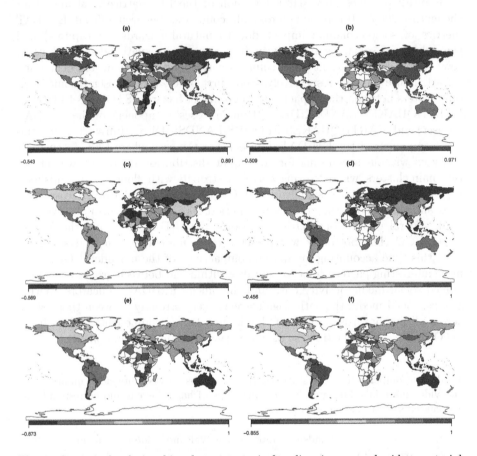

Fig. 3. Statistical relationships between topical online image and video material uploaded to the Yahoo! Flickr platform (2005–2014) and the following socio-economic indicators: (a) number of people affected (including *Dead, Injured* and *Homeless*) by any type of emergency taken place each year from 2005 to 2014, (b) economic losses (e.g., damage to infrastructure) due to any type of emergency taken place each year from 2005 to 2014, (c) number of people affected (including *Dead, Injured* and *Homeless*) by different types of hazards, occurring during the entire period 2005–2014, (d) economic losses (e.g., damage to infrastructure) due to different types of hazards, occurring during the entire period 2005–2014, (e) number of people affected (including *Dead, Injured* and *Homeless*) by different types of hazards, occurring during the entire period 2005–2014 *(accounting for spatial density of social media posts)*, (f) economic losses (e.g., damage to infrastructure) due to different types of hazards, occurring during the entire period 2005–2014 *(accounting for spatial density of social media posts)*.

directions of statistical relationships between official metrics and annual post-ings for all hazards (a) and (b), for each hazard during the entire 10-year period (*semantic volume*) ((c) and (d)), and for each hazard during the entire 10-year period (*semantic density*) ((e) and (f)). Here we can see that a number of coun-tries demonstrate strong correlation patterns across all hazards during each year; This can potentially suggest that structure of hazards on an annual basis has little variation and is likely to consist of the hazards whose impacts have already demonstrated high correlation levels with UGC during the previous steps in our analysis. This can be also confirmed by Fig. 3(c) and (d), which show similar patterns, with somewhat weaker correlations in the same locations. This can be explained by the bias introduced by the hazards, with weak/absent correlations with official impact indicators (e.g., volcanic eruptions), but also potentially by the different nature of the same hazards in different locations. For example, Canada and Australia are most likely to have the same structure of hazards presented in the scope of this study; however, in the case of Canada, they are more likely to occur in the same areas, whilst, in Australia, they exhibit a less structured pattern of emergence (Fig. 3(e) and (f)).

3 Appendix

3.1 EM-DAT Database

EM-DAT has been maintained since 1988 by CRED/University of Louvain (Belgium) as a worldwide database on disasters, and contains information about more than 19,000 disasters worldwide, dating back to 1900 [4]. Its content is daily updated and available for download every 3 months after validation. Emergencies are recorded at the country-level and contain such metadata and attributes as location, date, number of people killed/injured/affected, number homeless and estimated damage costs [4].

3.2 YFCC100M

We used the Yahoo! Flickr Creative Commons 100M (YFCC100M) dataset con-taining a list of images and videos uploaded to the Yahoo! Flickr platform between January 2005 and August 2014. All the audio-visual material provided in this database is licensed under one of the Creative Commons copyright licenses (CC:BY).

3.3 Methods

In this study we applied the standard feature interaction identification method (FII) widely used in machine learning [17] in order to determine whether rela-tionships exist between outputs of the standard empirical valuation methods of socio-economic impacts of the natural hazards and traces of human activities recorded online during outbreaks of such emergencies.

$$\rho_{X,Y} = \left(\frac{cov(X,Y)}{\sigma_X \sigma_Y}\right), \tag{1}$$

where cov is the covariance, σ_X is the standard deviation of X and σ_Y is the standard deviation of Y.

We exploited this technique in order to cover various angles of the possible dependencies between two main feature candidates (i) type of a hazard event (five types included) and (ii) location (any of the 176 countries, identified to upload hazard-related image and video material to Yahoo! Flickr platform during the period of study 2005–2014).

To match the empirically estimated indicators of human and economic losses over defined time intervals (one year in our case), we calculated the semantic propensity of hazard-related tags and keywords over the total amount of uploaded media during the same time frame:

$$\alpha_{(t_1-t)} = \frac{N_{hazards(t_1-t)} * 100}{N_{total(t_1-t)}} \tag{2}$$

In order to correct the total propensity of the semantic social media material geographically, we used the metric of standard distance (SD), which measures the compactness of a distribution of spatial point data, providing a single value representing the dispersion of features around the centre.

$$SD = \sqrt{\frac{\sum_{i=1}^{n}(x_i - \overline{X})^2}{n} + \frac{\sum_{i=1}^{n}(y_i - \overline{Y})^2}{n}}, \tag{3}$$

where x_i and y_i are the coordinates for the feature i, $(\overline{X},\overline{Y})$ represents the mean centre for the point features, and n is equal to the total number of features.

References

1. OECD: New Data for Understanding the Human Condition. OECD Global Science Forum Report on Data and Research Infrastructure for the Social Sciences (2013)
2. IPCC: Managing the risks of extreme events and disasters to advance climate change adaptation. Special Report of the Intergovernmental Panel on Climate Change (2012)
3. UNISDR: Global Assessment Report on Disaster Risk Reduction. World Risk Report. Bndniss Entwicklung Hilft, Berlin, Germany (2009)
4. Guha-Sapir, D., Hoyois, P.: Measuring the human and economic impact of disasters. Report produced for the Government Office of Science, Foresight project 'Reducing Risks of Future Disasters: Priorities for Decision Makers', Foresight (2012)
5. Gallina, V., Torresan, S., Critto, A., Sperotto, A., Glade, T., Marcomini, A.: A review of multi-risk methodologies for natural hazards: consequences and challenges for a climate change impact assessment. J. Env. Manag. 168, 123–132 (2016)

6. Tkachenko, N., Jarvis, S., Procter, R.: Predicting floods with Flickr tags. PLOS ONE (2017). doi:10.1371/journal.pone.0172870
7. Tkachenko, N., Procter, R., Jarvis, S.: Predicting the impact of urban flooding using open data. RSOS (2016). doi:10.1098/rsos.160013
8. Guthrie, R.: The catastrophic nature of humans. Nat. Geo. **8**(6), 421–422 (2015)
9. Wachinger, G., Renn, O., Begg, C., Kuhlicke, C.: The risk perception paradox - implications for governance and communication of natural hazards. Risk Anal. **33**(6), 1049–1065 (2013)
10. Earle, P.: Earthquake Twitter. Nat. Geo. **3**, 221–222 (2010)
11. Acar, A., Muraki, Y.: Twitter for crisis communication: lessons learned from Japan's tsunami disaster. Int. J. Web. Based Comm. **7**(3), 392–402 (2011)
12. Tang, Z., Zhang, L., Xu, F., Vo, H.: Examining the role of social media in California's drought risk management in 2014. Nat. Hazards **79**(1), 171–193 (2015)
13. Al-Saggaf, Y., Simmons, P.: Social media in Saudi Arabia: exploring its use during two natural disasters. Tech. Forec. Soc. Change **95**, 3–15 (2015)
14. Thomee, B., Shamma, D.A., Friedland, G., Elizalde, B., Ni, K., Poland, D., Borth, D., Li, L.J.: YFCC100M: the new data in multimedia research. ACM. Comms. **59**(2), 64–73 (2016)
15. Crooks, A., Croitoru, A., Stefanidis, A., Radzikowski, J.: Earthquake: twitter as a distributed sensor system. GIS. Trans. **17**(1), 124–147 (2013)
16. Granger, C.W.J.: Some properties of time series data and their use in econometric model specification. J. Econometr. **16**, 121–130 (1981)
17. Flach, P.: Machine Learning: The Art and Science of Algorithms that Make Sense of Data. Cambridge University Press, Cambridge (2012)
18. Popocatepetl Volcano (Mexico): largest eruption, 16 April 2012, heavy ash fall (2012). (Volcano Discovery: posted Monday 16 April, 2012, 21:45 PM)
19. Teigland, J.: Mega-events and impacts on tourism; the predictions and realities of the Lillehammer Olympics. Imp. Asses. Proj. Appr. **17**(4), 305–317 (1999)

What Can Software Tell Us About Media Coverage and Public Opinion? An Analysis of Political News Posts and Audience Comments on Facebook by Computerised Method

Yunya Song and Yin Zhang[✉]

Department of Journalism, Hong Kong Baptist University,
10/F Communication and Visual Arts Building, HKBU,
5 Hereford Road, Kowloon Tong, Hong Kong S.A.R.
zhangyin@hkbu.edu.hk

Abstract. In this exploratory study, we applied an automated linguistic analysis method (TextMind) to a social movement context by comparing a sample set of online news posts (N_1 = 13,434) with audience comments to the posts (N_2 = 1,998,095) on Facebook. The findings of this study revealed that there were, in fact, linguistic differences between the news posts by news media outlets and their corresponding audience comments. TextMind is able to detect such linguistic differences and their changes over time. Comparative findings suggest: (1) The linguistic choices of news reporting are affected by news media's (or journalists') political, ideological, and market orientations. (2) The language used by traditional newspapers is not necessarily more conservative or moderate in emotion than their online competitors. (3) Linguistic choices in news posts would change over periods of time. However, (4) the language patterns of news posts did not directly affect linguistic choices of audiences in opinion expression, which remained relatively consistent.

Keywords: Media coverage · Public opinion · Automated linguistic analysis · TextMind · Facebook

1 Introduction

Recent events and studies indicate that reading news on social media has become increasingly important because individuals are now engaged in large global virtual communities that produce and diffuse information quickly. The majority of adults in the U.S. get news on social media (68%), and many do so often (18%), according to a survey by Pew Research Center [1]. People are exposed to news content on social media and use their online networks to react to the reports. Yet knowledge about the relationship between the linguistic patterns of news and audience responses remains limited. In this exploratory study, we applied an automated linguistic analysis method to a social movement context by comparing a sample of news posts (N_1 = 13,434) and audience

© Springer International Publishing AG 2017
G.L. Ciampaglia et al. (Eds.): SocInfo 2017, Part II, LNCS 10540, pp. 230–241, 2017.
DOI: 10.1007/978-3-319-67256-4_18

comments to the posts (N_2 = 1,998,095) on Facebook. Our analysis is expected to shed light on the emotional profile of news writing and audience engagement on social media.

2 Literature Review

2.1 Emotion in News

Emotions are the glue of human societies [2, 3] and their influence on human behaviour is significant. Social media content often conveys information about the author's emotional state, his or her judgment or evaluation of a certain person or issue, or the intended emotional effect the sender wishes to have on the receiver during communication [4], which is generally termed as "sentiment".

Written text is inherently linked to emotion, and classic journalism studies indicate that news production is affected by ideological, cultural, institutional, and professional biases. Many of these studies focus on classifying the journalists' emotional state. However, little is known about the makeup of emotions during news reading on social media. Do reporters and audiences share the same feelings? If not, is the relationship between the news posts and emotions of the audience incidental, or are there recurring patterns? Previous studies have shown that affective information could be transferred through computer-mediated communication [5].

The connection between language and communication has been well established. Across academic disciplines, a number of analytical tools have been applied to political, social, and cultural discourses. There is more than one approach to assessing the emotion of written text. Examining linguistic patterns is an alternative to the traditional approach of interpreting a text's symbolic meanings and considering the text within a certain context. In this study, we aimed to explore this linguistic method as it relates to news reading on social media.

2.2 An Examination of Social Media Posts Using Automated Linguistic Analysis

Based on the assumption that political discourse can provide an accurate measurement of individual personality differences, a theoretical and methodological approach that measures personality through language in order to quantify linguistic differences has been developed. One computerised word count program called Linguistic Inquiry and Word Count (LIWC) was used to provide this measurement. LIWC and other word count programmes "assume that the words people use convey psychological information over and above their literal meaning and independent of their semantic context" [6]. Thus, the theoretical assumption in this study is that language can be categorised and quantified to make inferences about individuals' personalities, attitudes, or standpoints on a given issue.

This method involves classifying written samples by matching word stems with entries in the software's internal dictionary, and then placing the properly identified words into their respective categories. One advantage of this strategy is that a large number of written samples can be collected and analysed more quickly than with other methods, such as traditional discourse analysis or content analysis.

After initial research on personality traits manifested in the language of various populations, social scientists turned their attention to the political domain. Using computerised text analysis in previous studies, researchers have successfully identified significant differences in the speech of politicians and public figures. In previous studies, the research scope was not limited to the relationship between language and personality, but expanded to a comparison of the linguistic differences among several candidates – in connection with their personalities during election campaigns, under the assumption that the public and voters may be influenced by certain linguistic patterns [7–10].

The extent to which automated linguistic analysis is able to accurately identify, analyse, and categorise political discourse, especially idiomatic language with underlying pragmatic functions, is the major concern and critique of this approach, and additional studies are needed to extend the body of research. Moreover, the original LIWC programmes were developed for written text in English; whether and how can this method can be applied to other languages remains a practical and imperative issue for further research development. To address this research gap in this study, we adopted a Chinese-language version of LIWC called TextMind [11] to measure linguistic features in Chinese news posts. The lexicon of TextMind is referred to the English lexicon of LIWC2007 and the traditional Chinese lexicon of C-LIWC. It also integrates the word segmentation and part-of-speech tagging modules of both Natural Language Processing Information Retrieval (NLPIR) and Language Technology Platform (LTP).

This study aims to investigate to what extent TextMind can analyse political discourse in Chinese. We intended to find a case that can provide a longitudinal observation of both news posts and audience opinion expressions to these posts. Therefore, the Umbrella Movement happened in Hong Kong was selected as the case for empirical investigation, by studying the related news coverage on Facebook and audience responses to the news posts.

2.3   The Umbrella Movement (UM)

The Umbrella Movement was a 79-day civil disobedience campaign in Hong Kong that occurred between 28 September and 15 December 2014. The movement was widely called as "Umbrella Movement" (UM here after) by foreign media and local activists, for the recognition of the umbrella as a symbol of defiance and resistance against the police force. The protest demanded the institutionalisation of a "filterless" election for the Chief Executive of the Hong Kong Special Administrative Region (SAR) government in 2017. The idea to occupy the main streets in the financial district of central Hong Kong was proposed by a law professor in early 2013. The occupation was originally conceived as a non-violent and "highly disciplined" collective action that would involve people sitting on the ground and locking their arms to obstruct traffic. The occupation was not expected to last for more than a few days [12].

When student groups started a series of protests in late September 2014, about ten days before the planned starting date of the occupation, the dynamics of the protest movement changed. A series student-police conflicts and police arrests of student leaders, and the police firing tear gas into the protesting crowd on the first day of the occupation, led to not only the scaling up of the protest, but also to a more dispersed and increasingly decentralised campaign formation [13, 14]. Occupations were consolidated into three separate districts (i.e. Admiralty, Mongkok, and Causeway Bay). Many protesters sought to maintain control of public thoroughfares, which is a violation of law, in hopes that the Chinese central government and Hong Kong government would make major concessions. Even when courts ordered some streets to be cleared, those occupying have not always complied. However, the UM itself was very decentralised – the demands and perspectives of the protesters could not be unified from the beginning and even changed over time. The public opinion towards the movement also varied in the whole society. In Dec 2014, the occupied areas were cleared by police force. The protests, once lively with energy from the potential of tangible change, ended without any political concessions from the government.

Observers still believed that the UM has significant implications for the future of Hong Kong society and for the Greater China region. Ideological divisions of the society became more polarised; tension and conflicts increased between political camps (pro-establishment vs pro-democratic) and different generations. In the following years, the movement became an icon, even though perceptions of its symbolic meanings and related discussions varied among different political camps and stakeholders.

Against this background, media discourse changed in reaction to the social and political issues and incidents throughout the campaign itself as well as the post-movement periods. By identifying the specific language patterns of the news coverage and the public opinion through quantifiable text analysis, we believe we can better understand the public discourse surrounding this large-scale social movement. In this study, we are interested in how news media of different factions – liberal/democratic or pro-establishment – embody the changes? A linguistic analysis can reveal trend(s) in the portrayal of the movement by news media, as well as in audience responses to the news posts. This information may illustrate the relationship between news media and decentralised social movements.

Based on these conceptual discussions and the explication of the case, the following research questions guided the linguistic analysis of this study:

1. Do the political orientations of news media imply their linguistic choices in news reporting?
2. Are language choices by traditional newspapers more conservative than those by online news media?
3. Which characteristics, if any, are associated with the linguistic choices of news media?
4. Are the same characteristics found in the comments by social media audiences?

3 Research Design

This study used Facebook as the outlet for investigation. We chose Facebook is because it is currently the most dominant social media platform in Hong Kong, with more than 4.4 million local users, comprising more than 60% of the population [15]. Most pertinent to this study is the fact that many Hong Kong citizens, especially supporters of the UM, used Facebook to obtain information and communicate with others during that time [16, 17].

3.1 Data Collection

We used *R* to retrieve news posts that were published on the Facebook pages of five local news media, namely *Apply Daily, Ming Pao, Passion Times, Speak Out HK*, and *Wen Wei Po*. Three of these are traditional newspapers (*Apply Daily, Ming Pao, Wen Wei Po*) that provide both hard copies distribution and online news services; the other two (*Passion Times* and *Speak Out HK*) are online news sources that target the netizen market niche, especially the younger generation, and had recently emerged in the past few years. The sampling period was from September 2014 to December 2016.These five news media represent diverse points on the political spectrum, from radical anti-establishment (*Passion Times*) and typical pro-democratic (*Apply Daily*), to the centre and middle-class (*Ming Pao*), and to traditional pro-establishment (*Wen Wei Po*) and newly emerged for pro-establishment activsts (*Speak Out HK*).

This study used a series of keywords to search for news posts. The keywords were terms that people used to refer to the movement, including "zimling" (occupy), "zimzung" (occupy central), "zim ling gam zung" (occupy Admiralty), "zim ling hang dung" (occupy movement), "jyu-saan" or simply "saan" (umbrella), "ze-daa" (which literally means using the umbrella to fight), "bou pou syun" (fight for universal suffrage), "jyu saan gaak ming" (umbrella revolution), "wong si daai" (yellow riband – a symbol of the democratic movement), and "ngaan sik gaak ming" (colour revolution). Any news posts on the five Facebook pages that included one or more of these terms would be identified as part of the sample set, and the comments about these news posts on Facebook were also retrieved (as long as they fell within the timeframe).

A total of 13,434 news posts met the criteria and were retrieved directly from the news media Facebook pages; a total of 1,998,095 comments were also retrieved. The authors hoped that the collected news posts, as well as the comments to them, would provide a bigger picture about how news media portrayed the UM and the response to the incidents by a significant portion of the public.

In Hong Kong, people usually discuss socio-political issues based on news they have read and ongoing events at that time. Given that the media and public discourse are affected by the changing political atmosphere and emerging incidents, we further divide the study's timeframe into one movement period and three post-movement periods, which are as follows: (1) 28 Sept to 15 Dec 2014 (the movement period); (2) 16 Dec to 22 Nov 2015 (the district council election period); (3) 23 Nov to 9 Apr 2016 (transaction period); and (4) 10 Apr to 31 Dec 2016 (the legislative council election period). These classifications are event-based, and this level of detail in analysis may better reflect the changes of political discourse and sentiment during and after the large-scale social movement. The numbers of news posts and audience comments on each news media's Facebook pages during each period are presented in Table 1.

Table 1. Summary of number of posts and number of comments for five selected media during four time periods

	Period 1		Period 2		Period 3		Period 4	
	Post	Comment	Post	Comment	Post	Comment	Post	Comment
Apple daily	2,408	1,018,472	394	91,269	79	14,536	130	37,950
MingPao	2,888	159,650	1017	26,611	189	6,769	233	9,191
Passion time	4,228	465,392	961	56,612	181	8,279	177	5,604
Speak out HK	227	87,222	87	9,478	6	619	8	431
Wen Wei Po	126	4	31	2	13	2	51	2

3.2 Data Analysis

In analysing this data, we used TextMind to identify emotional cognitive lexicons, pronouns, exclamation marks, and past-present-future lexicons. The frequency of words and punctuation marks (number of occurrences divided by the total number of words in the text) determined their classification into a dimension or sub-dimension.

Three dimensions were analysed in the original news posts: affect, cognitive mechanism, and perspective. The affect dimension was measured through considering five sub-dimensions of emotion (i.e. positive emotion, negative emotion, anxiety, anger, and sadness). The cognitive mechanism dimension indicated the presence of rational thinking in addition to expression of emotion. The time consideration (perspective) dimension was defined by statements about the past, present, or future.

Three dimensions were also analysed in the comments: affect, self-identity, and exclamation. The affect dimension included the same five sub-dimensions as listed above. The dimension of self-identity was composed two sub-dimensions: "I" and "we". Finally, the dimension of exclamation categorises the strength of the tone used in audience comments.

The TextMind dictionary contained multiple words that were identifiable as belonging to particular categories. For example, the dictionary for "anger" encompassed words such as "annoyed", "argh", "bastard", etc.; the entry for "anxiety" contained words including "stressed", "terrifying", "uneasy", etc.; the classification of "sadness" included "agony", "depressed", "grief", etc. Based on the definitions of each dimension and sub-dimension, the software generated word count scores, the percentage of identified words that match the dictionary from the total number of words in the text. We compared the mean scores of news posts and audience comments for each dimension and sub-dimension by media source and across the identified time periods.

4 Results

A series of one-way ANOVAs were conducted to examine the differences among the five news media's news posts and related audience comments on Facebook. The analyses revealed that there were statistically significant differences among the five news media's coverage on the UM; significant differences were also found among audience comments to the posts. Moreover, these differences evolved during the four periods of time.

Table 2. Comparison of linguistic differences between news posts and audience comments in Period 1 (Umbrella Movement)

Post level	Apple daily	MingPao	Passion time	Speak Out HK	Wen Wei Po	F_Value (sig.)
PosEmo	0.0107000 a	**0.0218282 b**	0.0092663 c	0.0183553 d	0.0097371 ac	363.817***
OtherNegEmo	0.0025632 ac	**0.0031700 b**	0.0024086 c	**0.0039406 ab**	0.0029270 abc	5.783***
Anx	0.0012945 a	0.0016889 b	0.0011194 a	**0.0030204 c**	0.0018016 abc	15.371***
Anger	0.0032782 a	0.0043587 b	0.0031702 a	**0.0060226 c**	0.0058540 bc	17.133***
Sad	0.0010620 a	0.0014795 b	0.0009361 a	**0.0025741 c**	0.0018407 abc	15.521***
CogMech	0.0704186 a	**0.0920970 b**	0.0653103 c	0.1482895 d	0.0948105 b	319.656***
tPast	0.0008560 a	0.0015285 b	**0.0018780 c**	**0.0023019 bc**	0.0066221 d	49.102***
tNow	0.0016917 a	0.0021404 a	**0.0027743 b**	**0.0025265 ab**	0.0012010 a	14.470***
tFuture	**0.0006133 a**	**0.0007623 a**	0.0003696 b	0.0005962 ab	0.0010001 ab	9.443***
Comment Level						
PosEmo	**0.0369220 a**	0.0245767 b	0.0289243 c	0.0331473 d	0.0370370 abcd	1137.385***
OtherNegEmo	**0.0062413 a**	0.0054250 b	0.0051567 b	**0.0061257 a**	0.0000000 ab	73.577***
Anx	**0.0017631 a**	0.0015860 b	0.0012049 c	0.0014090 b	0.0000000abc	104.967***
Anger	**0.0072427 a**	0.0051732 b	0.0047433 c	0.0065898 d	0.0277778 abcd	346.669***
Sad	**0.0019880 a**	0.0016360 b	0.0015227 b	**0.0021055 a**	0.0000000 ab	62.949***
I	**0.0091200 a**	0.0075249 b	0.0083003 c	**0.0092413 a**	0.0000000 abc	130.045***
We	0.0020469 a	0.0014547 b	**0.0026528 c**	0.0018386 d	0.0000000 abcd	212.935***
Exclaim	**0.0432344 a**	0.0302669 b	0.0349289 c	0.0339995 d	0.0227273 abcd	1179.343***

Note: Results of the Tukey post-hoc analysis are shown through the use of subscripts (a, b, c, d). Means with the same subscript letter within each row are not significantly different, while means with different subscript letters within one row are significantly different at the $p < .05$ level.

Table 3. Comparison of linguistic differences between news posts and audience comments in Period 2 (district council election)

Post level	Apple daily	MingPao	Passion time	Speak out HK	Wen Wei Po	F_value
PosEmo	0.0108624 a	0.0132626 b	**0.0170598 c**	0.0159641 bc	0.0068792 a	28.283***
OtherNegEmo	0.0039525 ab	0.0031797 b	**0.0045545 a**	0.0036165 ab	0.0010081 ab	5.633***
Anx	0.0010834	0.0012934	0.0014786	0.0012808	0.0017930	1.243
Anger	0.0032032 a	0.0037338 a	0.0050636 b	**0.0058433 a**	0.0063787 ab	9.868***
Sad	0.0014765 ab	0.0014761 b	**0.0020826 a**	0.0017154 ab	0.0016671 ab	3.497***
CogMech	0.0804652 a	0.0904139 b	0.1115909 c	**0.1301156 d**	0.0910130 ab	81.727***
tPast	0.0038162 a	0.0033444 a	0.0035259 a	0.0034924 a	**0.0075994 d**	4.743***
tNow	0.0022513 a	0.0015147 b	0.0031006 c	0.0028910 ac	0.0010079 ab	21.792***
tFuture	0.0004877	0.0006705	0.0006265	0.0006763	0.0004032	0.568
Comment Level						
PosEmo	**0.0239682 a**	0.0214256 b	0.0211118 b	0.0224512 ab	0.0000000 ab	30.436***
OtherNegEmo	**0.0042177 a**	**0.0045964 a**	0.0047280 a	0.0041934	0.0000000 a	4.018***
Anx	0.0012251	0.0013166	0.0012619	0.0009598	0.0000000	1.910
Anger	0.0052966 a	0.0062215 b	0.0048645 c	**0.0083878 d**	0.0000000 abcd	39.591***
Sad	0.0014851 a	0.0015908 a	0.0018738 b	0.0017196 ab	0.0000000 ab	8.686***
I	0.0070070 a	0.0068494 a	0.0076407 b	0.0071931 ab	0.0000000 ab	7.169***
We	0.0009289	0.0009035	0.0009213	0.0010061	0.0000000	0.270
Exclaim	0.0304684 a	0.0261505 b	0.0276680 b	**0.0351001 d**	0.0000000 abcd	50.173***

Note: Results of the Tukey post-hoc analysis are shown through the use of subscripts (a, b, c, d). Means with the same subscript letter within each row are not significantly different, while means with different subscript letters within one row are significantly different at the $p < .05$ level.

Table 4. Comparison of linguistic differences between news posts and audience comments in Period 3 (transaction period)

Post level	Apple daily	MingPao	Passion time	Speak out HK	Wen Wei Po	F_value
PosEmo	0.0090980 a	0.0124384 a	**0.0172935 b**	0.0046713 a	0.0102986 ab	12.951***
OtherNegEmo	0.0045914	0.0031726	0.0055433	0.0065754	0.0032860	2.365
Anx	0.0003702 a	**0.0025438 b**	0.0015072 a	0.0000000 a	0.0016440 ab	6.473***
Anger	0.0064587 ab	**0.0100220 b**	0.0054121 a	0.0000000 a	0.0029838 ab	5.483***
Sad	0.0021679	0.0023156	0.0016966	0.0000000	0.0016013	1.077
CogMech	0.0711008 ab	0.0787633 b	**0.1057150 c**	0.0632980 a	0.0545247 a	32.018***
tPast	**0.0053010 a**	0.0022669 b	**0.0047554 a**	0.0000000 ab	0.0040985 ab	8.072***
tNow	**0.0022410 a**	0.0011374 a	0.0038005 b	0.0015723 ab	0.0000000 a	13.143***
tFuture	0.0012146	0.0005650	0.0005335	0.0000000	0.0000000	1.329
Comment Level						
PosEmo	0.0172496 a	0.0189914 a	**0.0223785 b**	0.0180708 ab	0.0000000 ab	17.162***
OtherNegEmo	0.0050955	0.0057264	0.0050959	0.0033011	0.0000000	1.685
Anx	**0.0015615 a**	**0.0017820 a**	0.0012494 b	0.0004741 c	0.0000000 abc	2.975***
Anger	0.0051130 a	**0.0072460 b**	0.0054357 a	0.0065214 ab	0.0000000 ab	7.890***
Sad	0.0016517	0.0015524	0.0016660	0.0016334	0.0000000	0.095
I	0.0062491	0.0065081	0.0069596	0.0062811	0.0000000	1.357
We	0.0006842 a	0.0009886 a	**0.0011025 b**	0.0005351 a	0.0000000 a	4.833***
Exclaim	0.0232363 a	0.0241908 a	0.0254164 a	**0.0300032 b**	0.0357143 ab	3.305***

Note: Results of the Tukey post-hoc analysis are shown through the use of subscripts (a, b, c, d). Means with the same subscript letter within each row are not significantly different, while means with different subscript letters within one row are significantly different at the p < .05 level.

Table 5. Comparison of linguistic differences between news posts and audience comments in Period 2 (legislative council election)

Post Levels	Apple Daily	Ming Pao	Passion Time	Speak Out HK	Wen Wei Po	F_value
PosEmo	0.0124128 a	0.0159297 bc	0.0172622 c	**0.0249900 d**	0.0120908 ab	6.200 ***
OtherNegEmo	0.0027020	0.0023663	0.0040004	0.0013298	0.0017843	2.217
Anx	0.0017733 a	0.0011253 a	**0.0008872 b**	0.0000000 a	0.0006045 a	2.517 ***
Anger	0.0044714 a	0.0041646 a	0.0041846 a	**0.0119921 b**	0.0030527 a	3.164 ***
Sad	**0.0024880 a**	0.0011104 b	0.0020837 ab	0.0000000 ab	0.0010051 ab	3.037 ***
CogMech	0.0783701 a	0.0804313 a	**0.0987473 b**	0.0715579 ab	0.0616756 ab	17.896 ***
tPast	0.0028093	0.0022773	0.0029560	0.0000000	0.0032792	2.179
tNow	0.0015735 a	0.0016880 a	**0.0025275 b**	0.0000000 a	0.0011264 a	3.921 ***
tFuture	0.0012607	0.0007093	0.0008662	0.0000000	0.0007683	1.002
Comment Level						
PosEmo	0.0198207 a	0.0188199 a	0.0199062 a	**0.0284933 b**	0.0000000 ab	4.626***
OtherNegEmo	**0.0054213 a**	0.0044407 b	0.0041156 b	0.0054368 ab	0.0000000 ab	5.180***
Anx	0.0010400	0.0013006	0.0011297	0.0013891	0.0000000	1.290
Anger	0.0049515 a	0.0061628 b	0.0047770 a	**0.0074071 ab**	0.0000000 ab	4.874***
Sad	0.0011912	0.0013243	0.0012934	0.0021579	0.0000000	1.083
I	0.0062848 ab	0.0056911 b	**0.0069401 a**	0.0060212 ab	0.0000000 ab	2.680***
We	**0.0007693 a**	0.0005040 b	**0.0008402 ab**	0.0011820 ab	0.0000000 ab	2.901***
Exclaim	0.0238530 ab	0.0224014 b	**0.0251009 a**	**0.0283526 ab**	0.0000000 ab	2.821***

Note: Results of the Tukey post-hoc analysis are shown through the use of subscripts (a, b, c, d). Means with the same subscript letter within each row are not significantly different, while means with different subscript letters within one row are significantly different at the p < .05 level.

4.1   News Posts

Affect. The analysis revealed that the newly emerged pro-establishment activist site (*Speak Out HK*) expressed the most intensely negative emotion towards the "chaos" created by the movement, including anxiety, anger, and sadness (see Table 2). The word count scores of *Speak Out HK* were significantly highest among the five news media. Such linguistic patterns were consistent with the site's anti-movement position. In contrast, *Ming Pao*, the centre and middle-class newspaper, was the most positive about the potential of political change during the movement. Such affect could be hardly found after the UM failed. During the post-movement periods, the radical anti-establishment news website (*Passion Times*) and the typical pro-democratic newspaper (*Apply Daily*) adopted an increasingly emotional tone in the post-movement periods, especially during the election periods (see Tables 3 and 5). These linguistic patterns reflected the two news media's frustration, disappointment, and even anger about the lack of political development.

Cognitive Mechanism. The analysis revealed that the centre and middle-class newspaper's (*Ming Pao*) reports were more rational and moderate during the movement period (see Table 2). In the post-movement periods, the radical anti-establishment news website (*Passion Times*) and activist pro-establishment news website (*Speak Out HK*) adopted similar cognitive processing linguistic patterns when reporting movement-related issues (see Tables 3, 4 and 5).

Time Consideration (Perspective).   Regarding the time consideration in reporting, the results revealed that the wording of *Apply Daily* mentioned more about the past in the first three periods and focused more on the future during the movement period. *Ming Pao* paid more attention to the future during the movement period, while did not show specific time consideration in later periods. *Passion Times* paid more attention to the present during the movement and the two elections periods. *Speak Out HK* only paid significantly more attention to the present and future during the movement period, while did not show specific time consideration pattern in their linguistic style later on.

4.2   Audience Comments

Affect. The analysis of audience comments showed that the wording of opinion expression in response to the typical pro-democratic newspaper (*Apply Daily*) were the most emotional during the movement period – the word count scores of the five sub-dimensions were all significantly highest (see Table 2). Comments on news posts by the centre and middle-class newspaper (*Ming Pao*) and the radical anti-establishment news website (*Passion Times*) became increasingly emotional in the first two post-movement periods (see Tables 3 and 4). The linguistic patterns of all these comments reflected the tendency of Facebook engagement to UM related news coverage. That is, the social media news posts remain a popular space for expressing their anti-establishment positions.

Self-identify. The results show that audience members of the two anti-establishment news media (*Apply Daily* and *Passion Times*) and the newly active pro-establishment news website (*Speak Out HK*) tended to comment with the wording "I" and "we", while commenters to the centre and middle-class newspaper (*Ming Pao*) used less first-person perspective (see Tables 2, 3, 4 and 5).

Exclamation. Regarding the tone of audience comments, results show that the audiences of the two anti-establishment news media (*Apply Daily* and *Passion Times*) and the newly active pro-establishment news website (*Speak Out HK*) tended to use a stronger tone when engaging with the selected news posts on Facebook, while commenters to the centre and middle-class newspaper (*Ming Pao*) used less exclamation (see Tables 2, 3, 4 and 5).

4.3   Associations Between News Posts and Audience Comments

From the above findings, we can see that the linguistic patterns of news posts may not directly affect the linguistic characteristics of audience comments. As shown in Table 2, 3, 4 and 5, the rankings and groupings of mean word count scores at post and comment levels did not match each other. However, the characteristics of the audiences were relatively consistent. By comparing the patterns in both the posts and comments, we observed that anti-establishment (or pro-democratic) and activist audiences on social media tended to express more emotion in their tone and maintain a stronger first-person perspective that reflects the identity as HongKonger.

5   Discussion

In a world of evolving digital media and online audiences, the dynamics of issue agendas are becoming more complex. Because both traditional and social media news outlets have online presences, they are equally accessible to time-series analysis. Therefore, systematic analysis of both news reporting and audience's opinion expression become increasingly important. In this study, we retrieve both news posts and related comments from Facebook for automated linguistic analyses. The exploratory results revealed that there were, in fact, linguistic differences existed among the news coverage on the UM, and the same was true of related audience comments to the news posts. The automated linguistic analysis method – TextMind – is able to detect these linguistic differences and their changes over time.

By comparing the word count scores of both news posts and audience comments on Facebook in four periods of time, the preliminary findings of this study can be concluded as follow: First, the linguistic choices of news reporting are affected by news media's (or journalists') political, ideological, and market orientations. With the help of computerised method, the wording of news reporting is now a quantifiable indicator to understand the affect, cognitive mechanism, and time consideration in news posts. Second, the language of traditional newspapers is not necessarily more conservative or moderate than their online competitors (i.e. online news websites). During particular circumstance (i.e. a large-scale social movement like the UM), traditional print media expressed stronger emotion in their news reporting, in response to the social atmosphere and development of social events. Third, within the context of the UM, linguistic choices in news posts would change over time. We found that, across the four periods of time, the news media's posts displayed different wording style. However, the language patterns of news posts did not directly affect linguistic choices of audiences in opinion expression. The linguistic style of audience comments remained relatively consistent. One possible explanation is that the news reading on social media is usually habitual. Hence, audiences' comment to the news posts they read on Facebook tend to consistently reflect their emotions and stands on the social issue.

6 Limitations

Although the longitudinal, multi-level, and cross-media results of this study contribute to the ongoing exploration of computerised method application in media text, public opinion, and social movement studies, this methodology has its quantitative and qualitative limitations. For instance, the construction and empirical basis for the formulas used in LIWC may have caused quantitative errors, especially when applying it to non-English (Chinese) written text. There are also qualitative constraints involved in using an automated linguistic analysis method to make inferences about the connection between the discourse and characteristics of either journalists or audiences. Dictionary-based programmes like LIWC/TextMind are notoriously noisy – this remains an inherent problem of this type and similar analytic methods. In order to verify the findings, we have randomly drawn a small sub-sample for manual coding (traditional content analysis). Compared to the results by TextMind, the sub-sample yielded similar results.

The above limitations could reduce the validity of the current method in political and media discourse analysis. Further validation tests that involve qualitative analysis (e.g. in-depth reading) or separate new sample(s) for software analysis would be encouraged. Interdisciplinary collaboration shall together improve the research design and generate more findings through broader research, and better understand the contextual language through a more sophisticated conceptual and theoretical framework.

Acknowledgment. We gratefully acknowledge the Research Grants Committee of Hong Kong for providing a generous research grant (HKBU 12632816) for a larger project on which this article is based.

References

1. Pew Research Center: News use across social media platforms (2016). http://www.journalism.org/2016/05/26/news-use-across-social-media-platforms-2016/. Accessed 20 May 2017
2. Durkheim, E.: The Division of Labor in Society. Free Press, New York (1893)
3. Collins, R.: Stratification, emotional energy and the transient emotions. In: Kemper, T. (ed.) Research Agendas in the Sociology of Emotions, pp. 27–57. Suny Press, New York (1990)
4. Bollen, J., Pepe, A., Mao, H.: Modeling public mood and emotion: Twitter sentiment and socio-economic phenomena. In: Adamic, L., Baeza-Yates, R., Counts, S. (eds.) Proceedings of the Fifth International AAAI Conference on Weblogs and Social Media, pp. 450–453. AAAI Press, Palo Alto (2011)

5. Harris, R.B., Paradice, D.: An investigation of the computer-mediated communication of emotion. J. Appl. Sci. Res. **3**(12), 2081–2090 (2007)
6. Pennebaker, J.W., Mehl, M.R., Niederhoffer, K.: Psychological aspects of natural language use: our words, our selves. Ann. Rev. Psychol. **54**, 547–577 (2003)
7. Pennebaker, J.W., Lay, T.C.: Language use and personality crises: analyses of major Rudolph Giuliani press conferences. J. Res. Pers. **36**, 271–282 (2002)
8. Pennebaker, J.W., Slatcher, R.B., Chung, C.K.: Linguistic markers of psychological state through media interviews: John Kerry and John Edwards in 2004, Al Gore in 2000. Analyses Soc. Issues Public Policy **5**(1), 197–204 (2005)
9. Slatcher, R.B., Chung, C.K., Pennebaker, J.W., Stone, L.D.: Winning words: individual differences in linguistic style among U.S. presidential and vice presidential candidates. J. Res. Pers. **41**, 63–75 (2007)
10. Kangas, S.E.N.: What can software tell us about political candidates? A critical analysis of a computerized method for political discourse. J. Lang. Polit. **13**(1), 77–79 (2014)
11. Gao, R., Hao, B., Li, H., Gao, Y., Zhu, T.: Developing simplified Chinese psychological linguistic analysis dictionary for microblog. In: Paper Presented at the 2013 International Conference on Brain and Health Informatics (2013)
12. Lee, F.L.F., Chan, J.M.: Media and the new/old logics of connective action: Hong Kong's Umbrella movement. Oxford University Press, New York (Forthcoming)
13. Cheng, E.W., Chan, W.: Explaining spontaneous occupation: antecedents, contingencies and spaces in the Umbrella movement. Soc. Mov. Stud. **16**(2), 222–239 (2017)
14. Tang, G.: Mobilization by images: TV screen and mediated instant grievances in the Umbrella movement. Chinese J. Commun. **8**(4), 338–355 (2015)
15. Go-Globe. Social media usage in Hong Kong – Statistics and trends (2015). http://www.go-globe.hk/blog/social-media-hong-kong/. Accessed 20 May 2017
16. Ma, W.K., Lau, H.C., Hui, Y.H.: 2014 news and social media use survey (2014). (in Chinese). Media Digest. http://app3.rthk.hk/mediadigest/content.php?aid=1960. Accessed 20 May 2017
17. Lee, F.L.F., Chan, J.M.: Digital media activities and mode of participation in a protest campaign: the case of the Umbrella Movement. Inf. Commun. Soc. **19**(1), 4–22 (2016)

Poster Papers: Opinions, Behavior, and Social Media Mining

GitHub and Stack Overflow: Analyzing Developer Interests Across Multiple Social Collaborative Platforms

Roy Ka-Wei Lee[(✉)] and David Lo

School of Information Systems, Singapore Management University,
Singapore, Singapore
{roylee.2013,davidlo}@smu.edu.sg

Abstract. Increasingly, software developers are using a wide array of social collaborative platforms for software development and learning. In this work, we examined the similarities in developer's interests within and across GitHub and Stack Overflow. Our study finds that developers share common interests in GitHub and Stack Overflow; on average, 39% of the GitHub repositories and Stack Overflow questions that a developer had participated fall in the common interests. Also, developers do share similar interests with other developers who co-participated activities in the two platforms. In particular, developers who co-commit and co-pull-request same GitHub repositories and co-answer same Stack Overflow questions, share more common interests compare to other developers who co-participate in other platform activities.

Keywords: Social collaborative platforms · Online communities

1 Introduction

Software developers are increasingly adopting social collaborative platforms for software development and making a reputation for themselves. Two of such widely adopted and studied social-collaborative platforms are *GitHub*[1] and *Stack Overflow*[2]. GitHub is a collaborative software development platform that allows code sharing and version control. Developers can participate in various activities in GitHub, for example, developers may *fork* (i.e., create a copy of) repositories of other developers. Stack Overflow is a community-based website for asking and answering questions relating to programming languages, software engineering, and tools. Although the two platforms are used for different purposes, developers can utilize both platforms for software development. For example, a developer who has interests in Java programming language may fork a Java project in GitHub and answer Java programming questions in Stack Overflow.

We broadly define the interests of a developer as the programming related topic domains of GitHub repositories and Stack Overflow questions that he or

---

[1] https://github.com/.
[2] http://stackoverflow.com/.

© Springer International Publishing AG 2017
G.L. Ciampaglia et al. (Eds.): SocInfo 2017, Part II, LNCS 10540, pp. 245–256, 2017.
DOI: 10.1007/978-3-319-67256-4_19

she has participated. For instance, when a developer answers questions tagged with *javascript*, *jquery*, and *angularjs*, we deduce that the developer is interested in the three technologies. Similarly, when a developer forked repositories in GitHub which description contains keywords such as *javascript* and *ajax*, we could estimate that the developer is interested in the two technologies.

The learning of developers' interests could provide new insights to how developers utilize the two social collaborative platforms for software development. For example, if developers share similar interests in GitHub and Stack Overflow, the two platforms may be used to complement each other for software development. Conversely, if the developers display differences between their interests in GitHub and Stack Overflow, the two platforms may have been used in a disjoint manner. The social and community-based element in GitHub and Stack Overflow also adds on to the dynamics when studying developer's interests; developers may find themselves sharing similar interests with other developers who also co-participated in a common repository or question. Thus, it would be interesting to investigate the interests of developers within and across the two platforms. In particular, we ask the following research questions: Does an individual developer share similar interests in his GitHub and Stack Overflow accounts? (**RQ1**), and does an individual developer share similar interests with other developers who co-participated activities in GitHub and Stack Overflow? (**RQ2**).

Our research in this paper is thus divided into two main parts: In the first part, we propose similarity scores to measure the developer's interests within and across social collaborative platforms. In the second part, we applied the propose measures on large GitHub and Stack Overflow datasets and conduct an empirical study to answer the two research questions listed earlier.

Contributions. This work improves the state-of-the-art of inter-network studies on multiple social collaborative platforms. Key contributions of this work include: Firstly, to the best of our knowledge, it is the first research attempt to study similarity of developer interests across GitHub and Stack Overflow using large datasets. Second, we proposed several scores to measure the similarity in developer interests within and across social collaborative platforms. The proposed similarity scores are also applied in an empirical study to quantify the similarity in developer's interests within and across Stack Overflow and GitHub.

2 Data Preparation

2.1 Dataset

There are two main datasets used in our study; we retrieve activities from October 2013 to March 2015 of about 2.5 million GitHub users and 1 million Stack Overflow users from open-source database dumps [5][3]. As this study intends to investigate developer interests across GitHub and Stack Overflow, we further identify developers who were using both platforms. For this work, we used

---

[3] https://archive.org/details/stackexchange.

the dataset provided by Badashian et al. [1], where they utilized GitHub users' email addresses and Stack Overflow users' email MD5 hashes to find the intersection between the two datasets. In total, we identify 92,427 developers, which forms our *base developer* set. Subsequently, we retrieved the platform activities participated by the base developers. In total, we have extracted 416,171 *Fork*, 2,168,871 *Watch*, 846,862 *Commit*, 386,578 *Pull-Request*, 277,346 *Ask*, 766,315 *Answer* and 427,093 *Favorite* activities. Our subsequent analysis will be based on this group of activities participated by the base developers.

2.2   Estimating Developer Interests

We estimate developer interests by observing the group of activities they participated in GitHub and Stack Overflow. To estimate developer interests in Stack Overflow, we use the descriptive tags of the questions that they asked, answered and favorited. For example, consider a question q related to mobile programming for Android smartphones which contain the following set of descriptive tags: {*Java, Android*}. If a developer d asked, answered, or favorited that question, we estimate that his interests include *Java* and *Android*. GitHub does not allow users to tag repositories but it allows users to describe their repositories. These descriptions often contain important keywords that can shed light to developer interests. To estimate developer interests from the repositories that a developer had participated, we first collect all descriptive tags that appear in our Stack Overflow dataset. Subsequently, we perform keyword matching between the collected Stack Overflow tags and a GitHub repository description. We consider the matched keywords as the estimated interests. We choose to use Stack Overflow tags to ensure that developer interests across the two platforms can be mapped to the same vocabulary.

We denote the estimated interests of a developer given a repository r that he or she forked, watched, committed or pull-requested in GitHub as $I(r)$. Similarly, we denote the estimated interests of a developer given a question q that he or she asked, answered, or favorited in Stack Overflow as $I(q)$. Since the estimated interests given a repository or a question is the same for all developers participated in it, we also refer to $I(r)$ and $I(q)$ as the interests in r and q. For simplicity, we also refer to them as r's interests and q's interests respectively. Developer d's overall interest in GitHub and Stack Overflow, denoted by $I^{GH}(d)$ and $I^{SO}(d)$, is the union of his/her interests over all the repositories and questions group of activities that d has participated in.

3   Measuring Developer Interests Similarity

3.1   Developer Interests Similarity Across Platforms

One way to measure the similarity in an individual developer's interests across platforms is to take the intersection of his interests in Stack Overflow ($I^{SO}(d)$) and his interests in GitHub ($I^{SO}(d)$). However, this simple measure considers all interests to have an equal weight. In reality, a developer may ask much more questions related to a particular interest than other interests. Similarly, a developer may fork repositories related to a particular interest than other interests. Thus, a finer way to measure the similarity in developer interests should consider the number of repositories and questions that belong to each interest.

To capture the above mentioned intuition, we propose *cross-platform similarity score*, which is denoted as $Sim^{SO\text{-}GH}(d)$. Given a developer d, we measure d's similarity in interests across Stack Overflow (SO) and GitHub (GH) by computing the *proportion* of d's repositories and questions that fall in d's *common interests* in Stack Overflow and GitHub (i.e., $I^{SO}(d) \bigcap I^{GH}(d)$). By denoting the repositories and questions that are related to d (i.e., d forked, watched, committed, pull-requested, asked, answered, or favorited these repositories or questions) as $d.R$ and $d.Q$, we can mathematically define $Sim^{SO\text{-}GH}(d)$ as follows:

$$CI(d) = I^{SO}(d) \bigcap I^{GH}(d) \tag{1}$$

$$Shared^Q(d) = \{q \in d.Q | I(q) \in CI(d)\} \tag{2}$$

$$Shared^R(d) = \{r \in d.R | I(r) \in CI(d)\} \tag{3}$$

$$Sim^{SO\text{-}GH}(d) = \frac{|Shared^R(d)| + |Shared^Q(d)|}{|d.R| + |d.Q|} \tag{4}$$

In Eq. 1, we define the common interests of developer d in both Stack Overflow and GitHub. Equation 2 defines the set of questions that falls into the common interests, while Eq. 3 defines the set of repositories that falls into the common interests. Equation 4 defines $Sim^{SO\text{-}GH}(d)$ as the proportion of repositories and questions of d that falls into the common interests. Please refer to Appendix 1 for an example that illustrate how *cross-platform similarity score* is calculated.

3.2 Developer Interests Similarity Among Co-Participated Developers

To study the similarity of interests among developers who co-participated in GitHub and Stack Overflow activities, we propose *co-participation similarity scores*, each focusing on a platform activity. Given a platform activity and a target developer d, we want to measure the similarity between d and *all other developers* who co-participated in the target activity for *at least one* common GitHub repository or StackOverflow question. For example, considering forking a repository as an activity of interest, we want to find developers who co-fork at least one common GitHub repository with d. Hence, given a developer d, we denote the set of other developers who co-participated in forking at least one common repository or question as $Co^F(d)$.

Intuitively, the more repositories or questions of common interests that d share with other developers in $Co^F(d)$, the higher the similarities should be. To compute the similarity in interests between d and $Co^F(d)$, we measure the average similarity in interests between d and each developer d' in $Co^F(d)$; for each of such pair, we measure their similarity by computing the proportion of d'''s forked repositories which share an interest with the interests of d in his/her forked repositories. Mathematically, we define the *co-participation similarity scores* for forking in Eq. 5.

$$Sim^F(d, Co^F(d)) = \frac{\sum_{d' \in Co^F(d)} \frac{|Shared^F(d,d')|}{|d'.RF|}}{|Co^F(d)|} \tag{5}$$

$$Sim^W(d, Co^W(d)) = \frac{\sum_{d' \in Co^W(d)} \frac{|Shared^W(d,d')|}{|d'.RW|}}{|Co^W(d)|} \tag{6}$$

$$Sim^C(d, Co^C(d)) = \frac{\sum_{d' \in Co^C(d)} \frac{|Shared^C(d,d')|}{|d'.RC|}}{|Co^C(d)|} \tag{7}$$

$$Sim^P(d, Co^P(d)) = \frac{\sum_{d' \in Co^P(d)} \frac{|Shared^P(d,d')|}{|d'.RP|}}{|Co^P(d)|} \tag{8}$$

$$Sim^A(d, Co^A(d)) = \frac{\sum_{d' \in Co^A(d)} \frac{|Shared^A(d,d')|}{|d'.QA|}}{|Co^A(d)|} \tag{9}$$

$$Sim^V(d, Co^V(d)) = \frac{\sum_{d' \in Co^V(d)} \frac{|Shared^V(d,d')|}{|d'.QV|}}{|Co^V(d)|} \tag{10}$$

In the above formulas, $d'.RF$ denotes the repositories or questions that d' forked. Furthermore, $Shared^F(d, d')$ denotes the set of repositories which are forked by d' and share common interests with d's forked repositories. Mathematically, it is defined as:

$$\{r' \in d'.RF | \left[I(r') \bigcap \bigcup_{r \in d.RF} I(r) \right] \neq \emptyset\}$$

In Eq. 5, we define the average similarity in interests between developer d and other developers who had co-forked at least 1 repository with d. The *co-participation similarity scores* for co-watch $(Sim^W(d, Co^W(d)))$, co-commit $(Sim^C(d, Co^C(d)))$, co-pull-request $(Sim^P(d, Co^P(d)))$, co-answer $(Sim^A(d, Co^A(d)))$, and co-favorite $(Sim^V(d, Co^V(d)))$ are similarly defined in Eqs. 6 to 10. Please refer to Appendix 2 for an example that illustrate how *co-participation similarity score* is calculated.

4   Empirical Study

In this section, we applied the developer interests similarity measures proposed in the previous section on GitHub and Stack Overflow large datasets. We also attempt to answer the two research questions that we have listed earlier in this empirical study **RQ1** and **RQ2**.

4.1 RQ1: Does an Individual Developer Share Similar Interests in His GitHub and Stack Overflow Account?

Figure 1 shows the distribution of the *cross-platform similarity scores* computed for the base developers. On average, the developers have a similarity score of 0.39. This suggests that on average, 39% of the GitHub repositories and Stack Overflow questions that a developer had participated shared similar interests. Also, close to half (49%) of the developers have scored 0.5 or higher, while 26% of the developers have their similarity scores equal to 0, i.e., the interests of these developers are totally different in GitHub and Stack Overflow. This suggests that although most developers do share high similarity in interests in GitHub and Stack Overflow, however, there are a group of developers who have totally different interest in GitHub and Stack Overflow.

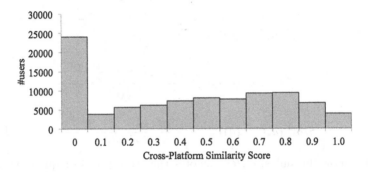

Fig. 1. Distribution of developers' *cross-platform similarity scores* in GitHub and Stack Overow

We further drill down to compare the similarity in developer interests for different types of activity across the two platforms. For example, we measure the similarity in developer's interests by only considering repositories that the developer has forked and questions that the developer has answered. Twelve different combinations capturing different pairs of activities across the two platforms are considered: *Fork-Ask, Fork-Answer, Fork-Favorite, Commit-Ask, Commit-Answer, Commit-Favorite, pull-request-Ask, pull-request-Answer, pull-request-Favorite, Watch-Ask, Watch-Answer* and *Watch-Favorite*.

Figure 2 shows the boxplots of *cross-platform similarity scores* for the 12 different activity pairs. The platform activity pairs have average similarity scores between 0.27 to 0.38, slightly lower than the overall average of 0.39. All the platform activity pairs also have significantly higher number of developers with scores of 0. This is as expected since by combining all platform activity pairs we have a larger pool of common interests. Among the 12 activity pairs, *pull-request-Answer* pair has the highest average similarity score. A possible explanation for this observation could be attributed to the nature of the platform activity; *pull-request* and *answer* not only reveal the interests of the developers but also demand the developers to have a certain expertise on the topics or programming languages of the participated repositories and questions. For example, a developer who is proficient in Java programming language would only *answer* Java programming related questions and submit *pull-request* for Java repositories but he could *watch* other programming language repositories or *favorite* questions from other topics for learning purposes.

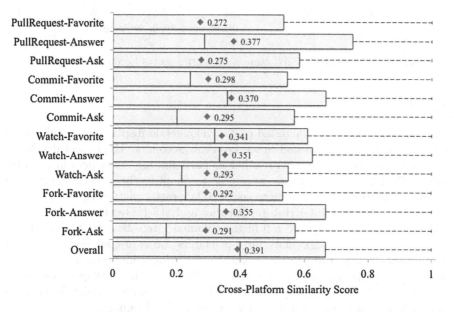

Fig. 2. Boxplots of interest similarity for different activity pairs

4.2 RQ2: Does an Individual Developer Share Similar Interests with Other Developers Who Co-Participated Activities in GitHub and Stack Overflow?

Figure 3 shows the boxplots of *co-participation similarity scores* of the base developers. We observe that an individual developer has average similarity scores between 0.45 to 0.86 with other developers who participated in at least one common platform activity. This means that given two developers who participated in a common platform activity, on average 45–86% of all repositories and questions that they participated in that platform activity shared common interests. Interestingly, we also observed that *commit, pull-request* and *answer* have higher average similarity score compare to the rest of the platform activities (0.81, 0.86 and 0.78 respectively). A possible reason for this observation could again be related to the expertise of the developers. We would expect that the expertise of the developers to be more specialized and less diverse than developers' interests, thus resulting in higher similarity scores for developers sharing a common *commit, pull-request* and *answer*.

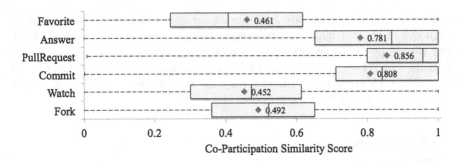

Fig. 3. Boxplots of *Co-Participation Similarity* scores for different activities

4.3   Discussion

Our empirical study has validated that developers do display some similarity in interests in their GitHub and Stack Overflow accounts (**RQ1**) and developers do share common interests with other co-participating developers in the platforms (**RQ2**). Furthermore, we were able to quantify the level of similarity in developer interests across different social collaborative platforms; we found that on average, 39% of the GitHub repositories and Stack Overflow questions that a developer had participated fall in the common interests. The findings in this research could also spark more inter-platforms software engineering research. For instance, when studying the evolution of developer interests, one could take a different perspective and investigate the differences in developer interests in multiple social collaborative platforms over time to observe how developers learn and pick up new interests (e.g., a new programming language).

The findings from our empirical study could be extended to build predictive analytics and recommendation application. As we learned that developers do share interest similarity across platforms (**RQ1**), intuitively we could predict a developer's activities in one platform using his or her interests displayed on another platform. For example, if we learn that a developer answer Java related questions in Stack Overflow, and he displays high similarity in interests across platforms, we can predict that the developer is likely to participate in Java related repositories in GitHub. Likewise in our empirical study, we found that developers do share similar interests with other developers who co-participated activities in GitHub and Stack Overflow (**RQ2**). With this insights, we could predict a developer' activities in a platform using the interests of other developers who had co-participated with him or her in the platform. For example, if we learn that a developer answers a Java related question in Stack Overflow, and we learn that other developers who answered the same questions also display strong interests in Android related questions, we can predict that the developer too, is likely to participate in Android related questions in Stack Overflow. We will look into extending our empirical study predictive analytics and recommendation systems in future works.

5 Related Work

There have been few existing inter-network studies on GitHub and Stack Overflow. These works did deepen our understanding of developer behaviors in the two social-collaborative platforms. Vasilescu et al. performed a study on developers' involvement and productivity in Stack Overflow and GitHub [13]. They found that developers who are more active on GitHub (in terms of GitHub commits), tend to ask and answer more questions on Stack Overflow. Badashian et al. [1] did an empirical study on the correlation between different types of developer activities in the two platforms. Their findings supported the findings of the earlier work by Vasilescu et al., that is: developers who actively contributed to GitHub, also actively answered questions in Stack Overflow. They observed overall weak correlation between the activity metrics of the two networks and concluded that developer activities in one network are not strong predictors for activities on another network. Both the works, however, did not consider intrinsic interests of the developers, although Vasilescu et al. did mention the possibility of extending their work to consider topic interests of the developers.

Stack Overflow and GitHub have also been studied for empirical works on developer interests. For example, there were research works that focused on analyzing topics asked by developers in Stack Overflow [2,3,10,15–17]. Similarly, there were also works on analyzing programming languages used by developers in GitHub and their relationships to GitHub contributions [4,6–9,11,14]. There are also studies characterizing social network properties of GitHub and Stack Overflow [12,15]. Our work extends this group of research by comparing developer interests in the two social collaborative platforms. To our best of knowledge, our work is the first inter-network study that examines cross-site developer interests in GitHub and Stack Overflow.

6 Conclusion and Future Work

In this paper, we studied the similarity in developer interests within and across GitHub and Stack Overflow. Our findings were based on data for 92,427 users who were active in GitHub and Stack Overflow. We first proposed similarity scores to measure similarity in developers' interests within and across social collaborative platforms. Next, we applied our proposed similarity scores in an empirical study on GitHub and Stack Overflow. We observed that on average, 39% of the GitHub repositories and Stack Overflow questions that a developer had participated fall in the common interests. The developers also do share common interests with other developers who co-participated activities in the platforms. For future works, we intend to we conducted experiments to predict the GitHub and Stack Overflow activities of developers using the insights gathered from our empirical analysis. For example, we can predict developer's GitHub activities using the interests learnt from his or her Stack Overflow activities, and vice versa. We also plan to conduct empirical studies to separate the expertises and interests of developers.

Acknowledgments. This research is supported by the National Research Foundation, Prime Minister's Office, Singapore under its International Research Centres in Singapore Funding Initiative.

Appendix 1: Example for Cross-Platform Similarity Score Calculation

Figure 4 shows an example for the calculation of *cross-platform similarity score* $Sim^{SO\text{-}GH}(d)$. Consider developer d who has participated activities in GitHub and Stack Overflow. d has forked 2 repositories; *Repository A* which description contains the tag set {*Java, Android*}, and *Repository B* which description contains the tag set {*Java*}, and watched *Repository C* which description contains the tag set {*C#*}. d also favorited 2 Stack Overflow questions; *Question D* which are tagged with {*Android*}, and *Question F* which are tagged with {*iOS*}, and answered *Question E* which are tagged with {*Java*}. We can estimate d's interests in GitHub (i.e. $I^{GH}(d)$) as {*Java, Android, C#*} and d's interests in Stack Overflow (i.e., $I^{SO}(d)$) as {*Android, iOS*}. The common interests of d (i.e., $CI(d)$) would be {*Java, Android*}. Therefore, $Shared^{R}(d)$ would include repositories A and B, while $Shared^{Q}(d)$ would include questions D and E. Thus, $Sim^{SO\text{-}GH}(d) = \frac{|2|+|2)|}{|3|+|3|}$.

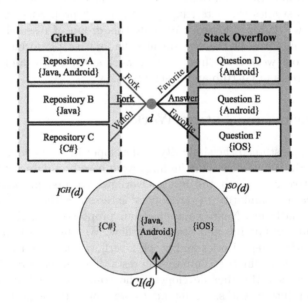

Fig. 4. Example of *cross-platform similarity score* calculation

Appendix 2: Example for Co-Participation Similarity Score Calculation

Figure 5 shows an example for the calculation of *co-participation similarity score* for watch activity $Sim^W(d, co^W(d))$ for developer d. Let us consider two developers d and d' and assume that there are no other developers. Developer d watched repositories A and B. Developer d' co-watched B with d. Thus, $co^W(d)$ is $\{d'\}$. In addition to B, developer d' also watched repositories C and D. $Shared^W(d, d')$ would then include B and C as both of the repositories share common interests with the repositories that d watched. $Sim^W(d) = \left[\sum_{d' \in Co^W(d)} \frac{|2|}{|3|} \right] / |1| = 0.67$.

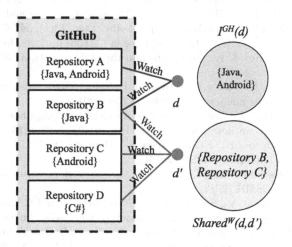

Fig. 5. Example of *co-participation similarity score* calculation for *watch* activity

It is important to note that the *co-participation similarity scores* only consider the similarity in interests between pairs of developers who have co-participated in at least one common repository or question with each other but the developers may have participated in many other repositories and questions different from each other. For example, developers d and d' only watched one common repository but they had watched many other repositories which were different from each other. Also, when computing the co-participation similarity measure between developers who participated in a particular activity, we only consider the interests of the developers in that target activity. For instance, when computing $Sim^W(d)$, we consider how similar are the interests between developers based only on the *watch* activities, i.e., we do not consider repositories forked by the developers or questions answered and favorited by the developers.

References

1. Badashian, A.S., Esteki, A., Gholipour, A., Hindle, A., Stroulia, E.: Involvement, contribution and influence in GitHub and stack overflow. In: CSSE (2014)
2. Bajaj, K., Pattabiraman, K., Mesbah, A.: Mining questions asked by web developers. In: MSR (2014)
3. Barua, A., Thomas, S.W., Hassan, A.E.: What are developers talking about? an analysis of topics and trends in stack overflow. Empir. Softw. Eng. 19(3), 619–651 (2014)
4. Bissyandé, T.F., Lo, D., Jiang, L., Réveillere, L., Klein, J., Traon, Y.L.: Got issues? who cares about it? a large scale investigation of issue trackers from GitHub. In: ISSRE (2013)
5. Gousios, G.: The GHTorrent dataset and tool suite. In: MSR (2013)
6. Jiang, J., Lo, D., He, J., Xia, X., Kochhar, P.S., Zhang, L.: Why and how developers fork what from whom in GitHub. Empir. Softw. Eng. 22(1), 547–578 (2017)
7. Kochhar, P.S., Lo, D.: Revisiting assert use in GitHub projects. In: EASE (2017)
8. Rahman, M.M., Roy, C.K.: An insight into the pull requests of GitHub. In: MSR (2014)
9. Ray, B., Posnett, D., Filkov, V., Devanbu, P.: A large scale study of programming languages and code quality in GitHub. In: FSE (2014)
10. Rosen, C., Shihab, E.: What are mobile developers asking about? a large scale study using stack overflow. Empir. Softw. Eng. 21(3), 1192–1223 (2015)
11. Sheoran, J., Blincoe, K., Kalliamvakou, E., Damian, D., Ell, J.: Understanding "watchers" on GitHub. In: MSR (2014)
12. Thung, F., Bissyandé, T.F., Lo, D., Jiang, L.: Network structure of social coding in GitHub. In: CSMR (2013)
13. Vasilescu, B., Filkov, V., Serebrenik, A.: StackOverflow and GitHub: associations between software development and crowdsourced knowledge. In: SocialCom (2013)
14. Vasilescu, B., Yu, Y., Wang, H., Devanbu, P., Filkov, V.: Quality and productivity outcomes relating to continuous integration in GitHub. In: FSE (2015)
15. Wang, S., Lo, D., Jiang, L.: An empirical study on developer interactions in Stack-Overflow. In: SAC (2013)
16. Yang, X.-L., Lo, D., Xia, X., Wan, Z.-Y., Sun, J.-L.: What security questions do developers ask? a large-scale study of stack overflow posts. J. Comput. Sci. Technol. 31(5), 910–924 (2016)
17. Zou, J., Xu, L., Guo, W., Yan, M., Yang, D., Zhang, X.: Which non-functional requirements do developers focus on? an empirical study on stack overflow using topic analysis. In: MSR (2015)

How Are Social Influencers Connected in Instagram?

Seungbae Kim[1], Jinyoung Han[2(✉)], Seunghyun Yoo[1], and Mario Gerla[1]

[1] University of California, Los Angeles, USA
{sbkim,shyoo1st,gerla}@cs.ucla.edu
[2] Hanyang University, Ansan, South Korea
jinyounghan@hanyang.ac.kr

Abstract. Due to the rapid growth of online social media, social influencers have attracted a great attention as new marketing channels. Brands such as NIKE or Starbucks try to advertise their products through social influencers who have expertise in specific areas and have a large number of followers with similar interests. In this paper, we analyze social relationships and interactions among influencers in Instagram. To investigate how social influencers manage social relationships with other influencers and how they share common followers, we conduct a measurement study on Instagram, and analyze the 218 social influencers who are followed by 8.9 M Instagram users. We find that influencers tend to have a large number of followers who are potential customers of brands, make reciprocal relationships with other influencers, and share common followers with other influencers. We also reveal that influencers who are connected each other tend to share common followers. We believe our work can provide an important insight for brands who would like to effectively hire a set of influencers and maximize their advertising effect.

1 Introduction

Social influencer marketing [1] that utilizes popular and influential users in online social media, dubbed as 'social influencers', recently has gained a great attention as a new marketing strategy [2–4]. Brands such as NIKE or Starbucks seek to advertise their products to potential customers through such social influencers who may be known as experts and thus can influence their followers [5,6]. Social influencers are often regarded as special individuals who can create valuable content and/or have high reputations in specific fields [7]. A recent McKinsey article reported that social influencer marketing plays a great role in attracting consumers to buy products [8]. Also, it has been reported that brands spent 121 billion U.S. dollars on influencer marketing in 2015 [9].

This in turn has led many researchers and firms to study various aspects of social influencer marketing. Bhatt *et al.* found that a future purchase can be affected by the adoption of the product by his/her friends, and this influence remains mostly local to first-adopters and their immediate friends [10]. Leskovec *et al.* showed that purchasing from recommendation follows a power-law distribution, and most person-to-person recommendations do not spread

© Springer International Publishing AG 2017
G.L. Ciampaglia et al. (Eds.): SocInfo 2017, Part II, LNCS 10540, pp. 257–264, 2017.
DOI: 10.1007/978-3-319-67256-4_20

beyond the initial purchase of a product [11]. Goodman *et al.* proposed a social media valuation algorithm that evaluates the defined index values for bloggers to determine whether the bloggers are influencers or not [12]. However, little effort has yet been paid to how social influencers interact each other. Understanding how social influencers manage their social relationships with other influencers and how they share common potential customers can provide a valuable insight for brands who would like to effectively hire a set of influencers and maximize the advertising effect.

This paper presents the first attempt to analyze social relationships and interactions among influencers in Instagram. By conducting a measurement study on Instagram, we collected and analyzed 218 social influencers, who are followed by 8.9 M users, and registered in *Popular Pays*, a popular influencer marketing platform that connects brands and influencers [13].

Using the collected dataset, we analyze (i) how social influencers establish relationships with others, in comparison to general users in Instagram, and (ii) how social influencers interact one another. We find that social influencers tend to (i) have a large number of followers who are mostly their fans and potential customers of brands, (ii) follow other influencers and make reciprocal social relationships with them, and (iii) share common followers with other influencers. By exploring social relationships and interactions among social influencers, we reveal that influencers who have higher node degrees and more bidirectional edges tend to have more common followers with other influencers. We also show that influencers with similar interests or same occupations tend to follow each other, have more interactions, and have more common followers.

2 Dataset

We collected the information of 218 social influencers, who had participated in marketing campaigns in the *Popular Pays* Instagram page. *Popular Pays* is a popular influencer marketing company that connects brands and influencers in Instagram. *Popular Pays* selectively posts advertising content created by their registered influencers. By crawling the *Popular Pays* page, we could obtain their 218 registered social influencers.

To examine the relationships among social influencers in *Popular Pays*, we first fetched the lists of followers and followees of the influencers. We collected 8.9 M followers and 167 K followees of the 218 influencers. We then downloaded the html files of Instagram pages of all the collected followers and followees to retrieve their profiles, e.g., their numbers of followers, followees, or posts. To analyze interaction among social influencers, we also collected all the comments on content posted by the influencers. We obtained 13 M comments from the 325 K posts in the influencers' Instagram pages. We also fetched the user profile pages of the influencers to classify them into four major occupations: (i) photographers, (ii) bloggers, (iii) designers, and (iv) others.

For the purpose of comparison, we randomly collected 948 Instagram users who have less than 10 K followers. These 'general' users have 378 K followers, 780 K followees, and 63 K comments in their 158 K posted content.

3   Influencers vs. General Users

We first investigate how social influencers maintain social relationships with other users via 'following'. Table 1 compares the influencers and the general users. Overall, as shown in Table 1, the social influencers show significantly different characteristics in terms of their connectivities or activities, in comparison with the general users. For example, influencers tend to create more number of content, and they are likely to be followed by more number of users than general Instagram users; influencers have 40 K followers and post 1,490 content while general users have 400 followers and 117 postings on average. While influencers are not likely to follow others, general users tend to have a large number of followees since they often use Instagram to see images of celebrities or popular brands.

Table 1. A comparison between the influencers and general users.

	Influencers	General
Number of users	218	948
Avg. followers	40,322	400
Avg. followees	765	823
Avg. posts	1,490	117
Total followers	8,790,208	378,069
Total followees	166,837	780,435
Common followers	1,104,999 (16.55%)	6,689 (1.81%)
Common followees	21,890 (20.16%)	55,084 (9.63%)
Distinct followers	6,676,252	369,255
Distinct followees	108,580	572,137
Reciprocal users	63,687	135,189
Avg. followers of followers	1,040	1,704
Avg. followers of followees	82,735	107,474
Avg. followers of reciprocal users	17,739	1,756
Avg. # comments with parasocial users	0.19	0.01
Avg. # comments with reciprocal users	7.60	0.23

We also examine how different influencers share common followers and followees. Two influencers, who share many common followers or followees, may have a strong tie in a network. As shown in Table 1, the influencers have 1.1 M common followers, which accounts for 16.55% of total number of unique followers, while only 1.81% of followers are common among general users. This implies that followers of influencers tend to also follow other influencers as well. We also find that Influencers have more common followees than general users; 20.16% of total followees are common across the influencers. Note that general users tend to have a relatively high common followees because they often follow specific famous celebrities or global brands who may have more than 1 M followers.

We next focus on how influencers have reciprocal relationships with others. People tend to have reciprocal relationships when they know each other or share similar interests. Thus, reciprocal users may have closer relationships and more interactions than parasocial users. The 218 influencers have reciprocal relationships with 64 K users, which indicates that 38.17% of influencers' followees are reciprocal users. However, only 0.72% of followers are also followed by the influencers. Considering the fact that 99% of followers of influencers are parasocial, most users who follow influencers can be regarded as their fans. Interestingly, general users tend to be more reciprocal with their followers than their followees, which implies that general users are likely to have reciprocal relationships with their friends and families, whereas general users may not be followed by their followees as they are often celebrities or popular brands.

We next analyze how influencers frequently interact with other users by investigating the number of comments on content posted by the influencers. As shown in Table 1, influencers tend to have more interaction with their followers and followees than general users. We also find that influencers have more interactions with reciprocal friends, who tend to have a large number of followers, than parasocial users.

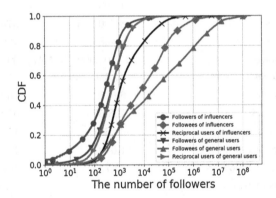

Fig. 1. Number of followers of influencers' or general users' followers, followees, and reciprocal (or bi-directional) users.

To investigate how followers, followees, or reciprocal (or bi-directional) friends of influencers have many numbers of followers, we plot the distributions of numbers of followers of influencers' followers, followees, and reciprocal users, respectively, in Fig. 1. We also plot the numbers of followers of general users' followers, followees, and reciprocal users, respectively, in Fig. 1. We find that followers of both influencers and general users have much smaller numbers of followers than followees of influencers and general users. This result confirms that followers are mostly fans of influencers, and both influencers and general users tend to follow famous people. Interestingly, the numbers of followers of reciprocal users for influencers and general users are substantially different. The distributions for general users' followers and reciprocal users are almost identical, whereas influencers' reciprocal users have a large number of followers. This reveals that influencers tend to have mutual relationships with other influencers.

4 Connectivities Among Social Influencers

In this section, we provide an in-depth analysis on how influencers are connected to each other. It has been reported that new links are attached to nodes in proportion to the its popularity [14], and users tend to connect to other users who are close in a network [15]. More specifically, we seek to answer the following question – How do two connected influencers share common followers? Answering such a question can provide important insight into homophily or synergy of connected influencers from a social influencer marketing perspective.

To investigate how social influencers are connected one another, we first define the notion of the *influencer network* where a node indicates an influencer and a directed edge represents 'following'. A weight on an edge from A to B represents the number of comments A writes on B's content. If A and B follows each other, the edge between A and B is bidirectional, and the weight on the bidirectional edge is the sum of the number of comments left in other's content.

Figure 2 illustrates the influencer network. Different node colors represent the influencer's occupations (e.g., photographer, designer, etc.). A larger node indicates the more number of followers the influencer has. The red edge between two influencer represents that one influencer follows the other influencer while they have a blue edge if they follow each other. The width of edges indicates the

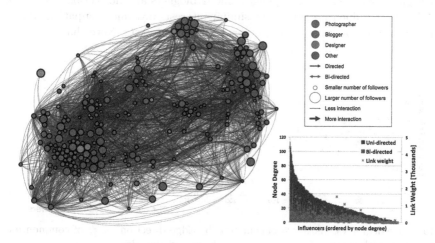

Fig. 2. An illustration of the influencer network. Influencers who participate in the marketing campaigns form a mesh-style social network. Among 218 influencers, 212 of them are connected among each other.

level of interaction, i.e., the number of comments. As shown in Fig. 2, influencers are highly connected to each other. When we look at the distributions of node degrees and link weights in Fig. 2, we find that some influencers have social relationships with more than 100 influencers, and nodes with higher degree tend to have larger link weight values. On average, an influencer follows 25 influencers and has written 322 comments.

To investigate how an influencer with different connectivities in the network share followers with other influencers, we plot the number of common followers shared by an influencer (with different degree) with others in Fig. 3(a). Each blue marker in Fig. 3(a) represents the number of total common followers that an influencer has. As shown in Fig. 3(a), if influencers have more connections to the other influencers, they tend to have more common followers.

We next examine how two influencers with parasocial (uni-directional) or reciprocal (bi-directional) relationships share common followers in Fig. 3(b). As shown in Fig. 3(b), two influencers who reciprocally follow each other have more common followers than those with parasocial relationships. This may be because the bi-directional relationship between two influencers may lead to expose postings to people who follow one influencer, which results in following the other influencer as well.

We finally investigate whether influencers with same occupations share more common followers than the ones with different occupations in Table 2. As shown in Table 2, among 218 influencers, 139 of them, which accounts for 64%, are photographers. The remaining influencers are composed of 37 bloggers, 13 designers, and 29 other occupations such as actors or sports stars. Except the photographers, influencers with same occupations have more common followers than influencers with different occupations. Bloggers have 2,477 common followers on average between two bloggers while they have 1,126 common followers with photographers. Also, 72% of total edges among bloggers are bidirectional ones. This implies that influencers who have similar interests or same occupations tend to share common followers, who may have similar interests. Note that nodes with

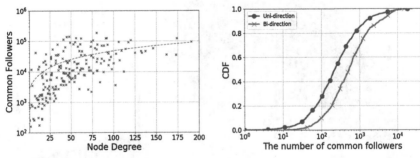

(a) Node degree vs. his/her # of common followers with others

(b) Edge direction vs. # of common followers on the edge

Fig. 3. Influencers' connectivities are associated with their common followers with other influencers.

Table 2. Influencers who have same occupation tend to share many common followers.

Edges from	Values	Edges to			
		Photographer(P)	Blogger(B)	Designer(D)	Other(O)
P	#Edges(Bi%)	2,838 (42.6%)	348 (64.9%)	193 (38.9%)	394 (40.6%)
	Avg. weight	12.9	12.9	7.5	14.7
	#Common	863.6	1,217.1	479.2	1,113.7
B	#Edges(Bi%)	446 (50.7%)	161 (72.0%)	47 (23.4%)	90 (33.3%)
	Avg. weight	11.1	18.7	3.7	4.5
	#Common	1,125.5	2,476.6	678.4	435.1
D	#Edges(Bi%)	134 (56.0%)	16 (68.8%)	8 (50.0%)	23 (43.5%)
	Avg. weight	12.5	19.9	30.0	17.2
	#Common	643.7	2,036.6	6,842.6	1,339.1
O	#Edges(Bi%)	363 (44.1%)	60 (50.0%)	20 (50.0%)	76 (47.4%)
	Avg. weight	14.0	8.3	7.8	13.5
	#Common	1,147.7	582.3	1,248.5	1,437.4

same colors (i.e., same occupations) tend to locate closely in the given network as shown in Fig. 2. Photographers show somewhat disparate patterns compared to others since their interests or topics could be diverse. For example, fashion photographers might have closer relationships with designers than food photographers.

In summary, influencers with similar interests or same occupations tend to follow and interact each other, and hence those influencers with same occupations are likely to have strong ties and form communities in the influencer network. The mutual ties between two influencers eventually lead to a greater number of common followers, which in turn results in their co-evolution in social influencer marketing.

5   Conclusion

We have studied how social influencers, who had participated in marketing campaigns in Instagram, maintain social relationships and interact with others. We summarize two findings as follows. First, we found that influencers tend to have a large number of fans, who are potential consumers of brands, whereas they tend to follow popular and influential people. Social influencers also tend to make reciprocal social relationships with other influencers, have more interactions, and have more common followers with them, compare to general users. Second, by analyzing social relationships and interactions among social influencers, we found that influencers, who have more connections and/or reciprocal relationships to other influencers, tend to have more common followers. We also revealed that influencers with same occupations tend to have more reciprocal influencers, more interactions, and more common followers, compare to influencers with different occupations. We believe our work can provide an important insight for marketers who would like to hire a set of effective influencers and maximize their advertising effect.

Acknowledgement. This work was supported by the National Research Foundation of Korea (NRF) grant funded by the Korea government (MSIP; Ministry of Science, ICT & Future Planning) (No. NRF-2017R1C1B5018199).

References

1. Gillin, P., Moore, G.A.: The New Influencers: A Marketer's Guide to the New Social Media. Linden Publishing, Chicago (2009)
2. Bakshy, E., Rosenn, I., Marlow, C., Adamic, L.: The role of social networks in information diffusion. In: 21st ACM International Conference on World Wide Web (WWW) (2012)
3. Han, J., Choi, D., Chun, B.G., Kwon, T.T., Kim, H.C., Choi, Y.: Collecting, organizing, and sharing pins in Pinterest: interest-driven or social-driven? In: ACM International Conference on Measurement and Modeling of Computer Systems (SIGMETRICS) (2014)
4. Kwak, H., Lee, C., Park, H., Moon, S.: What is twitter, a social network or a news media? In: 19th ACM International Conference on World Wide Web (WWW) (2010)
5. Goldenberg, J., Han, S., Lehmann, D.R., Hong, J.W.: The role of hubs in the adoption process. J. Mark. **73**(2), 1–13 (2009)
6. Guo, S., Wang, M., Leskovec, J.: The role of social networks in online shopping: information passing, price of trust, and consumer choice. In: 12th ACM Conference on Electronic Commerce (EC) (2011)
7. Cha, M., Haddadi, H., Benevenuto, F., Gummadi, P.K.: Measuring user influence in Twitter: the million follower fallacy. In: 4th AAAI International Conference on Weblogs and Social Media (ICWSM) (2010)
8. Bughin, J.: Getting a sharper picture of social media influence. McKinsey Q. **3**, 8–11 (2015)
9. Statista: Brand activation marketing spending in the united states in 2015, by type. http://www.statista.com/statistics/650998/brand-activation-marketing-spending-usa/
10. Bhatt, R., Chaoji, V., Parekh, R.: Predicting product adoption in large-scale social networks. In: the 19th ACM International Conference on Information and Knowledge Management (CIKM) (2010)
11. Leskovec, J., Adamic, L.A., Huberman, B.A.: The dynamics of viral marketing. ACM Trans. Web (TWEB) **1**(1), 5 (2007)
12. Goodman, M.B., Booth, N., Matic, J.A.: Mapping and leveraging influencers in social media to shape corporate brand perceptions. Corp. Commun. Int. J. **16**(3), 184–191 (2011)
13. Ha, A.: Instagram marketing startup popular pays raises $2 million. TechCrunch (2015)
14. Barabási, A.L., Albert, R.: Emergence of scaling in random networks. Science **286**(5439), 509–512 (1999)
15. Mislove, A., Koppula, H.S., Gummadi, K.P., Druschel, P., Bhattacharjee, B.: Growth of the Flickr social network. In: The First Workshop on Online Social Networks. ACM (2008)

Affinity Groups: A Linguistic Analysis for Social Network Groups Identification

Jonathan Mendieta[1,2]([⊠]), Gabriela Baquerizo[3], Mónica Villavicencio[1], and Carmen Vaca[1]

[1] Escuela Superior Politécnica del Litoral, 09014519, Guayaquil, Ecuador
{jonedmen,mvillavi,cvaca}@espol.edu.ec
[2] Facultad de Ciencias Naturales y Matemáticas, Guayaquil, Ecuador
[3] Universidad Casa Grande, 090112 Guayaquil, Ecuador
gbaquerizo@casagrande.edu.ec

Abstract. Socially cohesive groups tend to share similar ideas and express themselves in similar ways when posting their thoughts in online social networks. Therefore, some researchers have conducted studies to uncover the issues discussed by groups who are structurally connected in a network. In this study, we take advantage of the language usage patterns present in online communication to unveil affinity groups, i.e. like-minded people, who are not necessarily interacting in the network currently. We analyze 735K tweets written by 620 unique users and compute scores for 14 grammatical categories using the linguistic inquiry word count software (LIWC). With the LIWC scores, we build a vector for each user, apply a similarity measure and feed an affinity propagation clustering algorithm to find the affinity groups. Following the proposed method, clusters of religious activists, journalists, entrepreneurs, among others emerge. We automatically characterize each cluster using a topic modeling algorithm and validate the generated topics with a user study conducted with 200 people. As a result, more than 70% of the participants agreed on their selection. These results confirm that communities share certain similarities in the use of language, traits that characterize their behavior and grouping.

Keywords: Twitter · LIWC · Affinity propagation clustering · Linguistic clustering

1 Introduction

Because language is a basic element on the social process, some researchers have conducted studies to uncover the issues discussed by groups who are structurally connected in a network. However, the language patterns that emerge in online communication have not been considered yet to identify affinity groups, i.e. people with similar interests who might be already connected or not.

The purpose of this study is to analyze the use of language patterns that emerge on the Twitter social network; such patterns let us to discover affinity

G.L. Ciampaglia et al. (Eds.): SocInfo 2017, Part II, LNCS 10540, pp. 265–276, 2017.
DOI: 10.1007/978-3-319-67256-4_21

groups identified by the combinations of scores generated by the LIWC software (Linguistic Inquiry and Word Count). LIWC is a computerized text analysis program that counts words classifying them in grammar and psychologically meaningful categories that reveal information about writing patterns, psychology and individuals' behavior [13].

We collect 735K tweets written by 620 unique users to identify people who talk about the same issues and have the same interests; people who do not necessarily belong to an established virtual community or interact in the network currently. We show that affinity groups that exhibit similar language usage patterns clearly emerge from the analysis.

We uncover affinity groups starting from scores obtained for the grammatical and psychological dimensions in LIWC. This means that the grammar structure and writing style of the users -who are part of the affinity groups- are closely associated. Grammatical elements such as prepositions, articles and pronouns are features that characterize the formality or informality of the communication. In addition, these grammatical elements are used to express feelings, emotions, knowledge, thoughts, among others.

This paper is structured as follows. We present previous work on Sect. 2. Section 3 describes the dataset used for this study. Section 4 explains the methodology and algorithms used in this work. Section 5 presents the findings of this study and Sect. 6 the future direction of this research. Finally, we provide conclusions in Sect. 7.

2   Related

In recent years, a large number of research work have been conducted to discover relationships [1] or even the relationship strength [15] among people in the real world using the interactions that take place in the digital world. Most of the work have been focused on predicting links [2,5,19] using the topology of the networks resulting from the information exchange, modeling the content published by users [11] or studying the dynamics of content adoption [17].

A complementary line of research addresses the challenge to discover communities, i.e., *groups* of people who engage in discussions online, discussions about the climate [8] or about their political preferences [3], or share information after a disaster [12], among other scenarios.

In this work, we addresses a different problem, that is the discovering of groups formed by people who write in a similar way on a social network platform. It can be the case that the people in the *affinity groups* that we detect are not interacting already on the network. However, they exhibit similar characteristics in the syntactic patterns of language usage. We prove the relevance of our contribution in validating a set of affinity groups by performing a user study.

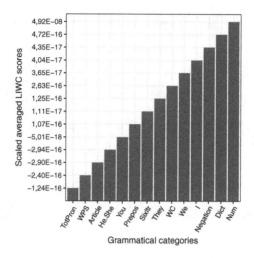

Fig. 1. Barplot of the 14 scaled grammatical categories in LIWC for our Dataset. It describes which categories the users communicate more within their ways of expressions.

3 Dataset

For our study, we recorded daily tweets from over 868 unique users during July 2016 using the Twitter Streaming API by using multiple accounts' tokens. We merged our dataset with one obtained in a previous research work [9], where tweets were collected from Ecuadorian users for the purpose of characterizing national political leaders. Since we wanted to land our study to Ecuador's dialect and ways of expressions, we filtered only the users who were Ecuadorian by looking at the location on their Twitter profiles. We filter the users manually with three annotators who read the user's profile description, his/her place and three random tweets. Consequently, our list of unique users -including the merging- was reduced to 620 Ecuadorian users. However, we needed a large user's corpus to be able to describe the use of language. Hence, our data was complemented with the users' timelines until each user had a minimum of 600 tweets. As a result, our dataset was comprised of 620 unique Ecuadorian users with a total of 735k tweets.

4 Methodology

The methodology followed in this study has three main phases: (A) Identification of affinity groups that emerge from social network users in a given country by using a text mining tool (i.e. LIWC) to analyze their language usage; (B) characterization, i.e. automatic annotation, of each affinity group by applying a topic modeling algorithm; and (C) validation of the generated topics through a survey.

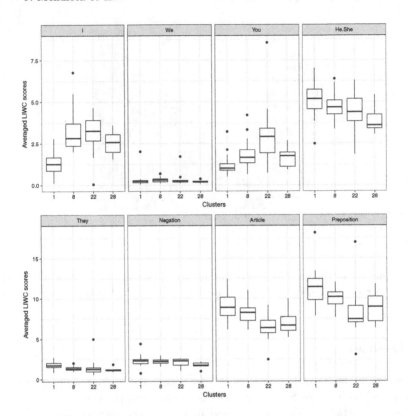

Fig. 2. Box-plots of differences between LIWC grammatical categories for the 4 largest clusters. This figure depicts the characterization of clusters by their applied vocabulary in the grammatical categories.

4.1 Affinity Groups Identification

For this phase, the linguistic inquiry word count software (LIWC) was used to obtain a linguistic profile per user. With LIWC, it was possible to obtain the distribution of words employed in tweets across grammatical categories described in [13] as linguistic processes. However, only 14 categories were found in our 2007 LIWC Spanish dictionary containing Word Count (WC), Dictionary Words (Dict), Negations, First Person Singular (I), First Person Plural (We), Numbers (Num), Third Person Plural (They), Six Letter Words (Sixltr), Prepositions (Prepos), Second Person Singular (You), Third Person Singular (He.She), Articles, Words per Sentence (WPS) and Total Pronouns (TotPron). Taking into consideration the methodology proposed by [20], all the tweets published by each user -over the studied time period- were concatenated into a single file to be scrutinized by LIWC. The same procedure was performed for every user of our dataset to obtain their linguistic profile. As this research was accomplished with Ecuadorian users, the language of our tweets was Spanish; therefore, we performed the analysis with the LIWC 2007 Spanish dictionary for every category under study. The user's profile is determined through a vector of 14 scores that represents each of the LIWC grammatical categories. Since not all the scores in the vector were of the same range, we scaled the data obtaining the Z-score described in Eq. 1.

$$\text{Z-score}_c^u = \frac{x_c^u - \mu_c}{\sigma_c} \tag{1}$$

Where x_c^u is the score for a user in the category c, μ_c is the mean score of all users in that category, and σ_c is the standard deviation of the score in that category. Figure 1 shows the average scores in each category once the data has been scaled. It's depicted in the figure that most of the users in this study uses more numbers in their tweets than any other category. The categories "I" and "We" are also highly used; these words provide insights about the ways of expressions that Ecuadorians use to communicate with each other. After scaling our data, the cosine similarity measure was applied to find groups of similar people in terms of language patterns. This measure has been applied before, where similarities between LIWC scores were analyzed to predict similarities of prolific weblog authors [14]. This measure was applied for each pair of users' vectors in our dataset, where the vectors were the user's LIWC category scores.

Next, to find the affinity groups, a clustering algorithm was fed with the matrix produced by applying the cosine similarity metric. The affinity propagation algorithm proposed by [6] was used with an objective function denoted as *netsimilarity* that iterates until it finds the best suitable number of clusters based on the similarity scores.

The number of clusters detected by the affinity propagation algorithm was 35, where each cluster varied on its size. The affinity propagation clustering returns the central nodes -called *exemplars*- for each cluster. The exemplars are based on the similarity they have with the rest of the data points within the cluster. We found that analyzing the *exemplars* was not relevant for our experiment due to the fact that we analyze the groups as a whole, and each data point within the cluster does not necessarily interact with their neighbors yet.

After identifying the clusters, we performed an statistical analysis to observe the differences between each cluster on the LIWC grammatical categories. Figure 2 shows the results of eight grammatical categories present in the clusters 1, 8, 22 and 28, which are the four largest clusters. The figure also depicts the differences of how people represented by the clusters communicate by using eight grammatical categories. For example, people from cluster 1 use more vocabulary in third person ("He.She" and "They") than any other cluster; the same happens with the use of Prepositions and Articles. This figure provides a better description of the users who pertain to a cluster, by differentiating each of them according to their vocabulary.

4.2   Characterization of Affinity Groups

To characterize the affinity groups represented in each cluster, we used the topic modelling technique NMF (Non-negative matrix factorization) proposed by [16], which is considered as a fast and resilient clustering algorithm for text mining [7]. Before feeding the algorithm, we cleaned our dataset by removing stop words, urls, usernames and applying stemming. The analysis of the topics of interest was performed automatically using NMF with a number of components equal to 5 that was chosen empirically; the algorithm was ran to identify one representative topic with the twenty most relevant words scored by NMF for each of the four largest clusters. Based on those relevant topics identified by our research team, the following apparent- topics were the following: phrases and thoughts (people who write motivational phrases and thoughts); soccer fans; people from TV shows and programs; and entrepreneurial people.

4.3   Validation of Topics

In order to validate the topics of interest identified by the researchers, a user study using the survey method was performed from mid-October to November 2016 with 200 participants. The instrument used for the survey was a questionnaire containing two sections, one for gathering general information about respondents, and the other for collecting topics of interest of the four clusters under analysis. The design of the second section of the questionnaire was based on the study reported in [4], in which the authors empirically investigated how close the automatic coherence metrics were with respect to human judgment. To do so, they asked CrowdFlower workers to choose - according to their opinions- the more coherent topic from a pair of topics.

In our case, we asked participants to choose one or two topics that better describe the twenty words of each cluster. The topics included in the survey were: sports, economics, politics, technology, journalism and media, entrepreneurship, health, religion, phrases and thoughts, entertainment, and other. In the last case, participants had to specify which other topic they were referring to. If participants were not sure about which topic to choose, they were allow to read a set of four tweets randomly taken from each cluster. The questionnaire was pilot-tested at the beginning of October 2016 with twelve university employees (teachers and assistants). As a result, the wording of the instructions to choose the topics was improved. For the survey, we used a purposeful sample considering students from two Ecuadorian universities registered in several programs (e.g. computer science, journalism, nursing, political sciences, social communication, economics, etc.) An example of one question of the survey can be read in Appendix A.

5   Results

In this section, the results are presented following the order of the research phases detailed in the previous section. The experiment reports a total of thirty five clusters. The largest affinity groups were cluster one, eight, twenty two and twenty eight.

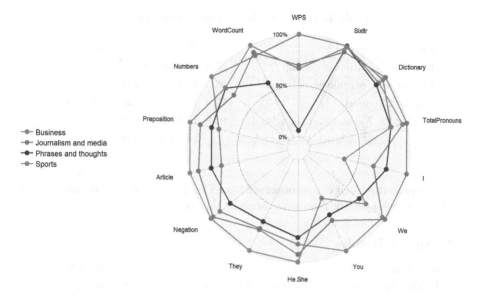

Fig. 3. Radar plot of LIWC grammatical categories for each identified affinity group.

5.1   Affinity Groups with LIWC

The identification of the affinity among users of a group was based on the language usage patterns. It means that we aim to detect similar people based on the use of the LIWC grammar categories such as personal pronouns (I, we, you, he, she and they), negation, articles and prepositions as shown in Fig. 3. According to Chung (2007), the use of pronouns reveals the focus of people when they talk. If they tend to self-focus, they use more singular pronouns and conjugate verbs in first - person. Opposite to this, when they use "we" (the third-person pronoun), it reveals a close relationship between users, more engagement and a positive relationship in a group (quality of the relation) [13]. This agrees with Chandra (2016), who said that social entrepreneurs rhetoric is focused on "we" (the third-person pronoun) when they talk to people because is more oriented to generate engagement with the stakeholders. Entrepreneurs use less the first person pronoun because it is related to a self-orientation (e.g., I, me, my, mine), which is not effective in strategic business communication.

The language style of journalism and media people and entrepreneurial people is characterized by the use of articles and prepositions. This result is positively related to high openness personality [10]. According to Five Factor Model personality traits, these are persons with active imagination, sensitiveness and inquisitive mind [18]. In the same way, openness trait is negatively correlated with second-person pronouns (i.e., you, your, yours). For that reason, journalism and media people use the third-person pronoun (i.e., we) to talk to others. Another finding reported in [10], reveals that negation words are negatively associated with agreeableness people trait. Finally, the number category refers to amount and quantity

Table 1. Topics of affinity identified per cluster

Clusters	Topic 1	%	Topic 2	%
Cluster 1	Entrepreneurship (*)	77.0	Economics	41.0
Cluster 8	Journalism and media (+)	82.5	Entertainment	73.0
Cluster 22	Sports (*)	97.0	Journalism and media	33.5
Cluster 28	Phrases and thoughts (*)	94.0	Entertainment	10.5

(*) Chosen by researchers   (+) Hard to tell

when people write. As it can be observed from Fig. 3, people in the business cluster are the ones who use the Numbers category the most.

5.2 Survey Results

The demographics of the 200 participants of the survey are presented in Appendix A. The majority of respondents were students aged less than 25 years old (95%) and predominantly female (62.5%). The sample considered students from 19 careers, where Social Communication was the one with more representativeness. Surprisingly, we found that only 48% of respondents use Twitter, meaning that young people apparently prefer Instagram and Facebook as social networks. Table 1 presents the two topics that best represent the affinity group of each cluster according to the opinion of participants (i.e. topics that describe the affinity among Twitter users that are part of the same cluster). The topics that include the symbol (*) are the ones that match with the opinion of our research team who manually reviewed each of the Twitter user accounts from each of the four clusters.

As it can be noticed, there is only one cluster (cluster 8) in which neither the surveyed students nor the researchers were completely sure about the topic of interest related to the cluster. Researchers found that the affinity among users from cluster 8 was sometimes related to TV shows and entertainment activities, while other times was related to local news. Something similar happened to university students who chose two topics to characterize this cluster: (1) journalism and media and (2) entertainment. This is understandable since two out of the twenty words that represented the cluster were related to a local TV channel.

6 Future Work

Despite the findings, we consider that the proposed methodology needs to be tested on different datasets in order to confirm its potential as a way to identify affinity groups. As a future task, we plan to make a comparison analysis of our affinity groups with the current social network graph (e.g. retweets, followers) as it could be related with some quantitative measures. As LIWC offers around 72 linguistic and psychological categories, we could improve our affinity group algorithm by filtering or adding more features into the analysis.

7   Conclusions

In this article, we present a methodology that takes advantage of the language usage patterns present in online communication. The methodology aims to identify and characterize affinity groups composed by people who are not necessarily interacting in a social network; instead, they share common interest and are like-minded. For the identification of affinity groups, we use a text mining tool (LIWC) with grammatical categories; and for the characterization, we employ a topic modelling technique (NMF).

By applying the methodology, similar language patterns among Twitter users were detected. Therefore, similarities and differences of linguistic characteristics from the affinity groups become apparent. For example, the use of formal language from journalists, and the use of the "We" pronoun from entrepreneurial people. Through the methodology, it is also possible to identify the topics that users are interested in. For example, the Sports affinity group identified in our study is interested mostly in soccer.

A   Appendix

A.1   Survey Example

According to your opinion, which of the following topics best describe the set of words presented below. Please, choose only one or two topics. Underline the words that justify your selection.

TOPICS
Sports ( ) Economics ( ) Politics ( )Technology ( )
Journalism and media ( ) Entrepreneurship ( )Health ( )
Religion ( ) Phrases and thoughts ( ) Entertainment ( )
Other: _____

WORDS (translated version)
More team Emelec player greeting BSC best thus only
Barcelona right be match Ecuador soccer day good
hello Esmerald game

If you are not sure about which topic to choose, please, read the four tweets located at the back of this page to help you to make a decision.

TWEETS
Tweet 1: #JuegaLIGA. #FutbolxDIRECTV. Inicio 2doT. Uno de los peores partidos de Hidalgo!! Le sent mal la renovacin de contrato!! Flojisimo

Tweet 2: para variar que malos dirigentes aparte que no le pagan

Tweet 3: Los culpables de esto es los Noboa, porque ellos contratan y no supervigilancia, ya quiero ver si en sus empresas es asi

Tweet 4: Siempre a su orden... Admirador de su inteligencia y belleza... Saludos desde Esmeraldas...

A.2   Participants' Demographics

From the surveyed people, we obtained the demographics described in the following Table 2:

Table 2. Demographics of respondents

Features	%
Degree	
Social communication	25.5
Multimedia	13.0
Computer science	12.5
Public relationships	12.5
Graphical design	12.5
Journalism	5.5
Others	18.5
Age	
Less than 20	50.0
Between 20 and 24	45.0
More than 24	5.0
Gender	
Female	62.5
Male	37.5
Social Networks	
Instagram	81.5
Facebook	80.0
YouTube	77.5
Snapchat	63.0
Twitter	48.0

References

1. Aiello, L.M., Barrat, A., Schifanella, R., Cattuto, C., Markines, B., Menczer, F.: Friendship prediction and homophily in social media. ACM Trans. Web (TWEB) **6**(2), 9 (2012)
2. Bliss, C.A., Frank, M.R., Danforth, C.M., Dodds, P.S.: An evolutionary algorithm approach to link prediction in dynamic social networks. J. Comput. Sci. **5**(5), 750–764 (2014)

3. Conover, M.D., Gonçalves, B., Ratkiewicz, J., Flammini, A., Menczer, F.: Predicting the political alignment of twitter users. In: 2011 IEEE Third International Conference on Privacy, Security, Risk and Trust (PASSAT) and 2011 IEEE Third International Conference on Social Computing (SocialCom), pp. 192–199. IEEE (2011)
4. Fang, A., Macdonald, C., Ounis, I., Habel, P.: Topics in tweets: a user study of topic coherence metrics for twitter data. In: Ferro, N., Crestani, F., Moens, M.-F., Mothe, J., Silvestri, F., Di Nunzio, G.M., Hauff, C., Silvello, G. (eds.) ECIR 2016. LNCS, vol. 9626, pp. 492–504. Springer, Cham (2016). doi:10.1007/978-3-319-30671-1_36
5. Fire, M., Tenenboim, L., Lesser, O., Puzis, R., Rokach, L., Elovici, Y.: Link prediction in social networks using computationally efficient topological features. In: 2011 IEEE Third International Conference on Privacy, Security, Risk and Trust (PASSAT) and 2011 IEEE Third International Conference on Social Computing (SocialCom), pp. 73–80. IEEE (2011)
6. Frey, B.J., Dueck, D.: Clustering by passing messages between data points. Science 315, 972–976 (2007). www.psi.toronto.edu/affinitypropagation
7. Godfrey, D., Johns, C., Meyer, C., Race, S., Sadek, C.: A case study in text mining: interpreting twitter data from world cup tweets (2014). arXiv preprint: arXiv:1408.5427
8. Pearce, W., Holmberg, K., Hellsten, I., Nerlich, B.: Climate change on twitter: topics, communities and conversations about the 2013 IPCC working group 1 report. PloS One 9(4), e94785 (2014)
9. Pita, O., Baquerizo, G., Vaca, C., Mendieta, J., Villavicencio, M., Rodríguez, J.: Linguistic profiles on microblogging platforms to characterize political leaders: the ecuadorian case on twitter. In: Ecuador Technical Chapters Meeting (ETCM), vol. 1, pp. 1–6. IEEE (2016)
10. Qiu, L., Lin, H., Ramsay, J., Yang, F.: You are what you tweet: personality expression and perception on twitter. J. Res. Pers. 46(6), 710–718 (2012)
11. Quercia, D., Askham, H., Crowcroft, J.: Tweetlda: supervised topic classification and link prediction in twitter. In: Proceedings of the 4th Annual ACM Web Science Conference, pp. 247–250. ACM (2012)
12. Sakaki, T., Okazaki, M., Matsuo, Y.: Earthquake shakes twitter users: real-time event detection by social sensors. In: Proceedings of the 19th International Conference on World Wide Web, pp. 851–860. ACM (2010)
13. Tausczik, Y.R., Pennebaker, J.W.: The psychological meaning of words: Liwc and computerized text analysis methods. J. Lang. Soc. Psychol. 29(1), 24–54 (2010)
14. Wienberg, C., Roemmele, M., Gordon, A.S.: Content-based similarity measures of weblog authors. In: Proceedings of the 5th Annual ACM Web Science Conference, pp. 445–452. ACM (2013)
15. Xiang, R., Neville, J., Rogati, M.: Modeling relationship strength in online social networks. In: Proceedings of the 19th International Conference on World Wide Web, pp. 981–990. ACM (2010)
16. Xu, W., Liu, X., Gong, Y.: Document clustering based on non-negative matrix factorization. In: Proceedings of the 26th Annual International ACM SIGIR Conference on Research and Development in Information Retrieval, pp. 267–273. ACM (2003)
17. Yang, L., Sun, T., Zhang, M., Mei, Q.: We know what@ you# tag: does the dual role affect hashtag adoption? In: Proceedings of the 21st International Conference on World Wide Web, pp. 261–270. ACM (2012)
18. Yarkoni, T.: Personality in 100,000 words: a large-scale analysis of personality and word use among bloggers. J. Res. Pers. 44(3), 363–373 (2010)

19. Yin, D., Hong, L., Davison, B.D.: Structural link analysis and prediction in microblogs. In: Proceedings of the 20th ACM International Conference on Information and Knowledge Management, pp. 1163–1168. ACM (2011)
20. Yu, B., Kaufmann, S., Diermeier, D.: Classifying party affiliation from political speech. J. Inf. Technol. Polit. 5(1), 33–48 (2008)

Deliberative Platform Design: The Case Study of the Online Discussions in Decidim Barcelona

Pablo Aragón[1,2(✉)], Andreas Kaltenbrunner[2], Antonio Calleja-López[3],
Andrés Pereira[4], Arnau Monterde[3], Xabier E. Barandiaran[5,6],
and Vicenç Gómez[1]

[1] Universitat Pompeu Fabra, Barcelona, Spain
pablo.aragon@upf.edu
[2] Eurecat, Technology Center of Catalonia, Barcelona, Spain
[3] Internet Interdisciplinary Institute, Universitat Oberta de Catalunya,
Barcelona, Spain
[4] ALabs.org, Madrid, Spain
[5] Ajuntament de Barcelona, Barcelona, Spain
[6] School of Social Work, UPV/EHU, University of the Basque Country,
Vitoria-Gasteiz, Spain

Abstract. With the irruption of ICTs and the crisis of political representation, many online platforms have been developed with the aim of
improving participatory democratic processes. However, regarding platforms for online petitioning, previous research has not found examples
of how to effectively introduce discussions, a crucial feature to promote
deliberation. In this study we focus on the case of Decidim Barcelona,
the online participatory-democracy platform launched by the City Council of Barcelona in which proposals can be discussed with an interface that
combines threaded discussions and comment alignment with the proposal.
This innovative approach allows to examine whether neutral, positive or
negative comments are more likely to generate discussion cascades. The
results reveal that, with this interface, comments marked as negatively
aligned with the proposal were more likely to engage users in online discussions and, therefore, helped to promote deliberative decision making.

Keywords: Human computer interfaces · Online deliberation · Civic
participation · Technopolitics · Online discussions · Discussion threads

1 Introduction

The crisis of representative democracy in the last three decades [26,28] has been
identified with the crisis of democracy itself [9,19]. Some authors have criticized
the technocratic tendencies operating in this period as signs of the rise of post-
democracy [8] or post-politics [25,31], while others, more precisely, have used the
term "post-representation", to refer to the emptying out (of power and meaning)
of representative institutions by dynamics ranging from globalization to growing
citizen mistrust [6,19]. Specially in the last years, this political crisis has led to

© Springer International Publishing AG 2017
G.L. Ciampaglia et al. (Eds.): SocInfo 2017, Part II, LNCS 10540, pp. 277–287, 2017.
DOI: 10.1007/978-3-319-67256-4_22

a period of fertile democratic innovation supported by an intensive and creative use of ICTs [7,27]. Thus, we are witnessing new forms of participatory and deliberative democracy based on computer mediated communication [11,14].

One of the recent institutional instantiations of this wider democratizing process is *Decidim Barcelona*[1], an online platform developed by the Barcelona City Council for supporting its participatory processes, e.g., the development of the Barcelona's strategic city plan. The strategic city plan defines objectives and actions to be carried out by the local government during the present legislature. The goal of this participatory process was to enroll the citizenry in a two month process of co-production, where citizens could discuss and support the proposals made by the government; and also make, discuss and support their own proposals. In total, more than 40 000 citizens participated in this process.

According to the functional specification of *Decidim Barcelona* [23], different pre-existing tools for participatory democracy were assessed, in particular, *e-Petitions Gov UK* (United Kingdom)[2], *Your Priorities* (Iceland)[3], *Cónsul* (Madrid)[4], and *Open Irekia* (Basque Country)[5]. On the one hand, these four tools share certain commonalities. First, they are web applications based on Free/Libre and Open Source Software (FLOSS). Second, they have been deployed in real environments by city, regional, or national governments. Third, they allow users to make online proposals. On the other hand, there are many differences among these four platforms. An important one is the way proposals are discussed by users. In *e-Petitions Gov UK*, proposals cannot be discussed and, therefore, this tool might be considered as enabling participatory but not deliberative democracy. *Your Priorities* allows users to publish comments either supporting the proposal (hereafter *positive comments*) or against it (hereafter *negative comments*). Positive and negative comments are displayed in two columns and sorted by the number of votes they receive to show the best arguments and, ultimately, to facilitate decision making. Although this strategy relies on comments, users do not engage in discussions, which might reduce the deliberative capabilities of the platform. In contrast, *Cónsul* corresponds to an opposite scenario given that users are able to discuss any proposal with a threaded interface without any visual indication of whether comments are positive or negative. Finally, the approach in *Open Irekia* allows users to indicate whether a comment is positive, negative or neutral. However, neutral, positive and negative comments are presented separately without applying a threaded discussion interface, as done in *Cónsul*. This heterogeneity received special attention in the design specification process of *Decidim Barcelona* [23] resulting in an interface which hybridizes the previous approaches. On the one hand, proposals are discussed in a threaded interface to promote online discussions and, consequently, online deliberation. On the other hand, users are able to establish when

---

posting a first level comment (i.e., a direct comment to a proposal) whether is positive, negative or neutral in relation to the proposal. In addition, authors of proposals and comments are notified when receiving replies.

Figure 5 (see appendix) shows a real proposal for the strategic city plan which requested a municipal ice skating rink in Barcelona. The discussion page shows two first positive (green) comments with no replies and a third negative (red) comment calling into doubt the adequacy of expending public funding on a winter sport facility in a Mediterranean city. As shown in Fig. 5, the negative comment triggered a discussion cascade among users.

This proposal is an illustrative example of the aim of this hybrid interface: users can engage in online discussion to promote deliberative processes while positive and negative comments are easily distinguishable to facilitate decision making. The combination of both approaches makes *Decidim Barcelona* an interesting case study for multiple reasons. First, recent studies have shown that conversation threading in online discussion platforms promotes the emergence of discussion cascades with higher levels of reciprocity [3] and online deliberation [5]. Second, given that users are able to mark the alignment of comments with the proposal (positive, negative and neutral), we can compare the typical network structures originated by the different types of comment alignment. According to [13], these structures can be used as proxies of very basic forms of deliberation. Given this particular scenario of *Decidim Barcelona*, the research question of this study is as follows:

– *Which are the structural differences of discussion cascades triggered by neutral, positive or negative comments on online proposals?*

As presented in the following section, despite the increasing research work on online petition plaforms, how to effectively introduce discussions is an open practical and research challenge [20]. We postulate that the combination in *Decidim Barcelona* of both conversation threading and comment alignment (in particular, explicitly negative comments to the proposal) should favor cognitive dissonance [10] in users, which would lead to a higher willingness to discuss the proposals, and, therefore, to deliberative practices of decision making.

The organization of the paper is as follows. In Sect. 2 we present related work on online petition platforms. We then describe in Sect. 3 our dataset of discussion threads from *Decidim Barcelona*. Next, we introduce the structural metrics of discussion threads for our analysis in Sect. 4 and the results of the study in Sect. 5. Finally, in Sect. 6, we discuss the implications of our findings for the design of online participation platforms.

2   Related Work

The interest in online petition platforms is reflected by the increasing attention from academia [24]. Some of the first studies analysed the platform developed by the German Parliament either to identify different types of users according to the frequency of participation [18] or to characterize the relationship between online participation and offline socio-demographic factors [21]. Indeed, much effort has been made to detect which factors affect the signing of online petitions [2,16,17,22,30].

Previous work has also examined the impact of platform design on the dynamics of online petitioning. A study of the UK government petitions platform showed that introducing trending information on the homepage increased the inequality in the number of signatures across petitions [15]. In relation to our research question, some papers have precisely assessed the role of the availability and design of discussion features. A study of online petition platforms launched by UK local authorities (Kingston and Bristol) [29] examined the performance of the online forums incorporated in these tools. Results indicated that most users did not visually identify the possibility to discuss proposals and just a few users published comments. Therefore, the study concluded that the discussion section for online petitions needed to be more appealing. A comparative analysis of four online petition systems (the aforementioned platform of the German Parliament and the platforms of the Scottish Parliament, the Parliament of Queensland, and Norwegian municipalities) also examined whether they integrate an online discussion forum [20]. Online discussions were available in every platform except for the case of Queensland. The study found little usage of these forums and concluded with the open research question about the function of these discussions and how to channel them into the political decision-making processes.

3   Dataset

Our dataset contains the discussion threads from the proposals in *Decidim Barcelona* for the development of the strategic city plan. To better understand the discussions that originated more activity we present in Table 1 (see Appendix) the most commented proposals, which are related to controversial topics in Barcelona like housing affordability and mobility.

Data were extracted through the Decidim API[6] to obtain a total of 10 860 proposals and 18 192 comments. 16 217 comments were first level comments (i.e., direct replies to the proposal) while 1 975 comments were replies to comments. As mentioned in the introduction, users were able to establish the alignment of first level comments with the proposal. Thus, 10 221 comments were marked as neutral (63.03%), 5 198 comments were marked as positive (32.05%), and only 798 comments were marked as negative (4.92%).

4   Structural Metrics of Discussion Cascades

Discussion threads are collections of messages posted as replies to either an initial message (the proposal) or another message (a comment). For this reason, discussion threads can be represented as a directed rooted tree. We present in Fig. 1 the proposal for a municipal ice skating rink (shown in Fig. 5) using a

---

[6] https://www.decidim.barcelona/api/docs.

radial tree visualization tool [4]. The black node is the proposal (root) and the nodes directly connected to the root are the first level comments (green colored if positive and red colored if negative). This tree structure allows to identify whether a first level comment triggers a discussion cascade, e.g., the red node on the right, which is the negative comment against expending public funding on a winter sport facility in a Mediterranean city, triggers several comments.

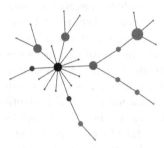

Fig. 1. Radial tree visualization of the proposal presented in Fig. 5. Black node (root) represents the proposal, green nodes are positive and red nodes negative first level comments. Comment nodes are sized by the indegree (number of replies to the comment). The visualization shows a cascade of comments triggered by a negative comment to the proposal (red node on the right). (Color figure online)

The structure of the discussion cascade of each first level comment can be characterized with typical metrics of tree graphs:

- size: number of nodes,
- width: maximum number of nodes at any level,
- depth: number of levels,
- h-index: maximum level h in which there are, at least, h comments [12].

In the discussion cascade originated by the aforementioned negative comment about public funding (red node on the right in Fig. 1), size is 9, width is 4, depth is 3, and h-index is 3.

With the exception of the size, which just quantifies the volume of the cascade, these metrics serve to inform about the network topology of a cascade. Morever, the last three metrics have been suggested to quantify the level of deliberation in online discussion threads [13]. This approach is based on the Madisonian conceptualization of deliberation as the conjugation of two dimensions: representation and argumentation [1]. Given that messages at any level often represent users within the discussion, width has been proposed to quantify the extent of representation of the online community in a discussion cascade. Because the exchange of arguments between users commonly occur as exchange of comments, the depth of the discussion cascade (i.e., the largest exchange of comments) has been proposed to capture argumentation. The last structural metric (h-index) both considers width and depth and, therefore, has been proposed to measure online deliberation in a discussion cascade [13].

5   Analysis of Discussion Cascades

The description of the dataset indicated that most of the first level comments were marked as neutral, an important fraction were marked as positive and just around 5% were marked as negative. To understand the structure of cascades triggered by comments from different alignments, we first examine the distribution of the cascade size depicted in Fig. 2. We observe a notably higher probability of triggering a cascade for negative comments. We also observe that, for every alignment, few cascades contain more than five comments.

Figure 2 reveals as well a larger preference for larger cascades triggered by negative comments. However, the size of the cascade is not an informative metric of the structure of the cascade. For this reason, we examine the probability of the alignment of the root (comment) of the cascade with different sizes and different values of the structural metrics (width, depth and h-index). Results are presented in Fig. 3 using heatmaps, i.e., the darker the more likely. We observe that, if a comment did not trigger any discussion cascade, that comment is probably neutral or positive. In contrast, when comments originated discussion, there is a higher probability that they are negative. Furthermore, the likelihood of negative comments increases when the value of the size and the structural metrics also increase.

These results suggest that discussion cascades occur more frequently due to negative messages and less frequently due to neutral messages. However, to perform a rigorous analysis we need to consider the following observations. First, we found by manual inspection that many neutral comments, despite being clearly positively or negatively aligned with the proposal, were not explicitly marked accordingly for some reason, e.g., problems of usability or perhaps a deliberate choice of the user. Second, we have to take into account the class imbalance

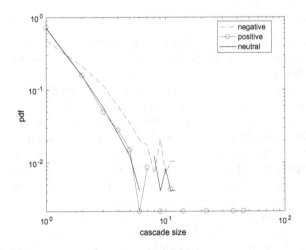

Fig. 2. Distribution of the cascade size triggered by the first level comments of each alignment (neutral, positive and negative).

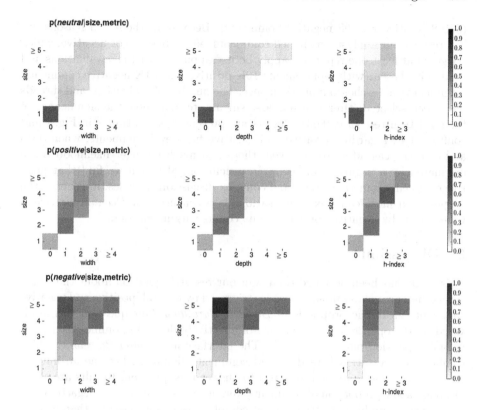

Fig. 3. Heatmaps of the probability of alignment (gray for neutral, green for positive and red for negative) of a first level comment given size and width, depth, or h-index of the cascade. Large values are aggregated in the top rows and rightmost columns. (Color figure online)

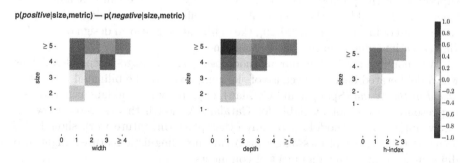

Fig. 4. Heatmaps of the probability of polar alignment (green for positive and red for negative) of a first level comment given the value of size and structural feature (width, depth, and h-index) of the cascade. Values are obtained with a statistical test of 10 K evaluations with 10 K random cascades each and shown if significant ($p < 0.05$). (Color figure online)

284 P. Aragón et al.

(5 198 positive vs. 798 negative comments). Because of these two reasons, we will restrict our analysis to aligned comments, either positive or negative, which triggered at least one reply. We apply bootstrapping, with 10 K evaluations and randomly chosen (with replacement) 10K positive and 10 K negative comments. Comments can be chosen more than once. The number of evaluations and threads have been selected, after multiple assessments, to guarantee the significance of the statistical test ($p < 0.05$). Results are presented as heatmaps in Fig. 4 and confirm that, regarding positive and negative first level comments, when deep and complex cascades are observed, there is a much stronger likelihood to be originated by a negative comment. In conclusion, although we find that positive comments sometimes triggered complex discussion cascades, in general, the deepest and most complex conversations between users in *Decidim Barcelona* were caused by negative comments, i.e., counter-argumentation.

6 Discussion

This study has been designed to answer our research question about the structural differences of discussion cascades triggered by neutral, positive and negative comments on online proposals in *Decidim Barcelona*. Our question was motivated by the open research challenge of effectively deploying online discussions in online petition platforms [20,29]. The interface in *Decidim Barcelona*, which combines conversation threading and comment alignment, became an innovative case study and an ideal scenario to answer this question. Results are clear: although a low proportion of comments were negative (about 5%), negative comments were more likely to trigger more complex discussion cascades than neutral and positive comments. We should note that users in *Decidim Barcelona* were notified when they received a reply. Therefore, authors of proposals were always aware of negative comments which might also increase their interest in engaging in discussion to advocate for their proposals. This is consistent with the basis of cognitive dissonance [10], i.e., negative comments usually contain new information which contradicts the idea of a given proposal and the author and supporters of the proposal will be likely to reply to it. We can conclude, thus, when trying to address the open challenge of effectively combining online petitioning and online discussion [20,29], the deliberative platform design of *Decidim Barcelona* introduces an innovative solution.

We should remark that our methodology was language-independent. This was a deliberated decision because of the complexity of the bilingual context of *Decidim Barcelona* (Spanish and Catalan), e.g., many natural language processing resources were not available for Catalan. Although this decision allows to easily apply our methodology on any other platform, future work should also focus on the content of messages to compare how linguistic features might also differ in relation to the alignment of comments.

Acknowledgments. This work is supported by the Spanish Ministry of Economy and Competitiveness under the María de Maeztu Units of Excellence Programme (MDM-2015-0502).

Appendix

Fig. 5. Discussion page of a proposal in *Decidim Barcelona* for building a municipal ice skating rink. The hybrid interface combines both conversation threading and coloring, i.e., positive and negative first level comments include green and red labels, respectively (the interface at that time colored the full text of positive and negative comments). (Color figure online)

Table 1. Top proposals in *Decidim Barcelona* by the number of comments. An English translation is indicated in parentheses.

Title	N. Comments
Noves llicàncies per a pisos turìstics (New licenses for tourist apartments)	337
Implantar el tramvia a la Diagonal (To build a tramway in Diagonal Avenue)	111
Cubriment de la Ronda de Dalt al seu pas per la Vall d'Hebrón (Roof for Dalt Road in Vall d'Hebrón)	108
Promoció de l'ús de la bicicleta, i millora i ampliació dels carrils bici (Promotion of cycling and improvement and expansion of bike lanes)	80
Regulació del mercat de lloguer (Regulation of the housing rental market)	77

References

1. Ackerman, B., Fishkin, J.S.: Deliberation day. J. Polit. Philos. **10**(2), 129–152 (2002)
2. Anduiza, E., Gallego, A., Cantijoch, M., San Martin, J.: Online resources, political participation and equality (2008)
3. Aragón, P., Gómez, V., Kaltenbrunner, A.: To thread or not to thread: the impact of conversation threading on online discussion. In: 11th International AAAI Conference on Web and Social Media, ICWSM 2017. The AAAI Press (2017)
4. Aragón, P., Gómez, V., Kaltenbrunner, A.: Visualization tool for collective awareness in a platform of citizen proposals. In: 10th International AAAI Conference on Web and Social Media, ICWSM 2016. The AAAI Press (2016)
5. Aragón, P., Gómez, V., Kaltenbrunner, A.: Detecting platform effects in online discussions. Policy Internet (2017, in Press). http://dx.doi.org/10.1002/poi3.158
6. Brito Vieira, M., Runciman, D.: Representation. Polity, Cambridge (2008)
7. Castells, M.: Communication Power. Oxford University Press, Oxford (2009)
8. Crouch, C.: Post-Democracy. Polity, Cambridge (2004)
9. Della Porta, D.: Can Democracy be Saved?: Participation, Deliberation and Social Movements. Wiley, Hoboken (2013)
10. Festinger, L.: A Theory of Cognitive Dissonance, vol. 2. Stanford University Press, Stanford (1962)
11. Fuchs, C.: Internet and Society: Social Theory in the Information Age. Routledge, New York (2007)
12. Gómez, V., Kaltenbrunner, A., López, V.: Statistical analysis of the social network and discussion threads in Slashdot. In: Proceedings of the 17th International Conference on World Wide Web, pp. 645–654. ACM (2008)
13. Gonzalez-Bailon, S., Kaltenbrunner, A., Banchs, R.E.: The structure of political discussion networks: a model for the analysis of online deliberation. J. Inf. Technol. **25**, 230–243 (2010)
14. Hague, B.N., Loader, B.: Digital Democracy: Discourse and Decision Making in the Information Age. Psychology Press, New York (1999)

15. Hale, S.A., John, P., Margetts, H., Yasseri, T.: Investigating political participation and social information using big data and a natural experiment. arXiv preprint arXiv:1408.3562 (2014)
16. Hale, S.A., Margetts, H., Yasseri, T.: Petition growth and success rates on the UK no. 10 downing street website. In: Proceedings of the 5th Annual ACM Web Science Conference on WebSci 2013, NY, USA, pp. 132–138 (2013). http://doi.acm.org/10.1145/2464464.2464518
17. Huang, S.W., Suh, M.M., Hill, B.M., Hsieh, G.: How activists are both born and made: an analysis of users on change.org. In: Proceedings of the 33rd Annual ACM Conference on Human Factors in Computing Systems, pp. 211–220. ACM (2015)
18. Jungherr, A., Jürgens, P.: The political click: political participation through e-petitions in Germany. Policy Internet 2(4), 131–165 (2010)
19. Keane, J.: The Life and Death of Democracy. Simon and Schuster, New York (2009)
20. Lindner, R., Riehm, U.: Electronic petitions and institutional modernization. International parliamentary e-petition systems in comparative perspective. JeDEM-eJournal eDemocracy Open Govern. 1(1), 1–11 (2009)
21. Lindner, R., Riehm, U.: Broadening participation through e-petitions? an empirical study of petitions to the german parliament. Policy Internet 3(1), 1–23 (2011)
22. Margetts, H.Z., John, P., Hale, S.A., Reissfelder, S.: Leadership without leaders? starters and followers in online collective action. Polit. Stud. 63(2), 278–299 (2015)
23. Monterde, A., Calleja-López, A., Pereira de Lucena, A.: Disseny del procés de participació digital del programa d'actuació municipal (PAM) i de districtes (PAD) 2016–2019, p. 93. Ajuntament de Barcelona, Barcelona, Spain (2015)
24. Panagiotopoulos, P., Elliman, T.: Online engagement from the grassroots: reflecting on over a decade of epetitioning experience in Europe and the UK. In: Charalabidis, Y., Koussouris, S. (eds.) Empowering Open and Collaborative Governance, pp. 79–94. Springer, Heidelberg (2012)
25. Rancière, J., Panagia, D., Bowlby, R.: Ten theses on politics. Theory Event 5(3) (2001)
26. Rosanvallon, P., Goldhammer, A.: Counter-Democracy: Politics in an Age of Distrust, vol. 7. Cambridge University Press, Cambridge (2008)
27. Toret, J., Calleja, A., Marín Miró, Ó., Aragón, P., Aguilera, M., Lumbreras, A.: Tecnopolítica: la potencia de las multitudes conectadas. el sistema red 15m, un nuevo paradigma de la política distribuida. IN3 Working Paper Series (2013)
28. Tormey, S.: The End of Representative Politics. Wiley, Hoboken (2015)
29. Whyte, A., Renton, A., Macintosh, A.: e-petitioning in Kingston and Bristol. International Teledemocracy Centre, Napier University, Edinburgh, UK (2005)
30. Yasseri, T., Hale, S.A., Margetts, H.: Modeling the rise in internet-based petitions. arXiv preprint arXiv:1308.0239 (2013)
31. Žižek, S.: The Ticklish Subject: The Absent Centre of Political Ontology. Verso, New York (2000)

Computational Controversy

Benjamin Timmermans[1], Tobias Kuhn[1(✉)], Kaspar Beelen[2], and Lora Aroyo[1]

[1] Vrije Universiteit Amsterdam, Amsterdam, Netherlands
t.kuhn@vu.nl
[2] University of Amsterdam, Amsterdam, Netherlands

Abstract. Climate change, vaccination, abortion, Trump: Many topics
are surrounded by fierce controversies. The nature of such heated debates
and their elements have been studied extensively in the social science literature. More recently, various computational approaches to controversy
analysis have appeared, using new data sources such as Wikipedia, which
help us now better understand these phenomena. However, compared
to what social sciences have discovered about such debates, the existing computational approaches mostly focus on just a few of the many
important aspects around the concept of controversies. In order to link
the two strands, we provide and evaluate here a controversy model that
is both, rooted in the findings of the social science literature and at the
same time strongly linked to computational methods. We show how this
model can lead to computational controversy analytics that cover all of
the crucial aspects that make up a controversy.

1 Introduction

On many topics people from different backgrounds have a shared understanding,
or at least have views that are not in contradiction to each other. On some questions, however, like global warming, gun control, the death penalty, abortion,
and vaccination, groups of people may strongly disagree despite lengthy interactions and debates [36]. Such situations are commonly called *controversies* and
nowadays unfold to a large extent on the Web via different social media, discussion forums, and news platforms. This digital nature has naturally led to many
computational approaches to capture and analyze controversy [3,6,15,20,30,40].
However, while the social sciences have studied the phenomenon of controversies extensively [11,21,23,26,32], there is a lack of a well-founded comprehensive
model of controversies for such computational approaches to rely on. For that
reason, existing computational approaches have mostly focused on a few hand-
picked aspects (such as polarity and emotions), which seems insufficient in the
case of the complex and multi-faceted nature of the concept of controversy. To
resolve this problem, we present and evaluate here a unified model for controversy, and show how the different relevant aspects can be computationally
captured and analyzed.

There are many situations where being able to understand the space of a
controversy is essential. For journalists, news agencies and media professionals

© Springer International Publishing AG 2017
G.L. Ciampaglia et al. (Eds.): SocInfo 2017, Part II, LNCS 10540, pp. 288–300, 2017.
DOI: 10.1007/978-3-319-67256-4_23

it is often difficult to present a clear picture of an issue from all perspectives. Governments need to make laws that deal with issues for which it is essential that they have a complete understanding of such issues from an unbiased source. For the general public, understanding a controversy can help prevent a filter bubble, a potentially biased situation where they are only presented with information that they want to see. These problems can be addressed by the computational discovery and analysis of controversies and their elements and aspects.

2 Controversy, a Disputed Concept?

2.1 Explaining Disagreement

Understanding why societies become divided around specific issues has been a major topic of interest for political scientists, communication specialists and linguists—to name just a few disciplines. To embed our work within this type of literature, this section reviews some of the crucial concepts that have influenced research on public disputes. The following chapter narrows its focus to dissect the "controversy" in its constitutive parts.

Communications scientists have explained disagreement in terms of diverging or opposing *frames*. According to Gamson and Modigliani [21]: "[a frame is] a central organizing idea or story line that provides meaning to an unfolding strip of events, weaving a connection among them. The frame suggests what the controversy is, [offering information] about the essence of the issue". Framing bears on how people perceive issues *and* how they are represented in discourse. Similar to essentially contested concepts, framing involves selection and salience, i.e. a frame tends to highlight one aspect (or a combination of aspects) at the expense of others. Or as Entman argues [16]: framing occurs in communication when aspects of a given problem are made more salient, thus promoting a "particular problem definition, causal interpretation, moral evaluation, and/or treatment recommendations". Dardis et al. [14] demonstrate how framing affects disagreement by distinguishing between conflict-reinforcing frames, which contain evidence-confirming information, and therefore amplify existing beliefs; and conflict-displacing frames that appeal to both sides of a dispute, and diminish the level of disagreement—changes the adversarial structure of a debate.

Political scientists often invoke the concept of an *ideology* to explain the adversarial positions actors take on public issues. Converse [12]—in one of the early groundbreaking papers on the topic—describes ideology as a "belief system [...] a configuration of ideas and attitudes in which the elements are bound together by some form of constraint or functional interdependence. This line of thinking emphasizes the systemic connections between beliefs. For example, it implies that we can predict attitudes toward gun control, given the opinions on abortion and environment. Freeden [18] develops a semantic approach: he perceives concepts, such as "liberty" and "justice" as the "building blocks" of political thought which acquire meaning by virtue of their position within a broader network of ideas: "ideologies are particular patterned clusters and configurations of political concepts." The meaning of the concepts, is always relational and contested in nature: "equality" and "social justice" might be related terms—in the sense that they "naturally" imply each other–for a Labour politician, but not for a conservative MP. "An ideology", Freeden continues, "is hence none other than the macroscopic structural arrangement that attributes meaning to a range of mutually defining political concepts". Freeden leans heavily on Gallie's [19] notion of "Essentially Contested Concepts" which have the following qualities (1) Appraisive, it signifies a valued achievement (i.e. "Liberty") (2) internally complex (3) contains "rivaling" descriptions of its component parts (4) Context dependent, can modified in the light of changing circumstances.

Linguists, especially the school of "Critical Discourse Analysis" (CDA) pointed to the dialectial relation between language and societal institutions: language use reflects as well as shapes relations of power and dominance, and therefore plays a crucial role in reproducing disagreement. Ideology, according to this tradition, is defined as common sense, or more precisely as a "pattern of meaning or frame of interpretation [...] felt to be commonsensical, and often functioning in a normative way" [43]. It is composed of "taken-for-granted" and therefore unquestioned premises that are shared within a specific community. This resembles the Kuhnean scientific paradigm. As [43] notices: "[paradigms are] specific ways of looking, based on taken-for-granted premises that are shared within a community or generation of scientists." Ideological disagreement therefore entails a contestation of these commonsensical norms and prescriptions held by specific segments of society.

Research of structuralist linguists—a movement which was prevalent during the seventies or eighties—attempted to unearth language patterns that elicit or reduce disagreement, by scrutinizing how conflict is initiated (the linguistic or communicational devices used) and how it develops [25]. This boiled down to an analysis of the structure of arguments and the sequential organization of disagreement. Brenneis and Lein 1977 [8] distinguished three argumentative sequences in role-played disputes among children: repetition, escalation, and inversion. In later, cross-cultural, studies they [27] encountered the same patterns in different countries, but also noted cultural differences related to the tolerance for overlaps and interruptions. Boggs [5] points to "contradicting routines" as the main device for performing disputes. Pomerantz [39] defines "dispreferred-action" turn shapes as triggers for dispute. These turns contain marked "dispreference" features such as "delays, requests for clarification, partial repeats, and other repair initiators, and turn prefaces". According to Millar et al. [35], "three consecutive one-up maneuvers" serve as a good predictor of verbal conflict: "a conflict results when speaker B's one-up response to speaker A's one-up statement is responded to with a one-up maneuver by speaker A."

2.2 Anatomy of Controversies

People of different ideologies, seeing the world through different frames, and possibly speaking different languages, thereby become divided by the public debates that are called controversies [11,23,26,32]. The participants in a controversy are typically varied and can be categorized as (1) core-campaigners, (2) occasional campaigners (3) participants encouraged by campaigners (4) sympathisers. It is through the interaction between core-campaigners and broader sections of the public (termed occasional campaigners and sympathizers) [32] that such debates spread: Scientific controversies involve non-scientists, as debates are also held outside the scientific laboratories and journals. These discussions usually involve (a combination of) several recurring points on which participants disagree, such as benefits, risks, fairness, economics, human rights, decision-making [32], but ultimately flow deeper rooted and persistent ideological divisions or opposing value systems [23,33].

Controversies have furthermore the characteristic property that they tend to become unsolvable and persist over time, but nonetheless experience clear punctuations, they "flare up and die down", or even follow a cyclical pattern [24]. Not only does the intensity of a controversy fluctuate over time, it also follows different rhythms depending on the arena of the debate. Issues can be low-key as a public debate, but heavily disputed among scientists, and of course vice versa. A controversial debate can be held in different platforms (among scientists [26,42] or experts [22]), but usually migrates to the public sphere through the media, through which it engages broad segments of the public [13,24].

Moreover, the increasing delineation of opposing views results in an ever widening disagreement or polarization [42]: the debate forces participant to develop coherent viewpoints and manage to navigate a debate by consistently picking the "right" side on each of the aspects. Polarization emerges as discussants develop increasingly well-defined but diverging perspectives—a dynamic propelled by core-campaigner who usually develop the templates [32]. Given that disputes flow from the beliefs and values participants hold dear, the exchange of opinions is not limited to the "facts", but invites strong emotions [28].

3   Related Work

In the last few years, many approaches and methods have been proposed to computationally analyze controversies, and many interesting insights have thereby been found. The OpinioNetIT [3] project, for example, attempts to computationally reconstruct public debates as an exchange of pro and con statements using person-opinion-topic triples. Other work measures the controversy of a topic by building "conversation graphs" using a set of Twitter retweets on a given hashtag [20]. Another approach uses Twitter to measure the controversy of events [40]. Their model principally relies on are linguistic, structural and sentiment features. Besides Twitter, Wikipedia has proven useful for modeling controversy on historic data. An example of this is Contropedia, where the metadata associated with Wikipedia pages such as the presence of edits and reverts were used [6]. It has furthermore been shown that controversial pages on the Web can be detected through mapping them to their closest Wikipedia pages [15].

Only a few approaches explicitly tackled the problem of detecting controversy in news articles. [30] measured which sentences trigger the largest responses in terms of tweets in order to locate the most controversial points in media coverage. [10] identified controversial topics by looking at which ones tend to invoke conflicting sentiment, and [34] analyzed news using a crowdsourced lexicon that comprises frequent content words for which participants were asked to judge their controversy. Our work aims to put such approaches onto a solid methodological foundation by measuring controversy in a manner that involved all aspects that have been found to be important in the literature on the topic.

4 Methodology

Based on the background provided above, we present here our methodology on what we call computational controversy. The main component is our unifying controversy model, which is linked to computational methods to retrieve, capture, and analyze such debates. We also show a generic architecture of how these different aspects can be brought together.

4.1 The CAPOTE Controversy Model

Our unifying model captures the different characteristic aspects of a controversy as identified in the varied literature on the topic. Based on that, a controversy can be generally defined as a *heated and polarized public debate by a multitude of actors persisting over time.* The key words in this definition that point to the different aspects are "heated," "polarized," "public," "actors," and "time." With some renaming and reordering, this leads us to claim that a Controversy is made from the key aspects of Actors, Polarization, Openness, Time-persistence, and Emotions, which we can show as an informal equation:

Controversy $\sim$ Actors + Polarization + Openness + Time-persistence + Emotions

As an acronym for this equation, we call our model CAPOTE. The key aspects of controversy are therefore:

- **Actors:** A controversy has many participating actors. We wouldn't call it a controversy if it had only a handful of participants.
- **Polarization:** Viewpoints are polarized and not uniform or scattered. We call something a controversy only if the participants are grouped in two or more camps that oppose each other, with few people positioning themselves somewhere in between.
- **Openness:** A controversy plays out in an open public space, such as the web. We wouldn't call it a controversy if it was all hidden and happening out of sight for society.
- **Time-persistence:** A controversy persists over longer stretches of time, typically years or more. A heated debate that is sparked and settled within a single day, for example, would hardly be called a controversy.

- **Emotions:** Strong sentiments or emotions are expressed and are an important driver. It is not a controversy if everybody discusses the matter with a cool head and with no personal emotional involvement.

Therefore, according to our model and definition, a set of opinions and arguments expressed in a debate can be called a controversy only if all five criteria above are satisfied. Importantly, all these five aspects can nowadays be algorithmically assessed and quantified based on a variety of techniques and data sources, as we will see below.

4.2 Computational Controversy

With modern techniques on natural language processing, machine learning, and network analytics, all five aspects of controversies according to the CAPOTE model can be computationally accessed. The prevalence of the Web furthermore means that most such data are digital-born and relatively easy to retrieve.

The *openness* of a controversy and the generality of the web allows us to use different types of web content mining [29] to retrieve pertinent data in the first place, in the form of newspaper articles, discussions, social media posts, and contents from collaborative platforms like Wikipedia. The openness criterion thereby establishes the entry point for computational controversy analysis. Based on these data, we can then identify the participating *actors* with techniques including named entity recognition [37] and social network analysis methods [41]. The *emotions* expressed by these actors can furthermore be detected and categorized with a wide array of existing sentiment analysis techniques [17,38]. Additionally, we can of course analyse the content of the posts and articles by extracting their topics and involved concepts. For this, we can apply methods such as topic modeling [4] and ontology learning [31]. These steps may be run independently, or they may depend on each other. For example, the extraction of emotions may depend on the information of extracted actors, or vice versa.

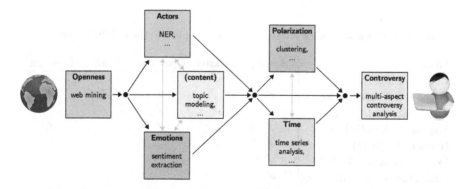

Fig. 1. A generic CAPOTE-based architecture. The black arrows denote the mandatory data flows for a fully CAPOTE-compliant architecture, whereas the gray ones denote optional data flows.

Based on this first round of analysis, we can investigate the remaining aspects of the CAPOTE model. The *polarization* of viewpoints can be assessed and quantified with clustering and network analysis techniques [1], taking as input the network of actors, their expressions, and the contained topics and emotions. The *time-persistence* aspect, finally, can be evaluated with time series analyses [7] and dynamic network models [9] on the same input (possibly including polarization and/or feeding its result to the polarization analysis).

All aspects of the CAPOTE model can therefore be extracted with established techniques, and this allows us in the end to combine the results and to analyze controversies in a complete and thorough manner. Figure 1 illustrates this general CAPOTE-based architecture of a system that allows for holistic, multi-aspect controversy analytics.

5 Evaluation

We evaluated our approach with a small qualitative study on related work, and a larger quantitative study on the accuracy of our proposed model.

5.1 Qualitative Study on Related Work

First we start with a small qualitative study of the approaches we introduced as related work on computational controversy analyses. We manually assessed which of the CAPOTE aspects were explicitly considered for each of these works. Table 1 shows the result. We see that all existing works on computational controversy cover at least three of our identified CAPOTE aspects, but none covers all five. While the Actors aspect was covered by all, Polarity and Time was covered by most, and Openness and Time was covered only by half of them. In aggregation, these studies had a good coverage, but in isolation each of them missed — or did not explicitly address — at least one of the aspects that our literature study identified as a crucial aspect of controversy.

Table 1. Classification of related work with respect to the CAPOTE model.

Work	Actors	Polarity	Openness	Time	Emotion
Choi et al. (2010) [10]	✓	✓	-	✓	✓
Popescu & P. (2010) [40]	✓	-	✓	✓	✓
Awadallah et al. (2012) [3]	✓	✓	✓	-	-
Mejova et al. (2014) [34]	✓	-	✓	-	✓
Borra et al. (2015) [6]	✓	✓	-	✓	✓
Dori & Allan (2015) [15]	✓	✓	-	-	-
Lourentzou et al. (2015) [30]	✓	-	-	✓	✓
Garimella et al. (2016) [20]	✓	✓	✓	-	✓

5.2   Design of Crowd Study

To evaluate the accuracy and completeness of our model we ran as our main study a crowdsourcing experiment using the CrowdFlower[1] platform. We wanted to find out whether our CAPOTE model aligns with what people would normally call a controversy and thereby whether it is a faithful model of the concept.

To assess the relevance of each of the five aspects, we showed newspaper articles to crowd workers and asked them whether these aspects apply to the given topic and whether they think it deals with a controversy. For this, we showed them the first two paragraphs from 5 048 Guardian newspaper articles together with five comments. We retrieved that data through the Guardian news API. Figure 2 shows the interface with the questions that was shown to the crowd workers. The questions correspond to the five CAPOTE aspects, with an additional question of whether the presented topic was controversial.

Fig. 2. The response section of the user interface of the crowd study

The collected annotations from this experiment were evaluated using the CrowdTruth methodology [2] for measuring the quality of the annotations, the annotators, and the annotated articles. This approach allows the measurement of ambiguity using a vector space. The ambiguity is computed by measuring the cosine distance between vectors of the annotators, where the features or dimensions of the vector represent the possible answers of the annotation task. The same measurement is then used to compare the vector of one annotator to the aggregated vector of all annotators for a single annotated article.

With the resulting data, we are then able to calculate a score between 0 and 1 for each article on these six dimensions, as an average of the workers' ratings. This in turn allows us to run a linear regression analysis to find out about the kind and extent to which the five aspects contribute to the degree to which a given topic is perceived as controversial or not. The five CAPOTE aspects serve as the independent variables in this regression analysis, with the score for conversy serving as the dependent variable to be predicted.

---

[1] http://crowdflower.com.

5.3   Results from Crowd Study

In the main experiment first a test was performed on 100 articles to measure how many annotators were required. Each article was annotated by 10 people, after which we found that using six workers would give the best results without significant changes. Following this, a total of 5 048 articles were annotated by 1 659 unique annotators resulting in a total of 31 888 annotations. This dataset is available for download at the CrowdTruth data repository[2]. Before we turn to the results of the main linear regression analysis, we can have a look at some descriptive results including Pearson correlation coefficients between the different aspects of the articles.

Table 2 show the results of the descriptive analysis. 43% of the individual judgment on the overall controversy aspect were positive, leading to a positive controversy classification in 50% of the articles if a simple majority vote is applied. Out of the five CAPOTE aspects, openness was the most prevalent (71% of the individual judgments), while time persistence was the least prevalent (44%). The openness scored highest with .915 for the relation clarity score, which indicates that it is the least ambiguous relation. In contrast, the actors, polarity, time and emotion aspect had similar lower clarity scores, indicating there is more disagreement between the annotators for these relations. The correlation values show the emotion aspect is most strongly correlated with controversy followed by polarity and time persistence, and with actors and openness showing the weakest correlation.

To find out whether these correlations together amplify, we can have a look at the regression results, which are shown in Table 3. The top part of the table shows the regression involving all five CAPOTE aspects to predict the controversy aspect. Overall the regression provides a good fit given the inherently noisy

Table 2. Results of the crowdsourcing experiment. For each answer the correlation with the other answers is shown, followed by the ratio of positive answers, the majority vote for yes and the average CrowdTruth relation clarity score as described in Sect. 5.2. Below that, the Pearson correlation scores are shown, which was computed by taking the ratio of occurrences for the relation in each article.

		Controversy	Actors	Polarity	Openness	Time	Emotion
Ratio of *yes*		0.43	0.62	0.57	0.71	0.44	0.49
Majority vote *yes*		0.50	0.81	0.73	0.88	0.52	0.62
relation clarity score		0.907	0.887	0.886	0.915	0.883	0.890
correlations:	C	1	0.4524	0.5520	0.4655	0.5796	0.6906
	A	0.4524	1	0.3848	0.5848	0.5428	0.4618
	P	0.5520	0.3848	1	0.4067	0.3868	0.4276
	O	0.4655	0.5848	0.4067	1	0.4564	0.4448
	T	0.5796	0.5428	0.3868	0.4564	1	0.5913
	E	0.6906	0.4618	0.4267	0.4448	0.5913	1

---

[2] http://data.crowdtruth.org.

nature of human annotations and social science concepts, with an adjusted R^2 of 59%. The effect of all variables is positive, and significant for all of them except Actors. Therefore, we do not have evidence so far that the Actors aspect contributes to the definition of a controversy.

If we look at all combinations of four aspects out of the five, however, we get a more nuanced picture, as shown in the bottom part of Table 3. No matter which four aspects we pick, they turn out to be all significant in predicting the controversy of a topic. Therefore, while the Actors aspect does not significantly add to the controversy concept when all other four aspects are present, it does deliver useful redundancy in the sense that it significantly contributes when one of the other aspects is lacking. These regression analyses furthermore confirm Emotions being the most important aspect. It increases the adjusted R^2 by more than 10%, followed by Polarity, which contributes 5%, while all other aspects contributing on their own less than 2%.

Table 3. Linear regression analysis on all five aspects (above) and on four of the five aspects (below)

ALL 5	(intercept)	Actors	Polarity	Openness	Time	Emotions
coefficient	-0.15386	0.00787	0.30629	0.10345	0.21832	0.47036
p-value	$< 10^{-15}$	0.64	$< 10^{-15}$	$3.1 \cdot 10^{-10}$	$< 10^{-15}$	$< 10^{-15}$
significant	*		*	*	*	*
adjusted R^2	0.5885					

4 OF 5	(intercept)	Actors	Polarity	Openness	Time	Emotions
coefficient	-0.15267		0.30687	0.10650	0.22040	0.47095
p-value	$< 10^{-15}$		$< 10^{-15}$	$1.7 \cdot 10^{-12}$	$< 10^{-15}$	$< 10^{-15}$
significant	*		*	*	*	*
adjusted R^2	0.5885					
coefficient	-0.09763	0.04465		0.16910	0.25043	0.53587
p-value	$< 10^{-15}$	0.012		$< 10^{-15}$	$< 10^{-15}$	$< 10^{-15}$
significant	*	*		*	*	*
adjusted R^2	0.5378					
coefficient	-0.12328	0.05008	0.32073		0.22726	0.48181
p-value	$< 10^{-15}$	0.00126	$< 10^{-15}$		$< 10^{-15}$	$< 10^{-15}$
significant	*	*	*		*	*
adjusted R^2	0.5848					
coefficient	-0.16247	0.07436	0.32261	0.12410		0.54804
p-value	$< 10^{-15}$	$6.7 \cdot 10^{-6}$	$< 10^{-15}$	$1.3 \cdot 10^{-13}$		$< 10^{-15}$
significant	*	*	*	*		*
adjusted R^2	0.5702					
coefficient	-0.14464	0.05969	0.39724	0.17575	0.43056	
p-value	$< 10^{-15}$	0.00154	$< 10^{-15}$	$< 10^{-15}$	$< 10^{-15}$	
significant	*	*	*	*	*	
adjusted R^2	0.4803					

6 Conclusions

Controversies are a frequent and important phenomenon of public discourse. Many approaches have recently been proposed to measure and analyze such controversies with computational means, but a principled framework has been missing. Based on an extensive literature study and supported by a crowdsourced study, we identified five key aspects that define a controversy: a multitude of involved actors, polarized opinions, open visibility of the debate, time persistence, and strong emotions. The results from our crowdsourced study indicate that each of these aspects is a positive indicator of controversy, but also that there is a clear difference in the extend of their influence. Most notably, the emotion aspect was found to be the strongest indicator, while the actors aspect had the weakest influence.

We can often feel that controversies around important issues, such as climate change, are holding us back to make progress on urgent problems. We think that our CAPOTE model can contribute to better understand these controversies and exploit the potential of computational approaches to their analysis. This, in turn, could be the first step towards breaking up the deadlock of long lasting controversial topics.

Acknowledgments. This publication was supported by the Dutch national program COMMIT/.

References

1. Andris, C., Lee, D., Hamilton, M.J., Martino, M., Gunning, C.E., Selden, J.A.: The rise of partisanship and super-cooperators in the us house of representatives. PLoS ONE **10**(4), e0123507 (2015)
2. Aroyo, L., Welty, C.: The three sides of crowdtruth. J. Hum. Computat. **1**, 31–34 (2014)
3. Awadallah, R., Ramanath, M., Weikum, G.: Opinions network for politically controversial topics. In: Proceedings of the 1st edn. Workshop on Politics, Elections and Data, pp. 15–22. ACM (2012)
4. Blei, D.M., Ng, A.Y., Jordan, M.I.: Latent dirichlet allocation. J. Mach. Learn. Res. **3**, 993–1022 (2003)
5. Boggs, S.T.: The development of verbal disputing in part-hawaiian children. Lang. Soc. **7**(03), 325–344 (1978)
6. Borra, E., Weltevrede, E., Ciuccarelli, P., Kaltenbrunner, A., Laniado, D., Magni, G., Mauri, M., Rogers, R., Venturini, T.: Societal controversies in wikipedia articles. In: Proceedings of the 33rd Annual ACM Conference on Human Factors in Computing Systems, CHI 2015, pp. 193–196. ACM, New York (2015)
7. Box, G.E., Jenkins, G.M., Reinsel, G.C., Ljung, G.M.: Time Series Analysis: Forecasting and Control. Wiley (2015)
8. Brenneis, D., Lein, L.: You fruithead: a sociolinguistic approach to children's dispute settlement. Child Discourse **49**, 65 (1977)
9. Casteigts, A., Flocchini, P., Quattrociocchi, W., Santoro, N.: Time-varying graphs and dynamic networks. Int. J. Parallel Emergent Distrib. Syst. **27**(5), 387–408 (2012)

10. Choi, Y., Jung, Y., Myaeng, S.-H.: Identifying controversial issues and their sub-topics in news articles. In: Chen, H., Chau, M., Li, S., Urs, S., Srinivasa, S., Wang, G.A. (eds.) PAISI 2010. LNCS, vol. 6122, pp. 140–153. Springer, Heidelberg (2010). doi:10.1007/978-3-642-13601-6_16

11. Clarke, A.E.: Controversy and the development of reproductive sciences. Soc. Probl. **37**(1), 18–37 (1990)

12. Converse, P.E.: The Nature of Belief Systems in Mass Publics. Survey Research Center. University of Michigan, Ann Arbor (1962)

13. Dalgalarrondo, S., Urfalino, P.: Tragic choice, controversy, and public decision-making: the case in france of random selection of aids patients for treatment ("lot-drawing"). In: Revue française de sociologie, pp. 3–40 (2002)

14. Dardis, F.E., Baumgartner, F.R., Boydstun, A.E., De Boef, S., Shen, F.: Media framing of capital punishment and its impact on individuals' cognitive responses. Mass Commun. Soc. **11**(2), 115–140 (2008)

15. Dori-Hacohen, S., Allan, J.: Automated controversy detection on the web. In: Hanbury, A., Kazai, G., Rauber, A., Fuhr, N. (eds.) ECIR 2015. LNCS, vol. 9022, pp. 423–434. Springer, Cham (2015). doi:10.1007/978-3-319-16354-3_46

16. Entman, R.M.: Framing: toward clarification of a fractured paradigm. J. Commun. **43**(4), 51–58 (1993)

17. Feldman, R.: Techniques and applications for sentiment analysis. Commun. ACM **56**(4), 82–89 (2013)

18. Freeden, M.: Political concepts and ideological morphology. J. Polit. Philosophy **2**(2), 140–164 (1994)

19. Gallie, W.B.: Essentially Contested Concepts. In: Proceedings of the Aristotelian Society, vol. 56, pp. 167–198. JSTOR (1955)

20. Garimella, K., De Francisci Morales, G., Gionis, A., Mathioudakis, M.: Quantifying controversy in social media. In: Proceedings of the Ninth ACM International Conference on Web Search and Data Mining, pp. 33–42. ACM (2016)

21. Garrison, W.A., Modigliani, A.: The changing culture of affirmative action. In: Equal Employment Opportunity: Labor Market Discrimination and Public Policy, vol. 373 (1994)

22. Hallberg, M., Rigné, E.-M.: Child sexual abuse-a study of controversy and construction. Acta Sociol. **37**(2), 141–163 (1994)

23. Horst, M.: Collective closure? public debate as the solution to controversies about science and technology. Acta Sociol. **53**(3), 195–211 (2010)

24. Jasper, J.M.: The political life cycle of technological controversies. Soc. Forces **67**(2), 357–377 (1988)

25. Kakavá, C.: Discourse and conflict. In: The Handbook of Discourse Analysis, pp. 650–670 (2001)

26. Kempner, J., Merz, J.F., Bosk, C.L.: Forbidden knowledge: public controversy and the production of nonknowledge1. In: Sociological Forum, vol. 26, pp. 475–500. Wiley Online Library (2011)

27. Lein, L., Brenneis, D.: Children's disputes in three speach communities. Lang. Soc. **7**(03), 299–323 (1978)

28. Levi, D.J., Holder, E.E.: Psychological factors in the nuclear power controversy. Polit. Psychol., 445–457 (1988)

29. Liu, B., Chen-Chuan-Chang, K.: Editorial: special issue on web content mining. ACM SIGKDD Explor. Newsl. **6**(2), 1–4 (2004)

30. Lourentzou, I., Dyer, G., Sharma, A., Zhai, C.: Hotspots of news articles: joint mining of news text & social media to discover controversial points in news. In: 2015 IEEE International Conference on Big Data (Big Data), pp. 2948–2950. IEEE (2015)
31. Maedche, A., Staab, S.: Ontology learning for the semantic web. IEEE Intell. Syst. 16(2), 72–79 (2001)
32. Martin, B.: The controversy manual. A practical guide for understanding and participating in scientific and technological controversies. Sparsnäs, Sweden, Reading, Massachusetts (2014)
33. Maynard-Moody, S.: Managing controversies over science: the case of fetal research. J. Public Adm. Res. Theor.: J-PART, 5–18 (1995)
34. Mejova, Y., Zhang, A.X., Diakopoulos, N., Castillo, C.: Controversy and sentiment in online news. arXiv preprint arXiv:1409.8152 (2014)
35. Millar, F.E., Rogers, L.E., Bavelas, J.B.: Identifying patterns of verbal conflict in interpersonal dynamics. West. J. Commun. (includes Commun. Rep.) 48(3), 231–246 (1984)
36. Misra, A., Walker, M.A.: Topic independent identification of agreement and disagreement in social media dialogue. In: Conference of the Special Interest Group on Discourse and Dialogue, p. 920 (2013)
37. Nadeau, D., Sekine, S.: A survey of named entity recognition and classification. Lingvisticae Investigationes 30(1), 3–26 (2007)
38. Pang, B., Lee, L., et al.: Opinion mining and sentiment analysis. Found. Trends® Inf. Retrieval, 2(1–2), 135 (2008)
39. Pomerantz, A.: Agreeing and disagreeing with assessments: some features of preferred/dispreferred turn shaped (1984)
40. Popescu, A.-M., Pennacchiotti, M.: Detecting controversial events from twitter. In: Proceedings of the 19th ACM International Conference on Information and Knowledge Management, pp. 1873–1876. ACM (2010)
41. Scott, J.: Social Network Analysis. Sage (2012)
42. Tarrow, S.: Polarization and convergence in academic controversies. Theory Soc. 37(6), 513–536 (2008)
43. Verschueren, J.: Ideology in Language Use: Pragmatic Guidelines for Empirical Research. Cambridge University Press, Cambridge (2012)

Evaluative Patterns and Incentives in YouTube

David Garcia$^{(\boxtimes)}$, Adiya Abisheva, and Frank Schweitzer

ETH Zurich, Weinbergstrasse 56/58, 8092 Zurich, Switzerland
dgarcia@ethz.ch

Abstract. Users of social media are not only producers and consumers of online content, they also evaluate each other's content. Some social media include the possibility to down vote or dislike the content posted by other users, posing the risk that users who receive dislikes might be more likely to become inactive, especially if the disliked content is about a person. We analyzed the data on more than 150,000 YouTube videos to understand how video impact and user incentives can be related to the possibility to dislike user content. We processed images related to videos to identify faces and quantify if evaluating content related to people is connected to disliking patterns. We found that videos with faces on their images tend to have less dislikes if they are posted by male users, but the effect is not present for female users. On the contrary, videos with faces and posted by female users attract more views and likes. Analyzing the probability of users to become inactive, we find that receiving dislikes is associated with users becoming inactive. This pattern is stronger when dislikes are given to videos with faces, showing that negative evaluations about people have a stronger association with user inactivity. Our results show that user evaluations in social media are a multi-faceted phenomenon that requires large-scale quantitative analyses, identifying under which conditions users disencourage other users from being active in social media.

Keywords: Social psychology · Incentives · YouTube

1 Introduction

The rise of the Social Web fundamentally changed the role of Information and Communication Technologies in the flow of information. The early platforms that connected mass media to wider audiences evolved into social media technologies that allow users to find content produced by other users [7]. While mass media focused on producing content of interest for their audience, social media became *participatory media* that encouraged users to produce content of interest for other users. Beyond this shift from audience to content producers, users of social media also became *evaluators* that can positively or negatively asses the content produced by others [24]. This new feature of social media is the source of one of the main challenges for the sustainability of online communities: the possibility of criticism and negative expression in social media can be a negative incentive

© Springer International Publishing AG 2017
G.L. Ciampaglia et al. (Eds.): SocInfo 2017, Part II, LNCS 10540, pp. 301–315, 2017.
DOI: 10.1007/978-3-319-67256-4_24

for user activity. Just few down votes, dislikes, or salty comments can be the cause behind a user abandoning an online community.

The way users interact in online participatory media depends, among other factors, on the design of the online platform they use [4]. This raises various questions about the mechanism design of a website, which are usually aimed to optimize user participation and involvement. A common question is the influence of the dislike button on user participation, which is currently excluded from the design of some of the leading social networking sites, like Instagram. Other sites, like Facebook, include a wider variety of buttons to express emotional reactions, but leave out the *"dislike"* option from the ways users can evaluate each other's content [6]. The rationale behind this decision is often attributed to the assumption that, when users receive explicit dislikes by other users, their participation decreases and might opt out from an online community. This *risk of the dislike button* leads various social media to only allow positive evaluations through the user interface, leaving any kind of criticism for comments or other kinds of textual interaction.

The risk of the dislike button heavily depends on the purpose and functionality of an online platform. As opposed to the above argument to exclude the dislike button, negative incentives can be critically necessary for social media that generate content aggregates, such as featured lists and front pages. An example of the *necessity of the dislike button* is the "Digg collapse" [37], in which a massive amount of users stopped using Digg to start using Reddit, following a platform redesign that disabled the option to down vote content [34]. Without the possibility to negatively assess content, the quality of the front page heavily suffered and the main functionality of the site was damaged. The role of explicit negative evaluations in social media is thus a multi-faceted phenomenon that requires a research approach that can distinguish the risks associated with the possibility to negatively evaluate other users' posts.

The above difference between the role of disliking on Facebook and Digg lies on the nature of the content posted in the online medium. While the content shared in Facebook is very close to the identity of the user that posts it (e.g. profile pictures or pictures of family and friends), the content shared in Digg is usually composed of web links that might even not be authored by the posting user. To understand the effect of negative evaluations in social media, we differentiate two evaluation scenarios: (i) *subject evaluation* when a person or group of people are salient in the evaluated content, and (ii) *object evaluation* when people are not salient in the content that is evaluated and objects, concepts, or events are at the center of the posted content. As it is not the same to dislike *something* as to dislike *someone*, this differentiation between object and subject evaluations is a potentially pivotal point in the effect of the dislike button.

We hypothesize that the difference between subject and object evaluation contexts affects the role of negative evaluations in user interaction. Users who evaluate are protected by their anonymity and are free to negatively evaluate any content they want, but some social and psychological factors that affect face-to-face evaluations might also appear online. First, when content represents a person in the subject evaluation context, the content has a closer resemblance to the evaluating user than in the object evaluation context. Implicit self-esteem [15] can generate biases towards positive evaluations when interacting with content that might resemble oneself, such as the name-letter effect [20]. In this case, users should be less likely to provide negative evaluations when people are salient (subject evaluations) than when people are not at the center of the evaluation (object evaluations). Inspired by this, we formulate the *negative subject evaluation avoidance hypothesis*: the tendency to receive dislikes in user content is lower when the content is about a person.

Second, negative evaluations can have stronger effects on user incentives when they happen in the subject evaluation context than in the object evaluation context. This principle is the assumption behind the risk of the dislike button, as allowing the negative evaluation of people poses a risk for user integration, motivation, and future activity levels. We formulate the *negative incentives hypothesis*: the probability of a user becoming inactive grows faster with negative evaluations to the content posted by the user when such content is about a person than when the content is not about a person.

To test the above hypotheses, we need to control for various inter-individual effects, including user popularity and demographic factors. A demographic factor that plays key importance in online behavior is gender [16,22]. In our negative evaluation scenario, gender might have two effects. First, subjective gender biases are linked to the perception of risks in technology [28] and could affect evaluation patterns depending on the gender of the posting user. Second, social forces might have stronger effects for female users [30], strengthening the disincentives associated to negative subject evaluations to content posted by female users. Our analysis takes into account gender in the analysis of online evaluations, assessing whether the role of negative evaluations might differ between male and female users.

Testing the above hypothesis has been a challenging task in previous research due to the difficulty to compare across content and platforms. Comparing negative evaluations across platforms can reveal statistical differences, but a threat to validity lies in the difficulty to single out the effect of context in disliking when various other differences in platform designs are present. Furthermore, due to the risk of the dislike button, not many platforms allow negative subject evaluations (e.g. disliking a Facebook profile picture), to avoid the risk of creating negative incentives to user activity. A notable exception is the case of YouTube, where negative evaluations are possible through the dislike button and users upload content that brings both object evaluations (e.g. videos about events) and subject evaluations (e.g. videoblogger selfie-like videos). We apply image processing to the images related to YouTube videos to operationalize a metric that distinguishes object from subject evaluation, to statistically analyze the link between disliking and user activity. This way, we provide a novel analysis that bridges the research gap that, to date, has prevented the evaluation of the hypotheses explained above. In the following we briefly outline the research background on the topic, followed by a description of the data and methods used to analyze evaluative patterns and incentives in YouTube.

1.1   Research Background

Evaluative patterns in social media have been subject of previous research. The appraisal of online content leaves digital traces in the form of up and down votes, likes and dislikes, or numeric star-ratings. Extended research has analyzed ratings of products in reviews communities like Amazon [23], often related to recommender systems and sentiment analysis [36]. Beyond products, previous works analyze the relationship between up an down votes in Reddit [24], finding a scaling pattern that also appears in other media like YouTube and Imgur [1]. Collective evaluations are useful to understand the social factors of spreading misinformation [10] and to analyze natural experiments about the factors that influence the success of content [21]. The nature and volume of user evaluations and attention has been found to depend on user gender, from popularity levels in Twitter [22,26] to variability in worker ratings of gig economy platforms [16]. Certain user actions are strongly correlated with negative evaluations and have been shown useful to analyze human behavior. Edit conflicts in Wikipedia show the burstiness and memory of disagreement [38], and the creation of negative social links shows the existence of structural balance patterns that reduce cognitive dissonance [33].

User incentives and churn in social media have been subject of extensive research. From individual decisions to leave online communities [19] to models that aggregate such behavior at the level of complete websites [12,29]. The decision of users to become inactive in an online community is a multifaceted choice that can reflect nonlinear behavior. For example, the tendency of Twitter users to become inactive shows a nonlinear relationship to their amount of followers, such that more followers not always means lower chances to become inactive [11]. Incentives can explain other user decisions beyond churn, for example when psychological biases appear in the creation of social connections [20] and in the evaluation of online content [14], or when economic incentives explain the sharing of links to malware [17].

Research on YouTube has shed light on various aspects of human behavior. The analysis of viewing patterns shows how video impact can be predicted [32] as well as the relationship of video popularity and demographic factors visible in other social media [2]. The temporal information provided by YouTube has been analyzed to identify the classes of collective responses of a society [9]. The large size of YouTube data allows further research, leading to the identification of a new collective response class not observed before [31]. The data on likes and dislikes of YouTube has been applied to analyze general patterns of polarization linked to the filter bubble [2], and allow the understanding of polarization in various contexts, from political campaigns [13] to anorexia-related content [27]. YouTube data has been a good alternative to Twitter and Wikipedia data, alleviating the model organism bias suffered by research on social media [35] and posing an alternative data source to further validate the findings of research in Computational Social Science and Social Informatics.

2   Materials and Methods

2.1   Data on YouTube Channels

As part of a larger analysis of YouTube data [2], we extracted detailed information on a set of YouTube channels. Starting from a large sample of random channels, we identified channels owned by individual users through the data provided by the YouTube API in 2013. These channels could be identified thanks to various fields related to the profile of the owner, such as age and gender. After applying this filter, we count with a sample of 1,556 user channels that were active in 2013, from which we can identify their gender as self-reported in earlier versions of the YouTube platform. In 2016, we performed a retrieval of all publicly available videos on the channel of each user in the dataset. This way we gathered more than 150,000 videos, including their count of views, likes, and dislikes. A descriptive summary of the dataset is presented on Table 1 and further descriptive statistics are reported in the Appendix.

Each YouTube video has an associated image that is used as a thumbnail to summarize the content of the video. We applied face recognition through the face++ API[1] to identify which videos contain a face and which ones do not. The face++ API is a tool that has been shown useful to detect faces in previous research [18,26] and is accurate enough [39] to have a valid approximation to the measurement of whether at least one person is salient in a video. We use the output of face++ to operationalize a variable that captures subject versus object evaluations. Subject evaluations are those directed to content where a person is salient ($Face = 1$), while object evaluations are given to content where people can be present but are not salient enough to be detectable in the image summarizing the video ($Face = 0$). Note that subject evaluations do not need to be evaluations directed to the user who posted the video, they are evaluations to videos in which at least one person is relevant, as opposed to videos not centered around people.

Table 1. Dataset summary. Total sample size of users and videos, counts of views, likes, and dislikes, and means and medians over the set of videos.

Users	1,556	Female	377	% Female	24.2%
Videos	157,661	With Face	48,366	% With Face	30.68%
Views	67,974,981,442	Mean	431,146.5	Median	30,129
Likes	666,168,168	Mean	4,225.3	Median	385
Dislikes	33,496,449	Mean	212.5	Median	24

---

[1] https://www.faceplusplus.com/.

2.2 Video Impact Models

To understand the interplay between video impact, evaluation context, and the gender of YouTube users, we apply regression models of the impact that videos have in terms of three variables: views, likes, and dislikes. More precisely, we define regression models for three dependent variables measured over each video: (i) the log-transformed amount of views of the video $log(views)$, (ii) the logarithm of the ratio of likes per view $log(L_R) = log(likes/views)$, and (iii) the logarithm of the ratio of dislikes per view $log(D_R) = log(dislikes/views)$. Log-transformations are applied to reduce skewness, as explained more in detail in the Appendix.

We analyze the views of a video through a mixed-effects regression model [5]:

$$log(views) = a_v + b_v \cdot Face + c_v \cdot Female + d_v \cdot Face \cdot Female$$
$$+ f_v \cdot log(D_R) + g_v \cdot log(L_R) + Z_v * u + \epsilon_v \tag{1}$$

where $Face = 1$ if a face was detected on the image of the video and 0 otherwise, $Female = 1$ if the user that posted the video is female and 0 if male, and u is a categorical variable that identifies each user. The fixed-effects parameter a_v measures the intercept of the model, while b_v measures the increase in views that can be attributed to subject evaluation, c_v to the gender of the posting user, and d_v to the statistical interaction between the $Face$ and $Female$ variables, i.e. the additional effect of subject evaluation for videos posted by female users. The fixed effect terms $f_v \cdot log(D_R)$ and $g_v \cdot log(L_R)$ are statistical controls to remove possible confounds with the likes and dislikes ratios. The vector Z_v contains the random effects of the model as an intercept per user, to correct for any inter-individual differences that can explain views. This way we solve a possible Simpson's paradox effect stemming from different popularity and activity levels of the users. The term ϵ_v is the residuals of the model, which are assumed to be normally distributed with zero mean and no relevant correlations to other terms of the model.

In a similar fashion, we model the logarithm of the likes ratio:

$$log(L_R) = a_l + b_l \cdot Face + c_l \cdot Female + d_l \cdot Face \cdot Female$$
$$+ f_l \cdot log(views) + g_l \cdot log(D_R) + Z_l * u + \epsilon_l \tag{2}$$

and of the dislikes ratio:

$$log(D_R) = a_d + b_d \cdot Face + c_d \cdot Female + d_d \cdot Face \cdot Female$$
$$+ f_d \cdot log(views) + g_d \cdot log(L_R) + Z_d * u + \epsilon_d \tag{3}$$

where the control terms have been set up to capture possible confounds with the other two impact variables. This last model of the dislikes ratio is of special interest, as the negative subject evaluation avoidance hypothesis implies that $b_d < 0$, with the parameter d_d quantifying the case of a difference on the effect between genders.

2.3   User Incentives Model

We analyze user incentives through an inactivity model that relates the probability of a user to become inactive with the dislikes received by the last video of the user, including the interplay between the content of the video and the gender of the user who posted it. We operationalize the inactivity of a user through the video variable I, which takes value 1 if the user did not post any videos for a period of two months after the video, and 0 otherwise.[2]

$$logit(P(I)) = (\beta + \beta_F \cdot Face + \beta_I \cdot Face \cdot Female + \beta_G \cdot Female) \cdot log(D_R)$$
$$+\alpha + \gamma \cdot log(views) + \delta \cdot log(L_R) + Z_I * u + \epsilon_I \qquad (4)$$

The above equation models a relationship between a logit transformation $(logit(x) = log(x/(1-x)))$ of the probability of a user becoming inactive after posting the video $P(I)$ with its dislike ratio for different $Face$ and $Female$ conditions. The parameter α quantifies the baseline tendency to become inactive independently of any video or user variable. The parameters β quantifies how inactivity depends on the dislike ratio, which we can expect to be positive if users respond to negative evaluations of others with higher inactivity tendencies. The parameter β_F quantifies how the role of the dislikes ratio depends on the video having a face and β_G and β_I how this depends on the gender of the user. The negative incentives hypothesis implies a value $\beta_F > 0$, which quantifies the increase in the relationship between the dislikes ratio and the tendency of users to become inactive for videos in the subject evaluation context. The terms $\gamma \cdot log(views)$ and $\delta \cdot log(L_R)$ quantify controls for other properties of the video, and we can expect that likes in particular, as positive evaluation signals, should have a negative effect on the probability to become inactive. The term $Z_I * u$ accounts for random effects of user levels in inactivity tendencies, and ϵ_I measures the model residuals.

Note that the models formalized in the above equations are designed to test the hypotheses explained in the introduction, not to serve as predictors for video impact or user churn. All variables, including views, likes, and dislikes, are measuring a long period after the video has been posted, and thus the models are a way to test association between variables rather than to formulate predictive methods. Our analysis focuses on robustly testing the hypotheses that motivate our research, and thus formulating accurate predictors for user activity or video impact is out of the scope of this research. We fit video impact models and the user incentives model with the lme4 R package [5]. We assess the validity of model assumptions through regression diagnostics on the distribution of residuals and their possible correlations with other model terms. To understand interaction effects, we analyze the *statistical effect* of independent variables on dependent variables by holding all controls constant to their average value. We assess the variance in these predictions by repeating the model fits on 1,000 bootstrap samples of the empirical data, as shown in the Results section.

---

[2] We replicated the analysis with alternative intervals of one and three months to determine inactivity, and regression models were qualitatively unchanged.

3 Results

3.1 Video Impact Analysis

The fit results of video impact models are shown on Table 2. Videos with a face and by female users receive more views and more likes. There is no significant interaction between *Face* and *Female* for the case of likes, but it is significant and positive for views. This indicates that the statistical effect of *Face* on views is higher for female users. The dislikes ratio model suggests that female users receive less dislikes per view than male users, as c_d is negative and significant. The dislikes ratio model supports the negative subject evaluation avoidance hypothesis, with an estimate of b_d significantly below zero. Nevertheless, the positive interaction term with *Female* shows that this is the case only for male users, as the terms b_d and d_d cancel out to a slightly positive value.

Table 2. Regression results of impact models. Videos with faces and posted by female users get more views and likes. Videos with faces get less dislikes for male users.

Term		Views model		Likes model		Dislikes model
Intercept	a_v	**2.128*****	a_l	**−2.525*****	a_d	**−2.828*****
Face	b_v	**0.064*****	b_l	**0.090*****	b_d	**−0.058*****
Female	c_v	**0.436*****	c_l	**0.267*****	c_d	**−0.205*****
Face · Female	d_v	**0.043***	d_l	−0.000	d_d	**0.072*****
$log(D_R)$	f_v	**−0.542*****	g_l	**0.151*****		
$log(L_R)$	g_v	**−0.574*****			g_d	**0.302*****
$log(views)$			f_l	**−0.166*****	f_d	**−0.315*****
AIC		501059.929		305887.837		414279.269
R^2		0.763		0.617		0.604
Num. obs		157661		157661		157661
Num. groups		1556		1556		1556

*****$p < 0.001$, ****$p < 0.01$, ***$p < 0.05$

To better understand the various interaction terms of the models, we performed an effect analysis of bootstrap samples, shown on Fig. 1. The statistical effects of *Face* and *Female* in the views and likes ratio models discussed above can be observed in the analysis of their respective models. The negative subject evaluation avoidance towards male users can be seen on the right panel, as the estimates of the dislikes ratio are lower for male users when the videos contain a face. The slightly opposite effect for female users confirms our observation that the negative subject evaluation avoidance effect does not exist for female users.

Model control terms reported on Table 2 show that, after accounting for other factors, views are negatively correlated with dislike and like ratios, and that the ratio of both evaluation metrics are positively correlated with each other.

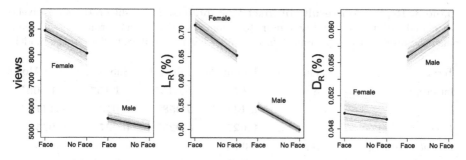

Fig. 1. User gender and video face statistical effect analysis. Fit estimated amount of views, L_R, and D_R as a function of the values of the *Face* and *Gender* variables when controls are set to their average value. Dark lines show the average estimates over 1,000 bootstrap samples of the empirical data, with the shaded lines showing all bootstrap results.

This points to the sublinear scaling of likes and dislikes with views previously reported in [1], and that polarization exists when positive and negative evaluations tend to coexist. The above inferences are coherent with the model assumptions explained in the Materials and Methods section, with normally distributed residuals and no relevant signs of heteroscedasticity.

3.2 Subject Dislikes and Inactivity

The results of the fit of the user incentives model are shown on Table 3. The first column shows the full model as expressed on Eq. 4, including controls and interaction terms. The negative incentives hypothesis is supported, as the estimate of β_F is positive and significant, i.e. the marginal effect of dislikes on the probability to become inactive is higher when the disliked video contains a face. In contrast to the dislikes model of the previous section, gender does not have any significant interaction and the hypothesis holds for both genders.

Regression results are qualitatively unchanged when fitting subsets of the variables, either ignoring controls or interaction terms with gender. Furthermore, a replication of the model with the value of I defined by one and three months instead of two months shed similar results, with β_F positive and significant. The positive and significant estimate of β in all models shows that higher dislikes ratios lead to higher chances for users to become inactive. The controls of the user incentives model show that the likes ratio is negatively associated with the probability of users becoming inactive, while the logarithm of the amount of views has a positive relationship with $P(I)$ when other variables are taken into account too. This suggests that likes incentivize users to stay active, and that views without likes are not the leading incentive for users to keep posting videos.

To understand interaction terms and incentives better, we fitted the model subset with the lowest Bayesian Information Criterion, reported on the last column of Table 3. We analyzed the estimate of $P(I)$ in the model as a function of *Face* and D_R in 1,000 bootstrap samples of the data. The results of this analysis

Table 3. Regression results of inactivity models. The dislike ratio is positively associated with the probability of users to become inactive, with a stronger association when the disliked videos contain a face. Gender has no significant effect in the model.

Term	Parameter	Full model	Subset 1	Subset 2	Best Model
Intercept	α	-1.513^{***}	-1.155^{***}	-1.157^{***}	-1.508^{***}
$log(D_R)$	β	0.143^{***}	0.058^{***}	0.059^{***}	0.141^{***}
$Face \cdot log(D_R)$	β_F	0.027^{***}	0.025^{***}	0.027^{***}	0.025^{***}
$Female \cdot log(D_R)$	β_G	-0.010		-0.007	
$Face \cdot Female \cdot log(D_R)$	β_I	-0.016		-0.014	
$log(views)$	γ	0.045^{***}			0.045^{***}
$log(L_R)$	δ	-0.109^{***}			-0.108^{***}
BIC		29884.423	29884.150	29907.510	29861.222
Cond. McFadden's R^2		0.34047	0.3394163	0.339429	0.3404538
Num. obs		157443	157443	157443	157443
Num. groups		1556	1556	1556	1556

$^{***}p < 0.001$, $^{**}p < 0.01$, $^{*}p < 0.05$

are shown on Fig. 2, where the trend of the probability of inactivity estimated by the model is shown in relationship to the dislike ratio for the cases of videos with faces and without faces. The negative incentives effect is present, as the trend for videos with faces grows faster with the dislikes ratio than for videos without faces. To formalize the test of the negative incentives hypothesis over the bootstrap samples, the right panel of Fig. 2 shows the histogram of the estimate of β_F over the 1,000 bootstrap samples. From all samples, only one had a

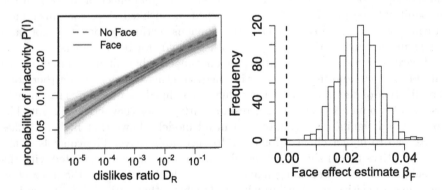

Fig. 2. Statistical effect of dislikes on inactivity. Left: Predicted probability of becoming inactive (I) as a function of the dislikes per view ratio (D_R) for videos with a face and without a face. Shaded lines show the results over 1,000 bootstrap samples of the dataset. Right: Histogram of estimates of the face effect parameter β_F in the 1000 bootstrap samples. The probability of becoming inactive grows faster with the dislike ratio for videos with faces than for videos without faces.

value slightly below zero, illustrating that the null hypothesis that $\beta_F = 0$ can be rejected with $p < 0.05$.

4   Discussion

To analyze the role of the dislike button in participatory media, we generated and analyzed a dataset with more than 150,000 videos from YouTube. We processed their related images with face detection to identify when people are salient in video content. Our views and likes models showed that videos being posted by women receive more likes and more views. This effect had an interaction with a video having a face in the views model, suggesting that YouTube users are more likely to watch videos about people if they have been uploaded by a woman. While it stays as an open question to study the gender of the faces related to the videos, this interaction between gender, faces, and views suggests that female-related images might be used to attract the attention of YouTube users.

Our analyses only focused on faces detected in images related to the videos, and we did not include a nuanced analysis of the full content of the video. While our results show a signal in the noise in the hypothesized directions, advanced video processing techniques offer the opportunity to extend and improve our work. Quantifying the amount of persons appearing in a video or the amount of time devoted to people is a promising avenue to have more precise measurements of the subject evaluation context. Furthermore, identifying the individuals depicted on each video can reveal which videos are centered around the user owning the channel, in which the negative incentive of receiving dislikes might have the strongest effect.

Our regression models show that videos with faces hinder the reception of negative evaluations (dislikes), but only for male users. Analyzing the probability of inactivity of users, we found that videos with high ratios of dislikes per view are associated with users becoming inactive, and that this effect is stronger when videos contain faces, as hypothesized. In our inactivity analysis we found no effect of gender, but our controls with other signals show that likes are negatively associated with users becoming inactive. Our results showed a surprising interaction between faces and gender in the amount of dislikes received by videos, which calls for further research to identify the reasons that drive users away from disliking videos posted by male users in the subject evaluation context.

While we identified post hoc correlations in our analysis, our conclusions are not directly applicable yet to the design of social media. Real-time analyses can shed light on whether the patterns that we identified are predictive of the inactivity of users. In the case of being consistent with our findings, future designs of social media interfaces should consider the risks of giving the possibility to dislike user-centered content. To ensure the sustainability and inclusivity of social media in the future, we need to further study which platform designs, conditions, and contexts lead to users disencouraging other users from being active in social media, as we found here in the case of dislikes in YouTube.

Acknowledgements. This research was funded by the Swiss NSF (Grant number: CR21I1_146499)

Appendix

As a preliminary step to fitting models and testing hypotheses, we survey descriptive statistics to guide the models explained in the previous section. The distributions of views, likes, and dislikes per video are shown on Fig. 3. The histogram of the left panel confirms our observations over the mean and median values of Table 1: all variables are right skewed. This skewness presents heavy right tails that, when eyeballing the plots, suggest the possibility that views, likes, and dislikes follow power-law distributions. Nevertheless, this possibility seems less plausible on the Complementary Cumulative Density Function (CCDF) shown on the right panel of Fig. 3, where the right tails decay faster than it would be expected for a power-law.

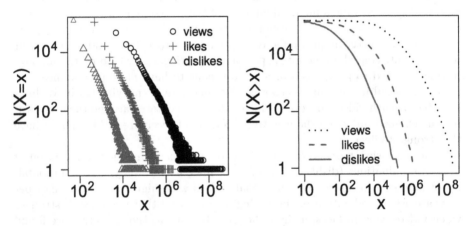

Fig. 3. Video impact distributions. Left: histogram of amount of views, likes, and dislikes over the videos of the dataset. Right: Complementary Cumulative Density Function (CCDF) of counts of videos with more than a certain amount of views, likes, and dislikes. While the histograms show right-skewness, the CCDF of counts show a decay faster than a power-law.

To have a better idea on whether the distributions of amount of views, likes, and dislikes might have scaling properties or diverging moments [25], we applied the method explained in [3] to verify that they do not follow a power-law distribution. We fitted power-law and log-normal distributions to the empirical data, comparing the fits in a log-likelihood ratio test. The results lend very strong evidence favoring the log-normal distribution over the power-law in all three cases: views ($LLR = 449.97, p < 0.01$), likes ($LLR = 275.7, p < 0.01$), and dislikes ($LLR = 159.99, p < 0.01$). This is an example of how informal statistics can be misleading in deciding whether distributions follow a power-law [3,8], suggesting that we should assume the distributions as log-normally distributed instead.

To ensure that we analyze the evaluative tendencies of videos and not their intrinsic correlation with video popularity, we divide likes and dislikes by the amount of views in the variables $L_R = likes/views$ and $D_R = dislikes/views$. These two variables and the amount of views are all roughly log-normally distributed, as it can be appreciated on the histograms of log-transformed values shown on the upper panels of Fig. 4. Some minor skewness can be attributed to integer approximations and boundary values. To cope with these possible deviations from normality in our models, we perform regression diagnostics to model fits to check that residuals are approximately normally distributed.

Figure 4D shows the distribution of the logarithm of the time between videos of the same user $log(\Delta t)$. A clear bimodality is present, but it disappears when normalizing over the average time between videos of each user $\langle t \rangle$. Figure 4E shows the distribution of $log(\Delta t/\langle t \rangle)$, where no bimodality can be observed. This points to the source of bimodality being a variable at the user level, i.e. the activity rate of each user, as the distribution of time intervals collapses to a unimodal distribution after normalization. In our mixed effects regression models of $P(I)$, we include random effects in the form of an intercept for each user that correct for this pattern, ensuring that our results are not a confound with idiographic properties of the users.

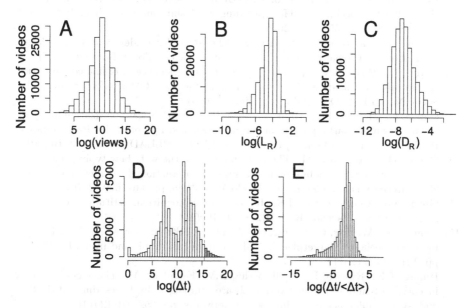

Fig. 4. Histograms of log-transformed video metrics. The upper panels (A,B,C) show the histogram of log-transformed amount of views, likes ratio (L_R), and dislikes ratio (D_R) over the videos of the dataset. Panel D shows the histograms of log-transformed time intervals between videos of the same user (Δt), in seconds. The vertical red line shows the threshold of inactivity of 2 months. Panel E shows the histogram of time intervals normalized over the average time between videos of the user.

References

1. Abisheva, A., Garcia, D., Schweitzer, F.: When the filter bubble bursts: collective evaluation dynamics in online communities. In: Proceedings of the 8th ACM Conference on Web Science, pp. 307–308 (2016)
2. Abisheva, A., Garimella, V.R.K., Garcia, D., Weber, I.: Who watches (and shares) what on YouTube? and when? using Twitter to understand YouTube viewership. In: Proceedings of the 7th ACM International Conference on Web Search and Data Mining, pp. 593–602 (2014)
3. Alstott, J., Bullmore, E., Plenz, D.: powerlaw: a python package for analysis of heavy-tailed distributions. PLoS ONE **9**(1), e85777 (2014)
4. Aragón, P., Gómez, V., Kaltenbrunner, A.: To thread or not to thread: the impact of conversation threading on online discussion. In: ICWSM, pp. 12–21 (2017)
5. Bates, D., Mchler, M., Bolker, B., Walker, S.: Fitting linear mixed-effects models using lme4. J. Stat. Softw. **67**(1), 1–48 (2015)
6. Cashmore, P.: Should Facebook add a dislike button? In: CNN articles (2010). http://cnn.it/2t7tu2h
7. Castells, M.: The Rise of the Network Society, vol. 1. Wiley, Hoboken (1996)
8. Clauset, A., Shalizi, C.R., Newman, M.E.J.: Power-law distributions in empirical data. SIAM Rev. **51**(4), 661 (2009)
9. Crane, R., Sornette, D.: Robust dynamic classes revealed by measuring the response function of a social system. Proc. Natl. Acad. Sci. **105**(41), 15649–15653 (2008)
10. Del Vicario, M., Bessi, A., Zollo, F., Petroni, F., Scala, A., Caldarelli, G., Stanley, H.E., Quattrociocchi, W.: The spreading of misinformation online. Proc. Natl. Acad. Sci. **113**(3), 554–559 (2016)
11. Garcia, D., Mavrodiev, P., Casati, D., Schweitzer, F.: Understanding popularity, reputation, and social influence in the Twitter society. Policy Internet (2017)
12. Garcia, D., Mavrodiev, P., Schweitzer, F.: Social resilience in online communities: the autopsy of friendster. In: Proceedings of the 1st ACM Conference in Online Social Networks (COSN 2013), pp. 39–50 (2013)
13. Garcia, D., Mendez, F., Serdult, U., Schweitzer, F.: Political polarization and popularity in online participatory media: an integrated approach. In: Proceedings of the 1st Workshop on Politics, Elections and Data - PLEAD 2012, pp. 3–10 (2012)
14. Garcia, D., Strohmaier, M.: The qwerty effect on the web: how typing shapes the meaning of words in online human-computer interaction. In: Proceedings of the 25th International Conference on World Wide Web, pp. 661–670 (2016)
15. Greenwald, A.G., Banaji, M.R.: Implicit social cognition: attitudes, self-esteem, and stereotypes. Psychol. Rev. **102**(1), 4 (1995)
16. Hannák, A., Wagner, C., Garcia, D., Mislove, A., Strohmaier, M., Wilson, C.: Bias in online freelance marketplaces: evidence from taskrabbit and fiverr. In: CSCW, pp. 1914–1933 (2017)
17. Huang, T.K., Ribeiro, B., Madhyastha, H.V., Faloutsos, M.: The socio-monetary incentives of online social network malware campaigns. In: Proceedings of the Second ACM Conference on Online Social Networks, pp. 259–270 (2014)
18. Karimi, F., Wagner, C., Lemmerich, F., Jadidi, M., Strohmaier, M.: Inferring gender from names on the web: a comparative evaluation of gender detection methods. In: Proceedings of the 25th International Conference Companion on World Wide Web, pp. 53–54 (2016)

19. Karnstedt, M., Hennessy, T., Chan, J., Hayes, C.: Churn in social networks: a discussion boards case study. In: 2010 IEEE Second International Conference on Social Computing (SocialCom), pp. 233–240. IEEE (2010)
20. Kooti, F., Magno, G., Weber, I.: The social name-letter effect on online social networks. In: International Conference on Social Informatics, pp. 216–227 (2014)
21. Lakkaraju, H., McAuley, J.J., Leskovec, J.: What's in a name? understanding the interplay between titles, content, and communities in social media. ICWSM 1(2), 3 (2013)
22. Magno, G., Weber, I.: International gender differences and gaps in online social networks. In: International Conference on Social Informatics, pp. 121–138 (2014)
23. McAuley, J., Leskovec, J.: Hidden factors and hidden topics: understanding rating dimensions with review text. In: Proceedings of the 7th ACM Conference on Recommender Systems, RecSys 2013, pp. 165–172. ACM (2013)
24. Mieghem, P.V.: Human psychology of common appraisal: the reddit score. IEEE Trans. Multimed. 13(6), 1404–1406 (2011)
25. Newman, M.E.: Power laws, pareto distributions and zipf's law. Contemp. Phys. 46(5), 323–351 (2005)
26. Nilizadeh, S., Groggel, A., Lista, P., Das, S., Ahn, Y.Y., Kapadia, A., Rojas, F.: Twitter's glass ceiling: the effect of perceived gender on online visibility. In: ICWSM, pp. 289–298 (2016)
27. Oksanen, A., Garcia, D., Sirola, A., Nsi, M., Kaakinen, M., Keipi, T., Rsnen, P.: Pro-anorexia and anti-pro-anorexia videos on YouTube: sentiment analysis of user responses. J. Med. Internet Res. 11(17), e2560 (2015)
28. Palmer, C.: Risk perception: another look at the 'white male' effect. Health, Risk Soc. 5(1), 71–83 (2003)
29. Ribeiro, B.: Modeling and predicting the growth and death of membership-based websites. In: Proceedings of the 23rd International Conference on World Wide Web, WWW 2014, pp. 653–664. ACM (2014)
30. Simmel, G.: Fashion. Am. J. Sociol. 62(6), 541–558 (1957)
31. Stommel, S., Garcia, D., Abisheva, A., Schweitzer, F.: Anticipated shocks in online activity: response functions of attention and word-of-mouth processes. In: Proceedings of the 8th ACM Conference on Web Science, pp. 274–275 (2016)
32. Szabo, G., Huberman, B.A.: Predicting the popularity of online content. Commun. ACM 53(8), 80 (2010)
33. Szell, M., Thurner, S.: Measuring social dynamics in a massive multiplayer online game. Soc. Netw. 32(4), 313–329 (2010)
34. Tassi, P.: Facebook Didn't Kill Digg, Reddit Did. In: Forbes (2012). http://bit.ly/2tx8e5C
35. Tufekci, Z.: Big questions for social media big data: representativeness, validity and other methodological pitfalls. In: ICWSM (2014)
36. Turney, P.D.: Thumbs up or thumbs down?: semantic orientation applied to unsupervised classification of reviews. In: Proceedings of the 40th Annual Meeting on Association for Computational Linguistics, pp. 417–424 (2002)
37. Walker, J., Ante, S.E.: Once a social media star, Digg sells for $500,000. The Wall Street J. (2012). http://on.wsj.com/2uv1AAS
38. Yasseri, T., Sumi, R., Rung, A., Kornai, A., Kertsz, J.: Dynamics of conflicts in Wikipedia. PLOS ONE 7(6), 1–12 (2012)
39. Zhou, E., Cao, Z., Yin, Q.: Naive-deep face recognition: touching the limit of LFW benchmark or not? arXiv preprint arXiv:1501.04690 (2015)

Beyond the Culture Effect on Credibility Perception on Microblogs

Suliman Aladhadh[1,2]([⊠]), Xiuzhen Zhang[1], and Mark Sanderson[1]

[1] Computer Science, School of Science, RMIT University, Melbourne, Australia
{suliman.aladhadh,xiuzhen.zhang,mark.sanderson}@rmit.edu.au
[2] College of Computer, Qassim University, Buraidah, Saudi Arabia

Abstract. We investigated the credibility perception of tweet readers from the USA and by readers from eight Arabic countries; our aim was to understand if credibility was affected by country and/or by culture. Results from a crowd-sourcing experiment, showed a wide variety of factors affected credibility perception, including a tweet author's gender, profile image, username style, location, and social network overlap with the reader. We found that culture determines readers' credibility perception, but country has no effect. We discuss the implications of our findings for user interface design and social media systems.

Keywords: Credibility · Social media · Microblog · Culture

1 Introduction

Social media provides an important information source for many people worldwide. Sixty-six percent of Facebook users and fifty-nine percent of Twitter users get some news from social media [13]. Over 85% of topics in Twitter are news [22]. Microblog posts, or tweets, provide a first alarm for news in emergency events such as an earthquakes [30]. In early 2011, Google started to incorporate people's social media status updates in its search engine results [12], indicating the importance of such content as socially relevant and timely sources of information.

In platforms built on user contributions, the information source on which the post is based cannot always be trusted. Social media suffers from unreliable data sources and rumors that can spread quickly, both of which can affect the credibility perception of social media platforms. Readers perceive the same content as less credible when it is posted on Twitter than on a website [31].

The way in which readers interact with social media to find information has changed over time. For instance, use of keyword search and hashtags to find information has increased. Such mechanisms allow readers to see content from previously unknown authors, which leads to credibility concerns [23].

The influence of culture on behavior has been well studied [18]. Readers' credibility perceptions are embedded in a specific social and cultural contexts, including individual and collective preferences, emotions, and other differences. Researchers have studied cultural differences in microblog credibility perception.

© Springer International Publishing AG 2017
G.L. Ciampaglia et al. (Eds.): SocInfo 2017, Part II, LNCS 10540, pp. 316–328, 2017.
DOI: 10.1007/978-3-319-67256-4_25

Yang et al. reported that readers from USA and China have significant differences in their credibility behavior [35]. However, these studies have examined a small numbers of countries, few readers or do not use the same microblog data for countries in their methodology. In this study, we aim to investigate the interrelationship of culture and country and their effect on Twitter readers' credibility perception. We found that readers from different cultures have different credibility perceptions, but those from countries sharing similar cultural characteristics have similar perceptions.

2   Related Work

Here, we describe current microblog credibility research, the research on culture and user's behavior in social media, and the gap in the current literature.

2.1   Microblog Credibility

Information credibility on the Web is commonly defined as a perception rather than as an objective measure of information quality [8]. Credibility is not about the information and sources as objects, but rather about how a reader judges information and source quality [9,10]. A number of researchers have tried to assess the credibility of tweets in different ways, focusing on tweets [4,5,15] or tweet authors [6,11,14]. Other researchers have focused on building topical authority recommendation systems [29,32]. Recent work has shown that credibility prediction results do not generalize well [3]; the classification accuracy of trained models has been overestimated. Understanding the factors that influence a reader's credibility judgment might improve model accuracy and increase generalization.

2.2   Microblog and Culture

Culture has a significant effect on behavior: culture was found to be a significant factor for predicting behavior in social questions and answers [36]. Previous research found significant differences in credibility judgments between microblog readers from the USA and China [35]. However, the research was not able to address if the measured credibility perception difference was due to country or culture.

Poblete et al. studied the behavior of millions of users from different countries using Twitter [28] considering use of hashtags, URLs, mentions, and retweets. The researchers found differences in use across countries of similar culture. Significant behavioral differences were found between users of different languages [33], even in languages of the same culture. Hong et al. compared users of different languages considering five behaviors: hashtags, URLs, mentions, retweets, and replies [19]. They found, for example that use of "Replies" varied within western culture, results were 50% for Dutch but only 36% for German, while within eastern culture, the results showed 59% for Korean and only 20% for Indonesian.

From the above studies we notice that there is ambiguity between the effect of culture and the effect of country on a social media user's behavior.

3 Methodology

We designed a study using a crowd sourcing platform to examine the credibility perception of readers of the American culture from the USA and of readers of the Arabic culture from countries located in the Middle East and North Africa where most people speak Arabic. The countries chosen are members of the League of Arab States:[1] Algeria, Egypt, Jordan, Morocco, Palestine, Tunisia, Saudi Arabia, and the United Arab Emirates. Saudi Arabia and the United Arab Emirates are representatives of the Arabic Peninsula region; Jordan and Palestine of the Levant region; Egypt of the Nile valley region; and Morocco, Algeria, Tunisia of the Maghreb. The populations of these eight countries make up 60% of all Arabic countries.[2] The countries historically share the same "Arabic culture" [7,17,25,34].

To examine the impact of culture and country on the credibility perceptions of readers in social media, we used metadata of tweet authors including gender, image, username, location, and network overlap. These features have previously been found to have significant effect on credibility perception [1,23].

3.1 Factors Examined

We next describe the author features used.

Gender. Gender has been studied previously in blogs [2] where male authors were perceived to be more credible than female authors. Morris et al. found gender influences reader credibility perception [23]. They found that readers perceived male authored posts to be significantly more credible than female, similar to another study [35]. To differentiate between the two genders, an image of a male or female was used and usernames were selected that were applicable for each gender.

H1: Male authored tweets will be more credible than female tweets.
H1a: Culture and country will change the user's overall behavior towards the gender of the author.

Profile Image. Profile pictures affect readers' judgments [21] as observed in many microblog platforms (Twitter and Reddit). Different types of profile images have different credibility judgment effects. In our study, we followed the methodology of [35] limiting images to two styles: a general (anonymous) image representing male or female, and real photos for both genders. All real photos pertained to each culture, showing the headshot of a young adult. For Arabic authors, we used real images for Arabian male and female, and for authors from the USA, we selected Caucasian male and female photos, as in Fig. 1.

H2: Real photos will be perceived as more credible than anonymous.
H2a: Photos indicating culture and country will affect credibility perception.

---

[1] http://www.lasportal.org/en/aboutlas/Pages/CountryData.aspx.
[2] https://en.wikipedia.org/wiki/Geography_of_the_Arab_League.

Username. The name presented next to an author profile image has been found to be effect readers' credibility perception. Pal and Counts found the perception of readers towards the quality of the content are often based solely on the author's name [27] and tweets with a username are rated more highly than anonymous tweets. In this study, two name styles were used: a topical username (e.g. Politics_News) and an Internet style name (e.g. Healthy_24), which is neither traditional nor topical.

H3: Topical usernames will be more credible than Internet style.
H3a: Usernames indicating culture and country will affect credibility perception.

Location. The author's location has been found to be an important factor for microblog credibility perception, especially in political topics [1]. Authors from the same country in which an event occurred were perceived as more credible by readers than those with no location indicated in their tweets. Another study used liberal and conservative locations to study the interaction between location of authors and user microblog credibility perception [35].

In our study we considered the size of a location: authors from large locations tend to share information more than those from small locations [21]. Each tweet identified the location of the author, including the name of a country/state and city. For Arabic tweets, we chose two large cities and two smaller cities for each country, For example, the large cities in Egypt were Cairo and Alexandria and the small cities were Damietta and Arish. For U.S. tweets, we adopted a methodology from past research [35]. We chose 16 states: two large cities were chosen from each of eight states and two small cities from each of the other eight. For example Seattle, Washington (large) and Manti, Utah (small). Wikipedia define large and small cities based on population.

H4: Tweets authored in large locations will be perceived as more credible than those authored in small locations.
H4a: **H4** will be affected by culture and country.
H4b: Location is a topic-dependent factor, as found by [1]. Location styles will vary based on the topic with significant interaction.

Network Overlap. Twitter provides a social network among users defined by users following other users. Poblete et al. studied social connections among Twitter users from ten different countries, and found the connectivity among users in some countries such as South Korea, Japan, and Canada was significant compared to other countries such as the USA [28].

We want to measure the effect of connectivity on the credibility perceptions of readers. We used two conditions: overlap and no overlap, inspired by [35]. We stated to readers "Imagine this is the number of your friends who are following this author". We generated a random number of friends, as shown in Fig. 1.

H5: Tweets authored by users with a network overlap will be more credible than tweets with no overlap.

H5a: Culture and country will make significant interaction with **H5**.
H5b: Overlapping styles will vary based on topic with significant interaction, this has been found in past work [35].

Fig. 1. Sample tweets: (a) USA, politics, male, real photo, Internet style username, large location, overlap. (b) USA, health, female, anonymous photo, topical style username, small location, no overlap. (c) Arabic, health, male, real photo, topical style username, small location, overlap. (d) Arabic, politics, male, anonymous photo, Internet style username, large location, overlap.

4 Experimental Design

We followed the methodology developed by Yang et al. [35]. We examined five different author factors: Gender, Location (large, small), User name (Topical, Internet), Profile image (general, photo), and Network overlap (overlap, no overlap). For each factor there were two conditions. Using a Latin Square design, the number of tweets will be 32 ($2 \times 2 \times 2 \times 2 \times 2$). For each language, we authored 32 political tweets and 32 health tweets, including two topics to study the interaction between topic and features across cultures. Each participant from each culture read only one type of tweet, either politics or health. Accordingly, we authored 128 tweets for the purpose of this experiment. All political tweets were about local events in the respective countries to make the tweet more relevant to the participants. The health tweets were written in English and the same tweets translated to Arabic [23,35].

Our experiment consisted of two parts: judging tweet credibility, and a survey on reader demographic information. When judging credibility, users were asked whether they thought "This tweet contains credible information". They answered using a 7-point Likert scale from strongly disagree to strongly agree. Each participant needed to complete 32 tweets on one topic and tweets were presented randomly.

4.1   Tweet Contents

In writing the simulated tweets, all tweets were false but plausible, thus eliminating participants' previous knowledge affecting their judgments. Groups of native Arabic and English speakers reviewed all tweets to ensure there were no grammatical mistakes that would affect user's credibility judgments. We repeated the checking and re-authoring process until all tweets were deemed ready and plausible. This method has been used by prior studies [1, 23].

All author features (gender, image, username, location and network overlap) were randomly combined for each tweet. Location and network overlap needed to be added to the tweet. Location was automatically generated and we added this manually in the exact way of a tweet appearance. We presented network overlap information next to location. Each username, photo and location was presented only once, so we prepared a sufficient set for each factor.

4.2   Experiment

We recruited participants via the CrowdFlower platform[3]. The platform gives an option to choose participant countries. We restricted participants to the nine studied countries. Note Palestine is as defined as a country by CrowdFlower. We specified language capability for the Arabic participants to be Arabic. Moreover, each participant was asked to specify his/her language. Only those who responded "Arabic" were further considered in this study. For participants from the USA, only those who nominated their first language as "English" were used.

5   Results

We received 30,336 judgments from 948 participants. Table 1a shows the spread of participants within the two cultures and the Arabic countries. Table 1b shows the distribution of participants across the two cultures was almost balanced, the gender, age distributions, and educational levels between the two cultures have the same ratio. We used a mixed design ANOVA (within and between predictors) to analyze and test the effect of all factors and interaction with credibility rating of tweets. We applied the mixed designed ANOVA twice, between cultures (Arabic and USA), and between the Arabic countries.

Table 2 shows ANOVA results for author factors and their interaction with culture, country, and topic. ANOVA analyses were performed to test all hypotheses and the impact of our experimental manipulations on users' credibility judgments, where the demographic variables of gender, age and educational level were controlled. We followed up with pairwise t-tests when appropriate and Bonferroni corrections were used to mitigate the effect of multiple comparisons.

For culture and country, we show the result of each hypothesis from the ANOVA model by presenting the means with p-value. Where the interaction was significant, we checked the direction of differences and report means with p

---

[3] https://www.crowdflower.com.

322   S. Aladhadh et al.

Table 1. Distribution and demographics of the participants

(a) Participants' distribution across cultures and countries

Culture	Freq.	Coun try	Freq.
Arabic	543	Saudi Arabic (SAU)	56
		United Arab Emirates (UAE)	35
		Jordan (JOR)	34
		Palestine (PSE)	22
		Egypt (EGY)	243
American	405	Morocco (MAR)	24
		Algeria (DZA)	78
		Tunisia (TUN)	51

(b) Participants' demographics across cultures and countries.

Demographic Item	Arabic (543)	American (405)
Male	72%	63%
Female	28%	37%
18-24	35%	35%
25-34	38%	37%
35-44	15%	17%
45-above	12%	11%
Less than high school	2%	1%
High school	14%	11%
Diploma	22%	32%
Bachelor	49%	44%
Master degree	11%	11%
PhD.	2%	1%

Table 2. Comparing culture (C) and Arabic countries(A). $^*p < 0.05$ and $^\dagger p < 0.001$.

Factor	Culture DF	Fvalue	P	Arabic cntry DF	Fvalue	P	Factor	Culture DF	Fvalue	P	Arabic cntry DF	Fvalue	P
C/A	1	9.45	0.002*	7	1.34	0.225	C/A*Topic	1	0.913	0.340	7	2.11	0.040*
Topic	1	88.17	0.000†	1	17.80	0.000†	Topic* Gender	1	8.47	0.004*	1	0.021	0.884
Gender	1	157.02	0.000†	1	31.77	0.000†	Topic*Image	1	0.886	0.347	1	0.110	0.741
Image	1	15.08	0.000†	1	43.44	0.000†	Topic*Username	1	0.886	0.690	1	3.08	0.079
Username	1	70.58	0.000†	1	20.59	0.000†	Topic*Location	1	8.07	0.005*	1	9.94	0.002*
Location	1	0.25	0.617	1	1.30	0.253	Topic*Network overlap	1	10.11	0.002*	1	59.05	0.000†
Network overlap	1	39.85	0.000†	1	2.13	0.145	C/A*Topic*Gender	1	17.02	0.000†	7	0.371	0.919
C/A*Gender	1	1.15	0.284	7	2.24	0.030*	C/A*Topic*Image	1	3.61	0.58	7	1.27	0.259
C/A*Image	1	84.18	0.000†	7	1.32	0.236	C/A*Topic*Username	1	12.35	0.000†	7	1.89	0.068
C/A*Username	1	0.002	0.962	7	0.735	0.642	C/A*Topic*Location	1	31.13	0.000†	7	0.838	0.556
C/A*Location	1	0.759	0.384	7	1.73	0.098	C/A*Topic*Network overlap	1	116.22	0.000†	7	1.71	0.103
C/A*Network overlap	1	5.98	0.015*	7	1.11	0.354							

value in tables for readability. We use the country's code of Arabic countries as in Table 1a, instead of their complete name.

5.1 Interaction of Culture with Author's Profile Features

Gender (H1: supported). Readers regarded tweets from males (mean $_{male}$ = 4.63) as more credible than female tweets (mean $_{female}$ = 4.34) with $p < 0.001$. **(H1a: Not supported).** The interaction between culture and gender was not significant ($p = 0.284$) and culture did not affect readers' credibility perceptions according to an author's gender. We explored the effect of topic interaction with gender and culture and found a significant interaction ($p < 0.001$). The two cultures in politics saw male authored tweets significantly more credible than female authored, while in the health topic American readers were more accepting of female tweets than were Arabic readers.

Table 3. Interaction culture with image and network overlap, *p < 0.05, †p < 0.001.

(a) Image vs. culture				(b) Network overlap vs. culture			
	Arabic	American	$P_{\text{two cultures}}$		Arabic	American	$P_{\text{two cultures}}$
Real	4.69	4.45	$0.000^{†}$	Overlap	4.61	4.48	0.03*
Generic	4.45	4.35	$0.000^{†}$	No_overlap	4.54	4.33	$0.000^{†}$
$P_{\text{two styles}}$	$0.000^{†}$	$0.000^{†}$	-	$P_{\text{two styles}}$	0.030*	$0.000^{†}$	-

Image (H2: supported). The difference in reader perception of credibility due to real or generic photos was significant (p < 0.001). People perceived tweets with real photos (mean $_{\text{Photo}}$ = 4.52) as more credible than those with generic (mean $_{\text{Generic}}$ = 4.45).

(H2a: supported). The interaction between culture and profile image was significant (p < 0.001). The real image was perceived significantly more credible by Arabic readers than American (Table 3a) while Americans were more accepting of the use of an anonymous image than Arabic readers.

Username (H3: supported). Tweets with a topical author name were judged to be more credible (mean $_{\text{Topical}}$ = 4.57) than tweets with an Internet style (mean $_{\text{Internet}}$ = 4.40, p < 0.001).

(H3a: Not supported). The interaction between culture and username was not significant (P = 0.962). However, adding topic to the interaction between culture and username made the interaction significant (P < 0.001). In politics, Arabic readers were more tolerant of the use Internet style than Americans, while the opposite behavior happened in health.

Location (H4: not supported). Tweets authored in large and small locations have no effect on readers' credibility perceptions (mean $_{\text{large}}$ = 4.49, mean $_{\text{small}}$ = 4.48, P = 0.617).

(H4a: Not supported). The interaction between location and culture was not significant (P = 0.384). However, the interaction between culture, location, and topic (p < 0.001) was significant. In Arabic culture, large locations were perceived to provide more credible tweets than small locations regarding the political topic, while small locations were the most credible in health topics. In both topics there was no difference between the two styles in U.S. culture.

(H4b: Supported): Interaction between location and topics is significant (p < 0.05) in politics, a large location was perceived to have a higher credibility than a small location, the two locations' styles showed no difference in credibility for the health topics, Table 4 refers.

Network Overlap (H5: supported). The difference between tweets authored by someone having or not having a friend connection was significant (mean $_{\text{overlap}}$= 4.54, mean $_{\text{no overlap}}$ = 4.43, p < 0.001).

Table 4. Location vs. Topic and Network overlap vs. Topic, *p < 0.05, †p < 0.001.

	Location			Network overlap		
	Large	Small	P two styles	Overlapping	No overlapping	Ptwo styles
Politics	4.26	4.20	0.014*	4.26	4.20	0.021*
Health	4.73	4.77	0.112	4.83	4.66	0.000†
Ptwo Topics	0.000†	0.000†	-	0.000†	0.000†	-

(H5a: supported). The interaction between cultural context and network overlap was significant (p < 0.05). Both cultures perceived authors with an overlap to be significantly more credible than those without, see Table 3b. However, American readers were more affected by network overlap than Arabic as they found that overlapped tweets were significantly more credible than non-overlapped, compared to less significant effect between the two styles in Arabic culture.

(H5a: supported). The interaction between network overlap and topic is significant (p < 0.01). In the health topic, there was a large difference between the two styles as overlapped tweets were more credible than those with no overlap. However, in politics the difference between the two styles was small when compared with the health topic, see Table 4.

5.2 Interaction of Arabic Countries with Author's Profile Features

Gender (H1: supported). Male authored tweets were more credible than female tweets (mean male = 4.68, mean female = 4.42, p < 0.001).

(H1a: supported). The interaction between country and gender was significant (p = .030). Credibility ratings differed significantly between male and female authors (p < 0.001) in some countries (DZA, EGY, SAU and TUN), other countries had the same gender credibility perceptions.

Image (H2: supported). Tweets from authors with a real image were more credible than tweets from authors with an anonymous image (mean photo = 4.66, mean generic = 4.44, p < 0.001).

(H2a: not supported). The interaction between country and profile image was not significant (p = 0.236), and the effect of tweets' topics on interaction between country and image was also not significant (p = 0.698).

Username (H3: supported). A topical username style was more credible than an internet username style (mean topical = 4.64, mean internet = 4.46, p < 0.001).

(H3a: not supported). The interaction with country did not show any significant difference (p = 0.642) and all countries were consistent with this finding.

Table 5. Location vs. Topic, Network overlap vs. Topic for Arabic, *p < 0.05, †p < 0.001.

	Location			Network overlap		
	Large	Small	P two styles	Overlapping	No overlapping	P two styles
Politics	4.42	4.27	0.000†	4.24	4.46	0.000†
Health	4.72	4.79	0.214	4.92	4.59	0.000†
P two Topics	0.004*	.000†	-	0.000†	.178	-

Location (H4: not supported). No significant differences were found between the two location types, Arabic readers viewed tweets from large and small locations as having the same credibility level (mean $_{large}$ = 4.57, mean $_{small}$ = 4.53, p = 0.098.

(H4a: not supported). The interaction of country with location was not significant (p = 0.192).

(H4b: supported). Interaction between location and topic was significant (p < 0.01). Large locations as sources were perceived as more credible than small locations significantly in political tweets, While both location types had the same credibility rating regarding the health topic, as shown in Table 5.

Network Overlap (H5: supported). Overlapping styles were rated at the same credibility level, (mean $_{overlap}$ = 4.58, mean $_{no\ overlap}$ = 4.52, p > 0.05).

(H5a: not supported). We found no effect of the difference in countries on the overlapping factor (p = 0.354).

(H5b: supported). The interaction between network overlap and topic was significant (p < 0.001), the overlapped tweets were perceived to be highly credible regarding the health topic, while no overlapped tweets were perceived highly credible in politics topic, as in Table 5.

6 Discussion and Conclusions

We examined the extent to which differences between cultures and countries interact with Twitter profile features (author's gender, profile image, user name, location, and network overlap) to affect readers' credibility judgment. All author's factors included in our study were shown to have a distinct effect on users' credibility judgments. The results of this study indicate that, regardless of country, culture has the main effect of users credibility assessment. We notice that the interaction between readers in Arabic countries and the factors (except gender) were not significant, even for three-way interactions (countries -vs- factor -vs- topic). Interaction of culture with the factors had a significant two- or three-way interaction. This finding confirms the hypothesis that culture has a strong influence on users' behavior in social questions and answers [36] and credibility perception of users in social media [35]. However, our results indicate that "culture" is not necessarily restricted to one country as two previous research findings, and many countries may be included under one culture.

At the two levels of our classification (culture and country), location and network overlap were topic-dependent factors. Location type was validated to be effective in support of user credibility perception in political tweets. This result confirms the finding of Aladhadh et al. that a tweet's location impacts credibility in political tweets [1]. Although few users include their location in their posts, location can be determined through analyzing tweets. This is an area of current research [16,24].

Network overlap was found to be an important factor in health tweets for Arabic readers, for Americans credibility for political tweets was important. Network overlap is culture and topic-dependent. Therefore, it is important to focus on such overlap to help users determine their credibility judgments. Topic might be the most influential factor on users' credibility judgments. It is necessary to build categories for proportion of features in different microblog topics and use that to enhance credibility of retrieved results in social media. This is similar to the categories of information distribution in different crises [20,26].

We sought to find readers' culture and country influence their credibility perceptions, and how the perceptions interact with different features common in social media. Culture can be used to customize social search engines to help assess content credibility, but including a country's attributes along with its culture can be more effective. Moreover, profile features have significant effect on credibility judgments by users. These findings will help designers of interfaces and algorithms about readers' needs. With the large impact of culture on users' credibility perceptions as found in this study, a number of limitations such as corporate accounts were not included in this study. Furthermore, studying the interaction between culture and other demographic factors in credibility perception can affect the behavior of readers. That is an area of future research.

References

1. Aladhadh, S., Zhang, X., Sanderson, M.: Tweet author location impacts on tweet credibility. In: Proceedings of the 2014 Australasian Document Computing Symposium, p. 73. ACM (2014)
2. Armstrong, C.L., McAdams, M.J.: Blogs of information: how gender cues and individual motivations influence perceptions of credibility. J. Comput.-Mediated Commun. 14(3), 435–456 (2009)
3. Boididou, C., Papadopoulos, S., Kompatsiaris, Y., Schifferes, S., Newman, N.: Challenges of computational verification in social multimedia. In: Proceedings of the 23rd International Conference on World Wide Web, pp. 743–748. ACM (2014)
4. Castillo, C., Mendoza, M., Poblete, B.: Information credibility on twitter. In: Proceedings of the 20th International Conference on World Wide Web, pp. 675–684. ACM (2011)
5. Castillo, C., Mendoza, M., Poblete, B.: Predicting information credibility in time-sensitive social media. Int. Res. 23(5), 560–588 (2013)
6. Counts, S., Fisher, K.: Taking it all in? visual attention in microblog consumption. ICWSM 11, 97–104 (2011)

7. Dedoussis, E.: A cross-cultural comparison of organizational culture: evidence from universities in the arab world and Japan. Cross Cult. Manag. Int. J. **11**(1), 15–34 (2004)
8. Flanagin, A.J., Metzger, M.J.: The role of site features, user attributes, and information verification behaviors on the perceived credibility of web-based information. New Media Soc. **9**(2), 319–342 (2007)
9. Fogg, B., Marshall, J., Laraki, O., Osipovich, A., Varma, C., Fang, N., Paul, J., Rangnekar, A., Shon, J., Swani, P., et al.: What makes web sites credible?: a report on a large quantitative study. In: Proceedings of the SIGCHI Conference on Human Factors in Computing Systems, pp. 61–68. ACM (2001)
10. Freeman, K.S., Spyridakis, J.H.: An examination of factors that affect the credibility of online health information. Tech. Commun. **51**(2), 239–263 (2004)
11. Ghosh, S., Sharma, N., Benevenuto, F., Ganguly, N., Gummadi, K.: Cognos: crowd-sourcing search for topic experts in microblogs. In: Proceedings of the 35th International ACM SIGIR Conference on Research and Development in Information Retrieval, pp. 575–590. ACM (2012)
12. Google Social Search: Official Blog (2011). http://bit.ly/2tm4LXJ
13. Gottfried, B.Y.J., Shearer, E.: News Use Across Social Media Platforms 2016. Pew Research Center 2016 (2016)
14. Gupta, A., Kumaraguru, P.: Credibility ranking of tweets during high impact events. In: Proceedings of the 1st Workshop on Privacy and Security in Online Social Media, p. 2. ACM (2012)
15. Gupta, A., Kumaraguru, P., Castillo, C., Meier, P.: TweetCred: a real-time web-based system for assessing credibility of content on Twitter. In: Proceedings of 6th International Conference on Social Informatics (SocInfo), Barcelona, Spain (2014)
16. Han, B., Cook, P., Baldwin, T.: Text-based Twitter user geolocation prediction. J. Artif. Intell. Res. **49**, 451–500 (2014)
17. Hofstede, G.: Cultures and Organizations: Software of the Mind (1991)
18. Hofstede, G.: Dimensionalizing cultures: the hofstede model in context. Online Readings Psychol. Cult. **2**(1), 8 (2011)
19. Hong, L., Convertino, G., Chi, E.H.: Language matters in twitter: a large scale study. In: ICWSM (2011)
20. Imran, M., Castillo, C.: Towards a data-driven approach to identify crisis-related topics in social media streams. In: Proceedings of the 24th International Conference on World Wide Web, pp. 1205–1210. ACM (2015)
21. Kang, B., Höllerer, T., O'Donovan, J.: Believe it or not? analyzing information credibility in microblogs. In: Proceedings of the 2015 IEEE/ACM International Conference on Advances in Social Networks Analysis and Mining 2015, pp. 611–616. ACM (2015)
22. Kwak, H., Lee, C., Park, H., Moon, S.: What is Twitter, a social network or a news media? In: Proceedings of the 19th International Conference on World Wide Web, pp. 591–600. ACM (2010)
23. Morris, M., Counts, S., Roseway, A.: Tweeting is believing?: understanding microblog credibility perceptions. In: CSCW, pp. 441–450 (2012)
24. Mourad, A., Scholer, F., Sanderson, M.: Language influences on Tweeter geolocation. In: Jose, J.M., Hauff, C., Altıngovde, I.S., Song, D., Albakour, D., Watt, S., Tait, J. (eds.) ECIR 2017. LNCS, vol. 10193, pp. 331–342. Springer, Cham (2017). doi:10.1007/978-3-319-56608-5_26

25. Obeidat, B., Shannak, R., Masa'deh, R., Al-Jarrah, I.: Toward better understanding for arabian culture: implications based on hofstede' s cultural model toward better understanding for arabian culture: implications based on hofstede' s cultural model. Eur. J. Soc. Sci. **28**(4), 512–522 (2012)
26. Olteanu, A., Vieweg, S., Castillo, C.: What to expect when the unexpected happens: social media communications across crises. In: Proceedings of the 18th ACM Conference on Computer Supported Cooperative Work and Social Computing, pp. 994–1009. ACM (2015)
27. Pal, A., Counts, S.: What's in a@ name? how name value biases judgment of microblog authors. In: ICWSM (2011)
28. Poblete, B., Garcia, R., Mendoza, M., Jaimes, A.: Do all birds tweet the same?: characterizing twitter around the world. In: Proceedings of the 20th ACM CIKM International Conference on Information and Knowledge Management, pp. 1025–1030. ACM (2011)
29. Rosa, K.D., Shah, R., Lin, B., Gershman, A., Frederking, R.: Topical clustering of tweets. In: Proceedings of the ACM SIGIR: SWSM (2011)
30. Sakaki, T., Okazaki, M., Matsuo, Y.: Earthquake shakes Twitter users: real-time event detection by social sensors. In: Proceedings of the 19th International Conference on World Wide Web, pp. 851–860. ACM (2010)
31. Schmierbach, M., Oeldorf-Hirsch, A.: A little bird told me, so i didn't believe it: Twitter, credibility, and issue perceptions. Commun. Q. **60**(3), 317–337 (2012)
32. Wagner, C., Liao, V., Pirolli, P., Nelson, L., Strohmaier, M.: It's not in their tweets: modeling topical expertise of twitter users. In: Privacy, Security, Risk and Trust (PASSAT), 2012 International Conference on and 2012 International Confernece on Social Computing (SocialCom), pp. 91–100. IEEE (2012)
33. Weerkamp, W., Carter, S., Tsagkias, M.: How People use Twitter in Different Languages, vol. 1, p. 1 (2011)
34. Wilson, M.E.: Arabic speakers: language and culture, here and abroad. Top. Lang. Disord. **16**(4), 65–80 (1996)
35. Yang, J., Counts, S., Morris, M.R., Hoff, A.: Microblog credibility perceptions: comparing the USA and china. In: Proceedings of the 2013 Conference on Computer Supported Cooperative Work, pp. 575–586. ACM (2013)
36. Yang, J., Morris, M.R., Teevan, J., Adamic, L.A., Ackerman, M.S.: Culture matters: a survey study of social Q&A behavior. In: Fifth International AAAI Conference on Weblogs and Social Media (2011)

Twigraph: Discovering and Visualizing Influential Words Between Twitter Profiles

Dhanasekar Sundararaman[1]([✉]) [iD] and Sudharshan Srinivasan[2] [iD]

[1] SSN College of Engineering, Chennai, India
dhanasekar312213@gmail.com
[2] SRM University, Chennai, India

Abstract. The social media craze is on an ever increasing spree, and people are connected with each other like never before, but these vast connections are visually unexplored. We propose a methodology *Twigraph* to explore the connections between persons using their Twitter profiles. First, we propose a hybrid approach of recommending social media profiles, articles, and advertisements to a user. The profiles are recommended based on the similarity score between the user profile, and profile under evaluation. The similarity between a set of profiles is investigated by finding the top influential words thus causing a high similarity through an Influence Term Metric for each word. Then, we group profiles of various domains such as politics, sports, and entertainment based on the similarity score through a novel clustering algorithm. The connectivity between profiles is envisaged using word graphs that help in finding the words that connect a set of profiles and the profiles that are connected to a word. Finally, we analyze the top influential words over a set of profiles through clustering by finding the similarity of that profiles enabling to break down a Twitter profile with a lot of followers to fine level word connections using word graphs. The proposed method was implemented on datasets comprising 1.1 M Tweets obtained from Twitter. Experimental results show that the resultant influential words were highly representative of the relationship between two profiles or a set of profiles.

Keywords: Twitter · Clustering · Profile modeling · Profile similarity · Multiple profiles connectivity

1 Introduction

The important characteristic of a successful social media is its large, engaged user base. Hence, every social media tries to improve its user base. Twitter is one such popular social media site providing microblogging service that has been an important representative of people's personal opinion in the past decade [1]. People use Twitter to share and seek information ranging from gossips to the news [19, 20], as its range of connectivity far greater than any other medium. Now Twitter has around 317 million users worldwide and about 500 million tweets posted per day. Though it has tons of information with monumentally large user-base, it is practically impossible for a user to find fellow users who share a common interest manually. There is a need for an

© Springer International Publishing AG 2017
G.L. Ciampaglia et al. (Eds.): SocInfo 2017, Part II, LNCS 10540, pp. 329–346, 2017.
DOI: 10.1007/978-3-319-67256-4_26

efficient user suggestion system that can group users with similar interests. An automated suggestion system [3] helps a user to find other users with similar interests, thus acquiring and sharing knowledge about a particular domain.

Now after an efficient recommendation system is built, a user develops his follower list. These followers would have followed the user based on his nature of the user's tweets. By nature, here we mean the topics used in the tweets. If the user is a guitarist and tweets were highly concentrated on acoustics, electrics and the brands of guitar, the followers of that user would probably have these topics in the majority. But when the user is a worldwide popular celebrity or politician, the nature of tweets may span several topics ranging from philosophy to cinema. Hence the followers of such a user may have followed that user for a range of topics found in his tweets. Though this is obvious, what if there is a way to find the important or influential words between a user and his follower group causing a person to be a follower. The method called *Twigraph*-Twitter suggestion and *word graph* would enable us to visualize the connectivity across profiles through words and vice versa (connectivity across words through profiles).

To summarize,

- We take approximately 3000 tweets of various users of domains like sports, politics, philosophy, and education from Twitter. We also take a large number of news and advertisement articles available online. Subsequently, we analyze, pre-process and store them efficiently.
- A profile under evaluation (user profile) is chosen, and top profiles similar to that of the user profile based on his nature of tweets are found (Explained in the upcoming sections).Article and advertisement suggestions are also made.
- Then, we analyze the top influential words between a profile and the gradually evolving user group (user profile and his followers) using *Influence Term Metric* (ITM) and a variant of clustering algorithm (proposed in Sect. 6).

The paper is organized as follows. Section 2 deals with the related works about the usage of Twitter as a social media data set in performing various tasks like document clustering and topic modeling. Section 3 talks about the collection of data from Twitter and preprocessing it. Section 4 gives a glimpse about the profile (Twitter profile) modeling and the distance measures used for finding the distance between profiles with an example. Section 5 explains the proposed hybrid suggestion system for advertisements, articles, and users. Section 6 performs a new clustering technique based on the user profile(query). Section 7 explains the method of finding influential words between a set of profiles using Influence Term Metric with great details and finally, Sect. 8 illustrates the visualization techniques namely *word graphs* to envisage the connection between profiles in words and we finally conclude with future works in Sect. 9.

2 Related Works

Analysis and recommendations for Twitter ranging from simple text mining to more complex learning algorithms have been proposed. The various ways and fields where Twitter data is used are summarized in the following.

Twitter as a source for text mining. Twitter is seen as an instant and short form of communication for users to share and seek information. Twitter provides large potentially useful data for purposes such as sentiment analysis, opinion mining, recommender systems, etc. The usage of social media like Twitter to share and seek day-to-day information and how this information can be analyzed is done in [1]. The increased usage of microblogging service in the recent years and how a large amount of data present in the form of tweets can be effectively used for text mining is well described in [2].

Twitter recommendations for users. Twitter has a monumentally large number of users. It is practically impossible to find users with similar interests manually as discussed in the introduction and hence there have been many works in building a user suggestion system. One such paper which describes how users with similar intentions connect with each other is shown [3]. Though Twitter provides a lot of information, the problem of finding followers with similar interests using various recommendation techniques is compared and contrasted in [4].

Twitter for Forecasting. The Twitter data in the form of tweets can not only be used for finding users and articles with similar interests, but it can also be used efficiently for forecasting. Twitter data based sentiment analysis can predict the mood of the users in the social media and thus enable a key factor for prediction. Two such works [5, 6] proposes the use of sentiment analysis on Twitter corpus data to effectively forecast elections results in advance.

Twitter profile modeling and similarity. A Document is modeled by identifying the keywords in it. Similarly, it can also be applied to a Twitter profile to find the words that are representative of the profile. TF-IDF have been used for finding word relevance and feature selection of terms in a document [7, 8] where the keywords of a document have been identified [7]. After modeling, it is worthwhile to find the similarity between two documents. This similarity can be achieved through a variety of similarity metric measures. Analysis of various distance measures for finding distances between two documents and the advantages and disadvantages of the same is emphasized [9].

Document clustering. After finding the keywords of a document, finding distances across documents, the possible next idea is to group similar documents together, which is achieved through clustering. An analysis of the various clustering methods for documents is done in [10, 11]. To be specific, it provides with a comparative study of agglomerative hierarchical clustering and K-means clustering. Clustering enables the searching of documents efficiently, and a technique for clustering text documents for browsing large document collections is done [12]. The TF-IDF and the clustering approach together for clustering English text documents that are more relevant are performed in [13]. The clustering of documents using TF-IDF scores at word levels for classifying the sentiment of the document as positive or negative is done [14]. In another work, the TF-IDF scores of words of different documents to perform clustering for the application of finding relevant search results for the user query using cosine distance is explained [15]. The above works details about document modeling, similarity, and clustering. An interesting work that uses the combination of TF-IDF and centroid-based clustering for summarizing multiple documents is conceptualized [16], and finally, the semantic similarity between texts using IDF as a metric is done in [17].

To summarize, there have been many works using the combination of TF-IDF with clustering for document topic modeling, stop words removal and document clustering for topic classification. We focus on finding the similarity between documents (profiles) and go to the next level in finding the words that are impactful between the two documents or a document with a set of another document causing the similarity. We propose a term Influence Term Metric (ITM) based on TF-IDF and a variant of clustering algorithm to achieve our case and finally propose a visualization paradigm in the form of word graphs and word paths that envisage the connection between Twitter profiles in the form of words and the profiles that are connected to a word.

3   Data Collection and Preprocessing

In this section, we first describe the Twitter data and then the process through which we collected tweets related to the domains of politics, sports, entertainment, education, and philosophy. Figure 1 illustrates the stage-wise filtering in the extraction of Twitter profiles data (pipeline). The data is obtained by using the official Twitter API, TweePy [18]. First, a huge list of Twitter profiles is created. Second, a Language filter is applied to extract only the profiles that share the common language. Language filter ensures

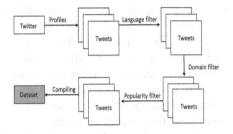

Fig. 1. Stage-wise extraction of Twitter data.

consistency across Twitter profiles in the choice of words as the same word written in the different language is perceived differently. Then a Domain filter is applied to extract profiles that come under five chief domains such as politics, sports, philosophy, entertainment, and education. Finally, Popularity filter is applied to ensure that the profiles have a minimum number of tweets. We extract approximately 3000 Tweets per user for various Twitter profiles of various domains. At an average of 120 characters per tweet, our data set comprises 1.1 M tweets with 130 M characters approximately. Next, Preprocessing effectively deals with replacing or removing a word. To avoid the case where the same word occurs twice in different forms, but convey the same because of acronyms, we preprocess the data with an acronym dictionary, by converting acronyms to their full form. For example, lol is translated to "laughing out loud". While in removing, words containing symbols such as '@,' '#' and words that are just numbers are removed. For our proposed methodology, it is essential that the tweets aren't just arranged as stand-alone strings but rather as profiles. Hence each tweet from a particular profile is merged to form one single profile document, which makes up a comprehensive data set.

4   Profile Modeling and Similarity

In this section, we first discuss profile modeling by finding the most representative words of that particular profile and then we find the similarity between profiles (Twitter profile) using the suitable distance metric by demonstrating a comparison between sets of profiles.

Profile modeling refers to the top words of a profile, by top we mean the most important words that often reflect the profile (document). If this importantness is quantified using the count of the words, then the articles and conjunctions like 'and' and 'if' becomes the top words most of the times. But these are mere stop words that don't reflect the characteristic of the profile in any way. Hence we calculate the TF-IDF of each word in the corpus. TF-IDF is the feature selection approach used in case of documents to find the words that are highly representative of the document and ignoring stop words that don't convey any meaning [8]. It is also used to find what words in a document that is favorable to use in a search query to fetch that document [7]. TF-IDF can be successfully used for stop words filtering in various subject fields including text summarization and classification. The document modeling for sample documents is shown in Appendix 1.

Now that the top words in a profile are identified using TF-IDF scores, the similarity between two profiles (Twitter profiles) can be calculated. There are various distance metrics such as Euclidean, Manhattan, Cosine, etc. to calculate this similarity. But Cosine distance is the apt choice [9] here as it avoids the bias caused by different document lengths evident from the TF-IDF scores as the inner product of the two vectors (sum of the pairwise multiplied elements) is divided by the product of their vector lengths. The resultant score is a value between 0 and 1. The similarity score is obtained by subtracting this value from 1. While calculating the distance between the user profile (query) and an another profile, the words contained in the user are alone taken. The TF-IDF scores corresponding to the words present in the user profile is used for cosine distance calculation. Next, the TF-IDF scores of these words in comparing profiles is compared with the TF-IDF scores of the user profile.

Let us consider the TF-IDF of the sample words namely 'immigrant', 'election', 'federal', 'twitter' and 'Washington' in the user profile document. A glimpse of handful picked terms from the user profile (HillaryClinton) is compared in both profiles 1 and 2 (realDonaldTrump and katyperry). In profile 1 (realDonaldTrump), all the words that are chosen from the user profile (HillaryClinton) have a positive TF-IDF scores, which indicate the mere presence of that word in profile 1 (realDonaldTrump), but not in profile 2(katyperry) with only two words having a positive score. More on this is discussed on Appendix 4. Though the number of words chosen here is a fraction of the total words of that profile, it is found that profile 1 (realDonaldTrump) is more similar to the user profile (HillaryClinton) than that of profile 2 (katyperry) using cosine distance. Like this, if the process is repeated for all the profiles with the user profile (query), the similarity can be sorted in decreasing order to find the most similar profile to the user profile and second most similar and so on.

5 Hybrid Suggestion System

A hybrid Suggestion system is a one which is capable of suggesting articles, advertisements, and profiles for a given user profile. Users would get their most similar profiles based on the nature of their profile to follow and most similar articles like news, entertainment, and research to read. Companies, on the other hand, would want to identify their potential customers by analyzing social media demographics instantly. We describe suggesting users in this section, for articles and users for companies in Appendix 3.

Suggesting users for a given user profile is explained in the previous section in great detail. As aforesaid, finding similar users can be a cumbersome task if done manually and automating this would be of utmost importance to gather people of similar interests. One of the works detail the architectural overview, and the graph recommendation algorithms for finding Twitter followers [3]. Another work suggests that, though

Table 1. Similar Users for each user profile

User profile	Top 3 users	Rank
HillaryClinton	THEHermanCain	1
	realDonaldTrump	2
	GovMikeHuckabee	3
Rihanna	lenadunham	1
	ddlovato	2
	souljaboy	3

Twitter provides a lot of information, one of the drawbacks is the lack of an effective method to find fellow users to follow and make friends [4]. As detailed in the previous section, we find the top 3 users for a profile. Table 1 gives the top 3 users for each of the profiles namely HillaryClinton, and rihanna. The top 3 users for HillaryClinton are THEHermanCain, realDonaldTrump, and GovMikeHuckabee who happen to share the common domain namely politics. For rihanna, the top 3 users are lenadunham, ddlovato and souljaboy who are singers in entertainment industry, since rihanna is a singer.

6 User Profile Based Single Source Clustering

After extracting tweets from different profiles, computing importance of terms in each profile, calculating similarity with each other (user profile and other profiles) and ranking them accordingly to each profile, we arrive at the final and key step, grouping similar profiles with each other. A comparative analysis of K-means and hierarchical clustering for documents is done [10]. An analysis of the various document clustering methods by showing the feature selection methods, similarity measures and evaluation measures of document clustering is done [11]. The use of clustering documents for browsing large document collections is presented in [12], document clustering for fetching relevant English documents in [13]. Clustering is also used for sentiment analysis in predicting the mood as positive or negative [14]. Finally, clustering is used for extracting key sentences from a paragraph based on the user query using the combination of TF-IDF and Cosine distance [15].

A key variant of the Hierarchical clustering algorithm is proposed for the grouping of profiles such that, the grouping does not take place across different profiles, but always showing prominence only on the user profile. Hence, a single source clustering algorithm is proposed as to focus on the user profile.

Single Source Clustering Algorithm
1 C   ←An array that stores TF-IDF scores of incoming profiles into the cluster
2 Profiles   ←TF-IDF scores of all profiles for each word in user profile
3 Profiles(q) ←TF-IDF scores of words in the user profile
4 Profiles(i) ←TF-IDF scores of user profile words in profile i
5 N, i=500 (Number of Twitter profiles taken)
6 **Start**:
7   Dist,P = inf
8   Count=0
9 **Loop**:
10   d=cosine distance(Profiles(q),Profiles(i))
11   **if** (d < dist) **then**
12   dist=d
13   P=i
14   Profiles(i) ← Profiles(i+1)
15   count ← count +1
16   **If** (count < N) **then**
17   **goto** Loop
18 profiles(q) ← (Profiles(q) + Profiles(P))/2
19 C.append(P)
20 Profiles.remove(P)
21 N ← N - 1
22 **If** (N > 0) **then**
23   **goto** Start

As mentioned in the algorithm, *profiles*(q) is the user profile (profile under query) that contains the TF-IDF scores of terms in that profile while *profiles* is the list with all the profiles that contain TF-IDF scores of user profile terms in each profile. All the remaining profiles in profiles except *profiles*(q) is iteratively compared with profiles(q) for shortest distance. Eventually, the closest profile to the user profile (which is also seen in Table 1 of the previous section) is added to the cluster. Then the TF-IDF scores of these profiles are averaged (Centroid). The centroid calculation enables the score of terms that occurs in both the profiles to be rewarded and scores of terms not in incoming profile (closest) to be penalized. The algorithm continues by finding the closest profile to the gradually forming cluster until *profiles* list is exhausted. In the first iteration, query user profile (Hilary) is merged with the most similar profile (THEHermainCain), thereby forming the first cluster. This cluster is formed, as the TF-IDF scores of these two profiles were similar enough for the profile (THE-HErmainCain) to be ranked first to user profile. Now the centroid of these two profiles is calculated as the cluster center. The next closest profile to this centroid score is then added to the cluster.

This way, the cluster is aggregated.

From Table 2, it is clear that the order in which the profiles enter into the cluster is not the same as the closest neighbors given in the previous section. It is because of the gradual change in scores of terms by averaging out the scores. The first profile to enter the cluster is the user profile's closest neighbor, the second

Table 2. Order of Entry for clustering(Hillary Clinton)

Profile	Entry number
THEHermanCain	1
realDonaldTrump	2
GovMikeHuckabee	3
newtgingrich	4
PeterBale	5

profile to enter is not the second closest neighbor, but the closest to the both the profiles in the cluster combined. This way, the diversity of terms is increased. For example, if the user profile is a politician who tweets only about politics, the first profile to enter will obviously be a politician. However, if the profile that enters has some percent of tweets related to the entertainment industry, the profiles related to entertainment industry soon has a chance to enter the cluster. It is evident from the word cloud generated based on the top influential words between a user group cluster and profile shown in Appendix 5.

7   Finding the Top Influential Words Between Profiles

In this section, we analyze the formation of clusters by finding influential words using *Influence Term Metric (ITM)*.

Influence Term Metric. The *Influence Term Metric* for a term uses the TF-IDF scores of the term in individual profiles and the global IDF score of the term. While the TF-IDF score of a term in a profile indicates the relative importance of that term in the concerned profile, the IDF score of that term indicates its importance in the entire corpus. The *Influence Term Metric* of a term indicates the importance of that term between a set of profiles. Here by 'set' we mean two profiles or between a cluster and profile.

$$ITM(X_{MN}) = T_{XM} * I_X * T_{XN} \tag{1}$$

$ITM(X_{MN})$ -> Influential Term Metric of term 'X' across profiles M and N
T_{XM} -> TF-IDF of term 'X' in document M
T_{XN} -> TF-IDF of term 'X' in document N
I_X -> IDF of term 'X' in the corpus.

The efficiency of the ITM for various cases of T_{XM} and T_{XN} are as follows.

Case 1: If both T_{XM} and T_{XN} is low, then obviously I_X is low as the term is less important in the corpus, then the ITM of that term is very low and proves to be less influential between the two documents.

Case 2: If T_{XM} is low and T_{XN} is high, that means that term has a high TF in document N overshadowing it's relatively less I_X, and in this case the ITM is mediocre. The same case occurs for the contrary case of high T_{XM} and low T_{XN}.

Case 3: If both T_{XM} and T_{XN} is high, indicating that the term is of high importance in both the documents and I_X is high, then the ITM is high. In a rare case, if T_{XM} and T_{XN} are high, but I_X is low (for the case where TF of that term overshadows the T_{XM} and T_{XN}), the ITM becomes mediocre as the I_X is low.

Table 3 shows the entry of profiles into the cluster based on the distance, initial profile being HillaryClinton which is realized [21]. That is the profiles with the shortest distance to the cluster formed so far enters the cluster. Our focus (as mentioned in the abstract) is to find the top influential words that caused the incoming profile to be the one with the shortest distance to the cluster. In other words, these are the common words between the cluster and the incoming profile and also were representative of the profile or cluster they belong. These words are found using the ITM. The different cases of

Table 3. Top 3 influential words between cluster and incoming profile(Distance based)

IP	Top 3 words	ITR
THEHermanCain	Hillary	1
	Bernie	
	Obamacare	
realDonaldTrump	America	2
	Mike_pence	
	Pennsylvania	
GovMikeHuckabee	Israel	3
	Abolish	
	Medicare	
Stephen_Curry	Science	75
	Newyorker	
	Universities	
Reillymj	Climate	104
	Warming	
	Global	
Faisalislam	Election	123
	Government	
	Amendment	
Number10gov	Secretary	144
	Investment	
	Economy	
DjokerNole	Tennis	268
	Practice	
	Tournament	

Notations used: IP- Incoming Profile,
ITR- Iteration.

TF-IDF scores of the words in the cluster and the incoming profile and their impact on the ITM are already detailed. Let us discuss them with few examples. In the first iteration, the term "flotus" has a high TF-IDF score in the user profile (HillaryClinton) and a good IDF score. It could have made it to the Top 5 words list had it had a good TF-IDF score in closest incoming profile resulting in the formation of the cluster (THEHermanCain). But the TF-IDF score of the term "flotus" in the incoming profile is 0, making the ITM of that term 0. The term "hillary" is the one with the highest TF-IDF score in the user profile (HillaryClinton), it also has a higher score in the closest profile (THEHermanCain) and the IDF of that term is high enough for it to be the top most influential word (Highest ITM). On the other hand, the term "obamacare" has a higher TF-IDF in incoming profile (THEHermanCain) than the term "bernie" and the IDF of "obamacare" is higher than "bernie" too. But it's TF-IDF in the user profile (HillaryClinton) is too low to beat the ITM score of "bernie" making it the second most influential between them. Many such scenarios can be explained, and the result is the words that have global importance and also importance in both the individual profiles.

On the other hand, the similar function can be performed for displaying the top influential words between the incoming profile and the existing cluster but not based on the distance but based on chronological order of entry (building of followers) to decompose a Twitter account using *Twigraph*. This is explained in Appendix 2.

This finding of influential words between profiles helps in grouping a large user base in social media together at the finest level, that is in words they have used in the social media. It also helps to analyze the gradual change in the topic or choice of words a profile has and the impact it has in connection with the other profiles. The relationship between two Twitter profiles in words can be visualized using *word graph* and *word path* combined forming *Twigraph*. *Word graph* denote the connection between two profiles in words, which in turn can be used to find profiles that are connected to a word. *Word path* denotes the tracing the *word graph* from one profile to another through to obtain a series of words. The word graph is explained in the next section.

8 Visualizing Word Graphs

In this section, we provide a visual representation and analysis of our proposed methodology *Twigraph*.

Notations used in Word graph for Figs. 2 and 3 are as follows.

Squared letter - Indicates an individual profile, **Squared number:** Indicates the cluster formed at that particular iteration. **Oval:** Represents the word connecting two profiles or a profile and cluster. **Blow-up bubble:** Represents the components of that particular cluster, i.e., the cluster in its previous iteration. **Dotted line**: Indicates that the word connecting two profiles or a profile and cluster, features among the top 20 words shared between them. **Dashed line:** Indicates that the word connecting the two profiles or a profile and cluster, does not feature among the top 20 words shared between them.

Dotted Dashed line. Represents the word that connects an incoming profile to a component in the blow-up bubble (used to identify if the previously entered profile share that word with the newly incoming profile.

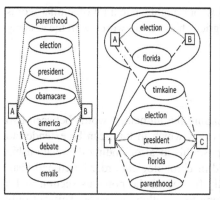 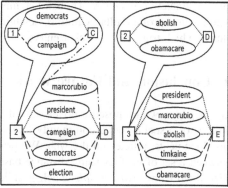

Fig. 2. Word graph for Iteration 1 and 2 of Clustering (Table 3)

Fig. 3. Word graph for Iteration 3 and 4 of Clustering

A lot of interesting analysis could be made out of Table 3 and Figs. 2 and 3 (word graph). In general, there are four possible scenarios that could be observed on the word path during the process of clustering:

Decreasing significance. This scenario is observed when a word initially features among the top 20 influential word list between a cluster and profile but loses its significance as we increase progress with the clustering process. An example of this scenario is the word "parenthood" which is a top 20 word between HillaryClinton and THEHermanCain. But with the entry of successive profiles into the cluster, the word loses its significance and moves out of the top 20 list.

Increasing significance. Contrary to the previous scenario, the word "marcorubio" is an example of this case where it doesn't make the top 20 between HillaryClinton and THEHermanCain but increases its significance with the successive entry of realdonaldtrump and GovMikeHuckabee thereby eventually making it to the top 20 list.

Maintaining significance. The word "president" is a perfect example of this scenario as it features in the top 20 list of the first 5 incoming profile thereby maintaining it's significance across several iterations.

Oscillating Significance. As the name suggests, it occurs when a particular word oscillates between high and low influential across several iterations. One such example is the word "timkaine" which didn't feature in the top 20 list between HillaryClinton and THEHermanCain but rose in significance and entered the list as realdonaldtrump entered. It again lost its significance with the entry of GovMikeHuckabee. These scenarios are extensively discussed in Appendix 6.

The scenarios mentioned above strengthen our stance behind the proposed methodology that every profile gets a fair chance of being clustered regardless of its distance from the user profile. This principle when extended, enables profiles which are further down the initially allocated distance list from Table 3, to get clustered out of order at a much sooner iteration. For instance, let us take the profile "GavinNewsom" as an example. According to Table 3, it is much closer to the user profile (HillaryClinton) than newtgingrich. But newtgingrich enters the cluster at iteration 3 which is way sooner than GavinNewsom's entry. Though GavinNewsom might share a lot of similar words with the user profile(HillaryClinton), newtgingrich shares more words with the existing cluster which triggers its quicker entry.

9 Conclusion and Future Work

In this paper, we proposed a novel way of finding the influential words between two profiles of a social media community like Twitter, which in turn, can be extended to any documents, articles on the web. We propose this idea for finding the relationship between a set of profiles using distance based or chronological order based and visualize them using *word graph* which is mildly briefed in the previous section and a comprehensive work on the same is being done for a follow-up paper. This not only enables us to find the similar profiles but goes to the finest level and finds the words that are responsible for the similarity of profiles. This enables to trace the connection of profiles through word path (list of words). These systems can be used to classify a large number of user profiles in a social media environment. One of the limitations of the current methodology is that it cannot comprehend the same word in different forms because of the lack of understanding of semantics. In the future, we would also use ontology and semantic based word recognition to prevent each word in different forms from appearing as different terms causing word redundancies.

Appendix 1

Document Modeling

Example of document modeling.
    TF: Term Frequency, which measures how frequently a term occurs in a document. Since every document is different in length, it is possible that a term would appear much more times in long documents than shorter ones. Thus, the term frequency is often divided by the document length (the total number of terms in the document) as a way of normalization. IDF: Inverse Document Frequency, which measures how important a term is. While computing TF, all terms are considered equally important. However, it is known that certain terms such as "is," "of" and "that," may appear a lot of times but have little importance.
    Document 1: data mining and social media mining
    Document 2: social network analysis
    Document 3: data mining
    Tables 4, 5 and 6 shows us the nomalized term frequency of each term in documents 1, 2, and 3 respectively. Table 7 shows us the IDF of all terms in document 1, 2 and 3. Table 8 shows us the TF-IDF of top words from document 1, 2 and 3. From Table 8, it is evident that TF-IDF is high for the important words in the document and how stopwords are ignored.

Table 4. Normalized TF of terms in document 1

	Data	Mining	And	Social	Media
TF	0.16	0.33	0.16	0.16	0.16

Table 5. Normalized TF of terms in document 2

	Social	Network	Analysis
TF	0.16	0.33	0.16

Table 6. Normalized TF of terms in document 3

	Data	Mining
TF	0.5	0.5

Table 7. IDF of terms in corpus

Terms	IDF
Data	1.176
Mining	1.176
and	1.477
Social	1.176
Media	1.477
Network	1.477
Analysis	1.477

Table 8. Term with top IDF scores in each document

Document	Top Words	TF-IDF
Document 1	Mining	0.388
Document 2	Network	0.487
Document 3	Data	0.588

Appendix 2

Influential Words Based on Chronological Order

Instead of using the distance as metric for the entry of the profile into the cluster, the chronological order of entry of profiles into the cluster is taken. The chronological entry is adopted to trace the influential words a profile possess that attracted a potential follower assuming the social media adopts the recommendation of users to follow based on the influential words between profiles we proposed. The technique can be used to blow down a Twitter profile with lot of followers to list of words and understand the relationship between that profile and followers (Table 9).

Table 9. Top 3 influential words between cluster and incoming profile(Chronological Based)

IP	Top 3 words	ITR
GovPenceIN	Govpencein	1
	Indiana	
	Governor	
WhoopiGoldberg	Romney	2
	People	
	Really	
jemelehill	Laughing	3
	Something	
	Always	

(continued)

Table 9. (continued)

IP	Top 3 words	ITR
paulwaugh	Election	75
	Abbott	
	News	
taylorswift13	Lenadunham	104
	Theellenshow	
	Mariska	
TwistedBacteria	Science	123
	Stories	
	Disease	
OwenJones84	Racism	144
	Defeat	
	Leadership	
KingJames	Kingjames	268
	Brother	
	Favorite	

This metric if used properly, would enable us to decompose a complex profile with a large follower-base like that of celebrities and detect the top influential words. By doing so, we can perform a detailed analysis on why people follow celebrities and which are the keywords that make a difference. Public relation officers and campaign managers for political candidates can use this analysis to target voting blocks.

Appendix 3

Hybrid Suggestion System (for Companies and Articles)

For companies or brands, personalized ad targeting based on the interest shown by the users would prove efficient as there is more possibility of a relevant user turning into a potential customer than a common user. Companies can use Twitter to display the most relevant ads to the respective users based on the nature of their tweets, performing personalized ad targeting. Table 10 gives the top 2 users for each of the brands namely Nike and BBC. The top 2 users for Nike happens to be footballers namely Alex Morgan and Wayne Ronney. While for BBC, a British news channel, the top user is number10gov which is the handle of UK prime minister; the second top user is a British referee Graham Scott (Table 11).

Table 10. Similar users for each company/brand

Brand	Top 2 users	Rank
Nike	Alex Morgan	1
	Wayne Rooney	2
BBC	number10gov	1
	Graham Scott	2

Table 11. Similar articles for each user profile

User profile	Top 2 articles	Rank
HillaryClinton	Alex Wallace to head Washington	1
	Brazil spied on US diplomats	2
Rihanna	Actors to watch this fall	1
	10 best dresses in movie history	2

Appendix 4

Profile Similarity

See (Tables 12, 13 and 14).

Table 12. TF-IDF of user profile terms (HillaryClinton)

Terms	TF-IDF
Immigrant	>0
Election	>0
Federal	>0
Twitter	>0
washington	>0

Table 13. TF-IDF of profile 1 terms(realDonaldTrump)

Terms	TF-IDF
Immigrant	>0
Election	>0
Federal	>0
Twitter	>0
Washington	>0

Table 14. TF-IDF of profile 2 terms(katyperry)

Terms	TF-IDF
Immigrant	0
Election	0
Federal	0
Twitter	>0
Washington	>0

Appendix 5

User Profile Based Single Source Clustering

Figures 4, 5, and 6 illustrate the word clouds formed based on the top impactful words between the closest incoming profile and the current formed cluster using the algorithm mentioned. The word clouds are made of words based on their importance between the current cluster and the incoming closest profile, calculated using the ITM (described in the next section). Figure 4 gives the word cloud between user profile (HillaryClinton) and the closest profile to the user profile (THEHermaineCain). Almost all of the words denote about politics, as these two profiles are politicians. Figure 5 illustrates the top

Fig. 4. Top Influential words between HilaryClinton and THEHermaineCain

Fig. 5. Top Influential words between the current Cluster and SpeakerRyan

Fig. 6. Top Influential words between the Cluster and JimmyFallon

words between the existing cluster (around 302 profiles including HillaryClinton and THEHermaineCain) and SpeakerRyan, while Fig. 6 illustrates the influential words between JimmyFallon and the existing cluster. It can be noted that the first two Figures are almost about politics while the last Figure is about entertainment.

Appendix 6

Visualizing Word Graphs

Decreasing significance. Taking the word "parenthood" as an example, we observe that it belongs in the top 20 influential words shared between the user profile (HillaryClinton) and her closest profile (THEHermanCain) as there is a high TF-IDF of that word in both their tweets. But when other profiles start coming into the equation as we progress with the clustering process, the word loses it's significance and moves out of the top 20 list because of its low usage amongst the newly clustered profiles. The same could be said for the word "democrats". HillaryClinton and THEHermanCain use that word with a very high frequency, and hence it makes the top 20 list of words shared between them. But due to its relatively low usage amongst the next incoming profiles, the word loses its significance.

Increasing significance. What happens if the influence for a particular word is very low for the first few incoming profiles but increases over several iterations? This leads to our second scenario where there is an increase in significance for a particular word with the progression of the clustering process. The word "marcorubio" can be used to describe this scenario perfectly. There is no usage of that word from THEHermanCain and hence it doesn't make the list of influential words. But there is some level of usage from realdonaldtrump and GovMikeHuckabee who are the third and fourth profile respectively. This ensures that the word enters the list of common words between existing cluster and incoming profile but not enough to push it to the top 20 influential words list. The word finally makes the top 20 list with the entry of newtgingrich as he had heavily used it in his tweets. The word "medicare" is another similar example.

Maintaining significance. This scenario is commonly observed when the usage of a word remains reasonably constant across several incoming profiles. One such example is the word "president". Since the first four closest profiles to HillaryClinton are all politicians, the word "president" is a common occurrence among their tweets. Hence it consistently features in the top 20 list across the first four iterations. Similarly, the word "america" follows the same scenario of maintaining its significance across iterations.

Oscillating Significance. This is the final scenario which can be observed from the progression of the clustering process. As the name suggests, it occurs when a particular word oscillates between high and low influential across several iterations. Every word will eventually follow this pattern if we are to increase the range of our observations across many iterations, but we are more interested with oscillations within a short range of iterations. For instance, the word "timkaine" helps us better understand this scenario. THEHermanCain didn't use this words in his tweets, resulting in it's absence from the list of common words for iteration one. But realdonaldtrump has such a high TF-IDF that it manages to make it to the top 20-word list. With the entry of GovMikeHuckabee, word falls out of the top 20 list again as he hasn't used that word in his tweets thereby decreasing it's score. The word "abolish" is another example which follows a similar pattern resulting in oscillating significance.

References

1. Java, A., et al.: Why we twitter: understanding microblogging usage and communities. In: Proceedings of the 9thWebKDD and 1st SNA-KDD 2007 Workshop on Web Mining and Social Network Analysis. ACM (2007)
2. Pak, A., Paroubek, P.: Twitter as a corpus for sentiment analysis and opinion mining. LREc **10**, 2010 (2010)
3. Gupta, P., et al.: WTF: The who to follow service at twitter. In: Proceedings of the 22nd International Conference on World Wide Web. ACM (2013)
4. Hannon, J., McCarthy, K., Smyth, B.: Finding useful users on twitter: twittomender the followee recommender. In: Clough, P., Foley, C., Gurrin, C., Jones, Gareth J.F., Kraaij, W., Lee, H., Mudoch, V. (eds.) ECIR 2011. LNCS, vol. 6611, pp. 784–787. Springer, Heidelberg (2011). doi:10.1007/978-3-642-20161-5_94
5. Kagan, V., Stevens, A., Subrahmanian, V.S.: Using twitter sentiment to forecast the 2013 pakistani election and the 2014 indian election. IEEE Intell. Syst. **30**(1), 2–5 (2015)
6. Tunggawan, E., Soelistio, Y.E.: And the Winner is...: Bayesian Twitter-based Prediction on 2016 US Presidential Election. arXiv preprint arXiv:1611.00440 (2016)
7. Ramos, J.: Using TF-IDF to determine word relevance in document queries. In: Proceedings of the First Instructional Conference on Machine Learning (2003)
8. Jing, L.-P., Huang, H.-K., Shi, H.-B.: Improved feature selection approach TFIDF in text mining. In: Proceedings of 2002 International Conference on Machine Learning and Cybernetics, vol. 2. IEEE (2002)
9. Huang, A.: Similarity measures for text document clustering. In: Proceedings of the Sixth New Zealand Computer Science Research Student Conference (NZCSRSC 2008), Christchurch, New Zealand (2008)
10. Steinbach, M., Karypis, G., Kumar, V.: A comparison of document clustering techniques. In: KDD Workshop on Text Mining, vol. 400(1) (2000)

11. Shah, N., Mahajan, S.: Document clustering: a detailed review. Int. J. Appl. Inf. Syst. **4**(5), 30–38 (2012)
12. Cutting, D.R., et al.: Scatter/gather: a clusterbased approach to browsing large document collections. In: Proceedings of the 15th Annual International ACM SIGIR Conference on Research and Development in Information Retrieval. ACM (1992)
13. Bhaumik, H., et al.: Towards reliable clustering of english text documents using correlation coefficient. In: 2014 International Conference on Computational Intelligence and Communication Networks (CICN). IEEE (2014)
14. Li, G., Liu, F.: A clustering-based approach on sentiment analysis. In: 2010 International Conference on Intelligent Systems and Knowledge Engineering (ISKE). IEEE (2010)
15. Kavyasrujana, D., Rao, B.C.: Hierarchical clustering for sentence extraction using cosine similarity measure. In: Satapathy, S., Govardhan, A., Raju, K., Mandal, J. (eds.) Emerging ICT for Bridging the Future - Proceedings of the 49th Annual Convention of the Computer Society of India (CSI) Volume 1. AISC, vol. 337, pp. 185–191. Springer, Cham (2015). doi:10.1007/978-3-319-13728-5_21
16. Radev, D.R., et al.: Centroid-based summarization of multiple documents. Inf. Process. Manage. **40**(6), 919–938 (2004)
17. Mihalcea, R., Corley, C., Strapparava, C.: Corpus-based and knowledge-based measures of text semantic similarity.In: AAAI, vol. 6 (2006)
18. Tweepy, https://github.com/tweepy/tweepy
19. Reuters Institute for the Study of Journalism. Digital news report 2015: Tracking the future of news (2015). http://www.digitalnewsreport.org/survey/2015/socialnetworks-and-their-role-in-news-2015/
20. Pew Research Center. The evolving role of news on twitter and facebook (2015). http://www.journalism.org/2015/07/14/the-evolving-role-of-news-ontwitter-and-facebook
21. Twigraph Source code. https://github.com/Dhanasekar-S/Twigraph_Source_Code

An Exploratory Study on the Influence of Guidelines on Crowdfunding Projects in the Ethereum Blockchain Platform

Vanessa Bracamonte$^{(\boxtimes)}$ and Hitoshi Okada

National Institute of Informatics, Tokyo 101-8430, Japan
{vbracamonte,okada}@nii.ac.jp

Abstract. In 2016, the DAO, a project which had raised $150 million in token sales in a crowdfunding campaign carried out on the Ethereum blockchain, was hacked using a vulnerability in its code. As part of the response to the incident, the Ethereum Foundation issued two guidelines: a security measure and a value limit. However, the characteristics of decentralized blockchain platforms make it difficult to establish or enforce new rules. In this paper, we investigate whether these guidelines had any influence on subsequent crowdfunding projects, by qualitatively analyzing the information provided by the projects' organizers. The results indicate that the Ethereum Foundation guidelines had some, although limited, influence on how the projects were conducted, in particular with regard to setting a value limit to the campaigns. They also provide some evidence of the influence of the community in the implementation and improvement of security measures related to the smart contracts. We discuss these results in the context of the challenges of governance of crowdfunding projects running in public blockchain platforms.

Keywords: Blockchain technology · Crowdfunding · Governance · Self-regulation

1 Introduction

In decentralized blockchain systems, created with the invention of Bitcoin [14], transactions between users are validated by participants in the system, rather than by a trusted third party. Some of these blockchain systems can also act as platforms for smart contracts. In the context of blockchain systems, a smart contract is "a program that runs on the blockchain and has its correct execution enforced by the consensus protocol" [13]. Participating nodes in the blockchain system independently validate the smart contract execution, instead of it being validated by a central system. In blockchains like Ethereum, smart contracts —also called decentralized applications— can be programmed to include complex logic.

The use of smart contracts makes it possible to implement crowdfunding campaigns on a blockchain system where contributions are made by buying tokens [1]. These "trustless crowdsales" [1] facilitate running direct crowdfunding campaigns [2] that do not rely on trusted third parties but can still provide important functions. For example, a basic crowdfunding smart contract can be programmed to automatically refund

© Springer International Publishing AG 2017
G.L. Ciampaglia et al. (Eds.): SocInfo 2017, Part II, LNCS 10540, pp. 347–354, 2017.
DOI: 10.1007/978-3-319-67256-4_27

participants' contributions if the minimum goal is not reached before a specified time, or to give control of the funds to the organizers if the campaign reaches the minimum goal [1].

Crowdfunding campaigns can also be conducted using more complex smart contracts. In 2016, a project called the DAO raised approximately $150 million in ether, the Ethereum native currency [3]. The DAO — a "distributed autonomous organization"— was an ambitious project designed to create a completely autonomous company. However, soon after the crowdfunding campaign had finished a vulnerability was discovered in its code, and approximately $50 million were drained from the DAO smart contract [3].

There were different responses to the incident from the community and other parties, but in this paper we focus on a particular response by the Ethereum Foundation, the non-profit organization in charge of the development of the Ethereum blockchain platform. The Ethereum Foundation made an announcement about the DAO incident in their official blog, and this announcement also included two guidelines for the creators of smart contracts [4], referring to code security and to a value limit for smart contracts. The guidelines are remarkable because public blockchain systems such as Ethereum are considered to be under no central authority who can restrict participation in the system or establish and enforce new rules [5], either for the blockchain system or for the smart contracts, although rules can be changed if the community can reach some level of consensus. This characteristic protects the blockchain system from unilateral changes, but it makes governance of the blockchain system and the decentralized applications that run on it a challenge.

Considering this, in this paper we investigate whether the Ethereum Foundation guidelines had any influence on crowdfunding campaigns that ran after the DAO incident.

2 Governance in Crowdfunding Projects

Centralized crowdfunding platforms, such as Kickstarter for example, can make use of price and non-price instruments to regulate the projects they host [6]. Belleflamme and Lambert [6] indicate that "crowdfunding platforms have a natural tendency to self-regulation," because it is favorable for the platform to attract quality projects and avoid possible scams. This in turn is also positive for the projects, because platforms with more quality projects can attract more contributors.

However, these instruments are difficult to apply to crowdfunding projects running in a public blockchain platform. For example, projects or users are not charged for using the Ethereum platform, although there is a cost, so price instruments are not applicable. Neither are non-price instruments such as quality control, because they would be difficult to implement without the possibility of enforcing rules.

Even public blockchain platforms can be negatively affected by the projects they host, as evidenced by the DAO incident, so it is in the interest of the system that projects do not run into critical problems. This fact that the Ethereum Foundation gave guidelines for smart contract authors can also be considered an evidence of this.

The question of how to regulate a blockchain systems has been addressed by previous research. One possibility considered is that government could exert regulatory pressure on the identifiable elements of the blockchain system, such as Bitcoin miners [9], exchanges [10] or other entities —although this is limited by the ability to fork the system [9]. This approach may also be possible for decentralized applications that run on blockchain platforms; in this case, the identifiable elements would be the crowd-funding project organizers. In a blockchain system, rules are enforced by the network, but people are involved in programming those rules [7, 8]. The same is true for smart contracts. In a similar way to Bitcoin miners and exchanges, regulators could also put pressure directly on the organizers of crowdfunding projects if they can identify them. However, this influence could be limited considering smart contracts can be easily replicated.

Another possibility is using the influence of the community. Decentralized applications are often developed as open source projects, which rely on their communities. The characteristics that community-managed governance can take —independence, pluralism, representation, decentralized decision-making, autonomous participation [11] — are not incompatible with public blockchain system community norms. Community also plays a part in the governance of crowdfunding projects that run on centralized platforms [12].

The Ethereum Foundation guidelines appear to be an attempt to regulate the behavior of projects. However, although the guidelines are not enforceable, it is difficult to consider the Ethereum Foundation as just another member of the community because of its role in the development of the system. As a first step to understand these guidelines in the context of governance, we investigate if and how they influenced the crowdfunding projects that ran after the DAO incident.

3 Analysis

In order to determine whether the Ethereum Foundation guidelines had any influence on the projects, we conducted a qualitative exploratory study of the information provided by the crowdfunding projects' organizers in their official websites and blogs.

First, we analyzed the content of the guidelines themselves. The guidelines were contained in a post in the official blog of the Ethereum Foundation, in an announcement related to the DAO smart contract incident [4]. In the blog post, a statement directed to smart contract authors indicated that they "should take care to (1) be very careful about recursive call bugs, and listen to advice from the Ethereum contract programming community (…) on mitigating such bugs" and "(2) avoid creating contracts that contain more than $\sim$ \$10 m worth of value", with some exceptions, "at least until the community gains more experience with bug mitigation and/or better tools are developed."

The first guideline refers to security measures, specifically to the mitigation of the type of bugs that had been used to attack the DAO smart contract: recursive call bugs. The smart contract of the DAO had been through external security audits and code reviews [3], but even so they had failed to identify this critical vulnerability. However, the vulnerability had been identified by members of the Ethereum community who were not directly related to the DAO project [3], which can explain why the call to "listen to advice from the Ethereum programming community" is included in the guideline.

The second guideline gives a limit for the value that smart contracts should hold ($10 million). The guideline indicates that this limit is temporary, although it does not specify clearly when it would no longer apply, and it also makes a reference to the experience of the community. In general, the first guideline can be said to refer to security measures and second guideline to a value limit for smart contracts, which include those used for crowdfunding.

We then gathered the information related to the campaigns. There is no authoritative source for a list of blockchain-related crowdfunding projects, so the list was obtained from third party websites that compile such information. We used four websites that included comprehensive lists of past projects, to compensate for biases in project selection. Only projects running on the Ethereum blockchain and whose campaigns had been conducted using Ethereum smart contracts were considered. In order to determine this, we reviewed the information about the project provided by the third party websites and conducted a preliminary check of the projects' official websites. From this list of Ethereum projects, we selected those with campaigns that had started after the date of the DAO incident and that had finished before the date the list was compiled, April 6, 2017. In one case, the website of a project that fulfilled the criteria was unavailable; this project was not included in the analysis. The final list contained 14 projects[1].

Next, we saved local copies of each project's official website and blog, if it existed. The data collection began on April 6, 2017 and ended on May 24, 2017. A preliminary check of these websites showed that information related to the crowdfunding campaign was no longer available in some cases. For these projects, online cached information was obtained. All data used for the analysis was publicly available data.

There were six variables of interest in the analysis: mentions of (1) the Ethereum Foundation guidelines, (2) the Ethereum Foundation itself, (3) the DAO incident, (4) effects of community influence, (5) a value limit for the campaign, and (6) implementation of security measures. We considered mentions of the Ethereum Foundation (variable 2) as a measure of both awareness and a certain willingness to acknowledge its influence. DAO incident mentions and effects of community influence (variables 3 and 4) are related to the potential regulatory effect of the community. Finally, mentions of a value limit and implementation of security measures (variables 5 and 6) are included as generalizations of the Ethereum Foundation guidelines. Each variable was associated with a list of keywords. The content of each project's websites was first searched for occurrences of these keywords, including spelling variations. Webpages that contained these terms were then manually analyzed to verify the context in which the mentions occurred. The results are summarized in Table 1.

---

[1] The list of projects is available on request.

Table 1. Results – Occurrence of variables of interest

	Guidelines	Ethereum foundation	DAO incident	Community influence	Value limit	Security measures	Note
P1	Y	Y	Y	Y	Y	Y	
P2			Y		Y	Y	
P3						Y	
P4		Y	Y		Y	Y	
P5			Y	Y			Refunded
P6						Y	
P7	Y	Y	Y	Y	Y	Y	
P8		Y			Y	Y	
P9							Refunded
P10			Y			Y	
P11							Abandoned
P12			Y		Y	Y	
P13		Y				Y	
P14		Y	Y	Y	Y	Y	

Projects ordered chronologically

4 Results

With regard to security measures, the majority of projects (11 out of 14) made some reference to measures to ensure the security of their smart contract code, through code audits, tests and/or bug bounties. However, only P10 made a reference to the specific type of bugs mentioned in the Ethereum Foundation blog post —recursive call bugs—, and the reference was made in the context of a smart contract code audit by an external party that had experience with this type of exploit, not in relation to the Ethereum Foundation guideline.

With regard to value limits, seven out of 14 projects established a monetary limit for their campaigns, ranging from $5.5 to $10 million. However, only P1 and P7 made explicit mention of the limit as related to the Ethereum Foundation guidelines. The start date of P1 was the closest to the DAO incident —just 5 days later— and the information from their sites indicates a change of plans in direct response to it. The Ethereum Foundation blog post containing the guidelines was referred to as having "received explicit warnings", and the content of these warnings was summarized as avoiding the "deployment of complex contracts with large volumes". In the case of P7, which start date was approximately 5 months after the DAO incident, the guidelines blog post was referred to as a "call to not create smart contracts holding more than $10 M". In P4 and P14, the reason for the value limit was mentioned to be strictly related to the amount needed for the project. No explanation for the value limit was found for P2, P8 and P12. In addition, time did not seem to affect this limit: P14, started 9.5 months after the DAO incident, included a value limit.

As for the projects without a monetary value limit, four projects (P3, P5, P6 and P13) still indicated a limit in the amount of tokens that could be purchased in the crowdfund. On the other hand, P9 and P10 indicated that they had no such limits. Only in one case (P11) no information could be found to determine whether there was a limit or not. Regardless of whether an explicit limit had been mentioned or not, none of the projects raised more than $10 million. The maximum amount raised was $8.6 million.

All projects with a monetary value limit also mentioned including some type of security measure. Projects where the opposite was not true still included a token limit, with the exception of one case (P10). Only three projects (P5, P9 and P11) did not make any mention of either a value limit or specific security measures taken for the project.

As Table 1 shows, only P1 and P2 made direct reference to the guidelines post, but references to the Ethereum Foundation and to the DAO incident were included in other projects. Ethereum Foundation mentions were related to its role in developing the Ethereum platform (P4 and P7) and in providing smart contract standards (P8, P13 and P14). In the case of the DAO incident, it was mentioned in relation to the security of smart contracts in most projects (P1, P2, P5, P7, P10), but it was also regarded as evidence of decentralization, in both a negative (P14) and positive (P4) way.

In three (P1, P7 and P14) of the five projects that explicitly acknowledged the influence of the community, it was related to the implementation or improvement of security measures. In P12, it was related to changes in the documentation. In the case of P5, concerns from the community about security issues and legal implications of the project affected the start date of the campaign, but no mention was found of particular security measures taken as a response. All other projects besides these five also provided different contact options for interaction with the community, such as through social media websites, but no indication could be found of specific ways community feedback had influenced their campaigns.

Finally, two projects (P9 and P11) did not make references to any of the variables in the analysis.

5 Discussion

The results show that only two projects out of 14 made direct reference to the Ethereum Foundation guidelines; in both cases, only the guideline regarding the value limit was mentioned. On the other hand, another five projects also set a value limit to their campaigns: two cited reasons related to the needs of their projects but the other three gave no specific reasons. In centralized crowdfunding platforms, it is usual for projects to set a minimum amount to be raised as well as a limited period of time in which it can be raised. However, although these platforms can have rules about limits, such as a maximum amount per pledge in the case of Kickstarter, there is usually no such rule for the total amount that can be raised. That crowdfunding projects in the Ethereum blockchain set a maximum amount for their campaigns suggests some awareness of the Ethereum Foundation guidelines, although there could be a reluctance to make the association explicit.

With regard to the guideline related to the recursive call bug, only one project mentioned the inclusion of measures to secure the smart contract against this particular bug, although most projects indicated the implementation of some type of security measure. However, this may be due to the fact that software projects usually consider verification of code quality. Therefore, it cannot be concluded that the implementation of security measures was necessarily a result of a generalization of the guidelines. In addition, feedback from the community was also referenced in relation to implementing or improving security measures, which is similar to the role of community participation in the improvement of quality of open source projects [11] as well as crowdfunding projects [12].

5.1 Limitations

There are a number limitations in this study. First, the number of crowdfunding projects is small and results cannot be generalized to future campaigns. Second, only official project websites and blogs were considered in the analysis; information posted in third party social media websites or user forums was not included and it was not possible to find the cached version of every unavailable webpage. Therefore, it is not possible to be certain of negative occurrences.

6 Conclusion

In this paper, we conducted a qualitative exploratory study on the influence of two guidelines given by the Ethereum Foundation after the DAO incident, applied to crowdfunding projects. In summary, the results indicate that the Ethereum Foundation guidelines had some, although limited, influence on how the projects were conducted, in particular with regard to setting a value limit to the campaigns. They also provide some evidence of the influence of the community in the implementation and improvement of security measures related to the smart contracts. These findings suggest it is possible that guidelines from an entity such as the Ethereum Foundation could function as governance mechanisms in conjunction with community based regulation.

However, the guidelines were given in the special circumstances of the DAO incident. Although the Ethereum Foundation provides smart contract templates as well as advice on best practices that are adopted by members of the community, it is not possible to say whether guidelines such as these —in particular the one related to monetary limits— would have been well received or implemented in normal circumstances.

The price and non-price regulatory instruments available to centralized crowdfunding platforms are difficult for public blockchain platforms to apply. Therefore, more research is needed on the role of community influence and self-regulation in preventing or limiting future incidents. In addition, the lack of mention of the specific type of vulnerability that affected the DAO should merit further investigation, in particular since the DAO itself implemented similar security measures as those mentioned by the projects in this study.

Acknowledgments. This research is part of the results of the joint project "Financial business applications of blockchain technology" (National Institute of Informatics and Sumitomo Mitsui Banking Corporation).

References

1. Ethereum Foundation: Crowdsale Raising funds from friends without a third party. (2017). https://www.ethereum.org/crowdsale. Accessed 31 Mar 2017
2. Bouncken, R.B., Komorek, M., Kraus, S.: Crowdfunding: the current state of research. Int. Bus. Econ. Res. J. **14**(3), 407–416 (2015)
3. Jentzsch, C.: The History of the DAO and Lessons Learned. slock.it, 24 August 2016. https://blog.slock.it/the-history-of-the-dao-and-lessons-learned. Accessed 07 Apr 2017
4. Buterin, V.: Critical Update Re: DAO Vulnerability (2016). https://blog.ethereum.org/2016/06/17/critical-update-re-dao-vulnerability/. Accessed 07 Feb 2017
5. Okada, H., Yamasaki, S., Bracamonte, V.: Proposed classification of blockchains based on authority and incentive dimensions. In: 2017 19th International Conference on Advanced Communication Technology (ICACT), pp. 593–597 (2017)
6. Belleflamme, P., Lambert, T.: Crowdfunding: some empirical findings and microeconomic underpinnings. Forum Financ.: Revue Bancaire et Financière **2014**(4), 288–296 (2014)
7. Lehdonvirta, V.: The blockchain paradox: why distributed ledger technologies may do little to transform the economy. Policy & Internet blog (2016). https://www.oii.ox.ac.uk/blog/the-blockchain-paradox-why-distributed-ledger-technologies-may-do-little-to-transform-the-economy/
8. De Filippi, P., Loveluck, B.: The invisible politics of Bitcoin: governance crisis of a decentralised infrastructure. Internet Policy Rev. **5**(3), 28 (2016)
9. Kroll, J.A., Davey, I.C., Felten, E.W.: The economics of bitcoin mining, or bitcoin in the presence of adversaries. In: The Twelfth Workshop on the Economics of Information Security (WEIS 2013), p. 21 (2013)
10. Böhme, R., Christin, N., Edelman, B., Moore, T.: Bitcoin: economics, technology, and governance. J. Econ. Perspect. **29**(2), 213–238 (2015)
11. O'Mahony, S.: The governance of open source initiatives: What does it mean to be community managed? J. Manage. Gov. **11**(2), 139–150 (2007)
12. Gerber, E.M., Hui, J.S., Kuo, P.-Y.: Crowdfunding: why people are motivated to post and fund projects on crowdfunding platforms. In: Proceedings of the International Workshop on Design, Influence, and Social Technologies: Techniques, Impacts and Ethics, p. 10 (2012)
13. Luu, L., Chu, D.-H., Olickel, H., Saxena, P., Hobor, A.: Making smart contracts smarter. In: Proceedings of the 2016 ACM SIGSAC Conference on Computer and Communications Security, pp. 254–269 (2016)
14. Nakamoto, S.: Bitcoin: a peer-to-peer electronic cash system, p. 9 (2008). www.bitcoin.org

Lost in Re-Election: A Tale of Two Spanish Online Campaigns

Helena Gallego[1,2(✉)], David Laniado[2], Andreas Kaltenbrunner[1,2],
Vicenç Gómez[1(✉)], and Pablo Aragón[1,2]

[1] Universitat Pompeu Fabra, Barcelona, Spain
helenag@mac.com, vicen.gomez@upf.edu
[2] Eurecat - Technology Center of Catalonia, Barcelona, Spain

Abstract. In the 2010 decade, Spanish politics have transitioned from bipartidism to multipartidism. This change led to an unstable situation which eventually led to the rare scenario of two general elections within six months. The two elections had a mayor difference: two important left-wing parties formed a coalition in the second election while they had run separately in the first one. In the second election and after merging, the coalition lost around 1M votes, contradicting opinion polls. In this study, we perform community analysis of the retweet networks of the online campaigns to assess whether activity in Twitter reflects the outcome of both elections. The results show that the left-wing parties lost more online supporters than the other parties. Furthermore, we find that Twitter activity of the supporters unveils a decrease in engagement especially marked for the smaller party in the coalition, in line with post-electoral traditional polls.

Keywords: Twitter · Politics · Political parties · Spanish elections · Online campaigning · Political coalition · Engagement · Political participation

1 Introduction

Social media are playing a key role in shaping public debate in political contexts, forming a new public sphere [6]; it is therefore increasingly important to understand their usage during political campaigns. Social media's function as a potential mirror of societal trends [5] and their strong impact on voters' perceptions and decision making make it important to understand their dynamics and influence [17], and their usage by politicians [1,22]. Although translating signals from the online to the offline world is not always straightforward, and previous studies aimed at predicting election results through the analysis of Twitter, e.g. [21], received many criticisms [7,11,15], it is undoubted that the analysis of social media as emerging political battleground can unveil important aspects of electoral campaigns. Indeed, a growing amount of research is devoted in particular to investigate multiple aspects of the usage of Twitter during elections, as illustrated in the systematic literature review presented in [14].

© Springer International Publishing AG 2017
G.L. Ciampaglia et al. (Eds.): SocInfo 2017, Part II, LNCS 10540, pp. 355–367, 2017.
DOI: 10.1007/978-3-319-67256-4_28

In this study, we focus on the Spanish general elections of 2015 and 2016 and compare Twitter activity during the two consecutive campaigns to assess whether and how it reflects changes in the engagement of the supporters of different parties. This case study is of special interest because the 2015 general elections marked the end of forty years of Spanish bipartidism. After the country was shaken by the economic crisis of 2008 and by the 15M (or *Indignados*) movement of 2011, with massive protests against major traditional parties [19], the elections in December 2015 were held in a very different scenario with respect to all previous elections [18]. The emergence of new political forces and the resulting fragmented parliament with no clear majority led, after six months of negotiation, to new elections in June 2016 [20].

The main parties involved in the elections and having a presence on the whole country are:

- Partido Popular (PP[1] - traditional, right);
- Partido Socialista Obrero Español (PSOE[2] - traditional, center/left);
- Izquierda Unida (IU[3] - traditional, left);
- Podemos (Pod[4] - new, left);
- Ciudadanos (CS[5] new, center/right).

It is also important to mention the organizations Compromís (Valencia), En Marea (Galicia) and En Comú Podem (Catalunya), regional confluences which included local bottom-up forces in coalition with Podemos.

From the election results in Table 4, we observe that the participation declined significantly from the first to the second election, suggesting a decrease in motivation of the electorate. They also show an increase in PP votes in 2016; this, combined with the participation drop, led to a significantly higher amount of representatives for this party. In the 2015 election, some of the main left parties ran together in a coalition formed by Podemos, En Comú Podem, Compromís and En Marea. Izquierda Unida decided to run alone, however in 2016 it joined the coalition which was re-named Unidos Podemos. The current Spanish electoral law, which penalizes small forces and gave IU only two representatives in the 2015 Congress after achieving almost one million votes, triggered the decision of the party to join the coalition in 2016. Although the sum of representatives of the coalition in 2016 was the same as the one achieved separately in 2015, the corresponding amount of votes dropped significantly (by around 1 million votes), contradicting several pre-election polls[6].

While the electoral results clearly indicate an increase or decrease in votes of each party between the two elections, they do not explicitly indicate voter migration between parties (or between parties and abstentionism), which is left

---

[1] https://en.wikipedia.org/wiki/People%27s_Party_(Spain).

[2] https://en.wikipedia.org/wiki/Spanish_Socialist_Workers%27_Party.

[3] https://en.wikipedia.org/wiki/United_Left_(Spain).

[4] https://en.wikipedia.org/wiki/Podemos_(Spanish_political_party).

[5] https://en.wikipedia.org/wiki/Citizens_(Spanish_political_party).

[6] http://datos.cis.es/pdf/Es3141mar_A.pdf.

to opinion polls. Several studies using post and pre-electoral polls tried to determine the voter transfers from one election to the other. According to a study [16], 73% from UP repeated their vote and the rest abstained. Also [10] estimated that the coalition managed to retain 74% of Podemos voters, but only six out of ten IU voters. This means that there were also differences in the distribution of voters within the coalition electorate. To complement opinion polls about voter migration between parties with evidence from social media activity, we formulate the following research question:

RQ1: *Can we observe from Twitter activity a migration of supporters between parties from the first to the second election?*

To answer this question, we consider the Twitter retweet network, perform a community analysis to identify clusters of political parties and characterize their structure following the methodology of [2]. As retweets generally represent endorsement, they have been proven useful in previous literature to detect clusters corresponding to political parties, both in the context of Spain [1,2] and other countries [8]. We will use the obtained clusters and study the migration of users between clusters. As we know from the electoral results that the parties who constituted Unidos Podemos lost more than 1 million voters, our hypothesis is that we will observe a drop in the users clustered around the accounts of these parties. We further expect the analysis to indicate which of the parties in the coalition lost most supporters in Twitter, and whether lost users started supporting other parties.

From 2015 to 2016, participation dropped significantly, showing a general demotivation or tiredness in the electorate. Several studies have examined the correlation between social media use and political engagement. Holt et al. [12] report that both political social media usage and attention to political news in traditional media increase political engagement over time, and suggest that frequent social media use among citizens can function as a leveler in terms of motivating political participation. Findings from [3] reveal that a variety of Internet uses are positively related to different forms of political participation, whereas the relationship between most uses of traditional media and participation are weak. Finally, Dimitrova et al [9] report only weak effects of digital media use on political learning, but find that the use of some digital media forms has appreciable effects on political participation. As we know that Twitter activity can be related to political engagement and there has been a motivation decrease between the two campaigns, the second question of this study is:

RQ2: *Is the demotivation of the electorate reflected in their Twitter activity/engagement?*

We will answer this research question analyzing the volume of activity per user in the two campaigns, and determining if there are notable differences between them. We will look separately at users supporting different parties, with a special attention towards Podemos and IU, the parties that lost more votes.

2   Dataset

This study relies on two different datasets collected from Twitter in relation to the electoral campaigns of the 2015 and 2016 Spanish national elections (December 4-20 2015 and June 10-26 2016). Tweets were collected if they either (a) were created by, (b) retweeted or (c) mentioned one of the official party accounts or party candidate accounts (listed in Table 2).

Table 1. Number of nodes (N_{2015} and N_{2016}) and edges (E_{2015} and E_{2016}) for the intra-network of each cluster in the retweet networks of 2015 and 2016.

Cluster	N_{2015}	E_{2015}	N_{2016}	E_{2016}
Podemos	16 114	33 488	9 771	12 818
IU	10 439	22 422	10 314	12 304
PP	8 345	28 677	5 614	11 682
PSOE	7 538	25 119	5 541	10 174
CS	7 200	24 110	5 458	9 501
ECP	1 412	2 925	1 791	2 868

To detect the Twitter organization of political parties, we build directed weighted graphs of users (nodes) and retweets (edges). Each weighted edge indicates the number of times the source user retweeted a message posted by the target user. We filter edges with weights lower than 3 to exclude anecdotal interactions as in [2]. The resulting network characteristics for 2015 and 2016 are presented in Table 3.

3   Network Analysis

We start showing some general results about our community discovery analysis for both election campaigns. We then analyze how the found clusters change between the two elections and conclude this section with a quantification of the change in political engagement.

3.1   Community Detection

Table 1 shows the clustering results obtained using the N-Louvain method[7] in both networks, showing only the largest clusters. For the four parties that formed the coalition –Podemos, En Comú Podem (ECP), En Marea and Compromís–, only two clusters are identified, corresponding to Podemos and ECP. The others, En Marea and Compromís, are effectively integrated in Podemos, while ECP forms a separate cluster. This separate cluster might be explained by the use of

---

[7] See Appendix A.1 for a description of the N-Louvain method.

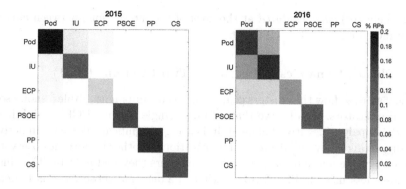

Fig. 1. Normalized weighted adjacency matrices of the 2015 (left) and 2016 (right) retweet networks aggregating nodes by party clusters.

different languages (Catalan instead of Spanish). We also observe that the IU party maintains its cluster despite merging with Podemos in the second election. The IU cluster is slightly bigger than the one of Podemos in the second election. This is noteworthy, since Podemos had by far a larger amount of votes in the first election, and one might expect the opposite effect in the network. In general, we conclude that the formation of the coalition for the 2016 elections *is not captured* by the observed communities, since Podemos, IU and ECP are associated to different clusters. Moreover, there is no obvious relation between the size of the identified communities and the electoral results, in terms of votes.

The analysis of the inter-cluster and intra-cluster density of edges provides a measure of how strongly are the interactions within and between the different parties in the different campaigns. Table 1 (second and fourth columns) shows that the amount of intra-cluster edges is smaller in 2016 than in 2015, with a decrease by almost 50%, indicating weaker connections in the second election.

What about the inter-cluster edges? We would expect some of these interactions to increase in the second election, as a consequence of the electoral coalition and of the synergies between the parties. To examine all the interactions between the parties, we consider the interaction matrix A, where A_{ij} is the normalized sum of all retweets that users from cluster i made for the tweets from users of cluster j displayed in Fig. 1 for both elections. Both matrices are diagonally dominant, since the vast majority of retweets were made between users from the same cluster in both elections, being this behavior more pronounced in 2015 than in 2016. Comparing the parties involved in the coalition, we clearly observe that their interactions increased in 2016, as the (yellow) off-diagonal elements indicate. Interestingly, the interaction between ECP and the other members of the coalition is not symmetric. This fact may be explained again by linguistic reasons, since ECP users retweet both messages in Spanish and Catalan, but most users in Podemos and IU clusters only speak Spanish and therefore do not retweet ECP messages in Catalan. We conclude that, despite the coalition is not captured at the clustering level (parties within the coalition do not merge into a single cluster), *it is captured* at the level of the interactions between clusters, which increased remarkably in 2016.

3.2   Cluster Dynamics Between the Two Elections (RQ1)

We now analyze how the clusters change between campaigns. Table 5 shows some general indicators. We observe that all but a single cluster (ECP) shrink in the second campaign (negative balance), indicating a significant decrease in activity and suggesting an overall decrease in motivation. Another important observation is that all clusters lose more than half of the users they had in 2015. The cluster that loses less users is PSOE (62%) while the one that loose more is Podemos (nearly 80%). This illustrates the high variability between the users assigned to the clusters in both campaigns. Podemos has the highest negative balance among all clusters, losing 6 324 users. Notice that IU, although being apparently the most stable cluster, is actually the second one that lost more members. The balance is explained because it also gained many new users from other clusters. Looking at the joint clusters of Unidos Podemos (UP), we see that it suffers a higher loss than the parties not in the coalition (69.6% of UP vs 62%–66%), indicating that not all the users migrate within the parties of the coalition.

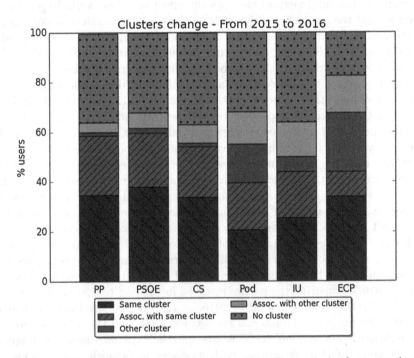

Fig. 2. Proportion of clustered users in 2015 who in 2016: remain in the *same cluster*; retweet mostly users from the same cluster (*associated with same cluster*); lie in an *other cluster*; retweet mostly users from another cluster (*associated with other cluster*); are not associated to any cluster (*no cluster*). (Color figure online)

To understand how users migrate between clusters, we apply the methodology described in Appendix A.2. Figure 2 shows the distribution of the different categories of users for each party cluster in 2015, providing a more detailed view of the (*lost*) users of Table 5 who correspond to the non dark-green regions in the figure. We analyze first the distributions of PP, PSOE and CS. They follow a similar pattern with around 35% of users remaining in the same cluster and around 25% of users associated with the same cluster. Despite losing the majority of users according to our clustering criteria, approximately 60% of their users do not change their support in 2016. The remaining ≈40% either do not have a cluster assigned in 2016 or by a small percentage migrated to other parties.

Regarding the UP clusters, Podemos has the smallest number of stable supporters (dark/light green) and ECP is the one with smallest proportion of users who do not fall in any cluster in 2016 (gray), which indicates that ECP users keep a high activity in the 2016 campaign. When viewed independently, Podemos, IU and ECP have a smaller proportion of users that stay in the same cluster or are associated to same cluster (dark/light green) than the other parties. However, when considered together in UP, this proportion increases and becomes comparable to the other parties. This suggests that migrations occur mostly within the clusters of the UP coalition. This is confirmed in Fig. 4, which shows the flow of clustered users between campaigns for the users clustered in both elections (either in the **same cluster** or in **another cluster**). It is noticeable that most of these users fall in the same party in both elections, indicating a strong political association. Clearly, Podemos is the cluster that suffers more changes, with a considerable amount of users that mostly migrate to IU and, to a lesser extent, to ECP. We do not see the same behavior in IU.

The following conclusions are extracted from the entire analysis on cluster changes: although the large variability observed initially in the compositions of the clusters, when the *associated* users are considered as well, the migration of parties is reduced, with exceptions within Unidos Podemos. It seems that users who actively participate in Twitter are usually very positioned towards one party and only retweet other parties very sporadically. In general, users that retweet the messages of a party tend to either keep supporting the same party, or stop participating actively in the campaign.

Unidos Podemos is the entity that loses more support from the first to the second election, as Table 5 and Figs. 2 and 4 show. The total balance between the two elections is negative and stronger than for the rest of the parties. However, when analyzing the nature of the cluster in 2016 and its changes in relation to 2015, this negative balance is not as high as expected from the electoral results (in relation to the other parties) and it does not seem to reflect the general demotivation which was interpreted from the electoral results. In Unidos Podemos, we have seen a strong migration of supporters from Podemos to IU, which did not happen in the opposite direction. The Spanish electoral law that favors bigger parties may have had an influence, pushing citizens closer to IU to vote and campaign for the bigger party Podemos in 2015.

3.3   Political Engagement (RQ2)

Twitter activity can be an indicator of political engagement. To characterize the activity of users in each cluster and in each election, we calculate the cumulative distribution function, or probability $P(X \leq x)$ that a user X retweets less than or x times, for those users that where present in both campaigns. Results are displayed for PP, PSOE, CS and Podemos in Fig. 3a. The solid curves (activity in 2016) lie above the dashed ones (activity in 2015), indicating a decrease of activity for all parties. These results confirm that political engagement decreased, perhaps due to the user fatigue after a long period of political activity.

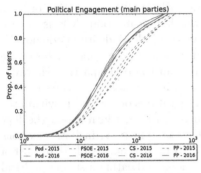
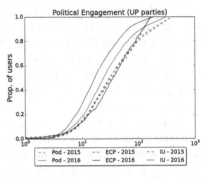

(a) Podemos, PP, PSOE and CS.   (b) UP clusters: Podemos, IU and ECP

Fig. 3. Cumulative distribution of the number of tweets per users who fall in the same party cluster in 2015 (dashed) and 2016 (continuous).

To analyze the engagement within the different parties that form the UP coalition, we break down the coalition and show in Fig. 3b the cumulative distribution functions for each UP cluster individually. First, we observe that all curves show a similar profile in 2015. However, in 2016 the picture changes. We observe that IU has much less activity than Podemos. Since our analysis includes the strongest supporters of the party only, a decrease in their activity suggests that those users might have been unhappy with the coalition and were demotivated during the second election. This result is in agreement with previous literature [20] and with the post-electoral study from Metroscopia [10], which reported that the UP coalition retained only three out of four Podemos voters (74%) and only six out of ten IU voters (60%). Moreover, the Catalan ECP shows the opposite effect than the rest of parties (it actually increases its activity in the second election), also in agreement with the electoral results in Catalonia, where Unidos Podemos lost fewer voters.

We can conclude that our proposed methodology that analyzes the activity distribution within the obtained clusters satisfactorily captures the observed behaviour with respect to engagement observed in the election.

4   Discussion

We have presented a methodology to analyze online Twitter campaigns based on several steps. First, we have used a robust community discovery method and matched automatically the user clusters across multiple executions of the Louvain method using the Jaccard coefficient. Second, we have proposed a characterization of the cluster composition dynamics in consecutive elections to reflect changes in party inclinations. Finally, we have analyzed political engagement by means of the Twitter activity distributions in the different clusters. Our proposed methodology can be seen as a refinement of similar approaches proposed recently for the analysis of online Twitter campaigns [2].

The analysis of user migration between party clusters (**RQ1**) reveals that several users have transitioned within the coalition. The results expose an important transfer of users associated to Podemos in the 2015 election to the cluster of Izquierda Unida in 2016. Those users might have been supporting the bigger party in the first election as a matter of utility when it came to getting representatives while actually feeling closer to the smaller party. The results also show a smaller proportion of users who remain in the UP clusters in 2016 compared to other parties, which may reflect the demotivation of its electorate, although this signal is weak compared to the large decrease in votes for UP.

Previous research has indicated how Twitter activity may be thought as an indicator of political engagement of the users [3,9,12]. Our study has also analyzed whether there is a relation between the motivation of the electorate and activity on Twitter (**RQ2**). Despite our analysis shows a lower activity in 2016 than in 2015 for all mayor parties, in line with the participation decrease, the results follow a very similar pattern for all parties although the electoral results were different for them. Moreover, the decrease in activity is not significantly higher for the users in the UP clusters, which lost the highest amount of votes. However our analysis reveled differences within the UP clusters, showing a much larger decay in activity for IU supporters. This may indicate that users strongly associated to IU were less appealed by the coalition, in agreement with existing studies [10,20].

Acknowledgments. This work is supported by the Spanish Ministry of Economy and Competitiveness under the María de Maeztu Units of Excellence Programme (MDM-2015-0502).

A   Methods

A.1   N-Louvain Method

The Louvian method [4] is widely used as a community detection algorithm because it is efficient and finds the correct clustering in certain types of networks. However, some care needs to be taken when applying this algorithm in our context. In particular, since the algorithm has a random component, different executions may typically produce different partitions for the same network.

To obtain robust results and find a reliable cluster assignment, we follow the method introduced in [2], which performs multiple executions of the Louvain algorithm and only considers nodes that fall almost all the times into the same cluster.

To identify each cluster across executions, we improve the previous method by applying the Jaccard index [13] to every pair of clusters c_i and c_j across different executions:

$$J(c_i, c_j) = \frac{|c_i \cap c_j|}{|c_i \cup c_j|}.$$

Thus, clusters across executions are matched if they are the most similar ones. This allows us to assess the proportion of times a node falls within the same cluster. Finally, the method assigns to each cluster all the nodes that appear in that cluster in at least a fraction $(1 - \varepsilon)$ of the partitions created, that is to say, ε represents the sensibility level of the algorithm ($\varepsilon = 0.05$ in this study). This procedure allows to validate the results of the community detection algorithm and to guarantee that all the nodes that are assigned to a cluster do actually belong to it with a given confidence. The remaining nodes, that cannot be assigned in a stable way to any of the main clusters, are left out from all the clusters.

A.2   Cluster Changes Between Networks

To characterize how users change between two consecutive networks, G_1 and G_2, we consider five possible categories, depending on how a user i that belongs to a cluster in G_1 is related to the clustering in G_2. Let $c_1(i)$ and $c_2(i)$ denote the cluster to which i belongs in G_1 and G_2, respectively. There are three main possible scenarios, either the user belongs to the same cluster in both networks,

1. $c_1(i) = c_2(i)$ (**Same cluster**),
2. it belongs to different clusters, $c_1(i) \neq c_2(i)$ (**Other cluster**),
3. or i does not fall robustly in any cluster of G_2. In this case, we can still assign a cluster to i depending on whether:
   (a) i retweeted users belonging to the same cluster $c_1(i)$ (we call this category **Associated with same cluster**), or
   (b) i retweeted users belonging to another cluster (**Associated with other cluster**).
   (c) Finally, if the level of activity of i does not reach the threshold to be included in G_2 (we only include interactions that occur at least three times), we assign i to the category **None**.

B   Supporting Information

Table 2. Twitter accounts of the selected political parties and candidates which were used to retrieve the datasets.

Party	Party account	Candidate account
PP	@PPopular	@marianorajoy
PSOE	@PSOE	@sanchezcastejon
Podemos	@ahorapodemos	@Pablo_Iglesias_
IU	@iunida	@agarzon
C's	@CiudadanosCs	@Albert_Rivera
En Comú Podem	@EnComu_Podem	@XavierDomenechs
Compromís	@compromis	@joanbaldovi
Equo	@Equo	@juralde
Marea-Anova-EU	@En_Marea	@tone_corunha
ERC-CATSÍ	@Esquerra_ERC	@gabrielrufian
DL	@ConvergenciaCAT	@franceschoms
EAJ-PNV	@eajpnv	@MikelLegarda
Bildu	@ehbildu	@ikerurbina1
CCa-PNC	@gnacionalista	@PabloRodriguezV

Table 3. Retweet network indicators for 2015 and 2016: number of retweets for the whole election (# tweets), number of nodes (N) and edges (E) in the network, clustering coefficient (cl) and average path length (ℓ).

Elections of	# tweets	N	E	cl	ℓ
2015	3 196 677	57 575	164 411	0.004	7.18
2016	1 602 528	72 269	168 135	0.0015	6.215

Table 4. Participation, percentage of obtained votes and parliament seats per party for the 2015 and 2016 elections. Pod+ stands for the sum of Podemos, En Comú Podem, En Marea, and Compromis. In 2016 IU is added to this sum as well.

Election	Participation	PP	PSOE	Pod+	IU	CS	Other
2015	69.67%	28.71%	22.01%	20.4%	3.68%	13.94%	11.26%
		123	90	69	2	40	26
2016	66.48%	33.01%	22.63%	20.79%		13.05%	10.52%
		137	85	71		32	25

Table 5. Main clusters per party. In columns: cluster sizes in 2015 and 2016, # of users present in the cluster in 2015 but not in 2016 (*lost*) and the corresponding percentage, # of users present in the cluster in 2016 but not in 2015 (*new*), difference (*balance*) between new and lost users. Last line (UP) is the sum of ECP, Podemos and IU

Cluster	size 2015	size 2016	*lost*		*new*	*balance*
CS	7 200	5 458	4 771	(66.3%)	3 029	−1 742
PP	8 345	5 613	5 446	(65.3%)	2 714	−2 732
PSOE	7 538	5 541	4 674	(62.0%)	2 677	−1 997
ECP	1 412	1 791	930	(65.9%)	1 309	379
Podemos	16 113	9 771	12 806	(79.5%)	6 464	−6 342
IU	10 439	10 313	7 792	(74.6%)	7 666	−126
UP	27 964	21 875	19 448	(69.6%)	13 359	**−6 089**

Fig. 4. Redistribution of cluster users: amount of users from a 2015 cluster (left) in the 2016 clusters (right). (Color figure online)

References

1. Aragón, P., Kappler, K.E., Kaltenbrunner, A., Laniado, D., Volkovich, Y.: Communication dynamics in Twitter during political campaigns: the case of the 2011 Spanish national election. Policy Internet **5**(2), 183–206 (2013)
2. Aragón, P., Volkovich, Y., Laniado, D., Kaltenbrunner, A.: When a movement becomes a party: computational assessment of new forms of political organization in social media. In: ICWSM 2016 - 10th International AAAI Conference on Web and Social Media. The AAAI Press (2016)
3. Bakker, T.P., De Vreese, C.H.: Good news for the future? Young people, internet use, and political participation. Commun. Res. **38**(4), 451–470 (2011)

4. Blondel, V.D., Guillaume, J.L., Lambiotte, R., Lefebvre, E.: Fast unfolding of communities in large networks. J. Stat. Mech. Theor. Exp. **2008**(10), P10008 (2008)
5. Caldarelli, G., Chessa, A., Pammolli, F., Pompa, G., Puliga, M., Riccaboni, M., Riotta, G.: A multi-level geographical study of Italian political elections from Twitter data. PloS One **9**(5), e95809 (2014)
6. Castells, M.: The new public sphere: global civil society, communication networks, and global governance. Ann. Am. Acad. Polit. Soc. Sci. **616**(1), 78–93 (2008)
7. Chung, J.E., Mustafaraj, E.: Can collective sentiment expressed on Twitter predict political elections? In: AAAI, vol. 11, pp. 1770–1771 (2011)
8. Conover, M., Ratkiewicz, J., Francisco, M., Gonçalves, B., Menczer, F., Flammini, A.: Political polarization on Twitter. In: ICWSM (2011)
9. Dimitrova, D.V., Shehata, A., Strömbäck, J., Nord, L.W.: The effects of digital media on political knowledge and participation in election campaigns: evidence from panel data. Commun. Res. **41**(1), 95–118 (2014)
10. Ferrándiz, J.P.: Fidelidades y fugas para explicar los resultados del 26j (2016). http://metroscopia.org/fidelidades-y-fugas-para-explicar-los-resultados-del-26j/. Accessed 10 June 2017
11. Gayo-Avello, D.: No, you cannot predict elections with Twitter. IEEE Internet Comput. **16**(6), 91–94 (2012)
12. Holt, K., Shehata, A., Strömbäck, J., Ljungberg, E.: Age and the effects of news media attention and social media use on political interest and participation: do social media function as leveller? Eur. J. Commun. **28**(1), 19–34 (2013)
13. Jaccard, P.: Etude comparative de la distribution florale dans une portion des Alpes et du Jura. Impr. Corbaz (1901)
14. Jungherr, A.: Twitter use in election campaigns: a systematic literature review. J. Inf. Technol. Politics **13**(1), 72–91 (2016)
15. Jungherr, A., Jürgens, P., Schoen, H.: Why the pirate party won the german election of 2009 or the trouble with predictions: a response to tumasjan, a., sprenger, to, sander, pg, & welpe, im "predicting elections with Twitter: What 140 characters reveal about political sentiment". Soc. Sci. Comput. Rev. **30**(2), 229–234 (2012)
16. Llaneras, K.: Qué votantes cambiaron su voto el 26-j (2016). http://politica.elpais.com/politica/2016/07/22/ratio/1469195845_977293.html. Accessed 10 June 2017
17. Metaxas, P.T., Mustafaraj, E.: Social media and the elections. Science **338**(6106), 472–473 (2012)
18. Orriols, L., Cordero, G.: The breakdown of the Spanish two-party system: the upsurge of Podemos and Ciudadanos in the 2015 general election. South European Society and Politics **21**(4), 469–492 (2016)
19. Peña-López, I., Congosto, M., Aragón, P.: Spanish Indignados and the evolution of the 15M movement on Twitter: towards networked para-institutions. J. Span. Cult. Stud. **15**(1–2), 189–216 (2014). http://dx.doi.org/10.1080/14636204.2014.931678
20. Simón, P.: The challenges of the new Spanish multipartism: government formation failure and the 2016 general election. South Eur. Soc. Polit. **21**(4), 493–517 (2016)
21. Tumasjan, A., Sprenger, T.O., Sandner, P.G., Welpe, I.M.: Predicting elections with Twitter: what 140 characters reveal about political sentiment. ICWSM **10**(1), 178–185 (2010)
22. Vergeer, M., Hermans, L.: Campaigning on Twitter: microblogging and online social networking as campaign tools in the 2010 general elections in the Netherlands. J. Comput. Mediated Commun. **18**(4), 399–419 (2013)

Beyond Item Recommendation: Using Recommendations to Stimulate Knowledge Sharing in Group Decisions

Müslüm Atas[✉], Alexander Felfernig, Martin Stettinger, and Thi Ngoc Trang Tran

Institute of Software Technology, Graz University of Technology, Inffeldgasse 16b/II, 8010 Graz, Austria
{muatas,afelfernig,mstettinger,ttrang}@ist.tugraz.at
http://ase.ist.tugraz.at/

Abstract. The intensity of domain knowledge exchange among group members is an important factor that directly influences group decision quality. The more frequent information is exchanged among group members, the higher the quality of the corresponding decision. In this paper we present results of an empirical study conducted with groups of students – the task of each group was to take a decision regarding the exam topics the group prefers. This group decision had to be taken on the basis of a group decision support environment with included recommendation functionality and a discussion forum that allows for information exchange among group members. Depending on the included variant of the group recommendation algorithm, groups received recommendations that varied in terms of recommendation diversity. The results of the study show that increased recommendation diversity leads to an increased degree of information exchange among group members.

Keywords: Group recommender systems · Group decision making · Decision quality · Information exchange

1 Introduction

Single user recommender systems focus on the recommendation of items to individuals [14,22]. In contrast, group recommender systems[1] determine item recommendations that fit the preferences of group members [12,18]. Table 1 provides an overview of example group recommendation environments. Jameson [13] introduces a prototype application that supports groups of users to elicit and aggregate user preferences with regard to holiday destinations. Masthoff [16] introduces concepts for television item sequencing for groups of users on

---

[1] The work presented in this paper has been conducted within the scope of the Horizon 2020 project OpenReq (Intelligent Recommendation & Decision Technologies for Community-Driven Requirements Engineering).

© Springer International Publishing AG 2017
G.L. Ciampaglia et al. (Eds.): SocInfo 2017, Part II, LNCS 10540, pp. 368–377, 2017.
DOI: 10.1007/978-3-319-67256-4_29

the basis of different models from social choice theory (see also [18]). O'Connor et al. [5] present a collaborative filtering based approach to movie recommendation that determines recommendations for groups of users. Ninaus et al. [10] demonstrate the application of group recommendation technologies in software requirements engineering scenarios where stakeholders are in charge of cooperatively developing, evaluating, and prioritizing requirements. Kudenko et al. [15] propose a system which helps a group of users while purchasing a product from an electronic catalog and mediates a group discussion with the goal to achieve consensus. McCarthy et al. [19] introduce a critiquing-based recommendation approach that supports groups of users in a skiing holiday package selection process. Finally, CHOICLA [25] is a group decision support environment which includes group recommendation technologies in a domain-independent fashion – related example application domains are personnel decisions and restaurant selection. For a detailed overview of existing group recommender applications we refer to Jameson and Smyth [12] and Boratto et al. [2].

Table 1. Example group recommender systems. For an in-depth discussion of group recommender applications we refer to [2,12]

System	Domain	Reference
TRAVEL DECISION FORUM	Tourist destinations	[13]
POLYLENS	Movies	[5]
INTELLIREQ	Software requirements	[10]
CATS	Ski holiday packages	[19]
CHOICLA	Domain-independent, e.g., personnel decisions	[25]

Also in the context of recommender systems, decision biases frequently occur and can lead to low-quality decisions [3,7,11]. Masthoff and Gatt [17] report possible approaches for the prediction of group member satisfaction with recommendations – in this context, *conformity* and *emotional contagion* are stated as major influence factors. Felfernig et al. [6] and Stettinger et al. [26] discuss the impact of *conformity* on group decision making and report an increasing diversity of the preferences of group members the later individual preferences are disclosed. Chen and Pu [4] show how emotional feedback of group members can be integrated in a music recommendation system. An outcome of their study is that emotional feedback can help to enhance the mutual awareness regarding the preferences of other group members.

Knowledge exchange between group members can have a major impact on decision quality [21]. The probability of discovering the relevant knowledge (knowledge of one group member not known to the other group members) to take a high-quality (if optimality criteria exist, also an optimal) decision increases with an increased frequency of information exchange between group members [27].

One possible reason for increased knowledge exchange between group members is *group diversity* (in terms of dimensions such as demographic and educational background). The higher the degree of diversity, the higher the probability of higher quality decision outcomes (measured, e.g., in terms of the degree of susceptibility to the framing effect [28]). Schulz-Hardt et al. [23] report the role of *dissent* in group decision making scenarios: the higher the dissent in initial phases of a group decision process, the higher the probability that the group manages to share the decision-relevant information. An initial study on selection criteria for preference aggregation in group decision making is reported in Felfernig et al. [8] – a major outcome is an observed shift from consensus-based strategies such as *average voting* to borderline strategies such as *least misery* in the case of high-involvement items such as apartments and financial services.

The major focus of our work is to analyze the impact of *recommendation diversity* on the frequency of information exchange between group members. We integrated different recommendation strategies with a varying degree of recommendation diversity into our group decision support environment [25] and analyzed the impact of recommendation diversity on knowledge interchange between users. The underlying idea is that too similar recommendations provide only a limited coverage of the whole item space (see, e.g., [20]) and increased diversity helps to introduce new alternatives and to trigger discussions/information exchange with regard to these alternatives.

In contrast to the mainstream in recommender systems research [14,22], we do not focus on improving the prediction quality of recommendation approaches. Our aim is to investigate possibilities to exploit recommendation technologies to foster intended behavior which can also be interpreted as a kind of persuasive technology. In group decision scenarios, it is often more important to increase the performance of the group and foster group members' information exchange, than predicting decisions that will be taken by the group. Based on this idea, we analyze the impact of recommendation diversity on the degree of knowledge exchange in a group. This paper (extended version of [9]) analyzes three different basic group recommendation heuristics (aggregation functions) (*min, avg,* and *max group distance*) with regard to their impact on the communication behavior (knowledge exchange) within a group.

The major contributions of this paper are the following. We show that recommendation diversity can help to increase the degree of information exchange in group decision making. Furthermore, a higher degree of information exchange also correlates with a higher preparedness to adapt initially articulated preferences. Finally, we discuss related open research issues.

The remainder of this paper is organized as follows. In Sect. 2 we introduce the different preference aggregation mechanisms used in our group recommendation approach that help to achieve different degrees of recommendation diversity. Thereafter, in Sect. 3 we introduce the hypotheses and present the results of our empirical study. In Sect. 4 we report open issues for future work. With Sect. 5 we conclude the paper.

2   Preference Aggregation Mechanisms

Different preference aggregation mechanisms were used in our study (see Sect. 3) that was conducted on the basis of our group decision support environment CHOICLA [25]. This system includes different group preference aggregation mechanisms from social choice theory [18] – GD_{min}, GD_{max} and GD_{avg} (see below) have been included for the purpose of the work presented in this paper. The mentioned aggregation mechanisms differ from each other especially with regard to the calculated diversity (see Formula 1). In this context, *diversity(d)* is interpreted in terms of the deviation of recommendations d (recommended evaluation of specific alternatives, i.e., exam modes) from the evaluations provided by individual group members (eval(u, s) where u is a user and s represents a specific alternative/item, e.g., an exam mode):

$$diversity(d) = \frac{\sum_{u \in Users} |eval(u, s) - d|}{\#Users} \tag{1}$$

The following group aggregation mechanisms were used within the scope of our study. First, the *minimum group distance* (GD_{min}) determines a rating d (rating scale [1..5]) that reflects the minimum distance to the individual preferences of the group members (see Formula 2). Consequently, Formula 2 implements a low-diversity recommendation approach that tries to take into account the initial preferences of group members.

$$GD_{min}(s) = arg \min_{d \in \{1..5\}} \left(\sum_{u \in Users} |eval(u, s) - d| \right) \tag{2}$$

Maximum group distance (GD_{max}) returns a rating d that represents the maximum distance to the preferences of individual group members (see Formula 3). Consequently, Formula 3 implements a high-diversity recommendation approach that often neglects the preferences of individual group members.

$$GD_{max}(s) = arg \max_{d \in \{1..5\}} \left(\sum_{u \in Users} |eval(u, s) - d| \right) \tag{3}$$

Finally, *average group distance* (GD_{avg}) represents a value between maximum and minimum group distance (see Formula 4) and thus can be considered as a compromise between minimum and maximum group distance.

$$GD_{avg}(s) = \frac{GD_{min}(s) + GD_{max}(s)}{2} \tag{4}$$

These aggregation functions were used as a basis for the user study discussed in the following section.

3 Empirical Analysis

Our user study on the impact of different aggregation functions on the preparedness of group members to exchange information has been conducted on the basis of the CHOICLA decision support environment [9,25]. A screenshot of the Android version of CHOICLA is depicted in Fig. 1. $N = 256$ computer science students (12% female, 88% male) participated in the study – all students were enrolled in a software engineering course (object-oriented analysis and design) and assigned to a group that had to implement a software within the scope of the course. Within the scope of our user study, each of these groups also had to choose a *preferred exam mode* for object-oriented analysis and design. An example of such an exam mode is: *1 theoretical question on State Charts (SC), 1 theoretical question on Sequence Diagrams (SD), and two practical exercises on Object-Relational Mapping (ORM)*.

All study participants were aware about the fact that there is no guarantee that the preferred exam mode will be taken into account in upcoming exams. The task of each group was to select a specific exam mode on the basis of the CHOICLA decision support environment. Figure 1 depicts example screenshots of the Android version of CHOICLA. The study participants had the chance to choose between $n = 15$ different exam modes which differ (1) in terms of the share of *practical exercises* (PE) and *theoretical questions* (TQ) and (2) in terms of the share of specific topics. For example, PE(2xSC, 2xORM) denotes an exam mode that includes only practical exercises (i.e., no theoretical questions) related to the topics of *state charts* (SC) and *object relational mapping* (ORM).

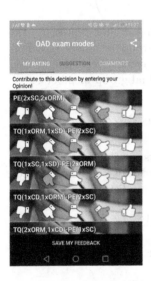
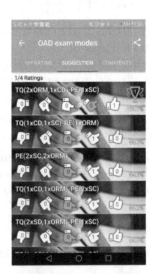

Fig. 1. CHOICLA group decision support environment [25] (Android version). Recommendations (suggestions) are determined on the basis of the different aggregation functions introduced in Sect. 2.

Within the scope of the study, each group member had to define his/her own preferences with regard to the available exam modes (see Fig. 1). Before a group member did not define his/her initial preferences, there was no possibility to see the preferences of the other group members (the underlying idea is to avoid anchoring biases that result from a too early preference disclosure [26]). On the basis of a short introductory statement before starting the decision process, study participants were encouraged to take a look at the group recommendations (tab *suggestion*) which was done by 91.41% of the participants at least once. An overview of the assignment of individual groups to specific CHOICLA versions that differ in terms of the used aggregation mechanism is depicted in Table 2.

Table 2. Assignment of preference aggregation mechanisms to groups.

Aggregation function	#groups	#participants
GD_{min}	17	92
GD_{avg}	12	69
GD_{max}	16	95
Total	45	256

The hypotheses analyzed within the scope of the empirical study were the following. H1: preference aggregation mechanisms with a higher resulting recommendation diversity increase the degree of knowledge exchange within a group. High-diversity recommendations can act as an anchor [1] and can also induce the feeling of dissent and a corresponding need to resolve the dissent. Increased knowledge exchange between group members can increase the probability of identifying the knowledge relevant for taking an optimal decision [21,27]. Examples of the different types of knowledge exchanged within the scope of a group decision processes are shown in Table 3. This table summarizes the total amount of messages exchanged between group members that can be assigned to one of the categories of *content-related*, *preference-related*, and *recommendation-related*. In the following we characterize these *categories* on the basis of related examples.

Content-related. A student only took a look at exercises related to a specific topic, e.g., *Object-relational Mapping (ORM)* and asks for further information regarding alternative topics. Another group member points out that there are only a few slides with very simple and understandable examples on the topic of state charts which are also very useful in industrial contexts.

Preference-related. A group member mentions that he/she prefers to include exercises related to the *Unified Process (UP)* compared to *State Charts (SC)*.

Recommendation-related. A participant does not like the group recommendation and he/she wants to discuss assignment topics that are more acceptable for the group as a whole.

Information units exchanged between group members were analyzed manually with regard to the three mentioned categories. In the context of recommendation-related information exchange, we evaluated the valence for recommendation-related comments, i.e., how positive/negative a recommendation was perceived.

H2: a higher degree of knowledge exchange provides more flexibility to change initial preferences afterwards. If more decision-relevant knowledge is exchanged between the members of a group, the amount of global decision-relevant knowledge is increased. This improves the individual capabilities of taking into account additional decision alternatives. Increased knowledge exchange between group members plays a key role to overcome a *discussion bias* (group discussions tend to be dominated by information group members already knew before the discussion [24]).

Hypothesis H1 can be confirmed, i.e., the degree of exchanged decision-relevant knowledge depends on the chosen aggregation function. The higher the diversity, the higher the number of exchanged decision-relevant knowledge (see Table 3). The number of the given comments for maximum group distance is highest (total number of comments for $GD_{max} = 278$, $GD_{avg} = 92$, $GD_{min} = 49$). Furthermore, also the overall time invested in taking a decision increases with the diversity of recommendations (see Table 4).

We can also confirm hypothesis H2. The flexibility of the group members to change their initial preference increases with the higher amount of knowledge exchange. Table 5 confirms hypothesis H2 which provides an overview of the changes of initial ratings depending on the supported aggregation mechanisms. The average degree of opinion adaptation of groups is highest with GD_{max}.

Table 3. Content-, preference-, recommendation-related comments (#comments, avg. #comments per group, and valence [−5 .. +5] (for recommendation-related comments)).

Function	Content		Preference		Recommendation		
	#comments	avg.	#comments	avg.	#comments	avg.	valence
GD_{min}	22	1.29	0	0	27	1.59	+4.2
GD_{avg}	31	2.58	26	2.16	35	2.92	+0.9
GD_{max}	79	4.93	91	5.69	108	6.75	−4.4

Table 4. Duration (endtime-starttime) and processing time (total time of system interaction) invested per group for decision task completion (i.e., rating of alternatives).

Function	Duration (h)		proc. time (min)	
	avg.	std.dev.	avg.	std.dev.
GD_{min}	71.06	13.05	210.71	20.19
GD_{avg}	85.64	26.58	234.56	17.67
GD_{max}	101.18	19.48	278.46	16.74

Table 5. Changes of initial ratings depending on included aggregation mechanism (difference between original rating and final rating).

Function	Degree of rating adaptation
GD_{min}	0.67
GD_{avg}	1.32
GD_{max}	2.46

Summarizing, the higher the diversity of preference aggregation, the higher the amount of knowledge exchange between group members. Thus, diverse group recommendations can help to increase the probability of identifying optimal solutions due to a higher probability of exchanging knowledge relevant for the optimal decision [23,24]. This can be considered as an important aspect to be taken into account by online decision support environments.

4 Future Work

A major focus will be the analysis of further aggregation mechanisms relevant in social choice scenarios [18]. Of major relevance in this context is to answer the question on the optimal degree of recommendation diversity that helps to optimize the parameters *degree of information exchange* and *perceived recommendation quality*. Tables 6 and 7 show that the satisfaction with group recommendations decreases with a higher degree of recommendation diversity.

Table 6. Diversity of group recommendations.

Function	GD_{min}	GD_{avg}	GD_{max}
Diversity	0.84	1.38	2.23

Table 7. Satisfaction with group recommendations.

Function	Very satisfied	Satisfied	Average	Unsatisfied	Very unsatisfied
GD_{min}	67	12	9	2	2
GD_{avg}	17	14	12	14	12
GD_{max}	2	1	15	25	52

5 Conclusions

This paper presents the results of an empirical study that focused on possibilities of increasing the amount of knowledge exchange in group decision scenarios. Thus, in contrast to the mainstream of recommender systems research, we focused on the application of recommendation technologies to improve decision processes per-se. The results of our empirical study show that recommendation diversity has an impact on the frequency of information exchange between group members – the higher the diversity, the more information is exchanged between group members. Furthermore, recommendations with a higher diversity can lead to an increased preparedness of changing initially defined preferences, i.e., these recommendations can be regarded as a mechanism to counteract discussion biases. We regard this work as a contribution to establish recommender systems as a core mechanism to improve the quality of group decision processes.

References

1. Adomavicius, G., Bockstedt, J., Curley, S., Zhang, J.: Recommender systems, consumer preferences, and anchoring effects. In: Decisions@RecSys2011 Workshop, Chicago, IL, USA, pp. 35–42. ACM (2011)
2. Boratto, L., Carta, S.: The rating prediction task in a group recommender system that automatically detects groups: architectures, algorithms, and performance evaluation. J. Intell. Inf. Syst. (JIIS) **45**(2), 221–245 (2015)
3. Chen, L., deGemmis, M., Felfernig, A., Lops, P., Ricci, F., Semeraro, G.: Human decision making and recommender systems. ACM Trans. Interact. Intell. Syst. **3**(3) (2013). Article no. 17
4. Chen, Y., Pu, P.: CoFeel: emotional social interface in group recommender systems. In: RecSys 2012 Workshop on Interfaces for Recommender Systems, Dublin, Ireland, pp. 48–55 (2012)
5. O'Connor, M., Cosley, D., Konstan, J., Riedl, J.: PolyLens: a recommmender system for groups of users. In: European Conference on Computer-Supported Cooperative Work, pp. 199–218. ACM (2001)
6. Felfernig, A., Zehentner, C., Ninaus, G., Grabner, H., Maalej, W., Pagano, D., Weninger, L., Reinfrank, F.: Group decision support for requirements negotiation. In: Ardissono, L., Kuflik, T. (eds.) UMAP 2011. LNCS, vol. 7138, pp. 105–116. Springer, Heidelberg (2012). doi:10.1007/978-3-642-28509-7_11
7. Felfernig, A.: Biases in decision making. In: International Workshop on Decision Making and Recommender Systems 2014, pp. 32–37. CEUR Proceedings (2014)
8. Felfernig, A., Atas, M., Tran, T.N.T., Stettinger, M., Erdeniz, S.P., Leitner, G.: An analysis of group recommendation heuristics for high- and low-involvement items. In: Benferhat, S., Tabia, K., Ali, M. (eds.) IEA/AIE 2017. LNCS (LNAI), vol. 10350, pp. 335–344. Springer, Cham (2017). doi:10.1007/978-3-319-60042-0_39
9. Felfernig, A., Stettinger, M., Leitner, G.: Fostering knowledge exchange using group recommendations. In: RecSys 2015 Workshop on Interfaces and Human Decision Making for Recommender Systems (IntRS 2015), Vienna, Austria (2015)
10. Ninaus, G., Felfernig, A., Stettinger, M., Reiterer, S., Leitner, G., Weninger, L., Schanil, W.: IntelliReq: intelligent techniques for software requirements engineering. In: European Conference on AI, Prestigious Applications of Intelligent Systems (PAIS) (2014)
11. Jameson, A., Willemsen, M.C., Felfernig, A., Gemmis, M., Lops, P., Semeraro, G., Chen, L.: Human decision making and recommender systems. In: Ricci, F., Rokach, L., Shapira, B. (eds.) Recommender Systems Handbook. LNCS (LNAI), pp. 611–648. Springer, Boston, MA (2015). doi:10.1007/978-1-4899-7637-6_18

12. Jameson, A., Smyth, B.: Recommendation to groups. In: Brusilovsky, P., Kobsa, A., Nejdl, W. (eds.) The Adaptive Web. LNCS, vol. 4321, pp. 596–627. Springer, Heidelberg (2007). doi:10.1007/978-3-540-72079-9_20
13. Jameson, A.: More than the sum of its members: challenges for group recommender systems. In: International Working Conference on Advanced Visual Interfaces, AVI 2004, Gallipoli (Lecce), Italy, pp. 48–54. ACM (2004)
14. Jannach, D., Zanker, M., Felfernig, A., Friedrich, G.: Recommender Systems: An Introduction. Cambridge University Press, New York (2010)
15. Kudenko, D., Bauer, M., Dengler, D.: Group decision making through mediated discussions. In: Brusilovsky, P., Corbett, A., Rosis, F. (eds.) UM 2003. LNCS (LNAI), vol. 2702, pp. 238–247. Springer, Heidelberg (2003). doi:10.1007/3-540-44963-9_32
16. Masthoff, J.: Group modeling: selecting a sequence of television items to suit a group of viewers. UMUAI 14(1), 37–85 (2004)
17. Masthoff, J., Gatt, A.: In pursuit of satisfaction and the prevention of embarrassment: affective state in group recommender systems. User Model. User-Adapted Interact. 16(3–4), 281–319 (2006). Springer
18. Masthoff, J.: Group Recommender Systems: Combining Individual Models. Recommender Systems Handbook, pp. 677–702 (2011)
19. McCarthy, K., Salamo, M., Coyle, L., McGinty, L., Smyth, B., Nixon, P.: Group Recommender Systems: A Critiquing based Approach. In: IUI 2006, pp. 267–269. ACM (2006)
20. McGinty, L., Smyth, B.: On the role of diversity in conversational recommender systems. In: Ashley, K.D., Bridge, D.G. (eds.) ICCBR 2003. LNCS (LNAI), vol. 2689, pp. 276–290. Springer, Heidelberg (2003). doi:10.1007/3-540-45006-8_23
21. Mojzisch, A., Schulz-Hardt, S.: Knowing other's preferences degrades the quality of group decisions. J. Personal. Soc. Psychol. 98, 794–808 (2010)
22. Ricci, F., Rokach, L., Shapira, B., Kantor, P.: Recommender Systems Handbook. Springer, New York (2011)
23. Schulz-Hardt, S., Brodbeck, F., Mojzisch, A., Kerschreiter, R., Frey, D.: Group decision making in hidden profile situations: dissent as a facilitator of decision quality. J. Personal. Soc. Psychol. 91, 1080–1093 (2006)
24. Stasser, G., Titus, W.: Pooling of unshared information in group decision making: biased information sharing during discussion. J. Personal. Soc. Psychol. 48, 1467–1478 (1985)
25. Stettinger, M., Felfernig, A., Leitner, G., Reiterer, S., Jeran, M.: Counteracting serial position effects in the CHOICLA group decision support environment. In: 20th ACM Conference on Intelligent User Interfaces (IUI 2015), pp. 148–157 (2015)
26. Stettinger, M., Felfernig, A., Leitner, G., Reiterer, S.: Counteracting anchoring effects in group decision making. In: Ricci, F., Bontcheva, K., Conlan, O., Lawless, S. (eds.) UMAP 2015. LNCS, vol. 9146, pp. 118–130. Springer, Cham (2015). doi:10.1007/978-3-319-20267-9_10
27. Wittenbaum, G., Hollingshead, A., Botero, I.: From cooperative to motivated information sharing in groups: moving beyond the hidden profile paradigm. In: Communication Monographs, pp. 286–310 (2004)
28. Yaniv, I.: Group diversity and decision quality: amplification and attenuation of the framing effect. Int. J. Forecast. 27, 41–49 (2011)

A Hierarchical Topic Modelling Approach for Tweet Clustering

Bo Wang[1](✉), Maria Liakata[1,2], Arkaitz Zubiaga[1], and Rob Procter[1,2]

[1] Department of Computer Science, University of Warwick, Coventry, UK
{bo.wang,m.liakata,a.zubiaga}@warwick.ac.uk
[2] The Alan Turing Institute, London, UK

Abstract. While social media platforms such as Twitter can provide rich and up-to-date information for a wide range of applications, manually digesting such large volumes of data is difficult and costly. Therefore it is important to automatically infer coherent and discriminative topics from tweets. Conventional topic models and document clustering approaches fail to achieve good results due to the noisy and sparse nature of tweets. In this paper, we explore various ways of tackling this challenge and finally propose a two-stage hierarchical topic modelling system that is efficient and effective in alleviating the data sparsity problem. We present an extensive evaluation on two datasets, and report our proposed system achieving the best performance in both document clustering performance and topic coherence.

Keywords: Tweet clustering · Topic model · Twitter topic detection · Social media

1 Introduction

In recent years social media platforms are increasingly being used as data sources to collect all kinds of updates posted by people. Updates that are of interest range from journalistic information that news practitioners can utilise for news gathering and reporting [14,25], as well as opinions expressed by people towards a broad range of topics. While social media is a rich resource to shed light on public opinion and to track newsworthy stories ranging from political campaigns to terrorist attacks, it is often difficult for humans to keep track of all the relevant information provided the large volumes of data. Automatic identification of topics can help to produce a manageable list that is easier to digest for users, enabling for instance identification of real-world events among those topics.

In contrast to the well-studied task of Topic Detection and Tracking [2], which is concerned with topic detection from newswire articles, detecting topics in social media such as Twitter poses the challenges of dealing with unmoderated, user-generated content. This presents caveats such as inconsistent vocabulary across different users as well as the brevity of microposts that often lack sufficient context. As a consequence, traditional document clustering approaches using

© Springer International Publishing AG 2017
G.L. Ciampaglia et al. (Eds.): SocInfo 2017, Part II, LNCS 10540, pp. 378–390, 2017.
DOI: 10.1007/978-3-319-67256-4_30

bag-of-words representation and topic models relying on word co-occurrence fall short of achieving competitive performance.

Recently a number of studies have employed various topic modelling approaches to tweets [26, 30, 36, 38], reporting mixed results and proving it to be a challenging task. In this work, we are motivated to effectively group tweets to a number of clusters, with each cluster representing a topic, story or event. Specifically, we propose a two-stage hierarchical topic modelling system shown in Fig. 1, which: (1) uses a collapsed Gibbs Sampling algorithm for the Dirichlet Multinomial Mixture model (GSDMM) [38] for tweet clustering; (2) aggregates each tweet cluster to form a virtual document; (3) applies the second stage of topic modelling to the virtual documents but this time incorporates word embeddings as latent features (LFLDA) [26]. This not only alleviates the noisy nature of tweets but also generates meaningful and interpretable topics. Finally we conduct extensive evaluation on two datasets, using clustering evaluation metrics as well as topic model quality metrics. We compare our proposed approaches with other clustering-based methods and topic models, reporting the best scores in both clustering performance and topic coherence.

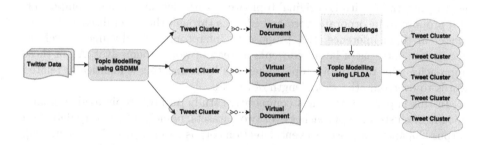

Fig. 1. Overview of the proposed topic modelling system

2 Related Work

Conventional topic models such as Latent Dirichlet Allocation (LDA) [6] have shown great success in various Natural Language Processing (NLP) tasks for discovering the latent topics that occur in long and structured text documents. Due to the limited word co-occurrence information in short texts, conventional topic models perform much worse for social media microposts such as tweets as demonstrated by Rosa et al. [32]. In this section we review the recent developments on Twitter topic modelling and how to tackle the sparse and noisy nature of tweets.

Earlier studies try to utilise external knowledge such as Wikipedia [30] to improve topic modelling on short texts. This requires a large text corpus which may have a domain issue for the task at hand. Since then four approaches have been studied in the literature to adapt conventional topic models for short texts such as tweets:

(1) Directly model the generation of word co-occurrence pattern (i.e. biterms) as demonstrated by Yan et al. [37]. However, such word co-occurrence information is still limited to the 140 characters of each tweet.

(2) Apply a document pooling strategy, to aggregate tweets to a number of virtual documents, based on authors [36], hashtags [21], conversation [3] or other metadata [11] such as timestamps and named entities. This strategy helps to overcome the limited context information in tweets, but pooling by such metadata can potentially have adverse effect on the subsequent topic modelling.

(3) [27] proposed a simple topic model, named Dirichlet Multinomial Mixture (DMM) model, based on the assumption that each document is sampled from one single latent topic. The DMM model has since then been used in many Twitter topic modelling studies for alleviating the data sparsity problem and reported to give more coherent topics [18,31,38,40], given that its underlying assumption is reasonable for short texts.

(4) Complement topic models which use the global word collocation patterns in the same document/tweet, with word embeddings that exploit the local word collocation patterns within a context window. [26] extend LDA and DMM to incorporate word embeddings as latent features. Such latent feature component is integrated with its original topic-word Dirichlet multinomial component. [18] propose to incorporate word embeddings through the generalised *Pólya urn* model in topic inference. [12] propose to infer topics via document-level co-occurrence patterns of latent concepts instead of words themselves. All of these approaches aim to improve topic coherence by connecting semantically related words to overcome the short length of tweets.

In this paper, we present a comparative study on both topic modelling and document clustering approaches over two datasets, namely a first story detection corpus [29] and a large-scale event detection corpus covering over 500 events [20]. Our proposed two-stage topic modelling system adopts three of the four strategies mentioned above, achieving not only the best performance measured in document clustering metrics but also topic coherence for its generated topics.

3   Methodology

In recent years we have witnessed various topic modelling studies tackling the challenge of clustering tweets into topics using several different strategies, and yet it is still proven to be a difficult task to solve. Inspired by the two-stage online-offline approach in Twitter event detection studies [5,39], we propose a two-stage hierarchical topic modelling system consisting of two state-of-the-art topic models, namely GSDMM [38] and LFLDA [26], with a tweet-pooling step streamlining the whole clustering process.

In the collapsed Gibbs Sampling algorithm for the Dirichlet Multinomial Mixture model [39] (GSDMM), the probability of a document belonging to a cluster is proportional to the cluster size and the frequency of each word of the document in the cluster. More specifically after the initialisation step where documents are randomly assigned to K clusters, at each iteration it uses three count variables to record the information of each cluster: n_z^w which is the frequency of word w in cluster z, n_z which is the number of words in cluster z and m_z which is the number of documents in cluster z. Given its proven record on clustering tweets, we use GSDMM as the first stage of topic modelling and set K to be a very large number which allows GSDMM to automatically infer the final number of clusters.

As shown in Fig. 1, we then assign every tweet to its corresponding cluster and aggregate each cluster to form a virtual document that consists of every tweet in that cluster. This pooling step is very similar to previous work [3,21,36], with the difference that it does not use any metadata which may not be available always (e.g. not every tweet mentions a hashtag or named entity).

Finally we apply the second stage of topic modelling to the previously generated virtual documents. Here we are motivated to take advantage of word embeddings [22] which have been shown to perform well in various NLP tasks, and combine it with topic models. [26] achieves this by replacing its topic-term multinomial distribution with a two-component mixture of a Dirichlet multinomial component and a word embedding component. We choose the better performing LFLDA model for our second-stage of topic modelling. Thus each tweet is assigned a topic with the highest topic proportion[1] given the virtual document cluster that it is in.

4   Datasets

We compare our proposed system with aforementioned approaches on two datasets, with different characteristics that help us generalise our results to different topic modelling tasks:

- A first story detection (FSD) corpus [29] collected from the beginning of July to mid-September 2011, containing 2204 tweets with each tweet annotated as one of 27 real-world stories such as "Death of Amy Winehouse" and "Terrorist attack in Delhi". It has some overlap of stories as well, e.g. four of the stories are related to the London riots in 2011, makes it also applicable to the task of sub-story detection.
- A large-scale event detection (ED) corpus [20], collected during October and November of 2012. Using Wikipedia and crowdsourcing as well as event detection methods [1,28], it generated 150,000 tweets over 28 days covering more than 500 events. Each event label represents a specific topic or story line, e.g. "British prime minister David Cameron and Scottish first minister Alex Salmond agree a deal". After retrieving 78,138 tweets we decide to use the first five days of data for evaluation, resulting in five sets of *tweets/labels*: *3330/32, 2083/41, 6234/48, 2038/36 and 3468/43.*

---

[1] Topic proportion: the proportion of words in document d that are assigned to topic t or the topic probabilities of a document, i.e. $p(t|d)$.

5   Evaluation

Experiments are conducted in two tasks. Moreover, document clustering metrics as well as topic model quality metrics are used for evaluation.

5.1   Experimental Setup

Compared Methods: Both topic modelling and document clustering methods are evaluated. The topic modelling methods are:

- **OLDA** [10]: An online variational Bayes (VB) algorithm for LDA, based on online stochastic optimisation.
- **TOLDA** [16]: An online version of LDA specific for tracking trends on Twitter over time. Due to the limitation of the FSD corpus, this method is only evaluated in the event detection data [20].
- **GSDMM** [38]: A collapsed Gibbs Sampling algorithm for the Dirichlet Multinomial Mixture (DMM) model, proven to work well for short texts.
- **LFTM** [26]: Consists of two models: **LFLDA** and LFDMM. We select the better performing LFLDA [12,19] to evaluate, which LFLDA is an extension of LDA by incorporating word embeddings.
- **LCTM** [12]: A latent concept topic model, where each latent concept is a localised Gaussian distribution over the word embedding space.

For the above models we assign the topic with the highest topic proportion to each tweet.

As for document clustering baseline methods, we use the learnt topic proportion from the above topic models as feature for each tweet and apply a clustering algorithm, e.g. **OLDA + HC**. Additionally, we also evaluate a tweet clustering approach [35] that uses character-based tweet embeddings (i.e. Tweet2Vec [8]) and outperforms the winner [13] of the 2014 SNOW breaking news detection competition[23] which was defined as a topic detection task. This method was named as **Tweet2Vec + HC**. All document clustering baselines employ a hierarchical agglomerative clustering algorithm as it is proven to be effective in [35].

The same preprocessing steps are applied to all methods to reduce the noise level. This includes removing hashtag symbols, URL links, user mention symbols and punctuation as well as lower-casing and the tokenisation of each tweet.

Experimental settings: GSDMM infers the number of clusters automatically based on a pre-defined upper bound, we set this initial number to 100 (which is a large number comparing to the true number of clusters). For all other topic models including the ones in our proposed system we set the number of topics, $K = 100$, even if they are in the second stage of topic modelling. We use *GloVe*[4] word embedding representation for **LFTM** and **LCTM**.

---

[2] http://www.snow-workshop.org/2017/challenge/.

[3] Their data is not evaluated due to its lack of annotated tweets.

[4] https://nlp.stanford.edu/projects/glove/.

For **LFTM** we empirically set $\beta = 0.2$, $\lambda = 0.6$ for processing tweets; and $\beta = 0.1$, $\lambda = 0.6$ for virtual documents in the second stage of topic modelling. The number of latent concepts S in **LCTM** is set to 500. The number of iterations in **GSDMM** is set to 100. Other parameters are kept to their default settings.

For **Tweet2Vec + HC** we directly use the Tweet2Vec model from [35] trained using 88,148 tweets, also the same hierarchical clustering algorithm implementation from *fast-cluster* library [23]. Hierarchical clustering requires to choose a distance metric, linkage method and criterion in forming flat clusters. We evaluate the performance of different linkage methods and a wide range of distance metrics, using the Cophenetic Correlation Coefficient (CPCC) [34] and pick the best performing combination. The mean Silhouette Coefficient [33], a cluster validity index, was found to be the most effective among 30 validity indices for measuring the quality of the produced clusters [4]. To avoid using the ground truth labels, we select the optimal criterion and distance threshold according to the Silhouette score in a grid-search set-up. This way we make sure our comparisons are reasonable and unbiased.

5.2 Tweet Clustering Evaluation

With topic models, we can represent each tweet with its topic distribution $p(topic|tweet)$. Hence we can evaluate the performance of each topic model on a document clustering task, by using the topic proportion directly as the final cluster assignment or indirectly as feature representations for a further round of clustering or topic modelling. We then compare the resulting clusters to the true cluster labels in two datasets. Normalised Mutual Information (NMI) is widely used for measuring the overlap between the cluster assignments and the ground truth labels. It ranges from 0.0 (worst) to 1.0 (best). We select NMI as our clustering evaluation metric.

Table 1 presents the performance of the different methods on both datasets. Among the standalone topic models, GSDMM consistently outperforms other methods except for day-2 of the event detection (ED) corpus where it is beaten by OLDA by a small margin. OLDA showing surprisingly good performance across the board, credits to the online nature of its optimisation. The models that incorporate word embeddings, namely LFLDA and LCTM, show inconsistent performance over the two datasets. Different to what is reported in [12], we found that LCTM performs worse than LFLDA in half of the cases[5], potentially caused by the noisy nature of tweets and its adverse effect on constructing latent concepts. In general the two online models perform reasonably well for this task. As for Twitter Online LDA (TOLDA), interestingly we observe it performs worse than OLDA on the ED corpus, due to the large number of clusters it assigns to the tweets.

We observe mixed results by employing hierarchical clustering using topic proportions as features. In many cases it is showing to give almost equivalent

---

[5] We have also evaluated LCTM with number of concepts setting to 600 and 1000, however we observed little difference in the performance.

Table 1. Document clustering performance (NMI only) on both datasets

Model	FSD		Day-1		Day-2		Day-3		Day-4		Day-5	
	N	NMI	N	NMI	N	NMI	N	NMI	N	NMI	N	NMI
OLDA	51	0.778	58	0.837	45	0.863	73	0.539	55	0.680	55	0.675
TOLDA			100	0.740	100	0.761	100	0.537	100	0.655	100	0.639
GSDMM	45	0.878	46	0.858	53	0.850	53	0.676	51	0.745	42	0.786
LFLDA	92	0.801	95	0.764	89	0.818	100	0.506	98	0.610	99	0.596
LCTM	93	0.721	94	0.726	83	0.804	100	0.512	99	0.632	97	0.617
OLDA + HC	42	0.799	39	0.828	40	0.859	64	0.529	45	0.684	49	0.669
TOLDA + HC			99	0.740	100	0.760	100	0.539	100	0.656	100	0.641
GSDMM + HC	45	0.878	46	0.859	53	0.851	53	0.677	51	0.745	94	0.771
LFLDA + HC	53	0.812	65	0.777	37	0.797	72	0.501	51	0.605	52	0.593
LCTM + HC	90	0.740	66	0.769	80	0.831	9	0.142	8	0.238	10	0.386
Tweet2Vec + HC	713	0.526	805	0.553	684	0.626	331	0.403	677	0.543	832	0.473
TOLDA + OLDA			32	0.819	34	0.847	35	0.613	38	0.696	35	0.755
TOLDA + LFLDA			48	0.814	46	0.845	40	0.577	41	0.706	35	0.718
TOLDA + LCTM			45	0.812	35	0.856	41	0.544	43	0.692	40	0.692
GSDMM + OLDA	36	0.891	26	0.870	34	0.872	38	0.694	25	**0.816**	26	0.793
GSDMM + LFLDA	30	**0.926**	28	**0.871**	29	**0.882**	34	**0.695**	27	0.773	22	**0.812**
GSDMM + LCTM	32	0.912	41	0.861	39	0.860	43	0.663	39	0.765	35	0.789

performance than using any topic model alone. This shows by simply using topic proportion as features for clustering is not a promising approach. We also observe by using Tweet2Vec neural embeddings with HC, it generates large number of clusters and thus very poor result.

Our two-stage topic modelling methods have shown to be rather effective in improving clustering performance, as only in 2 out of the 33 cases we have seen performance drop when comparing to either one of the topic models employed by the method (i.e. TOLDA + OLDA performs worse than OLDA at day-1 and day-2). This shows the promising result of using our proposed hierarchical topic modelling process with a pooling step. The proposed GSDMM + LFLDA proved to achieve consistent best performance over different datasets except at day-4 of the ED corpus it is beaten by GSDMM + OLDA.

5.3   Topic Coherence Evaluation

Here we examine the quality of our hierarchical topic modelling system by the topic coherence metric. Such metric measures to what extent the top topic words, or the words that have high probability in each topic are semantically coherent [7]. This includes using word intrusion [7], Pointwise Mutual Information (PMI) [24] and Normalised PMI (NPMI) [17]. We adopt the word embedding-based topic coherence metric, proposed in [9], which is shown to have a high agreement with humans and are more robust than the PMI-based metrics for tweets. In this paper we use two pre-trained word embedding models

Table 2. Averaged topic coherence for both corpora

Model	Topic coherence			
	FSD		Event detection	
	G-T-WE	W-T-WE	G-T-WE	W-T-WE
OLDA	0.217	0.123	0.302	0.135
TOLDA			0.329	0.141
GSDMM	0.277	0.121	0.363	0.132
TOLDA + OLDA			0.349	**0.154**
TOLDA + LFLDA			0.371	0.137
GSDMM + OLDA	0.282	0.142	0.349	0.150
GSDMM + LFLDA	**0.315**	**0.144**	**0.385**	0.142

learnt from Twitter data[6], resulting in two metrics G-T-WE (GloVe) and W-T-WE (Word2Vec). We also adopt the approach in [15], computing coherence for top-5/10/15/20 words and then take the mean over the 4 values.

For the ED corpus, we average all the results over the 5-day period for each model. As shown in Table 2, GSDMM + LFLDA achieves the best topic coherence in 3 out of 4 cases, with TOLDA + OLDA outperforming the others for W-T-WE on the ED data. When we compare the the two-stage topic modelling approach (i.e. TOLDA+* or GSDMM+*) to its respective topic model used in the first stage (i.e. TOLDA or GSDMM), we observe in 10 out of 12 cases its topic coherence has improved. Though our results for coherence are not perfect, it is demonstrated the usefulness of aggregating first round tweet clusters into virtual documents without the use of any metadata and then performing second round of topic modelling. As a result it is able to create not only more discriminative but also more coherent clusters.

5.4 Qualitative Evaluation of Topics

We also present a set of randomly selected example topics generated by the proposed system, GSDMM + LFLDA, on both data sets. Due to the limited space, these example topics are shown in Tables 3 and 4 of the Appendix.

6 Conclusions and Future Work

Inferring topics in tweets is hard due to the short and noisy nature of tweets. In this paper we proposed a two-stage hierarchical topic modelling system, named GSDMM + LFLDA, that leverages a state-of-the-art Twitter topic model, a topic model with word embeddings incorporated and a tweet pooling step without the

---

[6] The GloVe model was trained using 2 billion tweets while the Word2Vec model was trained on 5 million tweets using the skip-gram algorithm.

use of metadata in any form. We performed extensive experiments on two Twitter corpora. The experimental results show our proposed approach outperforms other clustering-based methods and topic models, in both clustering performance and topic coherence.

For future work, we plan to evaluate our system in tracking the same set of topics across adjacent time intervals, which is a different task to document clustering and topic detection.

Acknowledgments. This work is partly supported by The Alan Turing Institute. We would also like to thank Anjie Fang, Dat Quoc Nguyen, Jey Han Lau, Svitlana Vakulenko and Weihua Hu for answering questions regarding their work, respectively.

Appendix

We present a set of randomly selected example topics generated by GSDMM + LFLDA, on both the first story detection (FSD) corpus and the first day of the event detection (ED) corpus, as seen in Tables 3 and 4. Each detected topic is

Table 3. Example topics detected on FSD corpus

Detected topic	Corresponding topic description	Sample tweet
Amy winehouse rip amywinehouse die dead sad dy talent drug	Death of Amy Winehouse	Jesus, amy winehouse found dead. v sad #winehouse
Tottenham riot police news fire shoot car london north thur	Riots break out in Tottenham	RT @itv_news: Police cars set on fire in Tottenham, north London, after riots connected To the shooting of a young man by police on Thur ...
Mars water nasa flow found evidence may scientist saltwater liquid	NASA announces discovery of water on Mars	RT @CalebHowe: NASA reporting live right now that they have circumstantial evidence for flowing, liquid water on Mars.
House debt bill pass us vote ceiling the representatives raise	US increases debt ceiling	RT @politico: On Monday evening the House passed a bill to raise the debt ceiling, 269 to 161.
Delhi high blast court outside injured explosion attack kill bomb	Terrorist attack in Delhi	Bomb Blast outside of High Court Delhi just few minutes ago. http://t.co/MejKWlC
Pipeline fire kenya least kenyans people gasoline kill dead lunga	Petrol pipeline explosion in Kenya	RT @AKenyanGirl: RT @CapitalFM_kenya: Dozens suffer burns in Kenya #Pipeline fire in Lunga Lunga, Nairobi. Firefighters battling inferno ...

presented with its top-10 topic words, and is matched with the corresponding topic description or story from the ground truth (given by the creators of these data sets), as well as a sample tweet retrieved using the topic keywords.

As shown in Tables 3 and 4, words in obtained topics are mostly coherent and well aligned with a ground-truth topic description. We can also discover more useful information with regard to the corresponding real-world story, by simply looking at its topic words. For example, in the first topic of Table 3 we see the Twittersphere has mentioned 'Amy Winehouse' and 'death' along with the word 'drug'. This information may have been missed if one only chooses to read a set of randomly sampled tweets mentioning 'Amy Winehouse'.

Table 4. Example topics detected on ED corpus - day one

Detected topic	Corresponding topic description	Sample tweet
Merkel angela greece visit athens merkels greek chancellor protests protest	An estimated 25,000 protest in Athens as German Chancellor Angela Merkel visits Greece	Thousands protest merkel s greece visit http://t.co/sXGTX3jE
Syrian plane turkey passenger turkish land ankara force syria intercepts	A Syrian passenger plane is forced by Turkish fighter jets to land in Ankara due to the allegations of carrying weapons	BreakingNews: Turkish fighter jets force Syrian passenger plane to land in Ankara: Anadolu Agency
Malala yousafzai taliban activist pakistan shot girl attack bullet shooting	Malala Yousafzai, a 14 year old activist for women's education rights is shot by Taliban gunmen in the Swat Valley	Taliban Says It Shot Pakistani Teen, Malala Yousafzai, For Advocating Girls Rights... http://t.co/EjFR5in4
Lenovo hp pc top market battle spot computerworld gartner shipments	HP and Lenovo battle for top spot in PC market of Computerworld	HP, Lenovo battle for top spot in PC market - Computerworld http://t.co/zwzPdN8Q# googlenews
Merger eads bae systems aerospace plans talks cancel defence firms	BAE and EADS announce their merger talks are cancelled over political disagreements	BAE-EADS merger plans are 'off': Aerospace and defence firms BAE and EADS have cancelled their planned merger, t... http://t.co/UYFOiysX
Pussy riot court appeal moscow member one freed russian punk	A court in Moscow, Russia, frees one of the three Pussy Riot members at an appeal hearing	One Pussy Riot Member Freed by Moscow Court — News — The Moscow Times http://t.co/m60lwaWU# FreePussyRiot

References

1. Aggarwal, C.C., Subbian, K.: Event detection in social streams. In: Proceedings of the 2012 SIAM International Conference on Data Mining, pp. 624–635. SIAM (2012)
2. Allan, J.: Topic Detection and Tracking: Event-based Information Organization, vol. 12. Springer Science & Business Media (2012)
3. Alvarez-Melis, D., Saveski, M.: Topic modeling in twitter: aggregating tweets by conversations. In: ICWSM, pp. 519–522 (2016)
4. Arbelaitz, O., Gurrutxaga, I., Muguerza, J., Pérez, J.M., Perona, I.: An extensive comparative study of cluster validity indices. Pattern Recogn. **46**(1), 243–256 (2013)
5. Becker, H., Naaman, M., Gravano, L.: Beyond trending topics: real-world event identification on twitter. In: ICWSM 2011, pp. 438–441 (2011)
6. Blei, D.M., Ng, A.Y., Jordan, M.I.: Latent dirichlet allocation. J. Mach. Learn. Res. **3**, 993–1022 (2003)
7. Chang, J., Gerrish, S., Wang, C., Boyd-Graber, J.L., Blei, D.M.: Reading tea leaves: how humans interpret topic models. In: Advances in Neural Information Processing Systems, pp. 288–296 (2009)
8. Dhingra, B., Zhou, Z., Fitzpatrick, D., Muehl, M., Cohen, W.W.: Tweet2vec: character-based distributed representations for social media. In: The 54th Annual Meeting of the Association for Computational Linguistics, p. 269 (2016)
9. Fang, A., Macdonald, C., Ounis, I., Habel, P.: Using word embedding to evaluate the coherence of topics from twitter data. In: Proceedings of the 39th International ACM SIGIR Conference on Research and Development in Information Retrieval, pp. 1057–1060. ACM (2016)
10. Hoffman, M., Bach, F.R., Blei, D.M.: Online learning for latent dirichlet allocation. In: Advances in Neural Information Processing Systems, pp. 856–864 (2010)
11. Hong, L., Davison, B.D.: Empirical study of topic modeling in twitter. In: Proceedings of the First Workshop on Social Media Analytics, pp. 80–88. ACM (2010)
12. Hu, W., Tsujii, J.: A latent concept topic model for robust topic inference using word embeddings. In: The 54th Annual Meeting of the Association for Computational Linguistics, p. 380 (2016)
13. Ifrim, G., Shi, B., Brigadir, I.: Event detection in twitter using aggressive filtering and hierarchical tweet clustering. In: Second Workshop on Social News on the Web (SNOW), Seoul, Korea, vol. 8. ACM, April 2014
14. Jordaan, M.: Poke me, i'm a journalist: the impact of facebook and twitter on newsroom routines and cultures at two south african weeklies. Ecquid Novi: African Journalism Stud. **34**(1), 21–35 (2013)
15. Lau, J.H., Baldwin, T.: The sensitivity of topic coherence evaluation to topic cardinality. In: Proceedings of NAACL-HLT, pp. 483–487 (2016)
16. Lau, J.H., Collier, N., Baldwin, T.: On-line trend analysis with topic models: \# twitter trends detection topic model online. In: COLING, pp. 1519–1534 (2012)
17. Lau, J.H., Newman, D., Baldwin, T.: Machine reading tea leaves: automatically evaluating topic coherence and topic model quality. In: EACL, pp. 530–539 (2014)
18. Li, C., Wang, H., Zhang, Z., Sun, A., Ma, Z.: Topic modeling for short texts with auxiliary word embeddings. In: Proceedings of the 39th International ACM SIGIR Conference on Research and Development in Information Retrieval, pp. 165–174. ACM (2016)

19. Li, S., Chua, T.S., Zhu, J., Miao, C.: Generative topic embedding: a continuous representation of documents. In: Proceedings of The 54th Annual Meeting of the Association for Computational Linguistics (ACL) (2016)
20. McMinn, A.J., Moshfeghi, Y., Jose, J.M.: Building a large-scale corpus for evaluating event detection on twitter. In: Proceedings of the 22nd ACM International Conference on Information & Knowledge Management, pp. 409–418. ACM (2013)
21. Mehrotra, R., Sanner, S., Buntine, W., Xie, L.: Improving lda topic models for microblogs via tweet pooling and automatic labeling. In: Proceedings of the 36th International ACM SIGIR Conference on Research and Development in Information Retrieval, pp. 889–892. ACM (2013)
22. Mikolov, T., Sutskever, I., Chen, K., Corrado, G.S., Dean, J.: Distributed representations of words and phrases and their compositionality. In: Advances in Neural Information Processing Systems, pp. 3111–3119 (2013)
23. Müllner, D., et al.: fastcluster: Fast hierarchical, agglomerative clustering routines for R and python. J. Stat. Softw. 53(9), 1–18 (2013)
24. Newman, D., Lau, J.H., Grieser, K., Baldwin, T.: Automatic evaluation of topic coherence. In: Human Language Technologies: The 2010 Annual Conference of the North American Chapter of the Association for Computational Linguistics, pp. 100–108. Association for Computational Linguistics (2010)
25. Newman, N.: The rise of social media and its impact on mainstream journalism (2009)
26. Nguyen, D.Q., Billingsley, R., Du, L., Johnson, M.: Improving topic models with latent feature word representations. Trans. Assoc. Computat. Linguist. 3, 299–313 (2015)
27. Nigam, K., McCallum, A.K., Thrun, S., Mitchell, T.: Text classification from labeled and unlabeled documents using EM. Mach. Learn. 39(2), 103–134 (2000)
28. Petrović, S., Osborne, M., Lavrenko, V.: Streaming first story detection with application to twitter. In: Human Language Technologies: The 2010 Annual Conference of the North American Chapter of the Association for Computational Linguistics, pp. 181–189. Association for Computational Linguistics (2010)
29. Petrović, S., Osborne, M., Lavrenko, V.: Using paraphrases for improving first story detection in news and twitter. In: Proceedings of the 2012 Conference of the North American Chapter of the Association for Computational Linguistics: Human Language Technologies, pp. 338–346. Association for Computational Linguistics (2012)
30. Phan, X.H., Nguyen, L.M., Horiguchi, S.: Learning to classify short and sparse text & web with hidden topics from large-scale data collections. In: Proceedings of the 17th International Conference on World Wide Web, pp. 91–100. ACM (2008)
31. Quan, X., Kit, C., Ge, Y., Pan, S.J.: Short and sparse text topic modeling via self-aggregation. In: IJCAI, pp. 2270–2276 (2015)
32. Rosa, K.D., Shah, R., Lin, B., Gershman, A., Frederking, R.: Topical clustering of tweets. In: Proceedings of the ACM SIGIR: SWSM (2011)
33. Rousseeuw, P.J.: Silhouettes: a graphical aid to the interpretation and validation of cluster analysis. J. Comput. Appl. Math. 20, 53–65 (1987)
34. Sokal, R.R., Rohlf, F.J.: The comparison of dendrograms by objective methods. In: Taxon, pp. 33–40 (1962)
35. Vakulenko, S., Nixon, L., Lupu, M.: Character-based neural embeddings for tweet clustering. In: SocialNLP 2017, p. 36 (2017)
36. Weng, J., Lim, E.P., Jiang, J., He, Q.: Twitterrank: finding topic-sensitive influential twitterers. In: Proceedings of the 3rd ACM International Conference on Web Search and Data Mining, pp. 261–270. ACM (2010)

37. Yan, X., Guo, J., Lan, Y., Cheng, X.: A biterm topic model for short texts. In: Proceedings of the 22nd International Conference on World Wide Web, pp. 1445–1456. ACM (2013)
38. Yin, J., Wang, J.: A dirichlet multinomial mixture model-based approach for short text clustering. In: Proceedings of the 20th ACM SIGKDD International Conference on Knowledge Discovery and Data Mining, pp. 233–242. ACM (2014)
39. Yin, J.: Clustering microtext streams for event identification. In: IJCNLP, pp. 719–725 (2013)
40. Zhao, W.X., Jiang, J., Weng, J., He, J., Lim, E.-P., Yan, H., Li, X.: Comparing twitter and traditional media using topic models. In: Clough, P., Foley, C., Gurrin, C., Jones, G.J.F., Kraaij, W., Lee, H., Mudoch, V. (eds.) ECIR 2011. LNCS, vol. 6611, pp. 338–349. Springer, Heidelberg (2011). doi:10.1007/978-3-642-20161-5_34

Combining Network and Language Indicators for Tracking Conflict Intensity

Anna Rumshisky[1]([✉]), Mikhail Gronas[2], Peter Potash[1], Mikhail Dubov[3],
Alexey Romanov[1], Saurabh Kulshreshtha[1], and Alex Gribov[1]

[1] Department of Computer Science, University of Massachusetts Lowell, Lowell, USA
arum@cs.uml.edu
[2] Department of Russian, Dartmouth College, Hanover, USA
[3] Higher School of Economics, Moscow, Russia

Abstract. This work seeks to analyze the dynamics of social or political conflict as it develops over time, using a combination of network-based and language-based measures of conflict intensity derived from social media data. Specifically, we look at the random-walk based measure of graph polarization, text-based sentiment analysis, and the corresponding shift in word meaning and use by the opposing sides. We analyze the interplay of these views of conflict using the Ukraine-Russian Maidan crisis as a case study.

1 Introduction

Over the past decade, social media websites such as Twitter and Facebook (as well as their counterparts in other countries, such as Weibo in China or VKontakte in Russia) have become an integral part of social life in many locations around the world. In conjunction with the proliferation of social media use, a number of political conflicts and incidents of social unrest occurred around the world (for example, events associated with the "Arab spring" in Egypt and Tunisia in 2010 and 2011, Spanish 15-M movement of 2011–2012, and the Russian takeover of Crimea in 2014). As a result, substantial amounts of data have been accumulated regarding peoples behavior (both linguistic and extra-linguistic) in social media prior to and during such conflicts. We are now in a position to attempt a data-driven approach to conflict dynamics, detect internal logic, and analyze patterns in how conflicts originate and develop. In doing so, we follow in the footsteps of conflict sociologists such as Randal Collins who in his seminal 2012 paper outlined the dynamic processes involved in the initiation, development, and de-escalation of conflict [2].

In this paper, our goal is to look at the conflict dynamically as it develops. We hypothesize that as a complex phenomenon, conflict gets reflected in multiple related processes. Because conflict in our context is an inherently intra-human phenomenon, signals of its dynamics are likely present in common forms of communication, of which social media has become ubiquitous. If that is indeed the case, multiple conflict indicators derived from social media can be combined

© Springer International Publishing AG 2017
G.L. Ciampaglia et al. (Eds.): SocInfo 2017, Part II, LNCS 10540, pp. 391–404, 2017.
DOI: 10.1007/978-3-319-67256-4_31

into a composite measure of conflict intensity. We view conflict as a systemic and dynamic phenomenon, in which these indicators can be tracked over time to detect significant rapid changes. We argue that a typology of interaction dynamics for different indicators may be used to characterize the development of conflict over time.

For a composite measure to work, there should be a meaningful relationship between different components of a composite measure. In this paper, we investigate whether there is such a relationship between language-based and network-based measures of controversy. While previous work such as Garimella et al. [6] has substantially advanced the study of social media-based controversy, by providing the first empirical validation for the effectiveness (or ineffectiveness) of various network-based and language-based controversy measures, there has been no work so far that seeks to determine whether such controversy measures have a meaningful temporal relationship. In order to analyze the interplay between these two complementary views of conflict, we use the 2013–2014 Ukraine-Russia Maidan crisis as a case study. By having data collected over a year-long time period, we are able to calculate controversy measures at various intervals as the Maidan crisis evolves. This case study is based on the Russian-speaking social media during the Ukrainian events of 2014, where civil discontent and division led to protests in the streets, and eventually to armed violence.

We examine the network-based controversy measure using the user graph in which connections are induced by information-sharing/information-consuming patterns in the network. We build and examine network graphs in which an edge connects two users if they have liked the same social media post. For the language-based measures, we analyze the rhetorical patterns both quantitatively and qualitatively: the overall sentiment expressed by the opposing sides (determined using automated text-based sentiment analysis), and the shift in word meaning and use ("lexical drift") that happens, as the language used by opposing communities to describe events related to the conflict develops diverging semantic representations. We analyze the drift in word meaning using a word embedding model [13] that uses contexts of a word's occurrences in order to create dense vector space embeddings for individual words.

2   Related Work

The study of conflict and civil unrest is a highly interdisciplinary field at the intersection of philosophy, psychology, economics, sociology and political science, to name just a few. In the context of our study, especially relevant are big data oriented political science projects such as GDELT (Global Database of Events, Language, and Tone) and ICEWS (Integrated Crisis Early Warning System) that aim to predict and monitor civil conflicts on the basis of large-scale analysis of news sources. Distinct from such approaches, we focus on a social media representation of conflicts and network properties in the conflicting communities. Our approach focuses on the micro-analysis of the underlying social dynamics that lead to conflict, operating at the level of individual political opinions and allegiance.

In the field of theoretical political science and social psychology, Nowak et al. [17] and Deutsch et al. [3] have previously suggested that one of the defining properties of conflict is the shift and eventual alignment of the opposing opinions across the divisions between social groups. While our approach is based on similar underlying ideas, our model allows us to determine empirically and track such dynamic changes as they develop. Alternatively, the field of network science conceptualizes conflict in terms of polarization between user communities. Over the past few years, the problem of community detection in social networks has received a lot of attention. In 2006, Newman [16] defined the modularity metric Q that detects how separate two communities are from each other. Specifically, Q examines the clusters formed by two distinct community groups in a network, and how this clustering compares to a random network. The higher its value, the more modular the network is. Blondel et al. [1] proposed a community detection algorithm that tries to maximize Q in a given network. Furthermore, the algorithm generates a hierarchy of partitions: for each partition it makes, that partition has its own subpartitions. This view becomes more microscopic until each node is in its own community.

Peixoto [18] states that the metric of modularity does not take into account the possible statistical fluctuations of the null model, and notes that modularity can detect highly modular communities in random graphs [8]. Furthermore, Blondel et al.'s algorithm has difficulty detecting communities when the cluster sizes are small [5,12]. Another criticism of using the modularity metric for polarized community detection comes from the recent work by Guerra et al. [7], who note that modularity and related measures recover separate and autonomous communities, but not opposing user clusters. They propose a measure based on the notion of *popularity-at-boundary* in order to capture the polarization reflecting the opposition between user clusters.

There are several advantages and disadvantages to the graph-based measures proposed for quantifying controversy/polarization [6,7,15]. These measures analyze the interaction between to two communities in a graph, based on differing theories of how conflict/polarization manifests itself. Garimella et al. [6] have proposed the best experimental setup to quantify the best controversy measure. The authors do so by selecting both controversial and non-controversial topics, and show how well a given measure does at differentiating between the two types of topics. The authors show that a conflict measure based on random walks between the two communities (RWC) performs the best out of five methods tested [6,7,15]. Furthermore, the authors show that the standard deviation of sentiment is a strong linguistic marker of controversy, whereas average sentiment and divergence of the conflicting communities' vocabularies are not able to separate between conflicting and non-conflicting topics.

Volkova et al. [21] is another example of linguistic analysis during controversy. The authors used language analysis to study and predict the emotional response during the Maidan crisis. In contrast to their approach, we do not rely on noisy location data to create our corpus, but instead use self-labeled user groups relevant to the crisis.

3   Dataset

In this study, we used data from Russian-speaking online media, posted during the Ukrainian events of 2013–2014. We use the largest Russian social network "VKontakte" (VK)[1]. According to liveinternet.ru, VKontakte has 320 million registered users and is the most popular social network in both Russia and Ukraine. During the conflict, both pro-Russian and pro-Ukrainian side (also known as "Antimaidan" and "Pro-" or "Evromaidan") were represented online by large numbers of Russian-speaking users.

We have built a scalable open stack system for data collection from VKontakte using VK API. The system is implemented in Python using a PostgreSQL database and Redis-based message queue. VK API has a less restrictive policy than Facebook's API, making it an especially suitable social network for research. Our system supports such API methods as retrieving group members, retrieving all posts from a wall, retrieving comments and likes for a given post, and so on. Moreover, we are able to collect all posts (and its related attributes) by a user that are public.

In order to seed the data collection, we selected the most popular user groups from the two opposing camps, the Evromaidan group (154,589 members) and the Antimaidan group (580,672 members). We then manually annotated other groups to which the administrators of these two groups belonged, selecting the groups with political content. This process produced 47 Evromaidan-related groups with 2,445,661 unique members and 51 Antimaidan-related groups with 1,942,918 unique members. We retrieved all posts from these group walls, as well as all the users who have liked one of the posts.

We then selected the users who were reasonably active during the time period of interest. We defined *active users* as those who averaged 2 or more posts per 3 months at least once over the target time frame (Oct 1, 2013–Oct 1, 2014). This resulted in 745,880 users from the Antimaidan-related groups and 725,053 users from the Evromaidan-related groups. We retrieved all posts from these user walls, as well as all the users who have liked these posts. In order to restrict our data to politically-themed postings, we built a list of 45 political keywords, which included the names of political figures, locations, and derogatory terms used by both sides. This list was used to filter the wall posts of Evromaidan and Antimaidan users.

4   Methodology

Our work leverages the complementary views of networks and language when analyzing controversy. The first part of this section describes the quantitative methods that we use for measuring conflict. Because these methods are general and provide a single numeric value, they have the potential to be combined into a composite index. Next, we discuss our qualitative language-based method of lexical drift. We finish by discussing how to generalize our methodology to the analysis of other events.

---

[1] http://vk.com.

4.1 Network-Based Controversy

Our network-based controversy measure is the RWC measure from Garimella et al. [6]. For all graphs, nodes represent users. We create an edge between two users (nodes) if they have liked the same post. We use the python package NetworkX[2] to construct and manipulate graphs. Once we construct a graph, we extract the largest connected component. The RWC measure assumes that a given graph has two communities already identified – the graph has two clusters for the nodes. For the VK data, based on the data collection methodology, we have predefined communities based on whether the user came from an Antimaidan or Evromaidan group (see Sect. 3).

To compute the RWC measure on a graph, the first step is to identify the k nodes with highest degree in each community. These are referred to as the authoritative nodes. Generally speaking, the goal is to calculate the probabilities of starting a walk at a random node in a given community, and end at an authoritative node in same community, as well as ending at an authoritative node in the opposite community. In practice, these probabilities are calculated through inference as follows: (1) Randomly select 10% of nodes in each community, (2) For each node, perform a random walk until an authoritative node is reached in either community. We repeat steps 1 and 2 a thousand times to best estimate the target probabilities. For each random walk, we keep track of the counts related to starting on a given side and ending on a given side. The final formula for RWC is:

$$RWC = P_{XX}P_{YY} - P_{XY}P_{YX} \tag{1}$$

where

$$P_{AB} = P[start\ in\ community\ A|\ end\ in\ community\ B] \tag{2}$$

This measure will produce a real-valued score for a given graph, which in turn represents actions of users in a network.

4.2 Language-Based Controversy

The quantitative linguistic attribute we measure is the sentiment of language used in the posts from the VK data. Sentiment analysis produces a discrete label for a piece of text: positive, negative, or neutral, which we convert to an integer using the following mapping: positive $\rightarrow$ 1, neutral $\rightarrow$ 0, negative $\rightarrow$ −1. Since these values are given per piece of text (post), we compute aggregate statistics: average (mean) sentiment and standard deviation of sentiment. Garimella et al. [6] posit that the standard deviation of sentiment is a conflict indicator, like RWC. We apply language-based analysis to the data used to construct the user graphs. Thus, the exact posts we analyze is a subset of the overall data that has been collected.

Sentiment Analysis in Russian. In order to measure the sentiment for Russian, we used a Python port of the Sentimental system[3] for sentiment analysis.

---

[2] https://networkx.github.io/.
[3] https://github.com/Wobot/Sentimental.

Sentimental is a dictionary-based sentiment analysis system with basic capabilities of handling negated words. We used a lexicon which consisted of 7640 words with sentiment scores from -5 to 5. The overall sentiment score of a sentence is a sum of the scores of individual words, normalized be the length of the sentence. This system, along with the used lexicon, is publicly available on GitHub[4]. We threshold the output of the system to predict its label as follows: $> 0 \rightarrow$ positive, $= 0 \rightarrow$ neutral, $< 0 \rightarrow$ negative.

4.3 Quantitative Temporal Analysis

In order to analyze the temporal trends of our case studies, we segment the available data into time slices, which generally is dictated by what data is at our disposal. Based on the non-overlapping data segments, we calculate the following measures at each time slice: RWC, average sentiment, and standard deviation of sentiment. For the Maidan case study, the time slices are at monthly intervals. Between group and user wall posts, there is an average of 121,989 posts per time slice.

4.4 Qualitative Linguistic Analysis: Lexical Drift

Following the distributional hypothesis [4,9,14], the contexts in which words occur are indicative of their meanings. We trained word2vec embeddings [13] for each temporal slice of VK data, following the methodology outlined in [11]. A similar methodology has previously been used to analyze language during conflict [20]. Word2vec creates a mapping between words and vectors in $\mathbb{R}^n$, where n is fixed. Moreover, Mikolov et al. argue that the topology of the vector space is also *semantically* continuous – geometric proximity equates to semantic similarity. As new data is available at each time slice, allowing the model to continue training, the positioning of word representations in the vector space shifts as words begin to appear in different contexts. To compute distance between embeddings e_i, e_j, we use the following formula:

$$CosineDistance(e_i, e_j) = 1 - \cos(\theta_{e_i,e_j}) \tag{3}$$

where $\cos(\theta_{e_i,e_j})$ is the cosine of the angle between the embedding vectors e_i, e_j[5], which is in the range $[-1, 1]$, equaling -1 when the vectors point opposite directions and equaling 1 when the vectors point the same direction. Thus, a higher cosine distance translates to the meanings being farther apart. We use the Python package Gensim[6] to train word vectors.

---

[4] https://github.com/text-machine-lab/sentimental.
[5] https://en.wikipedia.org/wiki/Cosine_similarity.
[6] https://radimrehurek.com/gensim/.

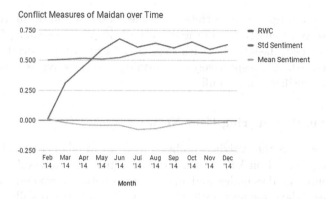

Fig. 1. Measures of conflict for Maidan, shown in monthly segments

4.5 Generalizability of Methodology

We argue that our method is generalizable across conflicts, given the presence of social media data (collected from a meaningful time period). We do note that the users of opposing sides should be in the same network and use the same language, or at least have familiarity with the opposing side's language. While our methodology uses joint liking to create edges between users, if Twitter data were to be used, one can use retweets, as Garimella et al. [6] suggest, instead. Secondly, the RWC measure requires the presence of two predefined communities. Although our data collection process is able to annotate this directly, one could use existing algorithms such as Metis[7] [10]. Lastly, our work requires a sentiment analysis tool. However, off-the-shelf sentiment tools for languages other than English may been difficult to come across. Annotated corpora for languages other than English are beginning to appear, such as for Arabic [19]. Even if annotated sentiment data is not available, one may use a dictionary-based approach such as ours.

5   Results and Discussion

In this section, we presents and discuss the quantitative and qualitative measures of the Maidan Crisis's temporal dynamics, based both on network and linguistic analysis. The interplay between the random walk controversy (RWC) measure and the dominating sentiment during the investigated time period is shown in Fig. 1. For our case study, the relationship between these two reflections of an ongoing conflict confirmed our initial hypothesis. Essentially, as the conflict intensifies, both the RWC measure and the standard deviation of overall sentiment expressed by the opposing groups (SenSTD) will increase in unison. And in fact, we found that RWC and SenSTD are positively correlated,

---

[7] We tested the Metis algorithm on our own data and found it recorded 80% accuracy predicting community membership.

with Pearson and Spearman correlation values of 0.674 and 0.745, respectively. We also observed that RWC and the average of the absolute value of the overall sentiment correlate negatively (with Pearson and Spearman correlation values of -0.598 and -0.291, respectively), confirming that negative sentiment accompanies the intensification of conflict.

5.1 Information-Sharing User Network

In order to visualize the evolving conflict during the Maidan crisis in Ukraine, we created graphs based on VK data from specific temporal intervals (See Fig. 2). Users are represented as nodes, and an edge exists between two users in a graph if they have liked the same post (either on user walls or on group walls). In order to induce graphs from specific time periods, we restricted a given graph to likes that occurred on posts that were created in a certain interval. We used a 12-month time period that started October 2013 and ended September 2014. In order to create the graph visualizations, we used the Python library NetworkX. The graph layout we have chosen is based on the Fruchterman-Reingold layout, which is a force-directed algorithm[8]. The algorithm simultaneously tries to minimize the distance between highly connected nodes while maximizing the distance between minimally connected nodes. Blue nodes represent pro-Maidan users, and red nodes represent anti-Maidan users.

As we proceed from the beginning of the conflict, we can observe the initial cluster formation, as a chaotic mass of users organizes into clearly defined clusters, based on the sources they like. By December 2013 (the month when support for the Maidan protest became widespread throughout Western and Central Ukraine), we see the formation of the Maidan cluster, still unopposed. Around January 2014, we observe the appearance of the counter-cluster, coinciding with the growing organization and ideological coherence of the anti-Maidan forces, primarily in the Eastern regions. As the conflict intensifies, the clusters grow more dense and modular, which corresponds to the increasing hostility between the opposing factions in real life and the flare up of the open military confrontation. Significantly, around January 2014, we also begin to observe the formation of a "bridge" between the two groups, i.e. a set of users who clearly like both groups of sources. Interestingly, these boundary, "bridge" users in this case seem to self-identify as anti-Maidan (they belong to the anti-Maidan user groups, and are correspondingly shown in red).

Essentially, in Fig. 2, you can see a clear reflection of the conflict dynamics described by Collins [2]. October and November 2013 graphs show a random arrangement of nodes in the absence of conflict, followed by an explosion that begins in December 2013 and January 2014. A bridge is formed and then disappears, as polarization increases and the conflict drives out the neutrals. The bridge begins to thin out around May 2014 and disappears completely in June 2014. As the bridge no longer exists, there is virtually no way for the representatives of the opposing sides to experience the discourse from the other side.

---

[8] https://en.wikipedia.org/wiki/Force-directed_graph_drawing.

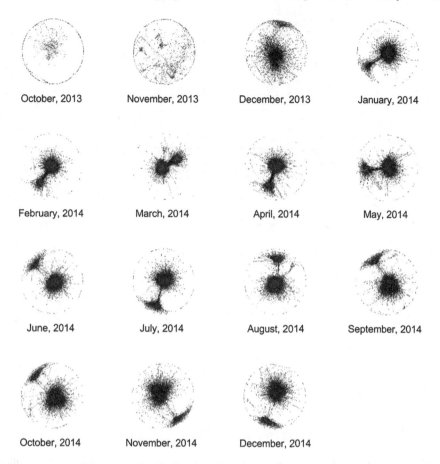

Fig. 2. Visualization of pro- and anti-Maidan VK user networks as conflict develops. Blue nodes represent Evromaidan users, and red nodes represent Antimaidan users. (Color figure online)

The network visualization in this figure thus clearly shows the logic hypothesized by Collins. This corresponds to the plateau observed in Fig. 1 that shows the random walk controversy measure for the Maidan data.

5.2   Lexical Drift

The change in the vector space embedding for the same word over time allows us to track word meaning drift as it happens during the conflict. Figure 3 shows the change in contextual distribution of important "drifter" words which changed meaning the most during the conflict. The graph shows the cosine distance between the initial vector space embedding in Feb 2014 and the embeddings for the following months.

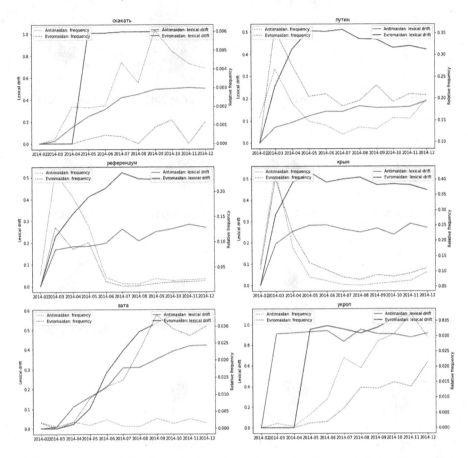

Fig. 3. Important "drifter" words that changed meaning the most during the conflict. The graph shows the cosine distance (left Y axis gives the scale) between the initial vector space embedding in Feb 2014 and the embeddings for the following months. Dotted lines show the relative frequency for each word, i.e., the percentage of posts wherein the word appears (right Y axis gives the scale). The following words are shown (left to right, top down): скакать (skakat') "jump", Путин "Putin", референдум "referendum", Крым (krim) "Crimea",вата (vata) "cottonballs", укроп (ukrop) "dill" or "Ukrainian nationalist".

The word "скакать" (skakat) (Fig. 3, top left), for example, became a popular taunt, a derogatory term applied by the anti-maidan movement to all various types of Ukrainian nationalist activities. This use of the verb originated in the viral YouTube video that captured a crowd of young Ukrainian nationalists braving the winter cold and trying to keep warm by hopping together and chanting "кто не пляшет тот москаль" , "who is not jumping is a moscovite". The chant became the object of ridicule among the "moscovites" and the word "скакать" (skakat) drifted towards new (political and anti-Ukrainian contexts).

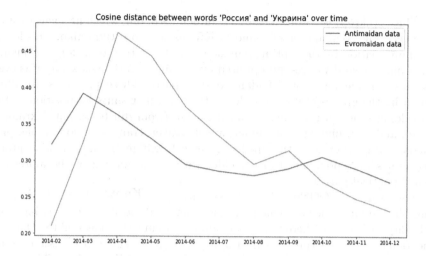

Fig. 4. Cosine distance between the words Russia and Ukraine in Evromaidan and Antimaidan data

Cosine distance plot for "skakat" suggests that the shift away from the original meaning for this word was the most pronounced amongst the words shown.

The graph for the word "Путин" (top right) shows a drastic increase in drift for Putins name among the Euromaidan users from the very start of the conflict. The corresponding drifting rise on the anti-maidan side is much flatter. This is explained by the singular importance of the Russian president in the conflict. In the eyes of Evromaidan community, he became the personification of the conflict (and of the evil in general). Putin became the personal enemy of the independence minded Ukrainians and the favorite object for taunts and insults – thus drifting from political contexts to such new embedding neighbours as "хуйло" (dick) in September 2014.

The word "вата" (vata) comes from the word "ватник" (vatnik), which is a type of heavy cotton jacket popular in rural Russia and often worn by soldiers, prisoners, and farmers. The word "vata" itself means "cotton balls". During the conflict, the term "vata" became a pejorative term picked up by the Evromaidan side as a way to taunt Russian nationalists and Russian-speaking Ukrainians (essentially the Antimaidan side), with the connotation somewhat similar to the usage of "redneck" in American English. This change in meaning is clearly visible in the corresponding lexical drift graph. Note that the term's use by the Antimaidan side has also shifted substantially (even if to a smaller relative extent compared to the Evromaidan side). Moreover, we are able to quantitatively capture the fact that this term was later re-appropriated to some extent by the Russian nationalists who started to use it as a pride badge of sorts. However, the frequency plot for "vata" shows that this takeover was still not comparable to the pervasive pejorative use by the Evromaidan side.

Укроп (ukrop) is a word meaning a garden herb, dill, which happens to start with the same combination of sound "UKR" as the word Ukrainian. This led to its appropriation by the Antimaidan side as a derogatory term for Ukrainians. Later on, the word was re-appropriated by Ukrainian nationalists, and was even used as a name for a pro-Maidan political party. These processes are illustrated by the graphs of semantic drifts: the word first shifts its position in the embedding space in the Antimaidan discourse (from dill to an anti-Ukrainian tease), and then undergoes a similar, albeit weaker, transformation among pro-maidaners. Furthermore, the up-tick in lexical drift in the Evromaidan graph that starts in September 2014 coincides with the formation of the aforementioned political party.

The words "референдум" (referendum) and "Крым" (krim; Crimea in English) see an immediate change in meaning (high positive slope) going from February to March as there were referendum votes in Crimea as well the Donetsk and Luhansk oblasts (provinces) in March that represented pro-Russian desire to secede from Ukraine and potentially join the Russian Federation. This change in meaning levels off, though, in the remaining months as the conflict continues.

This view of the lexical change also allows us to see relative drift in meaning of initially similar words. For example, consider the comparison in Fig. 4 which shows that the cosine distance between the words Russia and Ukraine in Euromaidan data increased drastically in April 2014. This rise coincides with the escalation of the conflict and the beginning of its military phase. On April 6, 2014, the Eastern separatists captured an administrative buildings in Donetsk and Lugansk regions and soon proclaimed independence. The occupation of Slavyansk by the pro-Russian forces led by Igor Strelkov began on April 12. Thus, in the Euromaidan discourse Russia became associated with the open aggression and intrusion into the Ukraines internal affairs. This lead to a drastic peak in the semantic drift that gradually subsides in the next few months.

6   Conclusion

We suggested methods for an analysis of the temporal dynamics of the political conflict as reflected in social media, using the 2014 Russian-Ukrainian conflict as a case study. We analyzed the interplay of the division of network-based vs. language-based measures of conflict, using Random Walk Controversy as a network measure and standard deviation of sentiment and semantic drift as verbal measures. We investigated the hypothesis that the network-based and the language-based measures of conflict intensity should correlate and provided a preliminary statistical confirmation for it. We also provided a data-driven illustration for Randal Collins' influential theory of conflict development. Specifically, we showed for that the major stages of conflict as described by Collins (explosion, plateau, dissipation) and some of the behavioral patterns he postulated (including driving out of the neutrals) may be observed and visualized in the social media data for the 2014 Russian-Ukrainian conflict. Finally, we performed a qualitative analysis of the semantic shift for key terms that typified the conflict.

References

1. Blondel, V.D., Guillaume, J.L., Lambiotte, R., Lefebvre, E.: Fast unfolding of communities in large networks. J. Stat. Mech: Theory Exp. **2008**(10), P10008 (2008)
2. Collins, R.: C-escalation and D-escalation: a theory of the time-dynamics of conflict. Am. Sociol. Rev. **77**(1), 1–20 (2012)
3. Deutsch, M., Coleman, P.T., Marcus, E.C.: The Handbook of Conflict Resolution: Theory and Practice. Wiley, Hoboken (2011)
4. Firth, J.R.: A synopsis of linguistic theory 1930–1955. In: Studies in Linguistic Analysis, pp. 1–32. Philological Society, Oxford (1957)
5. Fortunato, S., Barthélemy, M.: Resolution limit in community detection. Proc. Natl. Acad. Sci. **104**(1), 36–41 (2007)
6. Garimella, K., De Francisci Morales, G., Gionis, A., Mathioudakis, M.: Quantifying controversy in social media. In: Proceedings of the Ninth ACM International Conference on Web Search and Data Mining, pp. 33–42. ACM (2016)
7. Guerra, P.H.C., Meira Jr., W., Cardie, C., Kleinberg, R.: A measure of polarization on social media networks based on community boundaries. In: ICWSM (2013)
8. Guimera, R., Sales-Pardo, M., Amaral, L.A.N.: Modularity from fluctuations in random graphs and complex networks. Phys. Rev. E **70**(2), 025101 (2004)
9. Harris, Z.: Distributional structure. In: Katz, J. (ed.) Philosophy of Linguistics, pp. 26–47. Oxford University Press, New York (1985)
10. Karypis, G., Kumar, V.: Metis-unstructured graph partitioning and sparse matrix ordering system, version 2.0 (1995)
11. Kim, Y., Chiu, Y.I., Hanaki, K., Hegde, D., Petrov, S.: Temporal analysis of language through neural language models. In: ACL 2014, p. 61 (2014)
12. Lancichinetti, A., Fortunato, S.: Limits of modularity maximization in community detection. Phys. Rev. E **84**(6), 066122 (2011)
13. Mikolov, T., Sutskever, I., Chen, K., Corrado, G., Dean, J.: Distributed representations of words and phrases and their compositionality. In: Proceedings of NIPS (2013)
14. Miller, G., Charles, W.: Contextual correlates of semantic similarity. Lang. Cogn. Process. **6**(1), 1–28 (1991)
15. Morales, A., Borondo, J., Losada, J.C., Benito, R.M.: Measuring political polarization: Twitter shows the two sides of venezuela. Chaos: an Interdisciplinary. J. Nonlinear Sci. **25**(3), 033114 (2015)
16. Newman, M.E.: Modularity and community structure in networks. Proc. Natl. Acad. Sci. **103**(23), 8577–8582 (2006)
17. Nowak, A., Vallacher, R.R., Bui-Wrzosinska, L., Coleman, P.T.: Attracted to conflict: a dynamical perspective on malignant social relations. In: Understanding social change: Political psychology in Poland, pp. 33–49 (2006)
18. Peixoto, T.P.: Hierarchical block structures and high-resolution model selection in large networks. Phys. Rev. X **4**(1), 011047 (2014)
19. Rosenthal, S., Farra, N., Nakov, P.: Semeval-2017 task 4: sentiment analysis in Twitter. In: Proceedings of the 11th International Workshop on Semantic Evaluation (SemEval-2017). Association for Computational Linguistics, Vancouver, Canada, pp. 502–518. http://www.aclweb.org/anthology/S17-2088

20. Stewart, I., Arendt, D., Bell, E., Volkova, S.: Measuring, predicting and visualizing short-term change in word representation and usage in VKontakte social network. In: Proceedings of the 11th International AAAI Conference on Web and Social Media (ICWSM 2017), pp. 33–42 (2017)
21. Volkova, S., Chetviorkin, I., Arendt, D., Durme, B.V.: Contrasting public opinion dynamics and emotional response during crisis. In: SocInfo (2016)

Like Trainer, Like Bot? Inheritance of Bias in Algorithmic Content Moderation

Reuben Binns[1](✉), Michael Veale[2], Max Van Kleek[1], and Nigel Shadbolt[1]

[1] Department of Computer Science, University of Oxford, Oxford, UK
{reuben.binns,max.van.kleek,nigel.shadbolt}@cs.ox.ac.uk
[2] Department of Science, Technology, Engineering and Public Policy (STEaPP),
University College London, London, UK
m.veale@ucl.ac.uk

Abstract. The internet has become a central medium through which 'networked publics' express their opinions and engage in debate. Offensive comments and personal attacks can inhibit participation in these spaces. Automated content moderation aims to overcome this problem using machine learning classifiers trained on large corpora of texts manually annotated for offence. While such systems could help encourage more civil debate, they must navigate inherently normatively contestable boundaries, and are subject to the idiosyncratic norms of the human raters who provide the training data. An important objective for platforms implementing such measures might be to ensure that they are not unduly biased towards or against particular norms of offence. This paper provides some exploratory methods by which the normative biases of algorithmic content moderation systems can be measured, by way of a case study using an existing dataset of comments labelled for offence. We train classifiers on comments labelled by different demographic subsets (men and women) to understand how differences in conceptions of offence between these groups might affect the performance of the resulting models on various test sets. We conclude by discussing some of the ethical choices facing the implementers of algorithmic moderation systems, given various desired levels of diversity of viewpoints amongst discussion participants.

Keywords: Algorithmic accountability · Machine learning · Online abuse · Discussion platforms · Freedom of speech

1 Introduction

Online platforms, as 'curators of public discourse' [18] or digital extensions of the public sphere [12], have become important spaces for opinion and debate. While social media, news websites, and question–answer forums enable exchange of diverse viewpoints [19], aggressive, offensive or bullying comments can stifle debate, drive people away, and lead to intervention by regulators or law enforcement. Yet over-restrictive moderation can similarly send users elsewhere. Consequently platforms' terms of use, content policies and enforcement measures often attempt to bound acceptable discourse [23].

© Springer International Publishing AG 2017
G.L. Ciampaglia et al. (Eds.): SocInfo 2017, Part II, LNCS 10540, pp. 405–415, 2017.
DOI: 10.1007/978-3-319-67256-4_32

Moderation by employees, contractors, users or volunteers is an explicitly human endeavour. However quantity of content makes manually and rapidly vetting each item very costly, driving interest in automated content classification. Automatic detection used to require curated blacklists of banned words, but as these are difficult to maintain as language, norms, and gaming strategies change, more novel means involve training machine learning algorithms on large corpora of texts manually annotated for aggression, offence or abuse. According to the description of Google's 'Perspective API' [1], platforms might wish to predict the 'impact a comment might have on a conversation', giving 'realtime feedback to commenters or help moderators do their job'. Microblogging platform Twitter [35] and comment plug-in Disqus [27] are pursuing similar efforts.

While automating content moderation might lighten staff and volunteer burden, its norms hinge on raters' judgements within training data. Where multiple implicit or explicit communities exist — particularly where participation in labelling is not balanced — this might penalise content exhibiting particular views or vernacular. The global imposition of raters' norms might affect diversity and participation on the platform.

This paper explores methods for detecting of potential bias in algorithmic content moderation systems. We experiment with a series of text classifiers using an existing dataset of 100,000 Wikipedia comments manually scored for 'toxicity' (annotators' questions, Fig. 1a). To examine how differences between norms of offence might result in different classifications, we built different classifiers from demographically distinct subsets of the population responsible for labelling the training data. We focus on gender as a demographic variable potentially associated with differences in judgements of offence, primarily due to the ease of drawing balanced samples compared to other available variables (age, education). We do *not* intend to establish generalisable conclusions about gender and offence.

2   Background and Related Work

We do not attempt to define aggression, offence or harassment in this paper (for an overview of definitions, see [36]). Suffice to say, different logics for automated and semi-automated moderation exist, including the promotion of 'quality' comments online [13], the flagging of hate speech or bullying [6,17,29,34], or the maintenance of imagined 'networked publics' that 'allow people to gather for social, cultural, and civic purposes' [5].

Content moderation can have real and lasting effects on the direction of and participation in conversations in the digital public sphere. Norms of acceptability do not exist in a vacuum, as they are reinforced by prior standards, and they are also malleable. Previous research on online comments has found that by intervening in certain ways, news organizations can affect the deliberative behavior of commenters [31], altering the kinds of comments made (e.g. thoughtful or thoughtless) [32], and users' perceptions of the content they comment on [2].

Systems for automated content moderation began with primarily manually encoded rules and features, later becoming more inductively driven. Early work focussed on identifying abusive and hostile messages or 'flames' with manually crafted features (such as evaluated regular expressions or word lists) and decision trees [30]. These systems gave way to more general machine learning–based inferences, with bag-of-words and topic modelling both popular approaches. While newer machine learning techniques have been applied lately (see [26]), many relevant issues such as contextualisation are a bottleneck more widely across machine learning research [28].

As censorship and free speech are issues at the heart of democratic politics [15,25], inductive systems that seek to automatically reduce the visibility of certain contributions are unlikely to escape the scrutiny of those worried about 'algorithmic bias'. What (if anything) should be filtered is and has always been a matter for heated societal debate. Content considered 'abusive' by some might to others be partisan disagreement. Studying news platform comment moderation, Diakopoulos and Naaman found that media organisations acknowledge that moderators bring their own biases to the evaluation of standards [14].

Recent years have seen a rapidly intensifying focus on the way that bias enters computational systems, linked especially to the consequences of systems that 'profile' individuals and make decisions that relate to their lives. In these fields, efforts to understand and mitigate illegal bias or general unfairness in areas from loan acceptance to word embeddings have propagated [4,7,8,16]. Yet algorithmic content moderation has some distinctions from the current main trajectories of 'discrimination-aware data mining' (DADM). In particular, while DADM attempts to ensure fairness across individuals that share characteristics protected by anti-discrimination legislation, such as race, gender, religion, pregnancy, or disability, issues in algorithmic content moderation are not always of this type. While there might be instances where protected groups are directly affected — the filtering of African American Vernacular English, for example — practical issues seem more likely to relate to creating diverse, welcoming (and often legally compliant) places to be online. Here, some determined equitable distribution of *viewpoints* might be of more interest than representation of protected groups *per se*, although it is nonetheless likely that individuals within certain demographics share some norms of offence, gender being one example often studied [21,22,33].

In applied contexts, firms might be more interested in user-bases, political ideologies, or other platform-specific divides than protected characteristics — for example, avoiding classifiers that more often flag 'liberal' rather than 'conservative' comments. We might say this system is 'unfair' to some viewpoints. In the majority of cases, while it is unlikely these groups will be well-defined or self-declared, there may be practical methods for platform operators to segment users for analytic purposes. We focus in this paper on exploratory methods over defined groups, using gender as an illustrative example, but with the explicit caveat that gender will rarely be the prime grouping of interest.

3 Pragmatic Approaches for Exploring Biases by Altering Test and Training Sets

Our general question is: how do latent norms and biases affect the operation of offence detection systems? Specifically, do the norms of offence held by people who contributed the training data result in classifiers which systematically favour certain norms of offence over others?

The usual way to evaluate a classifier H is to define a loss function L, which measures the extent to which its predictions $\hat{Y}$ approximate the ground truth of the phenomena of interest Y. Normally, there is only one version of the ground truth, i.e. one set of labels for Y. In this case, we want to measure biases between classifiers relative to different *norms of offence*, which are characterised by sets of labels applied to a corpus of comments C in natural language $[c_1, c_2, ..., c_n]$ which score each comment along some axis, (e.g. 0 = 'not offensive', 1 = 'offensive'). If we take sets of ground truth we believe correspond to different norms, then applying chosen loss functions to the predictions $\hat{Y}$ and these ground truths help us better explore the nature of its 'bias' towards or against certain norms. There are other times where it is possible to alter the training data, but less easy to alter the test data. While the training dataset can always be split, this says little about performance where the domain is different — for example, where the classifier will be deployed on a website where comments have much less metadata. If the training data contain characteristics believed to be correlated with norms, a collection of classifiers $[H_1, H_2, ..., H_m]$ corresponding to m norms can be trained. Instead of evaluating a single classifier against several test sets, several classifiers (for example, labelled by those differing in inferred political standpoints) can be compared to a single, domain-relevant ground truth.

To demonstrate this approach, we examined an existing dataset of offence labels including demographic information about labellers. Our aim was to find a demographic variable likely to be associated with differences in attitudes about what texts are considered offensive. We chose to use gender because it was an easily understood, accessible demographic attribute of the labelling population, which enabled us to select large and equally sized sub-populations for new training sets, which (we hypothesised) would differ in their definitions of offence.

4 Data Sources and Methodology

We trained classifiers with an existing dataset from the Wikipedia Detox project (used in [37]). It features 100,000 annotations of Wikipedia talk page comments manually labelled by workers on the Crowdflower platform. Each comment is labelled by 10 workers for 'toxicity' (see Fig. 1a). Workers optionally provide demographic data, including age group, gender (restricted to male, female, other) and educational level. Noticeably, workers are not evenly distributed across reported gender (28.6% female, 55.6% male, 15.8% unreported/other), and there are fewer females per comment (see distribution in Fig. 1b). Comments without

Rate the toxicity of this comment

- *Very toxic* (a very hateful, aggressive or disrespectful comment that is very likely to make you leave a discussion)
- *Toxic* (a rude, disrespectful or unreasonable comment that is somewhat likely to make you leave a discussion)
- *Neither*
- *Healthy contribution* (a reasonable, civil or polite contributions that is somewhat likely to make you want to continue a discussion)
- *Very healthy contribution* (a very polite, thoughtful or helpful contribution that is very likely to make you want to continue a discussion)

(a) Question provided to raters

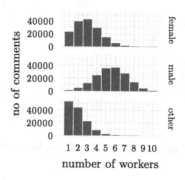

(b) Distribution of workers by gender

Fig. 1. Dataset statistics and rater question.

both male and female raters were excluded, as were raters not providing gender or the few selecting 'other'.

Considering the dataset before training classifiers, we measured agreement on toxicity within male and female annotators with Krippendorff's alpha (due to amenability to missing data, see [20]))[1], and average measures of how toxicity scores per comment differs between male and female annotators.

We then trained multiple text classifiers on various subsets of the original training data. Our model building process involved converting comments into *ngrams* (ranging from 1–2) at a maximum of 10,000 features, constructing a matrix of token counts, applying a TF-IDF vectoriser, before training a logistic regression model.[2] We first trained a classifier using all of the original training data (as used in the original study by [37]), to benchmark our modelling process against prior work and ensure that reasonable performance could be expected of classifiers built. We found that our models achieved an AUC score of 0.914 (the highest-performing classifier in [37] achieved a score of 0.96). We then used a bootstrapping method to sample new subsets of annotators in order to build various classifiers from these subsets. For each comment which had both male and female raters, we selected 10 male/female annotators at random with replacement. We then took the average score for these 10 sampled raters. 30 sets of training data were generated this way: 10 male, 10 female, and 10 a balanced mix. These data were used to train 30 different offensive text classifiers as above. Each set of classifiers was tested against unseen 'male', 'female' and 'balanced' rated test data, sampled in the same way as above.

---

[1] 95% bootstrapped CIs (500 replicates) were calculated with R's *rel* package [24].
[2] Code and data available at https://github.com/sociam/liketrainer.

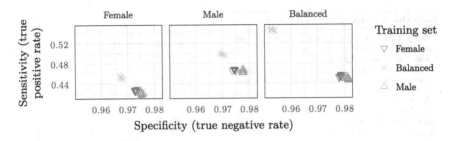

Fig. 2. Sensitivity and specificity, by training set (points) and test set (facets).

5   Results

We found evidence of difference between male and female annotators regarding the labelling of comments as 'toxic'. Firstly, inter-rater agreement (Krippendorff's alpha) was significantly lower for women (.468 [.457, .478 (95% bootstrapped CI)]) than for men (.494 [.484, .503 (95% bootstrapped CI)]); female annotators were less likely to agree with each other's offence scores than males. Furthermore, on average female annotators found comments less 'toxic' than male counterparts. By comment, average female toxicity scores were 0.043 [−0.048, −0.038 (95% CI)] lower than male ones.

Having established some gender differences in norms of offence, we proceeded to analyse if differences were also distinguishable in classifier performance on various test datasets. We found that both classifiers trained on male *and* those trained on female annotated data are less sensitive to female-labelled test data than to male-labelled test data (see Fig. 2 and Table 1a). True positive rates for female-labelled test data were 0.42 ('male' classifiers) and 0.43 ('female' classifiers), while true positive rates for male-labelled test data were higher at 0.46 ('male' classifiers) and 0.47 ('female' classifiers). We did not find such disparities in terms of specificity; 'male' and 'female' classifiers had similar true negative rates when tested on male and female-labelled data. In terms of the bias/fairness definition given above, both types of classifier could be considered 'unfair' to women, insofar as they exhibit more false positives when attempting to replicate *women's* collective judgments than *men's*. In other words, speech that female annotators collectively *did not* find offensive was more likely to be mis-classified as such by both 'male' and 'female' classifiers. We found that mixed-gender classifiers had higher sensitivity across all three test sets.

We also compared coefficients of the 'male' and 'female' classifiers. We took features used by the classifiers and calculated average coefficients across the 10 classifiers created for each gender. Selecting ngrams most strongly associated with offensive classifications (with a coefficient value of more than 2) for both 'male' and 'female' classifiers, we found significant overlap between 'male' and 'female' classifiers. The most offensive terms for 'male' classifiers however tended to be more strongly associated with offence than the same terms for 'female' classifiers.

Few terms were indicated to be more offensive to 'female' than 'male' classifiers, and for those that were, the margin was small (see Fig. 3).

6   Discussion

Online communities exhibit norms regarding acceptable speech. Who gets to define these norms is a contentious matter. It might be within the remit of company executives, or undertaken in consultation with users and other stakeholders. Large platforms often have teams dedicated to identifying and removing offensive content, while also relying on users flagging content, both as means of detection and as 'rhetorical justification' for censorship [11]. Moderation privileges may not be universal — volunteers may be self-appointed (e.g. Reddit), appointed through semi-democratic processes (e.g. Wikipedia), or implicitly through reputation (e.g. StackExchange). Whoever defines them, norms of acceptability are rarely static, consistent or uncontested. Discussion forum Reddit features many sub-fora exhibiting different norms, leading to frequent arguments between users, staff and executives across sub-fora over what kinds of posts should be allowed [9]. What counts as acceptable is therefore always a subjective matter.

It seems inevitable that introducing inductive automated content moderation systems risks amplifying these subjective norms and potentially exacerbating conflicts around them. These concerns may be compounded in cases where training data is decontextualised from the domain of application — increasingly common as more sophisticated classifiers, or classifiers for new or nascent communities utilise multiple external sources of data. The Perspective API, partly borne out of the Wikipedia Detox project, is now being used to moderate comments on the New York Times website [3]. One approach attempting to consider community differences is explored in [10]. Even if training data is only taken from where the moderation is occurring, it might introduce and reproduce historical biases or patterns incompatible with the changing nature of community norms. Where community standards are internally contested or in flux, automated content moderation will likely compound pre-existing platform conflicts.

In so far as the bounds of acceptable discourse are inherently contestable, we argue (relatively uncontroversially) that there can be no such thing as a 'neutral' classifier. Even in politically homogeneous environments with broad agreement about the offensiveness of all training data, an automated system would still constrain future speech on the basis of what has been deemed acceptable/unacceptable in the past. A healthy public sphere must also be capable of evolving, sometimes prohibiting speech which was previously acceptable and at other times relaxing prohibitions as social mores change.

At the same time, there can be no formula determining the extent to which different viewpoints need to be reflected in order for a classifier to be deemed fair. While anti-discrimination law might give anchoring to DADM methods, we cannot expect anything nearly so readily formalisable in this domain. Stakeholder norms differ — Some communities (or groups within them) might legitimately desire homogeneous 'safe spaces' in which otherwise offensive/inoffensive speech is permitted or prohibited; others might want to positively promote more diversity in discussion and thus aim to create classifiers which strike a balance between error rates which optimises diverse participation. In the latter case, one might aim to either minimise the false positive rates (making the conversation more permissive), or minimise the false negatives (less permissive), depending on whether subscribers to the under-represented norm are driven away primarily by over-zealous censorship or by exposure to comments they deem offensive.

While we use gender, as a common variable, it will often be that either protected characteristics are not the core concern, or that traits of concern are unavailable. Focussing on the training and test sets according to performance metrics of interest to find problematic patterns is a practical first step for platforms today given existing data, skillsets and methodologies. Going beyond gender, unsupervised methods such as clustering or manually identifying users by behaviour might help identify groups with conflicting views of offense. Finally, it is important to recognise that more civil discourse — if that is indeed a desirable goal — is unlikely to be achieved solely through moderation, whether manual or algorithmic; it also requires careful consideration of community dynamics, interface design, and rationales for participation.

7   Concluding Remarks

This case study aimed to illustrate methods and metrics for exploring bias in text classification tasks where learned concepts are inherently contestable, and to prompt reflection on the range of ethical considerations that should be taken into account by designers of algorithmic moderation systems, and the platforms that deploy them. While we do not conclude that automated moderation systems are 'sexist' (and did not seek to show this), we demonstrated how particular training sets may be biased in ways that are worth investigating prior to implementing such systems. Defining fairness in these systems strictly is likely impractical: these are highly complex, changing and contested concepts, and even were definitions arrived at, it would be unlikely that regular platforms held sufficient data on commenters and raters to operationalise them. Instead we illustrate an exploratory approach involving varying the test and training sets, which we believe to be a useful first step for organisations looking to implement automated content moderation, or test, monitor or evaluate technologies they are using.

As algorithmic content moderation approaches become more pervasive, platforms deploying them will face difficult choices with significant implications for the development of community discussions and digital public spheres. If individuals with certain viewpoints feel unwelcome, then polarisation online will likely continue to increase. People are drawn to online communities in part due to discursive norms and editorial policies, but algorithmic enforcement of those norms and policies could warp them in unforeseen ways. Platforms would therefore be advised to introduce such systems only with careful consideration and ongoing measurement; we hope that the methods discussed here can help.

Acknowledgments. Authors at the University of Oxford were supported under *SOCIAM: The Theory and Practice of Social Machines,* funded by the UK Engineering and Physical Sciences Research Council (EPSRC) under grant number EP/J017728/2. Michael Veale was supported by EPSRC grant number EP/M507970/1. The UCL Legion High Performance Computing Facility (Legion@UCL) supported part of the analysis. Thanks additionally go to three anonymous reviewers for their helpful comments.

Appendix

Table 1. Average performance by demographic of training and test sets.

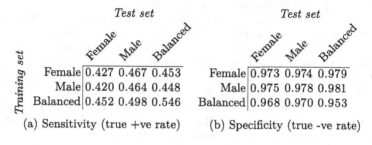

(a) Sensitivity (true +ve rate)   (b) Specificity (true -ve rate)

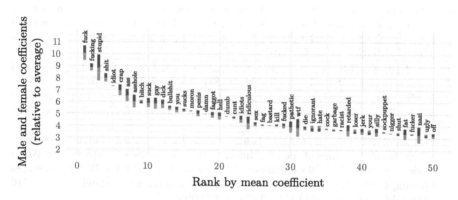

Fig. 3. Highest 50 average model coefficients greater than 2 by gender, ranked by average. Ends of blue and red lines indicate male and female coefficients. (Color figure online)

414 R. Binns et al.

References

1. Perspective API (webpage). http://perspectiveapi.com/. Accessed 04 Jul 2017
2. Anderson, A.A., Brossard, D., Scheufele, D.A., Xenos, M.A., Ladwig, P.: The nasty effect: online incivility and risk perceptions of emerging technologies. J. Comput.-Mediated Commun. **19**(3), 373–387 (2014)
3. Bassey, E.: The Times Sharply Increases Articles Open for Comments, Using Googles Technology. The New York Times. https://www.nytimes.com/2017/06/13/insider/have-a-comment-leave-a-comment.html
4. Bolukbasi, T., Chang, K., Zou, J.Y., Saligrama, V., Kalai, A.: Man is to Computer Programmer as Woman is to Homemaker? Debiasing Word Embeddings (2016). https://arxiv.org/abs/1607.06520
5. Boyd, D.: Social network sites as networked publics: affordances, dynamics, and implications. In: Networked Self: Identity, Community, and Culture on Social Network Sites, pp. 39–58. Routledge, London (2010)
6. Burnap, P., Williams, M.L.: Us and them: identifying cyber hate on Twitter across multiple protected characteristics. EPJ Data Sci. **5**(1), 11 (2016)
7. Calders, T., Žliobaitė, I.: Why unbiased computational processes can lead to discriminative decision procedures. In: Custers, B., Calders, T., Schermer, B., Zarsky, T. (eds.) Discrimination and Privacy in the Information Society. SAPERE, vol. 3, pp. 43–59. Springer, Heidelberg (2012). doi:10.1007/978-3-642-30487-3_3
8. Caliskan, A., Bryson, J.J., Narayanan, A.: Semantics derived automatically from language corpora contain human-like biases. Science **356**(6334), 183–186 (2017). http://science.sciencemag.org/content/356/6334/183
9. Centivany, A.: Values, ethics and participatory policymaking in online communities. Proc. Assoc. Inf. Sci. Technol. **53**(1), 1–10 (2016)
10. Chandrasekharan, E., Samory, M., Srinivasan, A., Gilbert, E.: The bag of communities: identifying abusive behavior online with preexisting internet data. In: Proceedings of the 2017 CHI Conference on Human Factors in Computing Systems, pp. 3175–3187. ACM (2017)
11. Crawford, K., Gillespie, T.: What is a flag for? social media reporting tools and the vocabulary of complaint. New Media Soc. **18**(3), 410–428 (2016)
12. Dahlberg, L.: The internet and democratic discourse: exploring the prospects of online deliberative forums extending the public sphere. Inf. Commun. Soc. **4**(4), 615–633 (2001)
13. Diakopoulos, N.: CommentIQ: Enhancing journalistic curation of online news comments. In: Proceedings of the 25th International Conference Companion on World Wide Web, WWW 2016 Companion, International World Wide Web Conferences Steering Committee, Republic and Canton of Geneva, Switzerland, pp. 715–716 (2016). https://doi.org/10.1145/2872518.2890099
14. Diakopoulos, N., Naaman, M.: Towards quality discourse in online news comments. In: Proceedings of the ACM 2011 Conference on Computer Supported Cooperative Work, pp. 133–142. ACM (2011)
15. Feinberg, J.: Offense to Others, vol. 2. Oxford University Press, Oxford (1985)
16. Feldman, M., Friedler, S.A., Moeller, J., Scheidegger, C., Venkatasubramanian, S.: Certifying and removing disparate impact. In: Proceedings of the 21th ACM SIGKDD International Conference on Knowledge Discovery and Data Mining, pp. 259–268 (2015)
17. Gagliardone, I., Gal, D., Alves, T., Martinez, G.: Countering Online Hate Speech. UNESCO Publishing, Paris (2015)

18. Gillespie, T.: The politics of platforms. New Media Soc. **12**(3), 347–364 (2010)
19. Halpern, D., Gibbs, J.: Social media as a catalyst for online deliberation? exploring the affordances of Facebook and YouTube for political expression. Comput. Hum. Behav. **29**(3), 1159–1168 (2013)
20. Hayes, A.F., Krippendorff, K.: Answering the call for a standard reliability measure for coding data. Commun. Methods Measures **1**(1), 77–89 (2007)
21. Jay, T.: Cursing in America: A Psycholinguistic Study of Dirty Language in the Courts, in the Movies, in the Schoolyards, and on the Streets. John Benjamins Publishing, Philadelphia (1992)
22. Johnson, F.L., Fine, M.G.: Sex differences in uses and perceptions of obscenity. Women's Stud. Commun. **8**(1), 11–24 (1985)
23. Ksiazek, T.B.: Civil interactivity: how news organizations' commenting policies explain civility and hostility in user comments. J. Broadcast. Electron. Media **59**(4), 556–573 (2015)
24. Martire, R.L.: REL: Reliability Coefficients (2017), rpackageversion1.3.0. https://CRAN.R-project.org/package=rel
25. Mill, J.S.: On Liberty. Broadview Press, Orchard Park (1999)
26. Pavlopoulos, J., Malakasiotis, P., Androutsopoulos, I.: Deep learning for user comment moderation (2017). https://arxiv.org/abs/1705.09993
27. Rohrer, K.: First steps to curbing toxicity. Discus Blog, April 2017. https://perma.cc/B7XE-7TD8
28. Schmidt, A., Wiegand, M.: A survey on hate speech detection using natural language processing. In: Proceedings of the Fifth International Workshop on Natural Language Processing for Social Media. Association for Computational Linguistics, Valencia, Spain, pp. 1–10 (2017)
29. Schrock, A., Boyd, D.: Problematic youth interaction online: solicitation, harassment, and cyberbullying. In: Computer-Mediated Communication in Personal Relationships, pp. 368–398 (2011)
30. Spertus, E.: Smokey: automatic recognition of hostile messages. In: IAAI-97 Proceedings, pp. 1058–1065 (1997)
31. Stroud, N.J., Scacco, J.M., Muddiman, A., Curry, A.L.: Changing deliberative norms on news organizations' Facebook sites. J. Comput.-Mediated Commun. **20**(2), 188–203 (2015)
32. Sukumaran, A., Vezich, S., McHugh, M., Nass, C.: Normative influences on thoughtful online participation. In: Proceedings of the SIGCHI Conference on Human Factors in Computing Systems, pp. 3401–3410. ACM (2011)
33. Sutton, L.A.: Bitches and skanky hobags. In: Hall, K., Buchholz, M. (eds.) Gender Articulated: Language and the Socially Constructed Self, pp. 279–296. Routledge, London (2001)
34. Tokunaga, R.S.: Following you home from school: a critical review and synthesis of research on cyberbullying victimization. Comput. Hum. Behav. **26**(3), 277–287 (2010)
35. Wagner, K.: Twitter says its going to start pushing more abusive tweets out of sight. Recode, February 2017. https://perma.cc/HKY7-ANR9
36. Wolak, J., Mitchell, K.J., Finkelhor, D.: Does online harassment constitute bullying? an exploration of online harassment by known peers and online-only contacts. J. Adolesc. Health **41**(6), S51–S58 (2007)
37. Wulczyn, E., Thain, N., Dixon, L.: Ex Machina: personal attacks seen at scale. In: Proceedings of the 26th International Conference on World Wide Web, pp. 1391–1399. International World Wide Web Conferences Steering Committee (2017)

Poster Papers: Proximity, Location, Mobility, and Urban Analytics

Modeling and Managing Airport Passenger Flow Under Uncertainty: A Case of Fukuoka Airport in Japan

Hiroaki Yamada[1(✉)], Kotaro Ohori[1,3], Tadashige Iwao[2,3],
Akifumi Kira[3,4], Naoyuki Kamiyama[3,5], Hiroaki Yoshida[1],
and Hirokazu Anai[1,3]

[1] Fujitsu Laboratories Ltd., 1-1, Kamikodanaka 4-chome,
Nakahara-ku, Kawasaki 211-8588, Japan
yamadah@jp.fujitsu.com
[2] Fujitsu Ltd., Shiodome City Center 1-5-2 Higashi-Shimbashi,
Minato-ku, Tokyo 105-7123, Japan
[3] Institute of Mathematics for Industry, Kyushu University,
744 Motooka, Nishi-ku, Fukuoka 819-0395, Japan
[4] Faculty of Social and Information Studies, Gunma University,
4-2 Aramaki-machi, Maebashi, Gunma 371-8510, Japan
[5] JST, PRESTO, 4-1-8 Honcho, Kawaguchi, Saitama 332-0012, Japan

Abstract. Airport terminal decision makers in recent years need to deal with unexpected and sudden congestion situations. Although various types of mathematical researchs has analyzed the congestion situations and have succeed to manage a subsystem, they cannot sufficiently describe the variety of phenomena observed in a real airport terminal, because they have not considered the interactions between subsystems of the real airport terminal. A simulation approach enables us to describe the interactions between facilities and passenger behavior in detail as a whole airport system and to find various types of possible congestion situations. The simulation approach, however, cannot directly lead exact prediction that can be useful in practical management and operation for difficulties of modeling a complex airport terminal system and acquiring complete input data. In this paper, (1) we modeled Fukuoka airport international terminal in Japan as Complex Adaptive System and built a passenger flow simulation based on the Discrete Event Model. Validity of the model was confirmed by experiments. Moreover, (2) we confirmed that it is possible to acquire simulation input data from discussing with stakeholders using the simulation. Therefore, we believe that it is possible to reduce uncertainty of the model systematically by continuing modeling, predicting, and discussing with stakeholders, repeatedly.

Keywords: Passenger flow simulation · Airport terminal · Complex adaptive system · Discrete event model · System design methodology

© Springer International Publishing AG 2017
G.L. Ciampaglia et al. (Eds.): SocInfo 2017, Part II, LNCS 10540, pp. 419–430, 2017.
DOI: 10.1007/978-3-319-67256-4_33

1 Introduction

Airport terminal decision makers in recent years need to deal with unexpected and sudden congestion situations. The unexpected congestions are caused by periodic or sudden condition change, such as passengers demand [2, 11], weather and equipment behavior [13], and also unintended and emerging effects of a variety of interventions conducted by multi-stakeholders [4]. In order to prevent congestions which cause delay of flights [9] and lowering of passengers' satisfaction [6], necessity of optimizing airport terminals in space-time high resolution and from holistic viewpoint is growing.

To predict and control the congestion situations, various types of mathematical researchs have analyzed the change of congestion situations from the viewpoint of planning the adequate capacity of facilities based on the estimation of passengers demands [21, 27], and designing landing slot auction based on peak-load pricing [19]. Although these studies have high practicability to the planning of a specific facility of an airport terminal, most models have not considered the interactions between many facilities of the terminal. As a result, they cannot sufficiently describe various phenomena observed in a real airport terminal. On the other hand, there is also simulation researchs that analyzed passengers flow and the optimal operation schedule [25]. The simulation approach enables us to describe the model of facilities and passengers behavior in detail as a whole airport system and to find various types of possible congestion situations that can be observed in the terminal. The simulation approach, however, cannot directly lead exact congestion prediction that can be useful for practical operation from the following two viewpoints: (1) modeling of a complex airport terminal system; (2) acquisition of complete input data.

The airport terminal system consists of plural subsystems such as baggage X-ray inspection facility, check-in facility, security checks facility, and departure examination facility, which are mutually connected to autonomously communicate with each other. The autonomous distributed system, which can be regarded as Complex Adaptive Systems (CAS) [14], has emergent properties such as percolation and phase transition [4, 5], and then causes various types of congestion situations due to the properties. In order to analyze practical issues in CAS, it is necessary to build a system model that can represent subsystems and the relationship among them in detail and to consider overall optimization of the whole system based on the model [14, 29].

The acquisition of complete input data is also a critical problem when using the simulation model for practical situation. Although the complex airport model can describe various types of situations observed in a real world, high accuracy and large amounts of input data is required to set the model parameters [19, 20]. It is difficult, however, to get complete data for setting about the model parameters from multi-stakeholders such as airlines, a security company and an airport building company at the airport terminals for the following two reasons. First, they cannot understand the effectiveness of simulation technique as a solution for reducing congestion without the explanation of simulation results. Second, they have high cost efforts in confirming their regulation relevant to information management so as to take the information outside. Hence, we need to consider a novel approach to gain the data for building a complex simulation model in multi-stakeholders situations.

The purposes of this paper are (1) to build an airport terminal model that has the features of CAS with appropriate level of abstraction, and (2) to consider a data collection process which systematically reduces the lack or the error of simulation input data through communication with multi-stakeholders in the airport.

2 Modeling and Managing Strategy

We select Fukuoka Airport International Terminal (FUK int'l terminal), which has the feature of CAS explained in the previous section, in Japan as a target field. This section describes a problem situation in FUK int'l terminal, and then states our research strategies for (1) building a FUK int'l terminal model in an appropriate level of abstraction and (2) collecting real data to input the model parameters systematically.

Fukuoka Airport is the third-largest airport after Haneda Airport and Narita International Airport in Japan, and has 20 million passengers per year in 2014. The number of inbound travelers is rapidly growing and congestion becomes serious. The terminal departure floor consists of baggage X-ray inspection facility, security checks facility, check-in facility, and departure examination facility. An airport security company operates the X-ray inspection and security checks facilities, airline companies controls the check-in facility and the immigration bureau controls the departure examination facility. So each stakeholder is required to handle passenger flow auton-omously in bottom-up management rather than top-down one, and then the whole system including the facilities has the feature of CAS. Since there are multi-stakeholders who have various types of information that cannot be opened to other ones due to the restriction of security and information system, it is difficult for each stakeholder to understand the congestion situation of facilities managed by other stakeholders (see Appendix 1). In the air port, the passengers adopt homogenous behavior without autonomous decision-making processes, but the characteristic are different in each passenger. For example, the passengers who ride on LCC carriers mainly consist of some tourist groups with many baggage items, while legacy carriers have a number of business passengers who have few baggage and travel by themselves. The difference of passengers' characteristics changes dynamically depending on the flight and season, which generates various types of congestion behavior and makes prediction in practical management.

To analyze the problem situations, we build the model of FUK int'l terminal departure floor. There have been various types of case studies that tried to analyze queuing behavior of customers based on a basic mathematical models, which consists of the customers' arrival process, the mechanism of service procedures and the rule of queue formation [1, 15, 21, 28]. Dunlay & Park [7] provided the queueing network model that can represent the structure of a series of service procedures in multiple facilities of FUK int'l terminal departure floor. However the queuing models cannot consider individual heterogeneity in detail and accordingly they cannot describe com-plex congestion behavior generated by the different types of passengers of our concern. On the other hand, simulation research with an individual model can represent the heterogeneity of passengers [8]. The simulation research is mainly classified into dis-crete event simulation (DES) and agent-based simulation (ABS) [3]. DES can represent that heterogeneous entities [8, 16], which do not have decision making capability, behave in pre-determined process, while ABS enable us to describe individual level decision making and interactions in detail [10, 17, 22, 26]. The passengers in FUK int'l terminal departure floor, advance in the pre-determined procedures, but have heterogeneous characteristics that affect the procedure time in each facility. Therefore, we select DES for building our model that represents facilities and passengers in FUK int'l terminal departure floor.

Next we explain the research process to consider the methodological issue to acquire complete data for the model parameters settings. As one of effective ways, in order to collect data for simulation models automatically, sensing devices have been examined [12, 18]. However, it is difficult to introduce the devices into FUK int'l terminal for developing the model due to cost and security related restrictions. As we explained in Sect. 1, we therefore need to acquire the data from multi-stakeholders who have enough domain knowledge about own facilities and passengers. Ohori et al. [23, 24] pointed out the communication with stakeholders through the simulation results is useful to extract their domain knowledge efficiently. We also focus on the usage of the simulation as communication tool, and then gradually extract the knowledge from them while repeating presentation of simulation analyses with various settings. As a result, we will be able to collect the complete data for model parameters, and thus to predict congestion situation exactly in the multi-stakeholder situations.

3 Model

We model all facilities and all passengers of the FUK int'l terminal departure floor based on the Discrete Event Model. There are four types of facilities which passengers are needed to pass, baggage X-ray inspection, check-in, security check, and departure examination. Baggage X-ray inspection, check-in, security check, and departure examination consist of several number of units or counters. And a check-in counter consists of several number of booths. The counter or the booth, the passenger uses, is predetermined by his/her flight. The time being needed to pass depends on number of people or number of baggages. If the passenger has more than one available the counters or the booths, he/she chooses not congested one. If the counter or booth is closed where the passenger queues, he/she goes another counter or booth. Passengers who are member of tour group have unique behaviors. They arrive at the airport at the same time, because they board same tour bus. They pass the baggage X-ray inspection and the check-in individually. But, they pass the security check with other tour members. Namely, they wait other tour members in front of the security check. Those behavior are represented by a Queueing Network and model parameters' values are collected by several ways (see Appendix 2).

The baggage X-ray inspection facility $B_n(B\_p_n, B\_s_n)$ has 2 parameters: processing speed B_p_n is the time being needed to inspect one baggage, operation schedule B_s_n is the timetable of operation. The check-in facility $C_{nm}(C\_cp_{nm}, C\_bp_{nm}, C\_s_{nm}, C\_t_{nm})$ has 4 parameters: check-in processing speed C_cp_{nm} is the time being needed making one person check-in. baggage processing speed C_bp_{nm} is the time being needed making one baggage check-in. operation schedule C_s_{nm} is the same as the baggage facility model's one, passenger type C_t_{nm} represents the booth for business class or the booth for economy class. The security check facility S_n has 2 parameters $S_n(S\_p_n, S\_s_n)$ and the departure examination facility E_n has 2 parameters $E_n(E\_p_n, E\_s_n)$. Those parameters are the same as the baggage X-ray inspection facility. n is unit number or counter number. A check-in counter consists of several number of booths, so m is booth number of counter n.

A group of passengers, such as a family or a group of friends, is a unit of passenger model. A group G_i has 7 parameters $G_i(G\_f_i, G\_a_i, G\_p_i, G\_cob_i, G\_cib_i, G\_s_i, G\_t_i)$: boarding flight G_f_i, arrival time at terminal G_a_i, number of people G_p_i, number of carry-on baggages G_cob_i, number of check-in baggages G_cib_i, type of seat (economy class passengers or business class passengers) G_s_i, and member of tour group or not G_t_i. The groups are generated by each flight. A flight F_j has 11 parameters $F_j(F\_ea_j, F\_ba_j, F\_ep_j, F\_bp_j, F\_eg_j, F\_bg_j, F\_ecob_j, F\_bcob_j, F\_ecib_j, F\_bcib_j, F\_t_j)$: arrival time distribution of economy passengers F_ea_j and business one F_ba_j, number of economy passengers F_ep_j and business one F_bp_j, group size distribution of economy passengers F_eg_j and business one F_bg_j, distribution of number of carry-on baggages of economy passengers F_ecob_j and business one F_bcob_j, distribution of number of check-in baggages of economy passengers F_ecip_j and business one F_bcip_j, and the number of tour group F_t_j. i is group number and j is flight number.

4 Experiment

4.1 Experiment 1

Outline. In order to validate the model, the experiment was conducted on every morning of February 21, 22, and 23, 2017. On Feb. 21, we adjusted security check facility's schedule based on simulation prediction. The temporal variation of each facilitie's queue lengths was measured. We used 95% prediction interval to evaluate predictability of the model. Prediction rate is defined by rate of the sample points correctly predicted by 95% prediction interval.

Result. Table 1 shows the result of experiment. The check-in have been well predicted, on the other hand, baggage X-ray inspection and security checks have been mis-predicted.

Table 1. The result of experiment 1.

	Feb. 21	Feb. 22	Feb. 23
Baggage X-ray inspection	57.81%	52.12%	52.12%
Check-in	80.99%	84.11%	83.33%
Security check	33.02%	46.67%	37.46%

Analysis. We hypothesized that the mis-prediction on the security check caused by seasonal difference of processing speed. Passengers wear coats only in winter season, thus additional operation time is required on security check compared with summer season. We observed two additional actions: inspectors direct passengers to remove coats, after that passengers remove their coats.

Table 2 shows the simulation result considering seasonal difference of processing speed. Figure 1 shows temporal variation of queue length of a counter. An unpredicted peak has become replicating. The result implies that seasonal difference of processing speed caused mis-prediction. Heidt & Gluchshenko [13] pointed out that change of equipment behavior causes change of congestion situation.

Table 2. The security check predictability without and with seasonal difference simulation.

	Feb. 21	Feb. 22	Feb. 23
Without seasonal difference ($\lambda = 1/13$)	33.02%	46.67%	37.46%
With seasonal difference ($\lambda = 1/17$)	56.61%	79.68%	74.60%

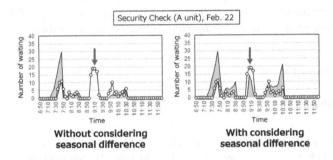

Fig. 1. Temporal variation of queue length of a unit. Grey area is 95% prediction interval, solid lien is the measured value.

Discussion with stakeholders. We discussed with a security company manager and airport building company managers based on the result. As a result of the discussion, the stakeholders recognized the importance of the security check processing speed data, and we reached a consensus on to measure processing speed and to provide it for experiment 2.

4.2   Experiment 2

Outline. Next experiment was conducted on April 12, 2017 morning. We predicted and measured queue length of the security check. There are two differences in Experiment 2 from Experiment 1: (1) Using actual processing speed of the security check counters ($\lambda = 1/14, 1/14, 1/38, 1/18, 1/14$). The data were collected from March 31, 2017 to April 11, 2017, (2) A full-body scanner, which conducts security check automatically, was introduced. A security check unit replaced by a full-body scanner on March 31.

Result. Figure 2 shows the result of experiment 2. The predictability has been increased.

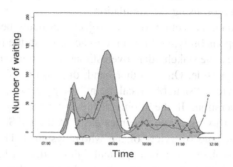

Fig. 2. The result of experiment 2. Grey area is 95% prediction interval, line (red) is average of the simulation of 100 trials, and line with points (blue) is the measured value. (Color figure online)

Discussion with stakeholders. In order to extract experts' domain knowledge, we conducted discussion with the security company manager.

Through the discussion, it was revealed that there are 10 factors causing irregular congestion. (1) Variation of Check-in speed is different for airlines, (2) Check-in speed is different for flights, (3) Check-in speed is different for staffs, (4) Check-in speed is different for passenger types, (5) Queue formation rule in check-in is different for flights, (6) Check-in schedule is variable, (7) Security check speed is different for staffs and seasons, (8) Passenger nationality is different for seasons, (9) Passenger behavior is different for flights, and (10) Number of passengers depends on travel campaigns.

Additionally, it was revealed that the manager has a way controlling above uncertainties. The manager controls uncertainties by a simple strategy: "planning based on the worst scenario, operating for cost reduction". The following is a planning and operating process adopted in practical situation. (i) The airport building and the airlines make flight plan in summer and winter. (ii) The security check manager estimates maximum number of passengers who arrive at each time, from departure time and number of seats of each flight, which are contained flight plan. And the manager makes schedule every month based on the estimated maximum passengers. (iii) The manager conducts everyday operation based on the schedule. But, if excess of the processing capacity becomes clear, the manager closes surplus facilities in the time. This simple strategy reduces the personnel cost, besides suppresses disturbance from uncertainties.

5 Discussion

The information and knowledge gotten from the discussion with stakeholders is unknown in advance. On the process gathering those information and knowledge, we found two remarkable phenomena in the discussion with stakeholders: facilitating cooperation and externalizing tacit knowledge. In the experiment 1, the stakeholders could make collective decision to cooperate for gathering processing data by the discussion using the simulation. In the experiment 2, the manager could externalize own tacit knowledge, 10 uncertainties factors and the strategy of controlling uncertainties, by the discussion using the simulation.

In the CAS, deciding and acting for new project is difficult, because, there is no one having authority, responsibility, and resource to accomplish the project [30]. By those organizational features, the stakeholders overestimate coordination costs and hesitate to take the information outside. On the other hand, discussion using explicit model and concrete results provides "sharable focal point" to perceive problem situation and cost-benefit of cooperation. If the problem and the necessity is obvious to every stakeholders, decision to cooperate becomes easy. In the CAS, it is also difficult for stakeholders to understand overview of the whole system [31]. Therefore the stakeholders can not recognize what is important information, what is unique domain knowledge, and which they have to provide it. Moreover, they are not familiar with system thinking. Explicit model and concrete results provide "mental model" to externalize experts' tacit knowledge. It is easier for experts to point out mistakes of model or parameter sets than express the correct situation from scratch.

We propose a system design methodology to develop a simulation of complex system and in multi-stakeholders situation. Under such situation, generally we cannot get enough knowledge and information because of organizational and social problems. Therefore, we need develop not only simulation but also stakeholders. We consider that by continuing modeling, simulating, and discussing repeatedly, it is possible to change technological and social aspect mutually (Fig. 3).

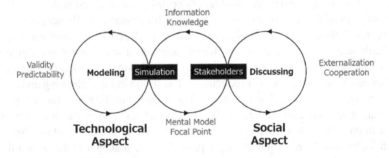

Fig. 3. Schematic view of design process of the simulation.

Acknowledgement. We appreciate to Fukuoka Airport Building Co., Ltd. for useful comments and considerable efforts. We are grateful to Mr. Daisuke Sunada and Mr. Kazuhiro Tokiwa for developing a simulator implemented our model. Naoyuki Kamiyama was supported by JST PRESTO Grant Number JPMJPR14E1, Japan. Akifumi Kira was supported in part by JSPS KAKENHI Grant Numbers 26730010 and 17K12644.

Appendix 1

In this appendix, we describe detail of the problem situation. Figure 4 shows passengers flow and management organizations of Fukuoka airport international terminal (FUK int'l terminal) departure floor in Japan. The baggage X-ray inspection consists of 6 inspection units, the check-in consists of 12 check-in counters and each counter having 8 booths, the security check consists of 5 inspection units, and the departure examination consists of 3 counters. The departure floor roughly divide in north area and south area. North-units of baggage X-ray inspection and from A counter to F counter of check-in are placed in north area. South-units of baggage X-ray inspection and from G counter to M counter of check-in are placed in south area. Each check-in counter are managed by each airline, and the passengers use own flight counter. The check-in booth is assigned for business class passenger or economy class passenger. If the passengers use north area check-in counter, they have to use north-units of baggage X-ray inspection. It is the same in the south area. The security checks counters and departure examinations are used by all passengers freely.

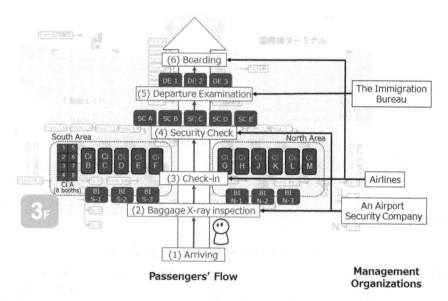

Fig. 4. Passengers' flow and management organizations of FUK int'l terminal departure floor.

The boarding process at the terminal departure floor is composed of the following steps: a passenger (i) has the examination of his/her check in baggage at the baggage X-ray inspection facility; (ii) checks in at the airport counter facility; (iii) gets the inspection of his/her body and carry-on baggage at the security checks facility; (iv) gets the inspections of his/her passport and flight ticket at departure immigration facility; and (v) proceeds to the boarding gate of his/her flight. In particular, most of passengers advance from the steps (i) to (iv) directly without visiting other facilities such as a restaurant and an exchange counter.

Appendix 2

In this appendix, we describe detail of the model. Figure 5 shows FUK int'l terminal departure floor represented by the Queueing Network. In this paper, we analyze only baggage X-ray inspection, check-in, and security checks. Because data about the departure examination could not be gathered for security reasons.

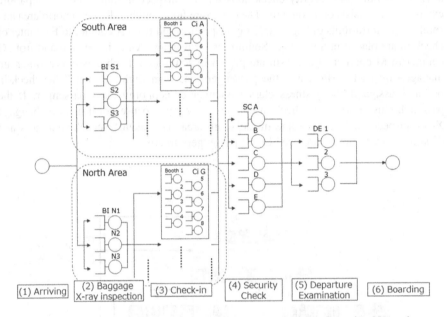

Fig. 5. FUK int'l terminal departure floor represented by the Queueing Network.

Tables 3 and 4 show values, source of values, and collected date of the each parameter.

Table 3. The values of the facilities' parameters.

Parameter	Value	Source of data	Date of collection
B_p_n	Exponential distribution ($\lambda = 1/25$)	Report from a manager	Summer of 2015
C_cp_{nm}, C_bp_{nm}	Exponential distribution (λ is different for each airline)	Counted processing speed	Summer of 2016
S_p_n	Exponential distribution ($\lambda = 1/13$)	Report from a manager	Summer of 2015
B_{s_n}, $C_{s_{nm}}$, $C\_t_{nm}S\_s_n$	Operation schedule	Actual operation schedule	About a month before
E_p_n, E_s_n	Not collectable	–	–

Table 4. The values of the flight's parameters.

Parameter	Value	Source of data	Date of collection
F_ea_j, F_ba_j	Estimated distribution	Counted queue length	Summer of 2016
F_ep_j, F_bp_j, F_t_j	Number of reservations	Reservation data	The day before
$F\_eg_j, F\_bg_j,$ $F\_ecob_j, F\_bcob_j,$ F_ecib_j, F_ecib_j	Empirical distribution	Interview and questionnaire to airport managers	Summer of 2015

References

1. Barbo, W.A.: The use of queuing models in design of baggage claim areas at Airports. Graduate Report. Institute of Transportation and Traffic Engineering, University of California, Berkeley (1967)
2. Beria, P., Laurino, A.: Determinants of daily fluctuations in air passenger volumes. The effect of events and holidays on Milan Malpensa airport. J. Air Transp. Manag. **53**, 73–84 (2016)
3. Borshchev, A., Filippov, A.: From system dynamics and discrete event to practical agent-based modeling: reasons, techniques, tools. In: Proceedings of the 22nd International Conference of the System Dynamics Society, Oxford, England (2004)
4. Bouarfa, S., Blom, H.A., Curran, R., Everdij, M.H.: Agent-based modeling and simulation of emergent behavior in air transportation. Complex Adapt. Syst. Model. **1**(15), 1–26 (2013)
5. Cook, A., Blom, H.A.P., Lillo, F., Mantegna, R.N., Miccichè, S., Rivas, D., Zanin, M.: Applying complexity science to air traffic management. J. Air Transp. Manag. **42**, 149–158 (2015)
6. Correia, A.R., Wirasinghe, S.C., de Barros, A.G.: Overall level of service measures for airport passenger terminals. Transp. Res. Part A: Policy Pract. **42**(2), 330–346 (2008)
7. Dunlay, W.J., Park, C.H.: Tandem-queue algorithm for airport user flows. Transp. Eng. J. ASCE **104**(TE2), 131–149 (1978)
8. Eilon, S., Mathewson, S.: A simulation study for the design of an air terminal building. IEEE Trans. Syst. Man Cybern. **3**(4), 308–317 (1973)
9. Eurocontrol: Impact Study of Landside Elements on Airport Capacity and Delays (2009)
10. Fayez, M.S., Kaylani, A., Cope, D., Rychlik, N., Mollaghasemi, M.: Managing airport operations using simulation. J. Simul. **2**, 41–52 (2008)
11. Gillen, D., Hasheminia, H.: Estimating the demand responses for different sizes of air passenger groups. Transp. Res. Part B: Methodological **49**, 24–38 (2013)
12. Gongora, M., Ashfaq, W.: Analysis of passenger movement at birmingham international airport using evolutionary techniques. In: IEEE Congresson Evolutionary Computation (CEC), pp. 1339–1345 (2006)
13. Heidt, A., Gluchshenko, O.: From uncertainty to robustness and system's resilience in ATM: a case study. In: Proceedings of the Third International Air Transport and Operations Symposium, Delft, Netherlands (2012)
14. Holland, J.H.: Studying complex adaptive systems. J. Syst. Sci. Complexity **19**, 1–8 (2006)
15. Horonjeff, R.: Planning and Design of Airports, 1st edn. McGraw Hill Book Company, New York (1962)

16. Jim, H.K., Chang, Z.Y.: An airport passenger terminal simulator: a planning and design tool. Simul. Pract. Theor. **6**(4), 387–396 (1998)
17. Ju, Y., Wang, A., Che, H.: Simulation and optimization for the airport passenger flow. In: International Conference on Wireless Communications, Networking and Mobile Computing (WiCom), pp. 6605–6608 (2007)
18. Kim, B., Lee, G.-G., Yoon, J.-Y., Kim, J.-J., Kim, W.-Y.: A method of counting pedestrians in crowded scenes. In: Huang, D.-S., Wunsch, Donald C., Levine, Daniel S., Jo, K.-H. (eds.) ICIC 2008. LNCS, vol. 5227, pp. 1117–1126. Springer, Heidelberg (2008). doi:10.1007/978-3-540-85984-0_134
19. Madas, M.A., Zografos, K.G.: Airport slot allocation: from instruments to strategies. J. Air Trans. Manag. **12**(2), 53–62 (2006)
20. Manataki, I.E., Zografos, K.G.: A generic system dynamics based tool for airport terminal performance analysis. Transp. Res. Part C: Emerg. Technol. **17**(4), 428–443 (2009)
21. Newell, G.F.: Application of Queuing Theory. Chapman and Hall, London (1971)
22. Odoni, A.R., de Neufville, R.: Passenger terminal design. Transp. Res. Part A: Policy Pract. **26**(1), 27–35 (1992)
23. Ohori, K., Kobayashi, N., Obata, A., Takahashi, A., Takahashi, S.: Decision support for management of agents' knowledge and skills with job rotation in service-oriented organization. In: 45th Hawaii International Conference on Systems Science (HICSS-45 2012), Proceedings, Grand Wailea, Maui, HI, USA, 4–7 January, pp. 1492–1501 (2012)
24. Ohori, K., Yamane, S., Kobayashi, N., Obata, A., Takahashi, S.: Agent-based social simulation as an aid to communication between stakeholders. In: Chen, S.-H., Terano, T., Yamamoto, R., Tai, C.-C. (eds.) Advances in Computational Social Science. ASS, vol. 11, pp. 265–277. Springer, Tokyo (2014). doi:10.1007/978-4-431-54847-8_17
25. Schultz, M., Fricke, H.: Managing passenger handling at airport terminals individual-based approach for modeling the stochastic passenger behavior. In: Proceedings of the 9th USA/Europe Air Traffic Management Research and Development Seminar, ATM 2011, pp. 438–447 (2011)
26. Takakuwa, S., Oyama, T.: Modeling people flow: simulation analysis of international-departure passenger flows in an airport terminal. Winter Simulation Conference, pp. 1627–1634. Louisiana, New Orleans (2003)
27. Tosic, V.: A review of airport passenger terminal operations analysis and modelling. Transp. Res. Part A: Policy Pract. **26**(1), 3–26 (1992)
28. Tosic, V., Babic, O., Janic, M.: Airport Passenger Terminal simulation, Annals of Operations Research in Air Transportation, Faculty of Transport and Traffic Engineering. University of Belgrade, pp. 83–103 (1983)
29. Wu, P.P.-Y., Mengersen, K.: A review of models and model usage scenarios for an airport complex system. Transp. Res. Part A: Policy Pract. **47**, 124–140 (2013)
30. McDermott, T., Rouse, W., Goodman, S., Loper, M.: Multi-level modeling of complex socio-technical systems. Proc. Comput. Sci. **16**, 1132–1141 (2013)
31. Park, H., Clear, T., Rouse, W.B., Basole, R.C., Braunstein, M.L., Brigham, K.L., Cunningham, L.: Multilevel simulations of health delivery systems: a prospective tool for policy, strategy, planning, and management. Serv. Sci. **4**(3), 253–268 (2012)

When Internet Really Connects Across Space: Communities of Software Developers in Vkontakte Social Networking Site

Olessia Koltsova[(⊠)] [ID], Sergei Koltcov [ID],
and Yadviga Sinyavskaya [ID]

Laboratory for Internet Studies,
National Research University Higher School of Economics,
55/2 Sedova Street, Saint-Petersburg, Russia
linis-spb@hse.ru

Abstract. Following the discussion on the role of Internet in the formation of ties across space, this paper seeks to supplement recent findings on prevalence of location-dependent preferential attachment online. We look at networks of online communities specifically aimed at development of location-independent ties. The paper focuses on the 25 largest communities of software developers in the leading Russian social networking site VKontakte, one of the communities being studied in depth. Evidence suggests that membership and friendship ties are overwhelmingly cross-city and even cross-country, while an in-depth analysis gives ground to assume that, commenting and liking in such communities might also be location-independent. This group case study provides some insights into a nature of professional networking and shows independence of the three networks: the friendship network as a means of group identification, the commenting network as an advice-giving tool, and the liking network as a result of approval by occasional visitors.

Keywords: Virtual communities · Software developers · Social networks sites · Internet · Social network analysis · SNA

1 Introduction

Do online communities really extend possibilities of offline groups by permitting them to cross space, time or by decreasing the cost of communication? Early reflections on the role of online communities and, more broadly, the Internet for societal bonds have expressed hopes that cyberspace may help people develop both common identities and interactions across space (Cairncross 1997). Recent works, however, discover dependence of online ties on geographic distance or transport connectedness (Goldenberg and Levy 2009; Takhteyev et al. 2012; Scellato et al. 2010; Kaltenbrunner et al. 2012; Traud et al. 2012). Takhteyev et al. (2012) and Scellato et al. 2010 find that people tend to make friends with those who are closer. Kaltenbrunner et al. (2012) specify that the probability of link formation drops dramatically after the distance reaches 30 km (exceeds commuting zone). However, all these conclusions are based on ego-networks

© Springer International Publishing AG 2017
G.L. Ciampaglia et al. (Eds.): SocInfo 2017, Part II, LNCS 10540, pp. 431–442, 2017.
DOI: 10.1007/978-3-319-67256-4_34

or, as in Kaltenbrunner's case, on the entire population of links of a social networking site, which is in fact similar to studying ego-networks. The latter might be thought of as naturally including those who are physically proximate. Traud et al. (2012) deal with a specific sample of students of 100 universities where location is dormitory and members are by definition not geographically far.

But certain kinds of communities may be more inclined to develop ties across space and may be even specifically aimed at it. Thus, worldwide social movements would be constrained only by language barriers, not by distance per se. For instance, Facebook groups have been critical in the spread of Occupy movement across the globe (Caren and Gaby 2011). Likewise, in the past decade people with rarely occurring diseases have tended to form very successful support communities online (Lasker et al. 2005). Recent research also shows that professional communities have proliferated particularly with certain kinds of occupations, such as medical workers, educators and software developers/IT professionals, as well as students of respective professions (Thompson et al. 2008; Duncan-Howell 2010; Ziovas and Grigoriadou 2008; Barcellini et al. 2005). These are professions that can potentially benefit from creating virtual communities, and it makes sense to expect them to be distance-independent.

Among those professionals, software developers are of special interest as they can literally collaborate online (Wu 2014), however, as Singer et al. (2014) have established, they also use social networks to stay aware of industry changes, to follow specific projects and to promote their own ones, as well as for learning, and for building professional relationships and networking. This latter function is particularly important: Wickramasinghe and Weliwitigoda (2011) find out that the number of networks of which an individual is a member and the frequency of interaction significantly predict job security and career advancement of software developers in Sri Lanka. Finally, it is known that online communities play an identity-building role for some professions that demand this identity to be strong (Hara and Foon Hew 2007; Goos and Bennison 2008). Software developers are among those whose identity is very strong (Marks and Scholarios 2007), which suggests that software developers would benefit from cross-space ties.

Thus, if we want to single out the long-distance connecting role of the internet it makes full sense to look for its space-crossing functions there where people are intentionally trying to make use of them, not there where they use it for local ties maintenance.

For instance, McGee et al. (2011), in line with other geographical research of the internet ties, find that people tend to have their Twitter connections situated at the distance of approximately ten miles; then, however, they find an additional and in fact a much stronger peak at the distance of 1000 miles, which is especially pronounced for the relations of unreciprocated friendships and mentionings. They conclude that different types of relations and communication develop at different distances, and, specifically, that long-distance connections are used for information dissemination more than for reciprocated strong friendship ties. For our purposes, therefore, it makes sense, first, to look at different types of connections, not only at static friendship/followship, but also at more dynamic communication patterns, such as commenting, liking or mentioning. Second, it makes sense to measure the inclination toward space-crossing connections not as a proportion of individual links, but as a proportion of links in a community that seeks to connect people independently of their location.

Such an attempt is made in this work, with same-city links being considered "local" and between-city links viewed as "space-crossing".

The rest of the article is structured as follows. In the next section we describe our data and justify the sample of 25 largest online groups of software developers. Section 3 presents the main results showing that group membership and friendship formation are location-independent over the entire sample. Section 4 is an in-depth case-study of the most location-independent group that finds no additional location dependencies in three types of networks – friendship, commenting and liking. We conclude with a summary of our findings and suggestions for future research.

2 Data and Sampling

We use data on communities from a social networking site (SNS)B for the purpose of comparability. VKontakte (VK) has been chosen as both the most popular SNS in the Russian-speaking community and the most open in terms of data access. For background comparisons, we use (Demyanenko 2011) and our own research of random samples of 150,000 groups (November 2014) and of 1,350,000 random users (April 2015). These data show that among many professional groups, software developers have been the most active. At the first stage we briefly examined all groups with over than 2,500 members finding 58 of them. Like in Facebook, communities in VK are divided into "pages" and "groups", the latter being either open or closed (that is, available to everybody or to the approved users only). Pages and closed groups allow very little participation of their subscribers or members respectively, so they were excluded from the analysis. Also, we excluded groups that were mere online replicas of offline commercial firms, ending up with 25 groups. We then downloaded all available metadata of group members and the data about friendships among the members of each group, which gave us the total of 265,952 users and 248,768 links. We also downloaded the "wall" (message board) of one of the largest groups, devoted to C#, for

Table 1. Basic features of the developers' groups

	Min	Max	Mean	Median
Users in group	2543	31038	9248	7541
Non-deactivated users (NDU) in group	1255	23057	7488	6705
Edges between NDU in group	300	36817	7606.6	3270
Cities in group	96	2033	981	1035
% of NDU having cities	53.1	96.2	84	85.3
Non-isolated (connected) NDU	317	7759	2556.3	1432
% of non-isolated NDU in sample	36.0	99.4	74.3	77.2
% of edges between non-isolated NDU in sample	34	97.4	73.5	74.2
Cities in sample	36	894	361.2	336
% of same-city links in sample among all links in sample	6.1	60.2	26	15.6
E-I index in sample	0.14	0.94	0.67	0.83
% of users from Moscow	0.95	13	5	4
% of users from Saint-Petersburg	0.32	7	3	2.6

qualitative in-depth analysis. In later stages of the analysis we also exclude all deactivated accounts. Table 1 shows descriptive statistics over the selected 25 groups.

3 Geography of Friendship in the Sample of 25 Groups

Space and ability/inclination to connect across space can be conceptualized in a number of different ways. For instance, they may be measured as exact distance between users. However, first, we do not know the distance between same-city VK users. Second, and most important: exact distance between cities in such spaces as Russia and post-Soviet world seems not the most relevant, since even "small" distances are most often too large to commute, transport connection is poor and expensive, and most kinds of "offline" social life tend to be clustered within cities or villages. That is why belonging to the same city was selected as a proxy for the geographical "sameness". Somewhat similar approach has been used in (Lengyel et al. 2015).

For the 25 selected groups, basic descriptive statistics and a number of network measures are presented in Table 1. On average, in these groups, 84% of non-deactivated users indicate their cities, but around 70% of the former are friendless. The subsets of linked pairs where both vertices have cities embrace on average 74% of all non-deactivated friended users and 73% of edges among the latter. Unavailability of the city usually depends on accounts' privacy settings: in closed accounts all user metadata (except gender and friends that can not be hidden) are concealed altogether. Therefore, we do not suspect that some types of cities lead their inhabitants to hide them more than others, and so no sample bias is expected.

The mere city count already shows that users are scattered across a large number of cities. Their distribution is highly skewed, but reflects the general VK city distribution that by the time of data collection was not yet affected by the Russian-Ukrainian crisis. Moscow and then St.-Petersburg clearly dominate; Kiev, Ukraine's capital, and Minsk, Belorussian capital can always be seen in the top, too, while the cities that follow present a mixture of Russian, Ukrainian and Belorussian places in the proportion close the general VK proportion. Most cities in the long tail are represented by a single user. Thus, if belonging to the same group is considered a tie, software-interested users clearly develop these ties irrespectively of their locations: they come to these groups even if no offline neighbors are there.

A stricter approach, however, is to look at friendship relations within these groups. Between-city links dominate over within-city links as 4:1, on average, although large variation is observed (see Table 1).

A widely known way to see if subgroups have more external links than internal ones is to compare within-city and between-city densities. Network density, however, is a ratio of all existing links to all possible links (Hanneman and Riddle 2005), while the latter grow in quadratic proportion compared to the former with the growth of a network. The same dependence is between the numbers of internal and external links (Hanneman and Riddle 2005). Since much more between-city links are theoretically possible in our networks, existing between-city links get strongly penalized when they are divided by possible between-city links, and between-city density is by definition always lower then within-city density.

A similar problem exists with methods involving comparison of existing systems of links to random graphs (such as QAP correlations and some other homophily tests), since the probability to get a link across the cities in a random graph is much higher simply because much more between-city links are possible, given our city distribution. This problem was acknowledged and addressed by Krackhardt and Stern (1988), where the authors proposed E-I index which for each a given subgroup (e.g. city) is computed as:

$$EI = \frac{EL - IL}{EL + IL} \tag{1}$$

where EL – the number of external links of a subgroup, IL – the number of internal links of a subgroup.

A global E-I index, although it is not described by Krackhardt and Stern (1988), is usually calculated as the mean of local indices (Hanneman and Riddle 2005). The index ranges from – 1 (no external links) to 1 (no internal links), and is equal to zero when all subgroups on average have the same number of external and internal links. This – although it does look obvious at the first glance – means that zero global EI corresponds to the global internal-external link ratio 2:1. This happens because each external link of subgroup i is also an external link for another subgroup j to which it leads, and thus is counted twice: in EI_i and in EI_j.. Thus, when globalized, EI keeps a "local vision" of the ratio of internal and external ties.

In our sample of VK groups, mean global EI (1) is 0.67 (median = 0.83), with 21 out of 25 groups having it over 0.5, but even for the group with 60% of internal links it takes a positive value of 0.14.

This is already a good confirmation of prevalence of between-city ties over within-city ties in the professional communities analyzed. However, the significance of the EI index observed value is usually checked through its comparison with the values calculated for a series of simulated random graphs – an approach that we have just criticized. The main limitation of this approach is that it sets unrealistic requirements – for instance, with our city distribution each user would have to establish around 95% of between-city links in order to exceed the probability of developing them at random. We suggest to pick up non-random, but sociologically grounded benchmarks for comparison in such cases. Thus, we do not claim that friendships are distributed randomly among cities; instead, we claim that inclination for cross-space ties is stronger in some social situations than in other – in particular, it is stronger than in ego-networks.

We therefore chose to compare the proportion of same-city links of individual users in their communities with the respective proportion in their ego-networks. Because downloading 266 thousand ego-networks through the available VK API would have taken months, we formed a random sample of 1,000 users. As T-test has shown, the difference was significant, although in absolute numbers it was not large (on average, 55% of between-city links in communities against 50% in ego-networks).

4 Case Study: C# Group and Its Networks

For in-depth analysis, we chose a group with the highest combination of size and EI index to check if the group indeed had no other signs of city-based homophily. All major parameters of the C# groups are summarized in Table 2. C# indicates its "location" in Ukraine, while the moderator is situated in Belarus, and the distribution of C# users over countries does not differ from other groups. Nearly all communication in the C# group is in Russian. By the time of data collection, the C# group contained 15,451 members, 895 posts, 1,392 comments and 1,595 likes on the wall. However, of 1,951 users who contributed to the wall only 806 (41.3%) were group members. Most activity in this group takes place on the wall.

Table 2. Basic features of group C#

Users total	15,452
Share of deactivated	34.15
Share of females, among non-deactivated	32.93
Share of Russia, among having country	61.83
Number of cities	1445
Ratio non-deactivated users to cities	7
Share of Moscow, among having city	10.2
Share of St. Petersburg, among having city	3.7
Edges total	35,396
Density	0.00043
Share of isolates, among non-deactivated	49.67
Mean degree, among non-deactivated	6.97
All possible friendships in sample	9 363 628
All possible same-city friendships in sample	543 338
All existing friendships in sample	28 034
All existing same-city friendships in sample	1 733
Total density in sample	0.0029
Overall within-city density in sample	0.00305
Between-city density in sample	0.00280
Possible same-city to possible non-same-city ratio*	0.06121
Existing same-city to existing non-same-city ratio	0.06656
Share of possible same-city links among all possible links	5.77
Share of all existing same-city links among all existing links	6.24
Users total	15,452

With deactivated accounts being filtered out, the friendship network has been clustered with Wakita and Tsurumi (2007) algorithm and it revealed a structure found in most other studied VK groups, and in fact in many other online graphs (Lescovec et al. 2008). It contains a single giant component with no clear underlying structure (modularity = 0.29), a small number of very little components and a large periphery of isolates that constitute the half of the active accounts.

Commenting and liking networks show a different structure (Figs. 3 and 4 of the Appendix). Since most contributors leave only one comment or like, these networks are collections of stars loosely connected by a minority of those who have chosen to leave 2-3 instances of feedback. This tendency especially visible in the liking network with its modularity of 0.85 against 0.4 in the commenting network. Half of the posts receive no comments, and 80% of them are never liked, so the networks are small. Contributing group members are not more, and even a little less central in the networks of friendship than silent members, which additionally suggests that communicative activity, on the one hand, and networking and self-identification with the group, on the other, are disconnected processes.

4.1   Friendship Network in C# Group

As mentioned above, C# group is the one with the higher EI index, that is, prevalence of inter-city ties in it is the strongest. However, it may be argued, that although users clearly prefer to connect beyond their own city, some pairs or subsets of cities may have preferential attachment to each other. To test this, we collapse all users from a given city into a single vertex and construct a weighted friendship graph where vertices are cities, and the number of individual inter-city links is edge weight. Trying to find densely connected subsets of cities we again perform community detection and find no cluster structure (modularity = 0.15). Instead of clustering, we again see a strong center-periphery differentiation with Moscow, Kyev and St.-Petersburg clearly being hubs that dominate in connecting to others.

Although the within-city density in C# friendship network is not much different from between-city density (0.00319 and 0.00298, respectively), the distribution of within-city densities might still be uneven, and a few cities might form dense sub-communities, while the overall low value of modularity might conceal this. Figure 1 shows that the distribution of in-city densities is a mixture of two distributions. A large proportion of cities with less than 20 users demonstrates zero density; when

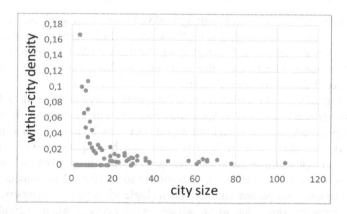

Fig. 1. Relationship between city size and friendship network density, C# group, four largest cities not shown

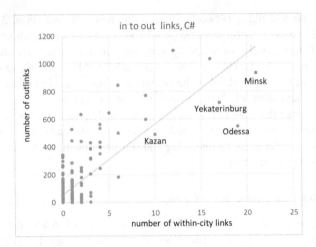

Fig. 2. In-city to out-city ratio distribution, C# group

they are filtered out, the remaining distribution is power-law ($y = 0, 6454x^{-1,268}$). That is, density is highly (and inversely) dependent of the city size, which, as mentioned in a previous section, happens just because it is calculated as the number of existing links divided by nearly squared group size (Hanneman and Riddle 2005). Thus, the studied sample follows the universal trend, and there are no outliers. This means that no unusually dense communities within any cities are observed.

We then hypothesized that, despite absence of unusually dense cities, there may be cities that are unusually disconnected from others. Figure 2 plots cities in the space of in-city and out-city friendships. It shows that most cities have less than five in-group links, while many possess a few hundreds of outlinks. Even those cities that are below the trend line have in-to-out ratio less than one (except a few with 1-4 users).

4.2   Commenting and Liking Features in C# Group

In VK groups several kinds of activity/feedback can be singled out: contribution through posts, comments, likes, and feedback received in comments to posts, likes to posts, and likes to comments. None of them correlates in the C# group, except commenting and liking, which means that users may be divided into posters, on the one hand, and feedback givers, on the other.

The subset of the commenting network for spatial analysis embraced 71% of edges and 62% of vertices (Fig. 3 of the Appendix). In-degrees in this network did not exceed 5, while top six commentators had out-degrees between 12 and 73 which means that the network was dominated by activity hubs, not by popularity stars. Hubs were connected through multiple users who had got commented by several of those active commentators, but had not left a single comment themselves. As commenters tend to be group members and posters are more often single-message non-members, the entire situation seems to correspond to an advice-giving network where a limited set of experts answers questions of occasional visitors.

Geographical analysis of commenting and liking networks is more difficult than that of friendship because the notion of the maximal number of possible links is not applicable: more than one edge between each pair of vertices may exist. Still, if the network that included all commentators and all commented posters was full, and each member could give only one comment, it would contain about 2.7% of same-city links. In real network, with self-comments being filtered out, only eleven same-city links remain, which constitutes 1.6% of the full network - actually lower than it could be expected even if each user could comment another user only once. Observation shows, however, that of the abundance job-seeking/offering posts most invite to connect via private messaging which might conceal the true proportion of within-city links.

In co-like network, with many likers being deactivated and cities of some users being unknown we could only analyze 569 out of 1 595 edges (36%) and 554 vertices. Among those, there were eight self-likes, and only 22 were same-city likes, 19 of which were within Moscow. This network, unlike commenting network, was dominated by popularity stars (like-receivers), while super-active like-givers were much fewer and much less manifest (Fig. 4 of the appendix). Most often, all nearly all likes were given to the same post of a user, which means that this was a network of occasional visitors leaving their only like (or their 2-3 likes) for an attractive message, not for its author. Only one user could be observed that got likes to really a multitude of posts: those were the posts written on behalf of the group itself (i.e. by its moderator).

5   Conclusion

Our research of 25 largest communities of software developers in the leading Russian SNS shows that members of such communities being the most active professionals in this SNS join these groups independently of their location. Each group contains a large number of cities, most of which are single-member, which means that most users do not find their offline neighbors in such groups. Since they still choose to join these groups, the observed power-law city size distribution (which of course prevents within-city linking) cannot be regarded as an external obstacle that hinders the desired geographical homophily; rather, this homophily is not desired, once users choose not to self-select based on location. Moreover, those of them who establish friendships, have more between-city ties than within-city ties. This trend is persistent across all studied communities: although the degree of prevalence of external links varies, internal links never prevail.

Whether this trend would sustain in other professional communities is a question for further research, however, we assume that it would – for relatively large communities, while smaller groups will be more differentiated. In our sample, the number of people per city decreases with the decrease of the group size, while there are no single-city-dominated groups. We think that among smaller groups the proportion of the same-city friendships will drop in one portion of groups, but another type of locally oriented groups will emerge. Actually, it does show up in the search results at the level below 2 500 members where one can find groups that indicate location in their very title (Kiev, St. Petersburg, Krasnoyarsk, Crimea being among the largest groups).

440   O. Koltsova et al.

Our case study also gives some insights into reasons why people in a professional community of software developers like to connect across space. Advice-seeking/ giving, and networking for finding jobs or freelance work and getting software development services dominate. These purposes can only benefit from absence of location-based homophily since the latter can dramatically narrow the range of advice givers or freelance opportunities.

Another interesting observation that is worth checking in a more representative research is absence of relationship between friendship, commenting and liking networks where central positions are occupied by different persons. These networks seem to serve different goals: friendship for identity building, commenting for advice seeking/giving and job seeking, and liking for short-term approval.

Summarizing our findings, we can say that they give a first glimpse at the issue of location-based homophily in online professional communities. They suggest that further worthy findings may be obtained by looking at differences in location-based homophily between different types of networks in various professional communities, on the one hand, and respective types of egonetworks of individual members of those communities, on the other. More reliable conclusions may be drawn from extending the research to other social networking sites and countries.

Acknowledgements. This research was supported by the Basic Research Program of the National Research University Higher School of Economics, 2014.

Appendix

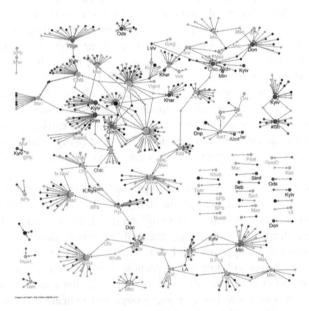

Fig. 3. Likes on posts, C# group. Vertices: individuals. Size: in-degree. Vertices with 0 in-degree not labeled. Arrows indicate direction of liking

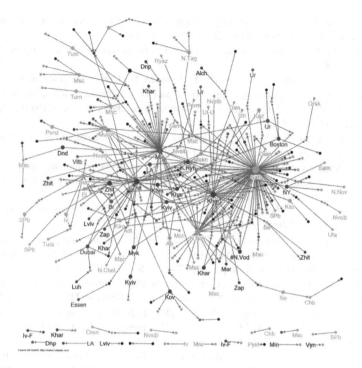

Fig. 4. Likes on posts, C# group. Vertices: individuals. Size: in-degree. Vertices with 0 in-degree not labeled. Arrows indicate direction of liking

References

Barcellini, F., Détienne, F., Burkhardt, J.M., Sack, W.: A study of online discussions in an open-source software community. In: Van Den Besselaar P., De Michelis G., Preece J., Simone C. (eds.) Communities and Technologies proceedings of the Second Communities and Technologies Conference, pp. 301–320. Springer, Netherlands (2005)

Cairncross, F.: The Death of Distance: How the Communications Revolution Will Change Our Lives. Harvard Business School, Cambridge (1997)

Caren, N., Gaby, S.: Occupy online: Facebook and the spread of Occupy Wall Street. SSRN Electron. J. **1943168** (2011). https://papers.ssrn.com/sol3/Papers.cfm?abstract_id=1943168. Last accessed 18 Nov 2016

Demyanenko, I.: Statistics on users' profiles in Vkontakte (2011). http://habrahabr.ru/post/123856/. Last accessed 25 Oct 2015

Duncan-Howell, J.: Teachers making connections: online communities as a source of professional learning. Br. J. Educ. Technol. **41**(2), 324–340 (2010)

Goldenberg, J., Levy, M.: Distance is not dead: social interaction and geographical distance in the internet era (2009). https://www.researchgate.net/publication/45857334. Last accessed 11 Nov 2015

Goos, M.E., Bennison, A.: Developing a communal identity as beginning teachers of mathematics: emergence of an online community of practice. J. Math. Teach. Educ. **11**(1), 41–60 (2008)

Hara, N., Foon Hew, K.: Knowledge-sharing in an online community of health-care professionals. Inf. Technol. People **20**(3), 235–261 (2007)

Hanneman, R.A., Riddle, M.: Introduction to Social Network Methods. University of California, Riverside (2005)

Kaltenbrunner, A., Scellato, S., Volkovich, Y., Laniado, D., Currie, D., Jutemar, E.J., Mascolo, C.: Far from the eyes, close on the web: impact of geographic distance on online social interactions. In: Proceedings of the ACM Workshop on Online Social Networks, pp. 19–24. ACM Press, New York (2012)

Krackhardt, D., Stern, R.N.: Informal networks and organizational crises: an experimental simulation. Soc. Psychol. Q. **51**(2), 123–140 (1988)

Lasker, J.N., Sogolow, E.D., Sharim, R.R.: The role of an online community for people with a rare disease: content analysis of messages posted on a primary biliary cirrhosis mailinglist. J. Med. Internet Res. **7**(1), e10 (2005)

Lengyel, B., Varga, A., Ságvári, B., Jakobi, Á., Kertész, J.: Geographies of an online social network. PLoS ONE **10**(9), e0137248 (2015)

Leskovec, J., Lang, K.J., Dasgupta, A., Mahoney, M.W.: Statistical properties of community structure in large social and information networks. In: Proceedings of the 17th International Conference on World Wide Web, pp. 695–704. ACM Press, New York (2008)

Marks, A., Scholarios, D.: Revisiting technical workers: professional and organizational identities in the software industry. New Technol. Work Employ. **22**(2), 98–117 (2007)

McGee, J., Caverlee, J.A., Cheng, Z.: A geographic study of tie strength in social media. In: Proceedings of the 20th ACM International Conference on Information and Knowledge Management, pp. 2333–2336. ACM Press, New York (2011)

Scellato, S., Mascolo, C., Musolesi, M., Latora, V.: Distance matters: geo-social metrics for online social networks. In: Proceedings of the 3rd Workshop on Online Social Networks, Paris, pp. 88–89. USENIX Association, Boston (2010)

Singer, L., Filho, F., Storey, M.A.: Software engineering at the speed of light: how developers stay current using twitter. In: Proceedings of the 36th International Conference on Software Engineering, Hyderabad, India, pp. 211–221. ACM Press, New York (2014)

Takhteyev, Y., Gruzd, A., Wellman, B.: Geography of Twitter networks. Soc. Netw. **34**(1), 73–81 (2012)

Thompson, L.A., Dawson, K., Ferdig, R., Black, E.W., Boyer, J., Coutts, J., Black, N.P.: The intersection of online social networking with medical professionalism. J. Gen. Internal Med. **23**(7), 954–957 (2008)

Traud, A.L., Mucha, P.J., Porter, M.A.: Social structure of Facebook networks. Phys. A Stat. Mech. Appl. **391**(16), 4165–4180 (2012)

Wakita, K., Tsurumi, T.: Finding community structure in mega-scale social networks: [extended abstract]. In: Proceedings of the 16th International Conference on World Wide Web, Banff, Alberta, Canada, pp. 1275–1276. ACM Press, New York (2007)

Wickramasinghe, V., Weliwitigoda, P.: Benefits gained from dimensions of social capital: a study of software developers in Sri Lanka. Inf. Technol. People **24**(4), 393–413 (2011)

Wu, Y., Kropczynski, J., Shih, P.C., Carroll, J.M.: Exploring the ecosystem of software developers on GitHub and other platforms. In: Proceedings of the Companion Publication of the 17th ACM Conference on Computer Supported Cooperative Work & Social Computing, Baltimore, MD, USA, pp. 265–268. ACM Press, New York (2014)

Ziovas, S., Grigoriadou, M.: Connecting communities through ICT: boundary crossing and knowledge sharing in a web-based 'community of communities'. Int. J. Web Based Commun. **5**(1), 66–82 (2008)

Inferring the Social-Connectedness of Locations from Mobility Data

Tristan Brugman, Mitra Baratchi$^{(\boxtimes)}$, Geert Heijenk, and Maarten van Steen

University of Twente, Enschede, The Netherlands
{t.w.r.m.brugman,m.baratchi,geert.heijenk,m.r.vansteen}@utwente.nl

Abstract. An often discriminating feature of a location is its social character or how well its visitors know each other. In this paper, we address the question of how we can infer the social contentedness of a location by observing the presence of mobile entities in it. We study a large number of mobility features that can be extracted from visits to a location. We use these features for predicting the social tie strengths of the device owners present in the location at a given moment in time, and output an aggregate score of social connectedness for that location. We evaluate this method by testing it on a real-world dataset. Using a synthetically modified version of this dataset, we further evaluate its robustness against factors that normally degrade the quality of such ubiquitously collected data (e.g. noise, sampling frequency). In each case, we found that the accuracy of the proposed method highly outperforms that of a state-of-the-art baseline methodology.

Keywords: Spatial profiling · Link prediction · Mobility data mining · Wi-Fi scanning · Mobility modeling

1 Introduction

Just like people, locations have a social profile. This profile reflects the social connectedness of people who visit those locations and it dynamically changes over time as people with different social ties enter and leave a location. Having knowledge about the social profile of a location before visiting it is a useful addition to location-based recommender systems. If we want to meet new people and make new friends, we may want to visit the most social pub among all the pubs in town. However, if we want to go to a quiet library for studying, a less social one may be more appropriate. Likewise, having knowledge about the social profile of a location helps to improve the services offered there. This has been shown to be important in, for example, elderly care facilitates [1–3].

To create social profiles for locations, in this paper, we design a method that can infer the social connectedness of that location from ubiquitously generated mobility data (such as GPS coordinates, Wi-Fi scans, or check-in records in location-based social networks). While research in spatial profiling [4] from mobility data has previously addressed characterizing locations from such data,

© Springer International Publishing AG 2017
G.L. Ciampaglia et al. (Eds.): SocInfo 2017, Part II, LNCS 10540, pp. 443–457, 2017.
DOI: 10.1007/978-3-319-67256-4_35

creating a social profile for locations has not been addressed before. In order to know how socially connected a location is, we investigate to what extent we can extract the social tie strength of people based on their visit to a single location. Previous research has mainly examined methods to infer the strength of social ties between pairs of individuals. This is achieved by using the global trajectory of mobile entities over *many* locations. We, however, consider characterizing *locations* rather than *individuals*. This means that, in our case the available input data is limited to that acquired from a single location.

Extracting the social context from visiting patterns of people in only a single location is a challenging problem. Mobility data is of limited social interaction content. For example, working in the same building does not guarantee that two people have strong ties or even know each other. Due to the inherent differences in the functionality of locations, the social context can be reflected in different features of visits. It is not yet clear which features of a visit can be used for this purpose. Furthermore, oftentimes additional data with strong social interaction content does not accompany mobility datasets. In most cases ground truth on social ties can only be collected from a small sample of visitors. To address these problems, in this paper, we propose a data-driven technique for extracting an aggregate measure for the social connectedness of a single location by detecting only the presence of people in that location. More specifically:

- We study a large number of features that can be extracted from mobility data acquired from presence of people in a single location.
- We propose a supervised method for selecting among this list of features and consequently learning social ties from them.
- We validate the performance of our method in predicting social tie strengths using a dataset of Wi-Fi mobility data. As ground truth, we use an estimate score of social tie strengths derived from the similarity of devices' SSID (Service Set IDentifiers) sets and show how the method performs by learning from a sample of these social tie indicators.

2 Related Work

There have been a number of previous studies that describe methods for inferring social ties between individuals from either Wi-Fi protocol-specific information, or more general mobility data.

Wi-Fi protocol-specific data: when Wi-Fi-enabled devices try to connect to nearby access points, they often broadcast *probe request* messages, which can be used to infer the social ties between the owners of devices. Detections of probe requests can be used to create a mobility trace representing timestamped presence of mobile devices near Wi-Fi access points (or scanners) [5]. Furthermore, probe requests contain the names of access points that the mobile device has been connected to before (SSIDs). Previous research has shown that it is possible to extract information about the social ties between device-owners from their similarity in SSID lists. The authors of [6] have examined different similarity metrics between the SSID lists of pairs of devices observing a high correlation between SSID lists and social tie strengths acquired by surveying device owners. The authors of [7] use SSID list similarity to extract a social network to confirm the sociological theory of homophily [8]. The study in [9] proposes a framework to use the social information acquired from the SSID list similarity and location visitation frequencies for calculating a venue reputation score. The method in [10] employs different techniques to infer social ties between device owners.

General mobility data: data acquired from location-based social networks, GPS, and cellular networks have also been used for extracting social information. Research presented in [11] describes a method to improve social tie prediction, focusing on user check-ins in location-based social networks. Two different mobility features are extracted for each pair of users that have visited the same location: the minimum place entropy across all venues they have both visited, and the sum of the inverse of each place entropy value. In [12] mobility data from cellular networks is used along with phone call communications to infer a reciprocal friendship social network. Authors of [13] use two information-theoretic indicators to infer social link types of people relying on similarities of their visits extracted from their GPS mobility data.

While the first group of research show that it is possible to infer social relationships from the SSID list, they have not investigated extracting such information purely from the mobility data acquired from probe requests. While SSID lists are specific to the Wi-Fi protocol, datasets made by the detection of probe requests can represent a more general class of mobility datasets such as those acquired from GPS, Bluetooth, cellular networks, etc. Our approach in this paper is to investigate to what extent mobility data acquired from probe requests can be used for extracting social information. The second group of studies, on the other hand, successfully makes use of mobility features to predict the existence of social relationships. By having access to the global trajectories, these methods are successful while only employing a limited number of mobility features. We, however, consider extracting the social context from mobility data collected from a single location. This is implied by our goal, which is characterizing *locations* rather that *individuals*.

3 Preliminaries

The goal of this study is to derive an aggregate social connectedness score for a location using mobility information collected from visitor's devices. In a specific location, we consider having a system that detects presence of visitor devices in it. Wi-Fi scanning [5] near a Wi-Fi scanner allows collection of such a dataset. Before explaining the problem, we define a number of terminologies used in the rest of the paper:

Definition 1. *A **location** is a defined spatial area where presence of devices can be detected. An example of a location is the area covered by a Wi-Fi scanner.*

Definition 2. *A **detection** in a location is a tuple* $\langle d, t \rangle$*, in which* d *represents the identifier of the visiting device and* t *represents the moment in time that the device is detected.*

Definition 3. *A **mobility trace**, denoted by* $\langle MT, t_{start}, t_{end} \rangle$*, is a collection of detections acquired in a timespan ranging from* t_{start} *to* t_{end}*.*

Definition 4. *The **pairwise social tie strength** between two device owners, denoted by* $\{s_{ij} | s_{ij} \in [0,1]\}$*, is the strength of the social tie between the owners of devices* i *and* j*.*

Definition 5. *The **social connectedness score**, denoted by* $\bar{s}$*, is the normalized social tie strength between a group of users. It is a score* $\bar{s} = \frac{1}{|D|} \sum_{i,j \in D} s_{ij}$ *for each set of devices* $D = \{d_1, d_2, ..., d_n\}$*, in which each* d_k *represents a different device.*

Problem: Given a mobility trace $\langle MT, t_{start}, t_{end} \rangle$ and a timestamp $t \in [t_{start}, t_{end}]$, we are interested to infer the aggregate social connectedness score $\bar{s}_t$ for the group of devices that are present in the location at time t.

4   Approach

In this section, we present our approach in extracting the social connectedness score of a location based on visits of people to only that location. Our approach is based on learning the relationship between mobility features and social tie strengths in a supervised manner. For this purpose, we train a model that identifies the relationship between mobility features and samples of social tie strengths. We explore a variety of possible mobility features and use a feature selection algorithm in order to identify a subset of important mobility features related to social ties. In order to determine an indicator for ground truth on social tie strengths, we consider the similarity between devices' Wi-Fi SSID lists. Based on the mobility dataset, other type of ground truth can also be used for this purpose.

4.1   Ground Truth Metric

In order to train a model, we need to obtain ground truth for the social tie strengths between pairs of devices. We take the approach of using the anonymized Wi-Fi SSID lists of each pair of devices, and computing a value that measures their overlap [6,7,9,10,14]. The general intuition is that elements of this list represent presence in places such as device owner's homes which are only probable to be shared when people have strong social ties. The more two lists share such kind of rare SSIDs, the probability that they have stronger ties increases. The research in [6] has compared a variety of similarity metrics, among which a modified version of Adamic-Adar metric known as Psim-3

performs best in determining social ties between individuals. This metric is calculated as $\sum_{z \in X \cap Y} \frac{1}{f_z^3}$, in which X and Y are the two SSID sets, and f_z is the
number of times that identifier z occurs in the dataset. This measure can be
normalized between zero and one based on the maximum strength found in the
whole dataset.

4.2   Method

Our method performs in two phases of learning and inference. During the initialization phase, the model is trained and its features are selected based on a
mobility trace and knowledge about the pairwise social tie strengths. This is
followed by the utilization phase, in which the mobility trace is supplied to the
model, inferring pairwise tie strengths. By combining these strengths with the
devices present at a given timestamp, an aggregate social connectedness score is
then calculated. Figure 1 provides an overview of the proposed method.

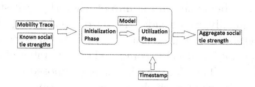

Fig. 1. High-level overview of the proposed method

4.3   Features

To train the model, we have selected 5 general feature classes leading to 124
mobility features which are extracted from each pair of devices. Table 2 provides
an overview of these features. This table can be interpreted using the notations
introduced in Table 1. The feature classes group the features by their source of
information; overlapping visits, devices themselves, and the environment. There
is no class related to the location only, because its features would be independent
of the pair of devices, and have the same values for each sample. These features
are:

- **Overlap Only** (51 features) These features characterize the mutual overlapping visits of the pair of devices to the location. Examples are the number
  and total length of the overlapping visits, and the average amount of time
  that one device waits before and after the other arrives.
- **Individual Only** (16 features) These features characterize the individual
  visits of each of the two devices to the location. They include the total number
  and length of visits by the devices, and their average and median visit lengths.

- **Overlap and Individual** (8 features) These features relate the overlapping visits to the individual devices' overall visiting pattern. For example, this group contains the ratio between overlapping visits and the total number of visits made by each device, or the ratio between overlap length and total visit length of each device.
- **Overlap and Location** (7 features) These features characterize the state of the location when the devices had overlapping visits to it. Specifically, it considers how busy the location was when the visit took place. Example features are the average and maximum number of devices present during overlapping visits.
- **Individual and Location** (42 features) These features characterize the state of the location during the individual visits of devices. Examples are the average and maximum popularity during individual visits.

The features are defined based on the mobility of any pair of devices i and j, such that $\{(i,j) \in \mathbf{D}\}$. For each of these devices, we consider the set of all of its n visits to the considered location, $\mathbf{V_d} = \{v_1, v_2, ..., v_n\}$ with d being the id of the detected device. Each v_p in this set is defined by tuples of the form $\langle s, e \rangle_{\mathsf{p},\mathsf{d}}$, with s and e being the timestamp of when the visit started and ended, respectively. Additionally, we consider the set of overlapping visits $\mathbf{O}_{i,j}$ of these two devices, by determining which visits in $\mathbf{V}_i$ took place during a visit in $\mathbf{V}_j$. The set $\mathbf{O}_{i,j} = \{ov_1, ov_2, ..., ov_m\}$ is composed of m number of overlapping visits these two devices had. Therefore, each ov_q is composed of tuples of the form $\langle s_i, s_j, e_i, e_j, s_o, e_o \rangle_q$, in which each element is a timestamp. The elements s_o and e_o are defined as follows: $s_o = max(s_i, s_j)$ and $e_o = min(e_i, e_j)$.

Finally, $\mathbf{Od}_{i,j}$ and $\mathbf{Od}_{j,i}$ are similar to $\mathbf{O}_{i,j}$, but each overlap is calculated from the point of view of a single device. For example, if a visit from device i starts during one visit of device j and ends during another, it counts as 1 overlapping visit for $\mathbf{Od}_{i,j}$ and as 2 for $\mathbf{Od}_{j,i}$. Table 1 defines a number of auxiliary functions that are required to compute the features. The function denoted by f generates seven statistical values from a given sequence of values, so it defines seven features.

Table 1. Function definitions

Function	Output	Definition
$length(v)$	$e - s$	Duration of the visit v
$present(t)$	$\{\mathsf{d} \in \mathbf{D} \mid (\exists v_\mathsf{p} = \langle s, e \rangle \in \mathbf{V_d} : (s \le t \le e))\}$	Id of devices present at time t
$max\_present(\mathbf{MT})$	$max(|present(t)|)_{t \in \mathbf{MT}}$	Maximum number of devices present in the location at any time
$f(x)$	$min(x), max(x), std(x), sum(x), mean(x), median(x), max(x) - min(x)$	Statistics applied on the set x

4.4 Initialization Phase

We use the above-mentioned features in the initialization phase. The first part of this phase is creating the input samples from available data and the second part performs feature selection and trains a model.

Creating samples: Input samples consist of $n = 124$ number of mobility features which are labeled with social tie strengths. In this paper, both the tie strength and mobility features are computed based on a data set of Wi-Fi access probe requests, in which each device is identified by its MAC address. The social tie strength is derived from SSID list similarity by calculating Psim-3, as described in Sect. 4.1. The mobility features are computed based on the timestamped Wi-Fi probe requests, which represent the presence of a device nearby a Wi-Fi scanner. The timestamps are recorded in discrete and irregular time intervals. In order to compute the mobility features, the start and end time of visits need to be detected from such timestamps. When the distance between two consecutive timestamps is shorter than a specific threshold tr they are grouped as a single visit. Otherwise, these timestamps are considered to be part of separate visits. We chose the gap length threshold tr such that it was higher than 95% of all gaps in the dataset (2 and 4 min). Algorithm 1 in the appendix provides algorithmic details on this procedure.

Table 2. Features extracted for each pair of devices i, j

Feature class	Indices	Feature definition
Overlap only	1	$|\mathbf{O}_{i,j}|$
	2	$\sum_i length(\mathbf{O}_{i,j})$
	3–16	$f(\{\langle s_o - s_k \rangle_{q,k} | ov_q \in \mathbf{O}_{i,j}, k \in i, j\})^{\text{a}}$
	17–29	$f(\{\langle e_k - e_o \rangle_{q,k} | ov_q \in \mathbf{O}_{i,j}, k \in i, j\})^{\text{a}}$
	30–36	$f(\{\langle s_o - min(e_i, e_j) \rangle_q | ov_q \in \mathbf{O}_{i,j}\})$
	37–43	$f(\{\langle max(e_i, e_j) - e_o \rangle_q | ov_q \in \mathbf{O}_{i,j}\})$
	44–51	$f(\{\langle (s_o - min(s_i, s_j)) + (max(e_i, e_j) - e_o) \rangle_q | ov_q \in \mathbf{O}_{i,j}\})$
Individual only	1–2	$\{|\mathbf{V}_k| | k \in i, j\}^{\text{a}}$
	3–16	$f(\{length(v_p) | v_p \in \mathbf{V}_k, k \in i, j\})^{\text{a}}$
Overlap and Individual	1–2	$\{|\mathbf{Od}_k|, k \in \langle i, j \rangle, \langle j, i \rangle\}^{\text{a}}$
	3	$|\mathbf{O}_{i,j}| / max(|\mathbf{V}_i|, |\mathbf{V}_j|)$
	4–5	$|\mathbf{O}_{i,j}| / |\mathbf{V}_k|, k \in i, j^{\text{a}}$
	6	$(\sum length(\mathbf{O}_{i,j})) / \sqrt{(\sum length(\mathbf{V}_i) * \sum length(\mathbf{V}_j))}$
	7–8	$(\sum length(\mathbf{O}_{i,j})) / (\sum length(\mathbf{V}_k)), k \in i, j^{\text{a}}$
Overlap and Location	1–7	$f(\{\langle |present(t)| / max\_present(\mathbf{MT}) \rangle_q | t \in \{range(s_o, e_o) | ov_q \in \mathbf{O}_{i,j}\}\})$
Individual and Location	1–14	$f(\{\langle |present(s)| / max\_present(\mathbf{MT}) \rangle_p | v_p \in \mathbf{V}_{k,k \in i,j}\})^{\text{a}}$
	15–28	$f(\{\langle |present((s + e)/2)| / max\_present(\mathbf{MT}) \rangle_p | v_p \in \mathbf{V}_{k,k \in i,j}\})^{\text{a}}$
	29–42	$f(\{\langle |present(e)| / max\_present(\mathbf{MT}) \rangle_p | v_p \in \mathbf{V}_{k,k \in i,j}\})^{\text{a}}$

[a] This feature is generated for both devices, leading to a pair of values. In order to make the order of those values independent from the order of the devices, the actual features are their maximum and minimum values

Feature selection and learning: In this phase, a number of features are selected and a model is trained to relate the input mobility features to the social tie strength. As we are interested in learning the social tie strengths as numerical values from numerical features, we are dealing with a regression problem. We initially select the important features in a greedy manner and continue to do so until no feature improves the quality of the regression [15]. Next we train the regressor using the selected set of features. Algorithm 2 in the appendix provides more detail on this procedure.

4.5   Utilization Phase

After the regressor has been trained, it can be used to predict the social tie strengths between each pair of devices from their mobility features, and those tie strengths can be used to determine the aggregate social connectedness score of the location. In this phase only mobility features are used and the actual ground truth indicator of social ties are not. While such ground truth is available in a special case for a dataset collected using Wi-Fi scanning, in other mobility datasets (e.g. GPS, Cellular networks) it is not and can only be collected in a small scale (e.g. through surveying visitors). Therefore, a utilization phase without such ground truth indicator is a valid approach. Algorithm 3 provided in the appendix shows the utilization phase in detail.

5   Evaluation

In this section, we present the result of two experiments to validate our method. Firstly, we evaluate the accuracy in prediction of social tie strengths using a dataset generated by Wi-Fi scanners in our university campus since the start of 2016 (both MAC addresses and SSIDs are anonymized through secure hashing and visitors are provided with an opt-out list). Secondly, we synthetically modified this dataset to analyze sensitivity of our method to various factors that degrade the quality of such datasets.

For each of the experiments we applied 10 fold cross-validation, by training both the proposed method and a baseline method and generating pairwise social ties as output. The generated score by the algorithms is then compared to the ground truth indicator acquired from SSIDs. The indicator of accuracy in these experiments is the coefficient of determination, which is defined as $R^2 = 1 - \frac{\sum_i (f_i - y_i)^2}{\sum_i (y_i - \bar{y})^2}$, in which y_i is the ith predicted result and f_i is the ith observed result. This metric describes which portion of the variation in the actual social tie strengths is explained by the predicted social tie strengths. The reason for choosing the metric was that we found that a high proportion of social ties measured are weak and relatively a much smaller proportion are strong. Compared to other alternative metrics (e.g. Mean squared error), this metric is not biased towards such unbalance in proportion of weak and strong social ties. The reasoning behind weak ties is better depicted by Fig. 2(a). This figure shows how the MAC addresses are distributed among the top 25 SSIDs. As seen, a large set of devices share one SSID. Plugging this number to Psim-3 indicator mentioned in Sect. 4.1 results in a week tie between all of these devices. Whereas, a much smaller number of devices share rare SSIDs leading to stronger ties.

Choosing a baseline: As mentioned before, none of the previous research has considered extracting social tie information from mobility data acquired of a single location. However, among the features used in previous research considering visits to multiple locations, the overlap feature calculated through measuring *co-occurrence probability* is the one that can also be calculated from a single location [10,11]. Therefore, as our baseline, we trained the regressor using this feature. For a pair of devices i and j this feature is calculated as $(\sum length(\mathbf{O}_{i,j})) / \sqrt{(\sum length(\mathbf{V}_i) * \sum length(\mathbf{V}_j))}$.

Table 3. Wi-Fi dataset statistics

Statistic	Value
Number of locations (scanner)	20
Data collection period	260 days
Number of unique MAC addresses	2,790,703
Number of non-random unique MAC addresses	281,562
Number of probes collected	130,279,931
Number of probes collected from non-random sources	126,807,946

5.1 Wi-Fi Dataset

In this section, we evaluate the accuracy of our proposed method in predicting SSID-derived social tie strengths, and compare it to the baseline's accuracy. Table 3 describes various features of this dataset. For each location, the timestamps, scanner IDs and anonymized MAC addresses are used to create the mobility trace, after the Organizationally Unique Identifier (OUI) field has been used to filter out randomized MAC addresses[1] (by examining the OUI field of addresses [16]). The anonymized SSIDs are solely used to infer the ground truth indicator of social tie strength between devices. As previously described in Sect. 4.1, we use the Psim-3 metric for this purpose.

Progression of the algorithm: We initially present the results on three locations (denoted by A–C) to demonstrate how the algorithm works. Figure 2(b) shows the performance of the methods during the progression of the feature selection algorithm (Algorithm 2). The algorithm keeps adding features and stops when no performance increase is observed. As seen, the proposed method reaches its optimal performance by using 7–14 features, reaching a coefficient of determination between approximately 0.3 and 0.45. Using a single feature the performance of the baseline is a constant value and significantly lower.

---

[1] This anonymization approach is taken by recent mobile phone operating systems.

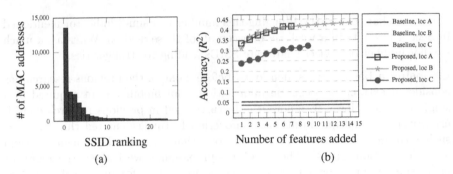

Fig. 2. (a) MAC addresses per SSID (b) Progression of performance by adding features

Figure 3(a) shows the distribution of performances of the regressors generated during the first round of the feature selection for location A (within Algorithm 2). The figure shows that in the first round features based on individual mobility patterns outperform those based on overlapping visits. This result is interesting as it is not intuitively expected that individual mobility features represent social ties. One possible reason for this is that **Individual** features act very strong in determining the social tie indicator of devices that are always present in the location. Examples of these would be stationary Wi-Fi enabled devices such as access points, and printers that have a social tie strength indicator close to zero. Figure 3(b) shows the same distributions for the second feature selection round, in which each regressor uses the feature from the previous round and a newly selected feature. The main difference with the previous graph is that the feature classes related to overlap seem to improve their performance. This is consistent with the idea that once static devices without real social ties are filtered out, overlap features could indicate which social ties are stronger. Finally, Fig. 4(a) shows how aggregate social connectedness score can be extracted from one of the locations over time. As seen, compared to the baseline method the score

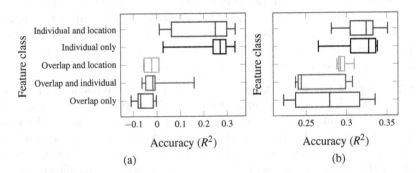

Fig. 3. Performance in location A after using (a) a single feature and (b) two features

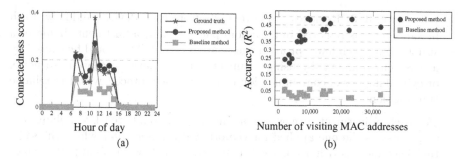

Fig. 4. (a) Aggregate connected score of one location (b) Accuracy of prediction over 20 locations

calculated using the proposed method is closer to the actual score acquired from the indicator acquired from SSIDs.

Results on the complete dataset: In order to compare the algorithm's performance for multiple locations, we trained regressors for all 20 locations separately for the best performing feature set on the previous locations (each dot represents results on a different location). Figure 4(b) shows the resulting scores, set out against the number of unique MAC addresses that visited the location. The figure shows a strong correlation between location popularity and the accuracy of the proposed method, but not with the accuracy of the baseline method. It also shows that the regressor performs well when a static feature set is used, instead of using the feature selection algorithm.

5.2 Sensitivity Test

In order to determine how sensitive our method is to different levels of uncertainties (noise, variability of probe request frequency, etc.), in this section we perform evaluations for several modifications of the original dataset. The modified datasets are generated by applying following adjustments to the original mobility trace **MT**:

- **Adjustment 1:** Removes probe requests received from each device by decreasing the probe frequency. For example, 50% of probe requests are removed by removing every second probe, and 75% is removed by only retaining the first, fifth, ninth, etcetera probe. This adjustment reflects an environment in which devices consistently broadcast fewer probe requests. This could be caused by different implementations of the 802.11 protocol leading to different probing frequency.
- **Adjustment 2:** Removes samples before supplying them to the regressor. This change reflects a decrease of data available to the method, which could be caused by running the initialization phase for a lower amount of time, by placing the scanner in a location where few people gather, or by a larger number of people enabling MAC address randomization.

- **Adjustment 3:** Removes probe requests from each device randomly. Each probe request is removed in a random pattern. This adjustment simulates a situation in which fewer probe requests are received. This could be caused by a noisy environment, by using scanners that are more susceptible to noise, or by making use of communication technology or protocols with less reliable transmission.

For each adjustment, a new set of samples was generated by applying the same process as the one applied for the original dataset, after which the same feature selection algorithm was used. Figures 5(a–c) show the final performance of the proposed method, which is the accuracy of the regressor after the feature selection algorithm has completed. Each figure shows this performance for different degrees of one of the three adjustment types, for each of the locations. For example, Fig. 5(a) shows the proposed and baseline performances when 0% (unadjusted), 50%, 75%, etc. of the probes have been removed by decreasing frequency. As expected, the proposed method performs better than the baseline in every case. Also, higher degrees of the adjustment decreases the performance of both methods in nearly every case.

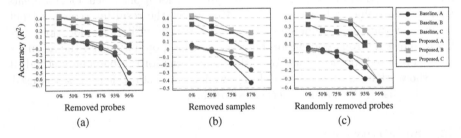

Fig. 5. Performance in different degrees of (a) adjustment 1 (b) adjustment 2 (c) adjustment 3

6   Conclusion and Future Work

In this study, we proposed a new method to characterize the social connectedness of a location based on the mobility traces acquired from it. The proposed method works by extracting and choosing from a large subset of mobility features. This method was evaluated on a real-world dataset and a number of modified versions of that dataset, in order to determine the method's sensitivity to various parameters that degrade the quality of such datasets. Our results show that it is possible to characterize the social connectedness of a location from the presence pattern of its visitors. While our evaluations were performed using a Wi-Fi dataset, the proposed method is also applicable to other types of mobility data (e.g. check-in records in location-based social networks and GPS tracks). Our future research entails studying the relationship between social connectedness and location attributes such as category of the location.

Appendix

In this section, we provide algorithmic details on the procedures of the initialization and utilization phase presented before in Sects. 4.4 and 4.5.

Algorithm 1. Initialization Phase, Sample Generation

Data: <mobility trace **MT**, social tie strengths **ST**>
Result: collection of samples **SC**
1   **SC** = [];
2   D = determineDevices(**MT**);
3   DP = computePairs(D);
4   **forall the** *pair in DP* **do**
5   **MF** = computeAllMobilityFeatures(pair, **MT**);
       /* set of values of all mobility features for this pair */
6   st = ST[pair]; /* the pairwise social tie strength   */
7   append(**SC**,⟨*st*, **MF**⟩);
8   return **SC**;

Initialization phase: Algorithm 1 shows the pseudo code for the first part of the initialization phase, in which the samples are generated. The inputs of this algorithm are the mobility trace (a collection of detections with form ⟨d, t⟩, with d being a device and t being a timestamp) and a collection of pairwise social tie strengths between some of the devices in the mobility trace. Its output is a collection of samples, each of which is a tuple ⟨st, **MF**⟩, with st being a pairwise social tie strength for some pair of devices, and **MF** being the set of values of all the mobility features for the same device pair, calculated in lines 4–7.

Algorithm 2 shows the pseudo code for feature selection and learning a regressor. The input of this algorithm is the collection of samples generated in Algorithm 1 and its output is a regressor trained using the combination of features as selected during feature selection. After computing the mobility features for each pair of devices, we need to determine which features should be supplied to the regressor. The feature selection algorithm performs as follows [15]. Initially the set of selected features is empty. The algorithm moves through the search space in a greedy manner by evaluating features (lines 10–21) and it halts when no new features improve the regression performance (line 18). The performance of the regressor is evaluated using 10-folded cross validation and determining the average of their mean squared errors (line 15). Once the features are selected we proceed to learning the regressor (line 22).

Utilization phase: Algorithm 3 shows the pseudo code for the utilization phase. The algorithm takes the regressor generated in Algorithm 2, the mobility trace, and a timestamp and outputs the aggregate social connectedness score for this mobility trace at that specific timestamp. The algorithm first determines which devices were present at the location at the specific moment in time (line 2).

It again uses device timestamps to determine visit starts and ends. After doing so, the method determines the value of mobility features that were given by the feature selection algorithm for each pair of devices present (line 5). Then, these feature values are supplied to the regressor, which predicts the tie strength for each pair (line 6). Finally, the tie strengths are averaged in order to obtain a score of aggregate social connectedness (line 8).

Algorithm 2. Initialization Phase, Feature Selection

    Data: collection of samples **SC**
    Result: regressor r
1 **FRC** = range(0, length(SC[0])); /* range of all feature indices */
2 **FIC** = []; /* current best feature indices overall   */
3 **BTFIC** = []; /* best feature indices for the current round   */
4 s = 0; /* overall best score overall   */
5 bts = 0; /* best score for the current round   */
6 sib = true; /* boolean indicating whether score has improved */
7 ftb = true; /* boolean indicating generation of best score   */
8 frb = true; /* boolean indicating completion of first round   */
9 **while** *sib* **do**
10   **forall the** *index in* **FRC do**
11   **if** *index in* **FIC then**
12   continue;
13   **TFIC** = union(**FIC**, [index]); /* feature indices to test */
14   **TS** = selectByIndices(**SC**, **TFIC**); /* samples to test   */
15   ts = 10FoldCrossValidateRegressor(**TS**); /* score from test */
16   **if** *ts >bts or ftb* **then**
17   bts = ts, **BTFIC** = **TFIC**, ftb = false;
18   **if** *bts >s or frb* **then**
19   s = bts, **FIC** = **BTFIC**, frb = false;
20   **else**
21   sib = false;
22 r = trainRegressor(**SC**, **FIC**); return r;

Algorithm 3. Utilization Phase

    Data: <regressor r, mobility trace **MT**, timestamp t>
    Result: aggregate social connectedness score as
1 **D** = computePresentDevices(**MT**, t);
2 **DP** = computePairs(**D**);
3 **PSC** = [];
4 **forall the** *pair in* **DP do**
5   **MF** = computeMobilityFeatures(pair, **MT**);
6   ps = predictTieStrength(regressor, **MF**);
7   append(**PSC**,ps);
8 as = computeAggregateTieStrength(**PSC**);
9 return as;

References

1. Seeman, T.E.: Social ties and health: the benefits of social integration. Ann. Epidemiol. **6**(5), 442–451 (1996)
2. Kawachi, I., Berkman, L.F.: Social ties and mental health. J. Urban Health **78**(3), 458–467 (2001)
3. Jylhä, M., Aro, S.: Social ties and survival among the elderly in tampere, finland. Int. J. Epidemiol. **18**(1), 158–164 (1989)
4. Baratchi, M., Heijenk, G., van Steen, M.: Spaceprint: a mobility-based fingerprinting scheme for public spaces. arXiv preprint arXiv:1703.09962 (2017)
5. Petre, A.C., Chilipirea, C., Baratchi, M., Dobre, C., van Steen, M.: WiFi tracking of pedestrian behavior. In: Smart Sensors Networks: Communication Technologies and Intelligent Applications. Elsevier (2017)
6. Cunche, M., Kaafar, M.A., Boreli, R.: Linking wireless devices using information contained in Wi-Fi probe requests. Pervasive Mob. Comput. **11**, 56–69 (2014)
7. Barbera, M.V., Epasto, A., Mei, A., Perta, V.C.: Signals from the crowd: uncovering social relationships through smartphone probes. In: Proceedings of the 2013 Conference on Internet Measurement Conference, pp. 265–276. ACM (2013)
8. McPherson, M., Smith-Lovin, L., Cook, J.M.: Birds of a feather: homophily in social networks. Ann. Rev. Sociol. **27**, 415–444 (2001)
9. Mashhadi, A., Vanderhulst, G., Acer, U.G., Kawsar, F.: An autonomous reputation framework for physical locations based on WiFi signals. In: Proceedings of the 2nd Workshop on Workshop on Physical Analytics, pp. 43–46. ACM (2015)
10. Cheng, N., Mohapatra, P., Cunche, M., Kaafar, M.A., Boreli, R.: Inferring user relationship from hidden information in WLANs. In: 2012–2012 IEEE Military Communications Conference on MILCOM, pp. 1–6. IEEE (2012)
11. Scellato, S., Noulas, A., Mascolo, C.: Exploiting place features in link prediction on location-based social networks. In: Proceedings of the 17th ACM SIGKDD International Conference on Knowledge Discovery and Data Mining, pp. 1046–1054. ACM (2011)
12. Eagle, N., Pentland, A.S., Lazer, D.: Inferring friendship network structure by using mobile phone data. Proc. Natl. Acad. Sci. **106**(36), 15274–15278 (2009)
13. Baratchi, M., Meratnia, N., Havinga, P.J.M.: On the use of mobility data for discovery and description of social ties. In: Proceedings of the 2013 IEEE/ACM International Conference on Advances in Social Networks Analysis and Mining, ASONAM 2013, NY, USA, pp. 1229–1236 (2013). http://doi.acm.org/10.1145/2492517.2500263
14. Di Luzio, A., Mei, A., Stefa, J.: Mind your probes: De-anonymization of large crowds through smartphone WiFi probe requests. In: IEEE The 35th Annual IEEE International Conference on Computer Communications, INFOCOM 2016, pp. 1–9. IEEE (2016)
15. Blum, A.L., Langley, P.: Selection of relevant features and examples in machine learning. Artif. Intell. **97**(1), 245–271 (1997)
16. Misra, B.: iOS8 MAC randomization analyzed! (2014). http://blog.mojonetworks.com/ios8-mac-randomization-analyzed/. Accessed 21 Nov 2016

Towards Simulating Criminal Offender Movement Based on Insights from Human Dynamics and Location-Based Social Networks

Raquel Rosés Brüngger[✉], Robin Bader, Cristina Kadar,
and Irena Pletikosa

Information Management Chair, D-MTEC, ETH Zurich, Zürich, Switzerland
{rroses,baderr,ckadar,ipletikosa}@ethz.ch

Abstract. Interest in data-driven crime simulations has been growing in recent years, confirming its potential to advance crime prevention and prediction. Especially, the use of new data sources in crime simulation models can contribute towards safer and smarter cities. Previous work on agent-based models for crime simulations have intended to simulate offender behavior in a geographical environment, relying exclusively on a small sample of offender homes and crime locations. The complex dynamics of crime and the lack of information on criminal offender's movement patterns challenge the design of offender movement in simulations. At the same time, the availability of big, GPS-based user data samples (mobile data, social media data, etc.) already allowed researchers to determine the laws governing human mobility patterns, which, we argue, could inform offender movement. In this paper, we explore: (1) the use of location-based venue data from Foursquare in New York City (NYC), and (2) human dynamics insights from previous studies to simulate offender movement. We study 9 offender mobility designs in an agent-based model, combining search distances strategies (static, uniform distributed, and Lévy-flight approximation) and target selection algorithms (random intersection, random Foursquare venues, and popular Foursquare venues). The offender behavior performance is measured using the ratio of crime locations passed vs average distance traveled by each offender. Our initial results show that agents moving between POI perform best, while the performance of the three search distance strategies is similar. This work provides a step forward towards more realistic crime simulations.

Keywords: Crime · Simulation · ABM · LSBN · Offender mobility · Human mobility patterns

1 Introduction and Related Work

Public safety has been a topic of concern for cities worldwide for many years. Recent technological developments and in particular the availability of novel data sources has shown potential towards addressing this problem by advancing crime prevention and this contributing to the safety of cities. As an approach, crime simulations can be applied to crime prevention to test the performance of various scenarios and derive

© Springer International Publishing AG 2017
G.L. Ciampaglia et al. (Eds.): SocInfo 2017, Part II, LNCS 10540, pp. 458–465, 2017.
DOI: 10.1007/978-3-319-67256-4_36

strategies for intervention at a very low cost [1]. In addition, these methods can be used to inform police forces about future crime events and thus support effective deployment of their patrols. Researchers investigating at the intersection between criminology and computational social science are building agent-based models (ABM) simulating crime with different purposes e.g. testing crime theories [2, 3], analyzing the performance of prevention strategies [4–6], and forecasting crime developments [7–9]. One of the main issues faced when building such models is not only related to the complexity of the phenomena itself, but to the lack of detailed information about offender movement in space [10]. There is no data tracking offender movement, which would provide insights into daily patterns and criminal target search strategies. A reason for the lack of such data is ethical, e.g. mobile user-data is not available for offenders but only for anonymized general population. Due to this limitation, in the field of criminology, attention has been paid mostly to the demographic characteristics of offenders (age, gender, ethnicity, etc.) and to their possible motivations for committing crimes, while research on movement patterns is still rather scarce. Previous crime simulation models include criminal agents who derive their movement behavior from Routine Activity Theory (RAT) [11], which describes certain aspects of offender behavior. According to RAT, offenders are believed to engage in criminal activities along their usual movement path (e.g. along their path to leisure activities), thus limiting the offender's movement between fixed points. Such activity areas, identified as attracting locations are disproportionally often located near areas with elevated criminal activity [12], confirming that the offenders' target selection strategy is largely influenced by the offenders' *awareness space*[1]. Following RAT, related work has simulated offender movement, based on offenders with known home and crime locations, to derive their possible trajectories [6, 8, 9]. The offender's travel-paths are then built between the fixed home location and other points, representing a reduced number of offenders and not being generalizable for the larger phenomena of crime.

In the current era, where large amounts of location-based user data are available providing detailed insights into human mobility patterns [13, 14], it seems natural, that gained knowledge could inform criminal offender's movement. Human mobility patterns have recently been studied using GPS-based user data [14, 15], and location-based social networks data e.g. gained from Twitter [16] and Foursquare[2] [17]. In this paper, we explore the use of (1) human dynamics insights from literature and (2) location-based social networks (LSBN), to inform offender mobility in an agent-based model. We hypothesize, that offender agents follow similar patterns to those of the general population. The contribution of our paper is twofold. First, we compare three approaches for step size calculation informed by human dynamic insights, i.e. a static, a uniform and a Lévy-flight distance trajectory, with the goal of determining the optimal strategy for calculation of the search area radius. Second, we leverage user-generated content from Foursquare (i.e. venues and check-ins) to inform offenders target selection. The aim of this comparison is to assess if unknown offenders can be realistically modeled in such a

---

[1] Area between usual activity nodes.

[2] Foursquare is a mobile application offering location-search-and-discovery for its users: https://foursquare.com/.

manner. In short, we study offender mobility using insights in human mobility patterns, historical crime data and Foursquare data for New York City (NYC), resulting in the design and implementation of 9 offender behaviors and the performance assessment of each behavior.

2 Offender Mobility

In this work, we study how to model offender mobility based on general human mobility patterns.

2.1 Problem Description

Our research is guided by the main hypothesis, that criminal offenders follow human mobility patterns identified for the general population (H1). This is derived from the notion, that crime is linked to a legal definition and does not provide information on, or define group behavior [18]. Traveling distances of humans have been identified in related work as following a scale-free random walk referred to as Lévy-flight [13, 14]. Thus, the distances traveled by humans follows a power-law distribution. Humans have a high probability to travel short distances and a low probability to travel long distances. This behavior is described in Eq. 1, where $P(\Delta r)$ is the distribution of displacement and $\beta < 2$ is the displacement exponent.

$$P(\Delta r) \sim \Delta r^{-(1+\beta)} \tag{1}$$

Furthermore, we hypothesize, that offenders move between Points of Interest (POI), meaning that the target of a movement path is a POI (H2), this is in line with general human attractors [19] as well as with research on the influence of POI for shaping offenders' awareness space [12, 20]. The path taken by offenders to any location, in this case POI builds up the space known by the offender (awareness space), increasing the probability for a crime to be committed in the same area, which is in line with RAT. In the same direction, we hypothesize, that offenders are strongly drawn to more popular POI (H3), following the general population patterns.

Formally, there is a set of Offenders O each traveling to a location $\ell \in \mathcal{L}$ within distance $r \in \mathbb{R}$ in the area $a \in A$ Our goal is to identify the right strategy for selecting ℓ and r to maximize the number of crime locations $c \in C$ on the actual travelled path.

To test the defined hypotheses, we design 3 distance selection strategies and 3 target selection algorithms, which combined make up 9 offender behaviors instantiated in our model. The distance selection strategies defines the search radius (H1), within which an offender selects a target. The search radius is optimized against the actual travelled distances, informed by human dynamics research (see Sect. 2.2 for more details). The first distance selection strategy uses a static search radius $r \in \mathbb{R}$. The second strategy, chooses its search radius from a continuous uniform distributed random variable, described by $R \sim U(0, 2r)$ so that $\mathbb{E}[R] = r$. For the third strategy we use Lévy-flight to determine the search radius r (see Eq. 1). We transformed the formula (see Eq. 2) to produce random radius $r \in \mathbb{R}$ following a power-law distribution within a probability range adapted to the area of study.

$$P(r) \sim r^{-(1+\beta)} \rightarrow r \sim \frac{1}{P(r)} \cdot e^{\frac{1}{1+\beta}} \tag{2}$$

In turn, the target selection algorithm defines the type of location ℓ an offender can select as a destination within r. The first ℓ type is any intersection, the second is a random POI and the third is a POI based on its popularity. The popularity of the venues is determined by the number of check-ins, influencing the probability to be chosen as a target POI, where the probability for choosing the target is given by Eq. (3).

$$P[\ell] = \frac{check - in}{check - ins \, total \, within \, r} \tag{3}$$

The performance of the 9 offender behaviors is assessed by an adaption of Predictive Accuracy Index (PAI), a standard measure developed for crime prediction models [21], which divides the hit rate by the area of study (see Eq. 4). For the purpose of this study, we adapt PAI to the simulation by dividing the hit-rate-crimes-passed by the total crimes in the study area. The larger the result, the better the performance of the index.

$$PAI = \frac{\left(\frac{c \, assed}{c \, otal}\right)}{\left(\frac{a \, traveled}{a \, total}\right)} \tag{4}$$

2.2 Dataset

We constructed a set of data to simulate the described problem. The simulation builds on the road network for NYC including 117,321 street segments collected from NYC open data portal[3]. Crime data was also obtained from the NYC open data portal, and includes anonymized felony crimes at street segment level (projected to the center) and intersection level, projected to the road network of the simulation. The crime data includes additional information such as type of crime, date, time, etc. The dataset includes the following types of crime: grand larceny, grand larceny of motor vehicle, robbery, burglary, and felony assault. For simulation purpose, we use crime data for 1 year (2015), to obtain an up-to-date overview of crime patterns for that period, resulting in 69,731 crime incidents mapped. Furthermore, we collected Foursquare data to gain information on popular venues attracting larger crowds of people, as proxy for human target preferences. The data was collected from the Foursquare API (in May and June 2016), including information about venues in the area of NYC: venue name, location, check-in count (cumulated over time), associated categories, etc. The set is composed of 273,149 venues in the proximity of every incident from the crime data set with over 122 million check-ins associated and categories ranging from Arts and Entertainment, College and University, Events, Food, Nightlife Spot to Shop and Service, etc.

---

[3] https://opendata.cityofnewyork.us/.

In this research, the foursquare venues are used as proxies for Points of Interest (POI), and the check-in and user-counts are used as proxies for human activity. All geographic data has been projected to NAD83/New York Long Island (ftUS) allowing measurement in foot for NYC area. Concrete human mobility pattern insights were gained from previous research and include the average trip length traveled by the New York State (NY) population [22].

3 Offender Simulation

The simulation model for offender mobility is implemented in the Java-based platform REPAST. The agent-based model is built on a geographic environment consisting of the road network for NYC (represented as a network graph, mapping roads to edges with information on crimes and intersections to nodes) and venue points from Foursquare (including venue type, check-in, and user-count information). The simulated criminal offenders travel on the road network from a random start point on an intersection to the most likely attractor (target), selecting the shortest path, weighted by road length. Thus, the agents perceive the geographic environment, select a radius to determine the travel distance, and move to a target within that distance. The model is set up in different scenarios, each running a different instantiation of offender behavior, to assess the best performing offender mobility design. The different offender behaviors are inspired by the hypotheses mentioned in Sect. 2.1. Grounded by findings in human mobility and criminology, the simulation scenarios have been shaped combining the following two behavior characteristics: (1) search space selection defines the search space radius in which the agent selects a target destination for its current movement. The average trip length for the simulation has been calibrated against the average trip length of 39,600 feet (average trip length for NY population) after completion of the 50 steps of the simulation. The optimal parameters for each search strategy are depicted in Table 1, while we have used the optimal parameter for Lévy-flight as described in previous research [13], we have adapted the probability interval to the size of NYC; and (2) target selection algorithm, defines the offenders' strategy to choose a target for its movement within the distance selected in the previous behavior and has been implemented as described in Sect. 2.1. The three target selection algorithms include: (a) random target selection, offering a choice of road intersections, (b) venue target selection, offering a choice of venues, and (c) priority venue target selection, offering a choice of venues, weighted by popularity.

Table 1. Search space selection strategy parameters

Static search	Uniform distributed search	Lévy-flight search
$r = 40,000$ feet[1]	$r = 80,000$ feet	$\beta = 0.6$

[1]The Lévy-flight (Eq. 2) is defined for km in literature, we transformed the output distance in feet in line with the projection of our data.

The model is run for 50 steps with 25 offender agents for each offender behavior, as an analogue to previous crime simulations [3]. This number of agents allows us to diffuse the impact of the starting location and therefore reduce the effects of path dependencies.

4 Simulation Results

The simulation model described in the previous section was used to generate various simulation scenarios, aiming to compare the performance of each offender implementation. In Table 2 we show the performance measure (see Eq. 4 in Sect. 2.1) for each agent type. In comparison, the search space selection strategies perform very similarly (the uniform strategy performs slightly better), while the target selection algorithm selecting POI as movement target performs best. Combined, the uniform distance selection strategy selecting POI as targets performs best, followed by the algorithm selecting popular POI. This confirms H2 and partly H3, stating that offenders travel to POI and popular POI, but does not confirm that offenders' movement distances follow a Lévy-flight (H1). In contrast, the uniform distribution seems to better capture offender mobility.

Table 2. Performance measurement, PAI

	Static strat.	Uniform strat.	Lévy strat.
Road al.	0.324	0.382	0.267
POI alg.	**0.439**	**0.519**	**0.425**
Popular POI alg.	0.347	**0.523**	0.283

5 Discussion and Implications

In summary, we have proposed designed and compared criminal offender movement behavior, distinguishing between search space and target selection. Our work has theoretical and practical implications.

On the theoretical side, we have shown that, offenders move similar to the general human population in some manner. The simulated target selection algorithm has shown, that offenders can be modeled traveling between POI's. In turn, the distance selection strategy did not show clear results. This could be due to the relatively small distances that agents can travel in NYC. Combined, these findings corroborate that offender behavior can be modeled using certain human mobility pattern insights, while these should still be further adapted to offenders.

On the practical side, our results especially show the potential of crowdsourced data (POI's and check-in information) for modeling offender behavior in crime simulations and can set a basis for modeling offender mobility in future crime simulations.

The main weakness of the model used in this study, is the limited amount of data used for the offenders target selection strategy. Ideally, the environment would hold additional information about attracting features.

In the future we plan to: (i) exploit additional types of data and compose new features to refine the target selection algorithm e.g. metro venues with user counts [20]; (ii) study other routing mechanisms; (iii) evaluate the performance of the offenders with additional metrics e.g. Euclidean and block distance of the traveled path to crime locations [12], and; (iv) study the performance of the implementation for different crimes types.

The presented simulation model can be refined and further developed to include criminal behavior. This would provide a fuller crime simulations to test prevention strategies and the opportunity to predict future crime.

References

1. Gerritsen, C., Elffers, H.: Investigating prevention by simulation methods. In: LeClerc, B., Savona, E.U. (eds.) Crime Prevention in the 21st Century. Insightful Approaches for Crime Prevention Initiatives. Springer, Cham, Switzerland (2017)
2. Brantingham, P.J., Tita, G.: Offender mobility and crime pattern formation from first principles. In: Liu, L., Eck, J. (eds.) Artificial Crime Analysis Systems. Using Computer Simulations and Geographic Information Systems, Information Science Reference, Hershey, N.Y., London (2008)
3. Birks, D.J., Townsley, M., Stewart, A.: Emergent regularities of interpersonal victimization. an agent-based investigation. J. Res. Crime Delinquency 51(1), 119–140 (2014)
4. Dray, A., Mazerolle, L., Perez, P., Ritter, A.: Policing Australia's 'heroin drought'. using an agent-based model to simulate alternative outcomes. J. Experimental Criminol. 4(3), 267–287 (2008)
5. Devia, N., Weber, R.: Generating crime data using agent-based simulation. Comput. Environ. Urban Syst. 42, 26–41 (2013)
6. Hayslett-McCall, K.L., Qiu, F., Curtin, K.M., Chastain, B., Schubert, J., Carver, V.: The simulation of the journey to residential burglary. In: Liu, L., Eck, J. (eds.) Artificial Crime Analysis Systems. Using Computer Simulations and Geographic Information Systems. Information Science Reference, Hershey, N.Y., London, pp. 281–299 (2008)
7. Gunderson, L., Brown, D.: Using a multi-agent model to predict both physical and cyber criminal activity. In: Proceedings of the IEEE International Conference on Systems, Man and Cybernetics. Cybernetics Evolving to Systems, Humans, Organizations, and their Complex Interactions, vol. 4, Piscataway, pp. 2338–2343 (2000)
8. Peng, C., Kurland, J.: The agent-based spatial simulation to the burglary in Beijing. In: Hutchison, D. et al. (eds.) Computational Science and Its Applications – ICCSA 2014. Lecture Notes in Computer Science, LNCS. Springer, Cham, pp. 31–43 (2014)
9. Malleson, N., Evans, A., Jenkins, T.: An agent-based model of burglary. Environ. Planning B Planning Des. 36(6), 1103–1123 (2009)
10. Malleson, N., See, L., Evans, A., Heppenstall, A.: Implementing comprehensive offender behaviour in a realistic agent-based model of burglary. Simulation 88(1), 50–71 (2012)
11. Cohen, L.E., Felson, M.: Social change and crime rate trends: a routine activity approach. Am. Sociol. Rev. 44(4), 588–608 (1979)
12. Reid, A.A., Frank, R., Iwanski, N., Dabbaghian, V., Brantingham, P.: Uncovering the spatial patterning of crimes. a criminal movement model (CriMM). J. Res. Crime Delinquency 51(2), 230–255 (2014)

13. Brockmann, D., Hufnagel, L., Geisel, T.: The scaling laws of human travel. Nature **439** (7075), 462–465 (2006)
14. Gonzalez, M.C., Hidalgo, C.A., Barabasi, A.-L.: Understanding individual human mobility patterns. Nature **453**(7196), 779–782 (2008)
15. Song, C., Qu, Z., Blumm, N., Barabasi, A.-L.: Limits of predictability in human mobility. Science (New York, N.Y.) **327**(5968), 1018–1021 (2010)
16. Jurdak, R., Zhao, K., Liu, J., AbouJaoude, M., Cameron, M., Newth, D.: Understanding human mobility from Twitter. PLoS ONE **10**(7), e0131469 (2015)
17. Noulas, A., Scellato, S., Lambiotte, R., Pontil, M., Mascolo, C.: A tale of many cities: universal patterns in human urban mobility. PLoS ONE **7**(5), e37027 (2012)
18. Tappan, P.W.: Who is the Criminal? Am. Sociol. Rev. **12**(1), 96–102 (1947)
19. Calabrese, F., Di Lorenzo, G., Ratti, C.: Human mobility prediction based on individual and collective geographical preferences. In: 2010 13th International IEEE Conference on Intelligent Transportation Systems - (ITSC 2010), pp. 312–317 (2010)
20. Kadar, C., Iria, J., Pletikosa Cvijikj, I.: Exploring Foursquare-derived features for crime prediction in New York City (2016)
21. Chainey, S., Tompson, L., Uhlig, S.: The utility of hotspot mapping for predicting spatial patterns of crime. Secur. J. **21**(1–2), 4–28 (2008)
22. New York State Department of Transportation. A Transportation Profile Of New York State (2012)

Poster Papers: Security, Privacy, and Trust

The Importance of Consent in User Comfort with Personalization

Jennifer Golbeck[(✉)]

University of Maryland, College Park, USA
jgolbeck@umd.edu

Abstract. Numerous research projects have documented concerns that users have with data commonly used by recommender systems. In this paper, we extend that work by specifically investigating the link between consent, explicitly given, and privacy concern. In a study with 662 subjects, we found that the majority of users would not consent to data from outside systems being used to personalize their experience, and sizable minorities object to even internal system data being used. Among those who said they could consent, found they are often uncomfortable with the data being used if they are not asked to consent, but become comfortable after they can explicitly give their consent. We discuss implications for recommender systems going forward, specifically with respect to incorporating data into algorithms when users are unlikely to consent to its use.

1 Introduction

Personalization and recommender systems must leverage data about their users in order to make predictions about what their future interests may be. Accessing personal data is easier than it ever has been, but users have varying levels of concern about how that data is used. Most systems are rather opaque regarding what data is used and generally do not allow users to explicitly consent to its use. As personalization becomes more prominent and drives profit, it becomes increasingly important to understand users' comfort with various types of data and the impact consent has on their comfort.

In this study, we address two main hypotheses:

H1: Those who would consent to a type of data being used will be more comfortable with its use than those who would not consent.
H2: Obtaining consent will increase users' comfort with the data being used.

Though H1 seems straightforward, it is important as a link between consent and comfort. H2 deepens our examination of that connection.

We conducted a survey of 662 people on Mechanical Turk. Subjects were presented with the description of a fictitious lifestyle website and app that personalizes a stream of data based on the user's interests. We asked subjects about a variety of types of personal data, ranging from behavioral analytics within the

© Springer International Publishing AG 2017
G.L. Ciampaglia et al. (Eds.): SocInfo 2017, Part II, LNCS 10540, pp. 469–476, 2017.
DOI: 10.1007/978-3-319-67256-4_37

app to sensitive information like location. They were asked if they would consent to such data being used for personalization, and how comfortable they would be with its use both when consent was obtained and when it was not.

Our results confirm both hypotheses. We found that consent was important in several ways. The opportunity to consent always improved people's comfort levels. Moreover, on the majority of data types, people who would consent were *uncomfortable* when the data was used without first obtaining consent, but *comfortable* with its use if they were given the opportunity to consent.

This emphasizes the importance of transparency regarding what data is being used, the ability for users to opt-out, and the value of building in explicit consent mechanisms to recommender and personalization systems. We hope these results will motivate deeper discussion about the importance of consent for recommender systems.

2   Related Work

Questions of privacy issues in recommender systems are not new; back in 2001 John Riedl edited a special issue of IEEE Internet Computing [6] that included a focus on the privacy risks associated with recommender systems and personalization. Articles, including [5], looked at risks to user privacy from these algorithms.

Work on users' experiences with recommender systems has highlighted the tension users feel when balancing the benefits of personalization and the desire to keep their personal information private [3]. Some privacy concerns are based in worries about *exposure* of personal information [7], though users may also have fundamental concerns about their personal data being collected and used even without the exposure risk.

User privacy preferences were analyzed in depth a decade ago in [1], which looked at how people's perception of information transparency related to their preferences regarding personalization. They found that those who wanted more transparency were, in turn, less willing to be profiled. The authors recommended companies focus on personalization for those who were more willing to be profiled, yet we have not seen such a discerning approach put into practice. No major systems limit personalization for more privacy-sensitive customers.

More recently, [2] looked at the various levels of concern that users had about different data points used in recommender systems. They found high levels of concern for data collected outside the system making the recommendations (e.g. a movie site using data from other sites, like social networks). We use the list of data points from this early study in the present work to analyze the relationship between consent and concern.

3   Methodology

3.1   Demographics and Subject Background

Subjects were recruited from Mechanical Turk. We required that subjects were located within the United States. While this limits the range of perspectives on

Table 1. Frequency distributions of subject demographic information

privacy, it also creates a more homogenous population to analyze. We expect there may be quite different results if subjects were recruited from other countries, particularly Europe, and this would be an interesting area for future work.

Subjects were paid $0.40 for completing the survey which worked out to an average hourly rate of $8/h.

After agreeing to the IRB-approved consent form for this study, we collected basic demographic information on subjects. This included age, gender, income level, and education level.

The median income was $40,000–49,999, median age was 25–34, median education level was a 4-year degree. Fifty-six percent of subjects were male, 43.4% were female, and 3 people (<0.1%) identified as "other". Table 1 shows frequency distributions for the demographic information.

3.2 Privacy and Consent Survey Instrument

We began by presenting subjects with the following scenario about a fictitious media company:

> Favoroo is a popular new lifestyle website and mobile app that shows you a personalized stream of information - images, blog posts, products, reviews, new stories, and ads 0 about your favorite topics (e.g. fashion, dogs, technology, landscaping, food, etc.). In Favoroo, you can read articles and also rate and review items.
>
> Because your stream is personalized, Favoroo needs to use some information about you to decide what to show next.
>
> Imagine you are a Favoroo user. At the top of each subsequent page, you will see a type of personal information listed (e.g. "My Favoroo Reviews"). Please answer the questions about how you feel about each type of information being used to personalize what you see on Favoroo.

We then presented subjects with a list of data types replicated from [2]. The complete list of data points can be seen in the results table, Table 2. For each type, subjects were asked the following questions:

- If asked, would you give Favoroo permission to use the data listed above to personalize your experience? (choosing Yes, I would give my permission or No, I would not give permission)

Table 2. User responses regarding concern about the use of various data points for personalization. Values are shown as mean (std. dev) except for the percentage of users would consent.

Data type	Consent %	WITHOUT consent		WITH consent	Mean change
		Non-Consenters	Consenters	Consenters	
My ratings of items in Favoroo	76.0%	−1.31	0.39	1.32	0.93
My reviews in Favoroo	75.0%	−1.42	0.31	1.29	0.98
The pages I have viewed in Favoroo	67.0%	−1.45	0.28	1.24	0.97
My profile information in Favoroo	62.0%	−1.53	0.14	1.18	1.05
Searches you have previously done on Favoroo	60.0%	−1.41	0.25	1.22	0.97
My friends' Favoroo ratings and reviews	40.0%	−1.38	0.12	1.13	1.01
My location	30.0%	−1.65	−0.53	0.93	1.45
My ratings of items taken from OTHER sites	27.0%	−1.49	−0.40	1.02	1.43
Products I have viewed on OTHER sites	22.0%	−1.48	−0.66	0.88	1.55
Data from my social media profiles	19.0%	−1.61	−0.68	0.81	1.49
Lists of my friends on social media	18.0%	−1.62	−0.36	0.9	1.26
Products I have purchased from OTHER sites	17.0%	−1.56	−0.77	0.89	1.66
My friends' Favoroo purchasing, browsing, and/or search history	17.0%	−1.61	−0.39	0.82	1.21
My web search history	8.0%	−1.73	−0.82	0.82	1.64
Information about my relationships with each of my friends, like who I trust most	7.0%	−1.71	−0.42	0.54	0.96
My phone contact list	5.0%	−1.83	−0.82	0.35	1.18

- If Favoroo used this data WITHOUT asking for your permission, how would you feel? (5 point Likert scale from Extremely uncomfortable to Extremely comfortable)
- (*If the subject said yes, they would grant permission*) How comfortable would you be with Favoroo using this data to personalize your experience AFTER you granted permission? (5 point Likert scale from Extremely uncomfortable to Extremely comfortable)

The order in which the various data points were presented was randomized to ensure no ordering effects. We pilot tested the survey with 50 mechanical turk subjects before releasing the survey to the bigger pool. The results from pilot testing are not included in our final data set. The survey also included an attention check question to ensure subjects were answering the questions properly.

4   Results

The attention check question eliminated 62 people from our sample, leaving us with valid answers from 662 subjects. Answers on the Likert scales were numerically coded from -2 (extremely uncomfortable) to $+2$ (extremely comfortable). Thus, negative numbers indicate some level of discomfort and positive values indicate comfort.

Overall, our comfort level results are generally consistent with an earlier study of users' privacy preferences [2]; data types that the earlier study found to be more sensitive was likely to receive ratings of higher discomfort in our study.

Results are shown in Table 2, including the percentage of users who would allow each data point to be used and the average comfort ratings for consenters and non-consenters. Central tendencies for Likert scale items are presented as means and generally treated as continuous values, as is common practice [8].

Data types that would be collected *within* Favoroo - a user's ratings, reviews, search history, browsing history, and profiles- was generally of lower concern for our subjects. The majority were willing to share this information. These "internal" data points were the only types of data that receive majority "yes" answers for willingness to consent to its use. Consenters all gave positive comfort scores regardless of whether their consent was obtained first, indicating they were generally comfortable about this data being used. Using friends' data within Favoroo received only a 40% yes vote. While the consenters' comfort ratings are still positive, they are close to 0 ($\mu = 0.12$).

The rest of the data points we asked about came from outside the Favoroo environment. The majority of users said they would not consent to this data being used and the average comfort rating - even among consenters - was negative when the data would be used without first obtaining permission. Among the most concerning data to our subjects was web search history, social data like trust, and their phone's contact list, with less than 10% of subjects consenting to this use.

For every data type we tested, subjects who would consent its use had significantly higher levels of comfort - even when they were not asked for permission - when compared with non-consenters. Both of these groups rated their comfort when a data point was used without first obtaining their permission. Their scores on each data point were compared using a 2-tailed Student's t-test. For every data point we looked at, consenters were significantly more comfortable for $p < 0.01$ with a Bonferroni correction to account for the multiple test run. The effect sizes were very large for all data points, with absolute values of Cohen's d > 8.0 for every data type. While it is not necessarily surprising that people who would consent are more comfortable than those who would not, it confirms the link between consent and comfort with data being used.

The ability to explicitly give consent also matters. We saw this manifest in differences in consenters' comfort levels when consent was and was not obtained. Among those who would consent to their data being used, their level of comfort increased dramatically when they were able to explicitly give consent. For each data point, the comfort levels *with* consent were significantly higher for $p < 0.01$, again after applying a Bonferroni correction. The effect sizes were similarly large, with absolute values of Cohen's d > 6.0 for every data type.

5 Discussion

As mentioned above, it is not especially surprising that we confirmed H1 - those who would not consent to a type of data being used have lower levels of comfort with its use. However, the results we found about their comfort levels do shed some new insight onto the issue of comfort and consent. Non-consenting subjects were deeply uncomfortable about the use of whatever data point was in question. All comfort ratings for non-consenters fall between "extremely uncomfortable" and "somewhat uncomfortable". And while they are a minority for many system internal data points, they are a large minority. A full 24% of subjects would not consent to their own ratings being used for personalization, and 40% would not consent to their history being used. The data points studied here are very common data points used for making recommendations and in personalization, and we should not dismiss the deep concern among these significant populations of users who do not want their information used this way.

The real importance of our results on consent arises when examining data from subjects who *would* consent. The fact that they would consent is not the same thing as actually consenting. As we see in this data, consenting subjects are uncomfortable with any data from outside the system being used for personalization without their consent first being explicitly obtained. Once consent is obtained, they move into the positive side of the comfort scale.

For example, consider the data point "Searches you have previously done on Favoroo". This was a borderline item, with 60% of subjects saying they would consent to its use and 40% saying they would not. Figure 1 shows the comfort level of non-consenters, consenters when the data is used *without* first obtaining consent, and consenters when the data is used *after* obtaining consent. Among consenters, we see a dramatic shift toward more comfort when they are allowed to give consent. This shows that the act of explicitly giving permission is very important to their comfort level. This pattern was repeated across all the data types in our survey.

This has practical implications for many systems. For example, when users log in through a social platform, like Facebook, website or app builders often get access to quite a bit of Facebook data. Users may be willing to share that data if asked, but if builders use it without asking, we can see that subjects will be uncomfortable with its use. The simple act of asking for consent moves those users to a better place.

Of course, asking permission carries the risk that subjects will not give it. This will likely encourage many organizations to go ahead and use the data without obtaining consent. We know that more information improves the accuracy of recommendations and personal information and that better results can mean more profit. This means there is a real cost that comes with obtaining consent (assuming the user's directive is to be respected). That tension makes this an especially critical time to be having these discussions as a community.

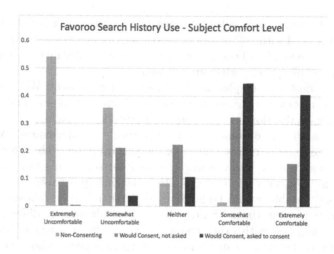

Fig. 1. Distribution of comfort levels among subjects who would refuse consent, who would consent but are not given the chance, and who would consent and are allowed to consent.

More work on consent, privacy preferences, and user comfort in recommender systems is necessary. However, this study and indicators from previous work show a clear level of concern with commonly used data, a growing concern about how their data is used, and the importance that consent plays in making users comfortable. Furthermore, as more sensitive data becomes available - like web browsing history, for example - we must ask as a community if it is ethical to keep using information that improves algorithm quality while violating the privacy preferences of the people the algorithms are targeting.

6   Conclusions

In this paper, we addressed the impact of consent on user comfort with different types of data used in personalization and recommendation systems. We found several insights about user comfort with data used in personalization systems overall, and that the opportunity to explicitly give consent was important in several ways.

We found that all data points pulled from outside the system were so sensitive that a majority of subjects would not consent to their use. Even data collected within the system was not given sharing consent by a sizable minority of users. Non-consenting users confirmed that they would be uncomfortable with this data being used to personalize their experiences. These data types are commonly used now, so the large populations of people who are uncomfortable with their use need to be considered. Our results replicated existing results with respect to the perceived sensitivity of different data points.

Furthermore, subjects who said they would consent to the data being used indicated that they wanted the opportunity to explicitly give that consent.

For many data points, this subset of consenting users was *uncomfortable* with the data being used without their permission but *comfortable* with its use if they could give permission. In all cases, user comfort significantly increased when they had the opportunity to explicitly give consent.

The large effect sizes emphasize the importance of consent. We believe these results should motivate increased discussion of the role of consent and user comfort in the personalization and recommender systems we build.

There are a number of limitations to this work. The Mechanical Turk population is not necessarily representative of the general public. The mere fact that they are technologically savvy enough to work on such a platform is likely to introduce bias. Generally, more work on the relationship between mturk workers and the broader public would be helpful. We further limited this study to people only located in the United States. The US has drastically different privacy regulations compared with other countries, especially in Europe. We suspect that there would be even greater concern among Europeans who have a greater expectation of their right to consent. More work is clearly necessary to gain a broader understanding of national variations in privacy, consent, and comfort.

References

1. Awad, N.F., Krishnan, M.S.: The personalization privacy paradox: an empirical evaluation of information transparency and the willingness to be profiled online for personalization. MIS Q. **30**, 13–28 (2006)
2. Golbeck, J.: User privacy concerns with common data used in recommender systems. In: Spiro, E., Ahn, Y.-Y. (eds.) SocInfo 2016. LNCS, vol. 10046, pp. 468–480. Springer, Cham (2016). doi:10.1007/978-3-319-47880-7_29
3. Knijnenburg, B.P., Willemsen, M.C., Gantner, Z., Soncu, H., Newell, C.: Explaining the user experience of recommender systems. User Model. User-Adap. Inter. **22**(4–5), 441–504 (2012)
4. Kumaraguru, P., Cranor, L.F.: Privacy indexes: a survey of westinÕs studies. Institute for Software Research International (2005)
5. Ramakrishnan, N., Keller, B.J., Mirza, B.J., Grama, A.Y., Karypis, G.: Privacy risks in recommender systems. IEEE Internet Comput. **5**(6), 54 (2001)
6. Riedl, J.: Personalization and privacy. IEEE Internet Comput. **5**(6), 29–31 (2001)
7. Lam, S.K., Frankowski, D., Riedl, J.: Do you trust your recommendations? an exploration of security and privacy issues in recommender systems. In: Müller, G. (ed.) ETRICS 2006. LNCS, vol. 3995, pp. 14–29. Springer, Heidelberg (2006). doi:10.1007/11766155_2
8. Sullivan, G.M., Artino Jr., A.R.: Analyzing and interpreting data from likert-type scales. J. Grad. Med. Educ. **5**(4), 541–542 (2013)
9. Watson, J., Lipford, H.R., Besmer, A.: Mapping user preference to privacy default settings. ACM Trans. Comput.-Hum. Interact. (TOCHI) **22**(6), 32 (2015)

Nudging Nemo: Helping Users Control Linkability Across Social Networks

Rishabh Kaushal[1]($\boxtimes$), Srishti Chandok[1], Paridhi Jain[2], Prateek Dewan[1], Nalin Gupta[1], and Ponnurangam Kumaraguru[1]

[1] Indraprastha Institute of Information Technology, Delhi, India
{rishabhk,srishti15061,prateekd,nalin14065,pk}@iiitd.ac.in
[2] American Express, Big Data Labs, Bangalore, India
paridhi.jain1@aexp.com

Abstract. The last decade has witnessed a boom in social networking platforms; each new platform is unique in its own ways, and offers a different set of features and services. In order to avail these services, users end up creating multiple virtual identities across these platforms. Researchers have proposed numerous techniques to resolve multiple such identities of a user across different platforms. However, the ability to link different identities poses a threat to the users' privacy; users may or may not want their identities to be *linkable* across networks. In this paper, we propose *Nudging Nemo*, a framework which assists users to control the *linkability* of their identities across multiple platforms. We model the notion of *linkability* as the probability of an adversary (who is part of the user's network) being able to link two profiles across different platforms, to the same real user. *Nudging Nemo* has two components; a *linkability* calculator which uses state-of-the-art identity resolution techniques to compute a normalized *linkability measure* for each pair of social network platforms used by a user, and a *soft paternalistic nudge*, which alerts the user if any of their activity violates their preferred *linkability*. We evaluate the effectiveness of the nudge by conducting a controlled user study on privacy conscious users who maintain their accounts on Facebook, Twitter, and Instagram. Outcomes of user study confirmed that the proposed framework helped most of the participants to take informed decisions, thereby preventing inadvertent exposure of their personal information across social network services.

Keywords: Privacy leakage · Identity resolution · Online social media

1 Introduction

Online Social Media (OSM) platforms are becoming popular among users of Internet. These platforms provide different types of services ranging from personal networks to interest based networks [1]. With so many social media platforms around, there are many reasons for users to register and maintain accounts (identities) across more than one OSM platform. According to statistics released

© Springer International Publishing AG 2017
G.L. Ciampaglia et al. (Eds.): SocInfo 2017, Part II, LNCS 10540, pp. 477–490, 2017.
DOI: 10.1007/978-3-319-67256-4_38

by Pew Research Center in 2016, more than half of online users (56%) use more than one OSM platform, a trend which has been consistent in the past few years [2]. A few of the reasons are (a) *type of content* being shared and (b) *type of network* being offered. Examples of varying type of content is that some OSMs promote sharing of images (like Flickr and Instagram) or videos (like YouTube) while others promote sharing of short messages (like Twitter) or combination of messages, video and images (like Facebook). For demonstrating different types of networks being provided to users, some OSMs provide access to professional network (like LinkedIn) while others provide access to a more personal network (like Facebook). These factors complicate and affects users' participation in these networks. For instance, an incoming friend request on a professional network tends to be accepted even if a requester is not personally known (referred as 'others') whereas on a personal network, a user would not like to accept such a request. Similarly, a user is likely to post about personal life events on a network like Facebook, but would probably refrain from doing the same on a professional network like LinkedIn.[1] Most instances discussed above are commonplace for a majority of social media users today. However, such instances give rise to a variety of privacy implications which are seldom addressed or acknowledged. Consciously or unconsciously, users tend to have a certain set of attributes and characteristics common across multiple social media platforms (for example, date of birth, city of residence, screen name, etc.), which enables third parties and adversaries to be able to link two profiles on different platforms to the same real world user. While some users may not be concerned about their profiles being linked and others might, in most cases, users are simply unaware of the phenomenon of any such *linkability* of their profiles online. Researchers have termed this concept of linking two online profiles to a user as *identity resolution*, and have demonstrated multiple techniques in the past where they have been able to correctly link profiles across platforms with a high success rate [4–11,13,15].

In this paper, we propose *Nudging Nemo*, a framework that allows users to learn about and control the linkability of their own profiles across different social media platforms. Our key contributions are as follows:

- We quantify linkability using a metric termed as *linkability score* which quantifies either separation or closeness between two identities belonging to the same user on different OSM platforms.
- We identify the factors (profile attributes) that contribute to the computed linkability score so that user is well informed to take remedial measures.
- We design and develop a soft paternalistic *linkability nudge* which alert users whenever their behavior results in change of linkability score beyond user-configured desired range.
- Lastly, we conduct a controlled lab study to evaluate effectiveness of the linkability nudge.

---

[1] We validated these claims by conducting an online pre-study survey as part of our work. Detailed results of the survey have been omitted from this manuscript due to space constraints.

2   Related Work

Numerous methods and techniques have been studied by researchers for performing identity resolution across multiple OSNs. Work from Zafarani et al. [4] exploited users' unique behavioral patterns that lead to information redundancies across sites to solve the problem of identity resolution. Bartunov et al. [5] proposed an approach based on conditional random fields which leverages profile attributes and social linkages. Carmagnola et al. [6] proposed an approach to identify users on different social networks using their public data. Jain et al. [7], for instance, divided the task of identity resolution into two steps namely, *identity search* and *identity match*. The author presented novel methods [8] for searching and linking multiple identities across OSNs. Their eventual aim was to aggregate the data related to same user across multiple sites by identifying users and retrieving their data. According to Liu et al. [9], the task of linking users across communities, comprises of two variants. In first variation, task is to find whether a set of usernames are owned by a single person and in second, the task is to find all usernames of a single person across multiple sites. Goga et al. [10] explored the innocuous activities of users namely in the form of geolocation attached to user's posts, timestamp of posts and writing styles of users to identify accounts that belong to the same user across different sites. Lim et al. [11] studied the cross-sharing behavior (which refers to the act of posting similar content across multiple sites) of users across six OSNs namely Flickr, Google+, Instagram, Tumblr, Twitter and YouTube. Zhang et al. [12] proposed canopying framework that performs linking of user profiles by using domain knowledge from online social networks. Li et al. [13] uses both personal and social identity features of users to develop better identity resolution techniques.

Besides above, we also draw ideas from prior work related to design of nudges particularly those related to privacy. Leenes et al. [14] in their work suggested segregation of audience for profile attributes of user on OSNs so that its visibility is controllable. Wang et al. [16] designed and implemented modifications to the Facebook web interface that would nudge user to consider the content and audience of their online disclosures. Wang et al. [17] had also earlier developed three types of privacy nudge, one was to provide the audience of a post, second was developed to introduce time delays before a post goes public and third was provided to obtain user feedback. Authors in [18,19] worked to understand and find out the set of actions that users perform over OSNs which they later regret which could be a good indicator of privacy leaks and need for nudging so that those actions don't get repeated in future. Ziegeldorf et al. [20] proposed a novel design paradigm called *comparison based privacy* in which a users can compare their privacy metrics with other groups of users to evaluate privacy disclosure levels. From works of [21,22], it can be seen that with widespread use of mobile devices, the ideas of privacy nudges are being applied on mobile platforms as well. To the best of our knowledge, there exist no prior work which provides a mechanism of nudging (or providing a feedback) users to prevent disclosures owing to the resolution of their multiple identities, which is the focus of our work.

3   Linkability Score

Linkability score quantifies the degree of closeness or separation between two identities on a pair of OSM platforms. Linkability score varies between 0 to 1, lower value would mean that the two identities are less linkable where high value would mean more linkable. Our approach to solution comprises of computing a function that takes a user's identities i_A and i_B on two OSM platforms A and B, respectively as input and compute linkability score between them as below.

$$LS_{i_A, i_B} \leftarrow f_{linkability\_score}(i_A, i_B) \tag{1}$$

Identity of a user u on OSM platform X is modeled as feature vector that is values $< v_1^X, v_2^X, ..., v_n^X >$ corresponding to n features $< f_1^X, f_2^X, ..., f_n^X >$. Given an identity pair $< i_A, i_B >$ as input, the function for computing the linkability score is weighted sum of appropriate *feature similarity metric (FSM)* between corresponding feature values of identity pair.

$$f_{linkability\_score}(i_A, i_B) \leftarrow \frac{1}{n} \sum_{i=1}^{n} FSM(v_i^A, v_i^B) \tag{2}$$

Weighted sum formulation was adopted after thoroughly evaluating other approaches (like probabilistic) on large dataset of similar and dissimilar identity pairs in our prior work, details of which are not included due to space constraints. In addition, we *rank* features based on their contribution to the linkability score.

3.1   Design and Implementation

In order to compute linkability scores between pair of identities of a user, we designed a web based application based on Django framework.[2] Figure 1 depicts the flowchart of the steps which are performed for computation of linkability scores.

On *client side*, there are two key steps as below.

1. User selects OSM platform, in our experiments as we shall discuss later, the options are Facebook, Twitter and Instagram.
2. User sends request for grant of access token so that our web application can get access to user's profile information.

On *server side*, following steps are performed.

3. After obtaining access authorization, web application collects user's data from the OSM platform's API endpoints.
4. Collected user data is passed as input to identity resolution algorithms which specifies various features, say $< f_1^X, f_2^X, ..., f_n^X >$.
5. Using the user's data, values of these features are computed on different OSM platforms, say $< v_1^X, v_2^X, ..., v_n^X >$.
6. Finally, using the feature vectors and algorithm (namely, Nemo, Hydra and Mobius), linkability scores for each pair of OSM platforms are computed using Eqs. 1 and 2.

---

[2] Django Framework, https://www.djangoproject.com/.

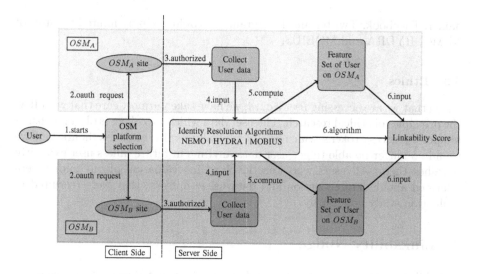

Fig. 1. Flowchart depicting the steps involved for computing linkability scores

3.2   Identity Resolution Methods

We leverage features from three well known Identity Resolution (IR) methods namely NEMO [7], HYDRA [15] and MOBIUS [4]. All these methods propose techniques using user's profile attributes and behavior in order to resolve user's identities across OSM platforms. However, our aim is to build upon these existing IR methods and propose a metric which we refer as *linkability score*, which quantifies the possibility of linkability or non-linkability of user's identities across OSM platforms. In the first IR method used, referred as **NEMO**, Jain et al. [7] have used four algorithms for identity resolution, namely profile search, content search, self-mention search and network search. In our work, we have used only *profile search* and *content search* algorithms. For computing linkability between two identities on different OSMs, we have considered five features namely username, name of user, location, profile image and post contents with suitable similarity measures. In second IR method that we use, referred as **HYDRA**, Liu et al. [15] have mainly considered user behavioral modeling, namely, User Attribute Modeling, User Style Modeling and Multimedia Content Generation. User Attribute Modeling considers textual attributes and visual attributes configured in their identities by user on different OSM platforms. To sum up, we use name of user, education, work, profile image, website, post contents and multimedia content (images) as the features. The third IR method, referred as **MOBIUS** and proposed by Zafarani et al. [4], is based on the fact that when individuals select usernames, they exhibit certain behavioral patterns, which often leads to information redundancy. We computed the top 10 most important features identified by Zafarani et al. [4] for username matching in the context of identity resolution. It may be stated here that due to restrictions in the endpoints offered by APIs and the number of attributes offered by OSM platforms namely Facebook, Twitter and Instagram, we could use only limited features of NEMO, HYDRA and MOBIUS.

3.3   Ethics

Given that we are accessing user's data, we have taken utmost care that we follow the principles of ethical research. The user data which we collect is obtained using temporary access tokens which would typically expire after few hours and we would no longer be able to get user data anytime in future unless user explicitly refreshes them. All users who were involved in evaluation of our nudge were informed about data collection and data usage upfront, they were recruited in evaluation study voluntarily.

4   Linkability Nudge

Linkability nudge is our proposed mechanism which introduces soft paternalistic interventions to user whenever user's behavior causes linkability score to change beyond the desired range configured by the user.

4.1   Architecture

We implement linkability nudge by developing a chrome browser *plugin* that can be installed on user's web browser.[3] This plugin monitors user's behavior in terms of the content being posted over OSM platforms and changes to profile attributes being made on OSM platforms. Architecturally, linkability nudge comprises of three main components namely browser extension, nudge server and linkability compute server, as depicted in Fig. 2.

Browser Extension: This is the only component where a user is required to install on Google chrome web browser. It performs a number of functions as follows: (1) Maintains user's identity and user context across the entire user session. (2) Captures user's posting activity and changes in profile attributes on all configured OSM platforms. (3) Also displays linkability nudge in various forms, discussed later.

Nudge Server: This is the component that is required to be installed on server side. It is an intermediary which sits between the *browser extension* and *linkability compute server*. It performs following functions: (1) Receives user's access token from browser extension and sends them to OSM servers to obtain user's data. (2) Stores user's data in a database temporarily. (3) Passes the information pertaining to user's activities like making a post or changing profile attribute to the linkability compute server. (4) Sends across the newly computed linkability scores to the browser extension from time to time based upon user's activities.

---

[3] Plugin shall be soon made available on Chrome Web Store for people to use and provide their feedback.

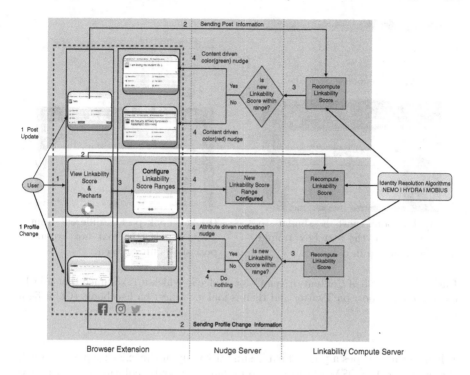

Fig. 2. Flow diagram of operation of Linkability Nudge depicting three key components namely browser extension (plugin), Nudge Server and Linkability Compute Server.

Linkability Compute Server: This is the component which performs most of the heavy computation involved in calculation of linkability scores and it is to be installed on server side. It performs following functions: (1) It implements the identity resolution methods to compute linkability scores. (2) It retrieves user's data from the database as input to compute linkability scores at initial setup time. (3) Subsequently, it receives every user activity's information (whether making a post or changing profile attribute), recomputes linkability scores and sends them back to nudge server.

4.2 Nudge Design

Inspired from the works of Schaub et al. [23] and Acquisti et al. [24] for designing privacy notices and nudges, in our proposed nudge design, we have focused on two types of nudges.

Content-driven Color Nudge: Users having identities across multiple OSM platforms often indulge in *cross posting* which means posting same or similar information across multiple OSM platforms. Such behavior increases similarity in their identities, thereby increasing the linkability score. Our first nudge design addresses this particular issue by nudging the user through use of color.

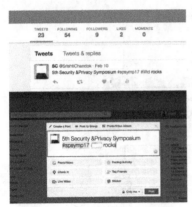

(a) Facebook post is similar to Twitter post, the text box around post shows up in red.

(b) Facebook post is different from Twitter post, the text box around post shows up in green.

Fig. 3. Illustration of Content-driven Color Nudge in which it is assumed that user has already made a post on Twitter and then is making a post on Facebook. (Color figure online)

Whenever user types a post which is similar to any of the existing posts made by the user on other OSM platforms, we nudge the user by coloring the post's text box border with red as show in Fig. 3a. Color is green as long as linkability scores are within their pre-configured ranges as shown in Fig. 3b. This is an indication to user that this post is an instance of *cross posting* which is going to increase user's linkability across OSM platforms. Nudge being only a soft paternalistic intervention, we leave the text box colored with red and let user decide whether user wants to continue making the post or refrain from making the post.

Attribute-driven Notification Nudge: User with multiple identities across OSM platforms maintain their identities such that there is overlap among the values of attributes specified by them on these OSM platforms. More the overlap, more similar the identities would be and higher would be the linkability scores. In fact, the initial linkability scores being computed when user grants authorization is mostly due to similar in profile attributes like name, username, location, profile picture and so on. Whenever user modifies value of any profile attribute over an OSM platform which causes change in linkability score such that the score goes beyond the pre-configured desired range, then the user is nudged. Nudge is delivered in the form of a pop-up notification on top right of screen with a short message saying *'Your linkability with Facebook has increased'* as show in Fig. 4. Again here, being only a soft paternalistic intervention, we allow user's change in attribute to take place and let user decide whether user wants to revert the change or not.

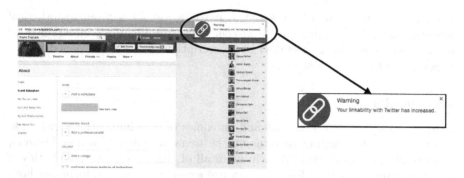

Fig. 4. Illustration of Attribute-driven Notification Nudge on top right of the Facebook page alerting user with a short message that 'Your linkability with Twitter has increased', similar notifications are present to user on interfaces of Twitter and Instagram. Also shown is the enlarged view of nudge notification.

5   User Evaluation and Results

In the last section, we present our approach for evaluating the system of linkability nudge by performing controlled lab study.

5.1   Participants

In order to gauge user's perceptions and opinions with respect to usage and linkability issues in a multi-OSM scenario, we engaged 40 participants in *pre-study questionnaire*. Subsequently, we filtered out and recruited only 12 participants for controlled lab study who had their accounts on all the three OSM platforms (namely Facebook, Twitter and Instagram) on which our proposed linkability nudge was designed. Participants were within the age group of 18–26 years, with 67% female and 33% male comprising of mostly undergraduate students studying computer science.

5.2   Study Design

We conducted controlled lab study in two phases namely

- *Control Period*: Participants are not exposed to linkability nudge. They are asked to perform tasks as outlined in next section.
- *Treatment Period*: Participants are subjected to linkability nudge. In this phase again, we ask the participants to perform the same tasks as performed in control period.

5.3   Tasks

In order to prompt user to perform some activities so that effect of linkability nudge could be observed, we designed two types of tasks: (a) Making *scenario based posts* in which users are asked to make a post for a given hypothetical scenario and (b) Changing *profile attributes* for the identities maintained by users on OSM platforms. Detailed task descriptions are not mentioned in this paper owing to space constraints.

5.4 Results

Here we present our observations and outcomes of user interactions with linkability nudge, the nudging patterns on the users, its impact on user behavior and overall user evaluation. To help us in all of these, we plotted activities of all participants on a time line from start of experiment till end including both control and treatment period, total of around one hour as depicted in Fig. 5.

Interactions with Nudge. The time line plot helped us in understanding user's interactions with linkability nudge (degree of participation) and vice-versa (nudging frequency).

Degree of Participation: Based on the amount of time spent and number of tasks performed (shown in Fig. 5) both during control and treatment period, we can divide participants among three categories. P1, P3 and P6 performed at least 8 or more tasks, taking into account both scenario based posts (shown in + symbol) and profile changes (shown in × symbol) during treatment period, we consider them *highly active*. While P4 and P5 also spent entire duration of one hour but they performed very less number of tasks during treatment period. P10 and P12 performed reconfigurations in their linkability scores (shown in ⋆ symbol) and were *moderately active*. While the remaining participants performed at least two tasks and were *least active*. We also recorded passive activities of participants in which they viewed their linkability scores (shown in ▷ symbol) and factors contributing to those scores in form of piechart (shown in ○ symbol).

Nudging Frequency: Participants were nudged during treatment period while during control period, they were not nudged (in Fig. 5, transition from control to treatment period is depicted by a | symbol). Content-driven color nudge is depicted by either ▽ (red) symbol or △ (green) symbol while Attribute-driven notification nudge is depicted by □ symbol. Participants who were *highly active* were also nudged the most, more specifically P1, P3 and P6 received nudges 10, 13 and 7 times, respectively. Participants who were *moderately active* received at least twice while the *least active* ones were nudged at least once.

Impact of Nudge on User Behavior. We may recall that nudge is an intervention which makes users more informed so that they may take better decisions. By design, nudges are suggestive and not binding on a user. Consequently, we observed that at times users did change their behavior while at other times they overlooked the nudge.

Impact of Content-driven Color Nudge: From Fig. 5, we see that both participants P11 and P12 in their last activities tried to make a post after which they

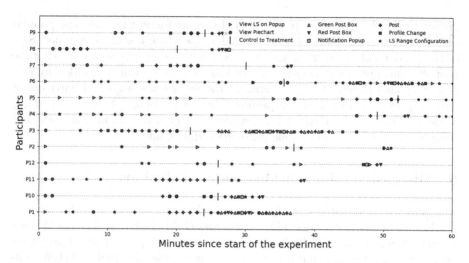

Fig. 5. Complete timeline of activities of all 12 participants who took part in controlled lab study performing various tasks in control and treatment period (Color figure online)

were prompted with a content driven red color nudge (+ symbol followed by ▽ (red) symbol) and they refrained from making the post. In contrast, participant P1 continued to make a post even when content driven red color nudge was displayed (+ symbol followed by ▽ (red) symbol which is again followed by + symbol indicating that participant continued to make the post).

Impact of Attribute-driven Notification Nudge: From Fig. 5, we see that participants P6 and P10 performed a profile change which triggered notification nudge which is immediately followed up by them to make change in linkability score range (× symbol followed by □ symbol followed by ⋆ symbol). In contrast, participant P3 made a number of profile changes and was shown notification nudge which was ignored (in other words linkability score were not reconfigured neither was profile change undone). P12 after having shown notification nudge only viewed linkability scores.

Implications of Nudge. To understand the overall impact of nudge, we assess its efficacy on two parameters namely in creating awareness and usefulness.

Awareness of Linkability: 58% of participants (7 out of 12) understood the concept of linkability either completely or most of it after using our proposed linkability nudge while the remaining 42% said that they understood a little bit about it. 42% of participants (5 out of 12) said that they are absolutely sure that they are more aware about linkability implications and better informed after using the nudge while another set of 5 respondents said that they are 'somewhat' more informed. Most of the participants (84%, 10 out of 12) said that they did notice the factors contributing to their linkability scores which itself suggest that participants were well informed about the causes for their linkability scores.

Nudge Utility: With respect to utility of nudge, we found that the most popular among users was the *Content-driven Color Nudge* which was liked by almost 84% of the participants (10 out of 12). This was followed by pie-charts showing the contribution of profile attributes towards linkability score which was liked by 75% of participants (9 out of 12). In terms of the overall assessment of participants with respect to *usability* of the proposed linkability nudge, 58% (7 out of 12) found it to be useful and easy to use, while 33% (4 out of 12) found it useful but complicated for use and only one participant didn't find it useful.

6   Discussions, Limitations and Conclusions

The purpose of linkability nudge was to help users understand the nuances involved in linkability of their identities across OSM platforms. The goal is that when they perform an activity (making a post or changing profile attribute), they are conscious of the fact that it may increase or decrease linkability of their identity with respect to their identities on other OSM platforms. Linkability nudge would be most beneficial to those who often make personal posts on one network and doesn't want their colleagues in another network to identity them on personal networks. Preventing linkability at the level of *profile* is quite challenging given that users would prefer to have similar values in their profile settings. However, our proposed linkability nudge goes beyond and takes into account linkability at the level of *content* being posted as well. Participants of user study exhibited varied level of participation and were intervened by all types of nudge designs during the controlled lab study. It is evidently clear that behavior of at least some of the participants did change when they were exposed to linkability nudge. They either refrained from making a post which is increasing their linkability or reconfigured the linkability score ranges. On other hand, behavior of some of the participants didn't change, which suggests that they were not concerned about linkability issues. We expected more activities from the participants and in future we would explore ways to improve it. Most of the participants liked the color nudge reinforcing the notion that simple designs make significant impact. Linkability nudge was able to make most of the participants more aware of the linkability issues. Some participants expressed concern over complicated usability, on further investigation, we found that it was mainly due to the time delay (2–5 s) which they experienced while making post during treatment period. This is because each word typed is sent back to server for re-computation of the linkability score causing the delay. We shall work to improve the engineering design so as to reduce the delay. In future, we plan to deploy our proposed system of linkability nudge in public domain and conduct a field study to understand its impact more extensively on a wider audience. To conclude, we may say that users maintaining multiple identities across OSM platforms were able to see, in quantifying terms, the linkability of their identities between each pair of OSM platform. Linkability nudge helped users to take corrective measures to avoid inadvertent disclosure of their personal information owing to increased linkability. User evaluation validates that linkability nudge is indeed quite helpful in making users understand the concept of linkability and helps them through soft interventions to remain within their desired linkability ranges.

References

1. HootSuite web application, https://blog.hootsuite.com/types-of-social-media/
2. Pew Research Center, Social Media Report, http://www.pewinternet.org/2016/11/11/social-media-update-2016/
3. Kumaraguru, P., Cranor, L.F.: Privacy indexes: a survey of Westin's studies. Technical report, Carnegie Mellon University CMU-ISRI-5-138 (2005)
4. Zafarani, R., Liu, H.: Connecting users across social media sites: a behavioral-modeling approach. In: Proceedings of the 19th ACM SIGKDD International Conference on Knowledge Discovery and Data Mining. ACM (2013)
5. Bartunov, S., et al.: Joint link-attribute user identity resolution in online social networks. In: Proceedings of the 6th International Conference on Knowledge Discovery and Data Mining, Workshop on Social Network Mining and Analysis. ACM (2012)
6. Carmagnola, F., Osborne, F., Torre, I.: User data distributed on the social web: how to identify users on different social systems and collecting data about them. In: Proceedings of the 1st International Workshop on Information Heterogeneity and Fusion in Recommender Systems. ACM (2010)
7. Jain, P., Kumaraguru, P., Joshi, A.: @ i seek'fb.me': identifying users across multiple online social networks. In: Proceedings of the 22nd International Conference on World Wide Web. ACM (2013)
8. Jain, P.: Automated methods for identity resolution across heterogeneous social platforms. In: Proceedings of the 26th ACM Conference on Hypertext & Social Media. ACM (2015)
9. Liu, J., et al.: What's in a name?: an unsupervised approach to link users across communities. In: Proceedings of the Sixth ACM International Conference on Web Search and Data Mining. ACM (2013)
10. Goga, O., et al.: Exploiting innocuous activity for correlating users across sites. In: Proceedings of the 22nd International Conference on World Wide Web. ACM (2013)
11. Lim, B.H., et al.: # mytweet via Instagram: Exploring user behaviour across multiple social networks. In: 2015 IEEE/ACM International Conference on Advances in Social Networks Analysis and Mining (ASONAM). IEEE (2015)
12. Zhang, H., Kan, M.-Y., Liu, Y., Ma, S.: Online social network profile linkage. In: Jaafar, A., Mohamad Ali, N., Mohd Noah, S.A., Smeaton, A.F., Bruza, P., Bakar, Z.A., Jamil, N., Sembok, T.M.T. (eds.) AIRS 2014. LNCS, vol. 8870, pp. 197–208. Springer, Cham (2014). doi:10.1007/978-3-319-12844-3_17
13. Li, J., Alan Wang, G., Chen, H.: Identity matching using personal and social identity features. Inf. Syst. Front. **13**(1), 101–113 (2011)
14. Leenes, R.: Context is everything sociality and privacy in online social network sites. In: Bezzi, M., Duquenoy, P., Fischer-Hübner, S., Hansen, M., Zhang, G. (eds.) Privacy and Identity 2009. IAICT, vol. 320, pp. 48–65. Springer, Heidelberg (2010). doi:10.1007/978-3-642-14282-6_4
15. Liu, S., et al.: Hydra: large-scale social identity linkage via heterogeneous behavior modeling. In: Proceedings of the 2014 ACM SIGMOD International Conference on Management of Data. ACM (2014)

16. Wang, Y., et al.: A field trial of privacy nudges for facebook. In: Proceedings of the SIGCHI Conference on Human Factors in Computing Systems. ACM (2014)

17. Wang, Y., et al.: Privacy nudges for social media: an exploratory Facebook study. In: Proceedings of the 22nd International Conference on World Wide Web. ACM (2013)

18. Wang, Y., et al.: From facebook regrets to facebook privacy nudges. Ohio State Law J. **74**, 1307 (2013)

19. Wang, Y., et al.: I regretted the minute I pressed share: a qualitative study of regrets on Facebook. In: Proceedings of the Seventh Symposium on Usable Privacy and Security. ACM (2011)

20. Ziegeldorf, J.H., Henze, M., Hummen, R., Wehrle, K.: Comparison-based privacy: nudging privacy in social media (position paper). In: Garcia-Alfaro, J., Navarro-Arribas, G., Aldini, A., Martinelli, F., Suri, N. (eds.) DPM/QASA -2015. LNCS, vol. 9481, pp. 226–234. Springer, Cham (2016). doi:10.1007/978-3-319-29883-2_15

21. Almuhimedi, H., et al.: Your location has been shared 5,398 times!: a field study on mobile app privacy nudging. In: Proceedings of the 33rd Annual ACM Conference on Human Factors in Computing Systems. ACM (2015)

22. Zhang, B., Xu, H.: Privacy nudges for mobile applications: effects on the creepiness emotion and privacy attitudes. In: Proceedings of the 19th ACM Conference on Computer-Supported Cooperative Work & Social Computing. ACM (2016)

23. Schaub, F., et al.: A design space for effective privacy notices. In: Eleventh Symposium on Usable Privacy and Security (SOUPS 2015). USENIX Association (2015)

24. Acquisti, A., et al.: Nudges for Privacy and Security: Understanding and Assisting Users Choices Online, 25 October 2016. SSRN, https://ssrn.com/abstract=2859227

Mediated Behavioural Change in Human-Machine Networks: Exploring Network Characteristics, Trust and Motivation

Paul Walland and J. Brian Pickering[✉]

IT Innovation Centre, Gamma House, Enterprise Road,
Southampton SO16 7NS, UK
{pww, jbp}@it-innovation.soton.ac.uk

Abstract. Human-machine networks pervade much of contemporary life. Network change is the product of structural modifications and not just participant relations. Taking citizen participation as an example, engagement with relevant stakeholders reveals trust and motivation to be the major objectives for the whole network. Using a typology to describe network state based on multiple characteristic or dimensions, we can predict possible behavioural outcomes in the network. However, this has to be mediated via attitude change rather than material or reputational reward predicted by social exchange models. Motivation for the citizen participation network can only increase in line with enhanced trust. The focus for changing network dynamics, therefore, shifts to the dimensional changes needed to encourage increased trust. It turns out that the coordinated manipulation of multiple dimensions is needed to bring about the desired shift in attitude.

Keywords: Humane-machine networks · Network dimensions · Typology · Trust · Motivation · Behavioural change · Modelling · Social exchange · Social networks · Virtual communities

1 Introduction

Human-machine networks[1] (HMNs) pervade contemporary life from social and family interactions to retail, online learning and eDemocracy. These HMNs display varying characteristics, offering many different ways to interact and achieve whatever the goals of participants might be [1]. But these networks can and do change as users alter their behaviours [2]; and attempts to account for network evolution often fail to appreciate user expectation and creativity when they engage, especially when explanations of dynamic change are reduced to theoretical models [3] or social exchange [4]. A more pragmatic approach might be to weigh user expectations and actions when using the network as it was intended, and then monitor how it changes. In so doing, we necessarily need to consider both intrinsic and extrinsic motivation [5]: is it the individual or the group which encourages participation [6] or the value of contributions [7]? In

---

[1] We use the terms human-machine network (HMN) and network interchangeably.

© Springer International Publishing AG 2017
G.L. Ciampaglia et al. (Eds.): SocInfo 2017, Part II, LNCS 10540, pp. 491–500, 2017.
DOI: 10.1007/978-3-319-67256-4_39

this paper, we examine different aspects of behavioural change in networks: the design of the network itself and the interaction between external and internal motivators.

2 Citizen Participation Networks

Given the reach of the Internet [8], it is no surprise that human-machine networks are also present within democratic processes [9, 10]. However, it is not clear how social network activity leads to participation in democracy [11]. On- and offline democratic processes do differ [8]: social network discussions do not necessarily translate directly into participatory behaviour [12]. eDemocracy and eParticipation tend to complement rather than replace traditional processes [9] extending debate rather than improving it [13]. Online discussion leads to a more refined understanding of a single issue, rather than shaping political decision-making [14], and as an inherently social activity [14] is influenced by social forces [15, 16]. In consequence, HMNs supporting citizen participation have to integrate social, political and technical factors if they are to succeed [9, 17]. There is therefore an inherent challenge in striking a balance between stakeholder expectations on the one hand, and socio-technical issues such as acceptability, system adoption and willingness, on the other [17]. Modelling online behaviour solely in terms of social exchange [18] underplays trust in the HMN itself [19], and the recognition that motivation changes over time in response to the interplay between intrinsic, social and extrinsic factors [6, 20]. To understand such interplay, we must first characterise the network and then return to the exploration of motivation.

3 Profiling Human-Machine Networks

Figure 1 summarises a set of eight characteristics or dimensions grouped into four abstract layers [21][2]. These dimensions allow individual aspects of the network to be examined; further, the interplay between each pair of dimensions within an abstract layer allows network dynamics to be explored [22, 23]. How this dynamism affects the network offers the opportunity to control and manipulate the network. To maintain participation for instance [7, 19, 20, 24], we use these limited dimensions to modify the network and encourage behavioural change [25].

Within an Analytical Layer, such as *Actors*, individual dimensions may be more or less independent of one another. Manipulating these dimensions will change network characteristics, either opening up additional opportunities or restricting others. For instance, if increasing the capabilities of the machine components allows human agents to do more then *Human* and *Machine agency* increase in tandem [22]. Further, the coordinated increase in Human and Machine agency is likely to increase participants' perception of self-efficacy: they can do more and possibly achieve more. Similarly, reducing *Network organisation* together with *Workflow interdependence* would increase autonomy for HMN participants. However, there may be other implications.

---

[2] See https://humane2020.eu/.

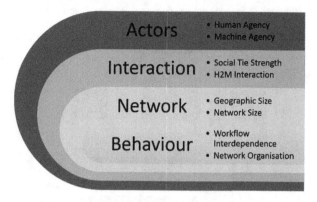

Fig. 1. Dimensions of a citizen participation human-machine network

Increasing autonomy in this way may lead to confusion about what can and cannot be done in the network, and therefore, reduce self-efficacy compromising motivation to engage with the network.

So the limited set of dimensions from the typology not only changes the structure of the network but also affects how actors in the network achieve their ultimate goals. It becomes important therefore to consider how those dimensions might affect generic, cross-cutting concerns such as motivation, trust and participation. To identify these intangible issues, or *meta-dimensions*, we propose to consider more than the structure of the network and its characteristics. To clarify how network dimensions may be used as controls in modifying network outcomes, we must engage directly with participants to establish what they need and expect from their HMN.

4 Identifying Stakeholder Perspectives

Figure 2 encapsulates a process for understanding the objectives of an HMN. Taking eParticipation as an illustrative example, stakeholders include policy makers, politicians, citizens and lobby groups each with their own priorities. From observation, discussion and questionnaire, we can surmise their respective goals[3]. Looking at the goals stakeholders aspire to, citizens want their voices to be heard; policy makers to understand what is important to the citizens and how they will respond to proposed legislation; and lobbyists to ensure that their point of view reaches the policy makers, and their objectives (and those of their members) met. At the same time, there are blockers or challenges to achieving those goals: citizens feel constrained to express what they truly feel, or lack trust that what they say will be taken into account; policy makers need to decide between opposing views and interests in formulating policy; and lobbyists need to demonstrate that they have faithfully represented those they serve *and* that there has been a positive effect [26].

---

[3] See https://humane2020.eu/2017/01/16/humane-roadmap-process/.

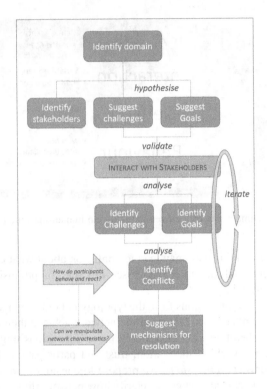

Fig. 2. Exploring participant perceptions

Validating these challenges and goals with the stakeholders allowed us to home in on how participants react. Monitoring their behaviours identifies what the relevant meta-dimensions for this network are. In a recent study, a small group of self-selecting actors involved in citizen participation [27] first ranked stakeholder roles in order of importance within the network: Citizen groups (most important), Non-Government Organisations (NGOs), Government, Policy makers, and IT Professionals and designers (least important). It is perhaps surprising to find Government and Policy makers ranked below Citizens themselves and NGOs. However, citizen engagement has been seen as more about debate and social interaction than necessarily establishing contact with Policy makers [13, 14, 17].

Turning to goals and challenges, the main goals of citizen participation networks turned out to be: (i) *Managing trust*; (ii) *Generating a culture of engagement*; (iii) *Encouraging open and transparent debate*; (iv) *Motivating participation from all parties*; and (v) *Accountability*. These relate particularly to **trust in the network** and **motivation**. Trust is affected by a number of different aspects of the network such as the technology involved and how competent individual users feel with the technology. Yet one of the challenges to network success is understanding the real role of technology. Further, looking at accountability and a call for open and transparent debate, trust is affected by perceptions of the process itself: does participation really make a difference, for example? Here again, one obstacle to achieving the overall network

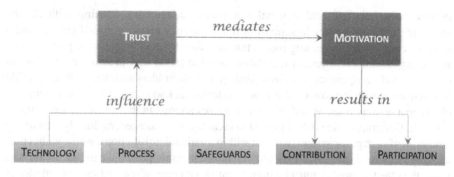

Fig. 3. A simple model of meta-dimensions in HMNs

goals was the desire to see outcomes being publicised and made available to all actors in the network. Finally, trust will be affected by whatever safeguards are in place to ensure accountability and protect open discussion.

Trust therefore is influenced by the factors summarised in Fig. 3. As an intrinsic factor, trust is not available for manipulation. However, it is possible to change network constructs like technology, process and safeguards. In this way, changes in trust as a consequence of manipulation of these factors will have an effect on motivation. Thus there is a mediating effect of trust: the underlying drivers of technology, process and safeguards encourage motivation. Stakeholders identified the need to generate a culture supportive of debate and to encourage participation and contributions from citizens. Motivation is precisely about driving active participation so that citizens and citizen groups provide input and contribute to the success of the network. So the way to facilitate these beneficial effects of motivation, we need to consider how we might affect the influencing factors which lead to changes in trust.

The two meta-dimensions, trust and motivation, are key components influencing behaviour and thereby the success of the network. In turn, they too are dependent on other constructs. For example, if trust is a willingness to expose oneself to vulnerability [28–30], then perceived risk and any regulation mitigating that risk will influence trust [23] and not the other way round [19]. Motivation on the other hand will relate to the willingness to participate driven externally by a social desire to engage [6, 14, 16], but equally there is an internal drive to demonstrate competence, affiliation and commitment [5, 31]. Importantly, though, how will the network dimensions engender trust and in turn motivation. We turn now to look at changes to individual dimensions and what effect this has on the meta-dimensions.

5 Manipulating Networks Through Controlling Network Dimensions

Given the simple model of human-machine networks, encouraging trust in the HMN to influence and improve motivation is not straightforward. Since the network dimensions do not directly affect trust, they must be applied to components in the network (technology), its outcomes (process) and external influences (safeguards). Starting with *Actors*, increasing machine agency in support of human agency encourages self-efficacy and a sense of competence increasing motivation and thereby a willingness for participation. Increasing Social Tie Strength facilitates communication and promote publication of outcomes and transparency as citizen participant stakeholders identified[4]. Raising H2M interaction strength improves self-efficacy via technical know-how. Using our example of eParticipation networks, as self-efficacy increases so trust in the overall process should improve. Geographic size is constrained to include only those geographically affected by outcomes of such participation (e.g. just within a national jurisdiction), whilst within that, as many individuals as possible should be enabled to participate. If the digital divide is an issue, then the technology must be implemented with ease of use and user experience as design principles. Workflow interdependence should attempt to lower perceived risk. This is where the interplay between different actors (e.g. policy makers and citizens) is most significant, and trust in the process is greatest, creating the system of government. Finally for Network organisation, a bottom-up evolution doesn't necessarily lead to participation in governance, as both *facebook* and *Twitter* have shown. Similarly, top-down creation of participation networks by government have also failed, since there is insufficient trust in the system [19], and poor communication of the objectives of the network [6]. Yet a purely bottom-up approach would lack the cohesion required to support constructive debate, and exposes the network to side-tracking by extremism. There is therefore a need to consider what the identification of an 'intermediate' organisation might be, and how a network that is neither bottom-up nor top-down might be created.

Since the analytical layers and network dimensions alter network characteristics, changing individual dimensions may bring about behavioural change. For, as the characteristics themselves are modified, so the behaviours associated with the network would be constrained or freed up to engage in different types of activity. If the model in Fig. 3 is correct, this indirect outcome – by manipulating network dimensions, which change trust levels, and in turn mediates motivation, leading to greater participation and so forth – reveals a process for behavioural change in networks. What we need to do now, though, is go one step further and identify the effects of multiple dimension changes at the same time.

6   Trust and Agency in Human-Machine Networks

In a recent study on how trust, human agency and machine agency might affect behaviour, Pickering et al. [23] modified previous work by Thatcher, McKnight and their colleagues on trust in technology [32, 33]. Figure 4 shows the research model Pickering and his colleagues proposed (with individual constructs in black), centred on the relationship between trust and behaviour. Briefly, *regulation* controls what can and cannot be done in a network, directly affecting human and machine agency; similarly, regulation will provide input to the estimation of any *perceived risk*. Together, they act as safeguards associated with the network. Interestingly, as regulation is typically

---

[4] See also [7].

external (linked with legislation and similar controls), so perceived risk tends to be internal (the result of some form of cognitive algebra). Only this internal factor affects trust and network behaviours directly, not external regulation. *Machine agency* allows human agents to achieve more in the network, and thereby increases *self-efficacy*, which will in turn affect network behaviours, along with trust in the network and *social norms*. This model summarises the effects we propose by manipulation of the network dimensions as outlined. But the model also makes clear that increasing trust is not simply about the aggregated effect of changes in technology, process and safeguards.

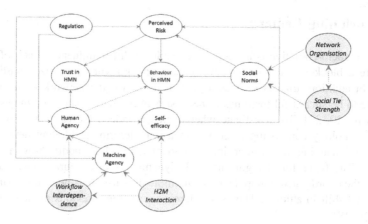

Fig. 4. Trust in human-machine networks

Taking this one stage further (the shaded constructs in Fig. 4), linking safeguards and agency with trust, self-efficacy and thereby network behaviours means that the model we propose may usefully be extended. The *interaction* and *behaviour* layers (see Fig. 1) affect different parts of the trust-behaviour model. To begin with, *Network organisation* can be expected to influence social norms: a bottom-up configuration would leave social cohesion outside the scope of the network, and therefore dependent solely on the individuals themselves. A top-down structure would impose uniformity on how human agents can interact and communicate with one another: the network would therefore constrain the possible effects of social norms. By contrast, *Workflow interdependence* will affect both *Human* and *Machine agency*: the more structured the workflow, the greater the machine agency, whilst human agency is constrained. With less structure, however, the opposite is not necessarily true.

Turning to the interaction layer, *Social tie strength* affects social norms: as individuals identify with other network participants, so social norms are determined by group identity. With weaker ties, social norms will be less influential since social identity among network users is less likely. At the same time, *H2M interaction* will influence *Self-efficacy*: as human network actors become more comfortable with what machine components do, so their perception of what they can achieve increases. First, for H2M interaction to have a significant, positive influence on Self-efficacy, Workflow interdependence would need to be less structured to enable greater Human agency and thereby increased Self-efficacy. Similarly, increased Social tie strength suggests less top-down Network organisation.

Coordinated network dimension change is needed if the goal is to increase trust for its mediating effect on behaviour in the HMN, or motivation for citizen participation. Behavioural change in human-machine networks is therefore not a simple issue of providing incentives, but the more complex effects of changing network characteristics as they influence non-deterministic motivation [34] and the meta-dimensions we propose.

7 Concluding Remarks

Trust is a socio-cognitive construct inaccessible to direct influence. Lack of trust is therefore a blocker to the future development and growth of a citizen participation HMN. In addition, trust is seen as a goal in itself: for the network to succeed and continue to be successful there has to be trust between participants and the associated process [6, 19, 33]. To investigate whether this is indeed the case, we have used a network typology comprising a set of dimensions describing different network characteristics. Changing these dimensions is a novel approach to modify how the network operates. The focus for changing network dynamics is to encourage increased trust. Further, the coordinated manipulation of multiple dimensions is needed to bring about the desired shift in attitude. This is a different focus from previous models of participation [6, 19].

Extending this discussion, a typology to describe network state based on multiple network characteristics or dimensions makes it possible to predict behavioural outcomes in the network. Directly modifying network dimensions represents a top-down intervention, an intentional manipulation which paradoxically may well undermine any beneficial effects: if network participants are aware that there is an attempt to influence them, say by financial incentive, then they may well withdraw co-operation. Indeed, any such incentive fails to recognise that altruism, for instance, is not about external reward [20, 35, 36]. Similarly, though, acknowledging network participant objectives without modifying the HMN to be able to support those objectives – participant aspirations emerging bottom-up – may simply lead to frustration and reduce motivation. How to resolve the tension between the top-down and bottom-up aspects of HMN change is the challenge we are now looking to address.

References

1. Tsvetkova, M., Yasseri, T., Meyer, E.T., Pickering, J.B., Engen, V., Walland, P., Lüders, M., Følstad, A., Bravos, G.: Understanding human-machine networks: a cross-disciplinary survey. ACM Comput. Surv. **50** (2017)
2. Viswanath, B., Mislove, A., Cha, M., Gummadi, K.P.: On the evolution of user interaction in Facebook. In: Proceedings of the 2nd ACM Workshop on Online Social Networks - WOSN 2009, p. 37. ACM Press, New York (2009)

3. Hellmann, T., Staudigl, M.: Evolution of social networks. Eur. J. Oper. Res. **234**, 583–596 (2014)
4. Borgatti, S.P., Everett, M.G., Johnson, J.C.: Analysing Social Networks. SAGE Publications (2013)
5. Ryan, R.M., Deci, E.L.: Intrinsic and extrinsic motivations: classic definitions and new directions. Contemp. Educ. Psychol. **25**, 54–67 (2000)
6. Vassileva, J.: Motivating participation in social computing applications: a user modeling perspective. User Model. User-Adapt. Interact. **22**, 177–201 (2012)
7. Rashid, A.M., Ling, K., Tassone, R.D., Resnick, P., Kraut, R., Riedl, J.: Motivating participation by displaying the value of contribution. In: Proceedings of the SIGCHI Conference on Human Factors in Computing Systems, pp. 955–958 (2006)
8. Dutt, P.K., Kerikmäe, T.: Concepts and problems associated with eDemocracy. In: Kerikmäe, T. (ed.) Regulating eTechnologies in the European Union, pp. 285–324. Springer, Cham (2014). doi:10.1007/978-3-319-08117-5_13
9. Coleman, S., Norris, D.F.: A new agenda for e-democracy (2005)
10. Co-operation and Development (OECD): Promise and problems of e-democracy: Challenges of online citizen engagement. OECD Publishing (2004)
11. Boulianne, S.: Social media use and participation: a meta-analysis of current research. Information. Commun. Soc. **18**, 524–538 (2015)
12. Panagiotopoulos, P., Sams, S., Elliman, T., Fitzgerald, G.: Do social networking groups support online petitions? Transform. Gov. People, Process Policy **5**, 20–31 (2011)
13. Loukis, E., Wimmer, M.: A multi-method evaluation of different models of structured electronic consultation on government policies. Inf. Syst. Manag. **29**, 284–294 (2012)
14. Kreiss, D.: The problem of citizens: E-democracy for actually existing democracy. Soc. Media + Soc. **1**, 11 (2015)
15. Ronson, J.: So You've Publically Shamed. Picador, Oxford (2015)
16. Stott, C., Reicher, S.: Mad Mobs and Englishmen?: Myths and Realities of the 2011 Riots. Robinson, London (2011)
17. Macintosh, A., Whyte, A.: Towards an evaluation framework for eParticipation. Transform. Gov. People, Process Policy **2**, 16–30 (2008)
18. Cropanzano, R., Mitchell, M.S.: Social exchange theory: an interdisciplinary review. J. Manage. **31**, 874–900 (2005)
19. Kim, J., Yoon, Y., Zo, H.: Why people participate in the sharing economy: a social exchange perspective. In: PACIS 2015 Proceedings, vol. 76. AIS Electronic Library (AISeL) (2015)
20. Paulini, M., Maher, M.L., Murty, P.: Motivating participation in online innovation communities. Int. J. Web Based Communities **10**, 94–114 (2014)
21. Eide, A.W., Pickering, J.Brian, Yasseri, T., Bravos, G., Følstad, A., Engen, V., Tsvetkova, M., Meyer, Eric T., Walland, P., Lüders, M.: Human-machine networks: towards a typology and profiling framework. In: Kurosu, M. (ed.) HCI 2016. LNCS, vol. 9731, pp. 11–22. Springer, Cham (2016). doi:10.1007/978-3-319-39510-4_2
22. Følstad, A., Engen, V., Haugstveit, I.M., Pickering, J.B.: Automation in Human-Machine Networks: How Increasing Machine Agency Affects Human Agency (2017)
23. Pickering, J.B., Engen, V., Walland, P.: The interplay between human and machine agency. In: Kurosu, M. (eds.) Human-Computer Interaction. User Interface Design, Development and Multimodality. HCI 2017. LNCS, vol. 10271, pp. 47–59. Springer, Cham (2017). doi:10.1007/978-3-319-58071-5_4
24. Vassileva, J.: Motivating participation in peer to peer communities. In: Petta, P., Tolksdorf, R., Zambonelli, F. (eds.) ESAW 2002. LNCS, vol. 2577, pp. 141–155. Springer, Heidelberg (2003). doi:10.1007/3-540-39173-8_11

25. Engen, V., Pickering, J.Brian, Walland, P.: machine agency in human-machine networks; impacts and trust implications. In: Kurosu, M. (ed.) HCI 2016. LNCS, vol. 9733, pp. 96–106. Springer, Cham (2016). doi:10.1007/978-3-319-39513-5_9
26. The Hansard Society: Audit of Political Engagement (2017)
27. Walland, P., Pickering, J.B.: A Roadmap for future human-machine networks for Citizen participation, https://humane2020.eu/2017/06/12/citizen-participation-are-human-machine-networks-the-solution/
28. Mayer, R.C., Davis, J.H., Schoorman, F.D.: An integrative model of organizational trust. Acad. Manag. Rev. **20**, 709–734 (1995)
29. Schoorman, F.D., Mayer, R.C., Davis, J.H.: An integrative model of organizational trust: past, present, and future. Acad. Manag. Rev. **32**, 344–354 (2007)
30. Rousseau, D.M., Sitkin, S.B., Burt, R.S., Camerer, C.: Not so different after all: a cross-discipline view of trust. Acad. Manag. Rev. **23**, 393–404 (1998)
31. Ryan, R.M., Deci, E.L.: Self-determination theory and the facilitation of intrinsic motivation, social development, and well-being. Am. Psychol. **55**, 68–78 (2000)
32. McKnight, D.H., Carter, M., Thatcher, J.B., Clay, P.F.: Trust in a specific technology: An investigation of its components and measures. ACM Trans. Manag. Inf. Syst. **2**, 12 (2011)
33. Thatcher, J.B., McKnight, D.H., Baker, E.W., Arsal, R.E., Roberts, N.H.: The role of trust in postadoption it exploration: an empirical examination of knowledge management systems. IEEE Trans. Eng. Manag. **58**, 56–70 (2011)
34. Michie, S., van Stralen, M.M., West, R.: The behaviour change wheel: a new method for characterising and designing behaviour change interventions. Implement. Sci. **6**, 42 (2011)
35. Batson, C.D.: In: Berkowitz, L. (ed.) Advances in experimental social psychology, vol. 20, pp. 65–122. Academic Press (1987)
36. Dickerson, P.: Social Psychology: Traditional and Critical Perspectives. Pearson Education (2012)

Hunting Malicious Bots on Twitter: An Unsupervised Approach

Zhouhan Chen[(✉)], Rima S. Tanash, Richard Stoll, and Devika Subramanian

Rice University, Houston, TX 77005, USA
{zc12,rtanash,stoll,devika}@rice.edu

Abstract. Malicious bots violate Twitter's terms of service – they include bots that post spam content, adware and malware, as well as bots that are designed to sway public opinion. How prevalent are such bots on Twitter? Estimates vary, with Twitter [3] itself stating that less than 5% of its over 300 million active accounts are bots. Using a supervised machine learning approach with a manually curated set of Twitter bots, [12] estimate that between 9% to 15% of active Twitter accounts are bots (both benign and malicious). In this paper, we propose an unsupervised approach to hunt for malicious bot groups on Twitter. Key structural and behavioral markers for such bot groups are the use of URL shortening services, duplicate tweets and content coordination over extended periods of time. While these markers have been identified in prior work [9,15], we devise a new protocol to automatically harvest such bot groups from live Tweet streams. Our experiments with this protocol show that between 4% to 23% (mean 10.5%) of all accounts that use shortened URLs are bots and bot networks that evade detection over a long period of time, with significant heterogeneity in distribution based on the URL shortening service. We compare our detection approach with two state-of-the-art methods for bot detection on Twitter: a supervised learning approach called BotOrNot [10] and an unsupervised technique called DeBot [8]. We show that BotOrNot misclassifies around 40% of the malicious bots identified by our protocol. The overlap between bots detected by our approach and DeBot, which uses synchronicity of tweeting as a primary behavioral marker, is around 7%, indicating that the detection approaches target very different types of bots. Our protocol effectively identifies malicious bots in a language-independent, as well as topic and keyword independent framework in real-time in an entirely unsupervised manner and is a useful supplement to existing bot detection tools.

Keywords: Bot detection · Social network analysis · Data mining

1 Introduction

In recent years, Twitter, with its easy enrollment process and attractive user interface has seen a proliferation of automated accounts or bots [11,13]. While a few of these automated accounts engage in human conversation or provide

© Springer International Publishing AG 2017
G.L. Ciampaglia et al. (Eds.): SocInfo 2017, Part II, LNCS 10540, pp. 501–510, 2017.
DOI: 10.1007/978-3-319-67256-4_40

community benefits [1], many are malicious. We define malicious bots as those that violate Twitter's terms of service [5] including those that post spam content, adware and malware, as well as bots that are part of sponsored campaigns to sway public opinion.

How prevalent are bots and bot networks on Twitter? Estimates vary, with Twitter [3] itself stating that less than 5% of its over 300 million active accounts are bots. Using a supervised machine learning approach with a manually curated set of Twitter bots, [12] estimate that 9% to 15% of active Twitter accounts are bots (both benign and malicious). An open question is how to efficiently obtain a census of Twitter bots and how to reliably estimate the percentage of malicious bots among them. In addition, it is important to estimate the percentage of tweets contributed by these bots so we have an understanding of the impact such accounts have on a legitimate Twitter user's experience. In particular, malicious bots can seriously distort analyses such as [14] based on tweet counts, because these bots cut and paste real content from trending tweets [9].

In this paper, we propose an unsupervised approach to hunt for malicious bot groups on Twitter. Key structural and behavioral markers for such bot groups are the use of shortened URLs, typically to disguise final landing sites, the tweeting of duplicate content, and content coordination over extended periods of time. While the use of shortened URLs and tweeting of duplicate content has been separately identified in prior work [9,15], we devise a new protocol that follows this up by verifying content coordination between bot groups over extended periods of time. Our bot detection protocol has four sequential phases as illustrated in Fig. 1. Our unit of analysis is a cluster of accounts. The initial clustering is based on duplicate text content and the use of shortened URLs. The final detection decision is made by examining the long term behavior of these account clusters and the extent of content coordination between them.

Our experiments with this protocol on actively gathered tweets with shortened URLs from the nine most popular URL shortening services shows a complex picture of the prevalence and distribution of malicious bots. Fewer than 6% of accounts tweeting shortened URLs are malicious bots, except for *ln.is* (27%) and *dlvr.it* (8%). The tweet traffic generated by malicious bot accounts using shortened URLs from *bit.ly*, *ift.tt*, *ow.ly*, *goo.gl* and *tinyurl.com* is under 6%. But malicious bots using *dlvr.it*, *dld.bz*, *viid.me* and *ln.is* account for 13% to 27% of tweets.

The gold standard for confirming bots is suspension by Twitter. However, as noted by [8,10], there is a time lag between detection of bots by researchers and their suspension by Twitter. If we had a reference list of bots, we could give recall and precision measures for our detection approach. In the absence of such a list, we can only provide a precision measure by comparing our bots with those detected by state of the art methods: a supervised learning approach called BotOrNot [10] and an unsupervised technique called DeBot [8]. We show that BotOrNot misclassifies around 40% of the malicious bots identified by our protocol. Unlike BotOrNot, our approach identifies entire bot groups by their collective behavior over a period of time, rather than using decision rules for classifying individual accounts as bots. DeBot is focused on the question of detecting

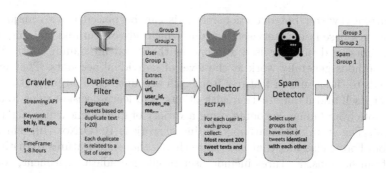

Fig. 1. The four phases of our bot detector architecture. Note the second round of tweet collection from a group of accounts that tweet near identical content and which use shortened URLs. This phase analyses the long term tweeting behavior of potential malicious bots.

groups of bots, not necessarily malicious ones, by exploiting coordinated temporal patterns in their tweeting behavior. Since we use duplicated content over a time period, and shortened URLs as primary behavioral markers, in contrast to synchronicity of tweeting, we find a far more diverse group of malicious bots than DeBot. Thus there is only a small overlap (7%) between bot groups found by our protocol and DeBot's, which mainly finds bots associated with news services rather than those that hijack users to spam, ad and malware sites.

In sum, our protocol effectively identifies malicious bots by focusing on shortened URLs and tweeting of near duplicate content over an extended period of time. It is language-independent, as well as topic and keyword independent and is completely unsupervised. We have validated our protocol on tweets from nine URL shortening services and characterized the heterogeneity of the distribution of malicious bots in the Twitterverse.

The remainder of the paper is organized as follows. Section 2 provides brief background on existing Twitter bot detection methods and the novelty and efficacy of our protocol. Section 3 describes and motivates each phase of our bot detection protocol. Section 4 introduces the tweet sets collected from nine URL shortening services used in our experiments, and provides results of our detection protocol on these sets. It also includes results of comparisons of our method with DeBot and BotOrNot. We conclude the paper in Sect. 5 that discusses our main results and directions for future exploration.

2   Background

There is a significant literature on detecting bots on Twitter and other social media forums – recent surveys are in [11,13]. Spam bots on Twitter are constantly evolving, and there is an ongoing arms race between spammers and Twitter's account suspension policies and systems. For instance, link-farming was a dominant category of spam bots in 2012. However, Twitter's new detection algorithms [2] have driven them to extinction.

Current Twitter bot detection methods can be placed in two major categories: ones based on supervised learning which rely on curated training sets of known bots, and unsupervised approaches that need no training data. Supervised methods generally work at the level of individual accounts. They extract hundreds to thousands of features from each account based on properties of the account itself and its interaction with others, and learn decision rules to distinguish bots from human accounts using a variety of machine learning algorithms [7,9,15]. The state of the art in this line of work is BotOrNot [10] which is a Random Forest classifier that uses more than a thousand features to distinguish bots from humans. Features include user profile metadata, sentiment, content, friends, network and timing of tweets. This method has two limitations. First, it makes decisions at the level of individual accounts and therefore fails to identify groups of accounts that act in concert. Second, it works only on accounts tweeting in English, and it is not adaptive; requiring re-training with new human-labeled data as new types of bots emerge.

The state-of-the-art in unsupervised bot detection is DeBot [8], which uses dynamic time warping to identify accounts with synchronized tweeting patterns. This protocol relies on tweet creation time and not its contents. Our results show that DeBot primarily finds news bots with temporally synchronized tweeting patterns. It does not capture malicious spam bots that are temporally uncorrelated, but that tweet duplicate trending content in order to hijack users to spam and malware sites.

Our unsupervised detection method fills a gap in Twitter bot detection research. The underlying features of bots identified by our method are accounts using shortened URLs and near duplicate content over an extended period of time. Because the method is unsupervised, it is not biased by any keyword, topic, hashtag, country or language. It does not require human labeled training sets, and can be deployed in a real time online fashion.

3   Our Methods

Our spam detection method consists of four components run sequentially: crawler, duplicate filter, collector and bot detector. The **crawler** collects live tweets from the Twitter Streaming API using keyword filtering [4]. We choose prefixes of the domain name of a URL shortening service as keywords. The **duplicate filter** selects suspicious groups of accounts for further analysis. It first hashes all tweet content extracted from the *text* field of the tweet's json representation and maps each unique tweet text to a group of users who tweet that content. The filter selects duplicate tweeting groups of size 20 or greater. This threshold of 20 enables us to focus on more significant bot groups. To make sure accounts do in fact violate Twitter's terms of service over a period of time, we perform a second level of tweet collection on each member of a suspicious group. The **collector** gathers the 200 most recent tweets of every account in each suspicious group using Twiter's REST API. This step ensures that we filter out innocent users who happen to tweet a few of the same texts as bots.

The **bot detector** clusters accounts in a group that have most of their historical tweets (200 most recent tweets) identical to each other. Given a group G of n accounts $a_1, \ldots, a_n$, sets $T(a_1), \ldots, T(a_n)$ of tweets where $T(a_i) = \{t_{i1}, \ldots, t_{i200}\}$ of the 200 most recent tweets for each account $a_i, 1 \leq i \leq n$, it constructs the set C of tweets that are tweeted by at least α accounts in the group. That is,

$$t \in C \iff |\{i \mid t \in T(a_i); 1 \leq i \leq n\}| \geq \alpha \tag{1}$$

In the next step, the detector measures the overlap between the tweet set $T(a_i)$ associated with an individual account and the set C of tweets for the group G that account a_i is a member of. The potential bots in the group, denoted by the set S, are identified as follows,

$$a_i \in S \iff \frac{|T(a_i) \cap C|}{|T(a_i)|} \geq \beta \tag{2}$$

Thus there are two parameters in our detection protocol: α, which we call *minimum duplicate factor*, which influences the construction of the most frequent tweet set C, and β, which we call the *overlap ratio*, which determines the ratio of frequent tweets in the tweet set associated with an account. Accounts that meet criteria (1) and (2) for a specific choice of α and β are identified as malicious bots in our protocol. In all of our experiments reported in the next section, we use $\alpha = 3$ and $\beta = 0.6$. These parameters were obtained after cross-validation studies which we do not have space to document here.

4   Experimental Evaluation

4.1   Landscape of Twitter Trending URLs

To justify the use of URL shortening as a marker in our bot detection protocol, we examined the distribution of all URLs in the Twitter stream to estimate the fraction of tweets containing URL shorteners. We first streamed more than thirty million live tweets using keyword *http*, extracted all URLs within each tweet, and sorted them by frequency of occurrence. While this is only a sample of all tweets with embedded URLs, we believe it is an unbiased sample since the Twitter Streaming API does not favor one particular region/language/account over another. Figure 2 shows top trending URLs on Twitter constructed with this sample. Shortened URLs clearly constitute a major fraction of tweet traffic.

4.2   Datasets and Results

Based on our analysis of the distribution of URLs on Twitter, we choose to study nine popular URL shortening services *bit.ly, ift.tt, ow.ly, goo.gl, tinyurl.com, dlvr.it, dld.bz, viid.me* and *ln.is*. In our sample, more than 24% of tweets with embedded URLs are generated from these nine service providers.

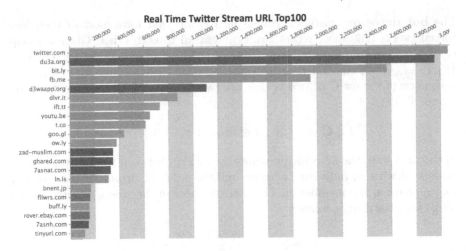

Fig. 2. Top trending URLs on Twitter (Green bars are social media websites, red bars are websites tweeting Quran verses, orange bars are URL shortening services, and blue bars are others. In this paper we focus on the orange bars. For real-time, complete top 100 trending URLs, visit our Twitter Bot Monitor [16].)

Table 1 shows the number and percentage of bot accounts identified by our detection protocol, the percentage of our bot accounts also identified by DeBot, and percentage of accounts that are identified by our protocol and later become suspended by Twitter. We note that the percentages of bot accounts vary greatly among the nine URL shorteners, ranging from 2.4% to 23%, and the percentage of tweets generated by these bot accounts vary from 2.7% to 26.65%, with an average of 10.51%. Four URL shorteners – *dlvr.it*, *dld.bz*, *viid.me* and *ln.is*, have more than 10% of their tweets generated by bot accounts, suggesting that those URL shorteners are more abused by malicious users than the other five.

4.3   Scaling Experiments

In July 2017, we performed a series of experiments on all nine URL shortening services in which we scaled the number of tweets gathered to around 500,000 in order to verify the robustness of our results in Table 1. Two of URL shorteners were no longer available: *ln.is* is suspended [6], while *viid.me* has been blocked by Twitter due to its malicious behavior. Table 2 gives the detailed statistics of our bot detection performance on the remaining URL shortening services.

Compared to our first set of experiments, we see an increase in the percentage of bot accounts in six out of seven URL shortening services, and increased percentages of tweets in all URL shortening services. The percentages of bot accounts range from 5.88% to 17.80%, and the percentage of tweets generated by these bot accounts vary from 14.74% to 56.46%. Together with Table 1, we find that the rate of bot account creation outpaces Twitter suspensions.

Table 1. Statistics of Twitter accounts from nine URL shortening services. Note the uptick in suspended accounts identified by us on `viid.me`

URL shortener	Total # of accts	Total # of bots	% bots we found	% tweets from bots we found	% our bots found by DeBot	% our bots susp. by Twitter until 6/10/17	% our bots susp. by Twitter until 7/17/17
bit.ly	28964	696	2.40%	4.44%	12.93%	3.74%	4.74%
ift.tt	12543	321	2.56%	3.54%	11.21%	2.80%	9.97%
ow.ly	28416	894	3.15%	3.22%	6.04%	45.30%	48.21%
tinyurl.com	20005	705	3.52%	5.70%	1.99%	5.39%	7.66%
dld.bz	6893	304	4.41%	13.36%	10.20%	8.22%	11.84%
viid.me	2605	129	4.95%	21.66%	22.48%	38.76%	55.81%
goo.gl	11250	710	6.31%	2.70%	8.73%	0.42%	3.24%
dlvr.it	15122	1194	7.90%	13.34%	22.86%	7.37%	9.13%
ln.is	25384	5857	23.07%	26.65%	3.57%	1.11%	1.25%

Table 2. Statistics of Twitter accounts from nine URL shortening services (10X scale experiments)

URL shortener service	Total # of accts	Total # of bots	% bots	% tweets from bots
bit.ly	193207	22938	11.87%	16.11%
ift.tt	75024	4415	5.88%	16.70%
ow.ly	182539	31416	17.21%	26.07%
tinyurl.com	49563	4644	9.37%	14.74%
dld.bz	11705	1036	8.85%	56.46%
goo.gl	177030	31515	17.80%	27.88%
dlvr.it	86830	6517	7.51%	18.58%
ln.is	N/A	N/A	N/A	N/A
viid.me	N/A	N/A	N/A	N/A

4.4   Comparison with Existing Bot Detection Methods

Twitter Suspension System. We revisited the account status of bots detected by our protocol to check if they have been suspended by Twitter. The last two columns in Table 1 show percentages of suspended accounts among all bot accounts identified by our protocol, one collected in June and the other in July. As of July, more than 56% of bot accounts using *viid.me* and 48% of accounts using *ow.ly* have been suspended. However, fewer than 15% of bot accounts that use the other seven URL shortening services have been suspended.

DeBot. We compare our results with DeBot in the following manner. For all Twitter accounts in the nine datasets, we queried the DeBot API to determine whether or not the account is archived in its bot database. Table 3 documents the number of bots identified by our method and by DeBot. The intersection of those two groups is small in all cases.

Table 3. Overlap of results from our Bot Detector and DeBot

URL shortener	# bot accts we found	# verified accts we found	# bot accts DeBot found	# verified accts DeBot found	Overlap in accts
bit.ly	605	2	1657	57	91
ift.tt	321	0	989	8	38
ow.ly	894	0	1500	34	55
tinyurl.com	705	0	826	9	14
dld.bz	304	0	473	2	31
viid.me	129	0	515	0	31
goo.gl	710	0	822	9	62
dlvr.it	1194	17	1843	19	281
ln.is	5857	0	2383	7	216

To investigate the low overlap in detected bots, we checked for verified accounts among the ones identified as bots by both methods. To determine the percentage of news bots (defined as an account that tweets at least once with a URL from a list of established news media URLs), we used the Twitter REST API to collect the 200 most recent tweets from these accounts. Table 4 shows that more than 50% of bot accounts identified by DeBot are news bots, compared to 15% based on our method.

Table 4. Comparison of percentage of news accounts

Protocol	Total bots	News bots	% News bots
Our protocol	696	102	14.66%
DeBot	1748	947	54.18%

Thus, what DeBot finds, but our method does not are news bots linked to large news media accounts. What both methods find are bot groups that tweet highly synchronously with duplicate content, and what our method finds but DeBot does not are bot groups using shortened URLs that do not tweet simultaneously.

BotOrNot. We also compared our results with BotOrNot, a supervised, account based Twitter bot classifier. BotOrNot assigns a score of 0 to 1 to an account based on more than 1000 features, including temporal, sentimental and social network information [10]. A score close to 0 suggests a human account,

Table 5. Bot accounts scores from BotOrNot

URL shorteners	Average Score	% bots with score in [0.4,0.6]
bit.ly	0.50	50.65%
ift.tt	0.56	50.46%
ow.ly	0.52	40.83%
tinyurl.com	0.56	66.08%
dld.bz	0.71	17.75%
viid.me	0.68	24.81%
goo.gl	0.53	68.99%
dlvr.it	0.49	44.43%
ln.is	0.44	56.81%

while a score close to 1 suggests a bot account. Like DeBot, BotOrNot also provides a public API to interact with its service. Table 5 shows the statistics of BotOrNot scores of all bots we identified in the nine datasets. In 5 out of the 9 datasets, more than 50% of the scores of accounts identified as bots by our protocol fall in the range of 0.4 and 0.6. We expect scores of bots detected by our protocol to exceed 0.6, so we interpret these results as misclassifications by BotOrNot.

5   Conclusions

In this paper we present a Twitter bot detection method that hunts for a specific class of malicious bots using shortened URLs and tweeting near duplicate content over an extended period of time. Our unsupervised method does not require labeled training data, and is not biased toward any language, topic or keyword. Arguably our method does not capture the most sophisticated bots out on Twitter, yet it is surprising that between 4% to 23% of the accounts we sampled from the streaming API satisfy our bot criteria and remain active on Twitter, generating 4% to 27% of tweet traffic. In the absence of identified bot lists, we resort to comparisons with two of the best bot detection protocols on Twitter to evaluate the effectiveness of our approach. Our work gives us a more nuanced understanding of the demographics of Twitter bots and the severity of bot proliferation on Twitter. Bot removal is a necessary step in any analysis relying on raw counts of collected tweets, so our work is useful for anyone with a Twitter dataset from which duplicates of trending tweets generated by malicious bots need to be eliminated. Our future work involves devising better approaches to evaluating bot detection tools, and developing new criteria for discovering more sophisticated bots that contaminate the Twitter stream. Malicious bot detection is an arms race between bot makers and social media platforms and we hope our work contributes to the design of better bot account detection policies.

References

1. Earthquakebot. https://twitter.com/earthquakebot?lang=en. Accessed 30 Mar 2017
2. Fighting spam with botmaker. https://blog.twitter.com/2014/fighting-spam-with-botmaker. Accessed 20 Mar 2017
3. Twitter Annual Report. http://files.shareholder.com/downloads/AMDA-2F526X/4335316487x0xS1564590-17-2584/1418091/filing.pdf. Accessed 22 Apr 2017
4. Twitter developer documentation. https://dev.twitter.com/streaming/overview/request-parameters. Accessed 20 Mar 2017
5. The Twitter Rules. https://support.twitter.com/articles/18311. Accessed 13 Jan 2017
6. We need you to help to get linkis back to work. http://blog.linkis.com/2017/06/02/we-need-you-to-help-to-get-linkis-back-to-work. Accessed 19 July 2017
7. Cao, C., Caverlee, J.: Detecting spam URLs in social media via behavioral analysis. In: Hanbury, A., Kazai, G., Rauber, A., Fuhr, N. (eds.) ECIR 2015. LNCS, vol. 9022, pp. 703–714. Springer, Cham (2015). doi:10.1007/978-3-319-16354-3_77
8. Chavoshi, N., Hamooni, H., Mueen, A.: DeBot: Twitter bot detection via warped correlation. In: Proceedings of the 16th IEEE International Conference on Data Mining (2016)
9. Chu, Z., Gianvecchio, S., Wang, H., Jajodia, S.: Detecting automation of Twitter accounts: are you a human, bot, or cyborg? IEEE Trans. Dependable Secure Comput. 9(6), 811–824 (2012)
10. Davis, C.A., Ferrara, V.E., Flammini, A., Menczer, F.: BotOrNot: a system to evaluate social bots. In: Companion to Proceedings of the 25th International Conference on the World Wide Web, pp. 273–274. International World Wide Web Conferences Steering Committee (2016)
11. Ferrara, E., Varol, O., Davis, C., Menczer, F., Flammini, A.: The rise of social bots. Commun. ACM 59(7), 96–104 (2016)
12. Ferrara, O.V.E., Davis, C.A., Menczer, F., Flammini, A.: Online human-bot interactions: detection, estimation, and characterization. arXiv preprint (2017). arXiv:1703.03107
13. Jiang, M., Cui, P., Faloutsos, C.: Suspicious behavior detection: current trends and future directions. IEEE Intell. Syst. 31(1), 31–39 (2016)
14. Montesinos, L., Rodrguez, S.J.P., Orchard, M., Eyheramendy, S.: Sentiment analysis and prediction of events in Twitter. In: 2015 CHILEAN Conference on Electrical, Electronics Engineering, Information and Communication Technologies (CHILECON), pp. 903–910, October 2015
15. Wang, D., Navathe, S., Liu, L., Irani, D., Tamersoy, A., Pu, C.: Click traffic analysis of short URL spam on Twitter. In: 2013 9th International Conference on Collaborative Computing: Networking, Applications and Worksharing (CollaborateCom), pp. 250–259. IEEE (2013)
16. Twitter Bot Monitor project on github. https://github.com/Joe--Chen/TwitterBotProject

Poster Papers: Tools and Methods

Exploratory Analysis of Big Social Data Using MIC/MINE Statistics

Piyawat Lertvittayakumjorn[1], Chao Wu[1], Yue Liu[1,2], Hong Mi[2],
and Yike Guo[1(✉)]

[1] Data Science Institute, Imperial College London, London SW7 2AZ, UK
{pl1515,chao.wu,l.yue,y.guo}@imperial.ac.uk
[2] School of Public Affairs, Zhejiang University, Zhejiang 310058, China
spsswork@163.com

Abstract. A major goal of Exploratory Data Analysis (EDA) is to understand main characteristics of a dataset, especially relationships between variables, which are helpful for creating a predictive model and analysing causality in social science research. This paper aims to introduce Maximal Information Coefficient (MIC) and its by-product statistics to social science researchers as effective EDA tools for big social data. A case study was conducted using a historical data of more than 3,000 country-level indicators. As a result, MIC and some by-product statistics successfully provided useful information for EDA complementing the traditional Pearson's correlation. Moreover, they revealed several significant, including nonlinear, relationships between variables which are intriguing and able to suggest further research in social sciences.

Keywords: Exploratory data analysis · Big social data · Maximal information coefficient · Correlation

1 Introduction

Exploratory Data Analysis (EDA) aims to understand the main characteristics of a dataset and, more importantly, find previously unknown relationships in the data. A well-known quantitative technique for EDA is using *Pearson's correlation* (also known as Pearson product-moment correlation coefficient denoted by r or ρ in literature) because it is easy to compute and, in the case of simple linear regression, its square (i.e., r^2) is a *coefficient of determination* telling noise level in a dependent variable predicted from an independent variable. However, a severe weakness of Pearson's correlation is that it can detect only linear relationships, but in real-world data sets, we are also interested in nonlinear relationships which may be missed if we use only Pearson's correlation to explore data.

In 2011, Reshef et al. proposed a nonlinear correlation measure called *Maximal Information Coefficient (MIC)* [8]. It was designed specifically for exploring large datasets with the ability to capture a wide range of associations regardless of their function types or whether they are formed by functional relationships.

© Springer International Publishing AG 2017
G.L. Ciampaglia et al. (Eds.): SocInfo 2017, Part II, LNCS 10540, pp. 513–526, 2017.
DOI: 10.1007/978-3-319-67256-4_41

By simulation, MIC gave similar correlation scores to equally noisy relationships of various types. In addition, the authors of MIC also proposed *MINE statistics* (Maximal Information-based Nonparametric Exploration) which are by-product statistics of MIC calculation that can provide us more information with regard to the variable pair besides the relationship strength reflected by MIC.

This paper aims to introduce Maximal Information Coefficient (MIC) and MINE statistics to social science researchers as effective EDA tools for big social data. By comparing the MIC scores of variable pairs in a multivariate dataset, we can easily detect the pairs with significant relationships that are worth to investigate in detail. In the case study, we used MIC/MINE statistics to explore a large-scale historical data of country-level indicators to find indicators which are strongly (and unexpectedly) related to two target indicators – *(i)* GDP per capita and *(ii)* Corruption Perceptions Index (CPI). We found that using MIC and MINE statistics provided useful information for EDA complementing the traditional Pearson's correlation. They also revealed several intriguing relationships between variables such as a relationship between CPI and time to import (days). With a relatively high MIC (rank 9, 0.594) and an insignificant $|\rho|$ (rank 62, |-0.608|) in 2014, it is expected to be a noticeably nonlinear relationship, whereas the reason "why it is" could be a future research topic in social sciences.

Overall, the main contribution of this paper is twofold: an experience-based case study of using MIC and MINE statistics for exploring big social data and general guidelines of employing these statistics for EDA based on what we learned from the case study.

2   MIC and MINE Statistics

As discussed earlier, MIC is a nonlinear correlation measure which is able to capture various types of significant relationships and allows us to compare the strength across all of them. The basic idea of MIC is that "if a relationship exists between two variables, then a grid can be drawn on their scatter plot to partition the data and encapsulate that relationship".

The following process is used to calculate the MIC of a bivariate data [8].

1. Create a scatter plot of the bivariate data.
2. Explore all possible grids placed on the scatter plot such that $n_x n_y < B$ where n_x and n_y are the number of the partition bins of the x- and y-axis respectively and B, called a maximal grid resolution, is a function of the number of data points n. The authors of MIC suggested B equal to $n^{0.6}$.
3. Calculate mutual information, I(X;Y), of each grid resolution (n_x-by-n_y) and partition placement (the position where a grid is placed) by

$$I(X;Y) = \sum_{y \in Y} \sum_{x \in X} p(x,y) log \frac{p(x,y)}{p(x)p(y)} \qquad (1)$$

where X and Y are discrete random variables by the partitions of x- and y-axis, $p(x,y)$ is a joint probability distribution function of X and Y, and $p(x)$, $p(y)$ are marginal probability distribution functions of X and Y, respectively.

4. Find the highest mutual information score for each resolution (n_x-by-n_y). Then normalise it using Eq. (2) to obtain a modified value between 0 and 1 and fill the value in a characteristic matrix $M = (m_{n_x,n_y})$.

$$m_{n_x,n_y} = \frac{I^*(n_x, n_y)}{log_2(min\{n_x, n_y\})} \tag{2}$$

where $I^*(n_x, n_y)$ is the best mutual information of the grid resolution n_x-by-n_y among all partition placements.

5. The statistic MIC is the maximum value in the characteristic matrix M.

MIC between two variables ranges from 0 to 1. It tends to 0 for a pair of statistically independent variables, whereas it tends to 1 for a variable pair forming a noiseless relationship, or a superposition of noiseless functional relationships. Also, by simulation, MIC approximately equals to the coefficient of determination r^2 relative to the respective noiseless function. In the case of non-function, MIC scores degrade when noise is added.

Additionally, four MINE statistics computed based on MIC and the characteristic matrix M are defined as follows [8, Supporting material]:

1. **Measure of nonlinearity** – Since MIC is general and roughly equals to r^2 on functional relationships, a measure of *nonlinearity* can be defined by MIC$-\rho^2$, where ρ denotes the Pearson's Correlation. If both MIC and ρ of a variable pair are high (i.e., MIC$-\rho^2 \approx 0$), the relationship is strongly linear. In contrast, in the case of high MIC but low ρ (i.e., large MIC$-\rho^2$), the relationship is strong but not linear.

2. **Maximum Asymmetry Score (MAS)** – MAS is helpful for detecting *deviation from monotonicity* as well as periodic relationships with unknown frequencies that vary over time. It is computed from cells in the characteristic matrix M using the equation below.

$$MAS = \max_{n_x n_y < B} |m_{n_x,n_y} - m_{n_y,n_x}| \tag{3}$$

MAS is never greater than MIC. The higher the periodic frequencies are, the larger the MAS is.

3. **Maximum Edge Value (MEV)** – MEV is defined by

$$MEV = \max_{n_x n_y < B} \{m_{n_x,n_y} : n_x = 2 \text{ or } n_y = 2\}. \tag{4}$$

It measures the degree to which the dataset appears to be sampled from a *continuous* function (i.e., closeness to being a function). Since MEV is chosen from a cell in the characteristic matrix, MEV$\leq$MIC.

4. **Minimum Cell Number (MCN)** – MCN is defined as

$$MCN(\epsilon) = \min_{n_x n_y < B} \{log_2(n_x n_y) : m_{n_x,n_y} \geq (1 - \epsilon)MIC\}. \tag{5}$$

It measures the *complexity* of the relationship, in terms of the number of cells (n_x-by-n_y) required to reach the MIC score. For noiseless functions, ϵ should

516 P. Lertvittayakumjorn et al.

Table 1. Eight data sources and the numbers of collected indicators

Data source	Description / Institution	No. of indicators
WDI[1]	World Bank Development Index (**Multidisciplinary**)	1,421
ILO[2]	International **Labour** Organization	1,122
OECD[3]	The Organisation for Economic Co-operation and Development (**Multidisciplinary**)	473
WTO[4]	World **Trade** Organization	107
WHO[5]	World **Health** Organization	93
Fund for peace[6]	**Failed State Index** and its relevant measures	14
ITU[7]	The International **Telecommunication** Union	7
Transparency[8]	**Corruption Perceptions Index**	2
Total number of indicators		**3,239**

[1] http://data.worldbank.org/indicator
[2] http://www.ilo.org/ilostat
[3] https://data.oecd.org/
[4] http://stat.wto.org/Home/WSDBHome.aspx
[5] http://www.who.int/gho/en/
[6] http://fsi.fundforpeace.org/
[7] http://www.itu.int/en/ITU-D/Statistics/
[8] http://www.transparency.org/

be set to 0. Otherwise, to provide robustness, the ϵ parameter is suggested to be a function of the MIC in question; for example, $\epsilon = 1 - \text{MIC}$. In any case, from Eq. (5), the range of MCN is $[2, log_2(B))$.

In summary, MINE statistics tell us other characteristics of the relationship – nonlinearity ($\text{MIC} - \rho^2$), non-monotonicity (MAS), continuity (MEV), and complexity (MCN) – apart from the relationship strength reflected by MIC.

3 A Case Study on Big Social Data

We conducted an interdisciplinary analysis of a large-scale historical data of country-level indicators. The objective of the case study is to find country-level indicators which are strongly and unexpectedly related to two target indicators – *(i)* GDP per capita (current US$) and *(ii)* Corruption Perceptions Index.

3.1 Dataset and Methodology

We collected country-level indicator data from eight trustworthy sources (listed in Table 1) which focus mainly on different aspects of countries such as agriculture, education, energy, finance, health, society, and technology. Regarding the target indicators, we chose GDP per capita (current US$) made available by

World Bank Development Index (WDI) and Corruption Perceptions Index by Transparency International [11]. We considered the relationships between these target indicators in a specific year and the values of other indicators in the previous year because these relationships will be helpful for one-year forecasting which we plan to do in the future. Two iterations of analysis were conducted. The first iteration studied the relationships between the target indicators in 2014 and other indicators, sometimes called explanatory variables, in 2013. The second iteration collectively studied the target variables from 2007 to 2014 and the explanatory variables in the previous year of target records.

MIC/MINE statistics can help us grasp lots of variable pairs in this large-scale dataset. However, computing MIC/MINE exhaustively takes very long time. So, we decided to use the approximate calculation software of MIC/MINE provided at http://www.exploredata.net. The software was implemented following *ApproxMaxMI* algorithm proposed by the authors of MIC/MINE.

3.2 Results and Interpretations

This section reports and interprets interesting EDA results from both iterations. Table 2 and Appendix 1's Table 4 list top 20 relationships (ranked by MIC score) between the target variable GDP per capita and explanatory variables in the first and second iteration respectively, while Appendix 1's Tables 3 and 5 present the same results but for Corruption Perceptions Index. The first and the last columns of these tables present the ranks of the explanatory variables with respect to their MIC and $|\rho|$, respectively. In addition, abbreviations used in these four tables (and following figures) are listed at[1].

To begin with, we can notice that there are two groups of indicators in Table 2. The first group consists of indicators originally related to the target, GDP per capita, by their definitions such as "GNI per capita" and "GDP per capita PPP". These indicators yielded really high MIC score and low MIC $- \rho^2$ meaning that they are strong linear relationships. In contrast, the other indicators such as "Fixed telephone subscriptions", "Agriculture; value added", and "Pupil-teacher ratio; primary" have surprised us because we could not imagine the obvious reasons why they are related to GDP per capita. Moreover, the relationships are not strongly linear as their $|\rho|$ measures were not so large.

To investigate more, we created interesting scatter plots from some of the top 20 relationships using Tableau [10] as shown in Fig. 1. Each dot represents indicator data of a country and its colour signifies the continent of that country. The association between GDP per capita and "Adjusted net national income per capita" (rank 1 in Table 2) displayed in Fig. 1(a) is a clear example of a linear relationship between two variables. On the contrary, the relationship between our target variable and "Agriculture; value added (% of GDP)" (rank 15), shown in Fig. 1(c), looks similar to a rectangular hyperbola. That is why its nonlinearity

---

[1] Abbreviations used in the tables and the figures: cap. = capita; c.US$ = current US dollar; c.int$ = current international dollar; 2011.int$ = constant 2011 international dollar; inhab. = inhabitants; consump. = consumption; pop. = population.

Table 2. Top 20 relationships ranked by MIC score for the target variable GDP per capita (current US$) (year: 2013 → 2014).

M #	Indicators (Unit)	MIC	MIC $-\rho^2$	MAS	MEV	MCN	ρ	$\|\rho\|$ #
1	Adjusted net national income per cap. (c.US$)	1.000	0.039	0.027	1.000	4.000	0.980	4
1	GDP per capita (c.US$)	1.000	0.003	0.027	1.000	3.585	0.999	1
1	GNI per capita; Atlas method (c.US$)	1.000	0.034	0.073	1.000	4.000	0.983	2
1	GNI per capita; PPP (2011.int$)	1.000	0.138	0.066	1.000	4.000	0.928	7
5	GNI per capita (2005.US$)	1.000	0.051	0.038	0.987	4.322	0.974	6
6	GNI per capita; PPP (c.int$)	0.981	0.134	0.036	0.971	4.585	0.921	9
7	Adj. net national income per cap. (2005.US$)	0.968	0.015	0.050	0.955	4.322	0.976	5
8	GDP per capita; PPP (c.int$)	0.964	0.108	0.028	0.964	4.585	0.925	8
8	GDP per capita; PPP (2011.int$)	0.964	0.117	0.022	0.964	4.585	0.920	10
10	GDP per capita (2005.US$)	0.961	−0.001	0.056	0.961	4.585	0.981	3
11	Health expenditure per cap.; PPP (2011.int$)	0.906	0.096	0.052	0.896	4.585	0.900	12
12	Household final consump. per cap. (2005.US$)	0.903	0.123	0.072	0.903	4.322	0.883	14
13	Health expenditure per capita (c.US$)	0.901	0.086	0.023	0.883	4.585	0.903	11
14	GDP per person employed (2011.PPP$)	0.893	0.101	0.051	0.893	4.459	0.890	13
15	Agriculture; value added (% of GDP)	0.817	0.530	0.045	0.817	4.459	−0.536	76
16	Fixed-telephone subscriptions per 100 inhab	0.815	0.381	0.156	0.800	4.459	0.658	38
17	Fixed telephone subscriptions per 100 people	0.787	0.315	0.120	0.787	4.585	0.687	35
18	Percentage of Individuals using the Internet	0.785	0.228	0.025	0.766	4.459	0.747	22
19	Electric power consumption (kWh per capita)	0.780	0.301	0.061	0.768	4.322	0.692	34
20	Pupil-teacher ratio; primary	0.770	0.491	0.070	0.754	4.322	−0.529	82

scores, MIC $-\rho^2$, is distinctively higher than other indicators. This demonstrates the ability of MIC to detect nonlinear relationships in big data. If we considered only the rank from $|\rho|$, we would miss interesting relationships.

The relationship between GDP per capita and "Fixed-telephone subscriptions per 100 inhabitants" (rank 16), shown in Fig. 1(d), got the highest MAS value in Table 2. It means that this relationship had the highest degree of non-monotonicity among the 20 relationships. It might be because we cannot decide definitely whether the right half of Fig. 1(d) shows the increasing or decreasing trend. In other words, it is unclear to state that this relationship is monotonic.

Comprehensive EDA not only tells us the shape of data but also guides us the proper means for further data analysis. For example, in Fig. 1(b) showing the relationship between GDP per capita and "Health expenditure per capita (current US$)" (rank 13), when the value on X-axis grows larger, the line of green dots (countries in Asia) is separate from the others and makes the plot seem like a superposition of two linear relationships. It suggests that if we create an OLS regression model for GDP per capita, we should have a linear term for health expenditure per capita and another term to control for location and capture different behaviours between continents.

With regard to another target variable – Corruption Perceptions Index (CPI), several measures in its top 20 relationships (ranked by MIC score) are also the top 20 s of GDP per capita. They are probably correlated as a group or a chain reaction. However, we found that the top 20 MIC scores of CPI are markedly lower than the ones of GDP per capita. This might be because CPI was not

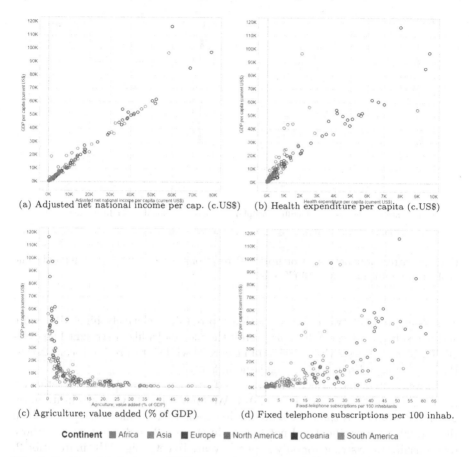

(a) Adjusted net national income per cap. (c.US$)   (b) Health expenditure per capita (c.US$)

(c) Agriculture; value added (% of GDP)   (d) Fixed telephone subscriptions per 100 inhab.

Continent ■ Africa ■ Asia ■ Europe ■ North America ■ Oceania ■ South America

Fig. 1. Scatter plots between GDP per capita (current US$) in 2014 (Y-axis) and some explanatory indicators in 2013 (X-axis).

computed from hard empirical data, but from surveys and assessments of corruption, gathered by various reliable institutions [11] causing higher uncertainty in CPI than GDP per capita.

Figure 2 shows two interesting scatter plots selected from the top 20 relationships of CPI. By definition, the lower the CPI is, the higher perceptions of corruption exist in that country. Figure 2(a) which looks like a linear or a logarithm function shows the relationship between CPI and the number of "Secure Internet servers" (rank 4). This relationship is unexpected because the number of secure Internet servers does not have a direct link to corruption. So, it is intriguing to figure out the reason behind this association. Besides, Fig. 2(b) illustrates an association between "Gross national expenditure deflator (base year varies by country)" and CPI (rank 10). This plot is interesting because most of the dots form a vertical straight line showing no relationships between the variables. The ρ of this relationship is close to zero because it shows neither increasing nor

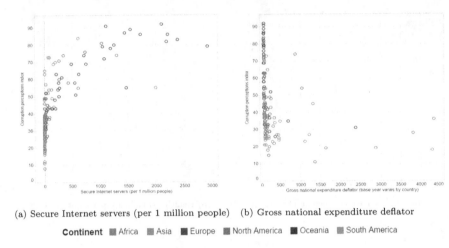

(a) Secure Internet servers (per 1 million people)   (b) Gross national expenditure deflator

Continent ■ Africa ■ Asia ■ Europe ■ North America ■ Oceania ■ South America

Fig. 2. Scatter plots between Corruption Perceptions Index in 2014 (Y-axis) and some explanatory indicators in 2013 (X-axis).

decreasing trend. However, this relationship obtains relatively high MIC score and it results in a large MIC $- \rho^2$ even if the plot looks like a straight line overall. This case suggests that we should be careful while interpreting the statistics. Please see more discussion on this issue in Sect. 4.

In iteration 2, we collectively computed MIC score and MINE statistics for the target indicators from 2007 to 2014. We found that MIC scores in iteration 2 were generally less than the scores in iteration 1. Also, many indicators from the top 20 s of iteration 1 did not appear in the top 20 s of iteration 2 as those relationships were strong for only a specific year. To get a high MIC in iteration 2, the indicators must correlate with the target for almost all of the analysed years which is quite difficult except for the indicators originally related by definitions.

On the whole, MEV (the continuity measure) and MCN (the complexity measure) did not play a significant role in exploring our interdisciplinary dataset in both iterations. We notice that MEV usually approximated to MIC. After creating a plot between MIC and MEV from all pairs of variables, we found that the plot was obviously linear with MIC $= 0.9779$ and $\rho = 0.9978$. The line of best fit is MEV $= 0.9953$MIC-0.0042 with $r^2 = 0.9957$. In other words, MEV $\approx$ MIC in this case study. Actually, MEV is not always a redundant measure of MIC. For instance, a noiseless circle with $n = 1,000$ yields MIC $= 0.71$ and MEV $= 0.32$ [8, Supporting material]. Nonetheless, this kind of relationships does not exist in our real-world dataset with more than thousand pairs of variables.

Considering MCN within each iteration, we cannot observe significant differences in complexity between scatter plots whose MCNs are unequal. However, the MCN values in iteration 1 are noticeably less than the ones in iteration 2. The ranges of MCN in iteration 1 and 2 are [3.58, 4.58] and [5.32, 6.49], respectively. This might be because iteration 2 has more dots than iteration 1. Hence, a more complex grid is required to capture the real-world relationships and reach the MIC scores, while the upper bound of MCN, which is $\log(B) = \log(n^{0.6})$, allows MCN to grow larger as n increases in iteration 2.

4   Discussions

Since MIC was intentionally designed for rapid exploration of multidimensional datasets, it performed well in the case study, capturing not only linear but also quadratic, logarithmic, and hyperbolic relationships. It seems that MIC is a perfect tool for EDA; however, it still has some limitations.

- Unlike Pearson's correlation (ρ), MIC does not imply the tone of relationship, i.e., whether it is increasing or decreasing.
- MIC, as well as ρ, supports only numeric data. We noticed different behaviours of continents in the case study not because of MIC but because of the different colours we set in the scatter plots.
- MIC is sensitive to noises and sometimes detects false-positive relationships. In other words, it sometimes gives a variable pair with no veritable association too high MIC score [9]. This might be the reason for the relatively high MIC score (as well as the high nonlinearity score) of Fig. 2(b). In our case study, even the lowest MIC value from both iterations is 0.0868 (8.68% from the perfect score), while the lowest $|\rho|$ is only 0.0003 (0.03%).

Based on what we learned from the case study and the limitations, we provide general guidelines for using MIC/MINE statistics to explore data as follows:

- Analyse MIC/MINE statistics with ρ to get more comprehensive information for the sketch of the relationship. Note that MIC does not totally replace ρ.
- Do not conclude the exact shape of the relationship from only the measures until seeing the scatter plot.
- Use MIC/MINE and ρ to help us select some (interesting) relationships to investigate graphically. The easiest way is selecting the relationships with a relatively high MIC score as we did in the case study. Another recommended way is plotting a scatterplot matrix (SPLOM) of the measures (as we show in Appendix 2) and manually selecting the relationships located in interesting areas of subplots in the SPLOM such as high MIC and MIC$-\rho^2$ or selecting the outlier dots compared to other relationships.
- Do not forget to use other visual variables of scatter plot such as shapes and colours to represent categorical features.

5   Related Work

Exploratory data analysis in social sciences – Several measures have been used as correlation measures in quantitative social research such as Lambda coefficient for nominal-level data, Kendall's and Spearman's correlation for ordinal-level data, and Pearson's correlation (ρ) for interval-level and ratio-level data. So far, however, there has been little discussion about nonlinear associations

522   P. Lertvittayakumjorn et al.

in social science research, even in recent research methodology textbooks [2,4]. Only a few papers turn to concern nonlinear associations such as the paper by Boutyline and Vaisey which used ρ for numeric variables and conducted general (not only linear) dependency analysis in an appendix using mutual information to confirm the results [3]. We hope that our paper will build more awareness of nonlinear relationships in social data among social science researchers.

Applications of MIC/MINE statistics – MIC has been employed in several data analysis studies. For example, Tan et al. conducted model selection based on the MIC between regression residuals and explanatory variables [6]. Zhao et al. combined MIC with affinity propagation clustering to perform feature selection [12]. MIC was also deployed to support construction and analysis of biological networks as it could capture a wide range of relationships [1,5,7]. Nonetheless, we have not seen any methodology or application papers using MINE statistics in their work. Moreover, even if a few papers tried applying MIC on social science datasets as small examples [8,12], to the best of our knowledge, this paper is the first study that places great emphasis on interpreting the meaning of MIC and MINE statistics for practical use in social science research.

6   Conclusion

This paper aims to use a case study of analysing a large-scale country-level indicator dataset to introduce MIC and MINE statistics for exploring big social data. Based on the case study, MIC was a powerful nonlinear correlation measure which detected several unexpected relationships and complemented the traditional linear correlation (Pearson's ρ). Also, two MINE statistics, MAS (for non-monotonicity) and MIC $- \rho^2$ (for nonlinearity), helped us imagine the scatter plots more accurately, while the other two statistics – MEV and MCN – did not show their full discrimination power in our big real-world dataset. To overcome some limitations of MIC/MINE statistics, we also provide general guidelines for using the statistics in this paper. For future work, we plan to conduct interdisciplinary forecasting of target indicators with the aid of MIC/MINE statistics. We believe that it could yield accurate prediction results as all related domains of country-level data are included in the model, not only the specific domain of target indicators.

Appendix 1: Supplementary Results

Table 2 in Sect. 3.2 and Appendix 1's Table 4 list top 20 relationships (ranked by MIC score) between the target variable GDP per capita and explanatory variables in the first and second iteration respectively, while Appendix 1's Tables 3 and 5 present the same results but for Corruption Perceptions Index. Each of the tables has nine columns. The first and the last columns present the ranks of the explanatory variables with respect to their MIC and $|\rho|$, respectively, as

Table 3. Top 20 relationships ranked by MIC score for the target variable Corruption Perceptions Index (year: 2013 → 2014).

M #	Indicators (Unit)	MIC	MIC $-\rho^2$	MAS	MEV	MCN	ρ	$|\rho|$ #
1	Corruption Perceptions Index	0.918	−0.074	0.041	0.918	4.000	0.996	1
2	Household final consump. per cap. (2005.US$)	0.721	0.015	0.114	0.701	4.170	0.840	7
3	Adj. net national income per cap. (2005.US$)	0.717	−0.001	0.113	0.700	4.170	0.847	4
4	Secure Internet servers (per 1 million people)	0.655	0.138	0.054	0.655	4.322	0.719	31
5	GNI per capita (2005.US$)	0.649	−0.058	0.050	0.623	4.170	0.840	6
6	Legitimacy of the State	0.645	−0.161	0.076	0.645	4.322	−0.898	2
7	Failed States Index Rank	0.602	−0.089	0.079	0.602	4.322	0.831	8
8	Failed States Index Total	0.601	−0.168	0.078	0.601	4.322	−0.877	3
9	Time to import (days)	0.594	0.224	0.117	0.594	4.322	−0.608	62
10	Gross national expenditure deflator	0.590	0.519	0.139	0.590	4.170	−0.267	261
11	GDP per capita (2005.US$)	0.587	−0.056	0.061	0.587	4.322	0.802	14
12	Health expenditure per capita (c.US$)	0.585	−0.003	0.066	0.585	4.322	0.767	25
13	Public services	0.585	−0.079	0.049	0.585	4.322	−0.815	11
14	Burden of customs procedure; WEF (1 to 7)	0.583	−0.070	0.053	0.583	4.170	0.808	13
15	GNI per capita; PPP (2011.int$)	0.581	0.064	0.046	0.581	4.170	0.719	32
16	Price level ratio of PPP conversion factor (GDP) to market exchange rate	0.581	−0.050	0.121	0.581	3.585	0.794	17
17	Improved water source (% of pop. with access)	0.578	0.234	0.036	0.578	4.322	0.587	70
18	Percentage of Individuals using the Internet	0.577	−0.033	0.071	0.577	4.322	0.781	22
19	Fixed-broadband subscriptions per 100 inhab	0.577	−0.042	0.131	0.577	4.322	0.786	20
20	Adj. net national income per cap. (c.US$)	0.575	−0.090	0.062	0.562	4.322	0.815	10

Table 4. Top 20 relationships ranked by MIC score for the target variable GDP per capita (current US$) (year: 2006–2013 → 2007–2014).

M #	Indicators (Unit)	MIC	MIC $-\rho^2$	MAS	MEV	MCN	ρ	$|\rho|$ #
1	GDP per capita (c.US$)	0.993	0.010	0.020	0.992	6.492	0.992	1
2	GNI per capita; Atlas method (c.US$)	0.974	0.015	0.019	0.973	6.459	0.979	3
3	Adjusted net national income per cap. (c.US$)	0.954	−0.001	0.020	0.954	6.358	0.977	5
4	GNI per capita (2005.US$)	0.946	−0.009	0.026	0.944	6.209	0.977	4
5	GNI per capita; PPP (2011.int$)	0.943	0.100	0.022	0.943	6.248	0.918	7
6	GDP per capita (2005.US$)	0.931	−0.036	0.026	0.931	6.459	0.984	2
7	GDP per capita; PPP (c.int$)	0.930	0.118	0.026	0.929	6.459	0.901	10
8	GDP per capita; PPP (2011.int$)	0.926	0.109	0.040	0.925	6.459	0.904	8
9	Adj. net national income per cap. (2005.US$)	0.925	−0.025	0.018	0.925	6.170	0.975	6
10	GNI per capita; PPP (c.int$)	0.918	0.110	0.018	0.917	6.459	0.899	11
11	Household final consump. per cap. (2005.US$)	0.863	0.047	0.028	0.863	6.209	0.903	9
12	Health expenditure per cap. (c.US$)	0.838	0.066	0.023	0.838	6.426	0.879	12
13	Health expenditure per cap.; PPP (2011.int$)	0.837	0.080	0.020	0.837	6.426	0.870	13
14	GDP per person employed (2011.PPP$)	0.821	0.074	0.026	0.819	6.392	0.864	14
15	Agriculture; value added (% of GDP)	0.780	0.494	0.056	0.780	6.392	−0.534	65
16	Electric power consumption (kWh per capita)	0.766	0.228	0.055	0.766	6.170	0.733	27
17	Automated teller machines per 100000 adults	0.713	0.291	0.077	0.713	6.358	0.650	42
18	Energy use (kg of oil equivalent per capita)	0.711	0.215	0.052	0.709	6.248	0.704	34
19	Air and GHG emissions - CO_2 (tonne_cap)	0.683	0.229	0.073	0.683	6.000	0.674	39
20	Fixed telephone subscriptions per 100 people	0.682	0.115	0.029	0.682	6.459	0.753	22

Table 5. Top 20 relationships ranked by MIC score for the target variable Corruption Perceptions Index (year: 2006–2013 → 2007–2014).

M #	Indicators (Unit)	MIC	MIC $-\rho^2$	MAS	MEV	MCN	ρ	$|\rho|$ #
1	Corruption Perceptions Index	0.865	−0.116	0.019	0.865	5.907	0.990	1
2	Household final consump. per cap. (2005.US$)	0.623	−0.101	0.042	0.620	6.044	0.851	5
3	Adj. net national income per cap. (2005.US$)	0.613	−0.122	0.049	0.613	5.907	0.857	4
4	Secure Internet servers (per 1 million people)	0.613	0.151	0.049	0.613	6.209	0.680	38
5	GNI per capita (2005.US$)	0.578	−0.142	0.036	0.578	5.954	0.848	6
6	Adj. net national income per cap. (c.US$)	0.568	−0.113	0.068	0.568	6.170	0.825	10
7	Public services	0.561	−0.142	0.046	0.557	6.209	−0.839	7
8	GDP per capita (2005.US$)	0.560	−0.103	0.059	0.560	6.248	0.814	13
9	Electric power consumption (kWh per capita)	0.554	0.142	0.084	0.551	6.044	0.642	49
10	Health expenditure per capita (c.US$)	0.553	−0.053	0.044	0.551	6.248	0.778	23
11	Failed States Index Total	0.551	−0.214	0.028	0.549	6.209	−0.875	3
12	Legitimacy of the State	0.540	−0.226	0.046	0.539	6.209	−0.875	2
13	Health expenditure per cap.; PPP (2011.int$)	0.536	−0.104	0.077	0.533	6.248	0.800	19
14	Agriculture; value added (% of GDP)	0.531	0.178	0.086	0.529	6.170	−0.595	64
15	GNI per capita; Atlas method (c.US$)	0.530	−0.128	0.040	0.530	6.209	0.811	16
16	Failed States Index Rank	0.529	−0.126	0.045	0.529	5.322	0.809	17
17	Percentage of Individuals using the Internet	0.520	−0.153	0.052	0.518	6.248	0.821	12
18	GNI per capita; PPP (2011.int$)	0.517	−0.008	0.045	0.517	6.087	0.725	31
19	GDP per capita (c.US$)	0.515	−0.111	0.042	0.513	6.248	0.791	21
20	Internet users (per 100 people)	0.514	−0.160	0.050	0.514	6.248	0.821	11

both measures reflect the relationship strengths (in different ways). The second column shows the variables' names and units of measurement. The third column reports the MIC scores of the relationships, whereas the fourth to seventh list their MINE statistics. The eighth column shows the Pearson's ρ scores ranging from −1 to 1. Lastly, abbreviations used in these tables are listed at[11].

Appendix 2: Relationships among the statistics

A scatterplot matrix (SPLOM) of measures in the case study (MIC, MIC-ρ^2, MAS, MEV, MCN, ρ, and $|\rho|$) is shown in Fig. 3. We can notice the linear relationship between MIC and MEV as well as the separation of MCN values of both iterations in this scatterplot matrix.

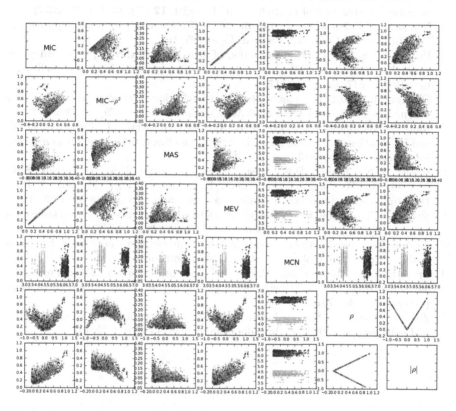

Fig. 3. A scatterplot matrix (SPLOM) of measures in the case study. Each dot represents a relationship of a variable pair. The blue dots are for the target variable GDP per capita (current US$). The red dots are for the target variable Corruption Perceptions Index (CPI). The light colours represent the relationship pairs from the first iteration, while the dark colours represent the relationship pairs from the second iteration.

References

1. Akhand, M., Nandi, R., Amran, S., Murase, K.: Gene regulatory network inference incorporating maximal information coefficient into minimal redundancy network. ICEEICT **2015**, 1–4 (2015)
2. Bhattacherjee, A.: Social science research: principles, methods, and practices (2012)
3. Boutyline, A., Vaisey, S.: Belief network analysis: a relational approach to understanding the structure of attitudes. Am. J. Sociol. **122**(5), 1371–1447 (2017)
4. Neuman, L.W.: Social research methods: qualitative and quantitative approaches, 7th edn. Pearson Education Limited, Essex (2014)
5. Paul, A.K., Shill, P.C.: Reconstruction of gene network through backward elimination based information-theoretic inference with maximal information coefficient. In: icIVPR 2017, pp. 1–5 (2017)
6. Qiuheng, T., Jiang, H., Yiming, D.: Model selection method based on maximal information coefficient of residuals. Acta Math. Sci. **34**(2), 579–592 (2014)
7. Rau, C., Wisniewski, N., Orozco, L., Bennett, B., Weiss, J., Lusis, A.: Maximal information component analysis: a novel non-linear network analysis method. Front. Genet. **4**, 28 (2013)
8. Reshef, D.N., Reshef, D.N., Reshef, Y.A., Finucane, H.K., Grossman, S.R., Mcvean, G., Turnbaugh, P.J., Lander, E.S., Mitzenmacher, M., Sabeti, P.C.: Detecting novel associations in large data sets. Science **334**, 1518–1524 (2011)
9. Simon, N., Tibshirani, R.: Comment on "Detecting novel associations in large data sets". In: Reshef., D.N., et al. Science, 16 December 2011. ArXiv e-prints (2014)
10. Tableau Software: Answer questions as fast as you can think of them with tableau (2016). http://www.tableau.com/trial/tableau-software
11. Transparency International: Corruption perceptions index 2016: Frequently asked questions (2017). https://www.transparency.org/news/feature/corruption_perceptions_index_2016
12. Zhao, X., Deng, W., Shi, Y.: Feature selection with attributes clustering by maximal information coefficient. Procedia Comput. Sci. **17**, 70–79 (2013)

Exploring Emerging Topics in Social Informatics: An Online Real-Time Tool for Keyword Co-Occurrence Analysis

Florian Cech[✉]

Centre for Informatics and Society, TU Wien,
Favoritenstrasse 9-11/187-1, 1090 Vienna, Austria
florian.cech@tuwien.ac.at
http://www.cisvienna.com
http://media.tuwien.ac.at

Abstract. In an academic field as diverse as Social Informatics, identifying current and emergent topics presents a significant challenge to individuals and institutions alike. Several approaches based on keyword assignment and visualizing co-occurrence networks have already been described with the goal of providing insight into topical and geographical clusters of publications, authors or institutions. This work identifies a few key challenges to the aforementioned methods and proposes an interdisciplinary approach based on qualitative text analysis to assign keywords to research institutions and quantitatively explore them by building interactive co-occurrence and research focus parallelship networks. The proposed technique is then applied to the field of Social Informatics by identifying more than a hundred organizations worldwide within that domain, coding them with keywords based on research group titles, online self-descriptions and affiliated publications, and creating an online tool to generate interactive co-occurrence, network neighbourhood and research focus parallelship visualizations.

Keywords: Keyword visualization · Co-Occurrence networks · Neighbourhood analysis · Research focus parallelship · Scientometrics · Social informatics

1   Introduction

Determining current and future trends in research foci is a challenging task, particularly so if the field in question is as diverse and interdisciplinary in nature as Social Informatics. Often enough, focusing on research output alone by analysing publications of relevant authors in the field provides only a partial view of emerging topics and can lead to a biased outcome. Furthermore, increased mobility of researchers and limited information about the research affiliation of authors at the time of writing make it difficult to geographically map certain trends. On the other hand, focusing on research institutions (as opposed to individuals)

© Springer International Publishing AG 2017
G.L. Ciampaglia et al. (Eds.): SocInfo 2017, Part II, LNCS 10540, pp. 527–536, 2017.
DOI: 10.1007/978-3-319-67256-4_42

as the primary sources of data presents a different challenge due to heterogeneous information sources (such as websites, promotional material or research group names). Overcoming these challenges would allow an accurate mapping of keywords to research institutions and provide rapid insights through established visualization techniques such as keyword co-occurrence or research focus parallelship (RFP) networks.

Within this work, we identify key challenges to established quantitative approaches in the field of Scientometrics and propose a mixed approach to collect and analyse institution-keyword mappings. Applying this technique to the field of Social Informatics, an online tool that allows interactive keyword co-occurrence, keyword neighbourhood and RFP network visualization and analysis is presented. Finally, a discussion of (dis-)advantages of the given implementation identifies key challenges and areas for improvement.

2   Related Work

The field of Scientometrics provides methods and tools to gain insight into the organization and topical clustering of scientific fields. Largely based on a quantitative analysis of (automatically) collected data, several approaches used scientific publication keywords (e.g. [4,30,33]), citations (e.g. [7,27]) or co-authorship (e.g. [19,21]) to produce networks of relations between keywords, authors or institutions. Building on these networks, graph visualization is the most common approach to extract domain knowledge from these networks, including co-occurrence visualization (e.g. [10,13,15,22,24,32]) and research focus parallelship (RFP) networks (e.g. [14,28,30]).

Although these approaches allow good insights into their respective domains, their real-world applicability is often limited to experts in the field due to the complex steps involved in collecting the data, generating and transforming the co-occurrence or RFP networks and visualizing the results via software tools such as Gephi [3]. In contrast, other fields such as Bioinformatics have already recognized this issue and demonstrated the value of user-friendly interactive (online) visualizations (e.g., [1,6,11,23,31]).

While the collection of keywords and relations through quantitative evaluation of scientific publications is a conveniently efficient approach, it also limits the options for data sources to structured content (such as already available online publication databases). For the use case of mapping institutions rather than authors alone, an approach based on publications presupposes a direct connection between the research output of an institution's affiliated research staff and the research focus of that organisation. In contrast, a purely qualitative approach is rarely feasible due to amount of data needed to be extracted, coded and categorized.

Recent advances in machine learning have produced promising results for keyword extraction, but their applicability to the often highly unstructured and heterogeneous textual data available through institution's websites is still limited (cf. [26] for a recent literature overview).

Given the challenges of qualitative approaches and the limitations of quantitative approaches, a mixed technique is proposed to extract keyword associations through qualitative text analysis and to quantitatively analyse and visualize the resulting data.

3 Data Collection

The goal of this study is the collection of research institutions relevant to Social Informatics, assignment of keywords to each individual institution and the visualization of relations between institutions based on their assigned keywords. The starting point for this collection was a list of more than 750 educational institutions listed in the latest *Informatics Europe* report on *Informatics Education in Europe* (cf. [20]). Given the report's limitation to European institutions, the list of surveyed institutions was extended to non-european institutions through notable publications and researchers related to already surveyed institutions.

A qualitative analysis of each institution's online self-descriptions was conducted, including *'about' pages, research focus outlines* as well as *research group names* and *publication titles* as textual sources. Loosely following Mayring's standard approach (cf. [18]) to qualitative content analysis, the full-text self-descriptions were *summarized* and *inductively categorized* with keywords extracted directly from the texts, and - where applicable - *explicated* with terms from supplementary sources such as research group names. The resulting first list of keywords and institutions was iteratively reduced via a process of standardisation to remove duplicate keyword entries and similar terms. Limiting factors that excluded institutions from the list were missing English or German translations or obviously outdated websites[1].

The final list of 116 institutions and 145 keywords was loaded into a web-application[2], and a Tableau[3] Web Data Connector (WDC) was implemented to facilitate data analysis within the Tableau software. Figure 1 shows a subset of the resulting keywords with their absolute number of occurrences.

4 Data Analysis

To allow an interactive and intuitive data analysis of the collected corpus of institutions and keywords, *co-occurrence, neighbourhood exploration* and *research parallelship* networks needed to be calculated and visualized in real-time. After some review of related literature (e.g. [25]), the SigmaJS[4] graph visualization library was chosen due to its ease of use and relatively good performance.

---

[1] A website was considered outdated if no changes had been done for more than 2 years.
[2] Available at http://orgs.cisvienna.com.
[3] cf. https://www.tableau.com/.
[4] cf. http://sigmajs.org.

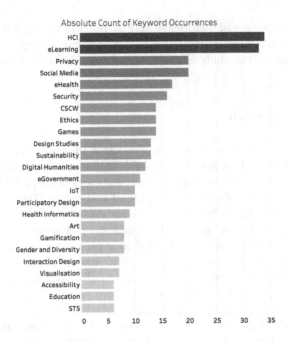

Fig. 1. Absolute count of keyword occurrences with threshold *count* > 6

4.1 Co-Occurrence and Neighbourhood Exploration

Following Rip and Courtial [24], a simple keyword co-occurrence matrix is constructed with co-occurrence k_{ij} defined as the sum of co-occurrences of keywords k_i and k_j within the same institution by first obtaining a keyword-institution matrix I with

$$I_{i,k} = \begin{cases} 1 & \text{if } keyword\ k\ in\ institution\ i \\ 0 & \text{otherwise} \end{cases} \tag{1}$$

The actual keyword-keyword co-occurrence matrix C is then calculated by multiplying I with its transposed matrix I^T as suggested by Sani et al. in [9, p. 310ff]:

$$C = I \times I^T \tag{2}$$

The resulting symmetrical matrix C is drawn as Graph $G = (K, E)$ with randomized starting positions for each node K representing a keyword and edges $E_{m,n}$ with weight $C_{m,n}$ for each co-occurrence of keywords m and n. Furthermore, the size of each rendered node K is representative of the total number of occurrences of that keyword to visualize their relative importance. The tool also provides an implementation of the *Force Atlas 2* algorithm (originally developed by Jacomy et al. (cf. [12]) for the Gephi software) and allows changing the algorithm's parameters, such as the *edge weight influence, Barnes-Hut optimizations* [2] for large graphs or *outbound attraction distribution*. Figure 2 shows an example output for the keyword co-occurence visualization after running the *Force Atlas 2* algorithm.

Given the large number of keywords and co-occurrences and to facilitate a more exploratory end-user experience, an alternative graph providing *neighbourhood exploration* functionality was implemented, allowing to identify related keywords for a central network actor. This graph is based on the same co-occurrence data as the original graph, but limits the shown keyword nodes to directly related nodes. The graph can be re-centered by clicking on any keyword, allowing an iterative exploration of connected keywords and the underlying complete graph. Figures 3 and 4 show the neighbourhood for the keyword 'Copyright' before and after running the *Force Atlas 2* layout algorithm.

Finally, to combat information overflow in the graph, two sliders filtering the display of graph nodes and edges by their respective weights were implemented. This allows a real-time, interactive reduction of the graphs to show only their most important nodes and edges as determined by their weights.

4.2   Research Focus Parallelship

To complement the keyword-centric visualizations of the co-occurrence matrix, an institution-centric research focus parallelship network (RFP, cf. [28]) is constructed. Instead of visualizing relations between the collected keywords themselves, the relations between institutions are calculated based on the assumption that two institutions that share keywords also share a research focus. Any institution O_i has a parallelship with another institution O_j, calculated through the number of shared keywords k and assigning the resulting sum value to the edge weight $W(E_{i,j})$:

$$W(E_{i,j}) = |k_i \cap k_j| \tag{3}$$

The resulting matrix was visualized similarly to the neighbourhood exploration graph, showing only a single institution's parallelship relations (cf. Fig. 5), and allows utilizing the same layout algorithm and user interactions as the other visualizations.

5   Results & Limitations

The resulting online tool allows a rapid and intuitive exploration of the collected data. Visual augmentation of graph nodes with contextual information ("Organisations with keyword [...]", "Keywords of organisation [...]") provide further insights into the collected data. Through adapting the parameters governing the *Force Atlas 2* layout algorithm, clustering of keywords and institutions can be observed for subsets of the data; where the algorithm fails to arrive at a solution (i.e. only minimal movement of nodes can be observed), the filtering options for the weights provide insight into the centrality of nodes and edges.

Given the number of keywords, institutions and their relations, the graphs - particularly the co-occurrence graph - can become overpopulated and limit their potential for insights. Alternative views like the neighbourhood analysis can balance this by providing a more focused view. These views provide a clear advantage over non-interactive visualizations: switching the central node for the neighbourhood view is as simple as clicking a different node - contrary to the same visualization rendered in dedicated desktop applications likex Gephi, where a set of filters must be (re-)applied every time a new central node should be considered.

While the naive implementation of centrality, neighbourhood and parallelship metrics shows the promise of interactive visualizations, more sophisticated approaches including *degree, between, closeness centrality, vertex similarity* and *biclique community detection* as outlined by Freeman, Brass and Burkhard, Su, Leicht et al. and Lehmann et al. (cf. [5,8,16,17,29]) could provide a more precise measure of influence for keywords and institutions in the graphs.

Furthermore, adding a temporal dimension to the analysis by recording changes to the institution and keyword database over time and providing a timeline to the visualization might produce better insights into *emerging* topics in particular, although the amount of effort involved in repeated qualitative analysis of institutional self-descriptions might not make this approach feasible.

Finally, the performance of the visualizations proved to be satisfactory; due to the nature of the technology stack (SigmaJS and JavaScript), the performance is dependent on the capabilities of the client computer rather than the performance of the server. Given the current performance of average desktop computers, this would only become an issue for viewing very large graphs - particularly on mobile devices: the resulting slower speed of animations would reduce interactivity and negatively affect the user experience. Optimisations in the way the data is handled could mitigate this issue and remain a future research topic.

6   Conclusion

Gaining insight into current and emerging topics within a scientific field to determine future research policy and directions is a challenging task for research institutions and individual researchers alike. Multiple previous approaches based on keyword co-occurrence of publication keywords focus on the automated collection of large amounts of data, but can be misleading for complex and multidisciplinary fields like Social Informatics. Choosing an approach grounded in qualitative text analysis can help mitigate the issues arising from synonymous keyword terms or unclear research affiliations and allow a high confidence in the results despite the small sample size of the resulting keyword space.

Visualization of co-occurrence and research parallelship networks has proven to be a valuable tool for the exploration of research topics within a given field. The limitations of pre-calculated graphs, the need for specialized software and the subsequent challenges of sharing and collaborating on the resulting visualizations can be addressed by using an online web application such as the one presented in this study. The design and implementation can be applied to any scientific field, and allows interactive exploration and collaboration on the resulting data, proving to be a valuable tool to researchers and institutions alike.

Appendix: Figures

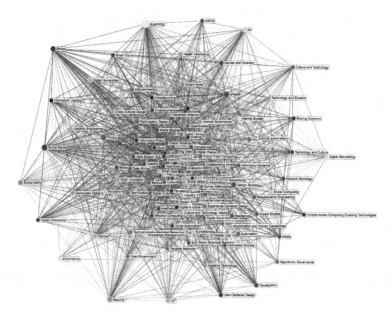

Fig. 2. Co-occurrence of keywords visualization after running *Force Atlas 2* with a *Barnes-Hut Theta* value of 0.5, *lin-log* mode and *outbound attraction distribution*.

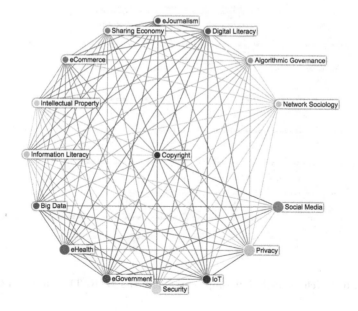

Fig. 3. Neighbourhood exploration of keyword 'Copyright' before the layout algorithm.

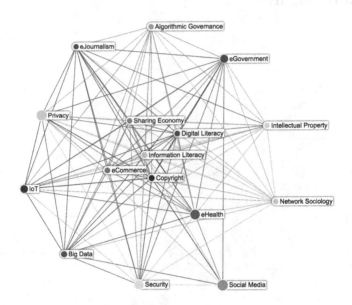

Fig. 4. Neighbourhood exploration of keyword 'Copyright' after the layout algorithm.

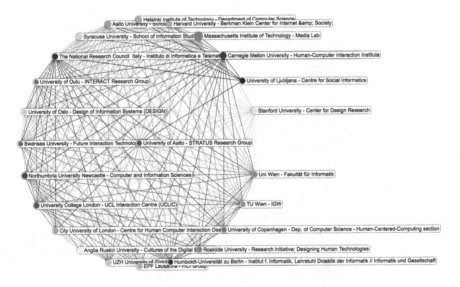

Fig. 5. Research Focus Parallelship centered on the 'STRATUS Research Group'

References

1. Abello, J., Van Ham, F., Krishnan, N.: ASK-graphview: a large scale graph visualization system. IEEE Trans. Visual. Comput. Graphics **12**(5), 669–676 (2006)
2. Barnes, J., Hut, P.: A hierarchical o(n log n) force-calculation algorithm. Nature **324**(6096), 446–449 (1986)
3. Bastian, M., Heymann, S., Jacomy, M.: An open source software for exploring and manipulating networks. In: Third International AAAI Conference on Weblogs and Social Media, pp. 361–362 (2009)
4. Bhattacharya, S., Basu, P.: Mapping a research area at the micro level using co-word analysis. Scientometrics **43**, 359–372 (2006)
5. Brass, D., Burkhardt, M.E.: Centrality and power in organizations. In: Networks and Organizations: Structure, Form, and Action, pp. 191–215 (1992)
6. Brown, K.R., Otasek, D., Ali, M., McGuffin, M.J., Xie, W., Devani, B., van Toch, I.L., Jurisica, I.: NAViGaTOR: network analysis, visualization and graphing Toronto. Bioinformatics **25**(24), 3327–3329 (2009)
7. Cambrosio, A., Keating, P., Mercier, S., Lewison, G., Mogoutov, A.: Mapping the emergence and development of translational cancer research. Eur. J. Cancer **42**(18), 3140–3148 (2006)
8. Freeman, L.C.: Centrality in social networks conceptual clarification. Soc. Netw. **1**(3), 215–239 (1978)
9. Goebel, R.: Lecture Notes in Artificial Intelligence Subseries of Lecture Notes in Computer Science LNAI Series Editors (2011)
10. Hu, M., Wongsuphasawat, K., Stasko, J.: Visualizing social media content with sententree. IEEE Trans. Vis. Comput. Graphics **23**(1), 621–630 (2017)
11. Hu, Z., Mellor, J., Wu, J., DeLisi, C.: VisANT: an online visualization and analysis tool for biological interaction data. BMC Bioinformatics **5**, 17–17 (2004)
12. Jacomy, M., Venturini, T., Heymann, S., Bastian, M.: ForceAtlas2, a continuous graph layout algorithm for handy network visualization designed for the Gephi Software (2014)
13. Kushima, M., Araki, K., Suzuki, M., Araki, S., Nikama, T.: Graphic visualization of the co-occurrence analysis network of lung cancer in-patient nursing record. In: 2010 International Conference on Information Science and Applications, pp. 1–8. IEEE (2010)
14. Lee, P.C., Su, H.N.: Investigating the structure of regional innovation system research through keyword co-occurrence and social network analysis. Innov.: Manage., Policy Pract. **12**(1), 26–40 (2010)
15. Lee, W.H.: How to identify emerging research fields using scientometrics: an example in the field of information security. Scientometrics **76**(3), 503–525 (2008)
16. Lehmann, S., Schwartz, M., Hansen, L.K.: Biclique communities. Phys. Rev. E **78**(1), P09008–9 (2008)
17. Leicht, E.A., Holme, P., Newman, M.E.J.: Vertex similarity in networks. arXiv.org, (2):P10012 (2005)
18. Mayring, P.: Qualitative Inhaltsanalyse (2010)
19. Melin, G., Persson, O.: Studying research collaboration using co-authorships. Scientometrics **36**(3), 363–377 (1996)
20. Pereira, C.: Informatics education in Europe: Institutions, degrees, students, positions, salaries. Technical report, Informatics Europe, Zrich (2016)
21. Persson, O., Beckmann, M.: Locating the network of interacting authors in scientific specialties. Scientometrics **33**(3), 351–366 (1995)

22. Peters, H.P.F., Vanraan, A.F.J.: Co-word-based science maps of chemical-engineering 1. representations by direct multidimensional-scaling. Res. Policy **22**(1), 47–71 (1993)

23. Reh, A., Gusenbauer, C., Kastner, J., Groller, M.E., Heinzl, C.: MObjects-a novel method for the visualization and interactive exploration of defects in industrial XCT data. IEEE Trans. Vis. Comput. Graphics **19**(12), 2906–2915 (2013)

24. Rip, A., Courtial, J.P.: Co-word maps of biotechnology: an example of cognitive scientometrics. Scientometrics **6**(6), 381–400 (1984)

25. Roy, S.: Effectiveness of JavaScript graph visualization libraries in visualizing gene regulatory networks (GRN) (2015)

26. Siddiqi, S., Sharan, A.: Keyword and keyphrase extraction techniques: a literature review. Int. J. Comput. Appl. **109**(2), 18–23 (2015)

27. Small, H.: Visualizing science by citation mapping. J. Am. Soc. Inf. Sci. **50**(9), 799–813 (1999)

28. Su, H.N., Lee, P.C.: Knowledge map of publications in research policy. In: PICMET: Portland International Center for Management of Engineering and Technology, Proceedings, pp. 2507–2516 (2009a)

29. Su, H.-N., Lee, P.-C.: Knowledge map of publications in research policy. In: PICMET 2009 - 2009 Portland International Conference on Management of Engineering & Technology, pp. 2507–2516. IEEE (2009b)

30. Su, H.N., Lee, P.C.: Mapping knowledge structure by keyword co-occurrence: a first look at journal papers in technology foresight. Scientometrics **85**(1), 65–79 (2010)

31. Wang, H., Azuaje, F., Black, N.: An integrative and interactive framework for improving biomedical pattern discovery and visualization. IEEE Trans. Inf. Technol. Biomed. **8**(1), 16–27 (2004)

32. Wu, W., Xu, J., Zeng, H., Zheng, Y., Qu, H., Ni, B., Yuan, M., Ni, L.M.: TelCoVis: Visual exploration of co-occurrence in urban human mobility based on Telco data. IEEE Trans. Vis. Comput. Graphics **22**(1), 935–944 (2016)

33. Zhu, L., Liu, X., He, S., Shi, J., Pang, M.: Keywords co-occurrence mapping knowledge domain research base on the theory of big data in oil and gas industry. Scientometrics **105**(1), 249–260 (2015)

Writer Profiling Without the Writer's Text

David Jurgens[✉], Yulia Tsvetkov, and Dan Jurafsky

Stanford University, Stanford, CA 94095, USA
{jurgens,tsvetkov,jurafsky}@stanford.edu

Abstract. Social network users may wish to preserve their anonymity online by masking their identity and not using language associated with any particular demographics or personality. However, they have no control over the language in incoming communications. We show that linguistic cues in public comments directed at a user are sufficient for an accurate inference of that user's gender, age, religion, diet, and even personality traits. Moreover, we show that directed communication is even more predictive of a user's profile than the user's own language. We then conduct a nuanced analysis of what types of social relationships are most predictive of users' attributes, and propose new strategies on how individuals can modulate their online social relationships and incoming communications to preserve their anonymity.

1 Introduction

Communication is the crux of online social platforms and the messages people write can reveal substantial information about their identity, such as their demographic attributes, personality, location, native language, or socioeconomic status. Knowledge of a person's identity benefits many downstream applications including commercial ones, which has led to a significant effort to develop methods that infer an author's latent attributes automatically from their writings. Most profiling and demographic inference methods focus on the text an individual writes. However, individuals also communicate directly with others, raising the question of how much *incoming* messages reveal about a recipient. Further, such directed speech also raises an important privacy concern: although people can opt to self-censor information to reveal less of their identity through the statements they make [2,62,63,85], a person does not control what their friends say to them, potentially exposing much about their identity. Such directed speech can be highly revealing of the individual's identity and social relationships, as shown in Fig. 1. Here, we measure to what degree incoming messages sent to an individual reveal their personal attributes and whether privacy-seeking individuals can obfuscate their own information when they cannot control the content they receive.

Prior work on demographic inference has largely focused on analyzing either the individual directly through the text they produce [20] or information from their social network, where friends are assumed to have similar attributes [1,3]. Here, we consider a third source of information from directed communications

G.L. Ciampaglia et al. (Eds.): SocInfo 2017, Part II, LNCS 10540, pp. 537–558, 2017.
DOI: 10.1007/978-3-319-67256-4_43

Congrats! @andyblack & @JulietSimmsALL on
the marriage!! & @ChrisABiersack congrats on
the new daughter-in-law . So happy for you
guys 🖤

Fig. 1. A real demographically-revealing directed message that conveys age, gender, marital status, and familial relations of the recipients.

to an individual. We hypothesize that directed communication affords multiple channels for revealing personal information, as it has been shown that peers construct a shared identity through language choice [17], that particular expressions are said more to particular social categories, e.g., biased language [25,33], and that language expresses an asymmetric social relationship linked with social differences, e.g., condescension [92]. Our work offers an important complementary approach to profiling and demographic inference that is applicable even when individuals reduce the amount of personally-identifying statements they make on social media [82,85] or even employ recent techniques to adversarially prevent their identity from being inferred [15,77,88,112,114].

Our work provides three main contributions:

- We establish that language in incoming communications is a highly-accurate source of demographic and personal information about an individual. To this end, we develop classifiers for five diverse demographic attributes: age, gender, religion, diet, and personality (Sect. 3). Our classifiers—trained on directed communications—learn to discriminate linguistic cues that are closely aligned with personal attributes of the individual to whom these messages are directed. These cues also have close correspondence with prior studies on profiling and demographic inference analyzing linguistic traits characteristic to the social group of the recipient.
- We establish, for the first time, a statistical relationship between (i) the efficacy of incoming communications in user profiling and demographic inference, and (ii) the strength of social ties of interlocutors (Sect. 4). We show that incoming communications from an individual's strong ties are more revealing of the individual's identity, but that this relationship only holds for publicly-visible aspects of the identity.
- We propose novel adversarial strategies for individuals to use for preserving their privacy (Sect. 5). We demonstrate that effective adversarial behavior is possible by strategic recruitment of new peers.

More broadly, our work captures the dual use of Natural Language Processing (NLP) techniques [50] by providing new demographic inference techniques that enable NLP for Social Good applications like mental health assessment [9], while also providing adversarial solutions for individuals who want to participate in social media but need to maximize anonymity for safety reasons [39].

2   Language and Identity

Individuals frequently reveal aspects of their social identity through their language choice and style. These choices help individuals associate themselves with a particular identity [17,37] and in conversation, language choice helps establish a social common ground and implicitly denotes mutual membership in a common social category [34,55]. Following, we outline some such demographic aspects and how they manifest in speech and social interactions.

2.1   Linguistic Signals of Personal Identity

Individuals make linguistic choices in order to signal their membership in social categories. These categories range from observable demographic attributes like age and gender to those associated with choice like diet and political affiliation. Here, we study five possible categories: gender, age, religion, diet, and extroversion. These categories capture a broad spectrum of possible attributes that affect language choice and include extrinsic, publicly-visible categories (age and gender) and intrinsic, private categories that are not necessarily publicly known by peers (diet, religion, extroversion). These attributes also reflect different computational tasks by including two binary variables (gender and extroversion[1]), two categorical variables (diet, religion) and a continuous-valued variable (age).

Gender. Gender is known to be one of the most important social categories driving language choice and its study has a long tradition within sociolinguistics [24,25,37,52,56,104,105]. More recent work has begun to examine how gender is expressed in platforms such as Twitter, where the lack of prosodic and nonverbal cues gives rise to other forms of linguistic variation; these purely textual signals have enabled large-scale studies of gender signaling [6,10,18,19,23,41,43, 78,87,94,111, *inter alia*]. These studies have found a broad range of style and content differences. For example, women are more likely to use pronouns, emotion words (like *sad, love,* and *glad*), interjections (*ah, hmmmm, ugh*), emoticons, and abbreviations associated with online discourse (*lol, omg*), while men tend to use higher frequency standard dictionary words, proper names (e.g., the names of sports teams), numbers, technology words, and links.

Age. Individuals make language choices that signal their age, which may be intended to convey the speaker's maturity or express the stage in life [35]. As with gender, textual communication on social media has allowed building computational models for predicting age from language usage, including Twitter [72,73,87], blogs [47,90], Facebook [93], and Netlog, a Dutch social network platform akin to Facebook [78]. The models show clear differences in linguistic choices, with younger individuals performing more stylistic variation like elongation and capitalization [7,47], grammatical differences in sentence length and

---

[1] We note that both gender and extroversion may also be considered along a spectrum [36,37]. We opt to study these as binary variables here due to lack of continuous-valued gender and extroversion ratings for social media users.

construction [49], and content choices to include more self-references, slang, and acronyms [73,87,90]. However, for older individuals these differences are less pronounced [74], which obstructs age inference solely from text.

Diet. Individuals adopt self-imposed dietary restrictions for a variety of medical, religious, or ethical considerations. The impact of this choice may expressed in the topics they discuss. Prior work has primarily focused on identifying vegetarians [8,38], suggesting such individual are identifiable from topical features.

Religion. Religious affiliation provides a social construct that individuals may identify with, akin to race or ethnicity [5,113]. Affiliations frequently provide metaphors and terminology that work their way into the regular lexicon, which automated methods have leveraged for classifying individuals in social media [21,75].

Extroversion. Extroversion is a strong predictor of social engagement with one's peers and increased social status [4], though the degree of extroversion or introversion has not been shown to affect the amount of self-disclosure [95]. Automated methods for personality detection have shown that extroverted individuals tend to use more terms describing social activities and concepts and colloquial language, whereas introverts refer to more solitary activities [30,45,53,86,96]

2.2   Social Identity in Communication

While an individual's own speech is predictive of their identity, the communication they receive is also potentially predictive due to the social processes that drive language selection. Following the principle of homophily, individuals tend to have social relationships with others similar to themselves in interests and demographics [66]; the communication within these relationships often focuses on the common ground [91], which can be used to identify their shared demographics. The process of revealing demographically-identifiable information is further supported by the tendency of individuals to reciprocate in self-disclosure in conversation, which provides more evidence of shared identity [29].

2.3   Online Identity and Privacy Protection

Public communication in social media can reveal significant information about a person, which has led some individuals to change their communication strategies to preserve privacy [102]. Individuals modulate these strategies relative to their closeness with the peer and are less likely to self-censor when talking with close friends [103]. In addition, anonymization strategies vary both demographically, e.g., females are more likely to use misinformation to preserve their privacy [77,114], and culturally, e.g., cultures with collectivist tendencies tend to censor less [89,109]. Despite these privacy efforts, an individual's identity may still be revealed by others' communication about or to them, e.g., parents compromising their children's privacy online by revealing their age and location [68], or friends revealing a person's religion or relationship status [108]. Our work extends this line of research by examining what can be inferred about a person from both explicit and implicit signals in the communications they receive.

3   Profiling via Incoming Communications

Given that a person's identity is expressed through language, we first examine to what degree *incoming* communications received by an individual are predictive of that user's personal attributes discussed in Sect. 2.1.

3.1   Data

Individuals for each demographic attribute were collected using targeted queries of the Twitter platform. For gender, we use fixed patterns on user profiles to find individuals who explicitly self-identify with a gender, e.g., "Writer in NY; she/her" or who identify with gendered social roles, e.g., "father to two girls." Age is identified using fixed patterns with aggressive filtering to remove noise. Diet was collected in a similar manner as in El-Arini *et al.* [38] by identifying individuals who report themselves as vegetarian, vegan, or paleo;[2] we sample an equal number of individuals not reporting these diets and treat them as being examples of the unrestricted diet class. We follow Chen *et al.* [21] and identify individuals' religious affiliations by searching for a fixed set of terms in the user profile for the following affiliations: agnostic, atheist, Buddhist, Christian, Hindu, Jewish, Muslim.[3] For personality, we adopt the approach of Plank and Hovy [83] for gathering Myers-Briggs personality type indicators and its Introversion/Extroversion labels, which have been shown to strongly load on the Extroversion dimension of the more-commonly used Big Five personality assessment [51,65].

Targeted queries were used to find all individuals with matching profiles or tweets during March 2016, except for Extroversion which was queried from January 2010 to December 2016 due to its relative sparsity. Tweets for identified individuals were then collected from a 10% random sample of Twitter from 2014 to 2016. The CLD2 language detector [64] was used to retain only English-speaking individuals. Finally, only those users with at least 100 tweets directed to them are included in the dataset. Table 1 summarizes the resulting dataset.

3.2   Personal Attribute Classifiers

Features. An individual's associated text is represented using content and stylistic features drawn from prior work. The broad themes are represented using a 100-topic LDA model [12], capturing both the average topic distribution for a

---

[2] We note that other diets are possible, such as kosher or halal; however, these are closely related to religion, which we also study, so we intentionally exclude them.

[3] Additional queries were formed for Sikhism and Jainism which did not return sufficient numbers of English speaking individuals to be included.

Table 1. Dataset sizes for each demographic attribute and frequencies of the majority classes.

Attribute	# of Tweets	Majority class	%
Gender	59800	Male	52.5
Religion	19940	Christian	65.8
Extroversion	24576	Introvert	63.0
Diet	9001	Unrestricted	41.0
Age	38134	21.3 (mean)	5.7 (s.d.)

message and the maximum probability a topic ever receives. A lexicon learned for each attribute was constructed by ranking all unigrams and bigrams using the weighted log-odds-ratio with an informative Dirichlet prior [70]. To construct binary classes for computing the log-odds of multiclass attributes, we chose one attribute relative to all the other attributes in the class; for age, lexicons were created by discretizing age into decade ranges (e.g., age 20–29) and computing the log-odds for that decade relative to the others. Content was additionally categorized using the Linguistic Inquiry and Word Count (LIWC) dictionary [106] and the average GloVe vector computed from all words received by an individual [81].

Stylistic features include pronoun usage, disfluencies, laughing expressions, question frequencies, average word length, usage of capital letters, word lengthening, and punctuation [7,23,47,73,80,87,90]. We also include emoji usage, which are language-independent signals that carry social status [60,107], a general lexicon for sentiment [69] and second sentiment lexicon focused on the extremes [61], which was shown to be effective for distinguishing different personality types, and lexicons with concreteness and abstractness ratings [16]. Ultimately, 2,625 features are used.

Models. Categorical attributes are predicted using random forest classifiers [14], an ensemble of decision tree classifiers learned from many independent subsamples of the training data; age is predicted using a random forest regressor. Random forest ensembles are particularly suitable for imbalanced multilabel setups such as ours and have been shown to be robust to overfitting when using many features [40]. Separate models were trained for each attribute. Models are evaluated using ten-fold cross-validation using Macro- and Micro-F1 for categorical attributes (see Appendix A) and the numeric age predictions are evaluated using Mean Squared Error and Pearson's r.

Baselines. We evaluate against two systems that use the same textual features but calculate them based on (1) the individual's outgoing language, rather than directed to them and (2) the language of the individual's peers, not necessarily directed towards the individual. For both baselines, we use the same ground truth individuals and recalculate the log-odds lexicons and topic models on their respective text. These models capture the information available through self-disclosure and from homophily, respectively, and are broadly representative of many related works for each attribute. To ensure a fair comparison with the incoming-text model, we evaluate each model on individuals that have 100 tweets authored by themselves or their peers, respectively. Finally, we include a baseline system that predicts the most frequent class or the mean numeric value.

3.3   Results

The language of incoming communications was highly predictive of recipients' demographic attributes, matching or surpassing the performance of the recipient's own speech and that of their peers for all attributes but age, as shown in Fig. 2. The performance of the directed speech classifier for each attribute is close to current state-of-the-art methods, e.g., [22], which typically also include features from the social network, biography, and other sources. Performance across attributes varied widely; the highest improvement relative to other forms of communication was seen for gender. This is expected, as individuals may be referred to by gendered categories in discourse. For example, the following tweets provide a clear lexical signal: "@User bro u don't even know my squad lol tf" and "@User Sounds great! Are you ladies going to #DisruptHRTO?". Our results build upon

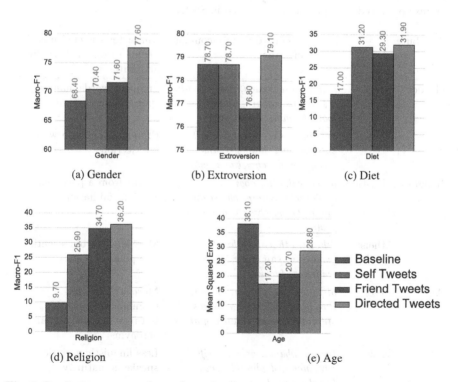

Fig. 2. Predictive accuracy for each attribute, reported as Macro-F1 and Mean Squared Error. Additional metrics are reported in Tables 4 and 5 in Appendix B.

multiple findings from sociolinguistics that directed speech can reveal significant information by individuals accommodating linguistic style of their peers [26,76], that individuals sharing the same attribute are more likely to use a common vernacular that indicate in-group status [67], and that dialog is conducive to self-disclosure [29].

Examining the feature importance for each attribute's classifier, we find that features based on the log-odds bootstrapped lexicons, topical differences, and the average word vector of received messages account for the majority of the most discriminative features. This trend matches the prior observation that machine-learned topic features are highly effective at distinguishing between demographics [79]. Examining the log-odds bootstrapped lexicons, the words most biased towards particular demographic attributes mirrored categories seen in self-speech, such as speech towards women including more emotion words and

Table 2. Examples of the most salient words used in directed speech (incoming communications) towards people with a particular attribute, learned from log-odds with a Dirichlet prior [70]. The right column lists what linguistic cues are expected to be observed in individual's texts (outgoing communications), based on prior work, summarized in Sect. 2.1. Strong linguistic and topical correspondence between outgoing and incoming communications enables training effective profiling classifiers without any text produced by a person, as proposed in Sect. 3.

Attribute		Most salient words in incoming communications	Characteristic cues used by people to signal their Own attributes
Gender	Male	*team, mate, coach, players, nfl, his, teams, games, player, football, man, matt, play*	Frequent words, names, sports teams.
	Female	*her, love, she, beautiful, gift, entered, girl, happy, thank, lovely, mom, christmas, cute*	Pronouns, emotion words, interjections.
Religion	Christian	*pjnet, catholic, obama, deplorable, trump, christian, amen, bless, church, america, prolife*	Words from a particular religious affiliation.
	Atheist	*atheist, atheism, atheists, evolution, shit, fuck, science, evidence, fucking*	More words from scientific and political topics.
Age	10–19	*birthday, happy, whooo, via, iloveyou, coolest, hemmings, stepfather, wvu, thanks, gotham*	More stylistic and grammatical variation, self-references, slang, and acronyms.
	30–39	*trump, obama, great, verified, win, news, deplorable, daily, latest, john, book, read*	Less linguistic variation, speaker's maturity

towards younger ages including more non-standard spellings and abbreviations. In addition, the log-odds lexicons captured topical preferences by gender, such as school terms for younger demographics, foods associated with the different diets, and religion-affiliated language. Table 2 shows examples of words from received communication that are most-biased towards particular demographic attributes. When an attribute's log-odds lexicon was highly weighted by the classifier, we found significant overlap with its most-biased words and the linguistic cues expected in self-speech when an individual signals their own social category. This overlap suggests that these demographically-biased words represent a common ground for two individuals with shared identity [17,37] and the relative importance of such words for classification indicates they are key features as individuals signal their identity in dialog.

As a follow-up experiment, we calculated the learning curve for each classifier to test how many peers are needed to obtain high performance. Curves were estimated by repeatedly sampling up to 100 peers for each user and estimating performance. Learning curves, shown in Fig. 3, reveal that most performance gains are seen with just a few peers and diminishing gains after 20 friends. These trends suggest that attributes can be reliably inferred from limited peer evidence, which substantially reduces the data collection effort needed to per user.

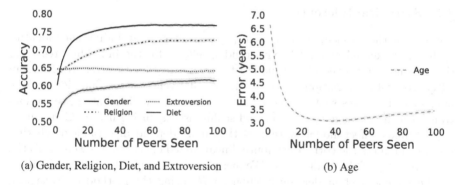

(a) Gender, Religion, Diet, and Extroversion   (b) Age

Fig. 3. Learning curves of how predictive accuracy changes relative to how many peers' communications are used for prediction. Shaded regions show bootstrapped 95% confidence intervals.

4 Demographic Inference and Tie Strength

Individuals engage with a variety of users on Twitter, from close friends to complete strangers; these different types of relationships can be categorized into strong and weak social ties [48]. Communication is driven in part by the strength of social ties [13]. For example, close friends may be more likely to discuss more intimate and immediate topics (e.g., dinner plans), whereas less-familiar acquaintances may use more formal language and relate to the person less as an individual and more as their social categories (e.g., gender, political affiliation) [57,84,100]. This observation motivates our research hypothesis that *the message content of close friends reveals more of the recipient's demographics than the more stereotypical language of socially-distant peers.* In this section, we use statistical inference to examine whether the directed speech generated from strong ties is more predictive of the recipient's identity.

4.1   Tie Strength

Tie strength in social relationships has many dimensions [54]. The four dimensions originally introduced by Granovetter are the amount of time in communication, intimacy, intensity, and reciprocity which characterize the tie [48]. Other dimensions were proposed later, for example social distance [58] and types of social relationships [42]. To capture the tie strength between the speaker and recipient, we use the following proxies, following prior work (also see Appendix C). **Communication frequency** [48] is operationalized by the number of tweets sent. **Explicit social relationships** [42] is captured by crawling the friend and followers edges of the individuals on the Twitter network. We consider four types of relationships: (1) the peer follows the individual, (2) the individual follows the peer, (3) both follow each other, (4) no edges.[4]

4.2   Statistical Inference

We test for the effect of social ties on predictiveness of an individual's identity by fitting mixed-effect models with random effects for the individual receiving the messages, and fixed-effects models for each proxy for tie strength. Random effects control for variation in the relative predictiveness across individuals. The number of messages sent by peers follows a power-law distribution, so we log-transform the message counts to avoid scaling issues during fitting. Generalized logistic mixed-effect models were fit to the binary dependent variable of whether the peer predicts the correct attribute; linear mixed effect models were fit to the absolute value of the error in age. We measure the amount of variance explained by the mixed-effect models by calculating R^2 using the method of Nakagawa and Schielzeth [71]; here, the marginal R^2 describes the proportion of variance explained by only the fixed effects (age and social distance); while the conditional R^2 measure variance from the fixed and random effects. To avoid data sparsity, we fit the models only with peers who send at least ten messages to a person.

4.3   Results

Results are summarized in Table 3. Our models reveal that increased tie strength is significantly associated with a peer's predictiveness for gender and age. However, no relationship was found for the other three attributes, religion, diet,

---

[4] Due to Twitter API rate limits, full edge information was gathered only for 1.7M pairs.

Table 3. Regression models showing the impact of increased tie strength (calculated via proxies discussed in Sect. 4.1) on a peer's predictive accuracy. The categorical variable for Relationship has the reference coding of "No Relationship" for all models. Note that since the Age regression is on Error instead of accuracy, its coefficients' interpretations are reverse of those of other attributes.

	Generalized logistic mixed-effects (Acc.)				Linear mixed-effects (Err.)
	Gender	Religion	Diet	Extroversion	Age
Communication frequency	0.032**	−0.049	0.147	0.105	−0.190***
Relationship: peer-follows	0.264***	0.365	0.303	−0.179	−0.051
Relationship: ego-follows	0.270**	0.336	−0.235	−0.263	0.085
Relationship: reciprocal	0.243***	0.556***	0.059	−0.056	−0.535***
Intercept	0.687***	0.384**	0.510**	1.584***	4.539***
Marginal R^2	1.713e-03	1.185e-03	8.123e-04	2.151e-04	3.617e-03
Conditional R^2	0.352	0.937	0.905	0.948	0.836
Observations	35,962	10,408	5,000	22,819	12,850

Note: *p<0.1; **p<0.05; ***p<0.01

and extroversion. We speculate that associations were found for gender and age because these attributes are more easily observable: they are frequently signaled by cues such as an individual's username or profile picture and therefore visible to both strong and weak ties. In contrast, religion, diet, and extroversion can be construed as more internal and not necessarily evident to an individual's ties, regardless of strength; because these attributes are less known, peers are less likely to modulate their speech on the basis of them.[5]

For gender and age, the majority of proxies for tie strength had a statistically-significant positive association with increased accuracy (gender) or reduced error (age), confirming our hypothesis that *stronger* ties are more predictive. For age and gender, more communication and having a reciprocal social relationship were consistently positively associated with demographic predictiveness, with additional significant effects seen for gender when individuals have any form of explicit relationship. The Marginal R^2 indicates that tie strength explains only a small part of the variance in predictive accuracy; however, the communications of a single peer alone are unlikely to be highly accurate (cf. the learning curve in Fig. 3), which limits establishing a larger fit from the fixed effects.

---

[5] One possibility for testing this hypothesis in future work is to identify a cohort of individuals who publicly signal these variables in an explicit way (e.g., including religious imagery in their profile picture) and then test for effects of tie strength on their peers' predictiveness.

5 Preserving Anonymity Through Adversarial Behavior

Online social platforms can serve a critical need for individuals to engage with others and obtain social, physical, and mental support [11,28]. When discussing sensitive or controversial topics, individuals often aim to maintain some degree of privacy online [27,97,115]. However, in Sect. 3 we have shown that even if individuals self-censor their content or employ adversarial strategies to mask their identity [2,62,63,85], the messages they receive can still reveal significant information about them.[6] This loss of privacy is potentially disastrous for individuals discussing politically-sensitive topics, as multiple reports have shown governments to pursue individuals when their identity is revealed [39].

Given the potential loss of privacy from other's incoming communications, we consider here how a user may still minimize what might be inferred about them. Under the reasonable assumption that an individual has no control over what their existing peers communicate to them (especially weak-tie peers), an alternative option a user has is to adversarially recruit new peers whose messages to them will mask the existing demographic signal. Without the ability to control what is said to them, an individual can no longer rely on adversarial stylometrics to hide their identity [2,62,63,85]. Following, we evaluate the effectiveness of adversarial strategies and then discuss key technical challenges for operationalizing these strategies in real platforms.

5.1 Adversarial Strategies

We model peer adoption strategies as a friend-of-a-friend recruitment, where individuals have the option of selecting a peer using two parameters: (i) who the peer is and (ii) who the peer is communicating with. For notational simplicity we refer to the individual recruiting a new peer as u_i; u_i can select another peer u_k who is communicating with peer u_j. Peer communication is simulated as if u_k communicated with u_i instead of u_j.

Four adversarial strategies are tested: three folk strategies that an individual might feasibly use on the basis of public information and one strategy that requires knowledge of the classifier.

1. **Random Peer:** the user chooses a random user u_j and then receives communication from a random friend of u_j.
2. **Different-Attribute Peer:** the user chooses the peer u_k of a user u_j who has a different demographic attribute than themself; e.g., a woman would choose the peer of a man.
3. **Topic Difference:** the user chooses the peer u_k whose messages to u_j are the most topically dissimilar from the topics seen in the current conversations to u_i.[7]

---

[6] This risk is valid even if the individual themselves does not engage with others, as platforms such as Twitter allow anyone to directly message another unless banned.

[7] We note that while we measure topical difference using our LDA model for messages, the peers selected by maximizing topical difference would be easily identified as such by the layperson (e.g., a peer discussing completely different topics).

4. **Feature Difference:** This strategy has knowledge of the exact features used by the classifier and the feature vector for the current individual. A new peer is chosen by selecting u_k whose messages to u_j would produce a feature vector that is maximally different from the vector for u_i.

When sampling multiple new peers, all strategies sample peers without replacement and the Topic Difference and Feature Difference strategies sample in decreasing order of distance (i.e., the most-different are chosen first).

5.2 Experimental Setup

We repeat the classifier and experimental setup from Sect. 3 with separate models for each attribute. The effectiveness of adversarial behavior is tested using ten-fold cross-validation where the test fold data alone is used for simulating adversarial behavior; i.e., all new peers selected by an adversarial strategy are chosen from within the test set, which prevents test-train leakage. During testing, we sample an increasing number of new peers for each user and compute the classifier's accuracy based on the percentage of new peers added relative to the number of prior peers.

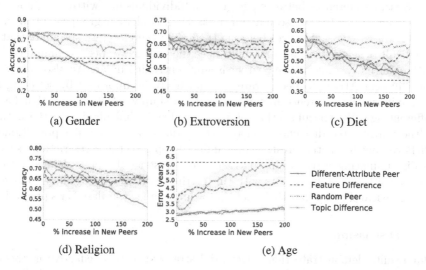

Fig. 4. Classifier accuracy for each adversarial strategy as new peers are chosen to communicate with an individual. Dashed red lines show the expected performance of randomly guessing for plots (a)–(d) and for guessing the mean age in (e). Shaded regions show 95% confidence intervals.

5.3 Results

Classifier performance, shown in Fig. 4, reveals that adversarial strategies can be effective at reducing performance to chance levels (denoted with a horizontal red line) and even at flipping the perceived attribute of the individual. However, the number of new peers needed to attain these goals varied substantially by strategy and attribute. With knowledge of the classifier's features, the Feature Difference strategy is able to effectively reduce performance to near chance for all but the diet and age attributes; as Figs. 4a, b, and d show, a 25% increase in the number of peers provides effective anonymity for those attributes.

Among the folk strategies, the Different-Attribute Peer and Topic Difference strategies are the most effective, though neither is able to consistently obtain at-chance performance. Both strategies are roughly equivalent for extroversion, diet, and religion, but diverge in their anonymization abilities for gender and age. For gender, Different-Attribute Peer is able to obtain at-chance performance with an 80% increase in new peers, while Topic Difference did not converge to at-chance even after tripling the number of peers a user has. However, for age, Topic Difference provides the highest effectiveness of any strategy. However, overall, folk strategies required far more new peers on average to be effective than the classifier-aware strategy, which is potentially prohibitive for users who already have a large cohort of peers messaging them.

Age and diet are difficult attributes to attain chance-level performance in our dataset. Age obfuscation is made difficult by the age distribution of the platform and textual differences between age groups. Individuals in Twitter are known to skew younger [31] (as also seen in our dataset) and older age groups are known to have fewer textual differences between them [73]; therefore, we speculate that it is difficult to select peers adversarially since there are fewer peers communicating with older individuals whose content is sufficiently dissimilar. We also note that the Different-Attribute Peer strategy could likely be improved by selecting u_j to maximize the difference in age, rather than simply selecting a u_j that has a different age. We speculate that obfuscating diet is difficult due to the nature of the unrestricted-diet class. Vegans, vegetarians, and paleo diet practitioners all have specific dietary restrictions and the topic of these restrictions serves as discriminating features; in contrast, the unrestricted diet is defined by the absence of these, so new peers with this attribute are much less likely to have a strong lexical signal about their diet that would change the classifier's prediction.

5.4   Discussion

Our results demonstrate that adversarial strategies can be effective in theory. However, implementing these strategies in practice faces two key challenges. First, our experiment simulates adding new peers as if the content they directed to u_j had been directed to u_i. This process assumes that new peers would still communicate with the same type of content as if they had been talking to u_j; e.g., if a female adds the peer of a male, the new peer would need to talk to her as if she were that male. In addition, new peers are expected to message with the same frequency, which is potentially unlikely when engaging with strangers.

Second, optimal adversarial behavior should be undetectable by the observing party. However, structural properties of the underlying social network of Twitter can potentially reveal the adversarially-added peers. Specifically, adding new peers would likely add individuals from distant parts of the network making them easier to detect. As a result, an adversarial user must add new peers whose placement in the social network is similar to that of their current peers, which could significantly restrict the available poor of new peers.

We speculate that for the truly adversarial, one option is to create and use sock puppet accounts. These accounts can easily be managed to control their content and to follow existing peers in order to seamlessly integrate into a user's social network. A second possibility for mitigating these challenges is changing the self-presentation signals of the account, such as selecting a gender-neutral profile picture and username. These strategies minimize the social signaling of identity in other domains (e.g., job applications, email) and are known to change peers' behaviors [46,101].

Finally, our findings have important implications for related work in differential privacy where, when releasing data about users, their privacy is preserved by strategically manipulating (or adding noise to) text that each produces [32]. Our work demonstrates that in order to preserve the anonymity of a person's demographic attributes, a differential privacy system would need to modify any queries requesting the directed speech to an individual as well—not just the individual's own speech.

6   Conclusion

We have long known that what you say on social media reveals your identity and may compromise your privacy. Our work shows that even ignoring what you say, just looking at what your friends say to you is generally even more informative, and allows us to guess your gender with 80% accuracy, as well as your age (71.2%), and even your private attributes like your religion (74.4%) and personality traits (67.3%). Moreover, your closer friends reveal more about your publicly-visible identity than more distant ones, but not about your private attributes. Strategic selecting new peers to communicate with can obstruct profiling, but more work needs to be done to safeguard privacy. Code and data used in the experiments are at https://github.com/davidjurgens/profiling-by-directed-speech.

Acknowledgments. We thank the anonymous reviewers, SocInfo organizers, the Stanford Data Science Initiative, and Twitter and Gnip for providing access to part of data used in this study. This work was supported by the National Science Foundation through awards IIS-1159679 and IIS-1526745.

Appendix

A   Classification Metrics

Macro-averaged F1 denotes the average F1 for each class, independent of how many instances were seen for that label. Micro-averaged F1 denotes the F1 measured from all instances and is sensitive to the skew in the distribution of classes in the dataset.

B   Additional Classifier Results

Table 4. Predictive accuracy for categorical attributes, reported as Micro-F1 and Macro-F1.

	Baseline		Self tweets		Friend tweets		Directed tweets	
Gender	52.0	68.4	75.2	70.4	71.7	71.6	**79.8**	**77.6**
Religion	63.2	9.7	71.5	25.9	**78.9**	34.7	74.4	**36.2**
Diet	51.3	17.0	55.7	31.2	54.2	29.3	**62.6**	**31.9**
Extroversion	64.8	78.7	65.3	78.7	64.2	76.8	**67.3**	**79.1**

Table 5. Predictive accuracy for age, reported Mean Squared Error and Correlation.

	Baseline		Self tweets		Friend tweets		Directed tweets	
Age	38.1	0.00	**17.2**	**0.27**	20.7	0.26	28.8	0.25

C   Additional Measures of Tie Strength

We initially considered two other potential proxies for tie strength based on textual analysis. First, we replicated the approach of Gilbert and Karahalios [44] which counted words occurring in ten LIWC categories to approximate intimacy in communication. Second, we attempted to measure social distance [58] by drawing upon Construal Theory [59,110] which conjectures that individuals with low social distance typically use more concrete language, whereas those with high social distance use more abstract language [98,99]; here, communication concreteness was measured using the word concreteness ratings of [16]. However, we found that the ratings for each approach did not match our judgments for their respective intended attributes and their use in the regression models produced non-significant results. Without ground truth for intimacy and social distance to validate their ratings, we therefore omitted these proxies based on our judgment of their unreliability to avoid drawing false conclusions about these dimensions of tie strength.

References

1. Al Zamal, F., Liu, W., Ruths, D.: Homophily and latent attribute inference: inferring latent attributes of Twitter users from neighbors. In: Proceedings of ICWSM (2012)
2. Almishari, M., Oguz, E., Tsudik, G.: Fighting authorship linkability with crowdsourcing. In: Proceedings of COSN, pp. 69–82. ACM (2014)
3. Altenburger, K.M., Ugander, J.: Bias and variance in the social structure of gender. arXiv preprint arXiv:1705.04774 (2017)

4. Anderson, C., John, O.P., Keltner, D., Kring, A.M.: Who attains social status? effects of personality and physical attractiveness in social groups. J. Pers. Soc. Psychol. **81**(1), 116 (2001)
5. Baker, W., Bowie, D.: Religious affiliation as a correlate of linguistic behavior. Univ. Pennsylvania Work. Pap. Linguist. **15**(2), 2 (2010)
6. Bamman, D., Eisenstein, J., Schnoebelen, T.: Gender identity and lexical variation in social media. J. Sociolinguist. **18**(2), 135–160 (2014)
7. Barbieri, F.: Patterns of age-based linguistic variation in American English. J. Sociolinguist. **12**(1), 58–88 (2008)
8. Beller, C., Knowles, R., Harman, C., Bergsma, S., Mitchell, M., Van Durme, B.: I'm a belieber: social roles via self-identification and conceptual attributes. In: Proceedings of ACL, pp. 181–186 (2014)
9. Benton, A., Mitchell, M., Hovy, D.: Multitask learning for mental health conditions with limited social media data. In: Proceedings of EACL (2017)
10. Bergsma, S., Van Durme, B.: Using conceptual class attributes to characterize social media users. In: Proceedings of ACL (2013)
11. Best, P., Manktelow, R., Taylor, B.: Online communication, social media and adolescent wellbeing: a systematic narrative review. Child Youth Serv. Rev. **41**, 27–36 (2014)
12. Blei, D.M., Ng, A.Y., Jordan, M.I.: Latent Dirichlet allocation. J. Mach. Learn. Res. (JMLR) **3**, 993–1022 (2003)
13. Bogardus, E.S.: A social distance scale. Sociol. Soc. Res. **17**, 265–271 (1933)
14. Breiman, L.: Random forests. Mach. Learn. **45**(1), 5–32 (2001)
15. Brennan, M., Afroz, S., Greenstadt, R.: Adversarial stylometry: circumventing authorship recognition to preserve privacy and anonymity. ACM Trans. Inf. Syst. Secur. (TISSEC) **15**(3), 12 (2012)
16. Brysbaert, M., Warriner, A.B., Kuperman, V.: Concreteness ratings for 40 thousand generally known English word lemmas. Behav. Res. Methods **46**(3), 904–911 (2014)
17. Bucholtz, M., Hall, K.: Identity and interaction: a sociocultural linguistic approach. Discourse Stud. **7**(4–5), 585–614 (2005)
18. Burger, J.D., Henderson, J., Kim, G., Zarrella, G.: Discriminating gender on Twitter. In: Proceedings of EMNLP, pp. 1301–1309 (2011)
19. Carpenter, J., Preotiuc-Pietro, D., Flekova, L., Giorgi, S., Hagan, C., Kern, M.L., Buffone, A.E., Ungar, L., Seligman, M.E.: Real men don't say "cute" using automatic language analysis to isolate inaccurate aspects of stereotypes. Soc. Psychol. Pers. Sci. **8**, 310–322 (2016)
20. Cesare, N., Grant, C., Nsoesie, E.O.: Detection of user demographics on social media: a review of methods and recommendations for best practices. arXiv preprint arXiv:1702.01807 (2017)
21. Chen, L., Weber, I., Okulicz-Kozaryn, A.: U.S. religious landscape on Twitter. In: Aiello, L.M., McFarland, D. (eds.) SocInfo 2014. LNCS, vol. 8851, pp. 544–560. Springer, Cham (2014). doi:10.1007/978-3-319-13734-6_38
22. Chen, X., Wang, Y., Agichtein, E., Wang, F.: A comparative study of demographic attribute inference in Twitter. In: Proceedings of ICWSM, vol. 15, pp. 590–593 (2015)
23. Ciot, M., Sonderegger, M., Ruths, D.: Gender inference of Twitter users in non-English contexts. In: Proceedings of EMNLP, pp. 1136–1145 (2013)
24. Coates, J.: Language and Gender: A Reader. Wiley-Blackwell, Oxford (1998)
25. Coates, J.: Women, Men and Language: A Sociolinguistic Account of Gender Differences in Language. Routledge, Abingdon (2015)

26. Danescu-Niculescu-Mizil, C., Gamon, M., Dumais, S.: Mark my words!: linguistic style accommodation in social media. In: Proceedings of WWW, pp. 745–754. ACM (2011)

27. De Choudhury, M., De, S.: Mental health discourse on reddit: self-disclosure, social support, and anonymity. In: Proceedings of ICWSM (2014)

28. De Choudhury, M., Kiciman, E.: The language of social support in social media and its effect on suicidal ideation risk. In: Proceedings of ICWSM, pp. 32–41 (2017)

29. Derlega, V.J., Harris, M.S., Chaikin, A.L.: Self-disclosure reciprocity, liking and the deviant. J. Exp. Soc. Psychol. **9**(4), 277–284 (1973)

30. Dewaele, J.M.: Individual differences in the use of colloquial vocabulary: the effects of sociobiographical and psychological factors. In: Learning Vocabulary in a Second Language: Selection, Acquisition and Testing, pp. 127–153 (2004)

31. Duggan, M.: Mobile messaging and social media 2015. Pew Res. Center, 13 (2015)

32. Dwork, C.: Differential privacy: a survey of results. In: Agrawal, M., Du, D., Duan, Z., Li, A. (eds.) TAMC 2008. LNCS, vol. 4978, pp. 1–19. Springer, Heidelberg (2008). doi:10.1007/978-3-540-79228-4_1

33. Eagly, A.H., Mladinic, A.: Gender stereotypes and attitudes toward women and men. Pers. Soc. Psychol. Bull. **15**(4), 543–558 (1989)

34. Eckert, P.: Jocks and Burnouts: Social Categories and Identity in the High School. Teachers College Press, New York (1989)

35. Eckert, P.: Age as a sociolinguistic variable. In: The Handbook of Sociolinguistics, pp. 151–167 (1997)

36. Eckert, P.: Variation and the indexical field. J. Sociolinguist. **12**(4), 453–476 (2008)

37. Eckert, P., McConnell-Ginet, S.: Language and Gender. Cambridge University Press, New York (2003)

38. El-Arini, K., Paquet, U., Herbrich, R., Van Gael, J., Agüera y Arcas, B.: Transparent user models for personalization. In: Proceedings of KDD, pp. 678–686. ACM (2012)

39. Elgin, B., Robison, P.: How despots use Twitter to hunt dissidents. Bloomberg-Businessweek (2016). https://www.bloomberg.com/news/articles/2016-10-27/twitter-s-firehose-of-tweets-is-incredibly-valuable-and-just-as-dangerous

40. Fernández-Delgado, M., Cernadas, E., Barro, S., Amorim, D.: Do we need hundreds of classifiers to solve real world classification problems. J. Mach. Learn. Res **15**(1), 3133–3181 (2014)

41. Flekova, L., Gurevych, I.: Can we hide in the web? large scale simultaneous age and gender author profiling in social media. In: Proceedings of CLEF (2013)

42. Friedkin, N.: A test of structural features of Granovetter's strength of weak ties theory. Soc. Netw. **2**(4), 411–422 (1980)

43. Garimella, A., Mihalcea, R.: Zooming in on gender differences in social media. In: Proceedings of the Workshop on Computational Modeling of Peoples Opinions, Personality, and Emotions in Social Media, pp. 1–10 (2016)

44. Gilbert, E., Karahalios, K.: Predicting tie strength with social media. In: Proceedings of CHI, pp. 211–220. ACM (2009)

45. Golbeck, J., Robles, C., Edmondson, M., Turner, K.: Predicting personality from Twitter. In: Proceedings of SocialCom, pp. 149–156. IEEE (2011)

46. Goldin, C., Rouse, C.: Orchestrating impartiality: the impact of "blind" auditions on female musicians. Technical report, National Bureau of Economic Research (1997)

47. Goswami, S., Sarkar, S., Rustagi, M.: Stylometric analysis of bloggers age and gender. In: Proceedings of ICWSM (2009)
48. Granovetter, M.S.: The strength of weak ties. Am. J. Sociol. **78**(6), 1360–1380 (1973)
49. Hovy, D., Søgaard, A.: Tagging performance correlates with author age. In: Proceedings of ACL, pp. 483–488 (2015)
50. Hovy, D., Spruit, S.L.: The social impact of natural language processing. In: Proceedings of ACL, vol. 2, pp. 591–598 (2016)
51. John, O.P., Srivastava, S.: The big five trait taxonomy: history, measurement, and theoretical perspectives. In: Handbook of Personality: Theory and Research, vol. 2, pp. 102–138 (1999)
52. Kendall, S., Tannen, D., et al.: Gender and language in the workplace. In: Gender and Discourse, pp. 81–105. Sage, London (1997)
53. Kosinski, M., Stillwell, D., Graepel, T.: Private traits and attributes are predictable from digital records of human behavior. Proc. Nat. Acad. Sci. (PNAS) **110**(15), 5802–5805 (2013)
54. Krackhardt, D., Nohria, N., Eccles, B.: The strength of strong ties. Netw. Knowl. Econ., 82 (2003)
55. Labov, W.: Sociolinguistic Patterns. University of Pennsylvania Press, Philadelphia (1972)
56. Lakoff, R.T., Bucholtz, M.: Language and Woman's Place: Text and Commentaries, vol. 3. Oxford University Press, USA (2004)
57. Lea, M., Spears, R., de Groot, D.: Knowing me, knowing you: anonymity effects on social identity processes within groups. Pers. Soc. Psychol. Bull. **27**(5), 526–537 (2001)
58. Lin, N., Ensel, W.M., Vaughn, J.C.: Social resources and strength of ties: structural factors in occupational status attainment. Am. Sociol. Rev., 393–405 (1981)
59. Liviatan, I., Trope, Y., Liberman, N.: Interpersonal similarity as a social distance dimension: Implications for perception of others actions. J. Exp. Soc. Psychol. **44**(5), 1256–1269 (2008)
60. Lu, X., Ai, W., Liu, X., Li, Q., Wang, N., Huang, G., Mei, Q.: Learning from the ubiquitous language: an empirical analysis of emoji usage of smartphone users. In: Proceedings of Ubicomp, pp. 770–780. ACM (2016)
61. Mairesse, F., Walker, M.A., Mehl, M.R., Moore, R.K.: Using linguistic cues for the automatic recognition of personality in conversation and text. J. Artif. Intell. Res. (JAIR) **30**, 457–500 (2007)
62. Marder, B., Joinson, A., Shankar, A., Thirlaway, K.: Strength matters: self-presentation to the strongest audience rather than lowest common denominator when faced with multiple audiences in social network sites. Comput. Hum. Behav. **61**, 56–62 (2016)
63. Marwick, A.E., Boyd, D.: I tweet honestly, i tweet passionately: Twitter users, context collapse, and the imagined audience. New Media Soc. **13**(1), 114–133 (2011)
64. McCandless, M.: Accuracy and performance of Google's compact language detector. Blog post (2010)
65. McCrae, R.R., Costa, P.T.: Reinterpreting the Myers-Briggs type indicator from the perspective of the five-factor model of personality. J. Pers. **57**(1), 17–40 (1989)
66. McPherson, M., Smith-Lovin, L., Cook, J.M.: Birds of a feather: homophily in social networks. Ann. Rev. Sociol. **27**(1), 415–444 (2001)
67. Milroy, J.: Linguistic variation and change: on the historical sociolinguistics of English. B. Blackwell (1992)

68. Minkus, T., Liu, K., Ross, K.W.: Children seen but not heard: when parents compromise children's online privacy. In: Proceedings of WWW, pp. 776–786. ACM (2015)
69. Mohammad, S.M., Turney, P.D.: Crowdsourcing a word-emotion association lexicon. Artif. Intell. **29**(3), 436–465 (2013)
70. Monroe, B.L., Colaresi, M.P., Quinn, K.M.: Fightin' words: lexical feature selection and evaluation for identifying the content of political conflict. Polit. Anal. **16**(4), 372–403 (2008)
71. Nakagawa, S., Schielzeth, H.: A general and simple method for obtaining R2 from generalized linear mixed-effects models. Methods Ecol. Evol. **4**(2), 133–142 (2013)
72. Nguyen, D., Smith, N.A., Rosé, C.P.: Author age prediction from text using linear regression. In: Proceedings of the Workshop on Language Technology for Cultural Heritage, Social Sciences, and Humanities, pp. 115–123. Association for Computational Linguistics (2011)
73. Nguyen, D.P., Gravel, R., Trieschnigg, R., Meder, T.: "how old do you think I am?" a study of language and age in Twitter. In: Proceedings of ICWSM (2013)
74. Nguyen, D.P., Trieschnigg, R., Doğruöz, A.S., Gravel, R., Theune, M., Meder, T., de Jong, F.: Why gender and age prediction from tweets is hard: lessons from a crowdsourcing experiment. In: Proceedings of COLING (2014)
75. Nguyen, M.T., Lim, E.P.: On predicting religion labels in microblogging networks. In: Proceedings of SIGIR, pp. 1211–1214. ACM (2014)
76. Niederhoffer, K.G., Pennebaker, J.W.: Linguistic style matching in social interaction. J. Lang. Soc. Psychol. **21**(4), 337–360 (2002)
77. Oomen, I., Leenes, R.: Privacy risk perceptions and privacy protection strategies. In: de Leeuw, E., Fischer-Hübner, S., Tseng, J., Borking, J. (eds.) IDMAN 2007. TIFIP, vol. 261, pp. 121–138. Springer, Boston, MA (2008). doi:10.1007/978-0-387-77996-6_10
78. Peersman, C., Daelemans, W., Van Vaerenbergh, L.: Predicting age and gender in online social networks. In: Proceedings of the 3rd International Workshop on Search and Mining User-Generated Contents, pp. 37–44. ACM (2011)
79. Pennacchiotti, M., Popescu, A.M.: A machine learning approach to Twitter user classification. In: Proceedings of ICWSM, pp. 281–288 (2011)
80. Pennebaker, J.W., Stone, L.D.: Words of wisdom: language use over the life span. J. Pers. Soc. Psychol. **85**(2), 291 (2003)
81. Pennington, J., Socher, R., Manning, C.D.: Glove: global vectors for word representation. In: Proceedings of EMNLP, vol. 14, pp. 1532–1543 (2014)
82. Phelan, C., Lampe, C., Resnick, P.: It's creepy, but it doesn't bother me. In: Proceedings of CHI, pp. 5240–5251. ACM (2016)
83. Plank, B., Hovy, D.: Personality traits on TwitterorHow to get 1,500 personality tests in a week. In: Proceedings of WASSA (2015)
84. Postmes, T., Spears, R., Lea, M.: Breaching or building social boundaries? SIDE-effects of computer-mediated communication. Commun. Res. **25**(6), 689–715 (1998)
85. Potthast, M., Hagen, M., Stein, B.: Author obfuscation: attacking the state of the art in authorship verification. In: Proceedings of CLEF (Working Notes), pp. 716–749 (2016)
86. Quercia, D., Kosinski, M., Stillwell, D., Crowcroft, J.: Our Twitter profiles, our selves: predicting personality with Twitter. In: Proceedings of SocialCom, pp. 180–185. IEEE (2011)

87. Rao, D., Yarowsky, D., Shreevats, A., Gupta, M.: Classifying latent user attributes in Twitter. In: Proceedings of the 2nd International Workshop on Search and Mining User-generated Contents, pp. 37–44. ACM (2010)
88. Reddy, S., Knight, K.: Obfuscating gender in social media writing. In: Proceedings of Workshop on Natural Language Processing and Computational Social Science, pp. 17–26 (2016)
89. Reed, P.J., Spiro, E.S., Butts, C.T.: Thumbs up for privacy?: differences in online self-disclosure behavior across national cultures. Soc. Sci. Res. **59**, 155–170 (2016)
90. Rosenthal, S., McKeown, K.: Age prediction in blogs: a study of style, content, and online behavior in pre-and post-social media generations. In: Proceedings of ACL, pp. 763–772. Association for Computational Linguistics (2011)
91. Rossi, L., Magnani, M.: Conversation practices and network structure in Twitter. In: Proceedings of ICWSM (2012)
92. Ryan, E.B., Hummert, M.L., Boich, L.H.: Communication predicaments of aging patronizing behavior toward older adults. J. Lang. Soc. Psychol. **14**(1–2), 144–166 (1995)
93. Sap, M., Park, G., Eichstaedt, J., Kern, M., Stillwell, D., Kosinski, M., Ungar, L., Schwartz, H.A.: Developing age and gender predictive lexica over social media. In: Proceedings of EMNLP, pp. 1146–1151. Association for Computational Linguistics (2014)
94. Schnoebelen, T.J.: Emotions are relational: positioning and the use of affective linguistic resources. Ph.D. thesis, Stanford University (2012)
95. Schrammel, J., Köffel, C., Tscheligi, M.: Personality traits, usage patterns and information disclosure in online communities. In: Proceedings of HCI, pp. 169–174. British Computer Society (2009)
96. Schwartz, H.A., Eichstaedt, J.C., Kern, M.L., Dziurzynski, L., Ramones, S.M., Agrawal, M., Shah, A., Kosinski, M., Stillwell, D., Seligman, M.E.S., Ungar, L.H.: Personality, gender, and age in the language of social media: the open-vocabulary approach. PLoS ONE **8**(9), e73791 (2013)
97. Shelton, M., Lo, K., Nardi, B.: Online media forums as separate social lives: a qualitative study of disclosure within and beyond Reddit. In: Proceedings of iConference (2015)
98. Snefjella, B., Kuperman, V.: Concreteness and psychological distance in natural language use. Psychol. Sci. **26**(9), 1449–1460 (2015)
99. Soderberg, C., Callahan, S., Kochersberger, A., Amit, E., Ledgerwood, A.: The effects of psychological distance on abstraction: two meta-analyses. Psychol. Bull. **141**(3), 525–548 (2015)
100. Spears, R., Lea, M.: Social influence and the influence of the "social" in computer-mediated communication. In: Lea, M. (ed.) Contexts of Computer-Mediated Communication, pp. 30–65. Harvester Wheatsheaf (1992)
101. Steinpreis, R.E., Anders, K.A., Ritzke, D.: The impact of gender on the review of the curricula vitae of job applicants and tenure candidates: a national empirical study. Sex Roles **41**(7), 509–528 (1999)
102. Strater, K., Lipford, H.R.: Strategies and struggles with privacy in an online social networking community. In: Proceedings of the 22nd British HCI Group Annual Conference on People and Computers: Culture, Creativity, Interaction, vol. 1, pp. 111–119. British Computer Society (2008)
103. Stutzman, F., Vitak, J., Ellison, N.B., Gray, R., Lampe, C.: Privacy in interaction: exploring disclosure and social capital in Facebook. In: Proceedings of ICWSM (2012)

104. Tannen, D.: You Just Don't Understand: Women and Men in Conversation. Virago, London (1991)
105. Tannen, D.: Gender and Conversational Interaction. Oxford University Press, Oxford (1993)
106. Tausczik, Y.R., Pennebaker, J.W.: The psychological meaning of words: LIWC and computerized text analysis methods. J. Lang. Soc. Psychol. **29**(1), 24–54 (2010)
107. Tchokni, S.E., Séaghdha, D.O., Quercia, D.: Emoticons and phrases: status symbols in social media. In: Proceedings of ICWSM (2014)
108. Thomas, K., Grier, C., Nicol, D.M.: unFriendly: multi-party privacy risks in social networks. In: Atallah, M.J., Hopper, N.J. (eds.) PETS 2010. LNCS, vol. 6205, pp. 236–252. Springer, Heidelberg (2010). doi:10.1007/978-3-642-14527-8_14
109. Trepte, S., Reinecke, L., Ellison, N.B., Quiring, O., Yao, M.Z., Ziegele, M.: A cross-cultural perspective on the privacy calculus. Soc. Media+ Soc. **3**(1), 2056305116688035 (2017)
110. Trope, Y., Liberman, N.: Construal-level theory of psychological distance. Psychol. Rev. **117**(2), 440 (2010)
111. Volkova, S., Bachrach, Y., Armstrong, M., Sharma, V.: Inferring latent user properties from texts published in social media. In: Proceedings of AAAI, pp. 4296–4297 (2015)
112. Wienberg, C., Gordon, A.S.: Privacy considerations for public storytelling. In: Proceedings of ICWSM (2014)
113. Yaeger-Dror, M.: Religion as a sociolinguistic variable. Language and Linguistics Compass **8**(11), 577–589 (2014)
114. Youn, S., Hall, K.: Gender and online privacy among teens: risk perception, privacy concerns, and protection behaviors. Cyberpsychol. Behav. **11**(6), 763–765 (2008)
115. Zhang, K., Kizilcec, R.F.: Anonymity in social media: effects of content controversiality and social endorsement on sharing behavior. In: Proceedings of ICWSM (2014)

Erratum to: Social Informatics

Giovanni Luca Ciampaglia[1](✉), Afra Mashhadi[2], and Taha Yasseri[3]

[1] Indiana University, Bloomington, IN, USA
gciampag@indiana.edu
[2] University of Washington, Seattle, WA, USA
[3] University of Oxford, Oxford, UK

Erratum to:
Chapter "Differential Network Effects on Economic
Outcomes: A Structural Perspective" in:
G.L. Ciampaglia et al. (Eds.): Social Informatics, LNCS 10540,
https://doi.org/10.1007/978-3-319-67256-4_5

The original version of the paper starting on p. 41 was revised. An acknowledgement has been added. The original chapter was corrected.

Erratum to:
Chapter "Attention Please!" in: G.L. Ciampaglia et al. (Eds.):
Social Informatics, LNCS 10540,
https://doi.org/10.1007/978-3-319-67256-4_15

In section 3.2 and 3.3. the last paragraphs are incorrect. They are located on page 174. They are corrected as follows:

Paragraph 3.2:
As a supplement to the 'discussion intensity' metric, we will also include a metric called editors' concentration. We define this as the number of contributors contributing to topic-related articles compared to the number of contributors contributing to non-topic related articles. Together with the discussion intensity, these metrics form a way of quantifying the aforementioned concept of attention management.

The updated online version of this book can be found at
https://doi.org/10.1007/978-3-319-67256-4_5
https://doi.org/10.1007/978-3-319-67256-4_15
https://doi.org/10.1007/978-3-319-67256-4

© Springer International Publishing AG 2017   E1
G.L. Ciampaglia et al. (Eds.): SocInfo 2017, Part II, LNCS 10540, pp. E1–E2, 2017.
https://doi.org/10.1007/978-3-319-67256-4_44

Paragraph 3.3:
We measure editors' concentration as the number of contributors working on Ukraine-related articles over the number of contributors working on non-Ukraine-related articles. See Eq. (2):

$$C_m^e = C_t/N_t \div C_n/N_n = (C_t * N_n)/(N_t * C_n) \tag{2}$$

In which C_m^e is the editors' concentration in a given month; C_t is the number of contributors working on topic-related articles; N_t is the number of articles on topic; C_n is the number of contributors working on off-topic articles; and N_n is the number of non-topic-related articles.

Additionally, the word **"editing concentration"** should correctly read **"editors' concentration"** throughout the entire contribution!

Author Index

Printed in the United States
By Bookmasters